SECURITIES REGULATION

IN CANADA

SECOND EDITION

by

Mark R. Gillen, B.Comm., M.B.A., LL.B., LL.M.
Associate Professor of Law, University of Victoria

CARSWELL
Thomson Professional Publishing

© 1998 Thomson Canada Limited

All rights reserved. No part of this publication may be reproduced, stored in a retrieval system, or transmitted, in any form or by any means, electronic, mechanical, photocopying, recording, or otherwise, without the prior written permission of the publisher.

This publication is designed to provide accurate and authoritative information. It is sold with the understanding that the publisher is not engaged in rendering legal, accounting or other professional advice. If legal advice or other expert assistance is required, the services of a competent professional should be sought. The commentary contained herein should in no way be construed as being either official or unofficial policy of any governmental body.

The paper used in this publication meets the minimum requirements of American National Standard for Information Sciences — Permanance of Paper for Printed Library Materials. ANSI Z39.48-1984.

Canadian Cataloguing in Publication Data

Gillen, Mark R., 1957–
  Securities Regulation in Canada
2nd ed.

Includes bibliographical references and index.
ISBN 0-459-26291-2 (bound)   ISBN 0-459-26289-0 (pbk.)

1. Securities — Canada.   I. Title.

KE1065.G55 1998   346.71'092   C99-930024-5
KF1070.G55 1998

CARSWELL
Thomson Professional Publishing

One Corporate Plaza,
2075 Kennedy Road,
Scarborough, Ontario M1T 3V4

Internet: www.carswell.com

Customer Service:
Toronto   1-416-609-3800
Elsewhere in Canada/U.S.   1-800-387-5164
Fax   1-416-298-5094
E-mail: orders@carswell.com

To my wife, Joyce, and my children, Lise and Torin, for their patience and to my parents for their guidance.

ACKNOWLEDGEMENTS

I owe many thanks to the efforts of my research assistants, Vance Goulding, Dawn Leroy, and Brad Vescarelli who assisted me on the first edition of the book and to Jamie Bless, Shannon Craig, Tara Gurr and Meredith Halbert who assisted me on the second edition of the book. I owe a great debt of gratitude to my secretary, Rosemary Garton, who patiently typed many versions of parts of the manuscript and provided much helpful advice on matters such as formatting and logistics in both the preparation of the manuscript for the first edition and the preparation of the many additions to the second edition.

PREFACE

The purpose of this book is to provide a brief introduction to securities law in Canada. It is primarily directed to students of law. However, it should also serve as an introduction to Canadian securities law for lawyers who do not regularly practice in the area, but who need to have some means of obtaining a general knowledge of the area to serve a particular client, or, to be generally aware of securities law issues. The book should be useful to persons engaged in the securities business who want to expand their knowledge of securities law. It may also be a useful introduction to securities law for business students who often graduate with a knowledge of finance, but with very little knowledge of the legal framework in which financing takes place. It is also hoped that the book will provide a source of information on securities law for economists in the finance field that will facilitate and promote empirical and theoretical research on securities law issues.

For law students, the purpose of the book is to provide them with an introduction to the law so that class time, which would otherwise be consumed conveying this information, can be freed for other uses. Students can get the basics of the law from the book so that class time can be spent on more in-depth discussions of the law on particular topics, applying the law to specific problems, or further pursuing policy analysis.

The book focuses on provincial securities legislation. It focuses on the "closed-system" statutes that have been enacted in Alberta, British Columbia, Nova Scotia, Newfoundland, Ontario, and Saskatchewan. The laws discussed are also generally similar to the substantially compatible securities laws of the province of Manitoba. Notational references are made to Quebec's compatible but different "closed-system" statute and to corresponding laws of Prince Edward Island, New Brunswick and the Territories. Footnote references are provided for guidance to relevant corresponding provisions in the various securities Acts. The cut-off date for these is August, 1998.

Securities administrators across Canada have endeavoured to make the laws of the various provinces and territories compatible to facilitate trading in securities at a national level. Consequently, the securities laws across the provinces and territories have a great deal in common. Since this book is intended as an introduction, it focuses on the common aspects of securities regulation across the country. Details of differences from jurisdiction to jurisdiction are generally not dealt with in the text, although some reference to outstanding differences is provided in notes to the text.

Chapters 1 to 3 of the book deal with introductory matters necessary to an understanding of securities law. Chapter 1 of the book provides an introduction to the institutional framework which securities laws seek to regulate. It is provided primarily for those who are not familiar with common types of securities and how they are traded. Chapter 2 provides an introduction to the valuation of securities and the concept of securities market efficiency which are essential to an understanding of securities law. Chapter 3 provides a brief history of securities regulation, its sources and underlying purposes.

This second edition of the book updates the more significant developments in Canadian securities laws from April, 1992 to August, 1998. Additions have been made to the types of securities that are traded, including a discussion of derivative securities and asset-backed securities. Academic literature on such matters as securities market efficiency, mandatory disclosure, insider trading and takeover bid regulation has also been updated. These additions have resulted in an increase in the size of the book. In the interests of maintaining the introductory nature of the book, choices had to be made concerning items that would have to be left out of the book. Some readers will have different views about the appropriateness of these choices. Feedback on these different views would be greatly appreciated. I have, however, resisted the suggestion that the broader policy discussions be excluded from the book. The book's primary audience is law students, many of whom are interested in such a perspective and who should consider such a perspective even if they have no other intention than to practice law upon graduation.

The reader should be aware that this book should not be used as a basis for making decisions on or providing advice with respect to securities law matters. Firstly, the book is an introduction to securities law, not a compendium of every aspect of the law one should be aware of to make decisions or provide advice. In particular, the summaries of the law on mutual funds and the regulation of brokers, dealers and advisors are very brief. Further, many jurisdictional, constitutional and charter issues are beyond the scope of the book and are not addressed. Secondly, as noted above, it focuses on the most common aspects of securities law. There may be differences in the laws of different jurisdictions which are not addressed in the book and which should be investigated to provide advice or make decisions. The notes to the statutory provisions are only a guide to similar statutory provisions in different securities Acts. The actual provisions often differ, in varying degrees, from the text and from jurisdiction to jurisdiction. There may also be other relevant statutory provisions beyond those cited in the notes. Thirdly, securities law is a rapidly changing area, such that what appears in the book may have been modified by the time the reader reads it. Indeed, several not insignificant developments occurred between the cut-off date for this second edition of the book and its final preparation for printing. Thus anyone with a potential securities law problem should consult a practicing lawyer for advice based on an in-depth analysis of the law and the kind of practical insights that come from years in a securities law practice.

TABLE OF CONTENTS

Acknowledgements v
Preface vii
List of Abbreviations xxxvii

CHAPTER 1:   BACKGROUND ON SECURITIES MARKETS

I.   Introduction 1
II.   The Purpose For Which Securities are Sold 1
III.   Common Types of Securities 3
       A. Debt Finance 3
           1. Trade Credit 4
           2. Bank Loan 4
              a. Short-term 4
              b. Long-term 4
           3. Commercial Paper 5
           4. Bonds/Debentures 5
              a. Call 6
              b. Sinking Fund 6
              c. Convertible 6
              d. Warrants 7
       B. Equity Finance 7
           1. Share Capital 7
           2. Common Shares 8
              a. The Right to Vote 8
              b. The Right to Dividends 8
              c. The Liquidation Right 9
           3. Preferred Shares 9
              a. Cumulative (vs. Non-cumulative) 10
              b. Participating (vs. Non-participating) . 10
              c. Redemption/Call Provision 11
              d. Retraction Rights 11
           4. Restricted Shares 11
           5. Rights 12

		6. Options	13
		7. Units in a Limited Partnership	13
		8. Units	14
	C.	Government Securities	14
	D.	Derivative Securities	15
		1. Warrants as an Example of a Derivative Security	16
		2. Derivative Securities as Risky or "Speculative" Investments	16
		3. The Use of Derivative Securities to Avoid (or "Hedge" Against) Risk	16
		4. Wide Variety of Derivative Securities	17
		a. Stock Index Options	17
		b. Interest Rate Caps	18
	E.	Asset Backed Securities	19
	F.	Summary	19
IV.		The Distribution of Securities	20
	A.	Introduction	20
		1. Direct Issue and Private Placements	20
		2. Bought Deal/Offer to Sell	21
		3. Best Efforts Underwriting	22
		4. Standby Underwriting	22
	B.	Distributions Through Underwriters	22
		1. Underwriting Agreement	22
		2. Syndicated Underwriting	23
		3. Banking Groups	23
		4. Selling Group	23
	C.	Summary	23
V.		How Securities are Traded	24
	A.	Introduction	24
	B.	Trading in Securities	25
		1. The Development of Stock Exchange Trading	25
		2. Trading Through the Facilities of an Exchange	27
		a. Communication	28
		b. Exchange	29
		(i) Payment	29
		(ii) Transfer of Ownership	29

     c. Simplifying the Process 34
       (i) Clearing Agency 34
      (ii) Broker Inventories and Certificate
          Depository 35
    d. The Computerization of Stock Exchanges and
      Securities Trading 36
  3. Trading Off the Exchange 37
    a. Private Trades 37
    b. The Upstairs Market 37
    c. Over-the-counter Trades 38
  4. Margin Trading 39
  5. Short Selling.............................. 40
C. Major Investors in the Canadian Securities
Market...................................... 41
  1. Banks 41
  2. Trust Companies 41
  3. Credit Unions and Caisses Populaire 41
  4. Life Insurance Companies 42
  5. Pension Funds 42
  6. Investment Funds 42
    a. Mutual Funds........................ 42
    b. Investment Companies 43
  7. Individuals 43
  8. The Importance of Institutional Investors 43
D. The Internationalization of Securities Markets..... 43

CHAPTER 2: SECURITY VALUES AND SECURITIES MARKET EFFICIENCY

I.   Introduction 47
II.   How Securities are Valued 47
  A. The Fundamentals of Security Values............ 47
    1. Source of Value 47
    2. Discounting 48
    3. Risk...................................... 49
      a. Generally 49
      b. Systematic and Unsystematic Risk 49
    4. Summary 50
  B. Approaches to Valuing Securities 51
    1. Fundamental Analysis....................... 51
    2. Technical Analysis......................... 51

III. Securities Market Efficiency 53
    A. What is Securities Market Efficiency? 53
        1. The Price of a Security as an Average of Estimates
            of the Value of the Security 53
        2. The Meaning of Securities Market Efficiency ... 53
        3. Factors that Affect the Efficiency of Securities
            Markets 54
    B. How Efficient are Securities Markets? 54
        1. Weak Form Efficiency (Patterns vs. Random
            Walks) 55
        2. Semi-Strong Form 56
        3. Strong Form Efficiency 57
        4. Problems with the Evidence on Securities Market
            Efficiency 58
            a. The Joint Hypothesis Problem 58
            b. Anomalous Results 60
            c. Fundamental vs. Informational Efficiency ... 60
            d. A "Noise" Theory of Deviations From
                Fundamental Values 61
            e. Application of the Evidence to Smaller
                Securities Markets and to Canada 63
    D. Securities Market Efficiency and Securities
        Regulation 63
        1. A Policy Perspective 63
        2. A Practical Perspective 65
    E. A Framework for the Analysis of Securities Market
        Efficiency 65

CHAPTER 3: CONSTITUTIONAL DIVISION OF POWERS, HISTORY, PURPOSE AND SOURCES OF SECURITIES REGULATION

I.   Introduction 67
II.   The Constitutional Division of Powers with Respect to
      Securities Regulation 67
III. A Brief History of Securities Regulation 70
    A. Early Developments in the United Kingdom 70
    B. U.S. Developments 73
    C. Canadian Developments 74
        1. Fraud Prevention Acts 74
        2. Prospectus Disclosure 75

　　　3. The *Kimber Report* . . . .　76
　　　4. The *Merger Report* and the "Closed System" . . . .　77
　　　5. Interprovincial Cooperation . . . .　77
　D.　Summary . . . .　78
IV.　The Purpose of Securities Regulation . . . .　79
　A.　Investor Protection, Confidence in the Market and
　　　the Efficient Allocation of Resources . . . .　79
　　　1. Investor Protection and Optimal Allocation of
　　　　Financial Resources . . . .　79
　　　　a. Investor Protection . . . .　80
　　　　b. Optimal Allocation of Financial
　　　　　Resources . . . .　80
　　　　c. Link Between Investor Protection and the
　　　　　Optimal Allocation of Financial
　　　　　Resources . . . .　81
　　　2. Achieving Objectives by Promoting Confidence
　　　　in the Market . . . .　82
　　　　a. Public Confidence-in-the-market . . . .　82
　　　　b. The Link Between Primary and Secondary
　　　　　Market Confidence . . . .　82
　　　　c. Allocation of Savings to Investment Promoting
　　　　　Economic Growth . . . .　82
　　　3. Not at Excessive Cost . . . .　83
　　　4. The Method of Achieving Public Confidence and
　　　　the Optimal Allocation of Financial
　　　　Resources . . . .　83
　B.　Confidence in the Market and Adverse
　　　Selection . . . .　84
　　　1. The Concept of Adverse Selection . . . .　84
　　　　a. Lower Quality Drives out Higher Quality . . .　84
　　　　b. Why There Are Undiscerned Differences in
　　　　　Quality . . . .　85
　　　2. Adverse Selection in the Securities Market . . . . .　85
　　　　a. Lower Quality Securities Tend to Drive out
　　　　　Higher Quality Securities . . . .　85
　　　　b. Why There Are Undiscerned Differences in
　　　　　the Quality of Securities . . . .　85
　　　3. Connection to Confidence in the Market . . . . . .　86
　　　4. Securities Regulation as a Response to Adverse
　　　　Selection . . . .　87

V.   Sources of Provincial Securities Regulation   87
     A.   Provincial Securities Acts   87
     B.   Provincial Regulations or Rules   88
     C.   Regulatory Bodies.   88
          1. Commissions and Administrators.   88
          2. Self-Regulatory Organizations   89
              a. Stock Exchanges   89
              b. Other Self-regulatory Organizations   90
              c. Securities Commission Review   91
     D.   Policy Statements   91
          1. National Policy Statements   91
          2. Uniform Policy Statements   92
          3. Local Policy Statements   92
          4. Securities Commission Jurisdiction to Make Rules,
              Issue Policy Statements and Blanket Orders, and
              Enter into Memoranda of Understanding   93
              a. Securities Commission Powers to Issue Policy
                  Statements and Blanket Orders, and Enter
                  into Memoranda of Understanding   93
              b. Commission Rule Making Power   94
              c. National Instruments   94
              d. Notice Requirements   95
              e. Policy Statements   96
              f. Blanket Orders   96
              g. Memoranda of Understanding   97
              h. Review of Legislation   97
     E.   Blanket Orders   97
     F.   Decisions and Rulings   98
     G.   Bulletins.   98
VI. The Scope of Securities Regulation in Canada and the
     Variation from Jurisdiction to Jurisdiction   98

CHAPTER 4:   THE PROSPECTUS REQUIREMENT

I.   Introduction   101
II. Overview of the Contents of a Prospectus   101
III. When a Prospectus is Required   105
IV. The Meaning of "Security"   106
     A.   The Definition of "Security" in the Act   106
          1. Common Types of Securities   107
          2. Less Common Securities   108

3. Catch-all Provisions   110
B. The Meaning of an "Investment Contract"   111
    1. *SEC v. C.M. Joiner Leasing Corporation*   112
    2. *SEC v. W.J. Howey Co.*   114
    3. *State of Hawaii v. Hawaii Market Center Inc.*   115
    4. *Pacifiic Coast Coin Exchange v. O.S.C.*   116
C. Summary   120
V.   The Meaning of "Trade"   121
A. Sale for Valuable Consideration   121
B. Trades on Behalf of Others   122
C. Pre-Sale Activities — Acts in Furtherance of a
    "Trade"   123
D. Open-ended Nature of the Definition   124
VI. The Meaning of "Distribution"   124
A. Trade in Securities not Previously Issued   124
B. Resale of Securities Returned to the Issuer   125
C. Sales by Control Persons   126
D. Deemed Distributions on Resale   127
VII. The Distribution Process   128
A. The "Waiting Period"   128
B. Vetting of the Preliminary Prospectus   128
C. Comment Letter and Clearance Period   130
D. Limitations on Selling Activities During the Waiting
    Period   130
E. Requirements on Distribution — Delivery of
    Prospectus and Cooling-Off Period   132
F. Amendment of Prospectus and Lapse of
    Prospectus   132
G. National Offerings   133
H. Canada-U.S. Multijurisdictional Offerings   134
I.   Blue-Sky (or "Merit") Discretion   134
VIII. Consequences of Failure to File or Deliver
Prospectus   137
A. Failure to Deliver a Prospectus   137
    1. Penal Sanction   137
    2. Administrative Sanctions   138
    3. Civil Sanctions   138
B. Failure to File the Prospectus   139
    1. Penal Sanction   139
    2. Administrative Sanctions   139

3. Civil Sanction 140
    a. Statutory Civil Sanction? 140
    b. Common Law Sanction 140

CHAPTER 5: STATUTORY LIABILITY AND DUE DILIGENCE

I.   Introduction 145
II.   The Common Law Position 145
       A.   Contractual Claims 145
       B.   Tort Claims 146
            1. Fraud 146
            2. Negligent Misstatement 147
III.   Statutory Civil Liability 149
       A.   Expansion on Common Law Liability 149
       B.   What the Plaintiff Must Show 150
       C.   Persons Liable 151
       D.   Defences 152
            1. Issuer's Defences 153
            2. Defences for Directors, Underwriters and Persons
               Signing the Prospectus 154
            3. Experts' Defences 155
            4. Damages 155
            5. Limitation Period and Common Law Rights 156
IV.   The Due Diligence Defence 156
       A.   Cases Considering the Due Diligence Defence 157
            1. *Escott v. BarChris* 157
               a. The Facts 157
               b. Expertised Portion is Not the Entire
                  Prospectus 158
               c. Liability of Directors and Officers 159
               d. Liability of the Underwriters 162
               e. Liability of the Auditors 162
            2. *Feit v. Leasco* 163
       B.   The Role of the Securities Lawyer 164
V.   Other Statutory Sanctions 167

CHAPTER 6:   CONTINUOUS DISCLOSURE

I.   Introduction 169
II.   Importance, Purpose and Competing Concerns........ 170
       A.   Increasing Emphasis on Secondary Market
            Disclosure 170
       B.   The Primary Purpose of Continuous Disclosure ... 170
       C.   Other Benefits of Continuous Disclosure 171
       D.   Competing Concerns 172
       E.   Summary..................................... 173
III.   Reporting Issuers 173
IV.   Financial Statements 175
       A.   Annual Financial Statements 175
       B.   Interim Financial Statements 176
       C.   Statements Prepared According to GAAP 176
       D.   Exemptions 177
            1   Deviation from GAAP 177
            2. Conflict with Laws of Another Jurisdiction 178
            3. Specific Omissions from Disclosure 178
            4. Consistency of Reporting 179
            5. General 179
V.   Proxy/Information Circulars 180
       A.   Proxy Solicitation Requirements 181
       B.   Information Required......................... 182
       C.   Exemptions 185
            1. Automatic Exemptions 185
                a. De Minimus 15 Shareholder Test.......... 185
                b. Compliance with Substantially Similar Laws
                    of Another Jurisdiction 185
                c. Registrants Forwarding Meeting Materials... 186
                d. Requests by Beneficial Owners of Execution
                    of Proxy by Registered Holders 186
            2. Discretionary Exemptions................... 187
                a. Conflict with Laws of Another
                    Jurisdiction 187
                b. Other Adequate Justification.............. 187
       D.   National Policy #41 189
VI.   Insider Reports 191

VII. Timely Disclosure — Reports on Material
      Information   192
      A.   Material Information Reporting Requirements   193
           1. Reporting of "Material Changes"   193
           2. Extension to "Material Facts"   194
           3. Determining What Must be Reported   197
      B.   Proposed Changes, Detrimental Information and
           Confidential Reporting   199
           1. Unduly Detrimental   200
           2. Proposed Changes   200
              a. Reasonably Probable Confirmation by the
                 Board of Directors   200
              b. Confidential Disclosure and Insider
                 Trading   201
      C.   The Process of Disclosure   202
VIII. Annual Information Forms and Management Discussion
      and Analysis   202
IX.   System For Electronic Document Analysis and Retrieval
      ("Sedar")   205
X.   Sanctions with Respect to Continuous Disclosure
      Requirements   208
      A.   Statutory Sanctions   208
      B.   Civil Liability   209
           1. No Statutory Civil Sanction   209
           2. Statutory Civil Liability Where Documents
              Incorporated by Reference in a Prospectus   211
           3. Civil Actions for Deceit or Negligent
              Misrepresentation and the "Fraud on the Market"
              Theory   211

**CHAPTER 7:   EXEMPTIONS FROM THE PROSPECTUS
              REQUIREMENT**

I.   Introduction   213
II.   The Closed System Concept   213
      A.   Weaknesses in the Preclosed System   214
           1. Uncertainty Associated with the Meaning of "to
              the public"   214
           2. Continuous Disclosure Requirements   216

B. The Closed System Response 217
    1. Response to Uncertainty and Gap in
        Regulation 217
    2. The Concept of the Closed System 217
        a. Trading Within the Closed Market 217
        b. Trading Outside the Closed Market 217
            (i) Prospectus Disclosure Followed by
                 Continuous Disclosure 217
            (ii) Resale Restrictions 219
C. Resale Restrictions 221
    1. Deemed Distribution 221
    2. The Conditions for Resale Without a Prospectus
        or Reliance on an Exemption 221
        a. Reporting Issuer Not in Default 221
        b. The Hold Period 223
        c. No Unusual Effort to Prepare the Market and
            No Extraordinary Commissions or
            Consideration 225
    3. Underlying Market Efficiency Concept 226
III. Exemptions and Their Underlying Principles 226
A. No Need to Know 227
    1. Sophisticated Investors 227
        a. Exempt Institutions 227
        b. Exempt Purchasers 229
        c. Large Purchases 229
        d. Registered Dealers 231
        e. Sale to Underwriters 231
        f. Consideration to Dealers or Underwriters . . . 232
        g. Other Sophisticated Investors 233
    2. Common Bonds 235
        a. Incorporators and Promoters 235
        b. Control Persons 237
        c. Purchase or Redemption 238
        d. Friends and Relatives 239
    3. No New Information 240
        a. Stock Dividend 241
        b. Dividends or Interest Used to Purchase
            Publicly Traded Securities 242
        c. Rights Offering 243

        d. Exercise of Conversion, Exchange or Purchase
           Rights 244
     4. Information Provided by Documents Other Than
       a Prospectus............................ 245
        a. Amalgamations and Reorganizations 245
        b. Takeover Bids......................... 246
        c. Stock Exchange Exemption 246
  B. Facilitate Financing by Smaller Issuers 247
     1. Private Issuers 247
     2. Small Number of Friends, Relatives and
       Sophisticated Investors 248
     3. Regulatory Barriers to Small Firm Finance and
       Suggested Reforms 248
  C. Regulated Under Another Regulatory Scheme 250
  D. Safe Investments 251
  E. Promotion of Specific Investments and Social
    Activities 253
     1. Educational, Charitable, Religious or Recreational
       Purposes................................ 253
     2. Prospecting Expeditions and Prospecting
       Syndicates 254
     3. Exchange Issuer Exemptions — B.C. 255
  F. Protection Provided by Active Markets: Prompt
    Offering Prospectuses, Shelf Offering Prospectuses
    and "Prep" Procedures 256
  G. Other Exemptions............................ 257
     1. Exemption Orders 257
     2. Blanket Orders 258

**CHAPTER 8: PROMPT OFFERINGS, SHELF OFFERINGS
           AND PREP PROCEDURES**

I. Introduction 259
II. The Prompt Offering Prospectus.................... 259
  A. The Problem to Which the POP System
    Responded................................. 259
  B. How the POP System Works 260
     1. The Annual Information Form ("AIF") 261
       a. The Initial AIF 261
       b. Subsequent AIFs 263
     2. Short-Form Prospectus 263

C. The Eligibility Criteria 264
  1. The General Criteria 265
    a. The Criteria 265
    b. The Reasons For the Criteria 266
  2. Alternative Criteria for Certain Issues of Debt or
    Preferred Shares 267
    a. The Criteria 267
      (i) Non-Convertible Debt or Non-Convertible
      Preferred Shares 267
      (ii) Guaranteed Non-Convertible Debt or
      Non-Convertible Preferred Shares 268
      (iii) Debt or Preferred Shares Convertible into
      Eligible Securities 270
  3. Alternative Criteria for "Substantial" Canadian
    Issuers 272
D. Implementation of the POP System 272
E. Exemptions for the POP Eligibility Criteria 272
III. The Shelf Offering Prospectus 274
A. The Problem to Which Shelf Offerings
  Responded 274
B. Description of the Shelf Offering Procedure 275
  1. A Brief Synopsis 275
  2. Eligibility 276
  3. Restrictions 276
  4. Disclosure 277
    a. The Annual Information Form 277
    b. The Short-form Shelf Prospectus 277
    c. Prospectus Supplements 279
  5. Variable Term Debt Securities 280
  6. Non-Fixed Price Offerings 280
  7. Civil Liability 282
IV. Prep Procedures 283
A. General Description 283
B. Eligibility 284
V. Assumptions and Concerns with the Pop System, Shelf
  Offerings and Prep Procedures 285
A. The Principle Behind the POP System 285

    B. Concerns with the POP System, Shelf Offerings and
        PREP Procedures 287
        1. Due Diligence and Statutory Civil Liability for
           Continuous Disclosure 288
        2. Favours Larger Issuers 288
        3. Favours Larger Underwriters 289
VI. The Multijurisdictional Disclosure System 289
    A. Reasons for the Multijurisdictional Disclosure
        System 289
    B. Permitted Offerings Using U.S. Documentation 290
    C. The Mechanics of an MJDS Offering 291
    D. Additional Canadian Disclosure 293

CHAPTER 9: MANDATORY DISCLOSURE AND MERIT DISCRETION: A RECONSIDERATION

I.   Introduction 295
II.   Some Evidence on the Effects of Mandatory
    Disclosure 295
    A. New Issue (or Prospectus) Disclosure 296
        1. Stigler 296
           a. Analysis of Price Effects 296
              (i) Method for Analysis of Price Effects 296
              (ii) Results on Price Effects 297
           b. The Analysis of the Effect on Risk 297
              (i) Method of Analysis of Effect on Risk ... 297
              (ii) Results of Analysis of Effect on Risk 297
        2. Jarrell 298
           a. Method 298
           b. Effects on Price 298
           c. Effects on Risk 298
        3. Simon 299
           a. Method 299
           b. Effects on Price 299
           c. Effects on Risk 300
    B. Secondary Market Disclosure — Financial
        Statements 300
    C. Comments on the Studies and Further Evidence... 301

III.   Some Critiques of Securities Regulation 303
     A.   Change in Emphasis 303
         1.   Focus on the Secondary Market and Sophisticated
            Investors 303
         2.   Future-Oriented and Market Disclosure 304
         3.   Change of Emphasis re Liability and
            Enforcement 305
         4.   Agency Cost Emphasis Not Accuracy
            Enhancement 306
         5.   Permitting Silence and Lying 307
     B.   No Need for Mandatory Disclosure 308
         1.   Adverse Selection Problem Can be Addressed by
            the Market 308
            a.   Independent Reviews of Issuer
                Representations 309
            b.   Purchase of Shares by Management 309
            c.   Taking on Debt 309
            d.   High Payout Policy 310
         2.   Issuers Will Have an Incentive to Make the
            Appropriate Level of Disclosure 310
         3.   Market Failures as a Justification for Mandatory
            Disclosure 311
            a.   The Market Failure Arguments 311
                (i)   Too Little Information 311
                (ii)   Investors Overinvest in Production of
                    Information 312
            b.   Responses to the Market Failure
                Arguments 313
            c.   Social Gains From Reducing Security Price
                Inaccuracies 314
            d.   Standardization of Information
                Presentation 316
     C.   Interest Group Theories 317
         1.   Possible Interest Group Influences 317
         2.   Interests Within Securities Regulatory
            Organizations 318
         3.   Use of Rhetorical Conventions 320
     D.   Further Research 320

IV.   Merit Discretion 321
      A.   Critique of Merit Discretion 321
      B.   An Interest Group Theory of Merit Discretion 322

CHAPTER 10:   INSIDER TRADING

I.   Introduction 323
II.   The Perceived Problem and the Approach of Canadian
      Securities Acts 323
III. Canadian Securities Acts and the Regulation of Insider
      Trading 325
      A.   What, When, Who and How? 325
           1. What is Prohibited? 325
           2. When is it Prohibited? 325
           3. Who is Prohibited? 325
           4. How the Prohibition is Enforced 328
               a. Penal Sanctions 329
               b. Civil Actions 333
               c. Actions by or on Behalf of the Reporting
                   Issuer 335
               d. Administrative Sanctions 337
                   (i)   Cease Trade Orders 337
                   (ii) Removal of Exemptions 337
                   (iii) Prohibition from Acting as a Director or
                         Officer 337
                   (iv) Administrative Penalty 338
               e. Insider Reporting 338
IV.   Enforcement Problems 338
      A.   Detection Problems 339
      B.   Enforcement Problems 340
           1. Circumstantial Evidence 341
           2. Penal Sanctions, the Burden of Proof and
               Compellability 342
           3. Civil Action for Damages 342
           4. Civil Action for Accounting 343
           5. Administrative Sanctions 343
      C.   Summary 344
V.   A Reconsideration of the Policy Regarding Insider
      Trading 344

A.   Do Investors Lose as a Consequence of Insider
    Trading? 345
    1. "Market Orders" 346
    2. "Limit Orders" 347
    3. Persons Trading in the Opposite Direction 347
B.   Is Insider Trading Detrimental or Beneficial? 348
    1. Superior Compensation 349
      a. Manne's Argument 349
      b. Responses to Manne and Replies 349
        (i) Windfalls 349
        (ii) Perverse Performance Incentives 350
        (iii) Hoarding 351
        (iv) Moral Hazard 351
        (v) Adverse Selection 352
    2. More Efficient Pricing 353
      a. The Argument 353
      b. Responses 354
      c. The Implications of Pre-regulation
        Non-prohibition 355
        (i) The Argument 355
        (ii) Responses and Replies 355
C.   An Interest Group Explanation of the Prohibition of
    Insider Trading 358
D.   Summary 359

**CHAPTER 11: TAKEOVER BID AND ISSUER BID
               REGULATION**

I.   Introduction 361
II.   Takeover Bid Regulation 361
  A.   Background 362
    1. What is a Takeover? 362
      a. Methods of Effecting a Takeover 362
      b. Friendly and Hostile Takeovers 362
        (i) Friendly 362
        (ii) Hostile 363
    2. What is a "Takeover Bid" (or "Tender
      Offer")? 363
  B.   Motivations for Takeovers 364
    1. Inefficient Management 364
    2. Synergy 364

3. Market Power 364
4. Tax Considerations 364
5. Undervaluation 365
6. Empire Building/Managerialism 365
7. Looting 365
8. Hubris 366
C. Reasons for Takeover Bid Regulation 366
1. Insufficient Information/Gap in Disclosure
Requirements 367
2. Insufficient Time to Respond 367
3. "First-Come First-Served" Offers Put Undue
Pressure on Shareholders to Tender Early 367
4. Lock-Up of Tendered Shares 368
5. Unequal Consideration 368
6. Looting 369
7. Other Concerns 369
D. An Outline of Takeover Bid Regulation 370
1. The Basic Rules 370
a. Provides Information — Disclosure
Requirements 370
b. Time to Assess the Information — Minimum
Bid Period 373
c. First-come First-served Offers Not Allowed —
Pro Rata Take-up 373
d. Lock-up Prevented — Withdrawal Rights ... 374
e. Unequal Consideration is Not Allowed 374
f. Looting — Formal Valuation
Requirements 375
(i) Corporate Law Constraints 375
(ii) Formal Valuations 375
(iii) Ontario Policy 9.1 377
g. Other Concerns Dealt With 379
2. When the Rules Apply 380
a. The Definition of "Takeover Bid" 380
b. Exceptions to the Application of the Takeover
Bid Rules 381
(i) Stock Exchange Bids 381
(ii) "Normal Course" Purchases 382
(iii) Control Block Purchase 383
(iv) Closely-Held Company Exemption 384

  (v) Limited Relevance to Jurisdiction 385
  (vi) Exemption Applications 386
 3. Anti-Avoidance Provisions 386
  a. Acting Jointly or in Concert 386
  b. Rights to Acquire Securities in the Future ... 387
  c. Direct or Indirect Offers 388
  d. Linked Bids 389
 4. "Early Warning" Disclosure 389
 5. Applications to a Securities Commission or
  Court 390
E. Takeover Bid Defences and Takeover Bid
 Regulation 391
 1. Some Typical Defences 391
 2. Validity of Takeover Bid Defences 393
  a. The "Proper Purpose" Test 393
  b. The "Best Interests" Test 394
 3. Reasonable in Relation to the Threat Posed and
  Shareholder Approval 395
 4. National Policy No. 62-202 396
 5. Securities Commission Response to Poison
  Pills 398
F. The Takeover Bid Regulation Policy Debate 399
 1. The Argument Against Takeover Bid
  Legislation 400
 2. Counterarguments by Proponents of Takeover
  Bid Regulation 403
  a. Non-socially Beneficial Takeovers 403
   (i) Undervaluations 404
   (ii) Reduced Competition 405
   (iii) Empire Building or Managerialism 406
   (iv) Hubris 407
   (v) Expropriation Theories 407
  b. Social Efficiency Benefits of Competitive
   Bidding 410
 3. Some Alternative Approaches to Takeover Bid
  Regulation 411
  a. The "Undistorted Choice" or "Sole
   Shareholder" Approach 411
  b. A Corporate Charter Approach 412
  c. Other Alternatives 415

III. Issuer Bid Regulation 415
      A. Reasons for Issuer Bid Regulation 415
      B. The Basic Rules 416
      C. Exemptions from Issuer Bid Requirements 418
          1. Pre-Arranged Acquisitions 419
          2. Security Holder Controlled Acquisition 419
          3. Employee Security Ownership 419
          4. Private Companies 420
          5. De Minimis Exemption 420
          6. Stock Exchange Issuer Bids 421
          7. Normal Course Purchases 421
          8. Exemption Order 421

CHAPTER 12: SECURITIES INDUSTRY REGULATION

I.   Introduction 423
II.   Securities Industry Participants 423
      A. Underwriters 424
      B. Brokers and Dealers 424
      C. Advisors 425
          1. Investment Counselling 425
          2. Market Commentaries 426
          3. Portfolio Management 426
      D. Securities Firms 426
III. Problems in Securities Industry Activities 426
      A. Financial Responsibility and the Risk of Securities
          Firm Business Failures 427
      B. Honesty 428
          1. Conflicts of Interest 428
              a. Churning 428
              b. Front Running 429
              c. Use of Inside Information 429
              d. Related Party Transactions and Other
                  Conflicts of Interest 430
          2. Market Manipulation 430
              a. Wash Sales 431
              b. Scalping 431
          3. Pressure Selling 431
      C. Professional Competence 432

IV. An Outline of Securities Industry Regulations 432
  A. Registration 432
    1. Who Must Register 432
    2. Subcategories of Registrants 433
    3. Application for Registration and the Discretion
       of the Administrator 435
    4. Renewals of Registration 436
    5. Continued Fitness for Registration 436
    6. Surrender of Registration 437
    7. Exemptions from the Registration
       Requirement 437
      a. Isolated Trades by Persons Who Are Not in
         the Securities Business 438
         (i) Executors, Administrators, Trustees,
            etc. 438
         (ii) Bank Realizations 439
         (iii) Trades Under Prospectus Exemptions . . . 439
         (iv) Exempt Advisors 440
         (v) Trades by Individual Investors 441
         (vi) Other Isolated Trades 441
      b. Regulated Under a Separate Regulatory
         Scheme 441
      c. Sophisticated/Common Bond Customer
         Exemptions 442
      d. Safe Security 443
    8. A Cautionary Note 444
  B. Response to Concerns Regarding Securities Market
    Actors 444
    1. Financial Responsibility/Business Failure 444
      a. Minimum Net Free Capital 445
      b. Bond 445
      c. Compensation Fund 445
      d. Know Your Client 445
      e. Competence 446
    2. Honesty and Integrity 446
      a. Conflicts of Interest 446
         (i) Churning 446
         (ii) Front Running 447
         (iii) Inside Information 447

         (iv) Related Party Transactions and Other
              Conflicts of Interest 447
       b. Market Manipulation 451
         (i) Wash Sales 451
         (ii) Scalping 451
       c. Pressure Selling 451
    3. Professional Competence 453
  C. Enforcement 454
    1. Penal Sanctions 454
    2. Administrative Sanctions 454
    3. Civil Actions............................. 454

CHAPTER 13:   MUTUAL FUNDS

I.   Introduction 457
II.   Background on Mutual Funds....................... 457
  A. Open-End (or Mutual) Funds and Closed-End Funds
    Distinguished 457
  B. Mutual Fund Organization 458
    1. The Manager 459
    2. Distribution 459
    3. Custodian................................ 459
  C. Types and Advantages of Mutual Funds.......... 460
    1. Types of Mutual Funds 460
      a. Income Funds 460
      b. Mortgage Funds 460
      c. Bond Funds 460
      d. Dividend Funds 461
      e. Growth Funds 461
      f. Balanced Funds 461
      g. Asset Allocation Funds 461
      h. Money Market Funds 461
      i. Specialty Funds 461
      j. International Funds 462
      k. Real Estate Funds 462
      l. Ethical Funds 462
    2. Advantages of Mutual Funds 462
  D. Purchases and Redemptions 463
    1. Methods of Buying Mutual Fund Securities 463
      a. Lump Sum 463
      b. Purchase Plans 463

         c. Dividend Reinvestment 463
        2. Sales Charges 463
    E. Mutual Fund Fees 464
        1. Trailer / Service Fees 464
        2. Management Fees 465
        3. Other Expenses 465
III. The Distribution of Mutual Fund Securities 465
    A. The Mutual Fund Prospectus 466
        1. Prospectus or Simplified Prospectus Option 466
        2. The Simplified Prospectus 467
        3. The Annual Information Form 469
        4. Pro-forma Simplified Prospectus and Pro-forma
           Annual Information Form 470
IV. Investment Requirements, Restrictions and Practices . . . 471
    A. Initial Investment in a New Mutual Fund 471
    B. Investment Restrictions 471
        1. Conflict of Interest Restrictions 471
        2. Investment Restrictions 474
        3. Investment in Mortgages and Hypothecs 476
    C. Disclosure of Investment Practices 477
V.   Approval of Changes 477
    A. Approval by Securities Administrators 477
    B. Approval by Securities Holders 478
VI. Contractual Plans 479
VII. Sale and Redemption 480
VIII. Management Fees 483
IX. Custodianship 484
X.   Advertising 485
XI. Insider Trading 485
XII. Private Mutual Funds 486
XIII. Mutual Fund Sales Practices 487
    A. Background 487
    B. Mutual Fund Sales Practice Concerns 487
        1. Trailer Fees 487
        2. Reciprocal Commissions 488
        3. Marketing Incentive Programs 489
        4. Trailer Fee Split Payments 489
        5. Trips and Other Non-Cash Sales Incentives 489
        6. Cooperative Advertising 490
        7. Bonus Commissions 490

8. Reimbursement of Expenses 490
C. Response to Mutual Fund Sales Practice
   Concerns 490
   1. The Broad Prohibition of Certain Sales
      Practices 491
   2. Permitted Sales Practices 492
      a. Commissions 492
      b. Trailer Fees........................... 493
      c. Cooperative Marketing Practices 493
      d. Mutual Fund Conferences or Seminars 494
      e. Payments of Representative Conference,
         Seminar or Course Registration Fees 495
      f. Non-monetary Benefits 495
      g. Reciprocal Commissions 496
      h. Other Sales Practices 497
   3. Prospectus and Point of Sale Disclosure 497

CHAPTER 14:   ENFORCEMENT MECHANISMS

I.   Introduction 499
II.   Sanctions 499
      A. Securities Acts............................. 499
          1. Penal Sanctions 499
             a. Offences 499
                (i) False Statement to Administrators,
                    Investigators or Auditors 499
                (ii) Failure to File 500
                (iii) Misrepresentation 500
                (iv) Contravention of Act or Regulations 500
                (v) Failure to Comply with a Decision Made
                    Under the Act 501
                (vi) Insider Trading or Informing 501
             b. Sanctions 501
             c. Due Diligence Defences 502
             d. Application to Officers, Directors and
                Others................................ 502
             e. Limitation Periods 503
             f. Costs of Investigation................... 503
          2. Administrative Sanctions 503
             a. Types of Orders 503
                (i) Compliance 503

         (ii) Cease Trade 504
        (iii) Denial of Exemptions 504
        (iv) Resignation or Prohibition from Acting as
            a Director or Officer 504
        (v) Prohibition of or Required Dissemination
           of Information 504
        (vi) Reprimand of Registrant or Suspension,
           Cancellation or Restriction of
           Registration 505
      b. Procedure 505
      c. Administrative Penalty 505
      d. The Scope of the Administrative Powers 506
    3. Civil Sanctions 508
  B. Common Law Civil Actions 508
III. Review and Appeal Procedures 508
  A. Review of Decisions by Securities Commissions ... 508
  B. Appeal of Decisions of Administrators 510
IV. Investigations and Audits........................ 511
V. Orders to Freeze Property 512
VI. Charter Issues 512

BIBLIOGRAPHY 515

INDEX 535

LIST OF ABBREVIATIONS

A.B.C.A.	Alberta *Business Corporations Act*, S.A. 1981, c. B-15 as amended.
A. Pol.	Policy Statements of the Alberta Securities Commission
A. Regs.	Regulations passed under the Alberta *Securities Act*
A.S.A.	Alberta *Securities Act*, S.A. 1981, c. S-6.1; as amended by 1981, c. B-15; 1982, c. 32; 1984, c. 64; 1985, c. R-21; 1988, c. P-4.05; 1989, c. 15; 1989, c. 17; 1989 c. 19; 1989, c. 31.1; 1991, c. 33; 1991, c. 33, c. L-26.5; 1992, c. 21; 1994, c. 23, c. C-10.5, c. G-8.5; 1995, c. 28, c. R-4.5; 1996, c. 28
B.C.C.A.	British Columbla *Company Act*, R.S.B.C. 1996, c. 62 as amended by 1997, c. 29
B.C. Pol.	Local Policy Statements of the British Columbia Securities Commission
B.C. Regs.	Regulations passed under the British Columbia *Securities Act*
B.C.S.A.	British Columbia *Securities Act*, R.S.B.C. 1996, c. 418, as amened by 1998, c. 7
C.B.C.A.	*Canada Business Corporations Act*, R.S.C. 1985, c. C-44, as amended
C.P.	Companion Policy — companion policies to national instruments adopted by the Canadian Securities Administrators
M. Regs.	Regulations passed under *The Securities Act*, Manitoba
M.S.A.	Manitoba, *The Securities Act*, R.S.M. 1988, c. S50, as amended by 1989-90, c. 54; 1991-92, c. 22; 1992, c. 35, c. 58; 1993, c. 4, c. 14, c. 29, c. 48; 1996, c. 50, c. 59, c. 73; 1997, c. 50

N.B. Regs.	Regulations passed under the New Brunswick *Security Frauds Prevention Act*
N.B.S.F.P.A.	New Brunswick *Security Frauds Prevention Act*, R.S.N.B. 1973, c. S-6; as amended by 1978, c. D-11.2; 1979, c. 41; 1980, c. 32; 1982, c. 3; 1983, c. 8; 1985, c. 4; 1985, c. 24; 1985, c. M-14.1; 1986, c. 4; 1986, c. 6; 1986, c. 8; 1987, c. 6; 1987, c. L-11.2; 1989, c. 21, c. 37; 1991, c. 27; 1992, c. 15; 1997, c. 26
Nfld. Regs.	Regulations passed under *The Securities Act*, Newfoundland
Nfld.S.A.	Newfoundland, *The Securities Act*, R.S.N. 1990, c. S-13, as amended by 1992, c. 39, c. 48; 1996, c. R-10.1
N.I.	National Instrument adopted by the Canadian Securities Administrators
N.P.	National Policy Statements adopted by the Canadian Securities Administrators
N.S. Pol.	Policy Statements of the Nova Scotia Securities Commission
N.S. Regs.	Regulations passed under the Nova Scotia *Securities Act*
N.S.S.A.	Nova Scotia *Securities Act*, R.S.N.S. 1989, c. 418, as amended by 1990, c. 15; 1996, c. 32
N.W.T. Regs.	Regulations passed under the Northwest Territories *Securities Act*
N.W.T.S.A.	Northwest Territories *Securities Act*, R.S.N.W.T. 1988, c. S-5, as amended by R.S.N.W.T. 1988, (Supp.), c. 8; 1994, c. 8
O.B.C.A.	Ontario *Business Corporations Act*, R.S.O. 1990, c. B.16, as amended
O. Pol.	Policy Statements of the Ontario Securities Commission
O. Regs.	Regulations passed under the Ontario *Securities Act*
O.S.A.	Ontario Securities Act, R.S.O. 1990, c. S.5, as amended by 1992, c. 18; 1993, c. 27; 1994, c. 11, c. 33; 1997, c. 10
P.E.I. Regs.	Regulations passed under the Prince Edward Island *Securities Act*
P.E.I.S.A.	Prince Edward Island *Securities Act*, R.S.P.E.I. 1988,

	c. S-3, as amended by 1985, c. 40; 1990, c. 59; 1994, c. 57; 1997, c. 58, c. 47
Q. Pol.	Policy Statements of the Quebec Securities Commission (Commission des Valeurs Mobilières du Québec)
Q. Regs.	Regulations passed under the Quebec *Securities Act*
Q.S.A.	Quebec Securities Act, R.S.Q. 1990, c. V-1.1, as amended by 1990, c. 77; 1992, c. 21, c. 35, c. 57, c. 61; 1993, c. 67; 1994, c. 13, c. 23; 1995, c. 33; 1996, c. 2; 1997, c. 36
S. Pol.	Policy Statements of the Saskatchewan Securities Commission
S. Regs.	Regulations passed under *The Securities Act*, Saskatchewan
S.S.A.	Saskatchewan The Securities Act, S.S.1988, c. S-42.2, as amended by 1989, c. 15; 1995, c. 32
U. Pol.	Uniform Act Policy Statements
Y. Regs.	Regulations passed under the Yukon *Securities Act*
Y.S.A.	Yukon Securities Act, R.S.Y. 1986, c. 158

Chapter 1

Background on Securities Markets

I. INTRODUCTION

The purpose of this introductory chapter is to provide a brief overview of common types of securities and the institutional framework within which they are sold. The subject matter of this chapter is the primary object of securities regulation and is thus fundamental to developing an appreciation of securities regulation.

Part II of this chapter begins by demonstrating the purpose of the sale of securities by way of a simple example. Part III introduces some of the more common types of securities and the kinds of rights commonly associated with those securities. Part IV discusses common methods through which securities are typically distributed to investors and Part V provides an introduction to how securities which have been distributed are traded amongst investors.

The subject matter covered in this chapter may already be familiar to you from a course of study or involvement in the securities market. If so, you may wish to proceed to Chapter 2.

The material in this chapter, and the book in general, does assume a basic knowledge of the workings of forms of business organization such as companies[1] and partnerships.

II. THE PURPOSE FOR WHICH SECURITIES ARE SOLD

Securities are sold primarily to raise funds for investment. In commercial activities, securities are sold to raise funds to purchase assets that will be used to produce goods or services for which there is a perceived demand sufficient to generate a level of profits compa-

---

[1] The term "company" is the British term for its American equivalent, the "corporation". The terms are used interchangeably throughout the text.

rable to that of other investment opportunities of similar risk. A person, or group of persons, may seek to start a new venture, or an established entity may either embark on a new venture or expand an existing venture. Securities will often be sold to raise the funds required for such ventures.

For example, suppose a group of individuals perceives an increased market demand for glass bottles in Canada. They decide to establish a new glass bottle production facility. This will require a building, the land on which the building will be situated, a variety of equipment, not the least of which will be a furnace to heat the materials for the production of the glass, office equipment, and so on. They decide to purchase the land, building and equipment. An inventory of supplies will be maintained. Some readily available funds, perhaps in the form of bank deposits or other assets readily convertible into cash (such as marketable securities), will be required to meet various regularly occurring expenditures such as the payroll and the purchase of supplies and materials for the production of glass bottles. It is also anticipated that some of the customers who buy the glass bottles will be permitted to buy on credit, thereby creating an asset, called accounts receivable, which will consist of claims for payment from these customers.

The various assets required to carry on the operation will have to be spelled out in some detail. However, the required assets might be summarized roughly as follows:

Cash	$ 750,000
Accounts Receivable	1,750,000
Inventories	4,000,000
Property, Plant, Equipment	21,000,000
Total Assets	$27,500,000

Funds will be required to finance the purchase of the land, building and equipment and the investment in inventory, accounts receivable and cash. The individuals who wish to engage in this venture do not themselves have sufficient funds to purchase these assets. Instead, the funds come from a variety of sources.

Some funds will be borrowed and will offer the lenders fixed periodic payments ("interest") on the amounts loaned and a promise to pay back the amount loaned within a specified period of time. This source of funds is typically referred to as "debt finance". Some funds will be raised by selling rights to share in (a) the distribution of profits remaining after the fixed payments on borrowed funds are made, and (b) the proceeds remaining after a sale of the assets of the business and repayment of amounts borrowed. This source of funds is typically referred to as "equity finance". The sources of funds for the glass bottle production operation might look something like the following:

Debts:

Accounts Payable	$ 1,700,000
Short-Term Loan	800,000
Long-Term Loan	1,000,000
Debentures	12,000.000

Equity:

Class A Shares ("common shares")	6,000,000
Class B Shares ("preferred shares")	6,000,000
Total Debt and Equity	$27,500,000

Part III briefly considers these sources of finance.

III. COMMON TYPES OF SECURITIES[2]

Equity obligations and many types of debt obligations sold to investors to raise funds for business activities, such as in the glass bottle example, are commonly referred to as securities. An issuer of securities can undertake any of a wide range of obligations, thereby creating a virtually infinite variety of securities.

Securities regulation is directed at a wide range of securities. Some of the more common types of debt and equity securities are discussed below.

A. Debt Finance

There are several sources of debt finance (or borrowing). The common methods of borrowing include trade credit, bank loans and

---

[2] The material in this section is based on, for example, *The Canadian Securities Course*, (Toronto: The Canadian Securities Institute, 1995), vol. 2, Chapters 5, 6, 7 and 8; J.C. Francis & E. Kirzner, *Investments: Analysis and Management*, 3rd ed., (Toronto: McGraw Hill Ryerson, 1988), Chapter 2; R. Brealey & S. Myers, *Principles of Corporate Finance*, (New York: McGraw-Hill, 1981), at 276-81; W.A. Klien & J.C. Coffee, Jr., *Business Organization and Finance: Legal and Economic Principles*, (Westbury, N.Y., The Foundation Press, 1996), Chapter 4.

the sale of bonds or debentures. Trade credit is not commonly described as a security. It is briefly discussed below for a more complete picture of the sources of funds used to finance business activities.

1. *Trade Credit*

The business, when in operation, obtains supplies from various sources and often buys on credit. It thus obtains the assets without paying for them for a period of time, maintaining a float of items bought on credit. In the glass bottle example above this item appears as "accounts payable".

2. *Bank Loan*

a. SHORT-TERM

To finance short-term fluctuations in cash flows,[3] funds are often obtained in the form of a short-term bank loan. Such short-term bank loans are often set up on a "revolving line of credit". A revolving line of credit allows the amount of the loan to fluctuate up and down as need requires with a limit on the maximum amount of the loan.

b. LONG-TERM

Other assets may be financed by longer-term bank loans. These bank loans will usually be given on terms which provide the bank with some protection against loss. Usually the bank will take a security interest in certain assets of the borrower, so that it can seize the assets in the event of bankruptcy or in the event that bankruptcy is imminent. There is often a set of events of default, which may include not only non-payment of the loan, but also a set of ratio tests based on the borrower's financial statements. The ratio tests (such as the ratio of short-term assets to short-term liabilities or the

---

[3] Cash (or other forms of payment readily converted to cash) is received (or "flows" in) primarily when amounts due to the business from the sales of goods or services are paid. Cash is expended (or "flows" out) to pay for goods sold and to pay expenses. Inflows and outflows of cash do not always match. There will often be times in a business when there are expenses that have to be paid before there is any cash inflow from the sales of goods or services. Funds will be required to pay these expenses.

ratio of total assets to total liabilities) attempt to identify situations in which there is a risk of bankruptcy. If the borrower fails to make a payment when it comes due, or if ratio tests are not met, the borrower will be in default on the loan and the bank will be entitled to certain rights, which will typically include a right to have the whole amount of the loan become due immediately and to seize the security taken under the loan agreement.

3. *Commercial Paper*

Short-term funding is often raised through the sale of commercial paper. Commercial paper carries an obligation on the part of the issuer to pay a specified amount (sometimes called the "face value") on a specified date (or "maturity date"). It may be purchased by various investors. Thus it is similar to getting a short-term loan from a bank, but the lenders are the various purchasers of the commercial paper.

Commercial paper may pay interest at a specified rate on the face value or it may be sold at a discount. The discounted price is less than the face value so that the investor's return (equivalent to interest) is the difference between the face value and the discounted price. The term to maturity varies from as little as a few days to as much as a year.

4. *Bonds/Debentures*

The individuals in the glass bottle example might also decide to borrow funds by selling bonds or debentures. A bond or debenture is simply an evidence of indebtedness; however, a distinction is occasionally made between the two terms. Bonds are said to be evidences of indebtedness which are secured by taking a security interest on one or more assets of the borrower, which may include assets that are subsequently acquired. Debentures, on the other hand, are often said to be evidences of unsecured indebtedness.

Bonds or debentures generally show a "face amount", which will be due to be paid at some future date (known as the "maturity date"), and will pay interest at regular intervals at a specified rate. For example, it might be a bond or debenture promising to pay $1,000 (the "face amount" or "par value") on a date ten years from now (the "maturity date") and paying interest at the end of each year until maturity at the rate of 10% (or $100 per year).

To encourage the sale of the issue, investors are often provided with some protection against loss. There is usually a document called a bond indenture which provides rights to the bond holders, which are similar to the rights a bank may retain under a loan agreement. Security may be taken and there will be a set of events of default. The events of default will generally be similar in character to those in a bank loan agreement.

Usually a trustee will be appointed to enforce the terms of the bond indenture. This is done because it would not be worthwhile for any individual bond holder to constantly monitor compliance with the terms of the indenture or enforce the terms in the event of a default.

Bonds or debentures, which represent contractual obligations, may carry a virtually infinite variety of special terms or features.

a. CALL

Bonds or debentures will often have a call feature which allows the borrower to repurchase the bond after a specified date for a specified price (usually at a premium to the face amount or par value). This allows the borrower to do a refinancing if interest rates fall and the borrower can raise the same amount of funds, but pay a lower rate of interest.

b. SINKING FUND

The indenture may provide for a fund to be built up each year to redeem some portion of the bonds before maturity or to meet the obligations to pay at maturity.

c. CONVERTIBLE

To improve the marketability of the bonds, or reduce the rate of interest at which the bonds are issued, the borrower may provide a right to convert the bonds into shares of the borrower. For instance, the bonds might provide that the holder is entitled to surrender a $1,000 face value bond to the company for 50 shares of the company. If the bonds have a market value of $1,000, this will mean that exercising the conversion right will be equivalent to paying $20 per share. This will be worthwhile if the shares have a market value substantially in excess of $20 per share. The conversion feature itself will have some value even if the shares have a market value of less than $20 per share at the time the bonds are issued. As long as there is some chance that the market value of the shares will increase to something in excess of $20 per share, the conversion feature will have some value.

d. WARRANTS

A warrant is another feature that is sometimes provided to improve the marketability of bonds or reduce the rate of interest at which the bonds must be issued. Warrants are sometimes issued in conjunction with a sale of common shares or preferred shares.

A warrant provides a right to buy securities (usually shares) from the issuer of the warrant for a specified price (called the "exercise price" or "striking price") during a specified period of time. For instance, a warrant may provide the holder of the warrant the right to buy one share of the company for $20 after August 31 and before the following April 30. If the shares are trading in the market for $25 per share, it will be advantageous to hold the warrant since it will allow one to buy a share trading for $25 at a cost of just $20. Even if the shares are trading at less than $20 per share, the warrant will have some value as long as there is a chance that the shares will trade at more than $20 per share before the last day on which the right provided by the warrant can be exercised.

B. Equity Finance

As noted above, equity securities grant rights to share in (a) the distribution of profits net of interest payments on debt and (b) the proceeds of a sale of the assets of the business net of payment of debts. The most commonly traded equity securities are shares in companies.

1. *Share Capital*

The persons in the glass bottle production example might decide to incorporate a company — GlassPro Ltd. Companies obtain equity finance through the sales of "shares". Shares usually entitle the owners of the shares to share in the distribution of profits of the company, net of interest payments on borrowed funds. These distributions of profits are referred to as "dividends". Shares also usually entitle the owner of the shares to a share in the proceeds, net of the payment of debts, on a sale of the assets of the company when the company is being wound up or dissolved.

Shares can be issued in classes. Each class of shares provides a bundle of rights to the holder of shares of that class. There can be a virtually infinite range of bundles of rights that might be provided by a class of shares. However, there are some bundles of rights that are more frequently used, the most common of which are discussed below.

2. *Common Shares*

The most frequently used bundles of share rights are typically referred to as "common shares". Common shares carry three essential rights: (i) the right to vote at shareholder meetings, (ii) the right to share in any dividends available for distribution on the common shares, and (iii) the right to share in a distribution of the proceeds from a liquidation of the company's assets on dissolution.

a. THE RIGHT TO VOTE

Common shares carry a right to vote at company meetings. This right to vote will include voting on such matters as the election of directors and major corporate decisions such as amalgamations, the sale or lease of substantially all the assets of the corporation or the creation of a new class of shares. The right to vote on the election of directors can be very important, since directors have the power to determine who will manage the company and how the company will be managed.

b. THE RIGHT TO DIVIDENDS

There is generally no obligation on the corporation to pay dividends. Dividends are paid when the directors of the corporation declare them. When dividends are declared, each common share carries a right to share pro rata with all the other common shares in any dividends available for distribution on the common shares.

When dividends are declared, there will not always be dividends available for distribution on the common shares since, as discussed below, there may be prior (or "preferred") claims on the dividends.

Dividends are usually paid in cash. However, occasionally dividends may be paid in the form of more shares of the company. This is called a "stock dividend". For instance, the company may have 1,000,000 common shares outstanding with a total market value of $10,000,000 or $10 per share. The company might declare a stock dividend of one new common share for every ten common shares held. There would then be 1,100,000 common shares outstanding. Of course nothing has happened to the assets of the company. They remain the same and should be expected to have the same value. Thus the total market value of the now 1,100,000 common shares outstanding will be $10,000,000 as it was before. However, the value of each individual share will be approximately $9.10.

c. THE LIQUIDATION RIGHT

On a liquidation the assets of the company are sold and the debts are paid, usually with the intention of dissolving the company. The common shares are entitled to share pro rata in any proceeds of the liquidation to the extent proceeds remain after the satisfaction of other claims.

3. *Preferred Shares*

These shares are "preferred" because they are given preference with respect to the distribution of dividends and often also with respect to the distribution of the proceeds on liquidation. For instance, the shares may provide that they will receive a specified amount, say $10 per share, in any given year before any dividends will be distributed to subordinate shares. Preferred shares are usually non-voting.

Preferred shares may carry any of a wide variety of special features. The most common features of preferred shares are cumulative dividend rights, participation rights, conversion rights, call rights and retraction rights.

a. CUMULATIVE (VS. NON-CUMULATIVE)

Preferred shares usually have cumulative rights regarding dividends. This means that if in any given year, dividends are either not declared or are not sufficient to pay the full amount of the annual preferred dividend on the preferred shares, then the amount unpaid carries over into the next year.

Take the glass bottle investment example (noted above) with 6,000,000 common shares issued for $1 per share and 60,000 preferred shares issued for $100 per share with a $10 per annum dividend. If, in year 1, dividends totalling $300,000 were declared, this would pay for a $5 dividend per share on the preferred shares. This would be $5 short of the annual dividend of $10. The unpaid $5 would carry forward such that, in the next year, $15 per share would have to be paid on the preferred shares before anything could be paid on the Class A common shares. Dividends totalling more than $900,000 (60,000 preferred shares x $15 per share) would have to be declared before anything would be available for distribution on the common shares.

If the preferred shares are non-cumulative, then the amounts unpaid in any year would not carry forward to the next year. In the example given above, the $5 unpaid in year 1 would not be carried forward to year 2 if the preferred shares were non-cumulative. In year 2, the amount that would be paid on the preferred shares before any payment on the Class A common shares would still be just $10 on each Class B preferred share. Not surprisingly, preferred shares that are non-cumulative are relatively rare.

b. PARTICIPATING (VS. NON-PARTICIPATING)

Preferred shares may occasionally be participating shares. That is, they participate in dividends beyond the specified preferred amount they are to receive in any given year. Suppose the Class B preferred shares in the glass bottle example were to participate on a pro rata basis in any dividends declared over those required to pay the preferred amount. If dividends totalling $1,206,000 were declared, then $600,000 would be consumed in paying the $10 per share preferred dividend on the preferred shares and the preferred shares would then be lumped in with the Class A common shares for the distribution of the remaining $606,000. Thus the remaining $606,000 would be distributed pro rata amongst

6,000,000 Class A common shares and 60,000 preferred shares for a dividend of $.10 per share ($606,000 / 6,060,000).

c. REDEMPTION/CALL PROVISION *company buys*

 Preferred shares may also be redeemable by the company. The company may want to facilitate a refinancing of the company by providing for a means of buying out the preferred shareholders. Consequently they may put in a redemption provision allowing them to buy back the shares from the shareholder at some future date for a specified price. The price is usually at a premium to the price for which the share is issued.

d. RETRACTION RIGHTS *stockholder sells*

 Preferred shares occasionally also have a retraction right. A retraction right permits the shareholder to tender the share to the company and the company has to buy it back at some price specified in advance.

4. *Restricted Shares* *voting rights restricted*

 A "restricted share" (sometimes called an "uncommon common" share) is like a common share in that it has a right to share pro rata in dividends and a right to share pro rata on a distribution of the proceeds of a liquidation of the assets of the company (subject, of course, to the preferred rights of any other classes of shares).[4] However, the voting rights of such shares are restricted.[5]

 Restricted shares allow a person holding sufficient voting shares for control of a company to raise capital with a sale of shares that are roughly equivalent to common shares without losing control over the company. They can retain control because restricted shares do not allow voting over such important matters as the election of directors.

---

[4] See the definitions of "restricted shares", "equity shares", "common shares" and "preference shares" in Ont. Pol. 1.3, Part I, para. 2. Preferred shares are often also described as "restricted shares". However, Ont. Pol. 1.3 distinguishes preferred shares from "restricted shares" that carry "a residual right to participate to an unlimited degree in earnings of the issuer and in its assets upon liquidation or winding up" but on which voting rights do not exist or are restricted in some way.

[5] See Ont. Pol. 1.3, Part I, para. 2.

Restricted shares also allow more capital to be raised out of what is essentially the same share structure. The reason for this is that for most shareholders the voting right is a useless right. A shareholder might have 100 votes out of a total 1,500,000 votes. Such a shareholder's vote would not have much influence in the greater scheme of things and would not be considered a valuable right by such a shareholder. Thus shareholders holding a relatively small number of shares could sell their voting shares and buy restricted shares and still have what for them would be effectively the same investment. As long as someone in the market finds the voting right valuable, the voting share should trade at a premium to the restricted share. The shareholder with only a few shares could, by selling common shares and buying restricted shares, have something worth just as much to them as the common share they sold and would have a net profit equal to the premium at which the common share traded over the restricted share.

5. *Rights*

Often companies will raise funds through granting "rights" to existing shareholders to buy additional shares in the company. Holders of a specified number of rights will have the right, exercisable within a specified period of time, to buy a share in the company for a predetermined price.

For example, rights issued on April 20 might entitle the holder of 10 rights to buy one class A share for $10 if exercised on or before May 15. Normally one right is granted for each share held. The period during which the rights may be exercised is normally four to six weeks. The price at which the rights can be exercised to buy a share (i.e. $10 in the example) is referred to as the "subscription price" or the "exercise price". It is normally set at a discount to the prevailing market price to encourage the exercise of the rights. Ensuring the exercise of a substantial portion of the rights assures the company that it will raise the amount of capital it is seeking through the issuance of additional shares.

Rights to buy shares of a public company[6] are normally free for trading. A shareholder who receives rights may hold the rights and exercise them before the exercise date or may sell the rights.

---

[6] Generally, a company whose securities have been sold to the public under a prospectus or are publicly traded by virtue of a listing on a stock exchange.

The use of rights on the issuance of additional shares is some-times required by a company's articles. Providing rights to existing shareholders to buy additional shares allows them to maintain their existing proportion of ownership in the particular class of shares being issued. Even where the company is not required to offer existing shareholders' rights to buy additional shares, it may use a rights issue. A rights issue accesses a ready market for its securities and may reduce the costs of distributing the issue by avoiding the costs of marketing it.

6. *Options*

An option contract gives the holder of the option a right to buy or sell the item specified in the contract. An option contract may be entered into with respect to a particular security such as a share or debenture. The option contract would give the holder of the option the right to buy or sell a specified quantity of a specific security within a specified period of time at a stated price.

A "call" option gives the holder of the option the right to buy. A "put" option gives the holder of the option the right to sell. The person who grants, or sells, the option is called the "writer" of the option. The buyer of the option pays the writer of the option a price called the "premium". For example, the buyer may pay $100 on March 1st for an option to buy 100 XYZ common shares on or before August 31st at $15 per share (the "exercise price" or "striking price"). Similarly, the buyer may pay $100 on March 1st for an option to sell ABC common shares on or before August 31st at $15 per share.

Options are also considered to be securities and trading in options is regulated under provincial securities regulation.

7. *Units in a Limited Partnership*

Another type of equity security that one should be familiar with is a unit in a limited partnership. A partnership involves two or more persons carrying on business in common. In a partnership each partner is personally liable for any debts incurred in the operation of the business. However, provincial legislation typically allows for the formation of a partnership in which some partners have limited liability. A limited partner's liability is limited to the investment of the limited partner. Often investment in a limited partnership is effected through the sale of "units" in the limited partnership. Each unit may represent an investment of a given amount. For example, each unit may represent an investment of $1,000.

There can be an income tax advantage to units in a limited partnership over shares in a corporation. When a corporation incurs a loss, it is an individual entity that incurs the loss. The loss means it will not pay tax and that loss may be carried forward to be applied against profits in future years. However, when a partnership suffers a loss, it is not a loss to any entity of partnership because a partnership is not considered to be a separate legal entity and is not treated as such for tax purposes. The loss is a loss to the individual partners, including the limited partners. The partners can then apply this loss to other income to reduce their taxable income in the year. In short, the loss can be used now and not at some indefinite point in the future when the business becomes profitable.

Units in a limited partnership are often issued when the business is starting up because the start-up phase frequently involves initial losses that may not be recouped if the business is not profitable. They have also frequently been used in businesses in which the government has provided incentives in the form of accelerated depreciation, which tends to create large paper tax losses in the early years of operation.

8. *Units*

Sometimes securities will be sold in "units". These units are bundles of securities that are sold together. For instance, an issuer may make a distribution of preferred shares with warrants. Each unit might then be one preferred share plus one warrant. The unit is a combination of securities, each having certain specified rights.

C. Government Securities[7]

The Government of Canada, provincial governments and municipalities raise funds through the sale of securities, in addition to

---

[7] With respect to government securities in Canada see, for example, *The Canadian Securities Course, supra* note 2, at vol. 2, pp. 5-5 to 5-12, and vol. 3, pp. 10-1 to 10-5; and H.L. Binhammer, *Money, Banking and the Canadian Financial System*, (Scarborough: Nelson Canada, 1988), 77-78.

raising funds through taxes. The Government of Canada sells Government of Canada bonds, which have characteristics similar to those described in the earlier discussion of bonds and debentures.[8]

The Government of Canada also issues Treasury Bills. These are short-term obligations to pay a specified amount at the end of a specified period. The amounts, or denominations, are large — usually $1,000 or more. The period between the time of issue and time of payment (or "maturity"), is usually 91, 182 or 364 days. Treasury bills do not pay interest. Instead they are sold at a discount to the amount to be paid at maturity. The difference between the discounted issue price and the price paid at maturity is the return the investor receives on the investment in the treasury bill.

The Government of Canada also issues Canada Savings Bonds. These are unique in that they cannot be traded on bond markets but can be cashed by the owner at any bank in Canada at any time. Canada Savings Bonds are sold for their face value. When they are redeemed the face amount is paid in addition to any accrued interest.

Provincial governments and municipalities also sell bonds or debentures. Provincial governments and municipalities also obtain short-term finance by selling short-term promissory notes. Provincial governments may also guarantee the bond issues of government commissions, government-owned corporations, municipalities, and, occasionally, private corporations.

D. Derivative Securities

Derivative securities have become increasingly prevalent in recent years. A derivative security is a security that derives its value from other underlying variables such as the price of a security or commodity or the level of an index such as stock exchange index. Some of these, such as warrants, rights and options, have already been discussed above.

---

[8] See Part III A 4, *supra*, except that they do not normally carry special features such as a conversion feature, sinking fund or warrants. Government of Canada bonds are generally referred to as bonds, rather than as debentures, even though they are unsecured.

1. *Warrants as an Example of a Derivative Security*

Consider a warrant, for example. Suppose the warrant provides the holder with the right to buy one share of the company for $20 after August 31 and before April 30 of the following year. Suppose further that the share is trading for $25. The warrant could be exercised allowing the holder to buy a $25 share for $20 providing a net gain of $5. If the share price goes up to $27, the warrant can be exercised to buy a share for $20 providing a net gain of $7. Thus an increase in the share price produces an increase in the value of the warrant. Similarly, if the share price goes down to $23, the warrant could be exercised to buy a share for $20 providing a net gain of $3. Thus a decrease in the share price produces a decrease in the value of the warrant. In short, the warrant "derives" its value from the value of the share. If the share price goes up, the value of the warrant goes up. If the share price goes down, the value of the warrant goes down. Corresponding analyses can be made with both options and rights.

2. *Derivative Securities as Risky or "Speculative" Investments*

Derivative securities can be very risky. Consider the example above. If you hold the share, a $2 increase in the value of the share is an 8% gain [=($27-$25)/$25 x 100%] and a $2 decrease in the value of a share is an 8% loss [=($23-$27)/$25 x 100%]. If you hold the warrant, a $2 increase in the value of the share can result in a 40% gain [=($7-$5)/$5 x 100%] and a $2 decrease in the value of the share can result in a 40% loss [=($3-$5)/$5 x 100%]. In short, holding the warrant is riskier because it subjects one to much greater percentage gains or losses than holding the share. A person who continues to hold the warrant on its own would be "speculating" on the value of the underlying share. The person would be speculating that the price of the share would go up.

3. *The Use of Derivative Securities to Avoid (or "Hedge" Against) Risk*

Derivative securities can, however, be used to avoid risk. Suppose you buy a share of a company for $25. If you also buy a put option (an option to sell the share), then gains and losses in the value of the share will be counterbalanced by losses and gains in the value of the option. Suppose you can buy a put option to sell the share at $27 over the next three months. If the value of the share goes down to $23, then the value of the put option will go up because the put option now allows you to sell a $23 share for $27 and someone would be willing to pay you at least $4 for that option. If the value of the share goes up to $27, there will be a decrease in the value of the option since it now simply allows you to buy a $27 share for $27. Thus the value of the share and the value of the option move in opposite directions reducing the fluctuations (or risk) in the investment. With the option to sell the share at $27, you will have locked in a gain on the share of $2. The net gain will be the $2 gain on the share less the cost of the option and any applicable brokerage fees. In other words, you can use derivative securities to provide a virtually risk free investment. Used in this way derivative securities can "hedge" risks to which an investor is exposed. Engaging in hedging for a large portfolio of investments can be much more complex than this simple example suggests and requires considerable expertise.

4. Wide Variety of Derivative Securities

A wide variety of derivative securities have been introduced in recent years. There are far too many derivative securities to describe them all here. Two examples should suffice.

a. STOCK INDEX OPTIONS

One interesting example of a derivative security that has become more prevalent in recent years is a stock index option. Index options are based on a stock index. A stock index consists of a list of selected stocks. It is usually a list of stocks trading on a particular exchange such as the Toronto Stock Exchange Index. The stock prices for stocks on a particular day are used as a base and assigned an index number — say 1000. Changes in the index are determined as the ratio of the sum of all prices of stocks on a subsequent day to the sum of the prices on the initial day times the base (i.e. the initial index number of 1000).

The stock index option is an option on the whole set of stocks that make up the stock index. Suppose a stock index is at 4000.

You might be able to buy a call option on the index at 4100 within a three-month period. The option *implicitly* gives you the right to buy the entire set of stocks that make up the index at prices that would produce an index value of 4100. If the index goes to 4200 within the three month period, then you could exercise the option buying the portfolio of stocks listed in the index at prices that would yield an index value of 4100, then sell the entire portfolio at the prices that led to the index value of 4200. Of course doing this for a stock index consisting of hundreds of stocks would be quite expensive (in terms of brokerage fees) and quite impractical. Consequently an index call option would not allow one to buy the entire set of stocks that make up the stock index. Instead the gain or loss is determined by taking the difference in the index and multiplying it by a particular amount expressed in the option contract. Usually this amount is $100 per contract. Thus if you bought one call option contract on the index for 4100 at a time when the index was at 4000 and the index went to 4200 then the contract would be closed out by having the writer of the option pay you $100 x (4200 – 4100) or $10,000.

b. INTEREST RATE CAPS

An interest rate cap is an example of a derivative security that can be used by borrowers for protection against interest rate fluctuations in a floating-rate loan. In a floating-rate loan, the interest rate varies with changes in prime rate of interest. The prime rate of interest is the rate banks provide for their best customers. The interest rate on a floating-rate loan is usually expressed as the prime rate plus some additional percentage (e.g. prime plus 1%). An interest rate cap specifies a maximum level to which the interest rate on the floating-rate loan can rise. If the interest rate on the loan goes above this cap, the seller of the cap pays the difference between the interest on the loan and the interest that would be paid on the loan if the cap rate applied.

Suppose a borrower received a floating-rate loan for $1 million at prime plus 1% per annum when the prime rate was 5% per annum. Suppose further that the borrower buys an interest rate cap contract that caps the interest rate on the loan at 7% per annum. If the prime rate goes to 8% per annum so that the interest rate on the loan goes to 9% annum for a six-month period during the life of the interest rate cap contract, then the seller of the interest rate cap would have to pay $10,000 [=$1 million x (9% - 7%) x 6 months/12 months]. Thus the value of the interest rate cap contract depends on the fluctuation in the interest rate on the floating-rate loan.

E. Asset Backed Securities

Another type of security that has been introduced in recent years is an "asset backed security". This involves taking a pool of assets that will produce a cash flow and selling interests in that cash flow to investors. For example, a company might have substantial accounts receivable due but needs cash for its operations sooner than it will be available from payments on the accounts receivable. The company could sell units to investors that would represent a percentage interest in the cash flows generated by the accounts receivable. The investors would pay money up front for the units which would provide the company with the needed cash for current operations. When amounts are paid on the accounts receivable, the proceeds would be distributed to the unit holders in proportion to the number of units held by each unit holder.

The process of converting cash generating pools of assets into securities to be sold to provide a more immediate cash flow to the issuer is known as "securitization". Many different types of cash generating assets have been "securitized". These may include such things as accounts receivable, mortgage payments due to a bank or other financial institution, or lease payments that will be due on residential or commercial space leased by a real estate developer.

F. Summary

Securities are sold to raise funds for investment in various business activities. Securities are also sold by federal, provincial and municipal governments to finance government expenditures.

A security provides the buyer of the security with a bundle of rights. These bundles of rights can be composed of any of a wide range of rights, resulting in a potentially infinite variety of securities. The most common types of securities are bonds or debentures, common and preferred shares, and warrants and rights sold in connection with bonds, debentures and shares. Securities regulation deals with the trading of securities such as the common types described above and other less common but similar instruments.

IV. THE DISTRIBUTION OF SECURITIES[9]

A. Introduction

Once it has been decided how an investment is going to be financed, steps must be taken to obtain the funds. Buyers must be found for securities that are being sold and the securities must be distributed to the buyers. Part IV provides an overview of ways in which securities are distributed and considers the roles of brokers and underwriters in the distribution of securities.

1. *Direct Issue and Private Placements*

One simple method of distribution is for the issuer to make contact with purchasers of the securities directly — without the assistance of anyone to help in finding purchasers. This is most common with respect to smaller issuers where the promoters of the issuer can raise sufficient capital simply by calling upon their own friends and relatives or upon various sophisticated investors.[10]

A direct issue is also common with a larger corporation that does a rights issue, since they are issuing securities to their existing group of shareholders and thus know who those shareholders are. With a rights issue the corporation can access potential purchasers from amongst their own shareholders and can avoid the cost of hiring someone to sell the issue of securities.

---

[9]See, e.g., D.L. Johnston & K.D. Rockwell, *Canadian Securities Regulation*, (Toronto: Butterworths, 1998), at 64-67; L. Loss, *Fundamentals of Securities Regulation*, (Boston: Little Brown, 1983), at 81-91; T.L. Hazen, *Treatise on the Law of Securities Regulation*, 3rd ed., vol. 1, (St. Paul: West Publishing, 1995), at 79-85.

[10]"Sophisticated" investors are those with sufficient investment knowledge or experience to assess the value of securities, without the full panoply of regulatory protection. If the investors are not co-promotors, directors, officers, friends, relatives or sophisticated investors, then the distribution is more likely to require the assistance of a broker See Chapter 7, Part III A.

A private placement is also a form of direct issue. In a private placement the securities are sold to institutional investors.[11] Bond issues, for example, are often done through private placements to a small group of institutional investors. A private placement may be arranged by the issuer, but is often arranged through a broker. The issuer may contact a broker about selling an issue of securities and the broker may say that the issue can readily be sold to a small group of investors whom they can interest in buying the securities.

The broker is used because the issuers themselves are not generally involved in the business of selling securities. They normally are not experts in identifying potential investors. Usually issuers will not have ready contacts with potential investors and will usually not have the skills best suited to soliciting and dealing with potential investors. They rely on the expertise of the broker in this regard.

2. *Bought Deal/Offer to Sell*

In a "bought deal", or "offer to sell" the issuer sells the securities to an underwriter. The underwriter then resells the securities to investors. The underwriter uses its own resources to locate investors interested in buying the securities. In this respect the underwriter's role is one of finding buyers for the securities. By buying the securities from the issuer, the underwriter relieves the issuer of the market risk associated with the potential variation in price of the security during the period in which the securities are being distributed.

The underwriting or insurance aspect of the bought deal can be of considerable assistance to the issuer. The issuer may need to raise a certain amount of funds to invest in a specific project. However, the issuer will generally lack expertise in assessing the risk associated with price fluctuations in securities markets and how the market will receive a particular issue of securities. If the price is much lower than expected, the issuer may not raise the amount of money needed, or may not sell the securities at the price anticipated, with the result that the investment, in retrospect, may not be worthwhile.

However, the market risk is usually shared. This is often done through a "market out" clause. This is a clause that says that if certain

---

[11] Institutional investors are investors such as banks, trust companies, life insurance companies, pension funds, and investment funds. See Part V C. below.

specified events occur such as a material change in the affairs of the issuer or if a cease trade order is issued by a regulatory body such as a securities commission, then the underwriter may not be obliged to take up the issue at the specified price.

3. *Best Efforts Underwriting*

In a best efforts underwriting, the underwriter does not buy the issue. The underwriter simply agrees to act as an agent in selling the shares for the best price it can get and agrees to pass on the proceeds, net of a commission, to the issuer. In a best efforts underwriting, the underwriter is not an underwriter in the strict sense of the word. By simply agreeing to give its best efforts in selling the securities, the underwriter is not providing any insurance with respect to the risk of fluctuations in the market price for the security.

4. *Standby Underwriting*

In a standby underwriting, the underwriter provides a partial insurance by agreeing to stand ready to take up all or some portion of an issue that cannot be sold above a certain price. This obligation on the part of the underwriter may also be qualified by a "market out" clause of the type described above with respect to the bought deal.

B. Distributions Through Underwriters

1. *Underwriting Agreement*

The issuer enters into an agreement with the underwriter which sets out the terms of their arrangement. This agreement is typically referred to as an "underwriting agreement". It sets out such matters as the obligations of the underwriter, various covenants and representations of the issuer, conditions pertaining to the underwriter's obligations and rights of termination (including a "market out" clause specifying circumstances under which the underwriter can be relieved of its obligations under the agreement).

2. *Syndicated Underwriting*

For larger issues of securities an underwriter may find that, because of the size of the issue, there may be a substantial risk associated with the issue. To reduce the risk to which the underwriting firm is exposed, the underwriting firm may choose to syndicate the underwriting. That is, it may find other underwriters willing to join in the underwriting of the issue. In a bought deal, this may mean other underwriting firms would become obligated to buy some portion of the issue from the issuer. In a standby underwriting, it may mean that other underwriting firms stand ready to take up a portion of the securities that are not sold at or above a given price.

3. *Banking Groups*

The underwriters in an underwriting syndicate may choose to further share the risk they have agreed to take with other underwriting firms that are not part of the syndicate. A given underwriter who has agreed to buy securities in a bought deal, or to take up securities in a standby underwriting, may form a group of other underwriting firms willing to buy some of the securities it has agreed to buy, or to take up some of the securities it has agreed to take up. The group of underwriting firms formed to share the risk in this way is known as a banking group.

4. *Selling Group*

The underwriting firm (or firms, as the case may be) will generally be a securities firm which provides a wide range of securities services, including the sale of securities. Thus the firm will often have clients who may be interested in buying the securities and may have other resources to devote to the sale of the securities. However, to further facilitate the sale of the issue, the firms underwriting the issue may contact other securities firms to assist in the sale of the issue. This can provide contact with a wider clientele and generally access a wider group of potential buyers of the securities.

C. Summary

Once the type of security to be issued is chosen, the security must be distributed to investors. This can be done directly, through

Diagram 1.a THE DISTRIBUTION PROCESS

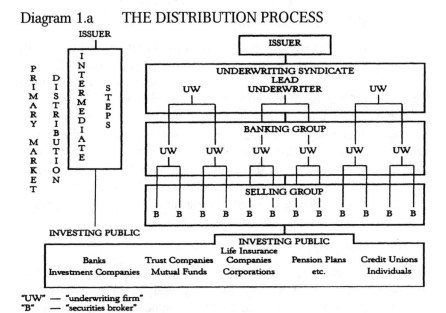

"UW" — "underwriting firm"
"B" — "securities broker"

a broker in a private placement, or with the assistance of an underwriter in a bought deal, stand-by underwriting or best efforts underwriting.

In a distribution assisted by an underwriter, the issuer and the underwriter will enter into an underwriting agreement. As depicted in diagram 1.a, above, the underwriter may syndicate the underwriting to spread the risk and members of the syndicate may form banking groups to further spread the risk of an underwriting. Securities firms involved in the underwriting syndicate or banking groups may also obtain the brokerage assistance of other securities firms to sell the issue.

V. HOW SECURITIES ARE TRADED[12]

A. Introduction

The distribution of securities by issuers through trades with investors is referred to as "primary market" trading. Once the secu-

---

[12] For material dealing with how securities are traded, see *The Canadian Securities Course, supra* note 2, at vol. 1, pp. 1-13 to 1-20, and 1-30 to 1-38 and W.F. Sharpe, G.J. Alexander, & J.V. Bailey, *Investments,* 5th ed., (Englewood Cliffs, N.J.: Prentice Hall, 1995), Chapters 2 and 3; Francis & Kirzner, *supra* note 2, at 41-55.

rities have been distributed to investors, they can be traded among investors. Trading amongst investors is referred to as "secondary market" trading. The issuer itself is generally not involved in these trades. An investor simply exchanges the securities (which represent obligations of the issuer) in return for payment from another investor. The object of this part of Chapter 1 is to provide an overview of trading in securities once they have been distributed.

B. Trading in Securities

To some extent trading in a security is very much like trading in anything else. A person interested in selling must identify a buyer and a person interested in buying must identify a seller. The buyer and seller must then negotiate the terms of the transaction. Once the terms of the transaction are set, the buyer and the seller must make the exchange. In terms of trading in securities, this is usually a transfer of the security in exchange for payment of the price agreed upon.

Although a person interested in selling a security might try to find a buyer on her own, the process of identifying a buyer is most often facilitated by a broker. The buyer will also usually seek the assistance of a broker. Brokers specialize in the purchase and sale of securities, and can save their client time and money selling or buying securities. They can also increase the likelihood that the securities will be sold.

1. *The Development of Stock Exchange Trading*

The following is typical of the development of many stock exchanges.[13] As the number of issuers of securities increases, trading in securities increases. More persons begin to act as brokers. When a broker cannot find a buyer (or seller) of a given security within their own clientele, the broker can contact other brokers to see if they have any clients that would be interested in buying (or selling). With the state of communications technology prevailing in the 19th

---

[13] This story of the development of stock exchanges is based on the development of various types of exchanges as described in Fernand Braudel, *Civilization and Capitalism, 15th-18th Century,* Vol. II: "The Wheels of Commerce", (London: Collins, 1982), at 97-114.

century, this meant visiting the other broker personally or sending a messenger.

These exchanges between brokers were often facilitated by meeting at a common place and time. For instance, various brokers might frequent the same coffee shop,[14] or meet regularly at the same lamppost[15] or tree.[16] This would present the opportunity to make inquiries of each other as to whether they had clients interested in buying or selling particular securities.

It was out of meetings such as these that many of today's stock exchanges developed. Business often turned out to be so brisk that these meetings (or trading sessions) could continue for the whole day. To allow time to meet and deal with their clients, brokers would need to send persons to the trading sessions while they dealt with their clients.

Problems did arise at these meetings of brokers at which securities were exchanged on behalf of investor clients. Some brokers might fail to honour obligations undertaken at the exchange meetings. Others might tend to engage in various sharp business practices. To deal with these problems, an agreement was reached, outlining the conditions which brokers would be required to meet in order to be allowed to participate in exchange meetings. In other words, certain conditions had to be fulfilled to become members of the "exchange". They also tended to agree on rules to govern their behaviour in trading on the exchange.

By bringing brokers into contact with one another, and therefore bringing buyers and sellers of shares into contact with one another, the exchange could greatly facilitate trading. Investors would tend to pay more for shares traded on an exchange because those shares could be more readily bought and sold. Issuers would want to have their shares traded on an exchange because it would increase the value of the shares and thus increase the amount of funds that could be obtained from an issue of shares. Exchanges began to charge fees for granting issuers the privilege of allowing trading in the issuer's shares on the exchange. The fees could be applied to cover

---

[14] For example, the Café de Bourse as the origin of the Paris stock exchange.

[15] As in the case of the American Stock Exchange.

[16] As in the case of the New York Stock Exchange.

the costs of administration of the exchange.[17]

The exchange might begin to develop a reputation. The willingness of investors to trade in shares listed on the exchange could suffer if the practices of member brokers were notoriously bad, or if the shares listed on the exchange were notorious for being associated with unsuccessful business ventures or frauds. Consequently, an exchange might be inclined to create further rules to govern the conduct of their members and create conditions which would have to be satisfied for listing on the exchange.

In spite of the complex array of rules that have developed to govern trading on the stock exchange, its basic function remains the same. It brings buyers and sellers together and facilitates the trading of shares.

2. Trading Through the Facilities of an Exchange

Trading through the facilities of a stock exchange is not unlike everyday trades made by individuals. A trade, whether a trade in a security or anything else, can be broken down into two elements. First, a communication between the buyer and the seller. Second, if the communication results in an agreement, there will be an exchange. A stock exchange facilitates the communication between brokers and thus facilitates communications between buyers and sellers.

Diagrams 1.b.1 to 1.b.3, below, show trading in shares with communication through the facilities of a stock exchange, and the steps

---

[17] Exchanges would have to pay for the space used by the exchange. Outdoor locations such as buttonwood trees (e.g., the New York Stock Exchange) or lampposts (e.g., the American Stock Exchange) may not have been conducive to trading when inclement weather struck. Thus the exchange would have to move indoors. Even indoor locations such as coffee shops may have been inclined to charge a fee for continued use of the shop.

If there were numerous securities trading at the same place brokers trading in one security might not be able to communicate over the din of other brokers trading in other securities. Separate places for trading in different securities would have to be set up. Thus each time a new security is added to those that are traded on the exchange there would be space implications. The exchange could thus not accommodate all securities and would tend to accommodate only those for which sufficient revenues from listing fees or commissions on trading would cover the costs of renting the space and of administration associated with the listing of the security.

involved in carrying out the exchange of shares and payment. The explanation begins with traditional floor trading for demonstrative purposes, even though trading on the floor of a stock exchange is becoming a thing of the past with the advent of computerized trading.

a. COMMUNICATION

The first step in the communication allows buyers to find sellers, and sellers to find buyers. An investor who wished to buy would call his or her broker. Suppose the investor told the broker that he or she wished to buy 1,000 class A shares of GlassPro Ltd. The broker would then call a person at a booth on the floor of the stock exchange (usually a person who worked on behalf of the brokerage firm), and notify that person of the order. The brokerage firm would usually also have someone trading on the floor of the exchange who would come to the booth to pick up orders. That person would then go back out onto the floor to the place where GlassPro class A shares were traded and attempt to strike a deal for the investor. The floor trader was, of course, under an obligation to effect the best deal possible for the investor.

At the other end, an investor would contact a broker and give an order to sell shares. For example, suppose the investor said that he or she wanted to sell 1,000 GlassPro class A shares.[18] The broker would call the firm's person at the booth on the exchange to communicate the order, and that person would relay the order to the floor trader, who would go to the place where GlassPro class A shares

---

[18] There are a wide variety of possible orders that can be given to the broker. For instance, in an "at the market" order, the broker will buy the shares at the best available offering price (or sell the shares at the best available price bid on the shares).

In a "limit order" the client specifies a price at which the transaction may be executed. For a buyer the broker would attempt to buy at the lowest price available but would not be authorized to pay more than the maximum price specified by the buyer. For a seller, the broker would attempt to sell at the highest possible price, but would not be authorized to accept less than the minimum price specified by the seller.

A "stop loss order" attempts to limit a loss by instructing the broker to sell the shares at the market when the price drops below a specified price. Similarly, a "stop buy" order instructs the broker to buy shares at the market if the price rises above a specified price.

were traded and attempt to strike a deal for the investor. By open outcry the brokers for buyers would bid for the shares (the "bid price") and the brokers for sellers would call out the price for which they would sell shares (the "asking price").

Once the floor traders agreed on the price and number of shares, they would communicate the agreed on trade to the clerks at the booths, who would then relay that notice to the brokerage firm. The brokerage firms would then notify their respective clients.

b. EXCHANGE

When the floor traders agreed on a price and the number of the particular shares to be traded, there would be an offer, an acceptance and consideration (money to be paid in return for shares). Thus, there would be a contractual arrangement binding on both the seller and the buyer. The next step would be to make the agreed upon exchange.

(i) Payment

Payment would be effected by having the buyer's broker pay the seller's broker. The buyer would then be indebted to his or her broker and the seller's broker would be obligated to pass on the payment received from the buyer's broker and would thus be indebted to the seller.

(ii) Transfer of Ownership

The ownership of the shares must also change hands. Over the years various mechanisms have been used for the transfer of ownership in securities such as shares. The transfer of shares in bearer form is the simplest to understand, and will thus be considered first. Then the somewhat more complex transfers of shares in registered form will be considered along with modifications that have greatly simplified the paper work involved in the transfer of shares in registered form.

Bearer Form

In the early days of share trading, shares were issued in bearer form. That is, the shares belonged to the bearer of the share certificate. The seller would transfer the bearer share certificates to his

Diagram 1.b.1   BEARER CERTIFICATE EXCHANGE

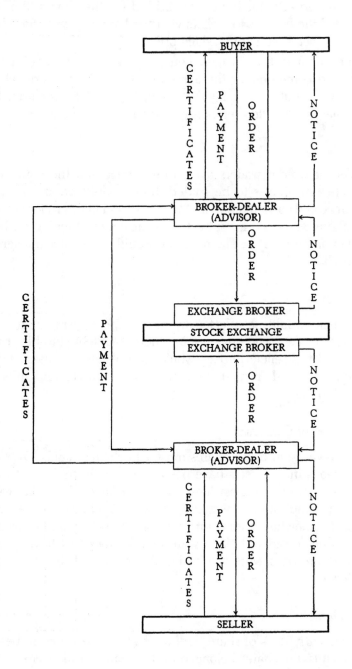

Diagram 1.b.2   REGISTERED CERTIFICATE EXCHANGE

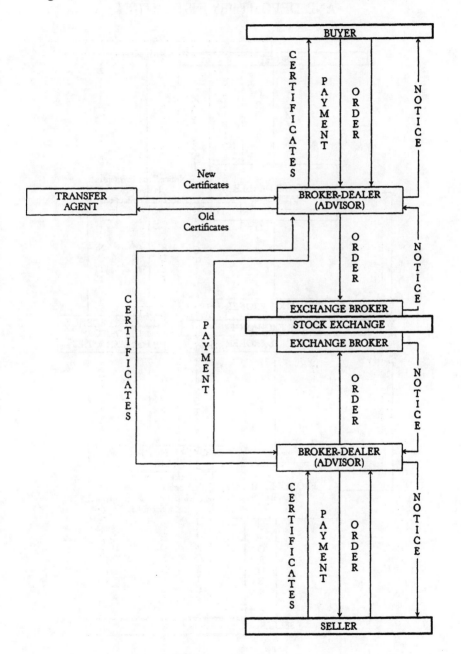

Diagram 1.b.3   EXCHANGE WITH CLEARING
                 AND DEPOSITORY INSTITUTION

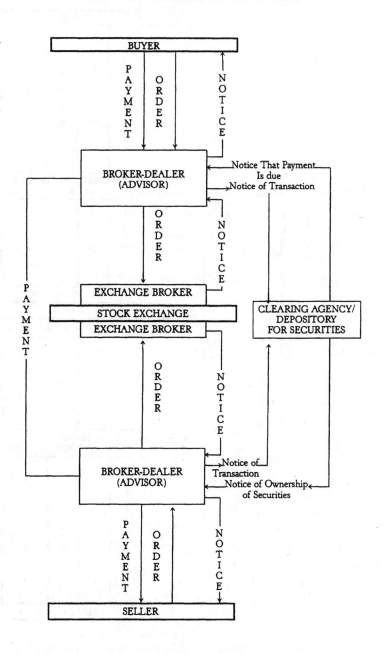

or her broker, who would transfer the certificates to the buyer's broker. The buyer's broker would then transfer the bearer shares to the buyer.[19] Diagram 1.b.1, above, shows the exchange process with bearer form certificates.

Registered Form

The transfer of shares in bearer form entails some risk. If the certificates are lost or stolen they can readily be traded by the thief or unethical finder. Others will quite reasonably believe the thief or finder is the bona fide owner because he or she is the bearer of the share certificate. To avoid such frauds, it became more common to use registered share certificates. That is, the name of the owner of the shares is shown on the certificate and that person is also registered in the books of the company (the shareholder register) as the owner of the shares.

These shares are transferred by the seller by putting an endorsement on the back of the share certificate assigning the rights in the shares to the buyer. The endorsement allows the buyer to present the shares to the company and ask for a new certificate in the name of the buyer. This makes it a bit more difficult for thieves or finders of lost certificates to sell the shares to innocent third party buyers because they have to take the additional step of forging the endorsement and running the risk that the company will identify the forgery and catch them in their fraud.

The transfer of shares in registered form is a bit more complicated than the transfer of shares in bearer form. The seller would deliver the shares to his or her broker, who would then transfer the certificates to the buyer's broker. The buyer's broker could then send the shares to the company to have the certificate in the seller's name cancelled and have the company issue a new certificate in the buyer's name. The new certificate could then go back to the buyer's broker who would then pass it on to the buyer. Diagram 1.b.2, above, shows the exchange process with registered form share certificates.

The process of verifying endorsements, issuing new certificates and keeping track of registered owners is a moderately complex

---

[19] The broker might continue to hold the bearer form share certificates and make a bookkeeping entry to the effect that the shares are held on behalf of the client.

administrative task, which companies engaged in manufacturing, mining, etc., have no particular expertise in. Consequently, it is common practice to have someone, typically called a "transfer agent", perform this function on behalf of the company.[20]

c. SIMPLIFYING THE PROCESS

The exchange of payment for shares is complex in two respects. First, it can result in an unnecessary number of payments and transfers of security certificates. Second, it creates a substantial volume of paperwork for the cancellation and reissuance of certificates in registered form.

Over the course of a day of trading, a broker may be involved in several transactions with another broker concerning the same security. In some of those transactions that broker may act on behalf of a seller, and in others that same broker may act on behalf of a buyer. For instance, broker A may have executed 100 buy orders for GlassPro class A shares with broker B acting for the seller in 20 of those orders. Broker A may have also executed 75 sell orders with broker B acting on behalf of the buyer in 15 of them. This will mean 20 separate payments to broker B by broker A and 15 separate deliveries of GlassPro class A share certificates to broker B. Conversely, broker B will make 15 separate payments to broker A and 20 separate deliveries of GlassPro class A share certificates to broker A. For the shares to be registered in the names of the buyers, the brokers would have to deliver the share certificates to the transfer agent for cancellation and reissuance in the names of the buyers.

(i) Clearing Agency

"Clearing agencies" were created to simplify this mass of transfers between brokers. Brokerage firms notify the clearing agency of their transactions. At the end of the day the clearing agency nets out all the transactions between, for example, broker A and broker B and then notifies them of their net obligation. That obligation may be an obligation to make a payment to another brokerage firm or to deliver certificates for shares of particular companies to another broker. For instance, it may be that brokerage

---

[20] Normally trust companies are engaged to act as transfer agents.

firm A must, at the end of the day, pay some amount to brokerage firm B and brokerage firm B must deliver some GlassPro class A share certificates to brokerage firm A. By netting out the transactions between broker A and broker B the clearing agency reduces the total number of payments and deliveries of certificates between brokers A and B.

(ii) Broker Inventories and Certificate Depository

The number of share certificate cancellations and reissuances was reduced by brokers holding inventories of shares. The certificates for the shares they held in inventory would be registered in the name of the broker. The broker could then just make a bookkeeping entry showing who the beneficial owner of the shares was. With this approach, if an investor bought shares, the brokerage firm could simply make an entry on its books showing that investor as the beneficial owner of the shares. If the investor sold some, or all, of the shares, the brokerage firm could make an entry reducing the investor's beneficial ownership of the shares.

This reduced the number of cancellations and reissuances of share certificates. However, brokers ended up carrying substantial inventories of shares. Furthermore, the net obligations between brokers still required delivery of share certificates and the cancellation and reissuance of certificates to reflect the changes in share ownership by brokerage firms. Thus broker B for example, would have to send GlassPro class A share certificates, registered in the name of broker B to broker A, which broker A would send to the transfer agent to be cancelled and reissued in the name of broker A. One solution to this problem was to have the securities issued in the name of a nominee owner. The securities would remain registered in the name of a nominee owner and bookkeeping entries would be used to keep track of the names of the persons on whose behalf the securities were held. With this approach broker B could fullfill the delivery obligation by notifying the nominee of the change in ownership from broker B to broker A and the nominee could make a bookkeeping entry to reflect the change in ownership.

The creation of a depository corporation for securities further simplified the process by providing for a single nominee registered security holder. A single depository corporation holds inventories of shares. The depository institution can also perform the clearing function. Thus brokerage firms notify the depository corporation of the trades and at the end of the day, the depository corporation notifies brokerage firms of their net payment obligations. For the transfers of shares, the depository corporation simply makes an entry in its books showing changes in which brokerage firms own which shares. Thus if broker B had a net obligation to deliver GlassPro class A shares to broker A, then the depository corporation would simply make an entry showing a reduction in the ownership of GlassPro class A shares by brokerage firm B and an increase in the ownership of GlassPro class A shares by brokerage firm A.

This avoids the need to submit the share certificates to the transfer agent for cancellation and reissuance in the name of another brokerage firm, since the shares are registered in the name of the depository corporation and the ownership by the various brokerage firms is simply shown as an entry on the books of the depository corporation. Since there is one institution holding the inventory instead of multiple brokers holding inventories, there is also a reduction in the number of inventories that must be held.

There are two primary depository institutions in Canada. One is the Canadian Depository for Securities Limited (or "CDS") which serves the Toronto Stock Exchange and the Montreal Exchange. The other is called the West Canada Depository Trust Company which serves the Vancouver Stock Exchange and the Alberta Stock Exchange. Diagram 1.b.3, above, shows the exchange process with a clearing agency and depository institution.

d. THE COMPUTERIZATION OF STOCK EXCHANGES AND SECURITIES TRADING

Computerization of stock trading has changed the nature of stock exchanges in recent years. Most stock exchanges no longer have trading on a trading floor. Now an investor can call the broker at the brokerage firm and simply tell the broker of his or her intention. For instance, the investor may be interested in buying GlassPro class A shares which trade on the Vancouver Stock Exchange. The broker can then call up information on trading in GlassPro class A shares on the Vancouver Stock Exchange and inform the investor of what is available and at what price. The investor then instructs the broker on the basis of the information the broker provides; the broker makes the trade accordingly.

A computerized trading system avoids the need to call a clerk at a booth on the exchange floor and to have a floor trader make the trade. Indeed, a member brokerage firm might have a broker located in Hong Kong, who takes the call and makes a trade on the VSE using the computerized trading system.

The clearing agency and depository functions for the settlement of the transaction (the exchange of money and shares) remains essentially the same. However, the computer allows for notification and record keeping (with respect to the transaction) to be completed soon after the broker makes the trade.

The growth of the Internet has permitted a computer interface between investors, brokers, stock exchanges and other securities markets further facilitating communication for the purpose of trading securities.

3. Trading Off the Exchange

Not all trading takes place on exchanges. There are trades, such as private trades and over-the-counter trades, which do not make use of the facilities of an exchange.

a. PRIVATE TRADES

Sometimes buyers and sellers can identify one another without relying on brokers or a stock exchange. The trade can take place directly between the buyer and the seller. This is usually referred to as a "private trade".

b. THE UPSTAIRS MARKET

Even where securities are listed on an exchange, large blocks of securities are often traded by way of private trades off the exchange. The market for these large block trades is often referred to as the "upstairs market". It usually involves trades by large institutional investors buying or selling securities in large volumes. A particular institutional investor seeking to sell a large block of securities may, usually with assistance of a broker, line up several other institutional investors to purchase the securities. These transactions are usually arranged and closed in offices in the upper floors of office buildings, hence the expression "upstairs market".

c. OVER-THE-COUNTER TRADES

As noted above, stock exchanges have a reputation to protect so that investors will be willing to trade in securities listed on the exchange. They often have listing requirements that provide some assurance of the viability of the operations of the issuer of the securities. The listing requirements also assure that the trading in the particular securities will generate enough business to justify the expenses of the exchange in supporting trading in the security.

Not all issuers of securities will be able to meet the listing requirements. It will not be possible to trade the shares of unlisted issuers on the exchange. Nonetheless, there may be people interested in trading the securities and the numbers may be sufficient to justify support of the trading by brokers. The shares can then be traded with the assistance of the brokers. This is called "over-the-counter" trading. The idea originated in the days of bearer shares when the share certificates would literally be passed over the counter.

In over-the-counter trading, the investor might contact a broker to buy shares of, for example, Limelite Ltd. If the broker's firm has an inventory of the shares, it could sell the shares to the investor out of the firm's own inventory. If the firm does not have an inventory of the shares, it could contact another broker who either has an inventory of the shares, or a client who has Limelite shares and is interested in selling them.

Information on some shares traded over-the-counter in Canada is available on the Canadian Dealing Network System (called the "CDN System"). This is a computerized quotation system that keeps track of prices of securities for unlisted securities that are traded over the counter. It was introduced in 1986. The system is actually operated by the Toronto Stock Exchange, but the securities traded on the CDN system are not traded on the Toronto Stock Exchange.

Bonds and debentures are not usually sold on exchanges. They are typically sold over-the-counter. Brokerage firms generally hold inventories of the major bond issues. The relatively large denominations of bonds and the investment nature of bonds means that they are less frequently traded.[21] Thus there may not be sufficient

---

[21] Since bonds and debentures usually offer fixed returns rather than a share in profits, they tend to be less prone than shares to fluctuations in price. Shares are thus more likely candidates for trading based on speculation with respect to variations in price. Shares may thus tend to trade more frequently. Bonds and

business from trading in bonds to justify the costs of exchange facilities. They are also often held in large quantities by institutional investors such as life insurance companies, banks, trust companies, and pension funds.

4. Margin Trading

A broker may loan funds to clients whom the broker considers to be sufficiently creditworthy. The loan is provided by allowing the client to pay less than the full amount required to purchase securities. For example, suppose an investor orders the purchase of 1,000 shares of GlassPro Ltd. at $10 per share. This would cost $10,000. However, the broker may allow the investor to pay just $6,000. The broker would then pay the remaining $4,000 required to purchase the shares; the $4,000 being considered a loan to the investor. The investor would be required to pay interest on the loan.

Brokers are subject to restrictions in the amounts they may loan to investors. The limit is usually expressed as the minimum percentage that the investor must pay. Thus a 40% margin requirement means that the investor must pay in at least 40% of the cost of securities purchased. Put another way, it means that the broker can only loan up to 60% of the cost of securities purchased.

Brokers are also subject to a requirement to maintain the margin to a certain percentage of the value of the securities. Suppose that the account must be maintained at 40% of the value of the securities held in an account. Put another way, it means that the loan by the broker cannot be more than 60% of the value of the securities held in an account. If the price of GlassPro Ltd. shares drops to $8 per share then the amount loaned ($4,000) would be 50% of the value of the 1,000 GlassPro Ltd. shares owned by the investor ($8 x 1,000 = $8,000). This would be above the required 40% minimum maintenance margin and no action by the broker would be required. However, if the price of GlassPro Ltd. shares dropped to $6 per share the amount loaned ($4,000) would be 67% of the value of the GlassPro Ltd. shares owned by the investor ($6 x 1,000 shares = $6,000). The broker would then make a "margin call" requesting the investor to either deposit cash with the broker to restore the

---

debentures, on the other hand, are more likely to be held as long-term investments and thus may tend to trade less frequently.

40% required maintenance margin, or the broker would sell GlassPro Ltd. shares and use the proceeds to reduce the amount of the loan. The maximum loan the broker could now make would be $3,600 ($6,000 value of GlassPro Ltd. shares x 60% maximum loan rate = $3,600). The investor would have to pay in $400 to reduce the loan from $4,000 to $3,600 or the broker would have to sell 67 shares of GlassPro Ltd. held for the investor to provide sufficient proceeds to reduce the loan to $3,600.

5. *Short Selling*

Brokers may also facilitate short sales by investors. A short sale involves the sale of securities by an investor which the investor does not actually own. By selling the securities, the investor takes on a contractual obligation to supply the shares in return for payment by the person purchasing the securities. To fulfill this contractual obligation the investor must, at some point, purchase the shares that the investor has already sold. Conceptually this is similar to a middleperson in the distribution of goods who promises to deliver, for example, so many tins of corned beef for a particular price at a time when the middleperson does not own any tins of corned beef. The middleperson will have to purchase tins of corned beef to satisfy the contractual obligation.

Brokers can support short sales by loaning the investor the securities required to fulfill the contractual obligation. For example, suppose an investor who owns no GlassPro Ltd. shares thinks that, at $10 per shares, the shares are overvalued and the price will fall in the near future. The investor sells 100 shares at $10 per share. The broker can assist the investor in meeting the obligation to deliver GlassPro Ltd. shares by delivering GlassPro shares held by the broker either on its own behalf, or on behalf of other investors, or by buying the requisite number of GlassPro Ltd. shares to meet the delivery obligation. If the price of GlassPro Ltd. shares drops to $8 per share the investor can purchase the GlassPro Ltd. shares to replace those loaned by the broker for just $8 per share and thus make a profit of $2 per share. However, the investor will lose $2 per share if the investor is required to replace the shares loaned by the broker and the price of GlassPro Ltd. shares has increased to $12 per share.

C. Major Investors in the Canadian Securities Market

The purchasers of securities in Canadian capital markets include both institutions and individuals. Institutions hold by far the majority of the securities traded in Canadian capital markets.[22] The institutions consist primarily of banks, trust companies, life insurance companies, pension funds, investment companies and mutual funds.

1. Banks

Banks raise funds through the sale of shares and debentures. However, major source of bank funding is through savings deposits of individuals, corporations and other associations, and through the issuance of certificates of deposit and other securities. The major assets of banks are mortgages and business and personal loans. A relatively small proportion of bank assets, in the order of 5%, are held in the form of provincial, municipal and corporate securities. Nonetheless, given the enormous size of bank assets, the dollar size of bank investments in Canadian securities is substantial.

2. Trust Companies

Trust companies raise funds through such devices as savings deposits, term deposits and guaranteed investment certificates. Trust companies invest these funds in stocks and bonds. They also act as trustees for corporations and individuals leaving them in charge of substantial portfolios of investments usually consisting primarily of stocks and bonds.

3. Credit Unions and Caisses Populaire

Concerns about the profits of chartered banks in the early part of the twentieth century led to the establishment of credit unions in English speaking Canada and Caisses Populaire in Quebec. These institutions typically seek member-depositors from persons with common interests such as similar ethnic backgrounds, residence in a given geographic area, or common social or business groups. They provide deposit and chequing services and make loans to members.

---

[22] See J.G. MacIntosh, "The Role of Institutional and Retail Investors in Canadian Capital Markets" (1993) 31 Osgoode Hall Law J. 371 at 373-74.

They also invest surplus funds making them significant investors in Canadian securities markets.

4. *Life Insurance Companies*

Life insurance companies obtain funds from premiums on various forms of life insurance, annuities, pensions, group medical and dental care programs. These companies invest these funds in government and corporate bonds and debentures and in corporate stocks.

5. *Pension Funds*

Pension plans are offered to the employees of many companies, Crown corporations, federal, provincial and municipal governments, and educational, professional and union organizations. Contributions, often made by both the employee and employer, create substantial funds. These funds are often managed by trust or life insurance companies and are invested in portfolios of stocks and bonds pending payouts under the plans to retired employees.

There are a number of significant pension funds in Canada. One of these is the Caisse de Depot et Placement. It administers the funds invested in the Quebec Pension Plan. Its very substantial funds make it a significant player in Canadian securities markets.

6. *Investment Funds*

Investment funds are of two types: so-called "open-ended" funds (or "mutual funds") and "closed-ended" funds (or "investment companies").

a. MUTUAL FUNDS

Mutual funds invest in a portfolio of stocks and bonds to produce income and capital gains. Mutual funds obtain their funds by selling shares to investors, which are redeemed by the mutual fund, on the demand of the investor, at the net asset value of the mutual fund's portfolio of investments.

b. INVESTMENT COMPANIES

Investment companies issue shares and invest the proceeds in a portfolio of securities to produce income and capital gains for their shareholders. A shareholder wishing to liquidate her or his investment is not entitled to have the shares redeemed by the company at the current net asset value of the company's portfolio of investments. Instead the shareholder must sell it in the market, as would the shareholders of other companies.

7. Individuals

As noted above, individual investors are not the dominant investors in Canadian securities markets. Although savings by individual investors are, in part, directly invested in stocks and bonds, the majority of the savings of individual Canadians is in the form of investments such as savings deposits at banks and trust companies, pension plan entitlements, life insurance, and so on. Banks, trust companies and life insurance companies reinvest the savings of individuals in securities, such as stocks and bonds, which are sold to raise funds for investment in assets used to produce goods and services. Thus they function as intermediaries through which the savings of individuals are ultimately invested in assets used to produce goods and services.

8. The Importance of Institutional Investors

The institutional investors discussed in subparts 1 to 6 above have grown significantly in size and importance in recent years in both Canada and the United States.[23]

D. The Internationalization of Securities Markets

One of the most significant changes in securities markets in recent years has been the trend to the "globalization", or "internationalization", of securities markets. North American companies have

---

[23]See, e.g., J.G. MacIntosh, "The Role of Institutional and Retail Investors in Canadian Capital Markets" (1993) 31 Osgoode Hall L.J. 371, at 373-74; and B.S. Black, "Shareholder Passivity Reexamined" (1993) 89 Mich. L.R. 520, at 567-70.

sought increasing amounts of capital overseas.[24] In Canada, for instance, the sales of new issues of securities to non-residents increased from $6.5 billion in 1978 to $22.3 billion in 1989.[25] The percentage of bonds placed in countries other than Canada or the United States by Canadian non-financial corporations increased from 0.9% in 1963-70, to 7.3% in 1971-80 and to 37.2% in 1981-87.[26] Similar figures for Canadian financial corporations were 0.6% in 1961-70, 21.8% in 1971-80 and 68.1% in 1981-87.[27] There have also been substantial increases in trading beyond national borders. For instance, in Canada sales of outstanding issues to non-residents grew from $2.6 billion in 1978 to $107.9 billion in 1989, and purchases of outstanding issues from non-residents grew from $3.0 billion in 1978 to $95.4 billion in 1989.[28]

Numerous factors have probably contributed to this trend.[29] One important factor has been advances in communications and com-

---

[24] In the U.S. the value of foreign trading in U.S. stocks grew from $75 billion in 1980 to $417 billion in 1990, an increase of 456%. From 1980 to 1990 foreign purchases of U.S. debt securities grew from $122.9 billion to $3.9 trillion, an increase of 3073%. Foreign companies raised $34 billion in capital in the U.S. in 1990, $48 billion in 1991 and $66 billion in 1992. In 1992 U.S. investors made $270.9 billion in trades in foreign securities. See Kellye Y. Testy, "Comity and Cooperation: Securities Regulation in a Global Marketplace" (1994) 45 Alabama L. Rev. 927, at 930.

[25] See H. Lazar, A. Mayrand and K. Patterson, "Global Competition and Canadian Federalism: The Federal Sector" (1992) 20 C.B.L.J. 1, at 5.

[26] *Ibid.*, at 7.

[27] *Ibid.*, at 7.

[28] *Ibid.*, at 5. For a general discussion of the internationalization of securities markets see, for example, B. Becker, "Global Securities Markets" (1988) 6 Int'l Tax & Bus. Lawyer 242; M.Q. Connelly, "Multinational Securities Offerings: A Canadian Perspective" (1987) 50 Law & Contemporary Problems 251, at 252-54; and Lazar et al., *supra* note 25, at 4-10.

[29] Factors affecting the globalization of securities markets are discussed in B. Becker, *supra* note 28, at 244; F. Kubler, "Regulatory Problems in Internationalizing Securities Markets" (1987) 9 Univ. of Pa. J. of Int'l. Bus. Law 107, at 107-11; A.L. Peters and A.E. Feldman, "The Changing Structure of the Securities Markets and the Securities Industry: Implications for International Securities Regulation" (1988) 9 Michgan Yearbook of Int'l. Legal Studies 19, at 21-22; M. Gruson, "The Global Securities Market: Introductory Remarks" [1987] Col. Bus. Law Rev. 303, at 304-6; and Josh Futterman, "Evasion and Flowback in the Regulation S Era: Strengthening U.S. Investor Protection While Promoting U.S. Corporate Offshore Offerings" (1995) 18 Fordham International Law J. 806, at 811-13.

puter technology. Information about securities being sold in any given jurisdiction can be disseminated to other jurisdictions much more quickly than was the case say thirty years ago. Trading instructions can be communicated to brokers in foreign jurisdictions much more quickly and cheaply than in the past. Advances in computer technology allow investors to access and process increasingly greater volumes of information much more quickly. They have also reduced the costs of making trades in securities and storing information required to facilitate trading.

Deregulation reducing barriers to trading in securities in foreign markets has also been an important factor in the internationalization of securities markets. For instance, many countries have reduced controls on foreign exchange, reduced foreign ownership restrictions, reduced restrictions on the extent of foreign investments individuals or institutions may hold, reduced withholding taxes, reduced or removed taxes on securities transactions (stamp duties), and removed restrictions on foreign firms listing on domestic stock exchanges.

International securities trading has also been facilitated by links between stock exchanges, extended trading hours, and advances in and standardization of the clearance and settlement of securities transactions across international boundaries. All of these changes, in conjunction with developments in investment theory that highlight the benefits of international diversification, have prompted many investors to diversify their investments internationally.[30]

The growth of institutional investment has also led to increased international investment. Institutional investors with large amounts to invest can more readily benefit from international diversification. Because of their size they have the capacity to gather and assess information on foreign securities markets at relatively lower cost per dollar invested than most individual investors can. The development of derivative securities has allowed investors, particularly institutional investors, to take advantage of diversification through foreign securities markets with smaller investments.[31]

The internationalization of securities markets raises a wide range of issues in securities law. These include concerns about conflicts in securities laws and whether the securities laws of different coun-

---

[30] The concept of diversification is discussed in Chapter 2, Part II A 3 b.

[31] A $3 option costs a lot less than a $20 share and provides a greater exposure to fluctuations in the foreign market than the $20 share.

tries should be harmonized, questions about the scope of jurisdiction of the securities laws of a particular country, questions about which of the conflicting securities laws of two or more countries should apply, and issues of coordination of investigations and enforcement.

CHAPTER 2

SECURITY VALUES AND SECURITIES MARKET EFFICIENCY

I. INTRODUCTION

Securities regulation is said to be intended to protect investors. Much of the regulation is designed to protect investors from paying more for securities than they are worth, or from selling securities for less than they are worth. In order to understand securities regulation as a response to this perceived problem, and not as just a set of obscure rules, it is necessary to know something about how securities are valued and how efficient securities markets are at setting prices that reflect the underlying value of securities.

Knowing about how securities are valued can provide a basis for understanding and criticizing regulations such as those providing for mandatory disclosure. Knowing something about how efficiently market prices reflect underlying values of securities provides a basis for understanding and criticizing the extent to which securities regulation relies on securities markets to protect investors. Thus the objective of this chapter is to provide, in Part II, an introduction to how securities are valued, and, in Part III, an introduction to the efficiency of securities markets.

II. HOW SECURITIES ARE VALUED[1]

A. The Fundamentals of Security Values

1. *Source of Value*

Suppose there was a company about which the following things are known in advance. It will have a 20-year life span. It will never

---

[1] This introduction to the valuation of securities is drawn from various sources. See *The Canadian Securities Course*, (Toronto: The Canadian Securities Institute,

pay a dividend or distribute earnings in any other way. At the end of the 20 years, the manufacturing plant, which is the company's only asset and is uninsured, will be completely destroyed. In other words, nothing will ever be paid back to investors on shares sold by the company. If such things were known in advance, the shares in the company would be worthless. An investor would not be willing to pay for the shares because the investor would not get anything in return for owning the shares. In short, securities, such as shares, derive their value from the future stream of cash flows that will accrue to the investor from owning the security.

2. *Discounting*

Cash flows expected to be received in the future are not worth as much as having cash in the present. This is because one can invest cash presently held in a relatively risk-free investment, such as a bank deposit, and earn a return in the form of interest on the cash invested. For instance, 62.4 cents invested at a rate of interest of 5% per annum for 10 years accumulates to $1. Thus the prospect of earning $1 10 years from now, would only be presently worth 62.4 cents to an investor who could earn 5% on a comparable investment. In other words, the "present value" of $1 to be received 10 years hence if one can invest at 5% per annum is 62.4 cents.

The calculation whereby one determines the amount that would have to be invested now, at a given rate of return, to accumulate to the projected future cash flow is known "discounting". The rate of return used in the calculation is known as the "discount rate". This same calculation could be made for each of the expected future cash flows. The sum of the discounted future cash flows that a security is expected to produce is the present value of the security. In principle at least, the value of a security to investors would be the present value of the stream of cash flows that the security will produce.

1995), vol. 3, Chapter 9; J.C. Francis & E. Kirzner, *Investments: Analysis and Management*, 3rd ed., (Toronto: McGraw-Hill Ryerson, 1988), Chapters 8, 9, 11, 14, 15, 17; W.F. Sharpe, G.J. Alexander & J.V. Bailey, *Investments*, 5th ed., (Englewood Cliffs, N.J.: Prentice-Hall, 1995); R. Brealey & S. Myers, *Principles of Corporate Finance*, (New York: McGraw-Hill, 1981), Chapters 2-4; J.F. Weston & T.E. Copeland, *Managerial Finance*, 9th ed., (New York: Dryden Press, 1992), Chapters 3, 10, 11.

3. Risk

a. GENERALLY

For some securities, the returns the security can be expected to provide are relatively certain. For instance, a Government of Canada treasury bill provides a reasonably certain return. It is unlikely that the Government of Canada will become unable to fulfill the obligation to pay the face amount of the treasury bill over its short time to maturity.[2] A share in a highly speculative mining venture, on the other hand, provides a far less certain return. The mining venture could lead to the discovery of a very rich body of ore and be enormously successful, or, it could be abandoned after failing to discover a commercially viable body of ore. If successful, the returns on the share could be substantial. If unsuccessful, there could be a substantial loss on the share. The share in the mining venture is thus a much riskier investment than the Government of Canada treasury bill.

Most people are inclined to avoid risk and demand compensation for taking risk. Consequently higher risk securities tend to provide higher expected returns. Thus in estimating the present value of the treasury bill one might use a 5% discount rate, while a 12% discount rate might be more appropriate for the share in the much riskier speculative mining venture.

b. SYSTEMATIC AND UNSYSTEMATIC RISK[3]

Some risks associated with a security will have no relation to risks associated with other securities. For instance, a risk such as the risk of loss due to an explosion at the XYZ Manufacturing Ltd.

---

[2] The short duration of the treasury bill also minimizes the risk that a change in interest rates will affect the value of the treasury bill. For instance, if interest rates go up, investors will no longer accept the lower rate implicit in the difference between the face value of the bill and the discounted price at which the bill initially sold. The price of the bill will go down to the point that the difference between the price of the bill and the amount to be paid at maturity, yields a rate of interest corresponding to the prevailing market rate.

[3] See Brealey & Myers, *supra* note 1, at 119-30; Francis & Kirzner, *supra* note 1, at 189-92; J.C. Francis, *Investments: Analysis and Management*, 3rd ed., (New York: McGraw-Hill, 1980), at 348-49; Sharpe et al., *supra* note 1, at 212-14, 276-77; F.J. Fabozzi, *Investment Management*, (Englewood Cliffs, N.J.: Prentice Hall, 1995), at 88.

plant in Toronto, is not likely to be correlated to the risk of ABC Mining Ltd. not finding a commercially viable body of ore after incurring substantial exploration costs on a site in British Columbia. Similarly, the discovery of a substantial cost-saving innovation at the XYZ Manufacturing Ltd. plant in Toronto is not likely to be correlated with the discovery of an extremely rich ore by ABC Mining Ltd. in British Columbia.

An investor can deal with these kinds of uncorrelated risks by buying and holding a portfolio of securities. By doing so, losses incurred due to unfortunate events concerning the issuers of some of the securities held by an investor, will be compensated for by the gains due to fortunate events concerning the issuers of other securities held by the investor. For instance, a plant explosion at XYZ Manufacturing Ltd. may be compensated for by the discovery of a rich body of ore at ABC Mining Ltd.

Risks that are not correlated to the risks of other securities in the market are referred to as "unsystematic" or "non-market" risks. Avoiding unsystematic risk by holding a portfolio of securities is referred to as "diversification".

Some risks associated with a security will tend to be correlated with the risks associated with other securities. For instance, fluctuations in the global or domestic economy may affect all securities in the market. A surge in the domestic economy may have a very significant effect on the earnings potential of XYZ Manufacturing Ltd. and may have a smaller, but nonetheless significant, effect on the earnings prospects for ABC Mining Ltd. Similarly, a recession may have a negative effect on the earnings potential for both XYZ and ABC. Where risks affect all securities in the market in a similar way, one cannot avoid the risk by holding a portfolio of securities since all securities will tend to move in the same direction in response to the event. Risks of this sort are referred to as "systematic" or "market" risks.

If investors can diversify, then unsystematic risks are not relevant to the underlying value of the security since they can be avoided. The relevant risk for investors who can diversify is the systematic, or market, risk because it cannot be avoided through diversification.

4. *Summary*

The fundamental elements of security values are thus risk and return. Securities derive their underlying values from the returns, or cash flows, which they are expected to produce. These future expected returns are discounted to the present at a rate that depends on the degree of risk inherent in the expected returns. The risk that is relevant in determining the appropriate discount rate is the systematic (or market) risk.

B. Approaches to Valuing Securities[4]

There are two general approaches to assessing whether a security is over- or under-priced. One method looks at the fundamentals of the underlying value of the security and is known as "fundamental analysis". The other method, known as "technical analysis", attempts to predict the future market price by reference to patterns in trading prices and volumes. An awareness of these radically different methods of evaluation can be useful in assessing the effectiveness of the kinds of disclosure mandated by securities laws.

1. *Fundamental Analysis*

Determining future returns and risk is normally not something that can be done with precision. Various factors relating to returns and risk must be assessed. It is the assessment of these factors that is referred to as "fundamental analysis". Those who do fundamental analysis assess potential future returns by looking at such factors as the market prospects for the issuer's business, the quality of the issuer's management, the degree of competition in the industry, the outlook for the economy as a whole, and many other factors. They assess the extent to which the returns will fluctuate with returns for the market as a whole in order to assess the degree of market risk associated with the security.

2. *Technical Analysis*

By contrast, there are other market analysts who look at patterns in past securities prices or trading volumes to determine future secu-

---

[4]See *The Canadian Securities Course, supra* note 1, vol. 3, Chapter 9; Francis & Kirzner, *supra* note 1, Chapters 15 and 17; Sharpe et al., *supra* note 1, at 844-54; R.A. Brealey, *An Introduction to Risk and Return from Common Stocks*, 2d ed., (Oxford: Basil Blackwell, 1983), Chapters 1-3.

rities prices. It is the analysis of these patterns that is referred to as "technical analysis" and the persons who do technical analysis are called "technical analysts". They use graphs and charts and mathematical models that search for previous trading patterns and patterns in previous prices. The analysis is based on the assumption that patterns exist and that patterns observed in the past will occur again.

For example, one pattern that has been observed is known as the "head and shoulders" pattern. If one observes this pattern developing, then it indicates when one should buy and sell the security. If the pattern is recognized by the time the price reaches the top of the second peak, then it is time to sell the security. When the price falls to the second valley, then it is time to buy the security again.

Other popular technical analysis theories include filter rule theories and the Dow Theory.[5] Filter rule theories are based on the notion that if a stock price goes up more than a given per cent then it is in the early stages of a longer term price increase. Thus, when the price increases by more than the pre-determined percentage, you buy. Similar filter rules would operate in the opposite direction and would lead to decisions to sell.

The Dow Theory was promulgated by Charles Henry Dow, the creator of the Dow Jones Index. The theory describes stock market prices in terms of three trends, primary trends, secondary trends and minor trends. Identification of primary trends is considered to be of substantial importance since these trends will continue for a prolonged period of time. One test of a primary trend postulates that when the Dow Jones Index goes above or below some predetermined amount, the whole market will continue to move dramatically forward in that direction. The theory became popular in the 1930s after it had correctly predicted the 1929 crash about six days before it occurred.

Whether technical analysis or fundamental analysis is a superior valuation technique has been a matter of some debate. The question has been addressed in the context of assessments of the efficiency of securities markets.

---

[5] There are also many other technical analysis theories such as moving averages, relative strength tests, and price and trading relationships. See Fabozzi, *supra*, note 3, at 217-20 and B.G. Malkiel, *A Random Walk Down Wall Street*, 5th ed., (New York: Norton, 1996), at 139-48.

III. SECURITIES MARKET EFFICIENCY

In an efficient market prices reflect any new information about the value of the items sold in that market very quickly. Whether or not the securities market is efficient is relevant to securities regulation from both a practical and policy perspective. This part of the chapter discusses the meaning of securities market efficiency, notes some of the evidence on securities market efficiency and problems with that evidence, then briefly highlights some aspects of the policy and practical significance of securities market efficiency for securities regulation.

A. What is Securities Market Efficiency?

1. *The Price of a Security as an Average of Estimates of the Value of the Security*

The price of a security reflects an average of views, both optimistic and pessimistic, on the value of a security. Those with optimistic views buy and those with pessimistic views sell. The price that prevails in trading in a security is a price that equates the number of units of a security demanded by those willing to buy and the number of units of a security supplied by those willing to sell. The price thus reflects an average of optimistic and pessimistic views. These views are based on the information available with respect to the value of the security.

2. *The Meaning of Securities Market Efficiency*[6]

The question of securities market efficiency is a question of the extent to which, and the speed with which, market prices reflect information about the value of securities. The more information the market prices appear to take into account and the more quickly market prices take information into account, the more efficient the market. Restating this, the efficiency of securities markets depends on (i) the amount of information available, (ii) the speed at which the information is disseminated to the market and assessed, and (iii)

---

[6]See the discussion of market efficiency in Brealey & Myers, *supra* note 1, at 257-63. See also R.J. Gilson & R.H. Kraakman, "The Mechanisms of Market Efficiency" (1984) 70 Virginia L. Rev. 549.

the extent to which that information comes to be reflected in the prices of securities.

3. Factors that Affect the Efficiency of Securities Markets

Two key factors that will affect the amount of information and speed with which information will be reflected in the market price of a security are the cost of gathering information with respect to the security and the value of the units of the security that are available for trading. With respect to the cost of information, more information is likely to be gathered where the information is less costly to gather.

The value of units of a security being traded affects the potential for recouping fixed costs associated with the gathering of information and for profiting from the gathering of information. There may be a substantial fixed cost element to gathering information about a security. That is, part of the cost of gathering information on a particular security will not vary no matter how many thousands or millions of dollars worth of the particular security are being traded. However, the greater the dollar value of trades in a particular security, the greater the potential for profit on information gathered on that security. Thus an investor may be more readily able to recoup the cost of gathering information where the dollar value of the security being traded is greater. The greater the dollar value of trading in the security, the more willing the investor will be to incur greater costs of gathering information and thus gather a greater amount of information. Thus one would predict that the market for smaller issues of securities would be less efficient than for larger issues since it is more worthwhile to gather information on a large issue security.

B. How Efficient are Securities Markets?[7]

How efficient is the market in pricing securities? Various hypotheses about the efficiency of securities markets have been

---

[7]See Francis & Kirzner, *supra* note 1, at 446-84; Brealey, *supra* note 4, Chapters 1-3; E.F. Fama, "Efficient Capital Markets: A Review of Theory and Empirical Work" (1970) 25 J. Fin. 383; E.F. Fama, "Efficient Capital Markets: II" (1991) 46 J. Fin. 1575; and K. Cuthbertson, *Quantitative Financial Economics: Stocks, Bonds and Foreign Exchange,* (New York: John Wiley & Sons, 1996), Chapters 5-8.

tested. These hypotheses focus on the type of information reflected in the market and the speed with which that information is reflected in market prices.

1. *Weak Form Efficiency (Patterns vs. Random Walks)*

One of these hypotheses is known as the weak form efficient market hypothesis. It postulates that stock prices follow a "random walk" and consequently there are no patterns in the movement of stock prices. In other words, previous prices or volumes of trading provide no information about the direction of future stock prices.

Early empirical tests tended to support this hypothesis. Various tests (runs tests,[8] serial correlation tests,[9] and trading rule tests)[10] provided little evidence of identifiable patterns in the behaviour of stock prices.[11] This evidence casts doubt on the validity of technical analysis which is based on the identification of patterns in trading prices.

---

[8] One type of test that has been done is referred to as a "runs test". Runs tests look at patterns of increases and decreases in stock prices and assess whether runs of increases and decreases are simply random or show clear patterns. The results are that the runs of increases and decreases in stock prices could have been the result of a totally random process. In other words, there were no discernible patterns.

[9] Serial correlation tests compare prices in one period with prices in several previous periods to determine whether there is any relationship between a price at a given point in time and previous prices. These tests found no significant evidence of such a correlation.

[10] Trading rule tests compare the profits obtained from using various popular trading rules (some of which are discussed above in Part II B 2) with the profits obtained by a "naive buy and hold strategy" under which stocks are chosen randomly and held (i.e., not traded). The evidence from these tests did, curiously, indicate profits from using trading rules that were greater, on average, than the profits from the naive buy and hold strategy. However, when the brokerage fees of buying and selling the stocks under the trading rules were deducted from the profits obtained by following the trading rules, the trading rules yielded lower profits than the naive buy and hold strategy.

[11] The evidence is reviewed in E.F. Fama, "Efficient Capital Markets: A Review of Theory and Empirical Work" (1970) 25 J. Fin. 383; J.H. Lorie, P. Dodd & M.H. Kimpton, *The Stock Market: Theories and Evidence*, (Homewood, Ill.: Dow Jones-Irwin, 1985), at 57-63; Brealey, *supra* note 1, at 615. More recent evidence is reviewed in Eugene F. Fama, "Efficient Capital Markets: II" (1991) 46 J. Fin. 1575.

More recent tests have examined the predictability of prices over longer horizons than earlier tests did. These tests have shown some, albeit weak, evidence of stock price patterns in which prices take large swings away from base prices and then slowly revert to those base prices.[12] Other more recent tests have also looked at whether variables other than stock prices and volumes, such as dividend yields (annual dividends divided by stock price) and earnings to price ratios, can be used to predict future stock prices. These tests have produced stronger results accounting for 25-30% of the variance in 2 to 5 year returns on stocks.[13] Further, earlier tests, such as serial correlation tests, tested for linear patterns in stock prices. More recent tests have provided some evidence of non-linear patterns in stock prices.[14] Collectively these more recent tests on the randomness of stock price movements suggest that stock price movements may not be entirely random. Thus previous stock prices, or other information such as dividend yields or earnings to price ratios, may provide some information about future stock prices, particularly over longer periods in the order of 2 to 5 years.

2. Semi-Strong Form

Even if the market is weak form efficient and prices follow a random walk, it may be that stock prices are very slow to reflect new information. Just how quickly do stock prices respond to new information?

One hypothesis that addresses this question is known as the semi-strong form of the efficient market hypothesis. It postulates that stock prices reflect all currently available public information. Tests of this hypothesis look at the response of stock prices to new publicly

---

[12] See Fama, "Efficient Capital Markets: II", *supra* note 11, at 1580-82, 1609.

[13] Ibid., at 1609.

[14] See Lawrence A. Cunningham, "From Random Walks to Chaotic Crashes: The Linear Genealogy of the Efficient Capital Market Hypothesis" (1994) 62 Geo. Wash. Law Rev. 546, at 571-81. Where there is a linear relationship a change in one variable (e.g., a change in the stock price at a given time) produces a proportionate change in another variable (e.g., a change in a stock price at a subsequent time). Where the relationship is non-linear a change in one variable may produce an exponential change in another variable (e.g., a two-fold change in price may produce a four-fold change at a subsequent time and three-fold change in price may produce a nine-fold change in price at a subsequent time).

available information. For example, tests have looked at the effect of announcements of earnings and of events such as stock splits, dividend changes, earnings announcements, new issues of common stock, takeover bids, mergers and sales of substantial assets. These tests have generally shown that securities markets react very quickly to new information, often within a matter of minutes.[15]

The amount of evidence gathered which directly or indirectly tests this hypothesis is voluminous and one review of the evidence concluded that "[t]he evidence has become so persuasive that it is fair to conclude that semistrong form market efficiency is now an accepted working assumption in financial economics research."[16] In short, there is considerable evidence that, for securities traded on the stock exchanges, the price responds to new publicly available information very quickly.

3. *Strong Form Efficiency*

Another hypothesis which addresses the question of how quickly the market responds to new information is known as the strong form of the efficient market hypothesis. It postulates that *all* information is fully reflected in the price. If this were true then no one (even insiders[17]) would have better information than that which is already reflected in the price.

Traces of stock prices in response to given events and tests of insider trading profits suggest that this level of efficiency does not exist. For instance, in tests of the market response to takeover bid announcements the stock price tends to move up before the public

---

[15] See generally Lorie et al., *supra* note 11, at 65-73; Brealey, *supra* note 4, Chapter 2; and Fama, "Efficient Capital Markets: II", *supra*, note 11, at 1599-1602. See also J.A. Patell & M.A. Wolfson, "The Intraday Speed of Adjustment of Stock Prices to Earnings and Dividend Announcements" (1984) 13 J. of Fin. Econ. 223.

[16] Lorie et al., *supra* note 11, at 73. After reviewing securities market reactions to several types of information Brealey, *supra* note 4, concludes, at page 46, that "[i]n each case, the predominant impression is that the stock price responds quickly and efficiently to the news".

[17] Insiders are persons such as senior officers (e.g., the president, vice-presidents, secretary, and treasurer), directors, and major shareholders of a company who will tend to have access to information about the company before it becomes publicly available.

announcement date.[18] This suggests that there is some trading going on in advance before the full effect of the information reflected in the price.[19] Other tests have looked at the profits made by insiders from trading and compared them to the profits that non-insiders would have been expected to make.[20] These tests have, for the most part, shown higher profits for insiders.

4. Problems with the Evidence on Securities Market Efficiency

There are several problems with the evidence on securities market efficiency. Several of these problems are briefly discussed below.

a. THE JOINT HYPOTHESIS PROBLEM

One of the problems with tests of the semi-strong form of the efficient market hypothesis is that they tend to test two hypotheses at once. This makes the results inconclusive. To understand this "joint hypothesis" problem it is necessary to briefly explain the concept behind most tests of the semi-strong form of the efficient market hypothesis.

Most tests of the semi-strong form of the efficient market hypothesis are of a type called an "event test". Event tests begin

---

[18] See G. Mandelker, "Risk and Return: The Case of Merging Firms" (1974) 1 J. of Fin. Econ. 303; A.J. Keown & J.M. Pinkerton, "Merger Announcements and Insider Trading Activity: An Empirical Investigation" (1981) 36 J. of Fin. 855. See also J.H. Lorie & V. Niederhoffer, "Predictive and Statistical Properties of Insider Trading" (1968) 11 J. of Law and Eco. 35.

[19] However, such pre-bid increases in price may be due to market anticipation of mergers or takeover bid announcements, see G.A. Jarrell & A.B. Poulsen, "Stock Trading Before the Announcement of Tender Offers: Insider Trading or Market Anticipation" (1989) 5 J. of Law & Org. 225.

[20] See J. Jaffe, "Special Information and Insider Trading" (1974) 47 J. of Bus. 410; J.E. Finnerty, "Insiders and Market Efficiency" (1976) 31 J. of Fin. 1141; H.N. Seyhun, "Insider Profits, Costs of Trading and Market Efficiency" (1986) 16 J. of Fin. Econ. 189; but see M.S. Rozeff & M.A. Zaman, "Market Efficiency and Insider Trading — New Evidence" (1988) 61 J. of Bus. 25; D. Givoly & D. Palmon, "Insider Trading and the Exploitation of Inside Information: Some Empirical Evidence" (1985) 58 J. of Bus. 69 suggesting that insiders make little or no abnormal profit on their reported trades.

with a model of, or hypothesis about, the behaviour of securities market prices. One of the models of securities market prices that is most frequently used for this purpose is the "capital asset pricing model". This model of securities prices relates the return on a security to a risk free rate of return plus an extra return (or "premium") that compensates for systematic (or "market") risk.[21] The concept behind an event test is that returns on securities, and their related prices, will track those predicted by the model until some event alters investor expectations of future cash flows. A favourable event, such as a takeover bid or a major ore discovery, will cause investors to expect higher cash flows. Higher cash flows will mean higher expected returns and investors will be willing to pay more for the security because it now produces returns that are greater than the risk free rate plus the market risk premium available on securities of similar risk. In other words, the event has caused returns greater than those the capital asset pricing model would have otherwise predicted. Investors will buy the security driving the price up to the point that the returns on the security once again correspond with the risk free rate of return plus the market risk premium. Event tests look at how quickly securities prices adjust so that they track the predictions of the underlying pricing model used in the event test.

The problem with event tests is that they have two hypotheses — one is that securities markets are efficient in the semi-strong form and the other is that securities market prices behave according to the model used in the test. A test that shows prices not responding quickly to an event could simply mean the market is not very efficient in its response to new information or it could mean that the model of securities prices used in the test is wrong. A test that shows prices adjusting quickly to an event could mean that the market is efficient in the sense that it responds quickly to new information or that the model of securities prices is wrong in a way that gives the impression that prices are reacting quickly to new information.

Thus evidence of the semi-strong form of the efficient market hypothesis based on event tests have an inherent flaw. Nonetheless, the enormous number of event studies that have yielded results that fit with predicted results, based on the assumption of efficient capital markets and pricing according to a particular pricing model, suggest

---

[21] On "systematic" or "market" risk see *supra* Part II A 3 b.

that these assumptions provide reasonable approximations of the behaviour of securities markets.

b. ANOMALOUS RESULTS

Another problem with the evidence on securities market efficiency is that there have been a number of tests of securities prices that reveal unusual features which are difficult to fully explain on a rational basis. For instance, most of the average daily return comes at the beginning or end of the day, returns on Mondays tend to be lower on average than returns on other days, returns are on average higher on the last trading day of the month and before a holiday, returns on small stocks are higher on average in January than in other months.[22] However, these anomalies tend to be small and are not sufficient to produce gains from trading net of brokerage costs that yield significantly higher returns than the market average for a given level of risk.[23] Further, the tests revealing these unusual features are typically event studies that have the joint hypothesis problem referred to above. The anomalous results may be evidence that the market is inefficient or simply evidence that the securities pricing model used in the test is not an entirely accurate model of how securities are priced.

c. FUNDAMENTAL VS. INFORMATIONAL EFFICIENCY

Another problem with the evidence on securities market efficiency is that the evidence does not support the proposition that securities prices reflect the underlying (or "fundamental") values of securities. The weak form, semi-strong form and strong form efficient market hypotheses are hypotheses about the type of information reflected in market prices and the speed with which that information is reflected in market prices. None of these hypotheses say that market prices for securities reflect the underlying value of securities. While the semi-strong form of the efficient market hypothesis, and the evidence supporting it, suggests that securities markets react very quickly to new publicly available information about securities, this

---

[22] See Fama, *supra* note 11, at 1586-89.

[23] See the conclusion in J.C. Francis, *Investments: Analysis and Management* (New York: McGraw-Hill, 1991) at 565-78 where several anomalies with respect to securities market efficiency are reviewed.

does not mean the resulting prices reflect underlying values. Thus securities markets may be "informationally efficient" in the sense that securities prices react quickly to new information. However, they may not be "fundamentally efficient" in the sense that securities prices reflect underlying securities values. In a securities market that is informationally efficient but not fundamentally efficient investors may be more concerned about what other investors will consider an appropriate price for a security rather than underlying factors that influence future cash flows on securities.

One approach to testing for whether stock prices track fundamental values has been to compare stock price variations to variations in what stock prices should have been. This has been done by gathering historical data on dividends and using that data to determine what the stock price should have been using standard stock valuation models. For example, one would determine what the stock price should have been in 1960 if one had known in 1960 of all of the dividends that would accrue from 1961-80. This approach showed actual variations in stock prices that are much greater than the predicted variations using the historical dividend data.[24] This suggests that while stock prices may follow the general pattern of movements in fundamental values, they may deviate substantially from fundamental values. It also suggests that markets may overreact to new information about stock prices.

d. A "NOISE" THEORY OF DEVIATIONS FROM FUNDAMENTAL VALUES

One view of these apparent deviations from fundmental values is that they are produced by "noise" — influences on securities prices that are not associated with rational expectations about securities prices. A number of psychological explanations of investor behaviour may account for this. For instance, there is a tendency of persons to make decisions on the basis of more recent, or vivid, and therefore easily recalled, information. This may account for anecdotal

---

[24]The evidence on the volatility of stock prices is reviewed in e.g. Fama, "Efficient Capital Markets: II", *supra* note 11, at 1586-89; K. Cuthbertson, *Quantitative Financial Economics: Stocks, Bonds and Foreign Exchange*, (New York: John Wiley & Sons, 1996), at 134-51; J.H. Cochrane, "Volatility Tests and Efficient Markets: A Review Essay" (1991) 27 J. of Monetary Economics 463. See also J.N. Gordon & L.A. Kornhausen, "Efficient Markets, Costly Information, and Securities Research" (1985) 60 N.Y.U.L. Rev. 761; and W.K.S. Wang, "Some Arguments that the Stock Market is not Efficient" (1986) 19 U.C. Davis L. Rev. 341.

evidence that investors tend to follow fads or chase trends. People also tend to overestimate their own abilities to assess information and make decisions discounting the element of chance. Thus they may underestimate risks associated with securities investments. There is also the so-called "endowment effect" in which there is a tendency to value what one has more highly than what one does not have. This may account for the apparent tendency of investors to hold stocks for longer than they otherwise would be expected to.[25]

Beyond the psychological explanations of "noise" there may be structural forces affecting securities markets that result in long term patterns the presence of which has been suggested by recent tests on the behaviour of stock prices.[26] These structural forces could include such things as changes in preferences with respect to savings and investment, possibly connected to demographic changes, or technological changes.[27] Even relatively small, and potentially difficult to measure, changes in these structural forces may have a significant cumulative impact on securities market prices. The cumulative combination of several of these structural forces may be quite complex and produce patterns in securities prices that are difficult to detect and even more difficult to predict.[28]

---

[25] See Donald C. Langevoort, "Theories, Assumptions, and Securities Regulation: Market Efficiency Revisited" (1992) 140 University of Pennsylvania Law Rev. 851, at 857-60.

[26] The potential for longer term structural patterns has been discussed in the context of "chaos" theory. Briefly, chaos theory says that events that appear to be random may in fact be related and have a non-random pattern. See the discussion of this in the context of capital markets in Cunningham, *supra* note 14, at 581-92. See also Cuthbertson, *supra* note 24, at 194-201.

[27] See Fama, *supra* note 11, at 1609 noting that "[r]ational variation in expected returns is caused either by shocks to tastes for current versus future consumption or by technology shocks." Fama goes on to note (at 1609-10) that "[w]e may never be able to develop and test a full model that isolates taste and technology shocks and their effects on saving, consumption, investment and expected returns. We can, however, hope to know more about the links between expected returns and the macro-variables."

[28] See Cunningham, *supra* note 14, at 581-92.

e. APPLICATION OF THE EVIDENCE TO SMALLER SECURITIES MARKETS AND TO CANADA

Even if securities markets with high volumes of trading can be said to be efficient in the semi-strong form (responding to new publicly available information very quickly), the same may not be true for securities markets with lower volumes of trading for the reasons noted in Part III A 3 above. For instance, evidence on the efficiency of Canadian securities markets have yielded results which suggest that the smaller Canadian securities markets may not be as efficient as the larger securities markets that have been considered in most of the U.S. studies on securities market efficiency.[29]

D. Securities Market Efficiency and Securities Regulation

An understanding of securities market regulation is important from both a policy and practical perspective.

1. *A Policy Perspective*

One reason for the importance of securities market efficiency from a policy perspective is that securities regulation is often justified on the basis of protecting investors from paying more than the value of a security when they buy and receiving less than the value of

---

[29] See e.g. G. Charest, "Returns to Dividend Changing Stocks on the TSE" (1980) 12 J. Bus. Admin. 1; G. Charest, "Returns to Splitting Stocks on the TSE" (1980) 12 J. Bus. Admin. 19; V.M. Jog & A.L. Riding, "Market Reactions of Return, Risk and Liquidity to the Creation of Restricted Voting Shares" (1989) 6(1) Can. J. Admin. Sci. 62; D.J. Fowler & C.H. Rorke, "Insider Trading Profits on the Toronto Stock Exchange" (1988) 5(1) Can. J. Admin. Sci. 13; J.M. Suret & E. Cormier, "Insiders and the Stock Market" (1990) 3(2) Cdn. Inv't. Rev. 87. See also the discussion in J.P. Williamson, "Canadian Capital Markets" in *Proposals for a Securities Market Law for Canada*, vol. 3, 1979, Chapter 1, at 30-32. However, these results may be due to statistical problems encountered with relatively thin trading often encountered in the trading of some stocks listed on exchanges in Canada rather than as a result of inefficiency. Less well-traded markets create problems for the kinds of statistical techniques that are normally used to test capital market reactions to information – see D.J. Fowler, C.H. Rorke & V.M. Jog, "Heteroscedascity, R^2 and Thin Trading on the Toronto Stock Exchange" (1979) 34 J. Fin. 1201; D.J. Fowler, C.H. Rorke & V.M. Jog, "A Note on Beta Stability and Thin Trading on the Toronto Stock Exchange" (1981) 8 J. Bus. Fin. Acct. 267; D.J. Fowler, C.H. Rorke & V.M. Jog, "Thin Trading and Beta Estimation Problems on the Toronto Stock Exchange" (1980) 12 J. Bus. Admin. 77.

a security when they sell. If the market is efficient in the sense that prices are fair estimates of the values of the securities, then investors buying at the market price will receive a security that, as best as can be determined at the time of purchase, is worth what they paid for it. Investors selling securities at the market price will receive a payment equal to what, at the time of sale, is a fair estimate of the value of what they are selling. Thus the more efficient the market the more likely it is that the market prices investors are trading on will be fair prices and thus the less the need for regulation to assure fair prices.

One of the key elements of securities regulation is mandatory disclosure of certain types of information. This has been justified on the basis that making more information available to the market will make the market more efficient thereby protecting investors by making securities prices more closely reflect the underlying values of the securities. This justification for mandatory disclosure assumes that the market would not otherwise disclose this information, that the benefits of such disclosure outweigh the costs, that market will respond to this information and that the information will be used by investors to assess the underlying value of the securities.

Another reason for understanding securities market efficiency from a policy perspective is that securities market efficiency concepts have often been invoked to justify or criticize securities regulation.[30] Many of these uses of the implications of efficient securities markets, or lack thereof, are considered in subsequent chapters. The importance of securities market efficiency in securities regulation over the

---

[30]See e.g. B.A. Banoff, "Regulatory Subsidies, Efficient Markets, and Shelf Registration: An Analysis of Rule 415" (1984) 70 Virginia L. Rev. 135, at 138; Merrit B. Fox, "Shelf Registration, Integrated Disclosure, and Underwriter Due Diligence: An Economic Analysis" (1984) 70 Virginia L. Rev. 1005, at 1008; R.J. Dennis, "Materiality and the Efficient Capital Market Model: A Recipe for the Total Mix" (1984) 25 Wm. & Mary L. Rev. 373; D.R. Fischel, "Efficient Capital Market Theory, the Market for Corporate Control, and the Regulation of Cash Tender Offers" (1978) 57 Tex. L. Rev. 1; J.R. Macey et al., "Lessons from Financial Economics: Materiality, Reliance, and Extending the Reach of *Basic v. Levinson*" (1991) 77 Virginia L. Rev. 1017; L.A. Stout, "The Unimportance of Being Efficient: An Economic Analysis of Stock Market Pricing and Securities Regulation" (1988) 87 Mich. L. Rev. 613; L.A. Stout, "Are Stock Markets Costly Casinos? Disagreement, Market Failure, and Securities Regulation" (1995) 81 Virginia L. Rev. 611.

past several years has also led to reassessments of securities market efficiency and its implications for securities regulation.[31]

2. A Practical Perspective

It is also important to understand securities market efficiency from a practical perspective. First, securities regulators often justify the regulation as, in part, serving to increase the efficiency of securities markets. Thus an understanding of securities market efficiency is important in terms of understanding what it is securities regulation is intended to accomplish.[32] Second, as discussed in a subsequent chapter, securities commissions often implicitly address the question of the efficiency of the market with respect to a particular security, or type of security, in exercising the discretion granted to them under securities acts. Thus an understanding of securities market efficiency can assist one in identifying issues that may need to be addressed in making arguments before securities commissions.

E. A Framework for the Analysis of Securities Market Efficiency

One way of analyzing securities market efficiency from a policy perspective is to break down the analysis into different aspects of efficiency.

One aspect of efficiency that one may want to consider is whether the market is efficient in the production of information. A market is efficient in the production of information if it produces information to the point that the last dollar spent on producing information produces a dollar worth of benefit to society. The market may be inefficient in this sense if issuers of securities, securities analysts and investors involved in gathering and disclosing information cannot capture all of the benefits of producing information or do not incur the full costs of producing information. If they cannot capture all of the benefits of producing information then they will not have an incentive to produce all the information that can be

---

[31] See e.g. R.J. Gilson & R.H. Kraakman, "The Mechanisms of Market Efficiency" (1984) 70 Virginia L. Rev. 549; Gordon & Kornhauser, *supra* note 24; and Wang, *supra* note 24; D.C. Langevoort, *supra* note 25; L.A. Cunningham, *supra* note 14.

[32] See, e.g., Chapter 7, Part II C 3 and Chapter 8, Parts II C 1 b and V A.

beneficially produced. If they do not incur the full costs of producing information then they may have an incentive to overproduce information. In either case the inefficiency in the production of information may justify a regulatory response. Claims of this sort concerning how efficient securities markets are in producing information are considered in Chapter 9 below where the need for mandatory disclosure is assessed.

Another aspect of securities market efficiency that can be considered is how quickly markets respond to information. For the reasons noted in Part III A 3 *supra*, markets with higher volumes of trading are likely to respond more quickly to information than markets with lower volumes of trading. The speed of a securities market response to new information can have implications for such matters as the need for, and length of, halts in securities trading while new information is being disseminated or the length of time an insider must wait before trading on information that is being made public. In focusing on the speed of response of securities markets to new information one might consider steps that would increase the speed of response such as reducing the costs of trading or the costs of gathering and assessing information about securities.

It is also important to assess whether the degree to which prices in a particular securities market reflect the underlying values of securities. This may be very difficult to assess. However, such an assessment is important in an appraisal of securities regulation since many aspects of securities regulation typically implicitly assume that securities markets, while perhaps not fully efficient in the production of information or in the speed of response to new information, do at least have some capacity to use information to reflect the underlying values of securities.[33]

---

[33] See the discussion in M.R. Gillen, "Capital Market Efficiency Assumptions: An Analytical Framework with an Application to Disclosure Laws" (1994) 23 Can. Bus. L. J. 346, at 359-77.

CHAPTER 3

CONSTITUTIONAL DIVISION OF POWERS, HISTORY,
PURPOSE AND SOURCES OF SECURITIES
REGULATION

I. INTRODUCTION

Part II of this chapter notes the constitutional position with respect to the regulation of trading in securities. Part III of this chapter provides a brief history of securities regulation to put it into historical context. Part IV notes the underlying theory on which securities regulation is based, so that the law discussed in subsequent chapters can be understood in terms of its intended purpose. Last, Part V summarizes the sources of law on securities regulation so that subsequent references to the sources can be understood and that those interested can further pursue the law from primary sources for themselves.

II. THE CONSTITUTIONAL DIVISION OF POWERS
WITH RESPECT TO SECURITIES REGULATION[1]

Although there is federal legislation affecting trading in securities,[2] it is primarily dealt with under provincial law. The provinces

_____

[1] For a more extensive discussion of the constitutional division of powers with respect to securities regulation and the potential powers for federal regulation of securities, see P. Anisman & P.W. Hogg, "Constitutional Aspects of Federal Securities Legislation", *Proposals for a Securities Market Law for Canada*, Vol. 3, (Ottawa: Minister of Supply and Services, 1979) at 135-220.

[2] See ibid., Anisman & Hogg, at 143-44; P. Anisman, "The Regulation of the Securities Market and the Harmonization of Provincial Laws" in R. Cumming, Research Coordinator, *Harmonization of Business Law in Canada*, (Toronto: University of Toronto Press, 1986), at 77. Various federal laws do touch on trading in securities. For instance, there are provisions in the *Criminal Code*, such as ss. 380(2), 382, 383, 384 and 400, which deal with trading in securities.

have enacted securities acts under their power to legislate with respect to "property and civil rights".[3] The "property and civil rights" power has been interpreted to include dealings in property, contracts, and the regulation of business, trades and professions.[4]

The courts have tended to uphold the validity of provincial securities laws.[5] Provincial securities law has been upheld even where there is some overlapping, but not conflicting, federal law.[6] Provincial securities laws affecting persons outside of the province have also been upheld.[7] This may be due, in part, to a concern with respect to the regulatory gap that could be created by not upholding provincial law when there is no corresponding federal law to fill the void.[8] Nonetheless, it is still arguable that provincial securities law does not apply to federal companies in some situations.[9] To some

---

[3] S. 92(13) of the *Constitution Act, 1982*, enacted as Schedule B to the *Canada Act 1982*, (U.K.) 1982, c. 11.

[4] See, generally, P.W. Hogg, *Constitutional Law of Canada*, loose-leaf ed. (Toronto: The Carswell Co., 1992), Chapter 21.

[5] See Anisman & Hogg, *supra* note 1, at 144 noting *Lymburn v. Mayland*, [1932] A.C. 318 (P.C.); *Re Thodas* (1970), 10 C.R.N.S. 290 (B.C.C.A.); *International Claim Brokers Ltd. v. Kinsey* (1966), 57 D.L.R. (2d) 357 (B.C.C.A.); *Woodson v. Russel*, [1961] Que. Q.B. 349 (C.A.); *Re Williams* (1961), 29 D.L.R. (2d) 107 (Ont. C.A.).

[6] See for example *Multiple Access v. McCutcheon*, [1982] 2 S.C.R. 161, 138 D.L.R. (3d) 1, 18 B.L.R. 138, 44 N.R. 181. See also *Duplain v. Cameron*, [1961] S.C.R. 693; *Smith v. R.*, [1960] S.C.R. 776; *Malczewski v. Sansai Securities Ltd.* (1974), 49 D.L.R. (3d) 629 (B.C.S.C.); *Gregory & Company Inc. v. Imperial Bank of Canada*, [1960] Que. S.C. 204.

[7] See Anisman & Hogg, *supra* note 1, at 145-46 noting *R. v. McKenzie Securities Ltd.* (1966), 56 D.L.R. (2d) 56 (leave to appeal denied, *sub nom. West v. R.*, [1966] S.C.R. ix) and *Gregory & Company Inc. v. Q.S.C.*, [1961] S.C.R. 584.

[8] Ibid., Anisman & Hogg, at 145.

[9] Federally incorporated companies are presumed to have objects other than provincial objects and are therefore presumed to have the capacity to operate throughout the country. It has therefore been held that they cannot be precluded from operating anywhere in the country — see for example *John Deere Plow Co. Ltd. v. Wharton*, [1915] 7 W.W.R. 706, 18 D.L.R. 353, [1915] A.C. 330 (B.C., J.C. P.C.). The application to federal companies of a power to refuse a licence to sell shares under the Manitoba *Sale of Shares Act, 1912* was struck down by the Privy Council in *A.G. Manitoba v. A.G. Canada*, [1929] 1 W.W.R. 136, [1929] 1 D.L.R. 369 (P.C.). The licencing requirement was said to sterilize the federal company from operating since it could not sell the necessary shares to begin operation. A similar provision of the Saskatchewan *Sales of Shares Act* had also been struck down

extent this potential gap has been addressed in the federal companies legislation.[10]

Although Parliament has not passed a statute such as the various provincial acts regulating trading in securities, there are several heads of constitutional power under which it might do so.[11] Given the interprovincial, and indeed international, nature of trading in securities, Parliament might justify the regulation of securities markets under the trade and commerce power.[12] The regulation of stock exchanges and automated trading systems, whose activities extend beyond provincial boundaries, might be justified under the trade and commerce power or the power to regulate with respect to interprovincial undertakings or works for the general advantage of Canada.[13]

---

by the Supreme Court of Canada insofar as its application to federal companies in *Lukey and A.G. Saskatchewan v. Ruthenian Farmers' Elevator Co.*, [1924] S.C.R. 56, [1924] 1 D.L.R. 706, [1924] 1 W.W.R. 577.

An Alberta securities act requiring sale of shares through a licenced broker was upheld in *Lymburn v. Mayland, supra*, note 5. The definition of "person" excluded "company". The prohibition against selling without a licence then applied not to the company, but to its officers or other employees. The requirement to sell through a licenced broker was said not to sterilize the federal company's operations since it could still sell shares. However, it is still arguable on the basis of *A.G. Manitoba v. A.G. Canada, supra,* and the *Lukey* case, *supra,* that some aspects of provincial securities laws would not apply to federally incorporated companies.

[10] The C.B.C.A. has provisions on takeover bids, insider trading, proxy solicitation and financial disclosure that, at least in their inception, were similar to provisions in provincial securities acts.

[11] See generally Anisman & Hogg, *supra* note 1, at 153-220.

[12] S. 91(2) of the *Constitution Act, 1982, supra* note 3. However, this may be difficult under the tests in *MacDonald v. Vapour Canada*, [1977] 2 S.C.R. 134 and *General Motors v. National Leasing*, [1989] 1 S.C.R. 641, since it may be difficult to argue that the regulation is not regulation of a particular industry (i.e., the securities industry) and that the provinces, jointly or severally, would be constitutionally incapable of enacting such legislation. See the discussion of the trade and commerce power in Hogg, *supra* note 4, Chapter 20, especially at p. 20.3.

[13] S. 92(10) of the *Constitution Act, 1982, supra* note 3. See Anisman & Hogg, *supra* note 1, at 218-19. Anisman and Hogg also note, but recommend against relying exclusively on, the use of such federal powers as the criminal law power (see pages 186-89) and the power "to make Laws for the Peace, Order, and good Government of Canada, in relation to all Matters not coming within the Classes of Subjects ... assigned exclusively to the Legislatures of the Provinces" (see pages 177-86).

III. A BRIEF HISTORY OF SECURITIES REGULATION

A. Early Developments in the United Kingdom

Securities regulation is a relatively recent phenomenon. Although there is evidence of the regulation of brokers in the City of London as early as 1285,[14] trading in stocks probably did not develop until many years later. In the post-renaissance period, new trading ventures, which were risky and involved large capital expenditures, encouraged risk sharing through loans and partnerships.[15] Eventually joint stock partnerships and companies based on Crown charters developed.[16]

Further developments of share capital companies were delayed by a fiasco concerning the "South Sea bubble".[17] The South Sea

---

[14] 13 Edward I, Statutes for the City of London. The reference in the statute is to brokers and not specifically to stock brokers. Just what these brokers traded in is not clear (although it seems unlikely that it was stocks). The reference to brokers is in the following passage,

> And Whereas divers Persons do resort unto the City, some from Parts beyond the Sea, and others of this Land and do there seek shelter and refuge, by reason of Banishment out of their own Country, or who for great offence or other misdeed have fled from their own Country; and of these some do become Brokers, Hostelers, and Innkeepers within the City, for Denizens and Strangers, as freely as though they were good and lawful Men of the Franchise of the City; and some nothing do but run up and down through the Streets, more by Night than by Day, and are well attired in Clothing and Array, and have their Food of delicate Meats and costly; Neither do they use any Craft or Merchandise, nor have they Lands or Tenements whereof to live, nor any Friend to find them: and through such Persons many perils do often happen in the City, and many evils, and some of them are found openly offending, as in Robberies, breaking of Houses by night, Murders, and other evil Deeds: ... And there shall be no Broker in the City, except those who are admitted and sworn before the Warden or Mayor, and Aldermen. ...

[15] See Fernand Braudel, *Civilization and Capitalism, 15th-18th Century,* Vol. II: "The Wheels of Commerce" (London: Collins, 1982), Chapter 4.

[16] See for example L.C.B. Gower, et al., *Gower's Principles of Modern Company Law,* 4th ed., (London: Stevens & Sons, 1979), at 23-27.

[17] The South Sea Company fiasco has been the subject of a plethora of literature. See for example Melville, *The South Sea Bubble* (London: Daniel O'Conner, 1921); W.R. Scott, *The Constitution and Finance of English, Scottish and Irish Joint-Stock Companies* (Cambridge: Cambridge University Press, 1912), Vol. 1, chs. XX and XXI; J. Carswell, *The South Sea Bubble* (London: The Cresset Press, 1960);

Company was organized in 1711 in response to the financial troubles of the English government. Government debt was exchanged for stock in the South Sea Company and a tax fund was established which could pay an annuity to the Company.[18] A monopoly in trade in the South Seas was given to the Company as an added inducement to investors.[19] Hopes for the cession by Spain, in the context of peace negotiations, of four "security ports", which would have provided a base for trading operations, were not realized. Instead they obtained the privilege of a contract for the supply of 4,800 negro slaves per year to Spanish possessions in America. This trade turned out not to provide much in the way of profit to the company's shareholders and eventually ceased by 1718.[20] New government debt reorganization plans in 1720 renewed speculation in the company's stock.[21] There was a lot of trading on margin (i.e., borrowing; buy now, pay later). Various events contrived to cause sales of shares of joint stock companies, including the South Sea Company.[22] Margins were called leading to further selling. The price rose from £128 on January 1st, 1720 to a peak of £1050 on June 24th (rising from £352 on May 13) and by December it had again fallen to a price of £128 (having dropped to a price of £290 by October 1).[23]

An attempt was made to maintain high prices for South Sea Company shares by preventing investment in other companies. This was done by passing a piece of legislation called the *Bubble Act* in 1720.[24] The Act prohibited the sale of shares in joint stock com-

---

V. Cowles, *The Great Swindle: The Story of the South Sea Bubble* (London: Collins, 1960); John G. Sperling, *The South Sea Company: An Historical Essay and Bibliographical Finding List* (Boston: Harvard Graduate School of Business Administration, Baker Library, 1962).

[18] See, for example, Sperling, *supra* note 17, at 1-2.

[19] Ibid.

[20] Ibid., at 2. On the problems with the negro slave trade contract see ibid., at 14-26.

[21] Ibid., at 27-32.

[22] Some of these events are discussed in Sperling, *supra* note 17, at 31-32.

[23] Ibid., at 31.

[24] 6 George I, c. 18.

panies unless the company was created by Crown charter.[25] Crown charters became much more difficult to obtain.[26] The result was that the raising of capital by the sale of shares in companies was constrained.[27]

The *Bubble Act* suppressed the formation of companies with share capital for roughly a century. However, by the 19th century, pressure for easier access to capital in the midst of the industrial revolution led to the repeal of the *Bubble Act* in 1825.[28] The pressure for easier access to capital in the industrial revolution led to the enactment of the *Companies Act* in 1844[29] which made it easier to organize in a company form. This led to a greater availability of shares for trading and thus greater potential for concerns to arise which could lead to some form of securities regulation.

One early type of securities regulation involved disclosure in a prospectus on the issuance of securities. This arose out of a concern as to the accuracy of statements in prospectuses for the sale of securities which was arguably mitigated by the decision in *Derry v. Peek*[30] in 1889. In *Derry v. Peek* an action based on a misrepresentation in a prospectus was dismissed on the basis that the plaintiff had to show fraud and had failed to do so. The court stated that fraud would be proven when it was shown that the misrepresentation was made (a) knowingly, or (b) without belief in its truth, or (c) recklessly, careless whether it be true or false.[31] This examination of intent made it difficult to sustain an action against directors for misrepresentations in a prospectus.

The constraints of *Derry v. Peek* with respect to misrepresentations in a prospectus were soon dealt with in the *Directors Liability Act, 1890*.[32] Directors, promoters and others who authorized the

---

[25] Ibid., s. 18. Brokers who traded in shares of the prohibited types of companies were subject to penalties of up to £500 (see s. 21).

[26] See, for example, Gower, *supra* note 16, at 31.

[27] Ibid.

[28] 6 Geo. IV, c. 91.

[29] 7 & 8 Vict., c. 110.

[30] (1889), 14 A.C. 337 (H.L.).

[31] See the decision of Lord Bramwell at 14 A.C. 350-53 and the decision of Lord Herschell at 14 A.C. 360-76.

[32] 53 & 54 Vict., c. 64. Ontario followed with a similar statute, the *Directors' Liability Act, 1891*, S.O. 1891, c. 34.

use of their name on the prospectus were liable to persons who subscribed for shares on the faith of the prospectus, if such persons had sustained loss or damage by reason of any untrue statement in the prospectus.[33] Directors, promoters and signers of the prospectus were liable, unless they could prove that they had reasonable grounds to believe the statements were true or that any copy of or extract from a report of an expert or official person was a fair copy or extract.[34]

B. U.S. Developments

In the U.S., states began legislating against securities frauds by the early 20th century.[35] Kansas passed the first state securities legislation in 1911.[36] The Kansas statute prohibited the sale of securities by an issuer in Kansas unless the sale of the securities was approved by the bank commissioner on the basis of the merits of the investment offered by the securities. Several other states followed the Kansas example by enacting similar statutes. A number of alleged stock market scandals and the crash of 1929 led to the U.S. federal *Securities Act of 1933*, which required registration statements for the sale of securities, and the *Securities Exchange Act of 1934*, which dealt with secondary market trading.[37]

---

[33] Ibid., s. 3.

[34] Ibid.

[35] See, for example, L. Loss, *Fundamentals of Securities Regulation* (Boston: Little, Brown & Co., 1983), at 8.

[36] Kans. Laws 1911, c. 133. The legislation allowed the state securities commissioner to pass on the merits of the particular securities before it could be registered for trading. State legislation of this type is known as "blue sky law", supposedly because its initial impetus was a concern about eastern industrialists selling "building lots in the blue sky in fee simple". See, for example, Loss, *supra* note 35, at 8; and T.L. Hazen, *Treatise on the Law of Securities Regulation*, 3rd ed., vol. 1 (St. Paul: West Publishing Co., 1995), at 6.

[37] See, for example, Hazen, *supra* note 36, at 7.

The emphasis in these statutes was disclosure.[38] This emphasis in the U.S. federal statutes appears to have had considerable influence on the development of Canadian securities laws.[39]

C. Canadian Developments[40]

1. *Fraud Prevention Acts*

Early statutes in Canada were directed at securities frauds. The Manitoba *Sale of Shares Act of 1912*,[41] modelled on the Kansas statute of 1911, required that any company not organized in Manitoba had to obtain a licence to sell shares in Manitoba and required that certain documents dealing with the financial status of the company be filed before a licence would be given.[42] Other provinces enacted similar legislation.[43] Ontario enacted *The Security Frauds Prevention Act*[44] in 1928 which required the licensing of stock brokers and provided for investigations into securities frauds.[45] "Fraud" was defined to include such things as intentional misrepre-

---

[38] See, for example, Hazen, *supra* note 36, at 7, "[t]he theory behind the federal regulatory framework is that investors are adequately protected if all aspects of the securities being marketed are fully and fairly disclosed"; see also Loss, *supra* note 35, at 7 noting that "there is the recurrent theme throughout these statutes of disclosure, again disclosure, and still more disclosure".

[39] The recommendations of the *Kimber Report* (see Part III C 3) with respect to disclosure, which were adopted in securities laws throughout most of Canada, emphasized disclosure of the type required by the *Securities Exchange Act of 1934*.

[40] On the development of Canadian securities law see, for example, J. Peter Williamson, *Securities Regulation in Canada*, (Toronto: University of Toronto Press, 1960), at 3-46; D.L. Johnston, *Canadian Securities Regulation*, (Toronto: Butterworths, 1977), 9-18; P. Anisman, "The Regulation of the Securities Market and the Harmonization of Provincial Laws", *supra* note 2, at 77-82; Notice, "Ontario's Proposed Securities Act: An Overview" [1975] Q.S.C.B. 235-70. For a very brief summary of the Quebec law see L. LaRochelle et al., "Bill 85, Quebec's New Securities Act" (1983) 29 McGill L.J. 88 at 92-94.

[41] S.M. 1912, c. 75.

[42] Ibid., s. 2.

[43] See *Sale of Shares Act*, S.S. 1914, c. 18; *Sale of Shares Act*, S.A. 1916, c. 18; *Sales of Securities Act*, S.N.B. 1923, c. 19; *Act respecting the powers of certain companies to issue and re-issue bonds, debentures and other securities*, S.Q. 1924, c. 64.

[44] S.O. 1928, c. 24.

[45] Ibid., s. 3.

sentations, unconscionable commissions, and conduct of business with intent to deceive.[46] The Act provided for injunctions, penal sanctions (of up to $2,000 for individuals and $25,000 for companies) and seizing of assets of offenders.[47] This form of legislation was adopted by most other provinces.[48]

2. Prospectus Disclosure

Ontario modified its legislation in 1945[49] and again in 1947.[50] The 1947 legislation required specified elements to be included in a prospectus for any distribution of securities to the public.[51] It also required delivery of the prospectus coupled with a right of rescission within seven days of receipt of the prospectus.[52] There was a statutory liability provision under which directors, promoters and others authorizing the issue of the prospectus were liable for any material false statement in a prospectus to any purchaser, whether fraudulent or not, and whether or not the purchaser relied on the representations made in the prospectus or even received the prospectus.[53] The statutory liability provision did not require the purchaser to show an intent on the part of the defendant to make a false statement. Instead, the provision made reasonable grounds for a belief in the

---

[46] Ibid., s. 2.

[47] Ibid., ss. 11,12, and 16.

[48] *Securities Frauds Prevention Act*, S.A. 1929, c. 10; *The Security Frauds Prevention Act, 1929*, S.P.E.I. 1929, c. 8; *The Security Frauds Prevention Act, 1929*, S.S. 1929, c. 68, revised S.S. 1930, c. 74; *The Security Frauds Prevention Act, 1930*, S.A. 1930, c. 8; *An Act to amend "The Security Frauds Prevention Act, 1929"*, S.M. 1930, c. 36; *The Security Frauds Prevention Act*, S.N.S. 1930, c. 3; *The Security Frauds Prevention Act, 1930*, S.P.E.I. 1930, c. 2; *Security Frauds Prevention Act, 1930*, S.Q. 1930, c. 88; *The Security Frauds Prevention Act*, S.N.B. 1935, c. 11.

[49] *The Securities Act, 1945*, S.O. 1945, c. 22.

[50] *The Securities Act, 1947*, S.O. 1947, c. 98.

[51] Ibid., ss. 43, 44, and 45. Specific prospectus requirements had been included in companies legislation in Ontario. See *The Ontario Companies Act*, S.O. 1907, c. 34, s. 99.

[52] Ibid., ss. 52 and 53.

[53] Ibid., s. 73. This brought the earlier Ontario *Directors' Liability Act, 1891*, S.O. 1891, c. 34 provision into comprehensive securities legislation.

truth of the statement a defence to an action by a purchaser.[54] This statute was followed by similar statutes in other provinces.[55]

The statute was quite different from the earlier fraud prevention statute in that it did not just try to deal with frauds (requiring a proof of intent) after the fact. It gave purchasers a statutory right of action in which they did not have to prove intent or reliance. It was presumably hoped that this would tend to more strongly deter fraudulent or negligent misstatements in prospectuses. However, the legislation dealt only with disclosure on the distribution of securities. It did not provide for ongoing disclosure of information to support secondary market trading.

3. *The Kimber Report*

Modern securities regulation in Canada has been considerably influenced by the Kimber Report[56] of 1965. The Kimber Report was one of several reports produced in the early 1960s that addressed the regulation of securities markets. These reports generally responded to specific problems that had arisen. Indeed, the Kimber Report got its impetus, in part, from the Shell Oil takeover of Canadian Oil, in which certain persons had used knowledge of the takeover to buy shares of Canadian Oil before the announcement of the takeover.[57] The Commission's mandate was primarily to look into insider trading and takeover bids, but its mandate also included generally addressing the degree of disclosure to shareholders. The Kimber Report recommendations included requirements for ongoing disclosure including the distribution of periodic financial statements, mandatory proxy solicitation and reporting of insider trading.[58] The Ontario *Securities Act of 1966*[59] adopted many of the Kimber

---

[54] Ibid., s. 73(1)(d).

[55] See *Securities Act, 1954*, S.S. 1954, c. 89; *Security Act, 1955*, S.A. 1955, c. 64; *Securities Fraud Prevention Act* (amended), S.N.B. 1955, c. 73; *Securities Act (Amendment)*, S.Q. 1955-56, c. 29; *Securities Act, 1962*, S.B.C. 1962, c. 55.

[56] "Report of the Attorney General's Committee on Securities Legislation in Ontario", (the "Kimber Report") (Toronto: Queen's Printer, March 1965).

[57] Notice, "Ontario's Proposed Securities Act", *supra* note 40, at 242.

[58] See the Kimber Report, *supra* note 56, Parts II, IV and VI.

[59] S.O. 1966, c. 142.

Report's recommendations and the Act (known as the "*Uniform Act*") was subsequently enacted in all of the western provinces.[60]

4. *The Merger Report and the "Closed System"*

By the time the western provinces had adopted the *Uniform Act*, Ontario had again reassessed the status of securities law. An influential report in this reassessment was the Merger Report of 1970. This reassessment ultimately led to the enactment of the "closed system" statute in 1978.[61] This statute was later adopted in most of the other provinces.[62] The key to the "closed system" statute is its very strong emphasis on ongoing disclosure for the purposes of secondary market trading. It allows trading amongst a select group of persons who are presumed not to need the protection provided by the extensive disclosure contained in prospectuses, financial statements, mandatory proxy solicitation, and so on. However, the concept is that, if trading is to be done beyond this select group, it must be supported by these various forms of mandatory disclosure. Most provinces have adopted the "closed system" form of statute with subtle variations on the Ontario model.

5. *Interprovincial Cooperation*

Cooperation between provincial securities administrators has been an important characteristic of the regulation of securities markets in Canada. Canadian securities administrators have met annually since the early 1950s[63] and semi-annually since 1963.[64] They have also cooperated in producing joint policy statements, undertaken joint studies of potential new policy developments, and

---

[60] *Securities Act, 1967*, S.A. 1967, c. 76; *Securities Act, 1967*, S.B.C. 1967, c. 45; *Securities Act, 1967*, S.S. 1967, c. 81; *Securities Act, 1968*, S.M. 1968, c. 57.

[61] S.O. 1978, c. 47.

[62] See the A.S.A.; B.C.S.A.; Nfld.S.A.; N.S.S.A.; and S.S.A. The Q.S.A., although substantially different in structure and wording, is also a "closed system" statute. See LaRochelle et al., *supra* note 40. For a description of the abbreviations of the statutes see the "Table of Abbreviations".

[63] See Anisman, *supra* note 2, at 79; and see Notice, "Ontario's Proposed Securities Act", *supra* note 40, at 240-41.

[64] Ibid., Anisman, at 79.

conducted joint hearings with respect to both policies and adjudicative proceedings.[65] The impetus for cooperation appears to be in part "a desire to avoid inconsistent requirements which would create impediments to the efficient functioning of the securities market and thus undermine rather than promote the ultimate purposes of the legislation, namely, enhancement of the raising of capital by corporate issuers".[66] Another impetus for interprovincial cooperation may be a desire to forestall any pressure for federal legislation of securities markets.[67]

A national regulation of securities markets has been suggested several times in the past.[68] However, attempts to provide for comprehensive federal securities regulation or to create a federal securities commission have thus far been unsuccessful. A proposal for a federal securities commission was first made in 1967.[69] In the late 1970s, a securities market law for Canada was prepared for the federal Department of Consumer and Corporate Affairs.[70] However, the federal government did not follow through on the proposal. A more recent proposal for a federal securities commission was developed in response to a First Ministers' meeting in December of 1993.[71] Under the proposed scheme a federal securities commission would take over the administration of securities laws passed by provincial legislatures. Interest in this proposal waned and, in spite of an attempt to revive it in the 1996 federal government throne speech, it has yet to be adopted.

D. Summary

Securities regulation – regulating brokers, requiring prospectus disclosure and various forms of disclosure directed at secondary

---

[65] Ibid., at 79-80.

[66] Ibid., at 80.

[67] Ibid.

[68] See, e.g., *Report of the Royal Commission on Price Spreads*, (Ottawa: King's Printer, 1935), at 41-2; *Report of the Royal Commission on Banking and Finance*, (Ottawa: Queen's Printer, 1964) (the "Porter Report"); and *Report of the Attorney General's Committee on Securities Legislation in Ontario*, (Toronto: Queen's Printer, 1965) (the "Kimber Report").

[69] See (November 1967) OSCB 61 at 65.

[70] See *Proposals for a Securities Market Law for Canada, supra* note 1.

[71] (1994) 17 OSCB 4401.

market trading — is a relatively recent phenomenon. Significant developments appear to have begun in roughly the mid-19th century, with the most significant developments occurring in the last 65 years. Most provinces have adopted the type of statutory scheme known as the closed system. Securities regulation in Canada has been marked by a growing degree of interprovincial cooperation. There has been a general move to making the regulation, while not identical, at least compatible across the provinces. Thus much of the legislation, regulations and policy statements that constitute securities regulation in the various provinces is very similar.

IV. THE PURPOSE OF SECURITIES REGULATION

A. Investor Protection, Confidence in the Market and the Efficient Allocation of Resources

The summary of the purpose of securities regulation which follows is based primarily on the Kimber Report.[72] The views set out in the Kimber Report are the basis of modern Canadian securities regulation. The views of the Kimber Report were echoed in other reports produced at about the same time as the Kimber Report and[73] were accepted in the subsequent Merger Report.[74]

1. *Investor Protection and Optimal Allocation of Financial Resources*

The two main objectives of securities regulation, as expressed in the Kimber Report, are investor protection and the optimal allocation of financial resources.[75]

---

[72] *Supra* note 56.

[73] For reports contemporary with the Kimber Report see "Report of the Royal Commission to Investigate Trading in the Shares of Windfall Oils and Mines Ltd.", (the "Kelly Report") (Toronto: Queen's Printer, 1965) and "Report of the Royal Commission on Banking and Finance", (the "Porter Report") (Ottawa: Queens Printer, 1964).

[74] "Report of the Committee of the Ontario Securities Commission on the Problems of Disclosure Raised for Investors by Business Combinations and Private Placements", (the "Merger Report") (Toronto: Ontario Securities Commission, February 1970).

[75] Kimber Report, *supra* note 56, at para. 1.06.

a. INVESTOR PROTECTION

The underlying purpose of securities regulation, it is said, is the "protection of the investing public".[76] However, the intention is not to provide paternalistic protection of the investor. According to the Kimber Report, although every effort must be made to ensure the public understands the normal business risks of success or failure,

> [t]his is not to suggest that the public must be protected against itself; rather, it is a matter of ensuring that the investing public has the fullest possible knowledge to enable it to distinguish the different types of investment activity available. In such circumstances, the public would have assurance that its losses are genuine economic losses, just as its gains are genuine economic gains.[77]

Thus the investor is to be permitted to incur a loss. However, the loss should be a genuine economic loss. In other words, the price at which an investor purchases or sells a security should be a fair estimate of the value of the future cash flows it will generate.

b. OPTIMAL ALLOCATION OF FINANCIAL RESOURCES

Another purpose of securities regulation is said to be the development of financial institutions which assure the optimum allocation of financial resources in the economy.[78] To promote this optimal allocation, there are two related objectives, namely, to ensure that

---

[76] Ibid.; see also the Merger Report, *supra* note 74, at para. 1.19. Similar statements have been made in a number of court decisions. For instance, in *W.D. Latimer Co. v. Ontario (Attorney General)* (1973), 2 O.R. (2d) 391 at 393 (Div. Ct.), aff'd (1974), 6 O.R. (2d) 129 (C.A.) Wright J. noted that, "[t]he Securities Act and the Commission are to protect the investing public in Ontario from grave and pressing perils ...". In *Gregory & Co. Inc. v. Quebec Securities Commission* (1961), 28 D.L.R. (2d) 721 at 725, [1961] S.C.R. 584 at 588, Fauteux J. said that,

> The paramount objective of the Act is to ensure that persons who, in the province, carry on the business of trading in securities or acting as investment counsel, shall be honest and of good repute and, in this way, to protect the public, in the Province or elsewhere, from being defrauded as a result of certain activities initiated in the Province by persons therein carrying on such a business.

See also *Gordon Capital Corp. v. Ontario (Securities Commission)* (1991), 1 Admin. L.R. (2d) 199 at 208 (Ont. Div. Ct.); and *Brosseau v. Alberta (Securities Commission)* (1989), 57 D.L.R. (4th) 458 (S.C.C.).

[77] Ibid., Kimber Report, at para. 1.12.

[78] Ibid., para. 1.06.

capital markets facilitate the mobility and transferability of financial resources and to provide facilities for the continuing valuation of financial assets.[79] In short, securities regulation should promote the efficiency of capital markets.

Theoretically, as the Kimber Report noted, the optimal allocation of financial resources could be achieved by the maintenance of a free and open securities market.[80] However, this, the Report noted, would depend on the existence of conditions such as perfect knowledge of the market and market opportunities by both buyer and seller, free access to the market and complete mobility of financial resources.[81] The Kimber Report noted that these conditions do not exist and concluded that securities regulation must be designed "not only to serve the purpose of reducing the imperfections in the free and open capital market, but also to assure the efficient operation of the market in achieving long-run economic objectives."[82]

c. LINK BETWEEN INVESTOR PROTECTION AND THE OPTIMAL ALLOCATION OF FINANCIAL RESOURCES

Investor protection and the development of financial institutions which assure the optimal allocation of financial resources are, according to the Kimber Report, closely linked:

> Establishment of the conditions and practices in the capital market which best serve the investing public will normally be consistent with the best interests of the whole economy. For example, disclosure of financial information which depicts adequately the operations and financial position of companies is vital to the investing public; such disclosure also provides the capital market with the information necessary to make a more satisfactory allocation of resources.[83]

---

[79] Ibid. See also the "Statement by the Honourable Eric A. Winkler, Minister of Consumer and Commercial Relations on the Introduction of the Securities Act, 1972 for First Reading, June 1st, 1972", Notice, [1972] O.S.C.B. 94.

[80] Ibid., para. 1.08.

[81] Ibid.

[82] Ibid., paras. 1.09 and 1.10.

[83] Ibid., para. 1.07.

2. *Achieving Objectives by Promoting Confidence in the Market*

a. PUBLIC CONFIDENCE-IN-THE-MARKET

Correction of market imperfections through securities regulation would create public confidence which, according to the Kimber Report, is "[o]ne of the strongest single forces in the complex process of raising capital ...".[84] Public confidence, it was said, "is largely based on the expectation of profits and knowledge of relevant facts necessary to permit the anticipation of such profits."[85]

Promoting confidence would thus involve providing knowledge of the relevant facts necessary to permit the anticipation of profits. This would protect investors by allowing the evaluation of the "worth" of investments[86] and thus providing investors with "reasonable assurance" that any losses would be "genuine economic losses".[87] By providing this confidence, investors will supposedly be willing to pay more for securities and will be inclined to direct more savings to investment.

b. THE LINK BETWEEN PRIMARY AND SECONDARY MARKET CONFIDENCE

The Kimber Report also emphasized the link between confidence in the secondary market and confidence in the primary market.[88] Investors will be willing to pay more for new issues of securities in the primary market if they are confident they will be able to subsequently sell the securities in the secondary market and will be able to do so at a price that is a fair estimate of the value of the security.

c. ALLOCATION OF SAVINGS TO INVESTMENT PROMOTING ECONOMIC GROWTH

With investors paying more for new issues of securities in the primary market, due in part to confidence in the secondary market,

---

84 Ibid., para. 1.11.

85 Ibid.

86 Ibid., para. 4.02.

87 Ibid., para. 1.06.

88 Ibid., para. 1.12.

more savings, it was said, would be channelled into investment. Better pricing of securities would improve the allocation of financial resources. The improved allocation of resources and increased investment would contribute to economic growth and the welfare of the nation.[89]

3. Not at Excessive Cost

The goals of investor protection and the optimal allocation of financial resources should not, it has been noted, impose excessive costs.[90] Regulatory requirements can impose substantial costs in terms of compliance and in terms of causing the market to shift to less efficient means of trading in securities or of financing operations. The desire to keep these costs down is often a partial explanation of the mitigation of more stringent requirements of securities regulation.[91]

4. The Method of Achieving Public Confidence and the Optimal Allocation of Financial Resources

Securities regulation seeks to provide investor protection, public confidence and an efficient market primarily through disclosure[92] and the regulation of persons such as brokers, dealers, underwriters, portfolio managers and advisors. Disclosure at the point of the distribution of securities in the primary market and, in response to the Kimber Report, continuous disclosure in support of secondary market trading, provides information for the purpose of assessing

---

[89] Ibid., paras. 1.13 and 1.14.

[90] See Johnston, *supra* note 40, at 1. The Merger Report, *supra* note 74, notes, at para. 1.19, that protection is to be "given to the investor in such fashion as to balance his rights and the obligations of the issuer so as to permit the capital market to function with maximum utility." A similar notion is implicit in the Kimber Report's (*supra* note 56) emphasis, at para. 1.06, on the maximum mobility and transferability of financial resources.

[91] This will be apparent in the analysis of various aspects of securities regulation in subsequent chapters.

[92] The Kimber Report clearly linked public confidence to disclosure, noting that "the substantial majority of its recommendations ... deal directly or indirectly with disclosure of information to investors, that is to say, with the factor of public confidence". (para. 1.17).

the returns and risks associated with securities.[93] It is intended to provide all investors with "equal access" to information.[94] The regulation of brokers, dealers, etc., is directed to providing public confidence by addressing concerns such as pressure selling, conflicts of interest, professional competence, and the risk of business failure.

B. Confidence in the Market and Adverse Selection

To further appreciate the concept of confidence in the market (or the lack thereof), and to understand some of the criticisms of mandatory disclosure, it is helpful to understand confidence in the market in terms of a concept called "adverse selection".

1. *The Concept of Adverse Selection*

a. LOWER QUALITY DRIVES OUT HIGHER QUALITY

Adverse selection is said to occur to the extent that buyers are unable to distinguish higher quality from lower quality products. In such circumstances the lower quality products will tend to drive out the higher quality products. This will occur because buyers, being unable to make the distinction between higher and lower quality, will not be willing to pay more than a price that represents an average of the value of the lower quality and the higher quality.[95] It is then not profitable to offer the higher quality product, since buyers will not be willing to pay a price equal to what the product is worth.[96]

---

[93] See ibid., the Kimber Report, at para. 4.02 where it notes that "[i]t is difficult for the ordinary investor, in the absence of adequate disclosure, to arrive at an informed opinion as to the worth of his investment."

[94] See, for example, National Policy #40, Part B.

[95] In this way the buyer's expected loss from getting the poorer quality version of the product is balanced by an equivalent chance of getting a better quality version of the product.

[96] See Ackerlof, "The Market for 'Lemons': Qualitative Uncertainty and the Market Mechanism" (1970) 84 Q.J. Econ. 488. The process described would presumably continue to force out higher quality products to the point at which distinctions in quality can be discerned. Initially a price is set at the average between higher and lower quality. It becomes no longer worthwhile to produce higher quality and the higher quality product is driven from the market. The market then sets a new average price that represents an average of the lowest identifiable quality

b. WHY THERE ARE UNDISCERNED DIFFERENCES IN QUALITY

Buyers may be unable to distinguish higher quality from lower quality because making the distinction will require a costly process of gathering and assessing information about the product. At some point the perceived cost of the information will outweigh the perceived gain from being able to make finer distinctions in quality. This will leave residual unidentified distinctions in quality.

2. Adverse Selection in the Securities Market

a. LOWER QUALITY SECURITIES TEND TO DRIVE OUT HIGHER QUALITY SECURITIES

In the context of the sale of securities, to the extent that investors are unable to distinguish higher quality (more valuable) securities from lower quality (less valuable) securities, the lower quality securities will tend to drive out the higher quality securities. Higher quality securities will sell at lower prices than they would if investors could properly determine their worth[97] and there will be less investment in these more valuable business activities than there otherwise would be (i.e., a misallocation of financial resources). Lower quality securities will sell for more than what they are worth and there will be more investment in these less valuable business activities (i.e., a misallocation of financial resources).[98]

b. WHY THERE ARE UNDISCERNED DIFFERENCES IN THE QUALITY OF SECURITIES

Investors will not gather and assess all the information necessary to distinguish higher quality from lower quality securities because the information gathering process is costly and at some point it will

---

and the average quality that could profitably be produced at the previous average price. At this new average price it is no longer profitable to produce product of the former average quality. These higher quality products are also driven from the market and on the process would go until only the lowest level of undistinguished quality would remain.

[97] In other words, if information were costless.

[98] See, for example, F.R. Easterbrook & D.R. Fischel, "Mandatory Disclosure and the Protection of Investors" (1984) 70 Virg. L.R. 669 at 673-74. Some higher quality securities, and the business activities they are associated with, may be driven from the market. The resources may be directed to less valuable substitute uses.

not be worthwhile to gather further information. This will leave some undiscerned differences in the quality of securities.

Issuers of higher quality securities might try to disclose information to assist investors in identifying the higher quality of their securities. However, this too will involve a cost and at some point further attempts by the issuer to signal the higher quality of their securities will no longer be worthwhile in terms of increasing the price of their securities in the market. Issuers may also withhold information to protect commercially valuable secrets, such as secret production processes. Some less than honest issuers may frustrate the information gathering process by making false statements that are costly to verify or by concealing significant information that is costly to reveal.[99]

3. *Connection to Confidence in the Market*

A restatement of the notion of public confidence in securities markets, in terms of adverse selection, might go something as follows. If investors could be given greater "confidence" in the accuracy of information disclosed by issuers and greater "confidence" that market prices are fair estimates of the values of securities, they would be willing to pay more for securities. If investors were more confident in their assessments of the quality of securities, then higher quality securities would be more likely to survive in the market. More of the available financial resources would be channelled into higher quality securities and the business activities associated with these securities, thus improving the allocation of financial resources. Confidence in the higher quality of securities (i.e., the prospect of higher returns for a given risk) would also encourage greater savings and the investment of those savings in securities.

In other words, creating confidence in the market would help to overcome the problem of adverse selection. Since adverse selection is due to a lack of information allowing distinctions between higher and lower quality securities, the solution to the problem requires providing additional information and improving the accuracy of information. Thus confidence would be created by providing additional information and improving the accuracy of information.

---

[99] Ibid., at 674.

4. *Securities Regulation as a Response to Adverse Selection*

Securities regulation, which requires disclosure for the purpose of increasing public confidence in securities markets in order to protect investors and improve the allocation of resources, can also be understood as a response to the problem of adverse selection. Providing information improves the identification of higher quality securities and thus increases the allocation of financial resources to higher quality securities.

While providing additional information through disclosure might improve the identification higher quality securities, the benefits of this mandatory disclosure may not outweigh the costs of providing the additional disclosure. This is a question that will be taken up in more detail in Chapter 9.

V. SOURCES OF PROVINCIAL SECURITIES REGULATION

Another piece of background information that is useful for anyone who wishes to pursue securities regulation further is a summary of some of the main sources of law with respect to securities regulation. The sources noted below are the provincial securities acts, the regulations and rules passed pursuant to those acts, policy statements, blanket orders, memoranda of understanding, notices and decisions of securities administrators and the by-laws, rules, policies and decisions of stock exchanges and other self-regulatory organizations.

A. Provincial Securities Acts

Each of the provinces has passed statutes dealing directly with securities regulation.[100] These provincial securities acts tend to set out the broad framework for the regulation of securities trading. Much of the detail, and indeed much of the policy, of securities regulations is found in regulations or rules passed pursuant to powers granted under provincial securities acts and in statements of policy as to how the securities commission, or other officials, will exercise the wide powers of discretion they are given.

---

[100]Cites to the provincial securities acts are set out in the Table of Abbreviations.

B. Provincial Regulations or Rules

Much of the detail for the regulation of brokers, the preparation of prospectuses, takeover bids and issuer bids, and so on, is set out in regulations or rules passed pursuant to securities acts. Many of the requirements are also found in "forms" included in the regulations or rules passed pursuant to securities acts. These forms set out, for example, details as to the contents of prospectuses, proxy circulars or takeover bid circulars. The forms also include the detailed contents of applications such as applications for registration for trading.

C. Regulatory Bodies

The securities acts and the regulations passed under the securities acts leave considerable adjudicative and administrative discretionary powers to panels of commissioners or an administrator. There are also self-regulatory organizations that have their own rules and decision making powers. The rules, decisions and policies of these regulatory bodies are an important part of the overall regulatory regime for securities.

1. *Commissions and Administrators*

The securities acts of the provinces of Alberta, British Columbia, Manitoba, Newfoundland, Nova Scotia, Ontario, Quebec and Saskatchewan create securities commissions.[101] The commissions are two-tiered structures. The first tier consists of a panel of commissioners.[102] The second tier consists of an administrative agency headed by a chief administrative officer.[103] This chief administrative officer is variously described as the "Executive Director" in Alberta and British Columbia, or the "Director" in Manitoba, Newfoundland, Nova Scotia, Ontario, and Saskatchewan. Given these various appellations, the more generic term "administrator" is used throughout the remainder of the book.

---

[101] A.S.A. s. 10; B.C.S.A. s. 4; M.S.A. s. 2; Nfld.S.A. s. 3; N.S.S.A. s. 4; O.S.A. s. 2; Q.S.A. s. 276; S.S.A. s. 3.

[102] Under the A.S.A. this tier is described as the "Board of the Alberta Securities Commission" (A.S.A. s. 10).

[103] A.S.A. ss. 13 and 13.1; B.C.S.A. s. 8; M.S.A. s. 4; Nfld.S.A. s. 7; N.S.S.A. s. 23; O.S.A. s. 6; S.S.A. s. 6.

The panel of commissioners, in provinces having securities commissions, makes orders and rulings and acts as an appeal tribunal from the decisions of the administrator. The securities commission also formulates policies and makes recommendations to government for changes in legislation or regulations. The administrator exercises the administrative functions assigned to the administrator under the applicable provincial act, and implements the decisions or directives of the commissioners.

The securities acts of New Brunswick, Prince Edward Island, the Northwest Territories, and the Yukon Territories do not create separate securities commissions. Instead, under these acts, the administrative responsibilities are assigned to government officials or administrators appointed under the Act.[104]

2. Self-Regulatory Organizations

There as several self-regulatory organizations whose rules, policies and decisions are an important part of securities regulation. Although this book contains some references to the rules or policies of these self-regulatory organizations, a detailed analysis of their rules and policies is beyond the scope of this book.

a. STOCK EXCHANGES

The stock exchanges are the major self-regulatory organizations with respect to the regulation of securities markets. Stock exchanges provide facilities for the buying and selling of securities of issuers whose securities are accepted for listing on the exchange. The four main stock exchanges in Canada are the Toronto Stock Exchange, the Montreal Exchange, the Vancouver Stock Exchange, and the Alberta Stock Exchange. These exchanges are non-profit organizations created by statutes to facilitate trading in securities through the members of the exchange. To carry on business as stock

---

[104]N.B.S.F.P.A. s. 2.1, 3 (the Minister of Justice is responsible for the administration of the Act and the Minister appoints an "Administrator"); N.W.T.S.A. s. 3 (a "Registrar of Securities" is appointed by the Commissioner). The P.E.I.S.A. vests administrative powers in either the Director of Corporations or a "Registrar". The Y.S.A. vests administrative powers in a "registrar".

exchanges in a province, they must be recognized by the relevant provincial securities commission.[105]

The exchanges pass by-laws and rules to govern the qualifications and continued fitness of members for membership in the exchange, set out requirements for the listing of securities of issuers and the conditions to be met by listed issuers to maintain their listing, and to govern the manner in which trading in listed securities is to be conducted by members. These by-laws and rules of the exchanges are important sources of applicable securities regulation for issuers that have their securities listed on the exchange or for members of the exchange.

Exchanges also issue policy statements providing guidelines as to how they will exercise the discretion left to them by their by-laws or rules. These stock exchange policy statements are also important sources of information for listed issuers and exchange members.

b. OTHER SELF-REGULATORY ORGANIZATIONS

Besides stock exchanges there are other self-regulatory organizations. For instance, membership in the Investment Dealers Association of Canada is required for registration as an investment dealer[106] and the Investment Dealers Association of Canada has rules governing the conduct of its members. Qualifications for registration to trade in, or provide advice with respect to securities requires the completion of courses administered by institutes,[107] the standards of which form part of the overall matrix of securities regulation. For instance, the Canadian Securities Course and the Canadian Investment Finance Course are prepared and conducted by the Canadian Securities Institute, the Canadian Investment Funds Course is prepared and conducted by The Investment Funds Institute of Canada, and the Canadian Financial Analysts Course is prepared and conducted by the Institute of Chartered Financial Analysts.[108]

---

[105]See A.S.A. s. 52; B.C.S.A. s. 25; M.S.A. s. 139; Nfld.S.A. s. 24; N.S.S.A. s. 30; O.S.A. s. 21; Q.S.A. s. 169; S.S.A. s. 25.

[106]See A. Rules s. 16; B.C. Rules s. 6(2); Nfld. Regs. s. 86; N.S. Regs. s. 13; O. Regs. s. 98; S. Regs. s. 10.

[107]See A. Rules ss. 40-45; B.C. Rules ss. 60-61; Nfld. Regs. ss. 111-14; N.S. Regs. ss. 41-44; O. Regs. ss. 124-27; S. Regs. ss. 37-39.

[108]See A. Rules 14; Nfld. Regs. s. 84; N.S. Regs. s. 11; O. Regs. s. 96; S. Regs. s. 8.

Clearing agencies and depository institutions are also important self-regulating organizations in the trading of securities.

c. SECURITIES COMMISSION REVIEW

The provincial securities commissions have the power to review and make decisions respecting a by-law, rule or other regulatory instrument or policy, or a direction, decision, order or ruling made under a by-law, rule or policy of a self-regulatory organization or stock exchange.[109] The provincial securities commissions may also review and make decisions on the procedures or practices of a self-regulatory organization or stock exchange, or may review and make decisions on the manner in which a stock exchange carries on business, the trading of securities on or through the facilities of a stock exchange, a security listed and posted for trading on a stock exchange, or issuers whose securities are listed and posted for trading on a stock exchange to ensure that the issuers comply with the securities act and regulations.[110]

D. Policy Statements

Securities commissions and administrators have wide discretionary powers. Policy statements provide guidelines on the way in which the discretionary powers of a commission or administrator will be exercised. There are three types of policy statements: national policy statements, uniform policy statements and local policy statements.

1. *National Policy Statements*

National Policy Statements are joint policy statements agreed to by the Canadian Securities Administrators. The Canadian Securities Administrators is composed of representatives of the various securities commissions (or other securities administrators) throughout the country.

---

[109] A.S.A. s. 52(3) and s. 53.1; B.C.S.A. s. 27; M.S.A. s. 139(2) (re stock exchanges); Nfld.S.A. ss. 21(2) and 24(2); O.S.A. ss. 21-21.7; S.S.A. ss. 21(6) and 25(2). Similar review powers are vested in the Quebec Securities Commission under Q.S.A. ss. 177-80.

[110] Ibid.

These National Policy Statements attempt to coordinate the efforts of securities commissions to reduce the amount of duplication encountered in compliance with multiple jurisdictions in matters in which the regulation of more than one province applies. They also represent joint responses to problems in securities markets with a view to making securities regulation more compatible from province to province.

2. Uniform Policy Statements

Uniform Policy Statements were joint policy statements of the western securities administrators (including Ontario, Manitoba, Saskatchewan, Alberta and British Columbia). These provinces had all passed the "uniform act" which was initially passed in Ontario in 1966.[111] That "uniform act" has since been replaced in Alberta, British Columbia, Ontario and Saskatchewan. Accordingly, the Uniform Act Policy Statements associated with the former *Uniform Act* are gradually being replaced with National Policy Statements. However, a few Uniform Act Policy Statements still remain in force.

3. Local Policy Statements

Local policy statements are the policy statements of local provincial securities commissions. Thus, for instance, the British Columbia Securities Commission has a number of local policy statements. The local policy statements of each province often have their counterparts in the local policy statements of other provinces.

---

[111] *The Securities Act*, S.A. 1967, c. 76; *Securities Act, 1967*, S.B.C. c. 45; *The Securities Act*, S.M. 1968, c. 57; *The Securities Act*, S.S. 1967, c. 81. The Ontario "uniform act", which was adopted in the western provinces, was *The Securities Act, 1966*, S.O. 1966, c. 142. Quebec also amended its *Securities Act* in 1973 (S.Q. 1973, c. 67) to include provisions on financial disclosure, takeover bids, and insider trading similar to those recommended by the Kimber Report and adopted in the *Uniform Act*.

4. Securities Commission Jurisdiction to Make Rules, Issue Policy Statements and Blanket Orders, and Enter Into Memoranda of Understanding

a. SECURITIES COMMISSION POWERS TO ISSUE POLICY STATEMENTS AND BLANKET ORDERS, AND ENTER INTO MEMORANDA OF UNDERSTANDING

In *Ainsley Financial Corp. v. Ontario (Securities Commission)*,[112] the scope of the Ontario Securities Commission's jurisdiction with respect to its use of policy statements was questioned. The Ontario Securities Commission attempted to regulate the sale of penny stocks by way of policy statement. The policy purported to provide guidelines as to how the Commission would exercise its discretion but the court held that the policy was "mandatory and regulatory in nature" and that the Commission had "exceeded its jurisdiction under its enabling legislation" in promulgating such a policy. Questions as to the validity of a particular National Policy Statement were also raised in *Pezim v. British Columbia (Superintendent of Brokers)*.[113] In the Supreme Court of Canada decision in *Pezim*, Mr. Justice Iacobucci said that,

> it is important to note that the Commission's policy-making role is limited. By that I mean that their policies cannot be elevated to the status of law; they are not to be treated as legal pronouncements absent legal authority mandating such treatment.[114]

The effect of these decisions was to cast doubt on the validity of many of the National Policy Statements and Local Policy Statements that were in effect. By questioning the scope of the jurisdiction of securities commissions to pass policy statements, these cases also raised questions about the validity of other ways in which securities commissions exercised their discretion, such as blanket orders and memoranda of understanding.[115] This was the impetus for the creation of a "Task Force on Securities Regulation" in Ontario which reviewed the role of the Ontario Securities Commission in the devel-

---

[112](1993), 14 O.R. (3d) 280, (1994) 1 C.C.L.S. 1 (Gen. Div.).

[113][1994] 2 S.C.R. 557, 114 D.L.R. (4th) 385.

[114][1994] 2 S.C.R. 557 at 596.

[115] See *Responsibility and Responsiveness: Final Report of the Ontario Task Force on Securities Regulation*, (Toronto: Queen's Printer for Ontario, 1994) (the "Ontario Task Force Report"), at 2.

opment of securities policy in Ontario. The Task Force recommended that the Ontario *Securities Act* be amended to expressly confirm the authority of the Commission to formulate and apply policy statements and to give the Commission a power to pass "rules" of a mandatory or regulatory character.[116]

b. COMMISSION RULE MAKING POWER

The main recommendations of the Ontario Task Force were followed in Ontario and there were similar responses to questions concerning the scope of securities commission discretion in Alberta, British Columbia, Manitoba, Nova Scotia, and Saskatchewan. The securities commissions in Ontario, Alberta, British Columbia, Manitoba, Nova Scotia may now make "rules"[117] with powers corresponding to those of the Lieutenant Governor in Council to make regulations.[118] In Saskatchewan the Lieutenant Governor in Council may authorize the Commission to make regulations.[119] The approach in British Columbia and Alberta has been to convert much of what were once regulations to rules.

c. NATIONAL INSTRUMENTS

To harmonize the adoption of rules on a national basis the Canadian Securities Administrators now issue "National Instruments" which can be adopted as rules or policies in each of the various securities regulatory jurisdictions. These National Instruments may be accompanied by "Companion Policies" which provide guidelines as to how the Canadian Securities Administrators interpret a particular National Instrument.

---

[116]See the Ontario Task Force Report, *supra* note 115, at iv-viii.

[117]B.C.S.A. s. 184; O.S.A. s. 143(1); N.S.S.A. s. 150; A.S.A. s. 196.1.

[118]See A.S.A. s. 196; M.S.A. s. 149.1(1); N.S.S.A. s. 150; O.S.A. s. 143(2). Under the B.C.S.A., the Commission's rule making powers are similar to those of the Lieutenant Governor in Council [B.C.S.A. s. 184]. However, there are some matters which can only be dealt with by the Lieutenant Governor in Council by regulation [see B.C.S.A. s. 184(4)]. There is a similar but less extensive constraint on the Alberta Securities Commission's rule making power [see A.S.A. s. 196.1(2)]. Note that the regulations prevail over the rules to the extent of any conflict. See A.S.A. s. 196.1(3); B.C.S.A. s. 186; M.S.A. s. 149.1(2); N.S.S.A. s. 150A(6); O.S.A. s. 143(13); S.S.A. s. 154(4).

[119]S.S.A. s. 154(1)(tt), (2).

d. NOTICE REQUIREMENTS

The Ontario *Securities Act* sets out a review and comment process for making, amending or repealing a rule. Subject to certain exceptions[120] the Commission must publish a rule it proposes to make[121] and must provide a period of at least 90 days for comments on the rule.[122] When the proposed rule is finalized it is delivered to the Minister of Finance who, within 60 days, either approves of the rule, rejects it or returns it to the Commission for further consideration.[123] A similar process of notice and ministerial approval is provided for in Saskatchewan.[124] Manitoba also has a minimum 60-day notice period.[125]

Under the Nova Scotia *Securities Act*, notice of the rule must be given to the Minister[126] and must be published in the *Royal Gazette*.[127] The rule is effective 75 days after the approval of the rule by the Commission unless, within 60 days, the Minister disapproves of the rule or returns it to the Commission for further consideration.[128] The Alberta *Securities Act* provides that the rule must be published in the *Alberta Gazette* in order for it to be valid.[129]

---

[120] O.S.A. s. 143.2(5).

[121] O.S.A. s. 143.2(1).

[122] O.S.A. s. 143.2(4). If changes are made to the proposed rule as a result of the consultation process the Commission must publish the proposed changes and provide a reasonable opportunity for comments [O.S.A. 143.2(7)-(9)].

[123] O.S.A. s. 143.3. The rule comes into force 15 days after it is approved by the Minister [s. 143.4(1)]. If the Minister does not approve of the rule, rejects it or returns it to the Commission for further consideration within the 60 day period, then the rule comes into force 75 days after it was delivered to the Minister [s. 143.4(2)].

[124] *The Securities Commission (Regulation Procedures) Regulations*, R.R.S. c. S-42.2, Reg. 2 (October 24, 1997). The notice period for comments is 45 days from the end of the month in which the regulation is published. The Minister then has 60 days to approve or reject the regulation or direct the commission to reconsider the regulation (ss. 5-7).

[125] *Rule-Making Procedure Regulation*, Man. Reg. 246/97.

[126] The Minister is the Attorney General or any other member of the Executive Council charged with the administration of the Act. See N.S.S.A. s. 2(x).

[127] N.S.S.A. s. 150A(2).

[128] N.S.S.A. s. 150A(3).

[129] A.S.A. s. 196.2. See also Alta. *Securities Regulation*, Alta. Reg. 11/95 as amended by Alta. Reg. 10/97, ss. 1-6 on the rule-making process.

In British Columbia the consent of the Minister is required for making or repealing a rule.[130]

e. POLICY STATEMENTS

Securities Commissions in Ontario and Saskatchewan have been expressly given the power to issue policy statements that set out (i) principles, standards, criteria or factors that relate to an exercise of discretion by the Commission under the Act, regulations or rules; (ii) how a provision of the Act, rules or regulations is interpreted or applied; or (iii) the practices of the Commission or administrator in carrying out their responsibilities under the Act.[131] In Ontario, the Act sets out a notice and comment period that is similar to that for the making of rules except that there is no requirement for approval by the Minister.[132] In B.C., the *Securities Act* also gives an express power to the B.C. Securities Commission to issue policy statements.[133] The lack of such a provision in other securities acts does not mean that securities commissions under those acts cannot issue policy statements. The jurisdiction of securities commissions to issue policy statements is implicit in both the *Ainsley* and *Pezim* decisions referred to above, although the scope of policy statements may be limited.

f. BLANKET ORDERS

In Ontario the Securities Commission make any orders or rulings of general application[134] and what were formerly blanket orders are now effected through the creation of a rule. In Nova Scotia, the Commission was given a separate power to make blanket orders exempting persons or companies, trades in securities or distributions of securities from the application of the Act or regulations.[135]

---

[130] B.C.S.A. s. 184(5). See also the *Rule-Making Procedure Regulation*, B.C. Reg. 195/97.

[131] O.S.A. s. 143.8(1); S.S.A. s. 154.1. This appears to enact what seems to have been the thrust of both the *Ainsley* and *Pezim* decisions. See also M.S.A. s. 149.5 and N.S.S.A. s. 19, which expressly permits the Commission to issue policy statements.

[132] O.S.A. s. 143.8(2)-(9).

[133] B.C.S.A. s. 188.

[134] O.S.A. s. 143.11.

[135] N.S.S.A. s. 151A.

g. MEMORANDA OF UNDERSTANDING

The Ontario *Securities Act* also has a provision dealing explicitly with memoranda of understanding ("MOU"s) or agreements entered into by the Commission. Any memoranda of understanding or agreements the Commission enters into with another securities or financial regulatory authority, a self-regulatory organization or any jurisdiction must be forwarded to the Minister who must approve of or reject the MOU within 60 days.[136]

h. REVIEW OF LEGISLATION

The Ontario Task Force also expressed concern with the responsiveness of securities legislation to the pace of developments in securities markets. To address this concern the Ontario *Securities Act* now provides that the Minister must appoint an advisory committee every five years to review the legislation, regulations and rules and the legislative needs of the Commission.[137]

E. Blanket Orders

Another source of securities regulation is contained in blanket orders and notices. Securities commissions or other designated administrators are given powers under securities acts and regulations to grant various orders. For instance, they open have powers to grant exemptions from the application of provisions of the Act or regulations. These orders are normally sought and provided on a case-by-case basis. However, when a similar order has been frequently requested, or when a new policy is developed for dealing with a particular situation, the commission may find it advantageous to grant a blanket order. The order applies to anyone who fits the terms of the order and they need not go to the commission to get a separate order. Blanket orders can substantially reduce the work load of a securities commission.

Notices are provided by securities commissions which contain information of interest to those who deal with securities regulation

---

[136] O.S.A. s. 143.10. If the Minister approves of the MOU it comes into force on the day it is approved [143.10(2)]. If the Minister rejects the MOU it does not come into force [143.10(5)], and if the Minister fails to approve of the MOU then it comes into force 60th day after its publication in the Bulletin [143.10(4)].

[137] O.S.A. s. 143.12.

on a regular basis. For instance, notices may advise of proceedings before the securities commission, of draft policies or blanket orders being considered, or of the effective dates of new policies.

F. Decisions and Rulings

Decisions and rulings of securities commissions and administrators form another important source of securities law. The decisions of courts hearing appeals from the decisions of securities commissions and applying the common law and statutes relating to securities are yet another source of securities law.

G. Bulletins

Provincial securities commissions publish important information about their activities. The information includes, for example, notices, blanket orders, decisions, orders and rulings of the securities commission, new policies, new legislation, cease trade orders, new issues of securities, and insider trading reports. These publications are usually referred to as bulletins,[138] but are referred to by different names in some provinces.[139]

VI. THE SCOPE OF SECURITIES REGULATION IN CANADA AND THE VARIATION FROM JURISDICTION TO JURISDICTION

Securities regulation in Canada requires disclosure on the initial distribution of securities and disclosure to support secondary market trading. It regulates trading and informing by insiders. It regulates bids for securities made for the purpose of effecting a takeover and bids for securities made by the issuer of the securities itself. It also regulates the persons who are involved in the activities of underwriting, brokerage, advising and portfolio management.

The securities acts of Alberta, British Columbia, Newfoundland, Nova Scotia, Ontario, and Saskatchewan are, for the most part, quite

---

[138] For example, the "Ontario Securities Commission Bulletin".

[139] For example, the "British Columbia Securities Commission Weekly Summary".

similar in structure and wording. These acts integrate the regulation of primary and secondary market trading through a concept known as the closed system. The book focuses primarily on securities regulation in these jurisdictions.

Quebec also has a closed system statute, which in many respects yields very similar results to the other above-mentioned statutes. However, the structure and wording of the Quebec statute is quite different from that of the above-mentioned statutes. Manitoba's statute only partially reflects the closed system approach. However, much of the Manitoba *Securities Act* is very similar to the securities acts of Alberta, British Columbia, Newfoundland, Nova Scotia, Ontario, and Saskatchewan. References to roughly corresponding provisions in these statutes are provided in the notes.

The securities acts of New Brunswick, Prince Edward Island and the Territories do not regulate takeover bids, issuer bids and insider trading. They also do not regulate secondary market disclosure to the extent it is regulated in the other provinces. References to corresponding provisions of these statutes are provided with respect to the regulation of initial distributions of securities and the regulation of persons engaging in securities market functions such as underwriting and brokerage.

CHAPTER 4

THE PROSPECTUS REQUIREMENT

I. INTRODUCTION

This chapter examines the requirement to provide a prospectus where securities are being distributed. The object is to provide the reader with a sense of when a prospectus may be required, and a sense of the regulatory process for the distribution of securities.

There are many possible approaches to explaining the disclosure requirements of provincial securities acts. This book begins with the disclosure required on the distribution of securities. This is consistent with following the disclosure required from a security's initial issuance to its subsequent secondary market trading. It is also consistent with the historical pattern of securities disclosure requirements in Canada, which initially focused on primary market disclosure.[1]

Part II of this chapter provides an overview of the contents of a prospectus. Part III notes some key definitions that must be understood in order to determine when a prospectus is required, namely, the definitions of "security", "trade", and "distribution". Parts IV, V and VI then examine the definitions of "security", "trade" and "distribution" respectively. Part VII provides a summary of the distribution process and Part VIII notes the consequences of a failure to provide a prospectus where one is required.

II. OVERVIEW OF THE CONTENTS OF A PROSPECTUS

A prospectus is a document which must be given to persons to whom securities are to be distributed. It is the document which

---

[1] The risk of this approach is that it may convey a false sense that the main focus of the legislation is on primary market disclosure, when it might be more accurate to say that it is secondary market disclosure that is the key to modern securities regulation in Canada.

is intended to provide information relevant to valuing the securities. The document follows a form which is set out in the forms provided, pursuant to the authority given in the securities acts. The most pertinent information may vary depending on the type of issuer involved in the distribution of securities. Consequently, there are separate forms for different issuers such as industrial issuers, finance companies, natural resource companies and mutual funds.[2]

The form for industrial issuers, for example, requires, among other things, that the following kinds of information be given:[3]

(i) the estimated proceeds of the issue and what they will be used for;

(ii) the loan and share capital structure;

(iii) a description of the issuer's business and the development of the business over the past five years;

(iv) attributes of the securities offered;

(v) occupations of directors and officers in the past five years, their backgrounds, and executive compensation;

(vi) factors which make the purchase of the security a risk or speculation; and

---

[2] See Alta. Forms 12-15; B.C. Forms 12-15; Man. Forms 9, 9A, 10, 12 and 12A (which includes separate forms for a mining company or a variable life insurance contract); N.B.S.F.P.A. s. 13(3); Nfld. Forms 12-15; N.S. Forms 12-15; N.W.T.S.A. s. 27 accepts the form of prospectus required in a province or in the Yukon Territory; Ont. Forms 12-15; P.E.I. Regs., s. 7-27; Que. Schs. I and II (which provide for a prospectus and a mutual fund prospectus respectively); Sask. Forms 13-16; Y. Regs., s. 18 and Schedules A, B and C.

"Industrial issuer", "finance company" and "natural resource issuer" (or corresponding terms) are defined in A. Regs. s. 1; B.C. Regs. s. 1(1); M. Regs. s. 1; N.B.S.F.P.A. s. 1 (except for "finance company" or "finance issuer"); Nfld. Regs. s. 2(2); N.S. Regs. s. 3(2); O. Regs. s. 1(2); P.E.I. Regs. s. 1; S. Regs. s. 2(1). Under the Q.S.A. separate requirements for natural resource companies and finance companies are set out in the form of prospectus in Sch. I of the Q. Regs.

There are also special disclosure requirements with respect to mutual funds. Prospectus disclosure for mutual funds is briefly considered in Chapter 13. There are additional disclosure guidelines in various policy statements, for example, with respect to restricted shares (e.g., O. Pol. 1.3; B.C. Pol. 3-37), prospectuses for mortgage and real estate investment trusts and partnerships (e.g., O. Pol. 5.3).

Other forms of disclosure documents are noted elsewhere in the book. For instance, statements of material facts and exchange offering prospectuses are briefly noted in Chapter 7. Short form prompt offering prospectuses and shelf offering prospectuses are considered in Chapter 8.

[3] See, for example, Ont. Form 12.

(vii) arrangements with underwriters.

The prospectus also contains recent financial statements of the issuer.

The disclosure in a prospectus is not limited to specific items. It is open-ended in that it requires full, true and plain disclosure of all "material" facts relating to the securities being offered.[4] A "material fact" is a fact that significantly affects, or would reasonably be expected to have a significant effect on, the market price or value of the securities.[5]

The information in a prospectus generally consists of verifiable existing facts. The inclusion of future oriented information is treated with caution. However, a securities administrator may permit the inclusion of a forecast in a prospectus, consisting of any or all estimates (such as an estimate of earnings or range of earnings, the most probable financial position or an estimate of changes in financial position that are based on assumptions about future economic conditions and courses of action that will be taken by the issuer).[6]

N.P.#48 addresses the circumstances in which securities administrators will allow future oriented financial information ("FOFI") to

---

[4] This is required by securities acts and by virtue of the certificates which must be set out in the prospectus and signed — see A.S.A. ss. 84, 90; B.C.S.A. ss. 63, 68, 69; M.S.A. ss. 41, 52, 53; N.B.S.F.P.A. s. 13(3)(xxxv); Nfld.S.A. ss. 57, 59; N.S.S.A. ss. 61, 63; O.S.A. ss. 56, 58, 59; P.E.I.S.A. s. 8.1(1); Q.S. Regs. s. 32 coupled with the definition of "misrepresentation" in s. 5 of the Q.S.A.; S.S.A. s. 61, 66; e.g., Y. Regs. Sch. C, items (ll) and (mm). Prospectus forms also require disclosure of all material facts — see, for example, Ont. Form 12, Item 32.

[5] See A.S.A. s. 1(1); B.C.S.A. s. 1(1); M.S.A. s. 108(1) (however this definition is set out in Part XI of the Act as a definition for that Part of the Act and thus may not apply to items in forms such as Form 9, Item 24 requiring disclosure of other "material facts"); Nfld.S.A. s. 2(1)(y); N.S.S.A. s. 2(1)(w); O.S.A. s. 1(1); S.S.A. s. 2(1)(z). The Q.S.A. does not define "material fact". However, the certificate required by s. 32 of the Regs. says that the prospectus should not contain any "misrepresentation likely to affect the value or the market price of the securities to be distributed" and "misrepresentation" is defined in s. 5 of the Act to be "any misleading information on a material fact as well as any pure and simple omission of a material fact". The N.B.S.F.P.A., N.W.T.S.A., P.E.I.S.A. and the Y.S.A. do not contain a definition of "material fact".

[6] The wording of the types of estimates allowed varies somewhat from province to province. A. Rules s. 112; B.C. Rules s. 115 and B.C. Pol. 3.02, Part 5; M. Regs. s. 35; Nfld. Regs. s. 48; N.S. Regs. s. 3(7); O. Regs. s. 60; Q. Regs. s. 50 and Q. Pol. Q-11; S. Regs. s. 86 and S. Pol. 4.6; and N.P. #48.

be included in a prospectus. It reflects the concern that the inclusion of such information in a prospectus is prone to abuse. It may be very difficult to prove that such information constituted a misrepresentation since it would require showing that the assumptions on which it was based were unreasonable at the time they were made. Thus there may be scope for overly optimistic projections that may not readily be brought within the scope of the statutory civil liability for misrepresentations in a prospectus.[7] Consequently, N.P. #48 reflects a cautious approach to FOFI.

For instance, FOFI is to be prepared in accordance with the recommendations of the Canadian Institute for Chartered Accountants Handbook.[8] FOFI based on projections for a business with less than two years of operations can be included in a prospectus but the prospectus must note in boldface that the projection is based on hypotheses and that there is a significant risk that actual results will vary, and may vary materially, from the results projected.[9] FOFI included in a prospectus must be accompanied by an auditor's report.[10] The auditor's consent letter filed with the prospectus must contain a reference to the auditor's report on FOFI contained in the prospectus.[11] When the issuer files subsequent financial statements prior FOFI must be compared to the actual results and the comparison must be disclosed by having it accompany the annual or interim financial statements required to be filed.[12] When a change occurs in the events or assumptions on which FOFI is based the change must be reported[13] and the FOFI must be updated.[14]

---

[7] See Chapter 5 on the statutory civil liability for misrepresentations in a prospectus.

[8] N.P. #48, para. 3.2.

[9] Ibid., para. 5.1.

[10] Ibid., para. 9.1.

[11] Ibid., para. 9.3.

[12] Ibid., paras. 6.1 and 6.2.

[13] Ibid., para. 7.1. See Chapter 6 on the requirements to report "material changes".

[14] Ibid., para. 7.2.

III. WHEN A PROSPECTUS IS REQUIRED

Most provincial securities acts provide that a person shall not distribute a security unless a preliminary prospectus and a prospectus respecting the security have been filed with the provincial securities administrator and the provincial securities administrator has given receipts for them.[15] For example, the Ontario *Securities Act* provides that,

> No person or company shall trade in a security on his, her or its own account or on behalf of any other person or company where such trade would be a distribution of such security, unless a preliminary prospectus and a prospectus have been filed and receipts therefore obtained from the Director.[16]

This provision contains some important defined terms. It says that a person or company shall not "distribute" a "security". The acts of most provinces have a definition of "distribution" that refers to a "trade" in a "security".[17] Thus, to determine whether a prospectus is required, it is first necessary to determine the meaning of "trade" and "security".

This list of definitions leads to the following logical progression of questions that need to be addressed:

(i) Does the transaction involve a "security"?

(ii) Does the transaction involve a "trade"?

(iii) Does the "trade" in the "security" constitute a "distribution"? This line of questioning should come to mind whenever a client suggests a business idea for which the client is seeking financing.

---

[15] A.S.A. s. 81; B.C.S.A. s. 61; Nfld.S.A. s. 54; N.S.S.A. s. 58; O.S.A. s. 53; Q.S.A. s. 11; S.S.A. s. 58. S. 8 of the P.E.I.S.A. does not refer to the "distribution" of a security as the other acts do. However it states that no person or company shall trade in a security unless a preliminary prospectus and a prospectus have been filed and receipts therefore have been obtained. The N.W.T.S.A. s. 27 and Y.S.A. s. 22 also refer to a "trade in a security". S. 37 of the M.S.A. and s. 13(1) of the N.B.S.F.P.A. are different from the provisions in other provinces in that they refer to a "primary distribution to the public". The effect of the distinction is discussed in Chapter 7.

[16] O.S.A. s. 53.

[17] See A.S.A. s. 1(f); B.C.S.A. s. 1(1); Nfld.S.A. s. 2(1)(m); N.S.S.A. s. 2(1)(l); O.S.A. s. 1(1); P.E.I.S.A. s. 1(6.1); Q.S.A. s. 5; S.S.A. s. 2(1)(r). The M.S.A. and the N.B.S.F.P.A. do not define "distribution". The reference is to "primary distribution to the public" in s. 37 of the M.S.A. or s. 13(1) of the N.B.S.F.P.A. On the definition of "primary distribution to the public" see Chapter 7. N.W.T.S.A., s. 27 and Y.S.A., s. 22 prohibit a "trade in a security" unless a prospectus is filed.

If the answers to each questions (i), (ii), (iii) are "yes", "yes" and "yes", then the client will need to produce a prospectus unless an exemption can be obtained.

The definitions of "trade" and "security" are also at the crux of another key requirement of provincial securities acts, namely, the requirement that one be registered to "trade in a security".[18] Discussion of the registration requirement is deferred to Chapter 12, where the regulation of securities dealers, underwriters and advisors is addressed. In this chapter the focus is on the prospectus requirement.

Having determined that the definitions of "security", "trade", and "distribution" are crucial, the next step is to consider the meaning of these terms.

IV. THE MEANING OF "SECURITY"[19]

A. The Definition of "Security" in the Act

The statutory definition of "security" might be said to take three sweeps at defining the kinds of items that should be considered secu-

---

[18] A.S.A. s. 54; B.C.S.A. s. 34; M.S.A. s. 6; N.B.S.F.P.A. s. 5; Nfld.S.A. s. 26; N.S.S.A. s. 31; N.W.T.S.A. s. 4; O.S.A. s. 25; P.E.I.S.A. s. 2; S.S.A. s. 27; Y.S.A. s. 3. The Q.S.A. does not specifically rely on the term "trade" in its registration requirement (Q.S.A. s. 148). However, one is required to register to act as a "dealer" and "dealer" is defined in s. 5 in terms of a person "trading in securities" or "distributing a security" and soliciting persons as part of such activities.

[19] On the meaning of "security" see, for example, V.P. Alboini, *Securities Law and Practice*, 2nd ed., (Toronto: Carswell, 1984), §INT.1.40. The definition of "security" in provincial securities acts is similar to the definition in the U.S. *Securities Act of 1933*, which itself was partly borrowed from definitions in earlier state securities acts. It is a definition that has been modified on an ad hoc basis over the years without a significant overhaul. Thus, much of the earlier literature on the definition of "security" continues to be useful. See J.P. Williamson, *Securities Regulation in Canada*, (Toronto: University of Toronto Press, 1960), at 105-16; D.L. Johnston, *Canadian Securities Regulation*, 2nd ed., (Toronto: Butterworths, 1998), at 25-34; F. Iacobucci, "The Definition of Security for Purposes of a Securities Act", *Proposals for a Securities Market Law for Canada*, (Ottawa: Ministry of Supply and Services, 1979), at 221. U.S. literature on the meaning of "security" is relevant because of the similarity between Canadian provincial act definitions and U.S. state and federal law definitions and because of the greater amount of jurisprudence on the point in the U.S. Thus one might wish to consult, for example, T.L. Hazen, *Treatise on the Law of Securities Regulation*, 3rd ed., (St. Paul: West Publishing,

rities for the purposes of the statute. First, the definition covers common types of securities. Second, it covers several other specific items which are not as common. Third, it contains several terms capable of taking on a very broad meaning and it is, by its terms, a non-exclusive definition.[20]

1. *Common Types of Securities*

The definition of "security" covers the typical kinds of securities discussed in Chapter 1. For instance, provincial securities acts typically provide that "security" includes "any bond, debenture, note *s. 1(1)* or other evidence of indebtedness, share, stock, unit, unit certificate, participation certificate, certificate of share or interest, preorganization certificate or subscription...".[21] This definition would cover

---

1995), at 28-61 or the materials collected in L. Loss, *Fundamentals of Securities Regulation*, (Boston: Little Brown, 1983), at 167-201.

[20] The potential scope of transactions that may be said to involve a "security", and therefore fall within the application of securities regulation, is highlighted by Hazen, *supra* note 19 at 28-9, in the opening words to his discussion of the definition of "security" as follows:

> "What do the following have in common: scotch whisky, self improvement courses, cosmetics, earthworms, beavers, muskrats, rabbits, chinchillas, fishing boats, vacuum cleaners, cemetery lots, cattle embryos, master recording contracts, animal feeding programs, pooled litigation funds, and fruit trees? The answer is that they have all been held to be securities within the meaning of federal or state securities statutes."

He provides notes to cases that have found transactions concerning each of the above items to involve securities.

[21] A.S.A. s. 1(v)(v); B.C.S.A. s. 1(1) "security" (a); M.S.A. s. 1(1) "security" (e); N.B.S.F.P.A. Regs. s. 2; Nfld.S.A. s. 2(1)(ss)(v); N.S.S.A. s. 2(1)(aq)(v); N.W.T.S.A. s. 1 "security" (e); O.S.A. s. 1(1) "security" (e); S.S.A. s. 2(1)(ss)(v); Y.S.A. s. 1 "security" (e). The Q.S.A. does not define "security". However the Q.S.A. does set out, in s. 1, the forms of investment to which the Act applies and s. 1(1) provides that it applies to "a share, bond, capital stock of an incorporated entity, subscription right or option to purchase". The P.E.I.S.A. s. 1(1) has a much abbreviated definition of "security". It provides that,

"'security' includes

    (i) any document, instrument or writing commonly known as a security,

    (ii) any document constituting evidence of title to or interest in the capital, assets, property, profits, earnings or royalties of any person or company,

    (iii) any document constituting evidence of an interest in an association of legatees or heirs,

    (iv) any document constituting evidence of an interest in any option given

the bonds, debentures, common shares, preferred shares, or any other shares discussed in Chapter 1.

The definition of "security" also includes "any document constituting evidence of an option, subscription or other interest in or to a security".[22] Warrants and rights would likely fall within the ambit of these words since warrants and rights provide the holder with an option to buy the security to which they relate.

The definition also includes "any instrument or writing commonly known as a security".[23] What is "commonly known" as a security would be determined by the character the instrument is given in commerce, the terms of the offer, the plan of distribution, and the economic inducements held out to the prospective purchaser.[24] This definition responds to potential changes over time as new types of securities are developed which come to be commonly used and commonly known as securities.

2. Less Common Securities

The definition sets out a number of other specific items all of which would normally involve an initial payment, which will be used to produce some future returns. For instance, the definition includes a certificate of interest in an oil, natural gas or mining lease,[25] an

---

upon a security, or

    (v) any document designated as a security by the regulations."

The N.B.S.F.P.A. s. 1 has a similar definition of "security".

[22] A.S.A. s. 1(v)(iv); B.C.S.A. s. 1(1) "security" (c); M.S.A. s. 1(1) "security" (d); N.B.S.F.P.A. s. 1 "security" (d); Nfld.S.A. s. 2(1)(ss)(iv); N.S.S.A. s. 2(1)(aq)(iv); N.W.T.S.A. s. 1 "security" (d); O.S.A. s. 1(1) "security" (d); P.E.I.S.A. s. 1(i)(iv); S.S.A. s. 2(1)(ss)(iv); Y.S.A. s. 1 "security" (d). With respect to the Q.S.A. see *supra* note 21. See *R. v. Hansen* (1973), 12 C.C.C. (2d) 368 (B.C. Prov. Ct.).

[23] A.S.A. s. 1(1)(v)(i); B.C.S.A. s. 1(1) "security" (a); M.S.A. s. 1(1) "security" (a); N.B.S.F.P.A. s. 1 "security" (a); Nfld.S.A. s. 21(1)(ss)(i); N.S.S.A. s. 2(1)(aq)(i); N.W.T.S.A. s. 1 "security" (a); O.S.A. s. 1(1) "security" (a); P.E.I.S.A. s. 1(i)(i); S.S.A. s. 2(1)(ss)(i); Y.S.A. s. 1 "security" (a). The Q.S.A. s. 1(1) provides that the Act applies to "any security recognized as such in the trade".

[24] See *SEC v. C.M. Joiner Leasing Corporation*, 320 U.S. 344 at 352-53 (1943) applied in *Re John T. Gelderman & Co. Inc.*, July, 1972, 3 Q.S.C. W.S. No. 65.

[25] A.S.A. s. 1(v)(x); B.C.S.A. s. 1(1) "security" (h); M.S.A. s. 1(1) "security" (i); N.B.S.F.P.A. Regs. s. 2; Nfld.S.A. s. 2(1)(ss)(x); N.S.S.A. s. 2(1)(aq)(x); N.W.T.S.A. s. 1 "security" (i); O.S.A. s. 1(1) "security" (j); S.S.A. s. 2(1)(ss)(x); Y.S.A. s. 1 "security" (i). The Q.S.A. s. 1 does not include a specific reference to an oil, natural gas or mining lease.

income or annuity contract other than one issued by an insurer,[26] a document constituting evidence of an interest in a scholarship or educational plan or trust,[27] an interest the value of which is based on a proportion of the value of a portfolio of assets (such as an interest in a mutual fund),[28] deposits to be repaid or treated as subscriptions,[29] and a collateral trust certificate.[30]

---

[26] A.S.A. s. 1(v)(xiii); B.C.S.A. s. 1(1) "security" (k); M.S.A. s. 1(1) "security" (l); N.B.S.F.P.A. Regs. s. 2; N.S.S.A. s. 2(1)(aq)(xiii); N.W.T.S.A. s. 1 "security" (m); S.S.A. s. 2(1)(ss)(xiii). In some provinces this part of the definition of "security" does not include income or annuity contracts which are regulated under separate investment contract acts — see Nfld.S.A. s. 2(1)(ss)(xiii); O.S.A. s. 1(1) "security" (m). Y.S.A. s. 1 "security" (m) simply says "any income or annuity contract" without words excluding income or annuity contracts issued by an insurer. The Q.S.A. s. 1 does not include a specific reference to an income or annuity contract.

[27] A.S.A. s. 1(v)(xv); B.C.S.A. 8.1(1) "security" (m); M.S.A s. 1(1) "security" (n); NfldS.A. s. 2(1)(ss)(xv); N.S.S.A. s. 2(1)(aq)(xv); O.S.A. s. 1(1) "security" (o); S.S.A. s. 2(1)(ss)(xv); Y.S.A. "security" (o). The N.B.S.A., P.E.I.S.A. and N.W.T.S.A. definitions of security do not set out this specific item. The Q.S.A. s. 1 does not make specific reference to investments in scholarship or educational plans.

[28] An exception is made for certain types of insurance contracts, regulated under insurance acts, which provide for payment at maturity of an amount not less than three quarters of the premiums paid by the purchaser for a benefit payable at maturity. See A.S.A. s. 1(v)(vi); B.C.S.A. s. 1(1) "security" (e); Nfld.S.A. s. 2(1)(ss) (vi); N.S.S.A. s. 2(1)(aq)(vi); O.S.A. s. 1(1) "security" (f); S.S.A. s. 2(1)(ss)(vi) (the S.S.A. provision does not make an exception for such contracts issued by an insurer). A guaranteed return of three quarters of the premiums was considered sufficient to approach in substance the traditional insurance contract — see V.P. Alboini, *supra* note 19, at §INT.1.40[f] and see *Re Variable Equity Insurance Contracts*, [1970] O.S.C.B. 46, 75, 128. This specific item is not set out in the definition of "security" under the M.S.A.; N.B.S.F.P.A.; N.W.T.S.A., P.E.I.S.A., or the Y.S.A. The Q.S.A. s. 1 does not specifically refer to this form of investment.

[29] A.S.A. s. 1(v)(vii); B.C.S.A. s. 1(1) "security" (f); M.S.A. s. 1(1) "security" (f); N.B.S.F.P.A. Regs. s. 2; Nfld.S.A. s. 2(1)(ss)(iv); N.S.S.A. s. 2(1)(aq)(vii); N.W.T.S.A. s. 1 "security" (f); O.S.A. s. 1(1) "security" (g); S.S.A. s. 2(1)(ss)(vii); Y.S.A. s. 1 "security" (f). The Q.S.A. s. 1 does not specifically refer to this form of investment.

[30] A.S.A. s. 1(v)(xii); B.C.S.A. s. 1(1) "security" (j); M.S.A. s. 1(1) "security" (k); N.B.S.F.P.A. Regs. s. 2; Nfld.S.A. s. 2(1)(ss)(xii); N.S.S.A. s. 2(1)(aq)(xii); N.W.T.S.A. s. 1 "security" (k); O.S.A. s. 1(1) "security" (l); S.S.A. s. 2(1)(ss)(xii); Y.S.A. s. 1 "security" (k). The Q.S.A. s. 1 does not specifically refer to this form of investment.

3. *Catch-all Provisions*

Recognizing the potential for a wide range of other creative financing techniques, the definition of "security" is also cast in very open terms. The definition is open-ended in that it:

(i) is non-exclusive because "security" is said to "include" the items listed and is thus not limited to the items listed;[31]

(ii) includes "a document evidencing title to, or an interest in, the capital, assets, property, profits, earnings or royalties of a person";[32]

(iii) "a profit sharing agreement or certificate";[33] and

(iv) includes "an investment contract".[34]

Interpretations of the definition of "security" have not gone outside the listed items probably because terms such as "an interest in property", "a profit sharing agreement", and "an investment contract" are sufficiently broad and vague enough to capture all that needs to be regulated under securities acts. Thus the non-exclusive nature of the definition has not been a factor in interpretations of the meaning of "security".

The term "interest in property" could potentially capture a wide range of daily transactions that could be severely impeded by compliance with securities acts, and for which the protection of securities acts may be considered either unnecessary or inappropriate. Thus in *Re O.S.C. Brigadoon Scotch Distributors (Can.) Ltd.* it was said that,

> The definition would not include documents of title which are bought and sold for purposes other than investment, for example, bills of lading

---

[31] See the provisions defining "security" cited, *supra*, note 21.

[32] A.S.A. s. 1(v)(ii); B.C.S.A. s. 1(1) "security" (b); M.S.A. s. 1(1) "security" (b); N.B.S.F.P.A. s. 1 "security" (b); Nfld.S.A. s. 2(1)(ss)(ii); N.S.S.A. s. 2(1)(aq)(ii); N.W.T.S.A. s. 1 "security" (b); O.S.A. s. 1(1) "security" (b); P.E.I.S.A. s. 1(i)(ii); S.S.A. s. 2(1)(ss)(ii); Y.S.A. s. 1 "security" (b). There is no directly corresponding provision in the Q.S.A.

[33] A.S.A. s. 1(v)(ix); B.C.S.A. s. 1(1) "security" (g); M.S.A. s. 1(1) "security" (h); N.B.S.F.P.A. Regs. s. 2; Nfld.S.A. s. 2(1)(ss)(ix); N.S.S.A. s. 2(1)(aq)(ix); N.W.T.S.A. s. 1 "security" (h); O.S.A. s. 1(1) "security" (i); S.S.A. s. 2(1)(ss)(ix); Y.S.A. s. 1 "security" (h). There is no directly corresponding provision in the Q.S.A.

[34] A.S.A. s. 1(v)(xiv); B.C.S.A. s. 1(1) "security" (l); M.S.A. s. 1(1) "security" (m); N.B.S.F.P.A. Regs. s. 2; Nfld.S.A. s. 2(1)(ss)(xiv); N.S.S.A. s. 2(1)(aq)(xiv); O.S.A. s. 1(1) "security" (n) (other than an investment contract under the *Investment Contracts Act*); Q.S.A. s. 1(7); S.S.A. s. 2(1)(ss)(xiv); Y.S.A. s. 1 "security" (n). The N.W.T.S.A. definition of "security" does not refer to an "investment contract".

and receipts for goods purchased for inventory or consumption purposes. Such an intention on the part of the Legislature can be inferred from the basic aim or purpose of the *Securities Act, 1966,* which is the protection of the investing public through full, true and plain disclosure of all material facts relating to the securities being issued.[35]

A "profit sharing agreement" is a potentially broad enough term to capture many of the other types of securities specifically referred to in the definition. In this respect it is somewhat redundant. It is also potentially broad enough to capture a wide range of other arrangements. However, the term has not received much attention and has not been defined in a way that goes beyond the term "investment contract". The Ontario Securities Commission commented in *Raymond Lee* that,

> We anticipate that situations will some day arise where an arrangement is found to constitute a "profit-sharing agreement" even though it is not also an "investment contract". We are not prepared to conclude that this is such a situation. Literal application of this clause on the basis advocated [by the Commission's counsel] would expand the application of the Act into realms limited only by the imagination of counsel.[36]

Thus the catch-all term that has received the greatest attention is "investment contract".

B. The Meaning of an "Investment Contract"

The term "investment contract" has received some attention in Canada and has been the focus of several decisions in U.S. courts. Canadian decisions have looked to the more extensive U.S. jurisprudence on the meaning of "investment contract".

While many U.S. cases have interpreted the statutory definition of "security", and in particular the meaning of the "investment con-

---

[35] [1970] 3 O.R. 714 at 716-17 (H.C.). See *R. v. Dalley,* [1957] O.W.N. 123 (C.A.) for an application of this branch of the definition to percentage interests in prospecting or drilling rights and *Parkdale Investment Syndicate,* March, 1958, O.S.C.B. 1 for an application to participation units in a trust to manage real property. For other cases addressing the application of this branch of the definition see e.g. *O.S.C. v. British Canadian Commodity Options Ltd.* (1979), 22 O.R. (2d) 278 (H.C.); *Raymond Lee Organization of Canada,* June, 1978, O.S.C.B. 119; *Prudential Trust Company Ltd. v. Forseths,* [1960] S.C.R. 210; *London Commodity Options,* April, 1977, O.S.C.B. 80.

[36] June, 1978, O.S.C.B. 125.

tract" part of the definition, the cases which have received the most attention are *SEC v. C.M. Joiner Leasing Corporation*,[37] *SEC v. W.J. Howey Co.*,[38] and *State of Hawaii v. Hawaii Market Center, Inc.*[39] While there have been several Canadian cases which have interpreted the meaning of the statutory definition of "security", the most significant with respect to the term "investment contract" is the decision of the Supreme Court of Canada in *Pacific Coast Coin Exchange of Canada et al. v. O.S.C.*[40] In *Pacific Coast*, the Supreme Court of Canada adopted the tests set out in the U.S. cases noted above. The discussion which follows focuses on the facts and decisions in these cases and should allow one to develop a sense of the potential scope of the definition of "security", and the approach of the courts in determining whether a given transaction constitutes a "security".

1. SEC v. C.M. Joiner Leasing Corporation

In *SEC v. C.M. Joiner Leasing Corporation*,[41] the SEC sought an injunction against C.M. Joiner Leasing Corporation with respect to assignments of leases. A Mr. Anthony had acquired leases on property in Texas in consideration of drilling a test well and of payment of $1 per year rental in the case of a delay in drilling.

---

[37] 320 U.S. 344 (1943).

[38] 328 U.S. 293 (1946).

[39] 485 P.2d 105 (Hawaii 1971).

[40] [1978] 2 S.C.R. 112, 2 B.L.R. 212, 80 D.L.R. (3d) 529, 18 N.R. 52, affirming (1976), 8 O.R. (2d) 257 (Ont. C.A.), which affirmed (1975), 7 O.R. (2d) 395 (Ont. Div. Ct.), Nov. 1974 O.S.C.B. 209. For other Canadian cases interpreting "investment contract", see, for example, *A.G. Alta. v. Great Way Merchandising Ltd.*, [1971] 3 W.W.R. 133; *British Columbia Securities Commission v. Bestline Products of Canada Ltd.*, [1972] 2 W.W.R. 287, affirmed [1972] 6 W.W.R. 245 (B.C.C.A.); *Farmex Enterprises Inc.*, March, 1974 O.S.C.B. 50; *Xantrex Management Corporation*, March, 1975 O.S.C.B. 93; *Re Western Ontario Credit Corp. Ltd.*, May, 1974 O.S.C.B. 87, affirmed (1975), 9 O.R. (2d) 93; *Re O.S.C. v. C&M Financial Consultants Ltd.* (1979), 23 O.R. (2d) 378 (H.C.); *Superintendent of Brokers v. Lazerman Investment Metals International Inc.* (1985), 62 B.C.L.R. 376 (C.A.); *Re Greymac Mortgage Corp.*, January, 1980 O.S.C.B. 21; *Re Shelter Corporation of Canada Ltd.*, January, 1977 O.S.C.B. 6; *R. v. Chering Service Inc.* (1990), 13 O.S.C.B. 5147 (Ont. Prov. Div.); *R. v. Ausmus*, [1976] 5 W.W.R. 105 (Alta. Dist. Ct.); *Re O.S.C. and British Canadian Commodity Options Ltd.*, *supra* note 35.

[41] *Supra* note 37.

Anthony transferred a substantial portion of the leases to Joiner who was to arrange financing for drilling which would be done by Anthony. They then engaged in a sales campaign whereby they tried to assign leases in the land, in parcels of 5 to 20 acres for prices of $5 to $15 per acre, with the promise that C.M. Joiner Corporation would drill a test well on or near the property leased so as to test the oil producing potential of the land covered by the lease.

The transaction was set up so that it was arguably just a sale of an interest in land. However, the court found that it was something more than that. It was not just a sale of an interest in property, but the sale of the prospect of gaining from the exploration exercise. The court took a purposive approach to interpreting the meaning of the word "security" and thus of the application of the Act. The court noted that the transaction "had all the evils inherent in the securities transactions which it was the aim of the *Securities Act* to end."[42]

The court noted that the structure of the definition is that it catches some specific and known types of securities, but goes on to use some more general terms.[43] The court also noted that these general terms should not be read down through the use of the *ejusdem generis* rule[44] or the *expressio unis*[45] rule. The Act must be able to respond to new, novel, uncommon, or irregular devices.[46] In short, in the court's view, the definition should be interpreted broadly to meet the purpose of the Act and should not be subverted by new security instruments designed to avoid the application of the Act or to frustrate the purpose of the Act.

---

[42] 320 U.S. 349.

[43] Ibid., at 350-51.

[44] This is a rule of interpretation which says that general words following an enumeration of particular persons or things should not be interpreted in their widest sense but should be interpreted as applying only to persons or things of the same type.

[45] The fuller expression is *expressio unius est exclusio alterius* and it is a rule of interpretation meaning that the expression of one thing implies the exclusion of other things. In other words, the argument in *Joiner* was that the list of items set out in the definition of "security" was exhaustive and if the transaction could not be fit within those terms, then it could not be considered a security.

[46] 320 U.S. 351.

2. SEC v. W.J. Howey Co.

In *S.E.C. v. W.J. Howey Co.*,[47] the Howey Company and Howey-in-the Hills Service Inc. were under common ownership. The Howey Co. owned large tracts of orange groves in Florida and also owned a hotel in Florida. The hotel's brochure mentioned the fine orange groves in the vicinity and the people who came to the hotel had the groves drawn to their attention as they were being escorted through the countryside. They were told that the groves were for sale and were given a sales talk if they expressed an interest in buying the groves.

The groves were sold in plots of about 1 acre each in long strips of land with orange trees running down the strip of land. The buyers of the land were advised that the land needed to be serviced and the services of Howey-in-the-Hills Service Inc. were recommended. The buyers were also told that returns of 20% per annum had occurred, but that they could expect average returns of about 10% per annum. Most of the purchasers bought the services of Howey-in-the-Hills Service Inc.

The court set out a test for the identification of "investment contracts" that has been applied in many subsequent U.S. decisions. The test, known as the "common enterprise" test, requires:[48]

(i) a contract, transaction or scheme whereby a person *invests*;

(ii) that the investment be in a *common enterprise*; and

(iii) that the person is led to *expect profits solely* from the efforts of a promoter or third party.

In the *Howey* case the court said there was more than just a sale of fee simple interests in land. The people, from distant locations, were attracted to the investment by the expectation of returns. The scheme would not work if the interests were not pooled in a common enterprise managed by Howey-in-the-Hills Service, Inc. because it would not be economical to cultivate and harvest such small plots of land. The transfer of land was just a convenient way of allocating the profits of the enterprise.[49] The court reiterated the point made in *SEC v. Joiner* that the definition is to be interpreted in a way con-

---

[47] *Supra* note 38.

[48] 328 U.S. 298-99, 301.

[49] Ibid., at 299-300.

sistent with the purposes of the Act and that it embodies a flexible principle.[50]

3. *State of Hawaii v. Hawaii Market Center Inc.*

In the *Hawaii Market Center* case,[51] the scheme involved a store in which only members could shop. The capital for the store was raised by the sale of founding memberships for which the members paid $320 or $820 for merchandise (a sewing machine and/or cookware) worth $70 or $140. They earned returns by selling other memberships and by commissions.[52]

The Securities Commission of Hawaii sought an injunction against the sales of these memberships on the basis that they constituted "investment contracts" and thus constituted "securities" under the *Securities Act.* The contention by Hawaii Market Center was that members had some control over their potential return by selling new memberships and thus they did not depend "solely" on others for their return as required by the *Howey* test.

The court said that the problem with the *Howey* test was the narrow focus on the mechanical test of "solely" thereby losing sight of the need to interpret the meaning of "investment contract" broadly to meet the purposes of the Act.[53] They set out a broader test often known as the "risk capital" test.[54] The test requires that:[55]

---

[50] Ibid., at 299.

[51] *Supra* note 39.

[52] For other cases involving pyramid selling schemes see *SEC v. Glen W. Turner Enterprises Inc.*, 348 F.Supp. 766 (1972), affirmed 474 F.2d 476 (9th Cir.), cert. denied 414 U.S. 821 (1973); *Georgia Market Centers Inc. v. Forston*, 171 S.E. 2d 620 (S.C.Geo. 1969); *Koscot Interplanetary Inc. v. King*, 452 S.W. 2d 531 (Tex. Civ. App. 1969). For Canadian cases involving pyramid selling schemes see *A.G. Alta. v. Great Way Merchandising Ltd.*, *supra* note 40 (in which such a scheme was held to be a security) and *British Columbia Securities Commission v. Bestline Products of Canada Ltd.*, *supra* note 40 (in which such a scheme was held not to be a security where the fee paid appeared to represent nothing other than the purchase of cleansing materials and other legitimate merchandising charges).

[53] See also *SEC v. Glen W. Turner Enterprises Inc.*, *supra* note 52, which took a liberal approach to the word "solely" in the *Howey* test.

[54] Another well known case which employed a "risk capital" approach is *Silver Hills Country Club v. Sobieski*, 361 P.2d 906 (1961). In the *Silver Hills* case golf club memberships sold to fund the development of a golf course were found to be securities even though only non-material benefits, instead of profits, were expected from the memberships.

[55] 485 P.2d 105 at 109.

(i)   the offerer furnish initial value;

(ii) a portion of the initial value is subjected to risks of the enter-prise;

(iii) the furnishing of the initial value is induced by promises or representations leading to a reasonable expectation or understanding that a benefit above initial value will accrue; and

(iv) the offeree does not have the right to exercise practical and actual control over the managerial decisions of the enterpnse.

Here the premium paid for the sewing machine and/or cookware set was the provision of initial value. The ability to recoup the initial investment and earn income to be generated by commissions depended on the success of the store. The fixed fees and commission were both benefits which were expected and which induced the purchase of the memberships and the investor did not have practical and actual control over the investment of the capital or the management of the store (and thus had no way to protect his or her investment).[56] As in the *Joiner* and *Howey* cases the court noted the need to interpret the definition broadly to meet the remedial purposes of the Act.[57]

4. *Pacifiic Coast Coin Exchange v. O.S.C.*

In *Pacific Coast Coin Exchange v. O.S.C.*,[58] customers could buy bags of silver coins through Pacific Coast Coin Exchange. For a commission, Pacific would buy coins and deliver them to customers who demanded delivery of silver coins *in specie*. The price at which Pacific sold silver coins to its customers was fixed by Pacific several times each day. The price was the market value quoted by Pacific plus commissions and other charges.

---

[56] Ibid., 109-11.

[57] Ibid., 108-9.

[58] *Supra* note 40. For other Canadian cases dealing with commodity agreements see, for example, *Re Xantrex Management Corporation, supra* note 40, and *Superintendent of Brokers v. Lazerman Investment Metals Inc., supra* note 40. For a recent case considering *Pacific Coast Coin Exchange* with respect to phantom stock see *Re George Albino*, [1991] 14 O.S.C.B. 365.

Customers were also allowed to purchase coins on margin. In fact, most of the coins sold by Pacific were sold on margin. It was this aspect of Pacific's business that was at issue in the case. With sales on margin there were loans to customers. The required margin was 35%. Thus the maximum loan Pacific would allow was 65% of the value of the silver coins. Consequently, one could buy 20 bags of coins and pay for only 7 bags. However, if the price of silver coins were to fall then the maximum amount of the loan allowed would also fall. The customer could be called upon to make a payment reducing the amount loaned to 65% of the prevailing value of the silver coins. If the customer failed to make the payment, the customer's interest in the silver coins could be reduced to restore the amount loaned to 65%.[59]

For example, a customer could purchase 20 bags of silver coins at $5,000 per bag for a total cost of $100,000 by paying just $35,000. If the value of a bag of silver coins then dropped to $4,000 per bag, the total value of the silver coins purchased would be $80,000. The maximum loan allowed on $80,000 worth of silver coins would be $52,000 (65% of $80,000). The initial loan of $65,000 would thus have to be reduced by $13,000. The customer would be asked to pay Pacific Coast $13,000. If the customer failed to do this then Pacific Coast could reduce the customer's interest in silver coins by an amount which would restore the maximum loan to 65% of the value of the customer's silver coins.

The customer was entitled to pay for the coins and take delivery of them or to close-out their position. Following the example noted above, if the price of the coins had increased to $6,000 per bag, then the customer could have paid off the $65,000 loan and taken delivery of coins worth $120,000. The customer would have made $20,000. Instead, the customer could simply closeout his or her position. The customer would be entitled to $120,000 worth of coins less the amount owed on the loan. Thus the customer would get $55,000 ($120,000 − $65,000). Since the customer initially paid $35,000 there would be a net gain of $20,000.

The satisfaction of the customers' rights by Pacific were arguably subject to certain risks. One risk was that Pacific might fail to maintain an adequate market for the coins. Another risk was that Pacific Coast might become bankrupt, in which case it would be

---

[59] See the discussion of margin trading in Chapter 1, Part V B 4.

unable to meet its obligations to its customers. In other words, Pacific might not be able to deliver the silver coins or might not be able to pay the customers off when the customers closed out their accounts. The solvency of Pacific depended on its efforts in hedging[60] its silver delivery obligations and in managing the general pool of funds obtained, in part, from the sale of silver coin contracts.

There was a potential for bankruptcy if Pacific had to satisfy obligations to a large number of successful customers. For example, suppose several customers bought 20 bags of coins when the coins were worth $5,000 per bag and then the market price of the coins increased to $6,000 per bag. For each customer who paid in full for the coins, Pacific could be obliged to deliver silver coins worth $120,000 when it had only been paid $100,000 by each customer. For each customer who bought coins on the 35% margin and closed out their position Pacific could be obliged to pay $55,000, which would be $20,000 more than the customer had paid in. If a sufficient number of such customers had demanded delivery or closed out their positions at the same time it could have led to bankruptcy for Pacific.

This would not have been a problem if Pacific Coast had kept an inventory of silver coins which corresponded to the amounts purchased by investors. However, Pacific only kept a small inventory of silver and used the remaining funds for other investments. It covered some of the remaining risk of its silver delivery obligations by buying futures contracts for silver (i.e., a right to buy silver for a specified price at some specified date in the future). Eighty-five per cent of the margin obligations were covered by the purchase of futures contracts. Pacific had a policy of covering not less than 95% of its margin obligations. The funds received from customers were mingled with the general funds of Pacific, some of which were used to buy futures contracts and some of which were used for Pacific's own investment purposes.

The majority decision of the Supreme Court of Canada, written by De Grandpre J., held firstly that U.S. case authority was appropriate and should be considered. The reasons for this, as De

---

[60] Hedging in these circumstances would involve the reduction of risk of fluctuations in the price of silver by either buying and holding silver, or, entering into a contract that allows one to buy silver at a specified price at a future time when one may have to satisfy an obligation to deliver silver.

Grandpre J. noted, were that (i) the definition of "security" in the U.S. *Securities Act of 1933* was similar to the definition in the *Ontario Securities Act*; (ii) both definitions referred to an "investment contract"; (iii) the purpose of the legislation was the same; and (iv) there was a dearth of Canadian authority on the meaning of the term "security".[61]

Secondly, the majority decision adopted both the *Howey* and *Hawaii* tests.[62] It expanded the concept behind the *Howey* test so that it would not be constrained by narrow interpretations of the words "common enterprise" and "solely". With respect to the meaning of "solely", it was said that the question is whether the efforts of the third party are undeniably significant for the success of the enterprise.[63] With respect to "common enterprise" it was said that one exists where the investor advances money while the success of the enterprise depends on the promoter.[64] According to De Grandpre J., "[t]here is no need for the enterprise to be common to the investors between themselves."[65] "The key to success of the venture" was, according to De Grandpre J., "the efforts of the promoter alone, for a benefit that will accrue to both the investor and the promoter."[66]

De Grandpre J. also noted that a broad purposive approach should be used in interpreting the meaning of the word "security". It must, he said, echoing the view expressed in U.S. cases, "be read in the context of the economic realities to which it is addressed."[67] He also quoted from the decision in the *Howey* case to the effect

---

[61] [1978] 2 S.C.R. 112 at 126 where De Grandpre J. noted that a similar approach had been taken in *Great Way Merchandising Ltd.*, *supra* note 40 and *Bestline Products of Canada Ltd.*, *supra* note 40.

[62] Ibid., at 127-31.

[63] Ibid., at 129 following the views expressed in *SEC v. Glen W. Turner Enterprises, Inc.*, 474 F.2d 476, 482 (1973).

[64] Ibid., at 129. Mr. Justice De Grandpre also accepted the statement in *SEC v. Glen W. Turner Enterprises*, Inc., 474 F.2d 476, 482 (note 7) (1973), that a "common enterprise" means "one in which the fortunes of the investor are interwoven with and dependent upon the efforts and success of those seeking the investment or of third parties" — see [1978] 2 S.C.R. 112 at 129.

[65] [1978] 2 S.C.R. 116 at 129-30.

[66] Ibid., at 130.

[67] Ibid., at 127 citing *Tcherepnin v. Knight*, 389 U.S. 332 (1967).

that the term "investment contract" must be interpreted to fulfill the statutory purpose of compelling full and fair disclosure relative to the issuance of instruments that fall within the concept of a security.[68]

With respect to Pacific Coast contracts, De Grandpre J. noted that there was a risk to the investor which depended on the success of the enterprise and the establishment of a true market.[69] The success of the enterprise depended on the efforts of the management of Pacific Coast in managing the pool of funds. In particular, it depended on how they invested the funds and the steps they took to reduce the risk of investment.

Chief Justice Laskin dissented. In his opinion, the risk to the customer depended solely on the solvency of Pacific. If so, there was no difference between this and other commercial contracts where the risk of bankruptcy could lead to non-performance of some contractual obligation. This, he thought, would extend the definition of "security" too far.[70]

C. Summary

As outlined above, discussion of the term "security" includes the following elements:

(i) describing common types of securities;

(ii) listing several specific but less common types of securities; and

(iii) using terms capable of taking on a very broad meaning, thereby allowing the application of securities acts to unusual and unanticipated types of transactions. The most widely used broad term is "investment contract".

The leading cases of *Joiner, Howey, Hawaii*, and *Pacific Coast* suggest that courts are inclined to take a purposive approach to the meaning of "investment contract", finding a transaction to involve an "investment contract", and therefore a "security", if it is the type

---

[68] Ibid. De Grandpre J. also noted a statement to similar effect from *Re Ontario Securities Commission and Brigadoon Scotch Distributors (Canada) Ltd.*, [1970] 3 Q.R. 714 at 717.

[69] Ibid., at 129.

[70] Ibid., at 119-20.

of transaction to which securities regulation was intended to be directed. Two key tests to determine whether a transaction involves an investment contract are the "common enterprise" test enunciated in *Howey*, and the "risk capital" test enunciated in *Hawaii*. Both these tests were accepted by the Supreme Court of Canada in *Pacific Coast*. The facts in these cases and the tests applied indicate a potentially wide scope for the term "investment contract" and thus a wide scope for the meaning of "security" and the application of securities acts.

V. THE MEANING OF "TRADE"

As with the term "security", "trade" is a key term in determining the application of the securities acts. The requirement to produce a prospectus depends on whether there is a "trade" in a "security" which constitutes a "distribution". The definition of "trade" is also essential to the requirement to be registered to "trade in a security".

Further, the term "trade" is at the heart of many jurisdictional questions which can arise in securities markets which are national or international in nature.

A. Sale for Valuable Consideration

A "trade" includes "any sale or disposition of a security for valuable consideration".[71] This applies "whether the terms of

---

[71] A.S.A. s. 1(x)(i); B.C.S.A. s. 1(1) "trade" (a); M.S.A. s. 1(1) "trade" (a); N.B.S.F.P.A. s. 1 "trade"; Nfld.S.A. s. 2(1)(uu)(i); N.S.S.A. s. 2(1)(as)(i); O.S.A. s. 1(1) "trade" (a); P.E.I.S.A. s. 1(k); S.S.A. s. 2(1)(vv)(i). Under the A.S.A., B.C.S.A., Nfld.S.A., N.S.S.A., O.S.A., and S.S.A. this branch of the definition of "trade" excludes transfers for the purpose of giving collateral for *bona fide* debts. However, a transfer, pledge or encumbrancing of securities of an issuer from the holding of a control person is defined to be a "trade" (see A.S.A. s. 1(x)(iv); Nfld.S.A. s. 2(1)(uu)(iv); N.S.S.A. s. 2(1)(as)(iv); O.S.A. s. 1(1) "trade" (d); S.S.A. s. 2(1)(vv)(iv)). Registration and prospectus exemptions are available for the pledge of collateral but the pledge will need a prospectus exemption to realize on the collateral (see Chapters 7 and 12). The N.W.T.S.A. and Y.S.A. have taken a different approach to the definition of "trade". The N.W.T.S.A. s. 1 defines "trade" as follows:

" 'trade' includes
    (a)   a purchase of a security, a solicitation or obtaining of a subscription to or purchase of a security, a sale or disposition of a security or a dealing or transaction in a security,
    (b)   in the case of a company, an allotment, issue or disposition of its

payment be on margin, instalment or otherwise". Since it covers any sale or disposition, it will cover both primary and secondary market trades. Indeed, primary market trades will normally be caught under this branch of the definition of "trade". Gifts of securities would probably not be considered trades under this branch of the definition, given that it applies to sales or transfers for valuable consideration. Under this branch of the definition, a "trade" does not include purchases of securities since, at least with respect to distributions of securities, it is the vendor that is the object of the regulation and it is the purchaser that the legislation is intended to protect.[72]

B. Trades on Behalf of Others

Other branches of the definition of "trade" are directed towards the regulation of persons involved in carrying out trades for others. Such persons are required to be registered and their activities are subject to extensive regulation.[73] Thus a "trade" is defined to include "participation as a trader in a transaction in a security ... on the floor of or through the facilities of an exchange".[74] It is also defined to include "the receipt by a registrant of an order to buy or sell a security".[75]

> own securities by option, agreement, sale, resolution, by-law or otherwise, and
>
> (c)   anything declared to be included in this definition by the regulations."

The definition of "trade" in s. 1 of the Y.S.A. is similar. The Q.S.A. does not use the term "trade" for the purposes of the prospectus requirement or the definition of a "distribution". Instead, in defining "distribution", it sets out situations that might be captured under the term "trade" in other Canadian securities acts.

[72] Ibid. The various securities acts generally provide under this branch of the definition that "trade" "does not include a purchase of a security". See, however, the definition of "trade" in the N.W.T.S.A. and the Y.S.A., *supra* note 71.

[73] See Chapter 12.

[74] A.S.A. s. 1(x)(ii); B.C.S.A. s. 1(1) "trade" (c); M.S.A. s. 1(1) "trade" (b); N.B.S.F.P.A. Regs. s. 3(1)(a); Nfld.S.A. s. 2(1)(uu)(ii); N.S.S.A. s. 2(1)(as)(ii); O.S.A. s. 1(1) "trade" (b); S.S.A. s. 2(1)(vv)(ii).

[75] A.S.A. s. 1(x)(iii); B.C.S.A. s. 1(1) "trade" (d); M.S.A. s. 1(1) "trade" (c); N.B.S.F.P.A. Regs. s. 3(1)(a); Nfld.S.A. s. 2(1)(uu)(iii); N.S.S.A. s. 2(1)(as)(iii); O.S.A. s. 1(1) "trade" (c); S.S.A. s. 2(1)(vv)(i). "Registrant" is defined to mean a person or company registered for trading or required to be registered for trading — see A.S.A. s. 1(1); B.C.S.A. s. 1(1) "registrant"; M.S.A. s. 1(1) "registrant"; Nfld.S.A. s. 2(1)(oo); N.S.S.A. s. 2(1)(al); O.S.A. s. 1(1) "registrant"; S.S.A. s. 2(1)(pp).

C. Pre-Sale Activities — Acts in Furtherance of a "Trade"

The sale process may involve a variety of pre-sale activities before the customer actually buys. The sales pitch may involve various pressure tactics and possibly subtle misrepresentations. There is a risk that the buyer may rely on these pre-sale representations or be influenced by pre-sale pressure tactics. To prevent the potential loss in confidence in the market from such activities, securities acts regulate these activities as well. To ensure that these activities will fall within the legislative scheme, "trade" is defined to include "any act, advertisement, solicitation, conduct or negotiation directly or indirectly in furtherance of" any of the activities described in the other branches of the definition.[76]

It is not clear whether the acts described under other branches of the definition need to eventually be completed before the notion of a "furtherance" can said to apply.[77] However, requiring that some form of "trade" must eventually be completed before a "furtherance" could be said to have occurred would unduly limit the legislative response to pre-sale activities. Such an interpretation might, for instance, prevent an injunction from being granted. Although the narrow reading is possible, the courts have shown their tendency to interpret securities legislation broadly[78] and might reasonably be

---

[76] A.S.A. s. 1(x)(v); B.C.S.A. s. 1(1) "trade" (f); M.S.A. s. 1(1) "trade" (d); N.B.S.F.P.A. s. 1 "trade"; Nfld.S.A. s. 2(1)(uu)(v); N.S.S.A. s. 2(1)(as)(v); O.S.A. s. 1(1) "trade" (e); P.E.I.S.A. s. 1(k); S.S.A. s. 2(1)(vv)(v).

[77] The question is discussed in D.W. Drinkwater, W.K. Orr and R. Sorell, *Private Placements in Canada*, (Toronto: Carswell, 1985), at 31-33.

[78] Courts have said repeatedly that the definition of "security" is to be read broadly to fulfill the purposes of the Act (see the discussion in Part IV above). Courts and securities administrators have also shown their willingness to take a broad approach to the meaning of "trade" in, for example, *R. v. Dalley*, [1957] O.W.N. 123 (C.A.); *R. v. Golden Shamrock Mines Ltd.*; *R. v. Langs*, [1965] 1 O.R. 692 (C.A.) and *Luccis & Co.*, June, 1962, O.S.C.B. 1; *Sanderson v. O.S.C.*, [1972] 3 O.R. 329 (C.A.) Thus they would likely not require a completion of the other activities covered under the definition, in order to say there has been a furtherance, if such an interpretation is considered necessary for the protection of the investing public.

The potential scope of the application of securities law through interpretation of the term "trade" is also apparent in *Gregory & Co. Inc. v. The Quebec Securities Commission*, [1961] S.C.R. 584; *R. v. McKenzie Securities Ltd.* (1966), 55 W.W.R. 157 (Man. C.A.); and *Midland Doherty Ltd. v. Zonailo* (1982), 36 B.C.L.R. 326, supplementary reasons at 36 B.C.L.R. 326 at 399 (S.C.), reversed on other grounds

expected to allow an injunction by not requiring, for instance, a completed sale before an act could be said to be in "furtherance".

D. Open-ended Nature of the Definition

The definition of trade is quite broad. "Trade" is defined to "include" the various matters noted above. Thus, the definition of "trade" has been left to be interpreted much more broadly, as the legislation requires.

VI. THE MEANING OF "DISTRIBUTION"

Once one has decided that the transaction in question involves a "security", then the sale of that security will, in most cases, fall within the branch of the definition defining a "trade" as a "sale or disposition of a security for valuable consideration". If the transaction can be said to involve a "trade" in a "security" the next question is whether the trade in the security constitutes a "distribution".

As noted in Part III above, a prospectus is required when one "distributes" a security. Thus the meaning of a "distribution" is fundamental to the prospectus requirement. Formerly Canadian securities acts required a prospectus when there was a "distribution to the public". Uncertainty associated with the meaning of the term made planning difficult and may have led to a number of issues being sold without a prospectus in situations where prospectus information and statutory liability might have been appropriate.[79] To rectify this, an approach known as the "closed system" has been adopted in most Canadian securities acts.[80] The "closed system" approach is to bring all distributions of securities within the ambit of securities regulation and then grant specific exemptions. Thus the definition of "distribution" is cast in broad terms.

A. Trade in Securities not Previously Issued

The most common distributions of securities will fall within the branch of the definition which provides that a "distribution" means

---

(*sub. nom. Midland Doherty Ltd. v. Zonailo; Midland Doherty Ltd. v. A.G.F. Management Ltd.*) (1983), 43 B.C.L.R. 138 (C.A.).

[79] See the discussion in Chapter 7.

[80] See Chapter 7 on the "closed system".

"a trade in a security of an issuer that has not been previously issued".[81] The term "issue" is not defined. However, with respect to securities, it is generally understood to mean the offer of securities for sale.[82] "Issuer" is a defined term and includes a person or company who issues a security.[83] In short, when a person or company offers a security for sale that has not previously been offered for sale, it will constitute a distribution and a prospectus will be required unless an exemption is available.

B. Resale of Securities Returned to the Issuer

Occasionally the issuer may buy back, or have returned as a gift, a security that they have previously issued. If the issuer were to resell the security, it may well have access to information that is not available to the public. Thus it may be appropriate to have the issuer provide information in the form of a prospectus if it resells securities that have been repurchased by it or returned to it. Accordingly, if the security is issued again, it will constitute a "distribution" under the branch of the definition that provides that a "distribution" means "a trade by or on behalf of an issuer in pre-

---

[81] A.S.A. s. 1(f)(i); B.C.S.A. s. 1(1) "distribution" (a); M.S.A. s. 1 ("primary distribution to the public"); N.B.S.A. s. 1 "primary distribution to the public" (a); Nfld.S.A. s. 2(1)(m)(i); N.S.S.A. s. 2(1)(l)(i); O.S.A. s. 1(1) "distribution" (a); P.E.I.S.A. s. 1(b.1)(i); S.S.A. s. 2(1)(r)(i). The N.W.T.S.A. and Y.S.A. do not use the term "distribution". Instead the N.W.T.S.A. s. 27 and Y.S.A. s. 22 refer to a "trade in a security". Under the Q.S.A. these types of distributions will be covered by the definition of "distribution" in s. 5 of the Q.S.A., particularly paragraphs (1) and (2) thereof which provide that a "distribution" means,

(1) the endeavour to obtain, or the obtaining by an issuer, of subscribers or acquirers of his securities;

(2) the endeavour to obtain, or the obtaining, by a firm underwriter, of purchasers for securities he has underwritten.

[82] "Issue": Black's Law Dictionary (5th) West Publishing Company; St. Paul, Minn. 1979.

[83] "Issuer" also includes a person or company which has outstanding securities or proposes to issue a security for reasons discussed in Chapter 7 below. A.S.A. s. 1(j); B.C.S.A. s. 1(1); M.S.A. s. 1 "issuer"; Nfld.S.A. s. 2(1)(u); N.S.S.A. s. 2(1)(s); O.S.A. s. 1(1); P.E.I.S.A. s. 1 (d.1); Q.S.A. s. 5 "issuer"; S.S.A. s. 2(1)(x)(ii). The N.B.S.F.P.A. does not define the term "issuer".

viously issued securities of that issuer that have been redeemed or purchased by or donated to that issuer".[84]

Such a distribution of previously issued securities will not occur with respect to shares in most Canadian corporations, since several corporate statutes require that shares which are redeemed cannot be held for resale (such shares often being described as "treasury shares") but must instead be cancelled.[85] Nonetheless non-Canadian corporations may sell shares in Canada and other instruments coming within the ambit of the term "security" might be repurchased or returned to the issuer and be subsequently offered for sale.

C. Sales by Control Persons

Sales of securities by persons in a position of control are also considered to be distributions because a position of control over the issuer will give persons having such control better knowledge of the issuer and an ability to alter the value of the issuer. A person (or persons) in a position to materially affect the control of the issuer may be in a position to influence the affairs of the issuer in such a way as to distort or conceal information in order to get as high a price as possible when selling securities of the issuer. Further, if the sale involves a substantial number of securities, it may have a substantial effect on the market price of the security. It may also mean that the control person, who may have been an important factor in the success of the issuer, will no longer be controlling the issuer.[86] The control person may also be a conduit for the distribution of securities to the investing public. Thus most securities acts

---

[84] A.S.A. s. 1(f)(ii); B.C.S.A. s. 1(1) "distribution" (b); M.S.A. s. 1(1) "primary distribution to the public" (b); N.B.S.F.P.A. s. 1 "primary distribution to the public" (b); Nfld.S.A. s. 2(1)(m)(ii); N.S.S.A. s. 2(1)(l)(ii); O.S.A. s. 1(1) "distribution" (b); P.E.I.S.A. s. 1(b.1)(ii); S.S.A. s. 2(1)(r)(ii). Under the Q.S.A. these types of distributions will be covered by paragraphs (1) and (2) of the definition of "distribution" in s. 5 (see *supra* note 81).

[85] Examples of this are the *Canada Business Corporations Act*, R.S.C. 1985, c. C-44, s. 39(6), the Ontario *Business Corporations Act*, R.S.O. 1990, c. B16, s. 35(6) and the Alberta *Business Corporations Act*, S.A. 1981, c. 15, s. 37(6). There are, however, still some exceptions such as B.C.C.A. s. 238.

[86] See *Report of the Committee of the Ontario Securities Commission on the Problems of Disclosure Raised for Investors By Business Combinations and Private Placements*, Dept. of Financial and Commercial Affairs, Ontario, February 1970, para. 4.04.

in Canada require the control person to produce a prospectus in order to provide information about the amount of securities sold and the effect of the sale on control of the issuer. The prospectus disclosure is also intended to provide equal access to information necessary to assess the value of the securities being sold. The acts do this by defining "distribution" to include trades in previously issued securities from the holdings of a "control person".[87] A "control person" is defined as a person (or group of persons) who has (have) sufficient control over voting rights to materially affect the control of the issuer.[88] A holding of 20% is deemed, in the absence of evidence to the contrary, to be sufficient to materially affect the control of an issuer.[89]

D. Deemed Distributions on Resale

Numerous exemptions to the requirement to produce a prospectus are provided in securities acts and securities regulations, or may be available pursuant to orders of securities commissions. These exemptions are provided where the prospectus requirement is, for one reason or another, deemed to be inappropriate. The prospectus requirement is often deemed inappropriate where the purchaser of the securities does not need the protection provided by prospectus disclosure. However, if such a purchaser resells the securities, the subsequent purchaser may be a person for whom the protection provided by prospectus disclosure is considered to be appropriate. Consequently these subsequent sales of securities that were previously exempt from the prospectus requirement are considered to be "distributions" and thus trigger the prospectus requirement.[90]

---

[87] A.S.A. s. 1(f)(iii); B.C.S.A. s. 1(1) "distribution" (c); M.S.A. s. 2(1) "primary distribution to the public" (b); N.B.S.A. s. 1 "primary distribution to the public" (b); Nfld.S.A. s. 2(1)(m)(iii); N.S.S.A. s. 2(1)(l)(iii); O.S.A. s. 1(1) "distribution" (c); P.E.I.S.A. s. 1(b.1)(iii); S.S.A. s. 2(1)(r)(iii).

[88] A.S.A. s. 1(c.2); B.C.S A. s. 1(1) "control person"; O.S.A. s. 1(1) "distribution" (c); S.S.A. s. 2(1)(k). See the definition of "distribution" in the Nfld.S.A. s. 2(1)(m)(iii) and in the N.S.S.A. s. 2(1)(l)(iii) and see the definition of "primary distribution to the public" in the N.B.S.F.P.A. s. 1 under paragraph (b) of the definition.

[89] Ibid. While 20% is deemed to be control in the absence of evidence to the contrary, less than 20% may nonetheless fit the definition of "control person" noted in the previous sentence.

[90] See A.S.A. s. 1(f)(v) and ss. 109-112; B.C.S.A. s. 1(1) "distribution" (e) and B.C. Rules ss. 140-143; Nfld.S.A. s. 2(1)(m) and s. 73(4), (5), (6) and (7); N.S.S.A.

VII. THE DISTRIBUTION PROCESS

A. The "Waiting Period"

If the transaction involves a "trade" in a "security" that constitutes a "distribution" then, unless an exemption is available, a prospectus is required. The process of distributing under a prospectus requires the filing of a preliminary prospectus followed, after a "waiting period",[91] by a final prospectus. The preliminary prospectus is intended to be the sole document containing representations about the security during the waiting period. Securities cannot be sold until the final prospectus is filed and a receipt for the final prospectus is obtained.[92] This gives potential investors an opportunity to consider many of the essential features of the investment which the security represents.

B. Vetting of the Preliminary Prospectus

The preliminary prospectus provides the specific items of disclosure required by the relevant prospectus form as well as "full,

---

s. 2(1)(l) and s. 77(5), (6), (7), (7A), (7B) and (10); O.S.A. s. 1(1) "distribution" and s. 72(4), (5), (6) and (7); Q.S.A. s. 5 "distribution" (3); S.S.A. s. 2(1)(r)(vii) and s. 81(6) and (8). Under the M.S.A. a subsequent sale of securities previously sold pursuant to an exemption from the prospectus requirement may be a "primary distribution to the public" (see s. 1(1)) and thus would be subject to the prospectus requirement under s. 37. The N.B.S.F.P.A. s. 13 and the s. 1 definition of "primary distribution to the public" would yield a result similar to the M.S.A. Under the N.W.T.S.A. s. 27, the Y.S.A. s. 22 and P.E.I.S.A. s. 8, a subsequent trade would constitute a "trade in a security" and would thus be subject to the prospectus requirement.

[91] B.C.S.A. s. 78; M.S.A. s. 38; Nfld.S.A. s. 66(1); N.S.S.A. s. 70; O.S.A. s. 65(1); P.E.I.S.A. s. 8.10; S.S.A. s. 73. The A.S.A. s. 99 speaks of a period between the issuing of a receipt for a preliminary prospectus and the receipt for the prospectus and outlines what can be done during the period but does not call it a "waiting period". S. 21 of the S.S.A. also speaks of this time frame but does not label it as the "waiting period". Q.S.A. s. 21 is similar to the A.S.A. and the S.S.A. in this regard. The N.B.S.F.P.A., N.W.T.S.A. and Y.S.A. simply refer to a receipt for a prospectus without a preliminary prospectus and prospectus and the intervening period.

The "waiting period" is also sometimes described as the "red herring" period owing to the statement which must be printed in red ink on the outside front cover of the preliminary prospectus (see, for example, A. Regs. s. 99; B.C. Rules s. 96(2); M.S.A. s. 39(3); Nfld. Regs. s. 38; N.S. Regs. s. 93; O. Regs. 38; P.E.I. Regs. s. 17; O. Regs. s. 74; S. Regs. s. 73).

[92] See *supra* note 15.

true and plain disclosure" of all material facts.[93] It need not contain information with respect to the price to the underwriter and the offering price of the securities or any other matters dependent upon or relating to the price.[94] Thus such matters as the price, maturity date, interest rate or dividend amount are often not set out until the final prospectus is prepared. These are matters that will be affected by prevailing market conditions that may well change in the period between the filing of the preliminary prospectus and the filing of the final prospectus.

When the preliminary prospectus is complete, it is filed with the administrator along with supporting documents such as an auditor's comfort letter, technical reports, consent letters, the underwriting agreement, material contracts, a resolution of the board of directors (or other governing body) approving the preliminary prospectus, the financial statements, and so on.[95] The administrator (assisted by a staff) gives a receipt for the preliminary prospectus if there has been substantial compliance with the filing requirements of the Act and Regulations.[96]

Once the receipt is given, the staff will begin to vet the prospectus. This vetting of the prospectus is not a passing on the merits of the securities offered nor is it a representation that the prospectus contains full disclosure.[97] The vetting process involves a determination of whether the required items of disclosure have been provided and whether there are any gaps in the information that are

---

[93] See Part II above.

[94] A.S.A. s. 82(2); B.C. Rules s. 96; M.S.A. s. 39(2); Nfld.S.A. s. 55(2); N.S.S.A. s. 59(2); O.S.A., s. 54(2); Q.S.A. s. 20 and O. Regs. s. 75; S.S.A. s. 59(2)(b).

[95] See, for example, O. Regs. ss. 23-25 and O. Pol. 5.1 and 5.7; B.C. Rules ss. 106, 108 and B.C. Pol. 3-02. See also A. Pol. 4.7 and 4.11. Other prospectus procedures such as provided for under the "POP System" or for shelf offerings or "PREP" procedures are considered in Chapter 8.

[96] A.S.A. s. 82(1), 83; B.C.S.A. ss. 63(2), 64, 65; O.S.A. ss. 54(1), 55. S. 64 of the B.C.S.A. says that the Superintendent may impose additional filing requirements and conditions if it is the public interest to do so, whereas O.S.A. s. 54 and A.S.A. s. 83 say that a receipt "shall" be issued "forthwith" upon the filing of a preliminary prospectus. See also M.S.A. ss. 39 and 37(2); N.B.S.F.P.A. s. 13; Nfld.S.A. s. 55(a) and s. 56; N.S.S.A. ss. 59(1) and 60; N.W.T.S.A. s. 27; P.E.I.S.A. s. 8(2) and s. 8(3); Q.S.A. s. 20; S.S.A. ss. 59(1) and 60; and Y.S.A. s. 22.

[97] See A. Regs. s. 100; B.C. Rules s. 98(1); Nfld. Regs. s. 39; N.S. Regs. s. 94; O. Regs. s. 39; Q. Regs. s. 30; S. Regs. s. 74. See also N.P. 13.

apparent from the material filed. This process can take up to several weeks.

C. Comment Letter and Clearance Period

When the vetting process is complete a "comment letter", or "deficiency letter" will be provided. The issuer will then have to clear up or respond to the deficiencies or inquiries of the administrator. This "clearance period" can take a few days to several weeks.

Once all the deficiencies are cleared, the final prospectus and supporting documents can be filed and a receipt obtained for them. It is only upon receiving a receipt for a final prospectus that the actual sales of the securities can begin.[98]

D. Limitations on Selling Activities During the Waiting Period

The period between the issuing of a receipt for the preliminary prospectus and the receipt for the prospectus is known as the "waiting period".[99] Amendments must be made to the preliminary prospectus to disclose any material adverse changes in the affairs of the issuer.[100] Material changes include changes in the business, operations or capital of the issuer that would reasonably be expected to have a significant effect on the market price or value of the securities.[101]

---

[98] The administrator can refuse to issue a receipt for the prospectus where it does not comply substantially with the appropriate requirements of the Act and regulations or contains a misrepresentation or a statement, promise, estimate or forecast that is misleading, false or deceptive. A.S.A. s. 96(2)(a); B.C. Rules s. 120(2)(a); M.S.A. s. 61(1)(a); Nfld.S.A. s. 62(2)(a); N.S.S.A. s. 66(2)(a); O.S.A. s. 61(2)(a); P.E.I.S.A. s. 8.8(2)(a); Q.S.A. s. 15(2); S.S.A. s. 70(2)(a).

[99] See *supra* note 91.

[100] A.S.A. s. 85; B.C.S.A. s. 66; M.S.A. s. 40(2); Nfld.S.A. s. 58(1); N.S.S.A. s. 62; O.S.A. s. 57(1); P.E.I.S.A. s. 8.3; Q.S.A. s. 26; S.S.A. s. 62. Since the N.B.S.F.P.A.; N.W.T.S.A. and Y.S.A. do not refer to a preliminary prospectus they do not have provisions with respect to the amendment of a preliminary prospectus.

[101] A.S.A. s. 1(k.1); B.C.S.A. s. 1(1) "material change"; Nfld.S.A. s. 2(1)(x); N.S.S.A. s. 2(1)(v); O.S.A. s. 1(1); P.E.I.S.A. s. 1(d.2); Q.S.A. s. 73; S.S.A. s. 2(1)(y). "Material fact" is defined in s. 108(1) of the M.S.A. but is confined to Part IX and would not apply specifically to s. 40(2).

Selling activities during the waiting period are constrained. The reason for this is that it would defeat the whole idea of having a prospectus with statutory liability for misrepresentations in a prospectus. If representations were allowed prior to the finalization of the prospectus the investor would not be protected by the statutory liability provision if the representations were false. Consequently, during the waiting period one can only identify the security, its price, and where it can be bought, give out the preliminary prospectus, and solicit expressions of interest in the purchase of the security.[102]

There are also limitations on the kind of advertising that can be done in the waiting period. Whether the ads are in newspapers, or on radio or television, all they can do is identify the security, the price, where it can be purchased and otherwise solicit expressions of interest.[103]

---

[102] A.S.A. s. 99; B.C.S.A. s. 78(2); M.S.A. s. 38(2)(a), (b) & (c); N.B.S.F.P.A. s. 20; Nfld.S.A. s. 66(2)(a), (b) & (c); N.S.S.A. s. 70(2); O.S.A. s. 65(2); P.E.I.S.A. s. 8.10(2)(a), (b) & (c); Q.S.A. s. 21(1), (2) & (3); S.S.A. s. 73(2). The N.W.T.S.A. and Y.S.A. do not have corresponding provisions. The dealer must maintain a record of the names and addresses of all persons to whom a preliminary prospectus has been sent — see A.S.A. s. 101; B.C.S.A. s. 63; Nfld.S.A. s. 68; N.S.S.A. s. 72; O.S.A. s. 67; P.E.I.S.A. s. 8.12; S.S.A. s. 75. This allows for sending any amendments of the preliminary prospectus to those persons who have received a copy of the preliminary prospectus. Amendments to the S.S.A., which became effective in 1996, have added a statutory civil liability sanction for misrepresentations in advertising or sales literature used in the course of a distribution (see S.S.A. s. 138.1).

[103] Uniform Act Pol. 2-13. See also draft N.P. #42 which deals with advertising on radio or television and restricts information to the name of the issuer, a concise statement of the issuer's business, the specific type of securities offered, the number offered, the price, special tax treatment, the name of the registrant placing the ad and instructions for obtaining a copy of the prospectus or preliminary prospectus. A warning is also required for advertisements placed in national publications (see N.P. 21). See also B.C. Pol. 3-39 and s. 2.4 of B.C. Pol. 3-03; Sask. Pol. 1.3; Ont. Notice (1987), 10 O.S.C.B. 2831 and Ont. Notice (1988), 11 O.S.C.B. 1098; Ont. Notice (1993), 16 O.S.C.B. 5776; and Que. Notice of June 20, 1986, Bulletin Hebdomadaire, Vol. XVII No. 25. See also Ont. Notice of July 7, 1989 concerning the use of "green sheets" (marketing documents) during the waiting period. It requests that issuers intending to use green sheets submit them to the Commission for review and notes that failure to do so runs the risk of a cease trade order on the use of the green sheets and a possible refusal of a receipt for the final prospectus.

In *Re Cambior*, [1986] O.S.C.B. 3225, the Ontario and Quebec Securities Commissions found that the issuer had engaged in a promotional campaign during the waiting period which was in contravention of restrictions on activities during the

E. Requirements on Distribution — Delivery of Prospectus and Cooling-Off Period

A dealer, upon receiving an order or subscription for a security offered in a distribution, must send the purchaser a copy of the prospectus before, or within two business days of, entering into a written confirmation of the sale of the security.[104] The purchaser of securities sold pursuant to a prospectus is entitled to a "cooling-off period". A purchaser who has agreed to buy the security has two business days from receiving the prospectus to withdraw from the obligation to buy the securities by giving notice of the intent not to be bound to the dealer from whom the security was purchased.[105] This provides a period within which the purchaser has the opportunity to examine the final version of the prospectus (and perhaps an opportunity for sober second thought).

F. Amendment of Prospectus and Lapse of Prospectus

During the period of the distribution, the prospectus must be amended to reflect any material changes.[106] The distribution of securities under the prospectus can continue for a period of up to 12 months from the date of the receipt for the preliminary pro-

---

waiting period. The issuer was only reprimanded, but the Ontario Securities Commission noted that it could make a cease trade order, refuse to issue a receipt for a prospectus, or seek penal sanctions for the violation of the Act. There may also be an action for rescission or damages where such promotional literature contains a misrepresentation.

[104] A.S.A. s. 105; B.C.S.A. s. 83(1); M.S.A. s. 64(1); Nfld.S.A. s. 72(1); N.S.S.A. s. 76(1); O.S.A. s. 71(1); P.E.I.S.A. s. 8.16(1); Q.S.A. s. 29; S.S.A. s. 79(1). There are similar prospectus delivery obligations under the N.B.S.F.P.A. s. 14; N.W.T.S.A. s. 28 and Y.S.A. s. 23.

[105] A.S.A. s. 106; B.C.S.A. s. 83(3); M.S.A. s. 64(2); Nfld.S.A. s. 72(2); N.S.S.A. s. 76(2); O.S.A. s. 71(2); P.E.I.S.A. s. 8.16(2); Q.S.A. s. 30; S.S.A. s. 79(3). The N.B.S.F.P.A., N.W.T.S.A. and Y.S.A. do not have a corresponding provision. The prospectus must contain a statement of the purchaser's withdrawal rights, and rights to rescission or damages where a prospectus, or any amendment of it, contains a misrepresentation — see A.S.A. s. 92; B.C.S.A. s. 63(3); M.S.A. ss. 64(9), 66; Nfld.S.A. s. 61; N.S.S.A. s. 65; O.S.A. s. 60; P.E.I.S.A. s. 8.7; Q. Regs. s. 29; S.S.A. s. 69. See also N.P. 35.

[106] A.S.A. s. 89; B.C.S.A. s. 67; M.S.A. s. 55; N.B.S.F.P.A. s. 13(8); Nfld.S.A. s. 58; N.S.S.A. s. 62; N.W.T.S.A. s. 27(4); O.S.A. s. 57; P.E.I.S.A. s. 8.4(1); Q.S.A. s. 25; S.S.A. s. 63; Y.S.A. s. 22(5).

$S.6\,2$

spectus.[107] After such a period the prospectus is said to have lapsed and no further distributions of the security can be made without a renewal of the prospectus.[108]

G. National Offerings

The process could be quite complicated in national filings if one had to respond to comments from each of the ten provinces as well as the two territories. Problems could arise with the timing and overlap of the comments from the various securities administrators. In response to this problem, the Canadian Securities Administrators released National Policy #1. Under National Policy #1 a principal jurisdiction is selected. This is normally done by the issuer.[109] The issuer files the preliminary prospectus and supporting materials contemporaneously with the administrator in each jurisdiction in which the securities are to be distributed.[110] The principal jurisdiction will then use its best efforts to review the material and issue a first comment letter within ten days.[111] This comment letter will be transferred to the other jurisdictions and the other jurisdictions will then use their best efforts to advise the principal jurisdiction of any additional comments within five days.[112] On the basis of the additional comments, the principal jurisdiction will then prepare a second comment letter to be sent to the issuer.[113] When the comments have been dealt with, the principal jurisdiction will issue a notice of acceptance for filing of the final material and the issuer can then proceed to contemporaneously file the final prospectus and supporting material.[114]

---

[107] A.S.A. s. 97 (subject to such shorter period as the executive director may order); B.C.S.A. s. 70 (subject to such shorter period as the executive director may order); M.S.A. s. 56; Nfld.S.A. s. 63(1); N.S.S.A. s. 67; O.S.A. s. 62; P.E.I.S.A. s. 8.9; Q.S.A. s. 33; S.S.A. s. 71.

[108] Ibid.

[109] N.P. #1, para. 1(b).

[110] Ibid., para. 1(a).

[111] Ibid., para. 1(c).

[112] Ibid., para. 1(d).

[113] Ibid., para. 1(e).

[114] Ibid., para. 1(i) & (j).

H. Canada-U.S. Multijurisdictional Offerings

Arrangements between Canadian and U.S. securities administrators have led to a "multi-jurisdictional disclosure system". This allows certain types of prospectus offerings by U.S. issuers to be made in Canada on the basis of disclosure documents prepared in accordance with the laws of the U.S., subject to the requirements of National Instrument 71-101.[115] Rules of the Securities and Exchange Commission in the U.S. also provide for certain prospectus offerings to be made in the U.S. on the basis of disclosure documents prepared in accordance with the laws of a Canadian jurisdiction.[116] These special types of prospectus offerings of securities are dealt with in more detail in Chapter 8 below.

I. Blue-Sky (or "Merit") Discretion

According to the Kimber Report, the idea was not that "the public must be protected against itself".[117] Investors would be protected by disclosure which would allow them to make informed investment decisions.[118] However, some discretion to assess the merit of securities offered under a prospectus has been an element of most securities regulation since its inception in the early part of the 20th century. This discretion with respect to the merits of the securities being offered is often referred to as "blue-sky" discretion. The term originated in the U.S. where states adopted securities laws that were said to protect investors against "eastern industrialists selling everything including the blue sky".[119]

The potential for review of the merit of securities offered by a prospectus is provided by the power of the Administrators to refuse to issue a receipt for a prospectus where it is in the public interest

---

[115] The types of securities that can be offered are limited as set out in National Instrument 71-101, s. 3.1 to 3.3.

[116] See Sec. Exch. Act Rel. No. 33-6902, [1991 Transfer Binder] Fed. Sec.L. Rep. (CCH) ¶84,812 (see June 21, 1991).

[117] *Report of the Attorney General's Committee on Securities Legislation in Ontario,* March 1965, para. 1.12.

[118] Ibid.

[119] Hazen, *supra* note 16, at 492.

to do so.[120] In most Canadian securities acts, the scope of the public interest discretion is delineated. For instance, the Administrator may refuse to issue a receipt for a prospectus where:

(i) an unconscionable consideration has been, or will be, paid or given for services, promotional purposes or the acquisition of property;[121]

(ii) the proceeds of the issue and the resources of the issuer are insufficient to accomplish the purpose of the issue;[122]

(iii) the issuer can't reasonably be expected to be financially responsible in the conduct of its business because of the financial condition of the issuer or of its officers, directors, promoters or control persons;[123]

(iv) the business of the issuer cannot be expected to be conducted with integrity in the best interests of security holders because of the past conduct of its officers, directors, promoters or control persons;[124]

---

[120] A.S.A. s. 96(1); B.C.S.A. s. 65(2); M.S.A. s. 61; N.B.S.F.P.A. s. 17(3); Nfld.S.A. s. 62(1); N.S.S.A. s. 66(1); O.S.A. s. 61(1); P.E.I.S.A. s. 8.8; Q.S.A. ss. 14, 15; S.S.A. s. 70(1).

[121] A.S.A. s. 92(2)(b); B.C. Rules s. 120(2)(b); M.S.A. s. 61(1)(b); Nfld.S.A. s. 62(2)(b); N.S.S.A. s. 66(2)(b); O.S.A. s. 61(2)(b); P.E.I.S.A. s. 8.8(2)(b); S.S.A. s. 70(2)(b). See, for example, *Harvard Growth Fund Ltd.*, Sept. 1965, O.S.C.B. 7.

[122] A.S.A. s. 96(2)(c); B.C. Rules s. 120(2)(c); M.S.A. s. 61(1)(c); Nfld.S.A. s. 62(2)(c); N.S.S.A. s. 66(2)(c); O.S.A. s. 61(2)(c); P.E.I.S.A. s. 8.8(2)(c); Q.S.A. s. 15(5); S.S.A. s. 70(2)(c). See, for example, *Loki Resources Ltd.* [1984] O.S.C.B. 583; *St. Anthony Mines Ltd.*, Oct., 1966, O.S.C.B. 23.

[123] A.S.A. s. 96(2)(d); B.C. Rules s. 120(2)(d); Nfld.S.A. s. 62(2)(d); P.E.I.S.A. s. 8.8(2)(d); S.S.A. s. 70(2)(d).

[124] A.S.A. s. 96(2)(e); B.C. Rules s. 120(2)(e); Nfld.S.A. s. 62(2)(e); N.S.S.A. s. 66(2)(e); O.S.A. s. 61(2)(e); P.E.I.S.A. s. 8.8(2)(e); Q.S.A. s. 15(4); S.S.A. s. 70(2)(e). See, for example, *Gogama Explorers Ltd.*, April 2, [1982] O.S.C.B. 13, 92C. In *Tex-U.S. Oil & Gas Inc.*, April 29, 1983 O.S.C.B. 773, a person who had been involved in the preparation of a prospectus had previously been charged with issuing a false prospectus, uttering a forged document and conspiracy to issue a false prospectus, but the charges were withdrawn. The person had been a co-promoter with others who were found guilty on similar charges. The Ontario Securities Commission held that the administrator (the "Director") could not refuse to issue a receipt because the person was entitled to be presumed innocent and his conduct was not to be defined by the conduct of others with whom he was in a solicitor-client relationship. In *Tricor Holdings Inc.*, [1988] O.S.C.B. 4059 there was evidence that Tricor was previously controlled by a convicted felon, but there was only circumstantial evidence that he continued to control Tricor. The majority of the Commission held that the Director could refuse a receipt.

(v) any escrow or pooling agreement considered necessary or advisable by the Administrator has not been entered into or the rights or restrictions on the securities the Administrator considers necessary or advisable has not been attached to the securities;[125] or

(vi) a person who has prepared or certified any part of the prospectus or who is named as having prepared a report or valuation used in or with the prospectus is not acceptable.[126]

The person who filed the prospectus is entitled to a hearing with respect to a refusal of a receipt for a prospectus.[127]

---

[125] A.S.A. s. 96(2)(f); B.C. Rules s. 120(2)(f); M.S.A. s. 61(1)(d); Nfld.S.A. s. 62(2)(f); N.S.S.A. s. 66(2)(f); O.S.A. s. 61(2)(f); P.E.I.S.A. s. 8.8(2)(f); S.S.A. s. 70(2)(f). In *Nipiron Mines Ltd.*, Jan., 1966 O.S.C.B. 10, the Ontario Securities Commission noted, at Jan., 1966 O.S.C.B. 11, that it was authorized:

> "to impose escrow restrictions for the reason that, at the date of the transfer of a mining property to a company, it is impossible to assess the true value of the property. It has been the practice to require that 90 percent of the vendor's shares be placed in escrow with the remaining 10 percent free from escrow. Under this arrangement, the free shares the vendor receives can be sold into the market for an immediate return, but the escrowed shares cannot be sold without the approval of both the company and the Commission. This ensures that the vendor takes a gamble on the future potential of the property he has sold to the company."

Escrow restrictions are usually only applied when an issuer files its first prospectus, particularly for junior resource and high-tech companies and when property is transferred to an issuer in exchange for shares. See also A. Pol. 4.2, Forms 16, 17; B.C. Form 16; Nfld. Forms 16, 17; N.S. Forms 16, 17; O. Pol. 5.9 and Forms 16, 17; Q. Pol. Q-8; S. Pol. 4.3 and Form 17.

[126] A.S.A. s. 96(2)(i); B.C. Rules s. 120(2)(i); Nfld.S.A. s. 62(2)(i); N.S.S.A. s. 62(2)(i); O.S.A. s. 61(2)(i); P.E.I.S.A. s. 8.8(2)(i); S.S.A. s. 70(2)(i). See, for example, *Rivalda Investments Corp*, Dec., 1965 O.S.C.B. 2; *Tricor Holdings Co. Inc.*, [1988] O.S.C.B. 4059; but see *Tex-U.S. Oil & Gas Inc.*, April 29, 1983 O.S.C.B. 773.

[127] A.S.A. 96(3); B.C.S.A. s. 65(3); M.S.A. s. 61(2); N.B.S.F.P.A. s. 37(3) (appeal to Court of Queen's Bench); Nfld.S.A. s. 62(3); N.S.S.A. s. 66(3); O.S.A. s. 61(3); P.E.I.S.A. s. 8.8(3); S.S.A. s. 70(3). Under the Q.S.A. s. 321 a decision to refuse a receipt for a prospectus may be reviewed and, under s. 312, the commission may conduct a hearing. The person filing the prospectus can appeal the decision of the commission to three judges of the Provincial Court (s. 324).

VIII. CONSEQUENCES OF FAILURE TO FILE OR DELIVER PROSPECTUS

There are penal, administrative and civil sanctions for failing to deliver the prospectus to a purchaser or for failing to file a prospectus where the filing of a prospectus is required.[128]

A. Failure to Deliver a Prospectus

1. *Penal Sanction*

As noted above, where securities are being distributed under a prospectus there is an obligation to deliver the prospectus to purchasers of the securities.[129] Failure to deliver the prospectus as required may expose the dealer,[130] who is required to deliver the prospectus, to a penal sanction of a fine or imprisonment.[131]

---

[128] The penal and administrative sanctions and procedural aspects of these sanctions are discussed in Chapter 14.

[129] See *supra* note 104.

[130] A dealer is a person who trades in securities as principal or agent. Normally securities distributed under a prospectus will be sold through dealers. The regulation of dealers and other securities market actors is dealt with in Chapter 12.

[131] A.S.A. s. 161(1)(e) ($1,000,000 or, for an individual, $1,000,000 or imprisonment for 5 years less a day or both fine and imprisonment); B.C.S.A. s. 155(1)(b) (depending on whether the word "record" includes a prospectus and on the interpretation of s. 155(1)(d) in conjunction with s. 155(1)(b)) ($1,000,000 or, for an individual, $1,000,000 or 3 years imprisonment or both a fine and imprisonment); M.S.A. s. 136(1)(c) ($1,000,000 or imprisonment for 2 years or both a fine and imprisonment); N.B.S.F.P.A. s. 41 ($5,000 for a company; $1,000 for a first offence, or $2,000 for a second offence or 6 months in prison in addition thereto for an individual); Nfld.S.A. s. 122(1)(c) ($1,000,000 or imprisonment for 2 years or both a fine and imprisonment); N.S.S.A. s. 129(1)(c) ($1,000,000 or imprisonment for 2 years or both a fine and imprisonment); N.W.T.S.A. s. 49(1)(c) ($2,000 or imprisonment for 1 year or both a fine and imprisonment, up to $25,000 for companies); O.S.A. s. 122(1)(c) ($1,000,000 or imprisonment for 2 years or both); P.E.I.S.A. s. 28 ($25,000 for a company; $1,000 for a first offence, or $2,000 for a second offence or 6 months in prison in addition thereto for an individual); Q.S.A. s. 195(3) ($500 to $10,000 for an individual; $500 to $25,000 for others − s. 202); S.S.A. s. 131(3)(c) ($1,000,000 or imprisonment for 2 years or both); Y.S.A. s. 46(1)(c) ($2,000 or imprisonment for 1 year or both; up to $25,000 for companies).

2. *Administrative Sanctions*

Failure to deliver the prospectus to purchasers may lead to any of several potential administrative sanctions imposed by a securities commission or administrator. For instance, it could result in an order directing compliance with the delivery obligation,[132] an order that trading in the securities cease,[133] a denial of exemptions from the requirements of the securities act or regulations,[134] or a reprimand or suspension, cancellation or restriction of registration for trading.[135] Under the B.C.S.A., N.S.S.A. or S.S.A., it may also lead to an "administrative penalty" of up to $100,000.[136]

3. *Civil Sanctions*

The securities acts also provide for a civil sanction for failure to deliver a copy of the prospectus. Where the prospectus is not delivered as required, the purchaser has a right of action for rescission[137] or damages against the dealer who failed to deliver the prospectus.[138] This right of action is subject to a limitation period. The action for rescission must, in most jurisdictions, be brought within 180 days of the date of the transaction that gave rise to the cause of action.[139] An action for damages must be brought before

---

[132] A.S.A. s. 164; B.C.S.A. s. 161(1)(a); M.S.A. s. 152; N.B.S.F.P.A. s. 23 (and s. 1 "fraud" (g)); Nfld.S.A. s. 126; N.S.S.A. ss. 133, 134(1)(a); N.W.T.S.A. s. 22(1)(b); O.S.A. s. 126; Q.S.A. s. 272.1; S.S.A. s. 133.

[133] A.S.A. s. 165; B.C.S.A s. 161(1)(b); M.S.A. s. 148; N.B.S.F.P.A. s. 18, 23; Nfld.S.A. s. 127; N.S.S.A. s. 134(1)(b); N.W.T.S.A. s. 37; O.S.A. s. 127; P.E.I.S.A. s. 19; Q.S.A. s. 265; S.S.A. s. 134(1)(b), (d); Y.S.A. s. 32.

[134] A.S.A. s. 166; B.C.S.A. s. 161(1)(c); Nfld.S.A. s. 128; N.S.S.A. s. 134(1)(c); O.S.A. s. 128; Q.S.A. s. 264; S.S.A. s. 134(1)(a). There is no similar provision under the M.S.A., N.B.S.F.P.A., N.W.T.S.A., P.E.I.S.A. or Y.S.A.

[135] A S.A. s. 56; B.C.S.A. s. 161(1)(f); M.S.A. s. 8; N.B.S.F.P.A. ss. 22, 23; Nfld.S.A. s. 28; N.S.S.A. s. 33; N.W.T.S.A. s. 10; O.S.A. s. 127; P.E.I.S.A. ss. 18, 19; Q.S.A. s. 273; S.S.A. s. 134(1)(i), (j); Y.S.A. s. 8(2).

[136] B.C.S.A. s. 162; N.S.S.A. s. 135; S.S.A. s. 135.1.

[137] Rescission involves an undoing of the contract from the beginning.

[138] A.S.A. s. 170(a); B.C.S.A. s. 135(a); N.B.S.F.P.A. s. 16 (a right of action for rescission but not damages); Nfld.S.A. s. 133; N.S.S.A. s. 141(1); N.W.T.S.A. s. 29 (an action for rescission but not damages); O.S.A. s. 133; P.E.I.S.A. s. 16.1; Q.S.A. s. 214; S.S.A. s. 141(2); Y.S.A. s. 24 (for rescission not damages).

[139] A.S.A. s. 175; B.C.S.A. s. 140; N.B.S.F.P.A. s. 16 (within 3 months of the

the earlier of 180 days after the purchaser first had knowledge of the facts giving rise to the cause of action or 1 to 3 years, depending on the jurisdiction, after the date of the transaction.[140]

B. Failure to File the Prospectus

1. *Penal Sanction*

Failure to file a prospectus where required, or distributing a security without having obtained a receipt for a prospectus as required, can lead to a penal sanction of a fine or imprisonment.[141]

2. *Administrative Sanctions*

Failure to file a prospectus where required, or distributing a security without having obtained a receipt for a prospectus as required, can lead to an order that trading in the security cease until the prospectus is filed and a receipt therefore is obtained.[142] It may lead to a denial of exemptions.[143] Under the A.S.A., B.C.S.A., N.S.S.A. or S.S.A., it may lead to an order that a person resign from any

---

date of serving a notice of intention to exercise the right of rescission); Nfld.S.A. s. 138(a); N.S.S.A. s. 141(4)(a) (2 years); N.W.T.S.A. s. 29 (within 3 months of service of the notice required by the section); O.S.A. s. 138(a); P.E.I.S.A. s. 16.2(a); Q.S.A. s. 234 (1 year); S.S.A. s. 147(a); Y.S.A. s. 24 (within 3 months of service of the notice required by the section).

[140] A.S.A. s. 175 (or 1 year after the date of the transaction); B.C.S.A. s. 140 (or 3 years after the date of the transaction); Nfld.S.A. s. 138(b) (or 3 years after the date of the transaction); N.S.S.A. s. 141(4)(b) (3 years after the date of the transaction); O.S.A. s. 138(b) (or 3 years after the date of the transaction); P.E.I.S.A. s. 16.2(b) (1 year after the plaintiff first had knowledge of the facts giving rise to the cause of action or 3 years after the date of the transaction); Q.S.A. s. 236 (3 years from the transaction); S.S.A. s. 147(b) (or 3 years from the date of the transaction). The N.B.S.F.P.A., N.W.T.S.A. and Y.S.A. do not provide a right of action for damages for failure to deliver a prospectus to a purchaser.

[141] See the provisions cited *supra* note 131. The applicable provision for B.C. would be B.C.S.A. s. 155(1)(d) the sanction for which is that set out *supra* note 131.

[142] A.S.A. ss. 164, 165 (a hearing is required); B.C.S.A. s. 161 or s. 164 (s. 164 provides that the order can be made without a hearing); M.S.A. s. 148; N.B.S.F.P.A. s. 18; Nfld.S.A. s. 127; N.S.S.A. s. 134(1)(b); N.W.T.S.A. s. 37; O.S.A. s. 127; P.E.I.S.A. s. 19; Q.S.A. s. 265; S.S.A. ss. 134(1)(b), (d) or 134.1; Y.S.A. s. 32.

[143] See the provisions cited *supra* note 134.

position as a director or officer of an issuer or be prohibited from becoming or acting as a director or officer of an issuer.[144] It may also lead to the reprimand of a registrant or suspension, cancellation or restriction of a registrant's registration.[145]

3. Civil Sanction

a. STATUTORY CIVIL SANCTION?

The statutory civil action noted above for rescission or damages for failure to deliver the prospectus,[146] might be thought to apply whenever a prospectus is required but has not been delivered. However, the statutory provisions setting out the obligation to deliver a prospectus refer to the "latest prospectus filed".[147] In *Jones v. F.H. Deacon Hodgson Inc.*,[148] the Ontario High Court held that the obligation to deliver the latest prospectus filed, only applies where a prospectus has been filed.[149] The B.C. provision was modified in 1995[150] to provide an action for recission or damages where a prospectus required to be delivered to a purchaser was either not sent or was not filed.[151]

b. COMMON LAW SANCTION

There may be an action at common law for a failure to provide a prospectus as required. The purchaser may succeed in an action

---

[144]A S.A. s. 166.1; B.C.S.A. s. 161(1)(d); N.S.S.A. s. 134(1)(d); S.S.A. s. 134(1)(h).

[145]See *supra* note 135.

[146]See the provisions cited *supra* note 138.

[147]See the provisions cited *supra* note 104.

[148](1986), 56 O.R. (2d) 540, 34 B.L.R. 1, 31 D.L.R. (4th) 455, 9 O.S.C.B. 5579 (H.C.).

[149]31 D.L.R. (4th) 464, 466. The court also held that since the statutory provision with respect to the obligation to deliver a prospectus did not apply, the limitation period associated with that statutory obligation also did not apply. The N.S.S.A. s. 141(3) has altered the result by giving an action for rescission or damages where the prospectus filing requirement has not been met. The Q.S.A. s. 214 also provides an action for rescission or damages for failure to comply with the prospectus filing requirement.

[150]S.B.C. 1995, c. 45, s. 40.

[151]B.C.S.A. s. 135(a) in conjunction with s. 83.

for a declaration that the contract is void and be entitled to recover the price paid for the securities. The action could be based on the general principle of contract law that a contract expressly or impliedly prohibited by statute is void. Thus the contractual sale of securities in violation of the prohibition against such a sale without a prospectus where one is required could be found to be void. However, while it is the general principle that a contract that is expressly or impliedly prohibited by statute is void, there are exceptions.[152] In assessing whether a contract in violation of a statute is void or voidable, it has been said that,

> The serious consequences of invalidating the contract, the social utility of those consequences, and a determination of the class of persons for whom the prohibition was enacted, are all factors which the Court will weigh.[153]

In 1926 in *Re Northwestern Trust Co., McAskill's* Case,[154] the Supreme Court of Canada held the sale of securities to be void where the company had not filed the documents and obtained the licence required by the *Manitoba Sale of Shares Act, 1912*,[155] for the sale of shares. However, in 1960 in *Meyers v. Freeholders Oil Co. Ltd.*,[156] the Supreme Court of Canada held that a sale made contrary to a statutory prohibition against calling at a private residence to trade in securities with the public, did not make the sale void since, in the view of the court, the penalty prescribed in the Act was intended to be the only remedy.

In 1973 in *Ames v. Investo-Plan Ltd.*,[157] the British Columbia Court of Appeal distinguished the *Re Northwestern Trust* case on the basis that the B.C. *Securities Act, 1967*[158] was "substantially different" from the *Manitoba Sale of Shares Act, 1912*, in question in

---

[152] For a discussion of the issue of the enforceability of contracts made in violation of a statute, see S.M. Waddams, *The Law of Contract*, 2d ed., (Toronto: Canada Law Book 1993), at paras. 554-56, 565-70.

[153] See *Royal Bank of Canada v. Groberman* (1977), 83 D.L.R. (3d) 415 (Ont. H.C.).

[154] (1926), 7 C.B.R. 440, [1926] S.C.R. 412, [1926] 3 D.L.R. 612.

[155] S.M. 1912, c. 75.

[156] [1960] S.C.R. 761, 33 W.W.R. 193, 25 D.L.R. (2d) 81.

[157] [1973] 5 W.W.R. 451, 35 D.L.R. (3d) 613, reversing [1972] 3 W.W.R. 443, 25 D.L.R. (3d) 581 (B.C.C.A.).

[158] S.B.C. 1967, c. 45.

Re Northwestern Trust.[159] The case involved a sale of shares made in violation of the prohibition against making a distribution to the public without first obtaining a receipt pursuant to the B.C. *Securities Act, 1967.* The Court concluded that it was not the intention of the Legislature to render void contracts made in violation of the prohibition against distributing securities to the public without first obtaining a receipt for a prospectus.[160]

In 1986 in *Jones v. F.H. Deacon Hodgson Inc.*,[161] the Ontario High Court held that a sale of shares made without filing a prospectus as required by the Ontario *Securities Act*[162] was void. The Court said that it was bound by *Re Northwestern Trust* and did not follow the *Ames v. Investo Plan* decision.[163] The Court held that the prospectus requirement was a fundamental element of the statutory scheme, the breach of which would render the contract void.[164] The investors were entitled to be paid back the purchase price of the securities. The *Deacon Hodgson* case was followed in *O.S.C. v. Consortium Construction Inc.* which held that agreements under which investors had advanced money were void for illegality.[165]

In summary, the current position appears to be as follows. For trades in the province of Ontario, a declaration that a contract, made in violation of the prospectus requirement, is void with a claim for return of the price paid for the security, is probably available on

---

[159] 35 D.L.R. (3d) 616.

[160] 35 D.L.R. (3d) 618. In fact a receipt for a prospectus had been obtained in Alberta and the Alberta prospectus had been provided to the investor. The Alberta and B.C. Securities Acts at the time were the uniform acts and it is thus likely that had the investor been given a prospectus for which a receipt had been given in B.C. it would have been identical to the Alberta prospectus the investor in fact did receive.

The situation in B.C. has since changed. B.C.S.A. s. 135 now provides a statutory civil action for rescission or damages for failure to file a prospectus. See *supra* notes 150 and 151 and the accompanying text.

[161] See *supra* note 148.

[162] R.S.O. 1980, c. 466.

[163] 31 D.L.R. (4th) 466.

[164] 31 D.L.R. (4th) 462, 467.

[165] (1993), 1 C.C.L.S. 117, at 139-40. *Jones v. F.H. Deacon Hodgson Inc.* has also been referred to in *Beer v. Townsgate Ltd.* (1995), 8 C.C.L.S. 256; *Campbell v. Sherman* (1993), 2 C.C.L.S. 156; and *Bossé v. Mastercraft Group Inc.* (1995), 7 C.C.L.S. 104.

the authority of *Jones v. F.H. Deacon Hodgson*. For trades in the province of British Columbia, in the face of the *Ames v. Investo Plan* case, it may be difficult to obtain a declaration that a contract made in violation of the prospectus requirement is void at common law, but a statutory civil action is now available.[166] Outside of Ontario and British Columbia, where neither the *Jones* nor *Ames* decisions would be binding authority, the situation is perhaps less clear. Suffice it to say that a declaration that a contract is void may be available where it relates to a distribution of securities for which a prospectus has not been filed.

---

[166] See *supra* notes 150 and 151 and the accompanying text.

CHAPTER 5

STATUTORY LIABILITY AND DUE DILIGENCE

I. INTRODUCTION

The incentive to provide "full, true and plain" disclosure in a prospectus is provided, in part, by a statutory civil sanction for misstatements or omissions. This statutory civil sanction expands upon the actions that would otherwise be available under the common law. However, common law remedies are preserved under the statutory civil liability provisions in provincial securities acts.[1] To understand the way in which the civil sanction provided by securities acts expands upon the common law remedies and what common law remedies may still be available, it is necessary to first consider what remedies were available at common law before the introduction of the statutory civil sanction.

II. THE COMMON LAW POSITION

A. Contractual Claims

Where there is a misrepresentation in a prospectus, the buyer of the security may be entitled to rescission even where the misrepresentation is innocent.[2] There is no right to damages on the basis

---

[1] See Part III D 5 below.

[2] See the discussion in A.G. Guest, *Anson's Law of Contract*, 26th ed. (Oxford: Clarendon Press, 1984) at 221-29, and in S.M. Waddams, *The Law of Contracts* 3d ed. (Toronto: Canada Law Book, 1993), at 279-80.

There may be circumstances in which there is a duty to disclose such that an action may lie for an omission of a material face from a prospectus. For a discussion of potential duties of disclosure, see S.M. Waddams, "Pre-Contractual Duties of Disclosure", in Peter Cane and Jane Stapleton, eds., *Essays for Patrick Atiyah*, (Oxford: Clarendon Press, 1991) at 237. For an example of a case where rescission of a contract involving a trade in securities was allowed on the basis of a failure to disclose see *MacLeod v. Ruck* (1985), 3 B.C.L.R. (2d) 35.

of an innocent misrepresentation.[3] However, if the buyer can establish the representation was intended to form part of the contract at the time of sale of the security, or was made in the course of the sale of the security for the purpose of inducing the purchase of the security and actually did induce the purchase, then an action for damages may be available for breach of contract.[4] Actions for damages on the basis of fraudulent or negligent misrepresentations that do not form part of the contract may be brought as actions in tort.

B. Tort Claims

1. *Fraud*

Tort claims based on misrepresentations in a prospectus were constrained by the decision of the House of Lords in *Derry v. Peek* in 1889.[5] The case involved a misstatement in a prospectus concerning a proposal for a tramway.[6] The House of Lords held that for the directors to be liable for a misrepresentation, it was necessary to show that the misrepresentation was fraudulent. This required showing that the defendant knew or ought to have known that the plaintiff would rely, and the plaintiff did rely to their detriment on a statement that was made "(1) knowingly, or (2) without belief in its truth, or (3) recklessly, careless whether it be true or false."[7]

Shortly after the decision in *Derry v. Peek,* Parliament passed the *Directors Liability Act,*[8] which made directors, promoters and others

---

[3] See the discussion in Guest, *supra* note 2, at 221 and in Waddams, *supra* note 2 at 286.

[4] See the discussion in Guest, *supra* note 2 at 110-14, and in Waddams, *supra* note 2, at 273-77. See also *Heilbut Symons & Co. v. Buckleton*, [1913] A C. 30 and *Dick Bentley Productions Ltd v. Harold Smith (Motors), Ltd.,* [1965] 1 W.L.R. 623.

[5] 14 A.C. 337, 58 L.J. Ch. 864, 61 L.T. 265.

[6] The prospectus asserted that the company was permitted to use steampowered cars. It was not so empowered at the time the prospectus was issued, but the directors believed they would get the consent as a matter of course. However, consent was never given and the company went into liquidation as a result.

[7] 14 A.C. 374. See the discussion in J.G. Fleming, *The Law of Torts*, 8th ed. (Sydney: The Law Book Company, 1992), at 629-39.

[8] 53&54 Vict. c. 64.

authorizing the issue of a prospectus liable for loss or damage sustained by reason of an untrue statement where shares or debentures were bought on the faith of the prospectus.[9] In defence the defendant could argue that he had reasonable grounds to believe and did believe that the statement was true.[10] Thus the proof of fraud by the plaintiff as required in *Derry v. Peek* was removed. This was adopted and expanded upon in Ontario in the *Securities Act, 1947.*[11] In part it expanded on the approach in the *Directors Liability Act* by providing that every purchaser of the securities to which the prospectus related was deemed to rely on the representations in the prospectus whether the purchaser had received the prospectus or not.[12]

2. Negligent Misstatement

These statutory developments in the area of securities law preceded common law developments with respect to negligent misstatements generally. However, the potential to maintain an action at common law for a misstatement was considerably expanded in the 1964 decision of *Hedley Byrne & Co. v. Heller & Partners Ltd.*[13] In *Hedley Byrne*, the House of Lords said that one could establish a claim for damages in tort on the basis of a negligent misstatement.

The dicta in *Hedley Byrne* has been applied in many subsequent cases to impose liability for negligent misstatements. In *Queen v. Cognos.*,[14] Mr. Justice Iacobucci set out five requirements for a claim of negligent misrepresentation:

(i) there must be a duty of care based on a "special relationship" between the representor and the representee;

(ii) the representation in question must be untrue, inaccurate or misleading;

(iii) the representor must have acted negligently in making [the] misrepresentation;

---

[9] Ibid., s. 3.

[10] Ibid., s. 3(a).

[11] S.O. 1947, c. 98.

[12] Ibid., s. 73.

[13] [1964] A.C. 465, [1963] 2 All E.R. 575.

[14] [1993] 1 S.C.R. 87, 99 D.L.R. (4th) 626, 14 C.C.L.T. (2d) 113 (S.C.C.).

(iv) the representee must have relied, in a reasonable manner, on the negligent misrepresentation; and

(v) the reliance must have been detrimental to the representee in the sense that damages resulted.[15]

Two approaches have been taken to the existence of a duty of care based on a "special relationship". One is a foreseeability test in which the person making the representation knew or ought to have known the other person would reasonably rely on the representation. The other approach is a voluntary assumption of responsibility test in which the person making the representation has expressly or by implication undertaken some responsibility.[16] Factors considered in the assessment of whether a duty exists include the skill of the representor, the skill of the representee and the nature of the occasion in which the representation was made. The greater the skill of the representor relative to the representee the more likely it is a duty will be found to exist. Representations made in informal or social circumstances are less likely to give rise to a duty than representations made in a professional or business context.[17]

In the context of disclosures in a prospectus the persons responsible for producing the prospectus, are likely to have greater skill and access to information than most prospective investors. Several persons responsible for producing the prospectus must also sign certificates in which they warrant that the information contained in the prospectus constitutes "full, true and plain disclosure".[18] An

---

[15] [1993] 1 S.C.R. 87 at 110; 99 D.L.R. (4th) 626; 14 C.C.L.T. (2d) 113 at 134. The judgment of Mr. Justice Iacobucci was concurred in on this point by the other five Supreme Court judges who heard the case.

[16] See L.N. Klar, *Tort Law*, 2d ed., (Scarborough, Ont.: Carswell, 1996), at 179-81. Klar comments (at 181) that, "it is difficult to envisage cases where characterizing the test one way or the other will alter the judicial result."

[17] On the influence of these factors see Klar, *supra* note 16, at 182-85.

[18] See A.S.A. ss. 84, 90; B.C.S.A. ss. 63, 68 and 69; M.S.A. ss. 41, 52, 53; N.B.S.F.P.A. s. 13(3)(xxxv); Nfld.S.A. ss. 57, 59; N.S.S.A. ss. 61, 63; O.S.A. ss. 56, 58, 59; P.E.I.S.A. s. 8.1(1); Q. Regs. s. 32 and the definition of "misrepresentation" in Q.S.A. s. 5; S.S.A. ss. 61, 66; Y. Regs. Sch. C, item (PR) and (mm). In *Montreal Trust Co. of Canada v. Scotia McLeod Inc.* (1995), 9 C.C.L.S. 97, the Ontario Court of Appeal dismissed an appeal of an order dismissing a claim against directors for a misrepresentation in a prospectus on the grounds that it did not disclose a reasonable cause of action. In the circumstances of the case, there was no basis for a statutory civil liability claim (on statutory civil liability see Part III, below). Consequently, a claim was made on the basis of the common law. Although the

investor who purchases a security on the faith of a prospectus does so in a serious business context.

The duty, when it arises, is a duty not to mislead.[19] Thus an accurate statement can be a misstatement if it misleads[20] (perhaps due to a failure to disclose other pertinent information necessary to make the statement not misleading). It may even extend to an opinion or belief as to the future.[21]

The persons to whom the duty is owed may be limited to persons who are members of the class of persons whom the defendant knows, or ought to know, will use and rely upon the statements of the defendant for the purpose for which the statements are to be used.[22] However, the duty may also extend to persons whose reliance on the statements could have been foreseen by the defendant.[23]

III. STATUTORY CIVIL LIABILITY

A. Expansion on Common Law Liability

The expansion of the common law in *Hedley Byrne v. Heller*, were it not for the statutory liability provisions already in place, would have greatly improved an investor's claim with respect to misrepre-

---

claim was dismissed for failure to disclose a reasonable cause of action the decision does not mean a claim for negligent misrepresentation against directors is not available. According to the Court of Appeal, the problem with the claim in the case was that it sought "to hold the directors vicariously liable for the negligence of the corporation". In other words, the pleadings did not allege separate acts of negligence against the directors. The claim was allowed to proceed against two officers of the corporation for whom the pleadings disclosed separate negligent misrepresentations.

In a negligent misrepresentation action against individual directors or officers of the corporation the concern that an action against such persons may amount to an "end run around the corporate veil" may have to be addressed. See, e.g., *Mentmore Manufacturing Co. v. National Merchandise Manufacturing Co.* (1978), 89 D.L.R. (3d) 195 (Fed. C.A.).

[19] See J.G. Fleming, *supra* note 7 at 648.

[20] Ibid.

[21] Ibid.

[22] See A.M. Linden, *Canadian Tort Law*, 6th ed., (Toronto: Butterworths, 1997), at 433-36, and Fleming, *supra* note 7, at 645-48.

[23] Ibid.

sentations in a prospectus. The investor would have to show that she relied on the misstatement, that the statement was negligently made and that she suffered some detriment due to reliance on the misstatement. The statutory civil liability for misstatements in a prospectus provided for in most Canadian securities acts goes considerably beyond the common law.[24] First, it applies to misstatements or omissions. Second, it makes the questions of reliance, negligence and causation defences rather than elements of the claim that the plaintiff must establish. This substantially reduces the burden of proof on the plaintiff.

B. What the Plaintiff Must Show

Statutory civil liability for misstatements in a prospectus can be briefly summarized as follows. The plaintiff must only prove[25] (i) a purchase of the security offered under the prospectus, (ii) that the purchase was made during the period of the distribution, and (iii) that there was a "misrepresentation" in the prospectus.

"Misrepresentation" is defined to be an untrue statement of a material fact or an omission of a material fact that is required to

---

[24] The discussion of the statutory civil right of action applies primarily to the provisions of the securities acts of Alberta, British Columbia, Newfoundland, Nova Scotia, Ontario, Prince Edward Island and Saskatchewan — see A.S.A. s. 168; B.C.S.A. s. 131; Nfld.S.A. s. 130; N.S.S.A. s. 137; O.S.A. s. 130; P.E.I.S.A. s. 16; S.S.A. s. 137. With respect to provisions of the securities acts of Manitoba, New Brunswick, Quebec and the Territories see *infra* note 25. In 1995 Saskatchewan added corresponding statutory civil liability provisions for misrepresentations in an offering memorandum (see, e.g., Chapter 7, Part III A 1 g) and in sales or advertising material used in connection with a distribution (S.S.A. ss. 138 and 138.1).

[25] A.S.A. s. 168(1); B.C.S.A. s. 131(1); Nfld.S.A. s. 130(1); N.S.S.A. s. 137(1); O.S.A. s. 130(1); P.E.I.S.A. s. 16(1); S.S.A. s. 137(1) The Q.S.A. s. 217 sets out similar requirements, namely, that the person subscribed for or acquired securities in a distribution effected with a prospectus containing a misrepresentation. The M.S.A. s. 65 provides a right of rescission for a purchaser who bought a security as a result of an offer in a primary distribution to the public, is still the owner of the security and who shows that the prospectus contained an untrue statement or omitted a material fact necessary in order to make any statement contained therein not misleading in light of the circumstances in which it was made. The M.S.A. s. 141 also provides an action for damages for purchases to which the prospectus relates if a material false statement is contained in the prospectus. The N.W.T.S.A. s. 30 and the Y.S.A. s. 25 provide an action for rescission similar to that in the M.S.A. s. 65 but do not provide an action for damages. The N.B.S.F.P.A. does not provide a statutory civil remedy for misrepresentations in a prospectus.

be stated or that is necessary to make a statement not misleading in light of the circumstances in which it was made.[26] Subject to various defences, the plaintiff is then entitled to rescission or damages.[27]

The plaintiff does not have to prove reliance. Instead, the plaintiff is deemed to have relied on the misrepresentation if it was a misrepresentation at the time of the purchase.[28] Since the action is provided for a purchase of the security offered under the prospectus during the period of distribution, it applies to secondary market purchases as well. Secondary market purchasers would have an action for damages.

C. Persons Liable

The persons liable for damages for misrepresentation in a prospectus are the issuer (or the selling security holder if it is a distribution from the holdings of a control person),[29] the underwriters,[30] the directors,[31] any expert who consented to the use of their expert

---

[26] A.S.A. s. 1(1)(m); B.C.S.A. s. 1(1); Nfld.S.A. s. 2(1)(aa); N.S.S.A. s. 2(1)(y); O.S.A. s. 1(1); Q. S.A. s. 5; S.S.A. s. 2(1)(cc). With respect to misrepresentations under the M.S.A., N.W.T.S.A. and Y.S.A. See *supra* note 25.

[27] A.S.A. s. 168(1), (2), (2.1); B.C.S.A. s. 131(1), (3); Nfld.S.A. s. 130(1); N.S.S.A. s. 137(1); O.S.A. s. 130(1); P.E.I.S.A. s. 16(1); Q.S.A. ss. 217, 218, 219; S.S.A. s. 137(1), (2). With respect to the M.S.A., N.W.T.S.A. and Y.S.A. See *supra* note 25.

[28] A.S.A. s. 168(1); B.C.S.A. s. 131(1)(a); M.S.A. s. 141; Nfld.S.A. s. 130(1); O.S.A. s. 130(1); P.E.I.S.A. s. 16(1); S.S.A. s. 137(1). See also Q.S.A. s. 137(1).

[29] A.S.A. s. 168(1)(a); B.C.S.A. s. 131(1)(b)(i); Nfld.S.A. s. 130(1)(a); N.S.S.A. s. 137(1)(a); O.S.A. s. 130(1)(a); P.E.I.S.A. s. 16(1)(a); Q.S.A. s. 218; S.S.A. s. 137(1)(a). The M.S.A. damages action (s. 141) does not apply to the issuer.

[30] Each underwriter who is required to sign the underwriter's certificate on the prospectus is liable − A.S.A. s. 168(1)(b); B.C.S.A. s. 131(1)(b)(ii); Nfld.S.A. s. 130(1)(b); N.S.S.A. s. 137(1)(b); O.S.A. s. 130(1)(b); P.E.I.S.A. s. 16(1)(b); Q.S.A. s. 218 ("dealer under contract to the issuer or holder whose securities were distributed"); S.S.A. s. 137(1)(b).

Underwriters who are in a contractual relationship with the issuer, or security holder, with respect to the securities offered under the prospectus are required to sign the underwriters' certificate − A.S.A. s. 91(1); B.C.S.A. s. 69(1); Nfld.S.A. s. 60(1); N.S.S.A. s. 64(1); O.S.A. s. 59(1); P.E.I.S.A. s. 8.6; S.S.A. s. 67(1). The M.S.A. damages action (s. 141) does not apply to underwriters.

[31] A.S.A. s. 168(1)(c); B.C.S.A. s. 131(1)(b)(iii); M.S.A. s. 141; Nfld.S.A.

opinion in the prospectus,[32] the chief executive officer, the chief financial officer and anyone else who signed the prospectus.[33] The issuer (or selling security holder in a distribution from the holdings of a control person) and the underwriters are subject to an action for rescission for misrepresentation in a prospectus.[34]

D. Defences

Several defences are available. These can be briefly summarized. Defendants can avoid liability by showing that:

(i) the person who purchased the securities had knowledge of the misrepresentation;[35]

(ii) he or she did not consent to the filing of the prospectus or that consent was withdrawn, with reasonable general notice

---

s. 130(1)(c); N.S.S.A. s. 137(1)(c); O.S.A. s. 130(1)(c); P.E.I.S.A. s. 16(1)(c); Q.S.A. s. 218 ("senior executive" which includes directors under the definition of "senior executives" in s. 5); S.S.A. s. 137(1)(c).

[32] Experts are liable only with respect to reports, opinions or statements that have been made by them — A.S.A. s. 168(1)(d); B.C.S.A. s. 131(1)(b)(iv); Nfld.S.A. s. 130(1)(d); N.S.S.A. s. 137(1)(d); O.S.A. s. 130(1)(d); P.E.I.S.A. s. 16(1)(d); Q.S.A. s. 219; S.S.A. s. 137(1)(d). The M.S.A. damages action (s. 141) does not apply to experts.

[33] A.S.A. s. 168(1)(e); B.C.S.A. s. 131(1)(b)(v); M.S.A. s. 141; Nfld.S.A. s. 130(1)(e); N.S.S.A. s. 137(1)(e); O.S.A. s. 130(1)(e); P.E.I.S.A. s. 16(1)(e); Q.S.A. s. 218 ("senior executives" which includes the president, vice-president, secretary, treasurer, controller, general manager, or similar function under the definition of "senior executive" in s. 5); S.S.A. s. 137(1)(e). The issuer's certificate in the prospectus must be signed by the chief executive officer, the chief financial officer (or their equivalent where the issuer does not have persons so named), two directors (or their equivalent where the issuer does not have persons so named), who are not the chief executive officer or chief financial officer, and each promoter of the issuer. See A.S.A. s. 90(1); B.C.S.A. s. 68(2); M.S.A. s. 52(1); Nfld.S.A. s. 59(1); N.S.S.A. s. 63(1); O.S.A. s. 58(1); P.E.I.S.A. s. 8.5; S.S.A. s. 66(1).

[34] The action for rescission against the underwriters is not limited to the underwriters who signed the underwriter's certificate in the prospectus, but extends to all underwriters for the distribution. See A.S.A. s. 168(2); B.C.S.A. s. 131(3); Nfld.S.A. s. 130(1); N.S.S.A. s. 137(1); O.S.A. s. 130(1); P.E.I.S.A. s. 16(1); Q.S.A. s. 217; S.S.A. s. 137(2). With respect to actions for rescission under the M.S.A., N.W.T.S.A. and Y.S.A. see *supra* note 25.

[35] A.S.A. s. 168(3); B.C.S.A. s. 131(4); Nfld.S.A. s. 130(2); N.S.S.A. s. 137(2); O.S.A. s. 130(2); P.E.I.S.A. s. 16(2); Q.S.A. ss. 217, 220(2); S.S.A. s. 137(3). This defence is also provided with respect to actions for rescission under the M.S.A. s. 65(3)(c); N.W.T.S.A. s. 30(3); Y.S.A. s. 25(3)(c).

of the withdrawal and the reason for it, prior to the purchase of the securities by the purchaser;[36]

(iii) the statement was not made by him or her and that he or she had no reason to believe and did not believe that it was wrong;[37]

(iv) he or she conducted a reasonable investigation to provide reasonable grounds for a belief that there was no misrepresentation and that he or she did not believe there had been a misrepresentation (often described as the "due diligence" defence);[38]

(v) the depreciation in value of the security was not caused by the misrepresentation.[39]

1. *Issuer's Defences*

Under securities acts in Canada providing for actions for damages or rescission against the issuer, the issuer is not entitled to either the defence that the statement was not made by the issuer or the defence of due diligence.[40] The issuer is thus effectively

---

[36] A.S.A. s. 168(4)(a), (b); B.C.S.A. s. 131(5)(a), (b); M.S.A. s. 141(a),(b); Nfld.S.A. s. 130(3)(a), (b); N.S.S.A. s. 137(3)(a), (b); O.S.A. s. 130(3)(a), (b); P.E.I.S.A. s. 16(3)(a), (b); S.S.A. s. 137(4)(a), (b).

[37] A.S.A. s. 168(4)(c), (d), (e); B.C.S.A. s. 131(5)(c), (d), (e); M.S.A. s. 141(d),(e); Nfld.S.A. s. 130(3)(c), (d), (e); N.S.S.A. s. 137(3)(c), (d), (e); O.S.A s. 130(3)(c), (d), (e); P.E.I.S.A. s. 16(3)(c), (d), (e); S.S.A. s. 137(4)(c), (d), (e).

[38] A.S.A. s. 168(5), (6); B.C.S.A. s. 131(6), (7); M.S.A. s. 141(c); Nfld.S.A. s. 130(4), (5); N.S.S.A. s. 137(4), (5); O.S.A. s. 130(4), (5); Q.S.A. s. 220(1); S.S.A. s. 137(5), (6). Except for the provisions under the M.S.A. and Q.S.A., the burden of proof in the provisions noted above may fall on the plaintiff because the provisions generally say that "no person is liable ... unless he failed to conduct a reasonable investigation ...". See R.L. Simmonds, "Directors' Negligent Misstatement Liability in the New Scheme of Securities Regulation in Ontario" in L. Sarna, ed., *Corporate Structure, Finance and Operations* (Toronto: Carswell, 1980) vol. 1, at 294-95.

[39] A.S.A. s. 168(8); B.C.S.A. s. 131(10); Nfld.S.A. s. 130(7); N.S.S.A. s. 137(7); O.S.A. s. 130(7); P.E.I.S.A. s. 16(7); S.S.A. s. 137(8). There is no corresponding provision under the M.S.A. or Q.S.A.

[40] A.S.A. s. 168(4), (5), (6); B.C.S.A. s. 131(8); Nfld.S.A. s. 130(3), (4), (5); N.S.S.A. s. 137(3), (4), (5); O.S.A. s. 130(3), (4), (5); P.E.I.S.A. s. 16(3), (4), (5); Q.S.A. s. 220(1); S.S.A. s. 137(4), (5), (6). With respect to the action for rescission under the M.S.A. s. 65, the N.W.T.S.A. s. 30 and the Y.S.A. s. 25, the issuer is entitled to the due diligence defence.

subject to strict liability. The defences available to the issuer are
that the purchaser had knowledge of the information[41] or that the
depreciation in value of the security was not caused by the misrepresentation.[42]

2. Defences for Directors, Underwriters and Persons Signing the Prospectus ·

Directors, underwriters and persons signing the prospectus are
entitled to claim all the defences listed above. With respect to these
persons, the defence that the statement constituting the misrepresentation was not made by the defendant relates to parts of the prospectus purporting to be made on the authority of an expert, by
an "official person" or purporting to be an extract from a "public
official document".[43] With respect to a claim that the representation
was made on the authority of an expert, the defendant must not
have had a belief, and must not have had reasonable grounds for
a belief, that there had been a misrepresentation, or, that that part
of the prospectus did not fairly represent, or was not a fair representation or extract from the expert's report.[44] With respect to statements made by an official person or in an extract from a public
official document, the defendant must show a belief, and reasonable
grounds for the belief, that it was a correct and fair representation
of the statement, or copy of, or extract from the document.[45] With
respect to statements not made on the authority of an expert, by
an official person or in an official document, the defence available
to directors, underwriters and persons signing the prospectus is the

---

[41] See *supra* note 35.

[42] See *supra* note 39.

[43] A.S.A. s. 168(4)(c), (e); B.C.S.A. s. 131(5)(c), (e); M.S.A. s. 141(d), (e); Nfld.S.A.
s. 130(3)(c), (e); N.S.S.A. s. 137(3)(c), (e); O.S.A. s. 130(3)(c), (e); P.E.I.S.A. s. 16(3)(c),
(e); S.S.A. s. 137(4)(c), (e).

[44] A.S.A. s. 168(4)(c); B.C.S.A. s. 131(5)(c); Nfld.S.A. s. 130(3)(c); N.S.S.A.
s. 137(3)(c); O.S.A. s. 130(3)(c); P.E.I.S.A. s. 16(3)(c); S.S.A. s. 137(4)(c). M.S.A.
s. 141(d) provides a similar defence.

[45] A.S.A. s. 168(4)(e); B.C.S.A. s. 131(5)(e); M.S.A. s. 141(e); Nfld.S.A.
s. 130(3)(e); N.S.S.A. s. 137(3)(e); O.S.A. s. 130(3)(e); P.E.I.S.A. s. 16(3)(e); S.S.A.
s. 137(4)(e).

defence of due diligence (i.e., that a reasonable investigation was made to provide reasonable grounds for making the statement).[46]

3. Experts' Defences

Experts liable to purchasers for a misrepresentation in a prospectus have available to them all of the defences listed above. With respect to the statements made on the authority of the expert, the expert can argue, in effect, that the statement was not their statement. This can be done by arguing that the misrepresentation in the prospectus was due to a failure to fairly represent the expert's report or opinion.[47] The expert must have believed and had reasonable grounds to believe, based on a reasonable investigation, that the expert's report or opinion was fairly represented.[48] Further, the expert must have advised the administrator of and given reasonable general notice of, the misrepresentation as soon as practicable after becoming aware of it.[49] Otherwise, with respect to statements made on the authority of the expert, the expert can attempt to establish a due diligence defence pointing to reasonable grounds for a belief in the statement based on a reasonable investigation.[50]

4. Damages

Where damages are claimed under the provision for statutory civil liability, the damages are limited to the price at which the secu-

---

[46] A.S.A. s. 168(6); B.C.S.A. s. 131(7); Nfld.S.A. s. 130(5); N.S.S.A. s. 137(5); O.S.A. s. 130(5); P.E.I.S.A. s. 16(5); Q.S.A. s. 220(1); S.S.A. s. 137(6). A due diligence defence is provided to directors under the damages action in s. 141(c) of the M.S.A. A due diligence defence is provided with respect to an action for rescission under the M.S.A. s. 65(3)(a); N.W.T.S.A. s. 30(3)(a); Y.S.A. s. 25(3)(a). Under some provincial acts it may be that the plaintiff must prove a lack of due diligence — see *supra* note 38.

[47] A.S.A. s. 168(4)(d); B.C.S.A. s. 131(5)(d); Nfld.S.A. s. 130(3)(d); N.S.S.A. s. 137(3)(d); O.S.A. s. 130(3)(d); P.E.I.S.A. s. 16(1)(d); S.S.A. s. 137(3)(d). Experts are not made liable under the damages action in s. 141 of the M.S.A.

[48] Ibid.

[49] Ibid.

[50] A.S.A. s. 168(5); B.C.S.A. s. 131(6); Nfld.S.A. s. 130(4); N.S.S.A. s. 137(4); O.S.A. s. 130(4); P.E.I.S.A. s. 16(4); Q.S.A. s. 130(4); S.S.A. s. 137(5). See *supra* note 47 regarding experts under the M.S.A. Under some provincial acts it may be that the plaintiff must prove a lack of due diligence — see *supra* note 38.

rities were offered to the public.[51] In a claim against an underwriter, the underwriter is not liable for more than the total public offering price represented by the portion of the distribution underwritten by the underwriter.[52] The liability of persons liable under the statutory civil action is joint and several.[53]

5. *Limitation Period and Common Law Rights*

The statutory civil right of action for misrepresentations in a prospectus is in addition to, and not in derogation of, any other right the purchaser may have.[54] This preserves the common law rights of action which may be of some value given the limitation periods on exercising the statutory right of action for rescission or damages. For instance, under the B.C.S.A. and the O.S.A., the limitation on an action for rescission is 180 days from the date of the transaction giving rise to the cause of action, or, in the case of an action for damages, the earlier of 180 days from the date the plaintiff first has knowledge of the facts giving rise to the cause of action or 3 years after the date of the transaction.[55]

IV. THE DUE DILIGENCE DEFENCE

The due diligence defence is the defence that the potential defendants under the statutory civil liability provision can lay the groundwork for in advance. This can be done by conducting a reasonable investigation to provide reasonable grounds for a belief that the prospectus does not contain a misrepresentation. This defence may account, in part, for the substantial amount of effort that is normally put into the preparation of the prospectus. Counsel for the

---

[51] A.S.A. s. 168(12); B.C.S.A. s. 131(13); Nfld.S.A. s. 130(9); N.S.S.A. s. 137(9); O.S.A. s. 130(9); P.E.I.S.A. s. 16(9); S.S.A. s. 137(11).

[52] A.S.A. s. 168(7); B.C.S.A. s. 131(9); Nfld.S.A. s. 130(6); N.S.S.A. s. 137(6); O.S.A. s. 130(6); P.E.I.S.A. s. 16(6); S.S.A. s. 137(7).

[53] A.S.A. s. 168(9); B.C.S.A. s. 131(11); Nfld.S.A. s. 130(8); N.S.S.A. s. 137(8); O.S.A. s. 130(8); P.E.I.S.A. s. 16(8); S.S.A. s. 137(9).

[54] A.S.A. s. 168(13); B.C.S.A. s. 131(14); Nfld.S.A. s. 130(10); N.S.S.A. 137(10); O.S.A. s. 130(10); P.E.I.S.A. s. 16(10); S.S.A. s. 137(12).

[55] B.C.S.A. s. 140; O.S.A. s. 138. See also A.S.A. s. 175; Nfld.S.A. s. 138; N.S.S.A. s. 146; P.E.I.S.A. s. 16.2; S.S.A. s. 147.

issuer, counsel for the underwriter, officers and directors of the issuer, employees of the underwriter, and experts are involved in conducting what is often called a "due diligence" investigation to assure that the prospectus is complete and accurate.

A. Cases Considering the Due Diligence Defence

The cases of *Escott v. BarChris* and *Feit v. Leasco*, which considered a statutory provision for civil liability under the U.S. *Securities Act of 1933* (which is very similar to that provided for under most Canadian securities acts) are discussed below.

1. *Escott v. BarChris*

a. THE FACTS

The standard of reasonableness is that of a prudent person in the circumstances of the particular case. The seminal case on what constitutes a reasonable investigation is the New York case of *Escott v. BarChris Construction Corporation*.[56] BarChris was a construction company that built bowling alleys. After a period of growth in the popularity of bowling upon the introduction of automatic pin placement, the bowling alley industry became overbuilt. Many alleys were forced to shut down. Many alleys built by BarChris had been built on credit. Delinquencies in payments caused financial difficulties for BarChris.

In the midst of these financial difficulties, BarChris sold an issue of debentures, which contained several misrepresentations in the registration statement[57] and prospectus. For instance, the prospectus under-represented contingent liabilities to a factor (a person who bought the right to receive amounts due from BarChris' customers at a discount). BarChris was contingently liable to the factor because the factor had recourse to BarChris where customers failed to pay. The contingent liability to the factor was represented as being 25%

---

[56] 283 F.Supp. 643 (S.D.N.Y. 1968).

[57] The U.S. federal *Securities Act of 1933* requires the filing of a "registration statement" containing information similar to that required in prospectuses that must be filed in Canada. The "prospectus" is the required selling document under the *Securities Act of 1933* and is a somewhat abbreviated version of the information contained in the registration statement.

of the amounts factored while in some cases the contingent liability was in fact 100% of amounts factored. There were overstatements of backlog orders for construction and some of these alleged backlog construction contracts were probably unenforceable. The prospectus failed to disclose that there were loans to officers and that one of the proposed uses of the proceeds of the debenture issue was to pay off officers' loans. The customer delays in payments were under-stated and the prospectus failed to disclose that BarChris had taken over some of the bowling alleys of delinquent customers and was thus in the business of operating bowling alleys. There were also sales of bowling alleys to BarChris subsidiary companies and these sales were not eliminated in the preparation of consolidated financial statements.

b. EXPERTISED PORTION IS NOT THE ENTIRE PROSPECTUS

The defendants were the signers of the prospectus (nine directors of BarChris and the controller), as well as the eight investment banking firms, led by Drexel & Co., that were the underwriters for the issue, and BarChris' auditors. The suit was based on s. 11 of the *Securities Act of 1933*. It was argued on behalf of the under-writers and signers of the prospectus that the entire prospectus was based on the authority of experts, being primarily the lawyers who had prepared the prospectus. This argument was not accepted. McLean J. stated that "[t]o say that the entire registration statement is expertised because some lawyer prepared it would be an unrea-sonable construction of the statute."[58] The only expert, "in the stat-utory sense" in the circumstances was the auditing firm.[59] It was also argued that all the figures in the prospectus were based on the authority of the auditors as experts. According to McLean J. the auditors were only experts with respect to the financial statements covered by their reports.[60]

---

[58] 283 F.Supp. 643 (S.D.N.Y. 1968) at 683.

[59] Ibid. Lawyers might, however, be experts if they had rendered a legal opinion and had consented to an extract or summary of that opinion being put in the pro-spectus. For instance, had there been a legal opinion on the questionable enforce-ability of some of the construction contracts in the *BarChris* case, it might have been considered to be an expertised portion of the prospectus.

[60] Ibid. at 683-84. There may be a practical lesson here for experts. They should be very careful about what it is they consent to in a prospectus. See also *In re Flight Transportation Corporation Securities Litigation*, 593 F.Supp. 612

c. LIABILITY OF DIRECTORS AND OFFICERS

The treasurer and chief financial officer, who was also a director of BarChris, was found liable for failing to conduct a reasonable investigation. It was said that he was in a position to know and must have known of many of the misrepresentations. His response was that he did not know what a registration statement was and that he relied on the lawyers and accountants to guide him. McLean held that he had not himself conducted a reasonable investigation and he could not avoid liability by placing the blame on the lawyers.[61] The chief executive officer was found to be aware of the relevant facts with respect to the misrepresentations, and it was held that he could not have believed that there were no untrue statements or material omissions in the prospectus.

The president and vice-president, who were also directors of BarChris and were the founders of the business, were also found liable. It was found that although their fields of responsibility in the business were limited, they were in a position to know enough that they could not have believed the prospectus contained no misrepresentations. It was also found that they had limited education and would have found the prospectus difficult reading. However, McLean J. said that "[t]he liability of a director who signs a registration statement does not depend upon whether or not he read it or, if he did, whether or not he understood what he was reading."[62]

The controller was also found liable. He was not a director nor was he a member of the executive committee. He was, according to McLean, J., "a comparatively minor figure in BarChris."[63] Nonetheless, it was found that although he may well have been unaware of several of the inaccuracies in the prospectus, he must have known of some of them. It was held that he could not have believed that the entire prospectus was true and, even if he did believe it to be true, he had not established his due diligence defence, as he

---

(D. Minn., 1984) at 613 and 616, noting that the prospectus is not expertised just because it has been prepared by, or reviewed by, accountants, lawyers or other experts.

[61] Ibid. at 685. A director or officer may, however, have a claim against a lawyer depending on the nature of the lawyer's engagement.

[62] Ibid. at 684.

[63] Ibid. at 686.

appeared to make no investigation and relied on others to supply accurate data.[64]

BarChris' in-house counsel had become a director after the date the prospectus was signed. He signed amendments to the prospectus and was also found liable for the inaccuracies in the prospectus. He kept the corporate minutes and so it was held that he must have known about several of the inaccuracies. He had advised that certain of the construction contracts were not enforceable and it was held that he must have known that some of the claims with respect to backlog orders were not accurate. With respect to inaccuracies he did not know of, he made no investigation and relied on others to get the prospectus right.[65]

There were other directors who were not officers of the company. These outside directors were also made liable for the misrepresentations in the prospectus. One of these was a chairman for a bank at which BarChris' did business. He became a director shortly after the filing of the registration statement and signed two amendments to the registration statement. The only investigation he had done was a credit check through Dun & Bradstreet and BarChris' banks before he became a director. He made no investigation of the accuracy of the prospectus. McLean J. concluded that he had not established his due diligence defence even though he only became a director "on the eve of the financing". McLean J. noted that,

> To say that such minimal conduct measures up to the statutory standard would, to all intents and purposes, absolve new directors from responsibility merely because they are new. This [would not be] a sensible construction of Section 11, when one bears in mind its fundamental purpose of requiring full and truthful disclosure for the protection of investors.[66]

---

[64] Ibid.

[65] Ibid. at 686-87. See also *In the Matter of Banco Resources Ltd.* (December, 1987), B.C. Corporate and Financial Regulatory Services Weekly Summary 1987, number 51, ch. 2, at 10 which involved the imposition of administrative sanctions arising out of several misrepresentations in a statement of material facts (a document substituting for a prospectus where the facilities of the exchange are used to distribute the securities).

[66] Ibid. at 688. A similar result obtained for another outside director, a civil engineer who was known to BarChris through previous dealings he had had with BarChris' chief executive officer. He became a director after the filing of the regis-

Legal counsel to BarChris, who prepared the registration statement, was also a director. He was sued in his capacity as a director and signer of the registration statement of BarChris. Although it was not found that he knew of inaccuracies in the prospectus, it was found that he had failed to establish his due diligence defence with respect to the non-expertised portion of the prospectus because he accepted the word of BarChris officers rather than doing at least rudimentary checks to confirm what he was told. For instance, he did not check the contracts with the factor which would have shown the misstatement as to contingent liabilities. He did not check the contracts for backlog orders that would have shown these were substantially overstated. He did not insist on the preparation of minutes of executive committee meetings, accepting that these meetings were "purely routine". A review of the minutes would have revealed the severity of customer delays in payments and the fact that BarChris was operating bowling alleys. He also failed to check on officers' loans to BarChris and on the use of the proceeds of the issue. McLean J. noted that while it would be unreasonable for the lawyer director involved in the preparation of the prospectus to do a complete audit, "a check of matters easily verifiable [would not be] unreasonable."[67] McLean appears to have imposed a higher standard on directors who are also company counsel. In his opinion the case "[did] not establish an unreasonably high standard in other cases for company counsel who are also directors. Each case must rest on its own facts."[68]

---

tration statement, but signed the amendments to it. He was found to have made no investigation into the accuracy of the registration statement. McLean cited *Adams v. Thrift*, [1915] 1 Ch. 557, aff'd [1915] 2 Ch. 21 where a director, who did not read the prospectus and knew nothing about it but simply relied on the managing director's statement that it was alright, was held liable for misstatements in a prospectus.

[67] Ibid. at 690. Generally with respect to the liability of the lawyer-director, see 689-92.

[68] Ibid. at 692. The extent of the standard that was imposed on the lawyer-director is perhaps highlighted by the question of the identification of officers' loans to BarChris. The lawyer-director had prepared a questionnaire, question 3 of which read:

"Describe briefly and state the approximate amount of any material interest, direct or indirect, of you, or any associate of you, in any material transactions during the last three years, or in any material proposed transactions, to which the Company or its subsidiaries were or are to be a party."

This, McLean J. said, could hardly have been understood by the president and

d. LIABILITY OF THE UNDERWRITERS

The underwriters were also found liable. The lead underwriter relied on its legal counsel to do the investigation. Counsel for the lead underwriter failed to examine most of BarChris' major contracts, failed to insist on the preparation and review of minutes of executive committee meetings that had not been drawn up, and accepted oral claims by the chief financial officer that officers' loans had been paid up and no further loans were contemplated, and that the delinquency problem was no longer as serious as it had been. It was found that, had a more effectual attempt at verification been made, many of the inaccuracies would have been found. The underwriters argued that they were entitled to rely on the statements of the company's officers. However, McLean J. noted that the purpose of making underwriters responsible under section 11 of the U.S. federal *Securities Act of 1933* was to protect investors, and that if underwriters were allowed to escape responsibility for the truth of the prospectus "by taking at face value representations made to them by the company's management, then the inclusion of underwriters among those liable under Section 11 affords the investors no additional protection."[69]

The lead underwriter was not excused on the basis that it had relied on its legal counsel. The other underwriters who did nothing but relied on the lead underwriter also did not escape liability.

e. LIABILITY OF THE AUDITORS

The auditors were also found liable for misrepresentations with respect to the financial statements on which they expressed their opinion in the auditor's report. It was found that some of the errors in the audited financial statements were immaterial and that a reasonable investigation had been made with respect to certain other errors. However, it was also found that the auditors should have known that BarChris was itself operating bowling alleys that were recorded as sales. It was further found that they did not make a

---

vice-president, who were of limited education, to call for information as to loans. See p. 691, note 21.

See also *In the Matter of Banco Sources, supra* note 65.

[69] Ibid. at 697. See *In re Software Toolworks Inc. Securities Litigation,* 50 F.3d 615 (9th Cir. 1994), where an underwriter's independent investigation was held to be sufficient to satisfy the due diligence defence.

reasonable investigation with respect to contingent liabilities. The review undertaken with respect to providing a comment letter, concerning changes in the financial position of BarChris in the four months between the date of the audited financial statements and the filing of the registration statement, was also found to be inadequate. The auditor's written program for the review engagement was found to conform to generally accepted auditing standards. However, it was found that several of the steps required in the program were not done. The auditor did not examine important financial records other than the trial balance. He did not read the minutes of executive meetings or the minutes of subsidies. He made no inquiry of factors as to customer delinquencies. He did not read the prospectus, the registration statement for which had been filed four months after the date of the audited financial statements. The person doing the review asked questions and accepted the answers given by officers of BarChris. McLean J. concluded that generally accepted accounting standards required a further investigation.[70]

2. Feit v. Leasco

The issue of what is required to meet the due diligence defence also arose in Feit v. Leasco Data Processing Equipment.[71] The case involved a takeover of Reliance Insurance Co. by Leasco. Leasco offered shares and warrants of Leasco in exchange for shares of Reliance. By offering shares in the bid, Leasco was required to file a registration statement, a document similar to a prospectus. The registration statement failed to disclose the amount of Reliance's so-called "surplus surplus", which consisted of liquid assets of an insurance company which were available for use in non-regulated enterprises. This may have caused Reliance's shareholders not to realize the value of the Reliance shares they were giving up in exchange for Leasco securities.

An action was brought against, among others, Leasco and its directors. Both Leasco and its directors were found liable. The court reiterated the views of Mr. Justice McLean in BarChris noting that "a completely independent and duplicate investigation is not required", however, "the defendants were expected to examine those

---

[70] Ibid. at 699-703.

[71] 332 F.Supp. 544 (1971 U.S.D.C., E.D. N.Y.).

documents which were readily available".[72] The court noted that "What constitutes 'reasonable investigation' and a 'reasonable ground to believe' will vary with the degree of involvement of the individual, his expertise, and his access to the pertinent information and data."[73]

With respect to directors generally, the court noted that "What is reasonable for one director may not be reasonable for another by virtue of their differing positions."[74] Thus a more lenient standard might be applied to outside directors, compared to that imposed on inside directors. With respect to inside directors, as compared to outside directors, the court noted that,

> Inside directors with intimate knowledge of corporate affairs and of the particular transactions will be expected to make a more complete investigation and have more extensive knowledge of facts supporting or contradicting inclusions in the registration statements than outside directors. ... BarChris imposes such stringent requirements of knowledge of corporate affairs on insider directors that one is led to the conclusion that liability will lie in practically all cases of misrepresentation. Their liability approaches that of the issuer as guarantor of the accuracy of the prospectus.[75]

B. The Role of the Securities Lawyer

One of the services of a lawyer in the preparation of a prospectus is to advise the client (the issuer or underwriter) with respect to the steps that should be taken to establish a due diligence defence. Also, the lawyer usually assists the client in carrying out the due diligence investigation. If the client is found liable for a misrepresentation in the prospectus, the client could sue the lawyer for negligent advice or assistance in the preparation of the prospectus.[76] The lawyer may also have a duty to the public requiring the lawyer to discourage the client from distributing securities under a misleading prospectus and possibly also requiring the lawyer to disclose, or

---

[72] Ibid at 577.

[73] Ibid. at 577.

[74] Ibid. at 577-78.

[75] Ibid. at 578.

[76] See V.P. Alboini, "Due Diligence and the Role of the Securities Lawyer" (1981-2) 6 C.B.L.J. 241, at 241.

"blow the whistle", where a client persists with the use of a misleading prospectus.[77]

The lawyer's role in the initial stages of prospectus preparation will be to ensure that the client fully understands the scope of the potential civil liability and the need to satisfy a due diligence standard of care.[78] The procedures that should be followed to establish a due diligence defence will vary depending on the circumstances.[79] The procedures could include such matters as:[80]

(i) meetings with the issuer's banker and major creditors concerning financing arrangements and any defaults;

(ii) contact with major customers or suppliers to determine any problems in their ongoing relationship with the issuer;

(iii) meetings with control block shareholders;

(iv) meetings with the auditors and the audit committee concerning the accounting system;

(v) meetings with experts providing reports or opinions to be included in the prospectus;

(vi) a review of the issuer's competitive position in the industry;

(vii) a review of the financial statements to be included in the prospectus;

(viii) a review of the backgrounds of directors and senior officers;

(ix) a review of recent press releases, articles and reports concerning the issuer;

---

[77] See the discussion in Alboini, *supra* note 76, at 243-55. See the remarks of R.J. Wright, Chair of the Ontario Securities Commission, September 26, 1990, on "The Changing Role of the O.S.C., Including the Relationship of The O.S.C. and Professionals" and see the "Submission to the Law Society of Upper Canada to the Ontario Securities Commission on Proposals for Amendments to the Securities Act", March 22, 1990 concerning proposed amendments to the O.S.A. which would give the O.S.C. the power, amongst other powers provided by the amendment, to order that a person (including a lawyer, accountant, engineer, valuator or other professional adviser) found to have engaged in misconduct in the marketplace not hold office in, or be a director of or be employed or retained by, or in any other way be associated with, any registrant or reporting issuer.

[78] See Alboini, *supra* note 71 at 261.

[79] See Alboini, *supra* note 71 at 241 and at 267.

[80] This partial list of steps that might be taken is drawn from Alboini, *supra* note 76, at 264-67. See also L.D. Soderquist, "Due Diligence Examinations" (1978) 24(2) The Practical Lawyer 33.

(x) a review of information circulars, annual reports, stock exchange filings, prospectuses, takeover circulars, etc.;

(xi) a review of the articles of incorporation of the issuer and significant subsidiaries of the issuer;

(xii) review of the minute books of the issuer and of important subsidiaries and amalgamating corporations;

(xiii) a review of certificates of status of the issuer and significant subsidiaries;

(xiv) a review of certificates of no bankruptcy of the issuer or its significant subsidiaries;

(xv) a review of share ownership registers and share transfer registers;

(xvi) a review of corporate extra-provincial licences;

(xvii) a review of other important licences;

(xviii) a review of important leases;

(xix) a review of material contracts including major supply agreements, labour contracts or collective agreements, executive management employment contracts, licencing and franchise agreements, debt instruments, loan agreements, major insurance policies, contracts or guarantees containing contingent liabilities, etc.;

(xx) a review of writs, appearances, statements of claim or statements of defence;

(xxi) a review of evidence of remuneration paid to senior officers and copies of pension plans and profit sharing plans;

(xxii) a review of employee share purchase plans, executive share purchase plans, dividend reinvestment plans, etc.;

(xxiii) confirmations of indebtedness to directors and officers;

(xxiv) title examinations with respect to important properties and trade mark and patent registrations;

(xxv) searches with respect to security interests.

Meetings should be conducted with the issuer's senior officers and directors and with members of the underwriter's staff to advise them of their statutory obligations.[81] These could be supported with

---

[81] See J.G. Coleman, Q.C., "Prospectus Preparation, Audit Committees and Advice to Potential Targets", prepared for the Canadian Bar Association Conference, May 9, 1980, entitled "Recent Securities and Corporate Law Developments — Advice to my Client".

letters to the persons involved in the prospectus preparation regarding their statutory obligations and duties.[82] The directors and senior officers could also be provided with a copy of the preliminary prospectus for review before filing.[83] The lawyer must exercise judgment as to procedures that should be undertaken in the particular circumstances.[84] The circumstances may call for any number of procedures beyond those listed above.

The lawyer should also consider maintaining a due diligence file as a record of what steps were taken by way of investigation and what actions were taken by the lawyer and the client in response to the findings of the due diligence investigation.[85] Such a file could assist the client in establishing a due diligence defence and could assist in showing that the lawyer took due care in advising and assisting the client.[86]

V. OTHER STATUTORY SANCTIONS

There are other statutory sanctions besides the statutory civil right of action. For instance, there are penal sanctions for misrepresentations in a prospectus.[87] There are also a range of administrative sanctions which can be imposed such as a cease trade order,[88] a removal of exemptions[89] or, under the B.C.S.A. and the N.S.S.A.,

---

[82] Examples of memoranda that might be sent are set out in Coleman, *supra* note 81.

[83] Suggestions as to steps that might be taken are provided in Coleman, *supra* note 81.

[84] See Alboini, *supra* note 76, at 267.

[85] See Alboini, *supra* note 76, at 263.

[86] Ibid.

[87] A.S.A. s. 161(1)(b); B.C.S.A. s. 155(1)(c); M.S.A. s. 136(1)(b); Nfld.S.A. s. 122(1)(b); N.S.S.A. s. 129(1)(b); N.W.T.S.A. s. 49(1)(b); O.S.A. s. 122(1)(b); P.E.I.S.A. s. 15(2); Q.S.A. s. 196; S.S.A. s. 131(3)(b); Y.S.A. s. 46(b).

[88] A.S.A. s. 165; B.C.S.A. s. 161(1)(b); M.S.A. s. 148; N.B.S.F.P.A. s. 18; Nfld.S.A. s. 127; N.S.S.A. s. 134(1)(b); N.W.T.S.A. s. 37; O.S.A. s. 127; P.E.I.S.A. s. 8.15; Q.S.A. s. 265; S.S.A. s. 134(1)(b), (d); Y.S.A. s. 32.

[89] A.S.A. s. 166; B.C.S.A. s. 161(1)(c); Nfld.S.A. s. 128; N.S.S.A. s. 134(1)(c); O.S.A. s. 128; P.E.I.S.A. s. 13(2); Q.S.A. s. 264; S.S.A. s. 134(1)(a). There is no similar provision under the M.S.A., N.B.S.F.P.A., N.W.T.S.A., or the Y.S.A.

an order for the correction of the misrepresentation,[90] or removal of a person as a director or officer under the A.S.A., B.C.S.A., N.S.S.A. and S.S.A.[91] There is also a *Criminal Code* provision imposing a penal sanction for the issuance of a false prospectus.[92]

---

[90] B.C.S.A. s. 161(1)(e); N.S.S.A. s. 134(1)(e).

[91] A.S.A. s. 166.1; B.C.S.A. s. 161(1)(d); N.S.S.A. s. 134(1)(d); S.S.A. s. 134(1)(h).

[92] *Criminal Code*, R.S.C. 1985, c. C-46, s. 400.

CHAPTER 6

CONTINUOUS DISCLOSURE

I. INTRODUCTION

The disclosure requirements do not stop with the production of a prospectus upon the issuance of securities. There are provisions for continuous disclosure in the form of periodic reporting, such as that provided by financial statements, proxy circulars, and insider trading reports, and "timely" reporting, such as that provided by material change reports. These continuous disclosure requirements are the subject of this chapter.

The reporting requirements discussed in this chapter are at the heart of modern securities regulation in Canada. A general awareness of reporting requirements is essential to an understanding of the "closed system" described in Chapter 7. Thus the objective of this chapter is to provide the reader with a general awareness of continuous disclosure requirements, the purposes these requirements are intended to serve and the competing concerns which form the basis for exemptions from continuous disclosure requirements. This should provide a starting point for assessing when reporting is required and when an exemption may be available.

Part II outlines the current importance of continuous disclosure in securities regulation, the purposes of continuous disclosure and competing concerns that suggest limits on the extent of disclosure. Part III briefly notes the concept of the "reporting issuer" who is the subject of continuous disclosure requirements. Parts IV, V and VI set out the financial statement proxy circular and insider trading reporting requirements respectively. Part VII notes timely disclosure obligations. Part VIII discusses the "System for Electronic Document Analysis and Retrieval", and Part IX notes the potential sanctions for failure to meet continuous disclosure requirements.

II. IMPORTANCE, PURPOSE AND COMPETING CONCERNS

A. Increasing Emphasis on Secondary Market Disclosure

Reports published in Canada in the early 1960s stressed the need for increased disclosure in secondary markets.[1] The *Porter Report* highlighted what it considered to be inadequacies in securities disclosure in Canada[2] and the *Kimber Report* recommended the amendment of securities laws in Ontario to provide for periodic disclosure through financial statements, proxy circulars and insider reports.[3] These recommendations were followed in the Ontario act in 1967 and adopted in several other Canadian provinces.[4] Timely disclosure in the form of material change reports, which had been required by the Toronto Stock Exchange since the late 1950s,[5] was required by securities commission policy statements by the late 1960s.[6] Timely disclosure in the form of material change reports became part of securities legislation through the 1980s[7] and has been expanded upon by National Policy #40. These developments are part of an increased emphasis on secondary market disclosure over the past 30 years.

B. The Primary Purpose of Continuous Disclosure

According to the *Merger Report* the purpose of disclosure in general is: to provide an equality of opportunity for all investors in the market place, sellers as well as buyers. The object is to make

---

[1] See *Report of the Attoney General's Committee on Securities Legislation in Ontario*, (the *Kimber Report*), 1965, Part I, paras 1.11, 1.12 and 1.16, and Paras II, IV, and VI; *Report of the Royal Commission on Banking and Finance* (the *Porter Report*) (Ottawa: Queen's Printer, 1964) at 349-52.

[2] *Porter Report, supra* note 1, at 349-52.

[3] *Kimber Report, supra* note 1, Parts II, IV and VI.

[4] See Chapter 3, Part III C 3.

[5] See W.M.H. Grover & J.C. Baillee, "Disclosure Requirements", *Proposals for a Securities Market Law for Canada* (Ottawa: Ministry of Supply and Services, 1979) 349 at 377.

[6] See O.S.C.B. (September, 1968), 192-94.

[7] See Chapter 3, Para. III C 4.

available on a timely basis all material facts the investor requires to make an informed investment judgment.[8]

Disclosure, it said, implements the broad objective of creating and maintaining confidence in Canadian capital markets by providing an information base from which investment decisions can be made and from which investment advice can be developed. Further, consistent with the notion of increasing the efficiency of capital markets, it said that "if securities are evaluated on the basis of complete and current information the pricing mechanisms of the capital markets operate in a more rational and accurate fashion."[9]

Thus disclosure was to provide information to allow the investor, investment advisors and the market in general to assess the value of the security.

C. Other Benefits of Continuous Disclosure

There as several other alleged benefits of disclosure generally and of continuous disclosure in particular. The availability of information allows the public to commend or condemn the performance of business enterprises.[10] This public response to business performance can occur in part through the demand for the securities of the business enterprise. It may also occur in part through the more effective use of voting, or other contractual or statutory rights of security holders.[11] It has been argued that disclosure provides the "healthy discipline" of ensuring that senior management of business enterprises are apprised of facts that must be disclosed.[12] It might also discourage "inappropriate corporate behaviour" and facilitate law enforcement by facilitating detection of improper behaviour.[13]

---

[8] *Report of the Committee of the Ontario Securities Commission on the Problems of Disclosure Raised for Investors by Business Combinations and Private Placements,* 1970 (the Merger Report) at 15.

[9] Ibid., at 15-16.

[10] See W.M.H. Grover & J.C. Baillie, *supra* note 5, at 384.

[11] Ibid., 389. In part public response could also come in a broader form through consumers or political pressures.

[12] Ibid. One might ask, however, whether market forces wouldn't encourage management to seek out and obtain helpful information to the extent it is cost-justified.

[13] Ibid.

Disclosure has also been said to dispel fears and reinforce public acceptability of existing societal institutions by providing an information base to refute charges of improper behaviour.[14] A further purpose of disclosure is to provide equality of opportunity by providing the information that is necessary to take advantage of opportunities.[15]

D. Competing Concerns

There are competing concerns that suggest limits on the extent of disclosure. First, there are benefits from the search for innovations, new markets and new products or services. These benefits might be lost if required disclosure of information allowed others to share in the gains and thereby reduce the incentive to search for such innovations, markets, products or services.[16]

Second, there is the cost of disclosure. The anticipated value of the disclosure should, presumably, be at least equal to the cost of the disclosure.[17] The balance between the value of disclosure and the cost may have shifted over time. Developments in computers and communications technology have probably lowered the costs of disclosure over the last several years. It may thus be that a greater amount of disclosure is justified than was previously the case.

Third, too much information can lead to an information overload. Like the proverbial needle in a haystack, more important information may be buried in a morass of insignificant information. Excessive disclosure can thus raise the cost of obtaining the more significant and valuable bits of information. This potential problem of information overload may have become less severe in recent years with improvements in computer hardware and software. These improvements have probably substantially reduced the costs of gathering and analyzing large volumes of information, thereby reducing the risk that significant information will be lost in a vast array of other information.

Further, there is a concern with respect to the timing of the release of information. Proposed business transactions may not ulti-

---

[14] Ibid., at 384-85.

[15] Ibid., at 385.

[16] Ibid.

[17] Ibid., at 388.

mately proceed. If information is disclosed about the transaction at an early stage before there is a reasonable probability it will proceed, then it may raise expectations which are not fulfilled. This may result in exaggerated fluctuations in prices[18] or in reduced confidence in the accuracy of disclosure generally.

E. Summary

Continuous disclosure is said to provide benefits in terms of increased information for the valuation of securities. It may provide other benefits such as increased public monitoring of business performance, increased enforcement of shareholder rights, constraints on and detection of improper management behaviour, increased confidence in business institutions, and the promotion of equality of investment opportunities. However, disclosure may cost more to produce than it is worth and excess disclosure can cause an information overload. In some instances disclosure may deter productive activity, or, if disclosure is premature, it may cause exaggerated fluctuations in price or reduced confidence in public disclosure.

III. REPORTING ISSUERS

The continuous disclosure obligations discussed below apply to issuers that are described in most provincial securities acts as "reporting issuers". Some issuers will not be reporting issuers and thus will not be subject to continuous disclosure obligations. The concept behind the distinction between issuers and reporting issuers is that the securities of reporting issuers are traded in markets in which some of the potential investors are persons who need to know the information provided by continuous disclosure.

The term "reporting issuer" is a key term in the concept of the "closed system".[19] It is a term that distinguishes between issuers whose securities are sold to those who are presumed to need to know and need access to the information that must be disclosed, and issuers whose securities are sold only to those who did not need to know or need access to the kind of information provided by dis-

---

[18] Ibid.

[19] The concept of the "closed system" is discussed in more detail in Chapter 7.

closure requirements. The closed system statutes of Alberta, British Columbia, Newfoundland, Nova Scotia, Ontario, Quebec,[20] and Saskatchewan are structured in such a way that securities sold by issuers that are not reporting issuers will only be sold to and traded amongst investors who either do not need to know, or do not need mandatory legislation in order to obtain access to, the kind of information provided by continuous disclosure.

To identify issuers whose securities trade in markets where potential investors include those who need access to continuous disclosure, the term "reporting issuer" is defined as an issuer that has issued securities under a prospectus or has its securities listed and posted for trading on an exchange in the province.[21] As discussed in Chapter 7, a prospectus is required where securities are sold to persons who need to know the kind of information contained in a prospectus. Once securities are sold under a prospectus, the securities can be freely traded and thus may be traded amongst persons who need to know information of the sort provided by continuous disclosure requirements. Securities listed and posted for trading on a stock exchange are also available for trading amongst investors who may need to know the kind of information provided by continuous disclosure requirements.

---

[20] The approach taken by the Q.S.A. is somewhat different, but the result of the act is very similar to that of the other closed system statutes.

[21] A.S.A. s. 1(t.1); B.C.S.A. s. 1(1) "reporting issuers"; Nfld.S.A. s. 2(1)(oo); N.S.S.A. s. 2(1)(ao); O.S.A. s. 1(1), and O.S.C. Pol. 3.1 B; Q.S.A. s. 5 "reporting issuer", and s. 68; S.S.A. s. 2(1)(qq). Issuers who have distributed securities under documents which substitute for a prospectus, such as an exchange offering prospectus, a statement of material facts, or a securities exchange takeover bid, are also considered to be reporting issuers (see the provisions cited above).

Securities of a reporting issuer corporation may be exchanged for securities of a non-reporting issuer corporation in the context of an amalgamation, merger, reorganization, or arrangement. In such a situation, security holders who were formerly shareholders of a reporting issuer corporation, and presumably in need of information, would become security holders of a non-reporting issuer corporation. Thus "reporting issuer" is defined to include the corporation with which the securities of the reporting issuer were exchanged. See B.C.S.A. s. 1(1) "reporting issuer" (d); O.S.A. s. 1(1).

For reasons noted in Chapter 7, issuers may also choose to become reporting issuers by filing a prospectus without distributing securities under that prospectus — see e.g., B.C.S.A. s. 1(1) "reporting issued" (b), s. 43; O.S.A. s. 1(1), s. 53(2).

Only the commission can provide relief from the status of "reporting issuer" — see e.g., B.C.S.A. s. 88; O.S.A. s. 82.

New Brunswick, Prince Edward Island and the Territories do not have secondary market disclosure requirements. Nonetheless, most issuers selling securities in those provinces will be required to provide continuous disclosure through corporate law requirements with respect to financial disclosure and proxy solicitation where the issuer is incorporated under the CBCA, provincial general incorporation statutes, and/or under stock exchange requirements where the issuer is listed on a stock exchange.

IV. FINANCIAL STATEMENTS

A. Annual Financial Statements

Securities laws require reporting issuers to provide regular financial disclosure. A reporting issuer must prepare annual financial statements within a specified period of time after the end of its financial year.[22] These statements must be audited.[23] They must be distributed to shareholders[24] and filed with the relevant securities administrators.[25] The annual financial statements must also provide comparative figures[26] for the previous year and must contain an income statement, a statement of retained earnings, a statement of changes in financial position and a balance sheet.[27] Stock exchanges

---

[22] A.S.A. s. 121(1) (140 days); B.C. Rule 145 (within 140 days); M.S.A. s. 120(1)(170 days); Nfld.S.A. s. 79(1) (140 days); N.S.S.A. s. 84(1) (140 days); O.S.A. s. 78(1) (within 140 days); Q.S.A. s. 75 (140 days); S.S.A. s. 87(2) (140 days). For financial disclosure requirements in the Territories, see N.W.T.S.A. ss. 39, 40 and Y.S.A. ss. 33, 34.

[23] A.S.A. s. 121(2); B.C. Rules 3(4); M.S.A. s. 119; Nfld.S.A. s. 79(2); N.S.S.A. s. 84(2); O.S.A. s. 78(2); Q.S.A. s. 75; S.S.A. s. 87(3). See National Policy #31 with respect to the change of auditors.

[24] A.S.A. s. 122; B.C. Rule 149; M.S.A. s. 134 (open to inspection at the offices of the commission); Nfld.S.A. s. 80; N.S.S.A. s. 85; O.S.A. s. 79; Q.S.A. s. 77; S.S.A. s. 88.

[25] A.S.A. s. 121(1); B.C. Rule 145(1); M.S.A. s. 120(1); Nfld.S.A. s. 79(1); N.S.S.A. s. 84(1); O.S.A. s. 78(1); Q.S.A. s. 75; S.S.A. s. 87(2).

[26] A.S.A. s. 121(1); B.C. Rule 145(1); M.S.A. s. 120(1); Nfld.S.A. s. 79(1); N.S.S.A. s. 84(1); O.S.A. s. 78(1); Q.Regs. s. 117; S.S.A. s. 87(2).

[27] A. Rules s. 151; B.C. Rule 145(2); M.S.A. s. 120(1); Nfld. Regs. s. 11; N.S. Regs. s. 147(1); O. Regs. s. 10; Q. Regs. s. 116; S. Regs. s. 125(1).

have similar requirements for issuers whose securities are listed on a stock exchange.[28]

B. Interim Financial Statements

Interim financial statements are to be prepared for interim periods during the year within a specified time after the end of the interim period.[29] The statements must also be distributed to shareholders[30] and filed with the relevant securities administrators.[31] However, these statements do not need to be audited.[32] The statements need only include an income statement and a statement of changes in financial position.[33] Stock exchanges have similar requirements for issuers with securities listed on a stock exchange.[34]

C. Statements Prepared According to GAAP

The details of financial statement presentation are dealt with by what is, in effect, a substantial subdelegation of regulatory power. The statements are to be prepared according to "Generally Accepted Accounting Principles" ("GAAP").[35] Generally accepted accounting

---

[28]See, e.g., T.S.E. By-laws 19.07 & 19.12; M.S.E. Rule 9159; V.S.E. Listing Agreement s. 3.4.

[29]A.S.A. s. 120(1); B.C. Rule 144(1); M.S.A. s. 129(1); Nfld.S.A. s. 78(1); N.S.S.A. s. 83(1); O.S.A. s. 77(1) (prepared for every 3 month period within 60 days of the end of the period); Q.S.A. "quarterly statements" s. 76; S.S.A. s. 86(1). See also, e.g., T.S.E. By-law 19.08; M.S.E. Rule 9160; V.S.E. Listing Agreement s. 3.4.

[30]A.S.A. s. 122; B.C. Rule 149; M.S.A. s. 129(5); Nfld.S.A. s. 80; N.S.S.A. s. 85; O.S.A. s. 79; Q.S.A. s. 78; S.S.A. s. 88.

[31]A.S.A. a 120(1); B.C. Rule 144(1); M.S.A. s. 129(1); Nfld.S.A. s. 78(1); N.S.S.A. s. 83(1); O.S.A. s. 77(1); Q.S.A. s. 76; S.S.A. s. 86(1).

[32]A. Rules s. 148; B.C. Rule 144(3); M.S.A. s. 119 (by implication); Nfld. Regs. s. 10; N.S. Regs. s. 146; O. Regs. s. 9; Q. Regs. s. 123; S. Regs. s. 124.

[33]A. Rules s. 146; B.C. Rule 144(4); M.S.A. 129(1)(b); Nfld. Regs. s. 8(1); N.S. Regs. s. 144(1); O. Regs. s. 7(1); Q. Regs. s. 121; S. Regs. s. 122.

[34]See, for example, A.S.E. By-law s. 23.08; M.S.E. Rule 9160; T.S.E. By-law 19.08 and T.S.E. Pol. Part I, para. 1.02.

[35]A. Rules s. 144(1)(a); B.C. Rule s. 3(3); N.B. Bus. Corp. Act s. 100(3); Nfld. Regs. s. 3(1); N.S. Regs. s. 8(1); O. Regs. s. 2(1); P.E.I. Regs. s. 2(1); Q.S.A. s. 80; S. Regs. s. 117(1). The M.S.A. ss. 121-29 sets out some specific requirements for the financial statement.

principles are defined to be the recommendations of the CICA Handbook.[36]

D. Exemptions

Exemptions from these financial reporting requirements are available, upon an order of a securities commission, where the commission is of the opinion granting the exemption would not be prejudicial to the public interest. The commission can grant an order subject to the terms and conditions it specifies being met. The available exemptions fall roughly into the following categories: deviations from generally accepted accounting principles, conflicts with laws of other jurisdictions, detriment to the issuer, and consistency of reporting. There is also a broad power to grant an exemption where it would not be detrimental to the public interest to do so.

1 *Deviation from GAAP*

An administrator can accept financial statements not prepared in accordance with generally accepted accounting principles where "it is not reasonably practicable for the issuer to revise the presentation in the financial statement to conform to generally accepted accounting principles".[37] A securities commission may also make an order allowing for deviation from generally accepted accounting principles where the deviation is "supported or justified by consider-

---

[36] A. Rules s. 6; B.C. Rules 2(1) & (2); Nfld. Regs. s. 2(3); N.S. Regs. s. 2(4); O. Regs. s. 1(3); P.E.I. Regs. s. 2(1); Q. Regs. s. 1 "g.a.a.p."; S. Regs. s. 2(2). See also National Policy #27.

[37] See A. Rules s. 144(4)(a); B.C. Rule 3(7) (can accept non-GAAP financial statements where "to do so would not be prejudicial to the public interest"); Nfld. Regs. s. 3(4)(a); N.S. Regs. s. 8(4)(a); O. Regs. s. 2(4)(a)(i); S. Regs. s. 117(4)(a).

The administrator can accept a financial statement deviating from GAAP where a deviation was previously allowed by an order of the commission and there has been no material change in the circumstances on which the order of the commission was based. See, for example, O. Regs. s. 2(4)(a)(ii).

Deviation from GAAP is also allowed where the issuer is incorporated or organized under another jurisdiction and has followed accounting principles prescribed by legislation of the jurisdiction or by an association equivalent to the Canadian Institute of Chartered Accountants, so long as a note to that effect is provided in the statements. See, for example, O. Regs. s. 1(4) (and O. Pol. 7.1 H regarding an exemption from the requirement to provide a note).

ations that outweigh the desirability of uniform adherence to generally accepted accounting principles."[38]

2. Conflict with Laws of Another Jurisdiction

Often the reporting issuer will have been incorporated or organized under the laws of another jurisdiction and may be subject to laws of that jurisdiction concerning statement disclosure. There may be a conflict between the laws of the incorporating or organizing jurisdiction and the laws of the applicable provincial securities act. To address this situation, most provincial securities commissions are given the power to make an order exempting the reporting issuer from financial statement disclosure requirements where the requirements of the incorporating or organizing jurisdiction conflict with the requirements of the provincial securities act.[39]

3. Specific Omissions from Disclosure

In some provinces exemptions are available with respect to disclosure of comparative statements for particular periods of time, sales or gross operating revenue, or basic or fully diluted earnings per share.[40] The exemption with respect to comparative figures may be appropriate, for instance, where the issuer changes its year end, such that the calculation of comparative figures would be difficult or unlikely to yield useful comparisons.[41] The exemption with respect to the disclosure of sales or gross operating revenue can be obtained where the disclosure of such information would be unduly detrimental to the interests of the reporting issuer.[42]

---

[38] A. Rules s. 144(4)(b); B.C. Rule 3(7) (can accept non-GAAP financial statements where "to do so would not be prejudicial to the public interest"); Nfld. Regs. s. 3(4)(b); N.S. Regs. s. 8(4)(b); O. Regs. s. 2(4)(b); S. Regs. s. 117(4)(b).

[39] A.S.A. s. 123(a); M.S.A. s. 131(2)(a); Nfld.S.A. s. 81(b)(i); N.S.S.A. s. 86(b)(i); O.S.A. s. 80(b)(i); S.S.A. s. 89(b)(i). B.C. Rule 3(7) has a general exemption provision allowing the executive director to grant an exemption where it is not contrary to the public interest to do so.

[40] M.S.A. s. 131(1)(a); Nfld.S.A. s. 81(a); N.S.S.A. s. 86(a); O.S.A. s. 80(a); S.S.A. s. 89(a). With respect to B.C. see *supra* note 39.

[41] See, for example, *Futurefund Shares Inc.*, [1986] O.S.C.B. 2939.

[42] M.S.A. s. 131(1)(a)(ii); Nfld.S.A. s. 81(a)(ii); N.S.S.A. s. 86(a)(ii); O.S.A. s. 80(a)(ii); S.S.A. s. 89(a)(ii). With respect to B.C. see *supra* note 39.

4. *Consistency of Reporting*

An exemption is available under most provincial acts where information is disclosed by the reporting issuer in a different form or at different times than required by the applicable provincial act.[43] An order might be granted in such circumstances in order to provide consistency and thus comparability of financial statements over time. In this respect, such an order would be consistent with providing information to security holders in a form allowing for improved valuation of the securities of the issuer.

5. *General*

Securities commissions typically have a more general power to provide an exemption where there is adequate justification for so doing.[44] While the commission would proceed on the assumption that required disclosure is for the benefit of the issuer's security holders and ought not to be lightly deviated from, there may be circumstances in which the potential cost of compliance or detriment to the issuer would outweigh the benefit to the issuer's security holders.[45] Accordingly, factors considered would presumably include the degree of deviation from the required disclosure, the number of security holders affected,[46] the degree of sophistication of existing security holders in interpreting the proposed disclosure, the cost of compliance, and the potential negative consequences of compliance to the issuer.[47]

---

[43] A.S.A. s. 123(b); M.S.A. s. 131(1)(c) (where there is "adequate justification"); Nfld.S.A. s. 81(b)(ii); N.S.S.A. s. 86(b)(ii); O.S.A. s. 80(b)(ii); S.S.A. s. 89(b)(ii). With respect to B.C. see *supra* note 39.

[44] A.S.A. s. 123(c); B.C. Rule 3(7) (where it is in the "public interest" to do so); M.S.A. s. 131(1)(c); Nfld.S.A. s. 81(b)(iii); N.S.S.A. s. 86(b)(iii); O.S.A. s. 80(b)(iii); S.S.A. s. 89(b)(iii). See also Q.S.A. s. 79 and s. 263.

[45] See, for example, *Denison Mines Ltd.*, [1980] O.S.C.B. 238 at 244.

[46] This is a factor that is noted in O. Pol. 7.1, Appendix A, paras. (3) and (6) with respect to exemptions for issuers that are reporting issuers only because of a listing on the Toronto Stock Exchange and which are not incorporated or organized in Ontario.

[47] Several cases concerning detriment to the issuer are discussed in V.P. Alboini, *Securities Law and Practice*, 2d ed., (Toronto: Carswell, 1984) at §18.6.1. Commissions appear to be likely to consider factors affecting a reduction in the issuer's revenues or an increase in the issuer's costs. For instance, where the issuer

V. PROXY/INFORMATION CIRCULARS

A form of proxy is a document which gives a person named therein (the "proxyholder") the power to exercise the vote of the person who signs the form of proxy.[48] The proxyholder must exercise the vote in the manner indicated in the form of proxy.[49] In the context of shares, a shareholder may, by a form of proxy, appoint a person to exercise the voting rights attached to the shares held by the shareholder.

In widely-held corporations it was common practice for management to solicit proxies. In other words, they would send a form of proxy, naming management's nominee as proxyholder, to shareholders and ask them to sign the form and return it. This allowed management to assure that sufficient shares would be represented at the shareholders' meeting to satisfy quorum requirements and thus ensure that the necessary business of the meeting would be completed. Occasionally a dissident shareholder, or group of shareholders, might seek to influence the voting on proposals for shareholder meetings by soliciting proxies.

Concerns arose with respect to the manner of solicitation of proxies by management or others which both corporate and securities legislation have responded to with requirements for the form of proxy and information that must be provided in a document called a "proxy circular" or "information circular".

---

has very few customers, reporting of gross operating revenues, or segmented revenue disclosure, might give the customer a bargaining power advantage. Similarly, requiring disclosure that competitors are not subject to may put the issuer at competitive disadvantage.

[48] The term "proxy" is often used to refer to the person who is appointed by a form of proxy (see e.g., *Black's Law Dictionary*, 5th ed.). However, corporate and securities legislation in Canada often define the term to mean a completed and executed form of proxy by means of which a security holder has appointed a person to attend and act for her or him at a meeting of security holders. See, for example, O.S.A. s. 1(1); C.B.C.A. s. 147.

"Form of Proxy" is typically defined as a written or printed form that, upon completion and execution by or on behalf of a security holder, becomes a proxy. See, for example, O.S.A. s. 1(1); C.B.C.A. s. 147.

[49] See *Re Dorman, Lang & Co.*, [1934] Ch. 635; *Patten v. Outerbridge* (1982), 37 Nfld. & P.E.I.R. 318 (Nfld. T.D.); *Oliver v. Dalgliesh*, [1963] 3 All E.R. 330 (Ch.D.); *Second Consolidated Trust v. Ceylon Amalgamated Estates*, [1943] 2 All E.R. 567.

A. Proxy Solicitation Requirements

The securities laws of most provinces require the management of a reporting issuer to send a form of proxy, by prepaid mail, to security holders in the province whenever voting security holders are given notice of a meeting of voting security holders.[50] A form of proxy sent by management, or anyone else who solicits proxies from the security holders of a reporting issuer who are resident in the province, must indicate whether or not it is solicited by or on behalf of management.[51] It must indicate and allow for the right of the security holder to appoint as proxyholder someone other than the person designated in the form of proxy.[52] The form must also allow the security holder to vote for or against each matter set out in the notice of meeting or information circular.[53]

Several securities acts provide that, at the meeting, the chair of the meeting may conduct a vote by show of hands instead of by ballot. These acts also generally provide that ballot is only required

---

[50] A.S.A. s. 127; B.C.S.A. s. 117(1); M.S.A. s. 101(1); Nfld.S.A. s. 86; N.S.S.A. s. 91; O.S.A. s. 85; Q.S.A. s. 81; S.S.A. s. 94.

[51] A. Rules s. 164(1)(a); B.C. Form 30, Item 2, Instruction #1; M.S.A. s. 104(a)(i); Nfld. Regs. s. 151(1); N.S. Reg. s. 165(1)(a); O. Regs. s. 177(1); Q. Regs. s. 141; S. Regs. 140(1).

[52] A. Rules s. 164(2); B.C. Form 30, Item 2, Instruction #3; M.S.A. s. 104(f); Nfld. Regs. s. 151(2); N.S. Regs. s. 165(2)(a), (3); O. Regs. s. 177(2), (3); Q. Regs. s. 142; S. Regs. 140(2)(a).

[53] A. Rules s. 164(3); B.C. Form 30, Item 2, Instruction #4; M.S.A. s. 104(b); Nfld. Regs. s. 151(4); N.S. Regs. s. 165(4); O. Regs. s. 177(4); Q. Regs. s. 144(2); S. Regs. s. 140(4). Such a form of proxy is often referred to as a "two way" or "for or against" proxy. This requirement does not apply with respect to the appointment of an auditor or the election of directors. However, the form of proxy must provide a means for the security holder to specify that the securities registered in the name of the security holder shall be voted or withheld from voting in respect of the appointment of an auditor or the election of directors — see, for example, O. Regs. s. 177(6).

Subject to specified conditions, the form of proxy may allow for discretionary voting on amendments or variations to matters identified in the notice of meeting or other matters which properly come before the meeting. See, for example, O. Regs. s. 178.

The form of proxy cannot provide authority to vote for a person proposed as director unless the person is named in the information circular, nor can it provide authority for voting on a matter other than at the specified meeting or any adjournment of that meeting. See, for example, O. Regs. s. 160.

where (i) it is demanded by a security holder in person or represented by proxy at the meeting or, (ii) there are proxies representing more than 5% of all the voting rights of securities entitled to be represented and voted at the meeting, which require that the securities represented by the proxies be voted against what would otherwise be the decision of the meeting.[54]

Every person who solicits proxies from security holders of a reporting issuer who are resident in the province must send an information circular to each security holder in the province whose proxy is solicited.[55] The information circular, the form of proxy and all other material sent in connection with the meeting must be filed with the relevant administrators.[56] "Solicit" or "solicitation" is broadly defined. It includes a management solicitation of proxies, any request for a proxy whether or not accompanied by a form of proxy, any request not to execute a form of proxy, or the sending of a form of proxy or any other communication to a security holder under circumstances reasonably calculated to result in the procurement, withholding or revocation of a proxy.[57]

B. Information Required

The information circular must provide specific information required by forms set out in the regulations passed pursuant to the

---

[54] A.S.A. s. 129(2); B.C.S.A. s. 118(2); M.S.A. s. 105; Nfld.S.A. s. 88; N.S.S.A. s. 93; O.S.A. s. 87; S.S.A. s. 96.

[55] A.S.A. s. 128(1)(a); B.C.S.A. s. 117(2); M.S.A. s. 102(1); Nfld.S.A. s. 87(a); N.S.S.A. s. 92(1); O.S.A. s. 86; Q.S.A. s. 82; S.S.A. s. 95.

[56] A.S.A. s. 124(1) & A. Rules s. 168; B.C. Rules 183, 184; M.S.A. s. 106(3); Nfld. Regs. s. 154; N.S. Regs. s. 168; O.S.A. s. 81 and O. Regs. s. 180; Q.S.A. s. 82; S. Regs. s. 143.

[57] A.S.A. s. 126(b); B.C.S.A. s. 116 "solicit"; M.S.A. s. 100 "solicit" or "solicitation"; Nfld S.A. s. 85(b); N.S.S.A. s. 90(b); O.S.A. s. 84; S.S. s. 93(b). However, the term is constrained so as not to make persons who respond to an unsolicited request for a form of proxy, or who perform professional services on behalf of another person who is soliciting proxies, subject to the proxy solicitation requirements.

various securities acts.[58] The information required includes, for example, such matters as:[59]

(i) the interest of persons making solicitation in the matters to be voted upon (where the solicitation is made by management, it is the interests of directors and senior officers that must be noted);

(ii) where known by the directors and officers of the reporting issuer, the names and holdings of persons having direct or indirect beneficial ownership of more than 10% of the voting rights;

(iii) information concerning persons proposed as directors;

(iv) details of executive compensation;

(v) indebtedness of directors and senior officers to the reporting issuer or its subsidiaries;

(vi) interests of insiders in material transactions;

(vii) the name of the person or company who has or will bear the cost of the solicitation of proxies;

(viii) details of management contracts under which a substantial degree of management functions are performed by persons other than the directors or senior officers.

The information circular must also provide details on matters to be voted on in sufficient detail to permit security holders to form a reasoned judgment concerning the matter.[60]

While other provinces have detailed requirements for the disclosure of executive compensation,[61] the required disclosure with respect to executive compensation is particularly detailed in both

---

[58] A. Rules s. 163, Form 30; B.C. Rules Form 30; M. Regs. s. 38, Form 13; Nfld. Regs. s. 150, Form 29; N.S. Regs. s. 164, Form 30; O. Regs. s. 156 and Form 30; Q. Regs. s. 150, Schedule VIII; S. Regs. s. 139, Form 28.

[59] Ibid.

[60] Ibid. For cases addressing the adequacy of disclosure in information circulars, see *Re National Grocers Co. Ltd.*, [1938] O.R. 142 (H.C.); *Garvie v. Axmith*, [1962] O.R. 65 (H.C.); *Re Ardiem Holdings* (1975), 67 D.L.R. (3d) 253 (B.C.C.A.), rev'g 61 D.L.R. (3d) 725 (B.C.S.C.); *Norcan Oils Ltd. v. Folger*, [1965] S.C.R. 36; *Charlebois v. Bienvenu*, [1967] 2 O.R. 635 (H.C.); *Re N. Slater Co.*, [1947] O.W.N. 226 (H.C.).

[61] See Alta. Form 40; Nfld. Form 39; N.S. Form 41; Q.S.A. Sch. VIII, Item 6; and Sask. Form 38.

Ontario and British Columbia.[62] The compensation disclosed for each individual must include all compensation "for services rendered by that individual in all capacities to the issuer or a subsidiary of the issuer or otherwise in connection with an office or employment of that individual with the issuer or the subsidiary of the issuer."[63] The individuals covered are the CEO, each of the issuer's four most highly compensated officers, other than the CEO, who were serving as executive officers at the end of the most recently completed financial year.[64] In addition, it includes any other individuals who were not serving as executive officers during the year but who are among the four most highly paid persons other than the CEO.[65]

The executive compensation information required in British Columbia and Ontario must be set out in tabular form.[66] It includes information on annual compensation such as salary and bonuses, and any other annual compensation.[67] It also includes information on long term compensation such as options on securities, payments of cash or issuances of securities based on an appreciation in the issuer's stock price, and any other long term incentive plan compensation.[68] Information on these types of compensation must be provided on a comparative basis for the issuer's three most recently completed financial years.[69] Estimated annual pension plan benefits payable on retirement must also be disclosed in tabular form.[70] The required information includes a performance graph comparing the annual return on each class of securities of the issuer with a broad market index.[71] The information must also include a report on executive compensation noting the compensation policies of a compensation committee, or of the board of directors if there is no such

---

[62] B.C. Form 41; Ont. Form 40.

[63] B.C. Form 41 Item I.7; Ont. Form 40, Item I.7.

[64] B.C. Form 41, Item I.3; Ont. Form 40, Item I.3.

[65] Ibid.

[66] B.C. Form 41, Items II to VI; Ont. Form 40, Items II to VI.

[67] B.C. Form 41, Item II; Ont. Form 40, Item II.

[68] Ibid.

[69] Ibid.

[70] B.C. Form 41, Item VI; Ont. Form 40, Item VI.

[71] B.C. Form 41, Item X; Ont. Form 40, Item X.

committee.[72] The report must include a discussion of the relationship of corporate performance to executive compensation.[73]

C. Exemptions

Some exemptions from the proxy and information circular requirements are automatic in the sense that they do not require an order from the relevant securities commission. Other exemptions are discretionary. The discretion is usually vested in the commission and an order from the commission is necessary.

1. *Automatic Exemptions*

a. DE MINIMUS 15 SHAREHOLDER TEST

Where persons other than management of the reporting issuer solicit the proxies of not more than 15 security holders, they need not comply with the requirement to send an information circular.[74] In these circumstances, there would presumably be little benefit from additional circular disclosure by a dissident group which is soliciting proxies. Indeed, requiring the dissident group to incur the cost of such disclosure is likely to deter such solicitation and thus arguably impede a useful constraint on management behaviour.

b. COMPLIANCE WITH SUBSTANTIALLY SIMILAR LAWS OF ANOTHER JURISDICTION

Where the reporting issuer is complying with substantially similar laws of the jurisdiction in which it was incorporated or organized, it is exempt from the proxy solicitation and information circular requirements described above.[75] Jurisdictions which are

---

[72] B.C. Form 41, Item IX.1; Ont. Form 40, Item IX.1.

[73] B.C. Form 41, Item IX.2; Ont. Form 40, Item IX.2.

[74] A.S.A. s. 128(2)(a); B.C.S.A. s. 117(3)(a); M.S.A. s. 102(2)(a); Nfld.S.A. s. 87(2)(a); N.S.S.A. s. 92(2)(a); O.S.A. s. 86(2)(a); Q.S.A. s. 83; S.S.A. s. 95(2)(a).

[75] B.C.S.A. s. 119(1); M.S.A. s. 103; Nfld.S.A. s. 89(1); N.S.S.A. s. 94(1); O.S.A. s. 88(1); Q. Regs. s. 157; S.S.A. s. 97(1). This exemption refers to the "reporting issuer" only and there is some doubt as to whether the exemption is available for other persons who solicit proxies and provide an information circular in compliance with substantially similar laws of the organizing jurisdiction — see V.P. Alboini, *supra* note 47, at 19-22.1 to 19-23. For greater certainty such persons should probably seek an order from the relevant securities commission.

accepted as being substantially similar for the purposes of this exemption are identified in the local policy statements of some provinces.[76] Where the requirements of the incorporating or organizing jurisdiction are substantially similar, there is likely to be little benefit in having the issuer incur the additional cost of complying with the requirements of the particular securities act.

c. REGISTRANTS FORWARDING MEETING MATERIALS

Brokers or their nominees are often registered holders of securities, but hold the securities on behalf of others.[77] They are required to forward any meeting materials they receive from an issuer to the beneficial owners of the security where the issuer or beneficial owner has agreed to pay the reasonable costs of delivery of the materials.[78] In doing so they could be considered to be sending or delivering a communication to a security holder under circumstances reasonably calculated to result in the procurement, withholding or revocation of a proxy and thus could be said to be "soliciting" proxies.[79] However, in performing this perfunctory task, they would not be intending to influence the votes of security holders and thus there is no purpose in subjecting them to the requirement of providing an information circular. Consequently, although the sending of the material could constitute a "solicitation", they are exempt from the requirement to send an information circular.[80]

d. REQUESTS BY BENEFICIAL OWNERS OF EXECUTION OF PROXY BY REGISTERED HOLDERS

Beneficial owners of securities might also request that the registrant execute a form of proxy on their behalf with respect to the

---

[76]See, for example, O. Pol. 7.1, para. F.

[77]The exemption described also applies to custodians of securities of mutual funds who are also obliged to forward meeting materials received.

[78]A.S.A. s. 79(2); B.C. Rule 182(2); M.S.A. s. 79; Nfld.S.A. s. 50(2); N.S.S.A. s. 55(2); O.S.A. s. 49; Q.S.A. s. 165; S.S.A. s. 55(3). The practical difficulties involved in the distribution of meeting materials to security holders is discussed in Part V D below.

[79]See Part V A above with respect to the definition of "solicit" and see the provisions cited in the accompanying notes.

[80]A.S.A. s. 128(2)(b); B.C.S.A. s. 116 "solicit" (f); M.S.A. s. 102(2)(b); Nfld.S.A. s. 87(2)(b); N.S.S.A. s. 92(2)(b); O.S.A. s. 86(2)(b); S.S.A. s. 95(2)(b).

securities that they beneficially own. Such a request to execute a form of proxy would constitute a "solicitation" as that term is defined. However, in requesting the registered holder to execute a form of proxy, they would not be attempting to influence the votes of other security holders and no purpose would be served in requiring them to provide an information circular. Thus an exemption from the requirement of sending an information circular is provided for a solicitation by beneficial owners in respect of securities that they beneficially own.[81]

2. Discretionary Exemptions

a. CONFLICT WITH LAWS OF ANOTHER JURISDICTION

Statutes governing the incorporation or organization of a reporting issuer often contain provisions with respect to proxy solicitation and the sending of proxy circulars. This is particularly so of general statutes of incorporation. In many cases, the provisions of the incorporating or organizing statute will be quite similar to the requirements of Canadian securities acts.[82] However, there may be conflicts between the provisions of the incorporating or organizing jurisdiction and the laws of a particular securities act. In these circumstances, most Canadian securities acts allow the commission to make an order, subject to such terms and conditions as the commission may impose, exempting a person or company from the proxy solicitation or information circular requirements of the securities act.[83]

b. OTHER ADEQUATE JUSTIFICATION

Commissions are also given the power to grant an exemption, subject to such terms and conditions as they might impose, where they are otherwise satisfied in the circumstances of the particular

---

[81] A.S.A. s. 128(2)(c); B.C.S.A. s. 117(3)(c); M.S.A. s. 102(2)(c); Nfld.S.A. s. 87(2)(c); N.S.S.A. s. 92(2)(c); O.S.A. s. 86(2)(c); S.S.A. s. 95(2)(c).

[82] See for example the provisions in C.B.C.A. ss. 147-54, Regs. ss. 32-43; O.B.C.A. ss. 109-14, Regs. ss. 27-28; B.C.C.A. s. 151-58 and Form 24.

[83] B.C.S.A. s. 119(2)(a); M.S.A. s. 103(2); Nfld.S.A. s. 89(2)(a); N.S.S.A. s. 94(2)(a); O.S.A. s. 88(2)(a); Q. Regs. s. 157; S.S.A. s. 97(2)(a).

case that there is "adequate justification" for so doing.[84] Presumably in assessing whether there is "adequate justification" for an exemption, the commission will have in mind the benefits perceived to be derived from proxy solicitation and information circular requirements, and will weigh the benefits likely to be derived in the circumstances of the particular case against the costs likely to be involved in compliance. The weighing of costs and benefits is apparent within the automatic exemptions discussed above. In each case it can be argued that there is little or no benefit from compliance with the proxy or information circular requirements for which the exemption is given. There is presumably no reason to force compliance where the costs of compliance more than offset any perceived benefits, such that security holders are left with a less valuable security.

The benefits perceived involve not just more knowledgeable exercise of voting rights, but also improved valuation of securities due to the disclosure of information. So, for example, where there are only a few voting security holders who are well informed about the issuer and are likely to exercise their votes in person, the commission might exempt the reporting issuer from the proxy solicitation requirement and the requirement to send an information circular to the voting security holders. However, if there are several non-voting security holders whose securities are regularly traded, the commission may be inclined to continue to require that the information circular be prepared and filed in order to provide information to the market as a basis for the valuation of the securities being traded.[85]

Mere inconvenience or cost may not be enough to obtain an order relieving the reporting issuer from the proxy and circular obligations, given the perceived benefits of proxy solicitation and information circular disclosure. However, where very little benefit would be derived from proxy solicitation or the sending of an information circular, the commission may be inclined to grant an exemption. Factors that a commission might consider in this regard include the

---

[84] B.C.S.A. s. 119(2)(b) ("not prejudicial to the public interest"); M.S.A. s. 103(2)(b); Nfld.S.A. s. 89(2)(b); N.S.S.A. s. 94(2)(b); O.S.A. s. 88(2)(b); Q.S.A. s. 263; S.S.A. s. 97(2)(b).

[85] See, for example, *Re Toronto Dominion Centre Ltd.*, April 1975 O.S.C.B. 139.

number of security holders affected,[86] the proportion of the securities held by security holders in the province to the total number of outstanding securities,[87] substitute forms of disclosure,[88] or the degree of complexity of the issues to be decided upon at the meeting.[89] It should be noted that where the particular reporting issuer has very few security holders it can apply to be relieved of its reporting issuer status.[90]

D. National Policy #41

The delivery of the form of proxy, the proxy circular and other security holder meeting materials is complicated by the modern techniques for the holding and delivery of securities. As noted in Chapter 1, securities are often held in the name of a depository institution or other nominee. Thus the security holders registered on the books of the issuer are primarily (and possibly even exclusively) just the nominee holders of the securities rather than the beneficial owners of the securities who are entitled to exercise any voting rights attached to the securities. The problem this creates is that if the issuer just delivers materials to its registered security holders, the materials may not ultimately be received by the beneficial owners of the securities who are, after all, the persons entitled to exercise the rights associated with the securities.

To address this problem the Canadian Securities Administrators developed National Policy #41 in 1987. Under NP #41 an issuer is required to set a record date that is at least 35 days before an upcoming meeting of security holders.[91] At least 25 days before

---

[86]See, for example, *Sulivan Resources Ltd.*, [1985] O.S.C.B. 4567 where a wholly owned subsidiary was exempted from filing and sending information circulars and financial statements.

[87]See, for example, *Sony Corporation*, July 25, 1974 O.S.C.W.S. 4A.

[88]See, for example, *Gotaas-Larsen Shipping Corp.*, March 27, 1981 O.S.C.B. 88B where the issuer was allowed to report information in its annual report that would otherwise have been required in its information circular.

[89]See, for example, *Consolidated Paper Corporation Ltd.*, July 1967 O.S.C.B.W.S. 11A where the only issue was a charge of name.

[90]See *supra* note 21.

[91]NP #41, Part IV, para. 1. For a discussion of NP #41, see P.H. Healy, "National Policy Statement No. 41: The First Year" in *Special Lectures of the Law Society of Upper Canada* (Toronto: De Boo, 1989) at 355.

the record date, the issuer must request and obtain from depository institutions the names of the various persons on whose behalf the depository institution holds the securities.[92] The persons on whose behalf the depository institution holds the securities are typically also nominee holders (referred to as intermediaries), such as securities brokerage firms, banks or trust companies. The issuer must then send a search card to the persons identified by the depository institution at least 20 days before the record date for the meeting.[93] Intermediary nominee holders of securities must respond to the search card within 3 days of receiving it.[94] In their response, they must request the number of sets of meeting materials they will need in order to deliver a set of materials to each of the persons on whose behalf they hold the securities.[95] The issuer must deliver the number of sets of materials required by each intermediary at least 33 days before the meeting date so that the intermediary can deliver the material to non-registered security holders no later than 25 days before the meeting.[96] Within 3 days of receiving the meeting materials, intermediaries are required to forward the materials to the non-registered owners of the securities.[97]

A card is included with the meeting materials which permits the non-registered owner of the securities to request that he or she be placed on an issuer's "supplemental mailing list".[98] This allows issuers to supply meeting materials directly to those non-registered security holders whose names are on the supplemental mailing list.

The intermediary nominees must send a document informing the non-registered security holder of their rights under NP #41 and a document requesting written instructions as to whether they wish to receive materials relating to annual or special meetings of security holders of the issuer.[99] The intermediary must not exercise any voting rights with respect to a security of which it is not owner and

---

[92] Ibid., paras. 2 & 3.

[93] Ibid., para. 4.

[94] NP #41, Part V, subpart IV, para. 1.

[95] Ibid.

[96] NP #41, Part IV, para. 6.

[97] NP #41, Part V, subpart IV, para. 2.

[98] NP #41, Part IV, para. 9.

[99] NP #41, Part V, subpart II.

the intermediary must vote the securities in accordance with the instructions of the non-registered owner of the securities.[100]

VI. INSIDER REPORTS

The reporting of insider trades is another part of secondary market disclosure obligations. The Kimber Committee was of the view that reporting of insider trading would serve as a deterrent to insider trading and would increase investor confidence in the securities market.[101] Accordingly, the Kimber Committee recommended that securities legislation provide for the reporting of insider trading.[102]

Under most provincial securities acts in Canada, insiders are required to file reports of ownership of and trading in securities of reporting issuers. Insiders are required to file an insider report, within ten days of becoming an insider of a reporting issuer, disclosing any direct or indirect beneficial ownership of, or control or direction over, securities of the reporting issuer.[103] Where the insider's direct or indirect beneficial ownership of, or control or direction over, securities of the reporting issuer changes, the insider is required to file a report, within ten days of the end of the month in which the change occurs, indicating the changes in ownership that occurred during the month and showing the insider's ownership of securities of the reporting issuer as at the end of the month.[104]

The term "insider" is typically defined to include the directors or senior officers of the issuer and persons having direct or indirect beneficial ownership of, or control or direction over, securities of the issuer carrying more than 10% of the voting rights attached to all the issuer's outstanding voting securities. It is also typically defined to include directors or senior officers of subsidiaries or of

---

[100] NP #41, Part V, subpart III.

[101] The *Kimber Report, supra* note 1, at para. 2.04.

[102] Ibid., at para. 2.17.

[103] A.S.A. s. 147(1); B.C.S.A. s. 87(2); M.S.A. s. 109(1), (2); Nfld.S.A. s. 108(1); N.S.S.A. s. 113(1); O.S.A. s. 107(1); Q.S.A. s. 96 (must disclose within ten days of becoming an insider); S.S.A. s. 116(1).

[104] A.S.A. s. 147(2); B.C.S.A. s. 87(4); M.S.A. s. 109(3); Nfld.S.A. s. 108(2); N.S.S.A. s. 113(2); O.S.A. s. 107(2); Q.S.A. s. 97 (report of any change in holdings within 10 days of the change — Q. Regs. s. 174); S.S.A. s. 116(2).

any person that is an insider by virtue of having direct or indirect beneficial ownership of, or control or direction over, securities of the issuer carrying more than 10% of the voting rights attached to the issuer's outstanding voting securities. It also includes the issuer when it holds its own shares.[105]

Directors and senior officers are also deemed to be insiders of other issuers in certain circumstances. Where an issuer becomes an insider of a reporting issuer, every director and senior officer of that issuer is deemed to have been an insider of the reporting issuer for the previous six months.[106] Where a reporting issuer becomes an insider of another reporting issuer, every director and senior officer of the latter reporting issuer is deemed to have been an insider of the former reporting issuer for the previous six months.[107] Such deemed insiders must file the reports referred to above for the previous six months within ten days of the date on which they are deemed to be insiders.[108]

VII. TIMELY DISCLOSURE – REPORTS ON MATERIAL INFORMATION

Besides the periodic reporting in the form of financial statements and information circulars discussed above, continuous disclosure is also provided through "timely" disclosure. "Timely" disclosure provides disclosure of significant events with respect to reporting issuers at the time of each particular event. It is intended to provide investors with access to up-to-date information which is equal to the access enjoyed by insiders, such as directors and senior officers, as well as by other persons with a sufficiently close connection to the issuer

---

[105] A.S.A. s. 1(1)(i); B.C.S.A. s. 1(1); M.S.A. s. 108; Nfld.S.A. s. 2(1)(s); N.S.S.A. s. 2(1)(r); O.S.A. s. 1(1); Q.S.A. s. 89; S.S.A. s. 2(1)(w).

[106] A shorter period applies where the person only became a director or senior officer within the previous six-month period. See A.S.A. s. 8(1); B.C.S.A. s. 2(2); Nfld.S.A. s. 2(8); N.S.S.A. s. 2(8); O.S.A. s. 1(8); Q.S.A. s. 94; S.S.A. s. 2(8).

[107] A shorter period applies where the person only became a director or senior officer within the previous six-month period. See A.S.A. s. 8(2); B.C.S.A. s. 2(3); Nfld.S.A. s. 2(9); N.S.S.A. s. 2(9); O.S.A. s. 1(9); Q.S.A. s. 95 (with respect to an amalgamation involving at least one reporting issuer); S.S.A. s. 2(9).

[108] A.S.A. s. 147(3); B.C.S.A. s. 87(5); Nfld.S.A. s. 108(3); N.S.S.A. s. 113(4); O.S.A. s. 107(3); Q.S.A. s. 98; S.S.A. s. 116(3).

to be able to obtain the information before it might otherwise be obtained by members of the investing public. It also provides the market with up-to-date information to improve the valuation of securities.

A. Material Information Reporting Requirements

1. *Reporting of "Material Changes"*

Reporting issuers must dispose "material changes" in the affairs of the reporting issuer by (i) filing a press release, as soon as practicable, which discloses the nature and substance of the change,[109] and (ii) filing a report of the material change as soon as practicable (and in any event within ten days).[110]

A "material change" is a change in the business, operations or capital of the issuer that would reasonably be expected to have a significant effect on the market price or value of any of the securities of the reporting issuer.[111] A "material change" includes a decision to implement a change made by either the directors of the issuer or by senior management of the issuer who believe that confirmation of the decision by the directors is probable.[112]

Stock exchanges in Canada also have rules with respect to the disclosure of material changes that apply to issuers that are listed on the stock exchange.[113] Stock exchanges reserve the right to either accept or not accept proposed material changes in the business or

---

[109] A.S.A. s. 118(1)(a); B.C.S.A. s. 85(1)(a); Nfld.S.A. s. 76(1); N.S.S.A. s. 81(1); O.S.A. s. 75(1); Q.S.A. s. 73; S.S.A. s. 84(2)(a).

[110] A.S.A. s. 118(1)(b); B.C.S.A s. 85(1)(b); Nfld.S.A. s. 76(2); N.S.S.A. s. 81(2); O.S.A. s. 75(2); Q.S.A. s. 73; S.S.A. s. 84(1)(b).

[111] A.S.A. s. 1(k.1); B.C.S.A. s. 1(1) "material change" (the B.C.S.A. definition refers to a change in the "business, operations, assets or ownership of the issuer"); M.S.A. s. 1(d.2); Nfld. s. 2(1)(w); N.S.S.A. s. 2(1)(v); O.S.A. s. 1(1); S.S.A. s. 2(1)(y). The description of "material change" under the Q.S.A. s. 73 is not confined to changes in the business, operations, assets or ownership of the issuer. It also does not deal with a decision to implement a change.

[112] Ibid.

[113] A.S.E. By-law 23.09(1) (see also Policy Circular No. 4); M.S.E. Rule 9153 (see also Policy No. I-6 and I-8); T.S.E. By-law 19.09 (see also T.S.E. Policies Part I); V.S.E. Listing Agreement s. 2 and Policy No. 10.

affairs of a listed issuer.[114] Proceeding with a change not accepted by the stock exchange can result in suspension from trading or delisting of the issuer's securities.[115] If the notice of the material change is accepted by the exchange, it gives notice of the change to its members and may also issue a press release.[116]

2. Extension to "Material Facts"

National Policy #40 purports to extend this reporting requirement to "material facts".[117] A "material fact" is a fact that significantly affects, or would reasonably be expected to have a significant effect on, the market price or value of the reporting issuer's securities.[118]

In *Pezim v. British Columbia (Superintendent of Brokers)*,[119] a majority of the B.C. Court of Appeal held that the requirement in the B.C.S.A. to report "material changes" could not be extended to include "material facts". Mr. Justice Lambert, writing for the majority, reasoned that because only the expression "material change" was used in the provision requiring reporting while both the expressions "material change" and "material fact" were used in the provision prohibiting insider trading, the legislature could not have intended the reporting provision to extend to "material facts".[120] If the legislature had intended the reporting requirement to extend to "material facts", it would have used that expression in the reporting

---

[114] Ibid.

[115] Ibid.

[116] Ibid.

[117] N.P. #40, para. B requires the disclosure of "material information" and para. D defines this as "any information relating to the business and affairs of an issuer that results in or would reasonably be expected to result in a significant change in the market price or value of any of the issuer's securities." Para. D goes on to say that "[m]aterial information consists of both material facts and material changes relating to the business and affairs of an issuer."

[118] A.S.A. s. 1(1); B.C.S.A. s. 1(1) "material fact"; Nfld.S.A. s. 2(1)(x); N.S.S.A. s. 2(1)(w); O.S.A. s. 1(1) "material fact"; S.S.A. s. 2(1)(z). The description of "material change" in s. 73 of the Q.S.A. is similar to the definition of "material fact" in the acts of the provinces noted above.

[119] (1992), 66 B.C.L.R. (2d) 257, 96 D.L.R. (4th) 137.

[120] (1992), 66 B.C.L.R. (2d) 265-69.

requirement provision.[121] The attempt by the Securities Commission to extend the reporting requirement to "material facts" by way of a policy statement amounted to an amendment to the *Securities Act* which was something only the legislature, and not the Commission, could do.[122]

The majority judgment of the B.C. Court of Appeal in *Pezim* went on to hold that significant assay results from a mining exploration site did not constitute a "material change" since assay results did not constitute a change in the "business, operations, assets or ownership of the issuer."[123] While the assay results might constitute a change in the value of assets they do not constitute a change in the assets themselves. Lambert J. reasoned that if a change in the value of assets were interpreted as a "material change" there would be no distinction between a "material change" and a "material fact".[124]

The B.C. Court of Appeal's decision was reversed on appeal to the Supreme Court of Canada in *Pezim v. B.C. (Superintendent of Brokers)*.[125] Iacobucci J., delivering the judgment of the court, did not disagree with Lambert J.'s view that the Commission could not amend a provision of the *Securities Act* by policy statement. Indeed, he stated that,

---

[121] (1992), 66 B.C.L.R. (2d) 270.

[122] Lambert J. acknowledged that the Commission may have a power to impose sanctions where it is in the "public interest" to do so. However, the Commission could not impose different and more exacting standards than the legislature in an area closely governed by legislative provisions. See (1992), 66 B.C.L.R. (2d) 270.

[123] The case involved, among other things, a failure to disclose the results of an allegedly very significant series of assay results. Lambert J. concluded that,

geological information of the nature obtained on a continuing basis as a result of a planned drilling program does not constitute a change in the business, the operations, the assets or the ownership of the issuer, no matter what information is obtained from the drilling results. Such information may constitute a basis for a perception that there has been a change in the value of an asset. But that is a far different thing than a change in an asset. [66 B.C.L.R. (2d) 268]

[124] According to Lambert J.,

if a "material change" encompasses a change in information on the basis that information is itself an asset then there would not be any difference in applicability between the definition of "material change" and "material fact". Every change of information would be both a change and a fact, ... [66 B.C.L.R. (2d) 269]

[125] [1994] 2 S.C.R. 557.

it is important to note that the Commission's policy-making role is limited. By that I mean that their policies cannot be elevated to the status of law; they are not to be treated as legal pronouncements absent legal authority mandating such treatment.[126]

However, Mr. Justice Iacobucci also held that considerable deference should be granted to the Securities Commission in determining what constitutes a "material change" since,

> the determination of what information should be disclosed is an issue which goes to the heart of the regulatory expertise and mandate of the Commission, i.e., regulating the securities markets in the public's interest.[127]

While Canadian Securities Administrators may not have the authority to amend securities acts to require reporting of "material facts" in addition to "material changes", their attempt to do so in National Policy #40 is a clear indication that they believe it is in the public interest to expand the scope of the statutory reporting requirement. With the degree of curial defence that the Supreme Court of Canada has said Securities Commissions should be accorded in determining what information should be disclosed, it is reasonable to assume that Securities Commissions will take a broad view of the meaning of "material change" that is not likely to be interfered with by courts on appeals from Securities Commission decisions. Thus while National Policy #40 may not validly amend the reporting requirement to include "material facts", it may be prudent, practically

---

[126] [1994] 2 S.C.R. 557 at 596.

[127] [1994] 2 S.C.R. 557 at 598. Mr. Justice Iacobucci thus concluded that the majority decision of the B.C. Court of Appeal was in error when it rejected the Commission's findings on whether the assay results constituted a material change [1994] 2 S.C.R. 557 at 599-600.

He also concluded that the majority decision of the B.C. Court of Appeal was clearly wrong in its findings on whether the assays results constituted a "material change" [1994] 2 S.C.R. 600. He quoted from G.C. Stevens & S.D. Wortley, "Murray Pezim in the Court of Appeal: Draining the Lifeblood from Securities Regulation" (1992), 26 U.B.C. L. Rev. 331, at 336-37.

To the geologist or the mining property valuator Lambert, J.A.'s statement is astonishing. Every mine starts from host rock. Every drill hole leads not merely to a change of perception of the asset: it is a piece in the puzzle that ultimately determines whether the asset is moose pasture or ore. Each new result may change the characterization of the asset from rock, to mineral deposit, to inferred ore, to probable ore and ultimately, with enough holes supported by a feasibility study, to proven ore.

speaking, for reporting issuers to treat the reporting requirement as extending to material facts and to carefully follow the guidelines set out in National Policy #40.

The reporting requirement for issuers that are listed on a stock exchange also extends to "material facts".[128] This extension to material facts by stock exchanges is within the authority of stock exchanges since it is a requirement they impose as a contractual term in exchange for listing the securities of an issuer on the exchange.

3. Determining What Must be Reported

It is the responsibility of the reporting issuer to determine what information is material and therefore should be reported.[129] The Canadian Securities Administrators have recognized that such decisions require careful subjective judgments.[130] They encourage reporting issuers to consult the relevant regulatory authority[131] or exchange when in doubt as to whether disclosure should be made.[132]

The concept that governs the responsibility of the timely reporting obligations of reporting issuers is that they should report on material information ("material changes" or "material facts") that has an effect on the prices of its securities that is unique or uncharacteristic of the effect experienced by other issuers engaged in the same business.[133] For instance, as noted in National Policy #40, a change in government policy that affects most issuers in a particular industry does not require an announcement, but if it affects only one or a few issuers in a material way, those issuers are expected to make an announcement.[134]

---

[128] A.S.E. By-law 23.09(1) and Policy Circular No. 4; M.S.E. Rule 9153 and Policies I-6 and I-8; T.S.E. By-law 19.09 and T.S.E. Policies Part I; V.S.E. Listing Agreement s. 2 and Policy No. 10.

[129] N.P. #40, para. D.

[130] Ibid.

[131] N.P. #40, para. A provides guidelines as to who is the relevant authority or exchange.

[132] N.P. #40, para. D.

[133] Ibid.

[134] Ibid.

National Policy #40 lists several developments that are likely to give rise to material information. It notes, for example, changes in issued capital, stock splits, redemptions, dividend decisions, changes in share ownership, changes in corporate structure (such as reorganizations and amalgamations), takeover bids and issuer bids, major corporate acquisitions or dispositions, changes in capital structure, borrowing of a significant amount of funds, development of new products or resources, entering into or loss of significant contracts, firm evidence of significant increases or decreases in near term earnings prospects, significant changes in management, significant litigation, and major labour disputes.[135] National Policy #40 also notes that when unusual market activity indicates that trading is being unduly influenced by rumour, the relevant securities administrators will request that the issuer make a clarifying statement and disclose the relevant material information if the rumour is correct in whole or in part.[136]

National Policy #40 notes that "[t]he materiality of the information varies from one issuer to another according to the size of its profits, assets and capitalization, the nature of its operations and many other factors."[137] Determining whether the information will have a significant effect on the price of the issuer's securities (i.e., determining materiality) is presumably a question of assessing the benefits and costs of disclosure. Benefits in terms of improved pricing of the securities and the effect on confidence-in-the-market of providing equal access to the information might be weighed against such costs as the cost of disseminating the information and the costs of gathering and assessing information where disclosure may contribute to potential information overload.

This weighing of costs and benefits cannot be done with any degree of precision. However, a rule of thumb that would serve as a helpful starting point would be whether an investor would alter his or her investment decision on the basis of the information. If an investor might alter his or her investment decision on the basis of the information, but he or she is still doubtful as to whether disclosure should really be required, he or she should consult with the securities authorities.

---

[135] Ibid. A.S.E. Pol. Circular No. 4(2.5); M.S.E. Pol. I-8(2); T.S.E. Pol. Part I, 1.01 B has the same list; V.S.E. Policy No. 10.

[136] N.P. #40, Para. E.

[137] N.P. #40, Para. D.

B. Proposed Changes, Detrimental Information and Confidential Reporting

In some circumstances, material information can be reported on a confidential basis. A report marked "confidential" must be filed with the commission together with written reasons for non-disclosure.[138] No press release is required.[139] After every subsequent ten-day period, the reporting issuer must advise the commission in writing if it believes the information should be kept confidential.[140]

Confidential reporting may be done where:

(i) in the opinion of the reporting issuer, disclosure would be unduly detrimental to the interests of the reporting issuer;[141] or

(ii) the material change involves a decision to implement a change made by senior management of the issuer who believe that confirmation of the decision by the directors is probable and senior management of the issuer has no reason to believe that persons with knowledge of the material change have made use of such knowledge in purchasing or selling securities of the issuer.[142]

---

[138] A.S.A. s. 118(2); B.C.S.A. s. 85(2); Nfld.S.A. s. 76(3); N.S.S.A. s. 81(3); O.S.A. s. 75(3); S.S.A. s. 84(2).

[139] Ibid.

[140] A.S.A. s. 118(3) [A.S.A. s. 118(4) − states that notwithstanding the fact that the reporting issuer can keep the material change confidential, the reporting issuer shall file, issue and publish the material change not later than 180 days from the day that the material change became known to the reporting issuer]; B.C.S.A. s. 85(3); Nfld.S.A. s. 76(4); N.S.S.A. s. 81(4); O.S.A. s. 75(4); Q.S.A. s. 74 allows for non-disclosure where disclosure would be seriously detrimental to the interests of the issuer, but states that when the circumstances which justified non-disclosure cease to exist, the issuer shall comply with s. 73 and file a press release; S.S.A. s. 84(3).

[141] A.S.A. s. 118(2)(a); B.C.S.A. s. 85(2)(a); Nfld.S.A. s. 76(3)(a); N.S.S.A. s. 81(3)(a); O.S.A. s. 75(3)(a); Q.S.A. s. 74; S.S.A. s. 84(2)(a).

[142] A.S.A. s. 118(2)(b); B.C.S.A. s. 85(2)(b); Nfld.S.A. s. 76(3)(b); N.S.S.A. s. 81(3)(b); O.S.A. s. 75(3)(b); S.S.A. s. 84(2)(b).

1. *Unduly Detrimental*

Consistent with the general approach of weighing the costs and benefits of the effect of disclosure on the confidence in the market, National Policy #40 notes that the,

> [w]ithholding of material information on the basis that disclosure would be unduly detrimental to the issuer's interests can only be justified where the potential harm to the issuer or to investors caused by immediate disclosure may reasonably be considered to outweigh the undesirable consequences of delaying disclosure.[143]

National Policy #40 also provides examples of different situations. For instance, confidential disclosure may be appropriate where the issuer's ability to pursue specific objectives is prejudiced, such as where premature disclosure of the purchase of a significant asset may increase the cost of the acquisition.[144]

Confidential disclosure may be appropriate where disclosure of confidential information would provide a significant benefit to competitors.[145] In this situation, confidential disclosure may be socially beneficial in that it may avoid a disincentive to investment in product or process innovations, or in market development that may result from use of the information by competitors.

Confidential disclosure may also be appropriate where disclosure of information concerning the status of ongoing negotiations would prejudice the successful completion of those negotiations.[146] This may be beneficial to the investors securities regulation is intended to protect, and to society as a whole, since otherwise the gains from a transaction being negotiated might be lost as result of a breakdown in negotiations caused by disclosure. When weighed against the gains from disclosure, this potential loss may justify non-disclosure.

2. *Proposed Changes*

a. REASONABLY PROBABLE CONFIRMATION BY THE BOARD OF DIRECTORS

A reading of corporate law statutes often suggests that corporations are governed by the directors of the corporation. However,

---

[143] N.P. #40, Para. G.

[144] Ibid.

[145] Ibid.

[146] Ibid.

corporations are said to be more often governed by the management of the corporation. The directors tend to merely rubber stamp the initiatives of management. Thus management may well propose a change that merely awaits what will, in effect, be a perfunctory approval by the board of directors. Accordingly, the definition of "material change" includes a decision to implement a change made by senior management of the issuer. However, it is also provided that senior management should believe that confirmation by the board is probable since otherwise there is a risk that information could be given to the market which later turns out to be incorrect when the change is not in fact implemented. Arguably, if a substantial number of disclosures turn out to be incorrect, the reliability of disclosure could be reduced.[147]

b. CONFIDENTIAL DISCLOSURE AND INSIDER TRADING

When disclosure is made confidentially, there is a risk that some persons who are aware of the information will take advantage of it by trading on the basis of the information before it is publicly disclosed. Such trades will tend to be made with members of the investing public who are unaware of and lack access to the information. The trades will also tend to be made on the basis of prices determined in a market that is unaware of and lacks access to the information. The policy reflected in securities regulation in Canada is that insider trading should not be allowed. Indeed, it is prohibited under most Canadian securities acts. However, to provide some additional protection against insider trades during the period of confidential disclosure, there is the added rider, with respect to confidential disclosure of proposed changes, that senior management should have no reason to believe that persons with knowledge of the material change have made use of that knowledge in purchasing or selling securities.[148]

National Policy #40 requires the issuer to make an immediate announcement with respect to confidentially disclosed information where it, or rumours of it, have been divulged.[149] Also, where there is unusual market activity indicating that news of the matter is being

---

[147]This concern with the effect of misleading announcements on the credibility of disclosure is reflected in N.P. #40, para. F.

[148]See the provision cited *supra* note 138.

[149]Ibid.

disclosed and that certain persons are taking advantage of it, the relevant securities administrator is to be advised and a halt in trading will be imposed until the issuer has made disclosure on the matter.[150]

C. The Process of Disclosure

The disclosure process, with respect to reports of material information, is intended to assure adequate dissemination of information so that there will not be a period during which some persons to whom the information has been disseminated are able to trade with the benefit of the information, while others have yet to receive the information. To assure adequate dissemination, the information is to be disclosed in a period during which there is no trading. Trading can resume after there has been adequate disclosure.

Consequently, with the approval of the relevant securities authorities, release of the information may be delayed until the close of trading. This will provide a period of non-trading during which the information can be disseminated. Where the information should be disclosed during trading hours, trading in the securities of the issuer may be halted for a period of time to allow for adequate dissemination of the information.[151]

VIII. ANNUAL INFORMATION FORMS AND MANAGEMENT DISCUSSION AND ANALYSIS

Certain reporting issuers are required to provide a document known as an annual information form ("AIF"). Reporting issuers that take advantage of the POP system or shelf offering procedures for prospectus offerings, discussed in Chapter 8 below, are required to file an AIF within 140 days after the end of each financial year.[152] In Ontario, the AIF filing requirement is not limited to reporting issuers using the POP system or shelf offering procedures. It extends

---

[150] Ibid.

[151] N.P. #40, para. E. The length of a trading halt depends on the significance and complexity of the announcement. However the duration of a trading halt is normally less than two hours.

[152] See NP 47, paras. 4.1 to 4.3 and Appendix A; and NP 44, paras. 2.4, 3.1.

to reporting issuers having equity or revenues, as reported in their annual financial statements, of in excess of $10,000,000.[153]

The AIF provides a cumulative source of information about the issuer. It provides information about the business of the issuer, financial information, information about subsidiaries, who the directors and officers are and their ownership of securities of the issuer, and other material information about the issuer.[154] It may incorporate by reference other information about the issuer that is contained in the issuer's most recent financial statements, proxy circular and material change reports.[155]

The AIF must also either include or incorporate by reference a management discussion and analysis ("MD&A") of the financial condition and results of operations of the issuer for the year.[156] MD&A accompanies the financial statements of the issuer (although it does not form part of the financial statements).[157] MD&A allows the management of the issuer to provide a narrative explanation of its current financial condition and its future prospects.[158] The intention is to give the investor "the ability to look at the issuer

---

[153] Ont. Pol. 5.10, Part I(3).

[154] For example, it contains information about the incorporation or organization of the issuer, the development of the business of the issuer over the last five years, a narrative description of each industry segment of the business (including a description of the principal products or services of the business, major customers and significant geographic regions where sales are made, sources and availability of raw materials, intangible properties such as brand names, copyrights or franchises, the extent to which the business is seasonal, and similarly important matters concerning other types of businesses such as mining, oil and gas, and banking), selected consolidated financial information, management discussion and analysis (set out or incorporated by reference), markets for the issuer's securities, and background on the directors and officers. See NP 47, Appendix A; Ont. Pol. 5.10, Part II.

[155] NP 47, Appendix A, Instructions (1); Ont. Pol. 5.10, Part I(7).

[156] NP 47, Appendix A, Contents of AIF, Item 5; Ont. Pol. 5.10, Part II, Specific Instructions, Item 5.

[157] NP 47, Appendix A, Schedule 2, Instructions (1); Ont. Pol. 5.10, Part III(1). The financial statements themselves would contain the report of the auditor on whether the financial statements fairly represented the financial position of the issuer. It would be unreasonable (and extraordinarily costly) for the auditor's opinion to extend to the management discussion and analysis.

[158] Ibid.

through the eyes of management" to better assess the issuer's performance and future prospects.[159]

In its MD&A management must discuss and compare the issuer's financial condition and its changes in financial condition and results of operations for the previous two financial years describing the causes for changes in the financial statements from year to year.[160] The results of operations are to be explained noting, for instance, any unusual or infrequent events or significant economic changes that materially affected income or loss from operations.[161] MD&A is also forward looking in that, for example, management is asked to describe any known trends or uncertainties that have had or that are reasonably expected to have a favourable or unfavourable impact on revenues or income or loss from operations.[162] The discussion must also consider the liquidity and capital resources of the issuer.[163] The discussion of liquidity focuses on the ability of the issuer to generate adequate amounts of cash (or cash equivalents) when necessary in both the short term and the long term.[164] In the discussion of the issuer's capital resources, management is asked to describe and quantify commitments for capital expenditures as of the end of the most recently completed financial year and note the anticipated source of funds to meet the commitments.[165] They must also quantify uncommitted but necessary expenditures to meet future plans discussed in the MD&A.[166]

With the increasing degree of integration between Canadian and U.S. securities markets many issuers have security holders in both Canada and the U.S. This creates the potential regulatory burden

---

[159] Ibid.

[160] NP 47, Appendix A, Contents of MD&A, Item 1; Ont. Pol. 5.10, Part III, Specific Instructions, Item 1(1).

[161] NP 47, Appendix A, Contents of MD&A, Item 3; Ont. Pol. 5.10, Part III, Specific Instructions, Item 1(4).

[162] Ibid.

[163] NP 47, Appendix A, Contents of MD&A, Item 2; Ont. Pol. 5.10, Part III, Specific Instructions, Item 1(3) and (4).

[164] NP 47, Appendix A, Contents of MD&A, Item 2; Ont. Pol. 5.10, Part III, Specific Instructions, Item 1(3).

[165] NP 47, Appendix A, Contents of MD&A, Item 2; Ont. Pol. 5.10, Part III, Specific Instructions, Item 1(4).

[166] Ibid.

of having to comply with the requirements of both Canadian and U.S. securities regulatory requirements with potentially conflicting requirements. Securities regulators in both Canada and the U.S. have attempted to reduce this potential regulatory burden to issuers that have securities trading in both Canada and the U.S. Since the U.S. has requirements similar to the Canadian AIF and MD&A requirements Canadian securities regulators have indicated that the AIF and MD&A requirements can be met by filing corresponding documents filed with the U.S. Securities and Exchange Commission ("SEC"). Thus an issuer that has securities registered for trading with the U.S. Securities and Exchange Commission may satisfy the AIF requirement by filing, and making available to security holders in Canada, its Form 10K or 20F filed with the SEC pursuant to the *Securities Exchange Act of 1934.*[167] Similarly the MD&A requirements can be satisfied by filing the corresponding document filed with the SEC.[168]

IX. SYSTEM FOR ELECTRONIC DOCUMENT ANALYSIS AND RETRIEVAL ("SEDAR")

In 1990, the Canadian Securities Administrators began developing an electronic filing system for securities filings.[169] It was felt that an electronic filing system would reduce the costs of storing, handling and searching through bulky paper records while providing investors with quicker and better access to more information.[170] It was also felt that, given the increasing integration of North American securities markets, a system should be developed in Canada similar to the U.S. Securities and Exchange Commission's development of the Electronic Data Gathering and Retrieval system ("EDGAR").[171]

---

[167] See NP 47, para. 5.4; Ont. Pol. 5.10, Part I(4).

[168] See NP 47, Appendix A, Contents of AIF, Item 5; Ont. Pol. 5.10, Part I(4).

[169] See "CSA Notice − An Electronic System for Securities Filings" (1994), 17 OSCB 2857; "Canadian Securities Administrators' Notice − SEDAR" (1995), 18 OSCB 1892; and "Request for Comments: SEDAR − Notice of Proposed National Instrument" (1996) 19 OSCB 2345 at 2345.

[170] See, e.g., "CSA Notice − An Electronic System for Securities Filings" (1994), 17 OSCB 2857; and "Request for Comments: SEDAR − Notice of Proposed National Instrument" (1996), 19 OSCB 2345 at 2347.

[171] Ibid.

While compliance with SEDAR requirements might increase filing costs for issuers,[172] it was felt that the benefits of SEDAR would outweigh the costs.[173] Issuers would be able to file in all Canadian jurisdictions through one electronic filing as opposed to filing multiple copies of paper documents in multiple jurisdictions. It would also allow for an extended period of filing beyond the normal business hours of the securities commission offices. The Canadian Securities Administrators felt that SEDAR would facilitate the review of, and response to, securities filings. Investors would have better access to the information, possibly through Internet access. This would allow them quicker access to information. The use of electronic search procedures could permit investors to find and analyze information more quickly.[174]

Consequently, several securities commissions now require that continuous disclosure documents be filed electronically. The documents are then stored and made available to the public in a system called the "System for Electronic Document Analysis and Retrieval", otherwise known as "SEDAR". This computer-based electronic filing and retrieval system is operated by CDS Inc., a subsidiary of the Canadian Depository for Securities Limited.[175] The system was introduced in 1996 by way of a National Instrument that could be implemented as a rule, regulation or other instrument in each of the provinces.[176]

Under the National Instrument annual and interim financial statements, material change reports, proxy circulars, and management discussion and analysis are to be filed electronically.[177] The documents must be prepared in either WordPerfect or Microsoft

---

[172]For instance, it could require issuers to train staffs to prepare documents for electronic filing, or the hiring of agents to prepare and file documents on their behalf. There would also be the fees for electronic filing and the licencing fee for the electronic filing software. See "Request for Comments: SEDAR — Notice of Proposed National Instrument" (1996), 19 OSCB 2345 at 2347.

[173]Ibid., (1996), 19 OSCB 2347-8.

[174]Ibid.

[175]See "Request for Comments: SEDAR — Notice of Proposed National Instrument" (1996), 19 OSCB 2345 at 2345 and the letter of accord with CDS Inc. [set out in (1996), 19 OSCB 2473-89].

[176]The National Instrument is set out at (1996), 19 OSCB 2350-60.

[177]NI para. 2.2 and Appendix A.

Word[178] and must then be transmitted to CDS Inc. using a software package licenced to the issuer by CDS Inc.[179] Detailed instructions on how to make electronic filings is provided in a SEDAR Filer Manual available from CDS Inc.[180]

All issuers, other than foreign issuers, are required to comply with the electronic filing requirement unless they are exempted from the requirement.[181] A temporary exemption can be obtained for short term technical difficulties.[182] Under this temporary exemption the issuer files a form with the paper filing indicating that the paper filing is being made in reliance on the temporary exemption. The particular document filed in paper form must later be filed in electronic form to ensure that the electronic database of public filings is complete. A continuing exemption may also be available on the basis of hardship.[183] This requires a written application to the appli-

---

[178]SEDAR Filer Manual, para. 7.2(b) [(1996), 19 OSCB 2397].

[179]NI para. 2.4 and the SEDAR Filer Manual, para. 4.4.

[180]An early version of the SEDAR Filer Manual is available in the Ontario Securities Commission Bulletin (1996), 19 OSCB 2378-2472. One may prefer to consult the abbreviated version in a song sung by Doris Day entitled "K-SEDAR, SEDAR".

[181]See the National Instrument on the System for Electronic Document Analysis and Retrieval (hereinafter "NI"), para. 2.1. A "foreign issuer" is defined as an issuer that is not incorporated or organized under the laws of Canada or a province or territory of Canada. However, even if the issuer is not incorporated or organized under the laws of Canada or a province or territory of Canada, it will still be subject to the electronic filing requirement if it has a class of its securities listed and posted for trading on a stock exchange in Canada and does not have any of its securities listed and posted for trading on a stock exchange or quoted in a published market in any other country. An issuer that is not incorporated or organized under the laws of Canada or a province or territory of Canada can also be subject to the electronic filing requirement if the voting securities carrying more than 50% of the votes for the election of directors are held by persons or companies whose last address as shown on the books of the issuer is in Canada and either the majority of the senior officers or directors of the issuer are citizens or residents of Canada, assets of the issuer that represent more than 50% of the value of all assets of the issuer are located in Canada, or the business of the issuer is administered principally in Canada. See NI para. 1.1 "foreign issuer". A foreign issuer may opt to use electronic filing, and if it does so it may also opt to cease using electronic filing. See NI para. 2.1.

[182]NI para. 3.1 and SEDAR Form 3 set out in the SEDAR Filer Manual, Appendix N [see (1996), 19 OSCB 2462-4].

[183]NI para. 3.2.

cable securities regulators. If granted, the exemption may allow for filing in a paper format with no requirement to subsequently file in an electronic format.[184]

Paper documents must be filed in some instances. An obvious example is the filing of a material change report with a request that it be kept confidential.[185] An electronic filing of the report in SEDAR would make the report publicly available.

X. SANCTIONS WITH RESPECT TO CONTINUOUS DISCLOSURE REQUIREMENTS

There are several possible sanctions for the failure to comply with continuous disclosure requirements or for misrepresentations contained in documents filed pursuant to continuous disclosure requirements. Some of the sanctions are provided for in the various provincial statutes. Otherwise there is potential for a common law civil action and, in some circumstances a potential statutory civil action.

A. Statutory Sanctions

A failure to comply with the continuous disclosure requirements can lead to penal sanction.[186] Also, a misrepresentation in the required disclosure document can also lead to a penal sanction.[187] Compliance orders can be obtained.[188] A commission could also

---

[184] Ibid.

[185] See NI para. 2.3(1). On the confidential filing of material change reports see *supra*, Part VII B.

[186] A.S.A. s. 161(1)(d)(e), (2); B.C.S.A. s. 155(1)(d) & (f); M.S.A. s. 136(1)(c); Nfld.S A. s. 122(1)(c); N.S.S.A. s. 129(1)(c); O.S.A. s. 122(1)(c); Q.S.A. s. 195(3) and s. 202; S.S.A. s. 131(3)(c).

[187] A.S.A. s. 161(1)(b), (2); B.C.S.A. s. 155(1)(c); M.S.A. s. 136(1)(b); Nfld.S.A. s. 122(1)(b); N.S.S.A. s. 129(1)(b); O.S.A. s. 122(1)(b); Q.S.A. s. 197 and s. 202; S.S.A. s. 131(3)(b).

[188] A.S.A. s. 164; B.C.S.A. ss. 157, 161(1)(a); M.S.A. s. 152; Nfld.S.A. s. 126; N.S.S.A. ss. 133, 134(1)(a); O.S.A. ss. 127(1), (5), 128(3); Q.S.A. s. 272.1; S.S.A. s. 133.

make a cease trade order[189] or remove an issuer's right to use the various exemptions provided in the Act.[190]

The power to enforce the extension of timely disclosure to material facts through National Policy #40 may be problematic. The penal sanctions apply to a breach of the timely disclosure requirement in the various acts. However, the timely disclosure requirement in the securities acts refers to "material changes" and not "material facts". Thus the penal sanction would presumably not be available. This problem might be addressed, as noted above,[191] by giving a broad scope to the meaning of "material change". The administrative sanctions might be said to be available on the basis that the extension of the application of the timely disclosure requirements to "material facts" is "in the public interest". If so, then it falls within the discretion of a securities commission to impose an administrative sanction where it "considers it to be in the public interest"[192] to do so.[193]

B. Civil Liability

1. No Statutory Civil Sanction

There is no statutory civil liability for misrepresentations in secondary market disclosure documents such as financial statements, proxy circulars, material change reports and insider trading reports. Proposals for a statutory civil liability sanction for misrepresentations

---

[189] A.S.A. s. 165(1)(a), (b); B.C.S.A. ss. 161(1)(b). 146; M.S.A. s. 148; N.B.S.F.P.A. s. 18; Nfld.S.A. s. 127; N.S.S.A. s. 134(1)(b); O.S.A. s. 127(2); Q.S.A. s. 265; S.S.A. s. 134(1)(b).

[190] A.S.A. s. 165(1)(c); B.C.S.A. s. 161(1)(c); Nfld.S.A. s. 128; N.S.S.A. s. 134(1)(c); O.S.A. s. 127(3); Q.S.A. s. 264; S.S.A. s. 134(1)(a).

[191] See *supra* notes 119-127 and the accompanying text.

[192] This is the standard provided for the exercise of most administrative powers under most provincial securities acts — see, for example, B.C.S.A. s. 161.

[193] See, for example, *Re Canadian Tire Corp Ltd. (sub nom. Canadian Tire Corp. v. C.T.C. Dealer Holdings Ltd.)*, [1987] 10 O.S.C.B. 857, 35 B.L.R. 56, aff'd (1987), 10 O.S.C.B. 1771, 59 O.R. (2d) 79 *(sub nom. CTC Dealer Holdings Ltd. v. O.S.C.)*, 35 B.L.R. 117, 23 Admin. L.R. 285, 37 D.L.R. (4th) 94, 21 O.A.C. 216 (Div. Ct.), leave to appeal to the Ont. C.A. refused (1987), 35 B.L.R. xx (note) (Ont. C.A.) for a case which gave a broad scope to the "public interest" test not requiring that a breach of the Act or regulations occur. See Chapter 14, Part II A 2 d.

in continuous disclosure documents have been made in the past.[194] These proposals have been supported on the notion that without a statutory civil liability provision for secondary market disclosure there will be discrepancies between the standard of care given to the preparation of primary and secondary market disclosure documents and the remedies available for misrepresentations in primary and secondary market disclosure documents.[195] The proposals were also supported on the basis of advancing the goal of integrating primary and secondary market disclosure and on the basis of the importance of secondary markets, reliance on secondary market disclosure and the consequent need to promote investor confidence in secondary market disclosure.[196] However, concerns such as the scope of potential plaintiffs, issuers to whom liability should extend, the extent of liability for directors, officers and experts, the types of disclosure documents to which liability should extend, whether there should be a limit on the amount of damages, whether liability should be based on negligence or fraud, and whether liability for the issuer should be strict, have discouraged the implementation of such proposals.[197]

Saskatchewan has enacted a provision providing for disability for verbal misrepresentations "to a prospective purchaser of a security".[198] The provision is not, on its face, confined to distributions of securities and may thus extend to secondary market transactions. It is similar in structure to the statutory civil liability for a misrepresentation in a prospectus in that there is a deemed reliance and defenses such as showing the plaintiff knew of the misrepresentation or that the defendant could not reasonably have known that his or her statement contained a misrepresentation.

---

[194] "Civil Liability for Continuous Disclosure Documents Filed Under the Securities Act — Request for Comments", 7 O.S.C.B. 4910 (November 23, 1984). See also *Proposals for a Federal Securities Market law for Canada*, Vol. I (Ottawa: Minister of Supply and Services Canada, 1979) s. 13.09 at 89-90 and see the accompanying commentary in Vol. II at 264-66. See also J.E. Gresham, "The POP System, Dissemination and Civil Liability: A Proposed Alternative to the Closed System" in *Special Lectures of the Law Society of Upper Canada* (Toronto: DeBoo, 1989) at 385; and Toronto Stock Exchange report, "Responsible Corporate Disclosure: A Search for Balance" (March 18, 1997).

[195] 7 O.S.C.B. 4910 (November 23, 1984) at 4910 to 4913.

[196] Ibid.

[197] Ibid., at 4914.

[198] See S.S.A. s. 138.2.

2. Statutory Civil Liability Where Documents Incorporated by Reference in a Prospectus

In spite of the lack of specific statutory civil sanctions for misrepresentations in secondary market disclosure documents, there can be statutory civil liability for misrepresentations in secondary market disclosure documents if the secondary market disclosure document is incorporated by reference in a prospectus. The incorporation of secondary market disclosure documents in a prospectus is provided for with respect to the prompt offering prospectus procedure and the shelf offering prospectus procedure discussed in Chapter 8 below. When secondary market disclosure documents are incorporated by reference in a prospectus, any misrepresentations contained in those documents become subject to the civil liability provisions for misrepresentations in a prospectus discussed in Chapter 5 above.[199]

3. Civil Actions for Deceit or Negligent Misrepresentation and the "Fraud on the Market" Theory

In cases other than those in which secondary market disclosure documents are incorporated by reference in a prospectus, the civil liability sanction will be the common law sanction for deceit or negligent misrepresentation. These common law civil actions were briefly discussed in Chapter 5 above.[200]

One of the elements of either the action for deceit or negligent misrepresentation that will be difficult to establish is that the plaintiff relied on the misrepresentation. For some investors it may stretch the credulity of the court to argue that the investor actually read the particular disclosure document, understood it and invested on the basis of it. Several U.S. cases have dealt with this problem by basing reliance on a "fraud on the market" doctrine.[201] The concept

---

[199] Chapter 5, Part III.

[200] Chapter 5, Part II.

[201] Several cases have considered and applied the fraud on the market theory; see, for example, *Blaikie v. Barrack,* 524 F.2d 891 (1975), cert. denied, 429 U.S. 816 (1976); *Ross v. A.H. Robbins Co.,* 607 F.2d 545 (1979), cert. denied 446 U.S. (1980); *Panzirer v. Wolf,* 663 F.2d (1981); *T.J. Raney & Sons, Inc. v. Fort Cobb, Oklahoma Irrigation Fuel Authority,* 717 F.2d 1330 (1983), cert. denied 465 U.S. 1026 (1984); *Lipton v. Documentation, Inc.,* 734 F.2d 740 (1984), cert. denied,

behind the fraud on the market doctrine is that the market is efficient in the semi-strong form, or at least approximates this degree of efficiency.[202] Therefore the market price will quickly reflect information disclosed in disclosure documents. The investor is said to rely on the accuracy of the market price. Thus any misrepresentations in information disclosed to the market will be implicitly relied on by the investor.[203] This is an argument which could be tried where it is difficult to establish the element of reliance more directly.[204]

---

469 U.S. 1132 (1985); *Harris v. Union Electric Co.*, 787 F.2d 355, cert. denied 107 S.Ct. 94 (1986); *Peil v. Speiser*, 806 F.2d 1154 (1986); *Basic Incorporated v. Levinson*, 108 S.Ct. 978, 99 L. Ed. 2d 194 (U.S. Ohio, 1988).

There is extensive academic literature on the fraud on the market theory. For differing views see Black, "Fraud on the Market: A Criticism of Dispensing with Reliance Requirements in Certain Open Market Transactions" (1984) 62 N.C.L. Rev. 435; J.R. Macey, "Good Finance, Bad Economics: An Analysis of the Fraud on the Market Theory" (1990) 42 Stan. L. Rev. 1059; R.J. Thomas, "The Fraud-on-the-Market Theory: A Basically Good Idea Whose Time has Arrived" (1989) 29 Indiana L. Rev. 1061.

[202] The semi-strong form of the efficient market theory is discussed in Chapter 2, Part III C. As the court expressed it in *Peil v. Speiser*, 806 F.2d 1154, at 1160-61,

> The fraud on the market theory is based on the hypothesis that, in an open and developed securities market, the price of a company's stock is determined by the available information regarding the company and its business.

In *Basic v. Levinson*, 108 S.Ct. 978, 99 L.Ed. 2d 194 (U.S. Ohio, 1988) at 99 L.Ed. 2d 218 the U.S. Supreme Court affirmed the fraud on the market theory noting that,

> [r]ecent empirical studies have tended to confirm Congress' premise that the market price of shares traded on well-developed markets reflects all publicly available information, and, hence, any material misrepresentations.

[203] In *Blaikie v. Barrack*, 524 F.2d 891 at 907 (9th Cir. 1975) the court stated that the investor,

> relies generally on the supposition that the market price is validly set and that no unsuspected manipulation has artificially inflated the price, and thus indirectly on the truth of the representations underlying the stock price — whether he is aware of it or not, the price he pays reflects material representations.

[204] The "fraud-on-the-market" theory was considered in *Kripps v. Touche Ross & Co.* (1992), 69 B.C.L.R. (2d) 62, 94 D.L.R. (4th) 284 (B.C.C.A.) but concluded that the theory would not assist the plaintiff in the particular case.

CHAPTER 7

EXEMPTIONS FROM THE PROSPECTUS REQUIREMENT

I. INTRODUCTION

We have already examined the prospectus requirement (Chapter 4) and the continuous disclosure requirements that apply once a prospectus has been issued (Chapter 6). However, not all distributions require the issuance of a prospectus. In fact, there are numerous exemptions from the prospectus requirement.

In providing for exemptions, most Canadian securities acts have adopted the concept of the "closed system". In the closed system, resales of securities purchased under an exemption are subject to specific resale restrictions. To fully appreciate the nature of the exemptions and the related resale restrictions, one must begin with an understanding of the concept of the closed system. Part II of this chapter outlines the closed system concept.

Part III of the chapter provides a summary of prospectus exemptions and related resale restrictions in the context of principles which underlie the exemptions and restrictions. As this is intended to be an introductory text, the objective is not to give precise detail or provide a comprehensive manual on prospectus exemptions. Rather, by looking at principles underlying the exemptions in the context of the closed system, the object is to provide a conceptual guide upon which one can develop a sense of when a specific exemption and related resale restriction apply, or, when an exemption may be available from a securities commission.

II. THE CLOSED SYSTEM CONCEPT

The closed system is most readily understood as a response to perceived weaknesses in the scheme of mandatory disclosure that predated the closed system.

213

A. Weaknesses in the Preclosed System

Under the disclosure system that prevailed prior to the adoption of the closed system, a prospectus was required where there was a "primary distribution to the public".[1] In some circumstances an exemption could be obtained where the distribution was a primary distribution to the public.[2] However, these pre-closed system acts generally did not restrict the resale of securities purchased under an exemption.[3] This created two problems. First, there was uncertainty associated with the meaning of the phrase "a primary distribution to the public" which was the basis on which a prospectus was required.[4] Second, continuous disclosure, required where securities were distributed under a prospectus, might not be present to support secondary market trading where securities were not distributed under a prospectus.[5] A distribution under a prospectus was not required either where an exemption was available or where the distribution was not a "primary distribution to the public".

1. *Uncertainty Associated with the Meaning of "to the public"*

Although courts did occasionally grapple with the meaning of the words "to the public", they were unable to give them a precise meaning. One of the leading cases addressing the meaning of the words "to the public" was *SEC v. Ralston Purina.*[6] Ralston Purina instituted an employee share ownership plan under which shares of the company were made available to "key employees". However, shares were offered to any employee who expressed an interest in the shares. Shares were sold to employees in several different states and included such employees as a chuck loading foreman, a clerical assistant, a stock clerk and a production trainee. The United States

---

[1] See, for example, *The Securities Act*, S.O. 1966, c. 142, s. 35. This Act was known as the "*Uniform Act*" and was adopted in all of the western provinces.

[2] See ibid., s. 58.

[3] See the discussion in Chapter V of the *Report to the Committee of the Ontario Securities Commission on the Problems of Disclosure Raised for Investors by Business Combinations and Private Placements* (the *Merger Report*), February, 1970, esp. pp. 59-61.

[4] Ibid., Chapter III, 37-39.

[5] Ibid., 66-67.

[6] 346 U.S. 119, 73 S.Ct. 981 (1953).

Supreme Court held that the sales constituted a distribution to the public and thus were subject to the *Securities Act of 1933*. In discussing the meaning of "to the public" the court noted that the security need not be made available to the whole world[7] and that "to the public" applies whether the offer is made to many persons or to only a few persons.[8] The key question, in the view of the court, was whether the persons who are offered the security need to know the kind of the information that the prospectus would provide.[9]

In *R. v. Piepgrass*,[10] a leading Canadian case, $50,000 worth of capital was sought by soliciting farmers, most of whom were known by the promoter from previous business dealings. The Alberta Court of Appeal upheld the trial decision which held that sales to the persons solicited constituted a distribution to the public. The Court of Appeal noted that the persons sold to "were not in any sense friends or associates of the accused, or persons having common bonds of interest or association".[11] The court did not expand on the reason for this test. However, the concept appears to be that one is not likely to take advantage of friends, associates or persons who have common bonds of interest or association. Also, persons having common bonds of interest or association may have access to the kind of information that would appear in a prospectus. Such persons would thus not need the protection provided by prospectus disclosure accompanied by withdrawal rights and civil liability.

The tests set out in these cases are known respectively as the "need to know" test and the "common bonds" test. Although these two tests provided some guidance as to the meaning of the expression "to the public", there remained considerable ambiguity as is to whether a distribution constituted a distribution "to the public". Thus it was often not clear whether a prospectus was

---

[7] 346 U.S. 123.

[8] 346 U.S. 125.

[9] 346 U.S. 126-27.

[10] (1959), 29 W.W.R. 218, 23 D.L.R. (2d) 220, 125 C.C.C. 364, 31 C.R. 213 (Alta. C.A.).

[11] Ibid., 29 W.W.R. 228. It was also noted that the company, through the appellant, had "put on a vigorous selling campaign to certain members of the public, members who had no common bonds of interest or association with the appellant." [29 W.W.R. 228].

required. Cautious solicitors resolved this doubt by seeking an exemption order from the Securities Commission. There were numerous applications to the Commission for clarifying orders.[12]

2. Continuous Disclosure Requirements

In response to recommendations of the Kimber Commission, provincial securities acts required continuous disclosure in the form of financial statements and proxy circulars. It is apparent from the Kimber Report that such additional disclosure was intended to promote confidence in secondary markets.[13] However, under the preclosed system disclosure scheme, secondary market trading involving members of the investing public could, in some circumstances, occur without the support of continuous disclosure.

If a distribution did not constitute a "primary distribution to the public" or if the distribution was made under an exemption, then no prospectus was required.[14] If no prospectus was required, and if the issuer was not listed on a stock exchange in the province, there would be no subsequent requirement to provide continuous disclosure through financial statements and proxy circulars.[15] However, persons who purchased securities in such distributions were generally not prohibited from reselling those securities to whomever they chose.[16] Thus the securities could be sold to members of the investing public who might be described as persons who needed to know the kind of information that would be provided in a prospectus.[17] This gap in continuous disclosure requirements meant that some secondary market trading in securities was supported by continuous disclosure while other secondary market trading was not.

---

[12] See the *Merger Report*, *supra* note 3, at 38-39.

[13] See generally paras. 1.11, 1.12, 1.14, 1.16, 4.03.

[14] See *supra* notes 1 and 2.

[15] See, for example, *The Securities Act*, S.O. 1966, c. 142, ss. 120, 129, and the definition of "corporation" in s. 118 with respect to financial statements, and s. 102 and the definition of "corporation" in s. 100 with respect to proxy circulars.

[16] See *supra* note 3.

[17] A sale under an exemption followed by a resale shortly thereafter to a member of the "public" was known as a "backdoor underwriting".

B. The Closed System Response

1. *Response to Uncertainty and Gap in Regulation*

The closed system was a response to the uncertainty associated with the meaning of the words "a primary distribution to the public" and the gap in continuous disclosure requirements. Under the closed system all "distributions" of securities are subject to the application of the act. The system is closed in the sense that there are no openings for unregulated distributions of securities. It is also closed in the sense that when distributions do occur without a prospectus, pursuant to an exemption, any subsequent secondary market trading is confined to a narrow group of persons who do not need to know the information contained in a prospectus. This narrow group of persons constitutes a closed market for secondary market trading in securities not supported by continuous disclosure.

2. *The Concept of the Closed System*

The concept of the closed system is that securities will only be allowed to trade outside of this closed secondary market if that trading is supported by adequate continuous disclosure. This is depicted in Diagram 7.a which shows all distributions of securities being directed into a box which constitutes the closed market.

a. TRADING WITHIN THE CLOSED MARKET

Secondary market trading within the closed market can occur only in reliance on an exemption from the prospectus requirement. It is the requirement that one rely on an exemption that ensures that trading remains in the closed market. The exemption will be available only where the purchasers are persons who do not need to know the information contained in a prospectus. This is depicted in Diagram 7.a as an arrow (marked in the middle with the word "exemptions") within the closed market box.

b. TRADING OUTSIDE THE CLOSED MARKET

(i) Prospectus Disclosure Followed by Continuous Disclosure

Trading outside of the closed market can only occur where adequate information has been provided to the investing public. There

Diagram 7.a

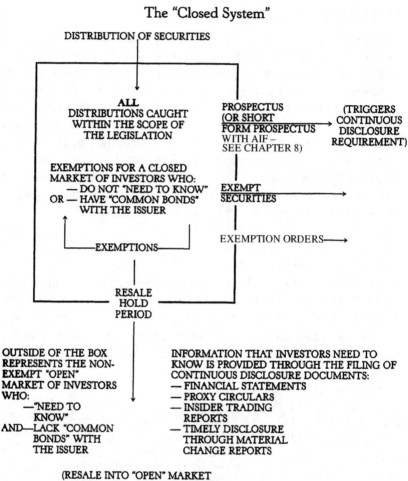

The "Closed System"

DISTRIBUTION OF SECURITIES

ALL
DISTRIBUTIONS CAUGHT
WITHIN THE SCOPE OF
THE LEGISLATION

PROSPECTUS
(OR SHORT
FORM PROSPECTUS
WITH AIF –
SEE CHAPTER 8)

(TRIGGERS
CONTINUOUS
DISCLOSURE
REQUIREMENT)

EXEMPTIONS FOR A CLOSED
MARKET OF INVESTORS WHO:
— DO NOT "NEED TO KNOW"
OR — HAVE "COMMON BONDS"
WITH THE ISSUER

EXEMPT
SECURITIES

EXEMPTIONS

EXEMPTION ORDERS—→

RESALE
HOLD
PERIOD

OUTSIDE OF THE BOX
REPRESENTS THE NON-
EXEMPT "OPEN"
MARKET OF INVESTORS
WHO:
—"NEED TO
KNOW"
AND—LACK "COMMON
BONDS" WITH
THE ISSUER

INFORMATION THAT INVESTORS NEED TO
KNOW IS PROVIDED THROUGH THE FILING OF
CONTINUOUS DISCLOSURE DOCUMENTS:
— FINANCIAL STATEMENTS
— PROXY CIRCULARS
— INSIDER TRADING
REPORTS
— TIMELY DISCLOSURE
THROUGH MATERIAL
CHANGE REPORTS

(RESALE INTO "OPEN" MARKET
ONLY IF CONTINUOUS DISCLOSURE
REQUIREMENTS FULFILLED)

are two ways in which adequate information can be provided to
the investing public. The first way is by providing a prospectus.[18]
Once securities have been sold under a prospectus any subsequent
secondary market trading will be supported by continuous disclosure

---

[18] When an issuer sells securities to the "public" for the first time under a
prospectus, it is referred to as "going public".

which is required where securities have been distributed under a prospectus.[19]

(ii) Resale Restrictions

The second way in which adequate information is provided to the investing public is through the use of resale restrictions. Resale restrictions allow a person who purchased under an exemption to sell to members of the investing public as long as certain conditions assuring adequate continuous disclosure have been met. These conditions generally assure that the issuer has been providing continuous disclosure for a sufficient period of time to provide an adequate base of information. The purpose of this is to protect investors by providing (i) access to information for those investors who care to gather it themselves, (ii) information as a basis for professional investment advice, or (iii) a base of information for professional traders whose trading will cause the market price of the issuer's securities to reflect their underlying values. This method of escaping the closed market is depicted in Diagram 7.a by an arrow, marked by the words "resale hold period", extending from the exemptions within the closed system box to the open unrestricted secondary market trading area outside of the box.

For example, suppose XYZ Ltd. wanted to raise $5 million through the sale of common shares. Under the closed system statutes, an offering of these securities would constitute a trade in securities that had not been previously issued. It would thus be a distribution of securities and a prospectus would be required unless an exemption from the prospectus requirements were available. Thus one option to XYZ Ltd. would be a distribution of the shares under a prospectus following the process outlined in Chapter 4. However, another option would be to sell the securities pursuant to an exemption. For instance, XYZ Ltd. might arrange to sell the whole $5 million issue to an insurance company. Such a transaction would be exempt from the prospectus requirement on the basis that the insurance company would be a relatively sophisticated investor that would not need to know the kind of information that would be contained in a prospectus.

The way in which the closed system statutes have the created the closed market is to define the resale of securities purchased

---

[19] The continuous disclosure requirements are discussed in Chapter 6 above.

under an exemption as a distribution. Thus if the insurance company sought to resell the XYZ Ltd. shares, such sales would constitute a distribution. Consequently, a prospectus would be required unless an exemption could be relied upon.

If XYZ Ltd. was providing continuous disclosure in the form of financial statements, proxy circulars and material change reports, then the insurance company would have another option. It could hold on to the securities for the period required by the Act or regulations and resell the securities at the end of the period without having to produce a prospectus or rely on an exemption. The "hold period" specified in the Act or regulations is presumed to be of sufficient length to allow an adequate build up of information about the issuer and the particular security to support secondary market trading.

This closed system approach is the system set up under the A.S.A., B.C.S.A., Nfld.S.A., N.S.S.A., O.S.A., Q.S.A. and S.S.A. The M.S.A., N.B.S.F.P.A., N.W.T.S.A., P.E.I.S.A. and the Y.S.A. do not use the closed system approach.[20]

---

[20] The M.S.A. effects a similar result in many cases since a prospectus is required where a "trade in a security" is "in the course of a primary distribution to the public of the security" and "primary distribution to the public" means,

"trades that are made for the purposes of distributing to the public securities issued by a company and not previously distributed to the public."

If securities previously distributed do not constitute trades to the public, then subsequent trades may still fall within the definition of "primary distribution to the public". Also, a resale restriction scheme on subsequent trades of securities sold under certain exemptions is set up by M. Regs. s. 93.

The N.B.S.F.P.A. requires a prospectus where there is a "primary distribution to the public" and thus it follows the pre-closed system approach with respect to secondary market trading (except where the vendor of the security is a control person — see N.B.S.F.P.A. s. 1 "primary distribution to the public"). Exemptions are provided under N.B.S.F.P.A. s. 13(12) and s. 7.

The N.W.T.S.A., P.E.I.S.A. and Y.S.A. require a prospectus where there is a "trade" in a security. "Trade" is broadly defined along the lines discussed in Chapter 4, Part V. Under the P.E.I.S.A., several types of trades in securities are exempt from the prospectus requirements. However, there are no secondary market disclosure requirements to provide a base of information to support secondary market trading without prospectus type disclosure. Therefore trades in securities must either be supported by prospectus disclosure or must rely on an exemption. See also the exemptions under Yukon Registrar's Order, March 1, 1980.

C. Resale Restrictions

With this concept of the closed system in mind, and the resale restrictions that make it work, one can consider, in somewhat greater detail, how the resale restrictions work.

1. *Deemed Distribution*

The restriction on the resale of securities purchased under an exemption is effected by deeming such a resale to be a "distribution".[21] By deeming the resale to be a "distribution" the resale of the security will be subject to the prospectus requirement.[22] Thus the resale of the securities requires either that a prospectus be provided or that an exemption be relied upon. However, the provisions deeming such resales to be distributions go on to provide that these resales will not be deemed to be distributions if certain conditions are met.

2. *The Conditions for Resale Without a Prospectus or Reliance on an Exemption*

Briefly, the conditions under which a resale of securities previously purchased under an exemption will not be deemed to be a distribution are that (i) the issuer must be a reporting issuer not in default of any requirement of the applicable act or regulations, (ii) the securities have remained within the closed market for a specified minimum period of time (called the "hold period"), and (iii) no unusual effort has been made to prepare the market or create a demand for the securities nor has any extraordinary commission or consideration been paid in respect of the trade.

a. REPORTING ISSUER NOT IN DEFAULT

In order for a security purchased under an exemption to be traded without a prospectus or reliance on another exemption, the

---

[21] See, for example, A.S.A. ss. 109, 109.1, 110 & 111; B.C. Rules ss. 140-43; Nfld.S.A. s. 73(4), (5), (6) & (12); N.S.S.A s. 77(5), (6), (7), (7A), (7B) & (10); O.S.A. s. 72(4), (5) & (6) and Reg. s. 19; Q.S.A. s. 5 "distribution" (3); S.S.A. s. 81(6) & (8).

[22] See Chapter 4.

issuer must be a reporting issuer. Reporting issuers are required to provide continuous disclosure in the form of financial statements, proxy circulars, reports with respect to material information concerning the issuer and insider trading reports.[23] This continuous disclosure provides information which is similar to the kind of information that is provided in a prospectus. Its availability allows the investor, or, more realistically, sophisticated investors, to assess the value of the securities of the issuer. With access to information provided by continuous disclosure that is similar to that which would be contained in a prospectus, a prospectus is considered to be no longer necessary for the protection of investors.

However, if the reporting issuer is in default of a requirement of the Act or regulations, it may mean that some important information is not available to the market. For instance the reporting issuer might be in default of a requirement under the Act or regulations for the filing of a financial statement, proxy circular or material change report. Therefore, some information may be missing which could affect the decision of an investor to buy the security. Thus, either the default would have to be corrected or a prospectus would have to be provided to supply the missing information.

The requirement that the issuer not be in default of any requirement of the Act or regulation is, under the law of some provinces and with respect some exemptions, only a condition if the selling security holder is an "insider" of the issuer,[24] or in some provinces if the selling security holder is in a "special relationship" with the issuer.[25] The reason for so qualifying the condition is that presumably it will only be an "insider", or more generally, a person

---

[23] See Chapter 6.

[24] See, for example, B.C. Rules s. 140(1)(b); Q.S.A. s. 58. S.S.A. ss. 81(7)(b), 8(b) & (10)(b) provide that if the vendor is an "insider", the vendor must have reasonable grounds to believe that the issuer is not in default. For the definition of "insider" see Chapter 6, Part VI.

[25] See, for example, Nfld.S.A. s. 73(15); O. Regs. s. 21. The qualification only applies to exemptions such as those with respect to stock dividends, reorganizations, amalgamations, exchanges of securities by an acquirer for securities of a target in a takeover, tenders on a takeover or issuer bid, to employees or in securities of a company that was formerly a private company. On the meaning of "special relationship" see Chapter 10, Part III A 3. A similar provision in N.S.S.A. s. 77(9) applies with respect to securities exchange takeover bids but says that the vendor must have reasonable grounds to believe that the issuer is not in default.

in a "special relationship" with the issuer, who will have access to information that may not be disclosed to the public as a result of the reporting issuer's default. It will thus only be these persons who, in making a trade, can take advantage of the undisclosed information.

b. THE HOLD PERIOD

Most exemptions are subject to a resale hold period requirement. A security previously purchased under such exemptions cannot be sold without a prospectus or reliance on an exemption unless a specified minimum period of time has elapsed from the later of the time the issuer became a reporting issuer or the time the security was first traded under an exemption.[26] The reporting issuer must be a reporting issuer for a sufficient period of time to allow for a build up of information about the issuer through financial statements, proxy circulars, material change reports and insider trading reports. The issuer may have been a reporting issuer for a sufficient period on the day the security was first traded under an exemption. However, this does not mean the securities can be traded immediately thereafter. The securities must also be held for a sufficient period to allow the investors, especially sophisticated investors, to assess information about the issuer and the security itself. This is why the period during which resales are restricted runs from the later of the time the issuer became a reporting issuer and the time the securities were first traded under an exemption.

The applicable time periods set out in securities acts and regulations are not consistent. For instance, British Columbla has a 12-month hold period that can be reduced to 4 months in certain circumstances.[27] Other provinces require a 6-month period for securities which meet certain conditions.[28] First, the securities must

---

[26] See, for example, A.S.A. s. 109(3); B.C. Rules s. 140(2); Nfld.S.A. s. 73(4); N.S. Regs. s. 132; O.S.A. s. 72(4); Q.S.A. s. 58; S.S.A. s. 81(7). See also M. Regs. s. 93.

[27] See, for example, B.C. Rules ss. 140-43, and B.C. Blanket Order #97/12 and Interim Policy No. 3-27 (see also Blanket Order #97/11 reducing the hold period on Eurobond issues to 40 days); N.S. Regs. s. 132(1). See also M. Regs. s. 93 with respect to a 12-month hold period for certain exemptions in the regulations and under certain conditions.

[28] See, for example, A.S.A. s. 109(3)(a) & (b); Nfld.S.A. s. 73(4)(b)(i) & (ii); O.S.A. s. 72(4)(b)(i) & (ii); S.S.A. 81(7)(c)(i) & (ii). A similar time period applies with respect to "gilt edged" securities under Q.S.A. s. 58.

either be bonds, debentures or other evidences of indebtedness, or preferred shares, or they must be listed and posted for trading on a recognized stock exchange. Second, the securities must comply with certain statutory restrictions on insurance company investments.[29] The concept here is that because these securities are available for institutional investor investments they will tend to be widely traded and closely followed so that less time will be necessary for the assessment of information about the issuer and the particular security.

If the securities do not meet the conditions noted above, but are listed and posted for trading on a recognized stock exchange or are bonds, debentures or other evidences of indebtedness issued or guaranteed by a reporting issuer whose securities are listed on a recognized stock exchange then the hold period is 12 months.[30] In this situation the fact that the securities are not available for investment by institutions, such as insurance companies, suggests that they are not likely to be as closely followed as securities which do qualify for insurance company investment. It may then take a somewhat longer period for the investors to assess the information concerning the issuer and the particular security.

If the securities involved do not meet the conditions set out above, then the securities are likely to be somewhat less widely traded and less closely followed. Consequently, information about the securities may be less quickly disseminated to and assessed by investors. Accordingly, where the securities involved do not meet the condition noted above, the requisite hold period is 18 months instead of 6 or 12 months.[31]

There are some exemptions where the securities involved, given the nature of the exemption, have been trading in the public domain for some time[32] or where prospectus type disclosure is made in the

---

[29]See, for example, the *Insurance Act*, R.S.O. 1990, c. I.8, s. 433(1)(m), (n). See also Q. Regs. s. 3 with respect to "gilt edged" securities under Q.S.A. s. 58.

[30]See, for example, A.S.A. s. 109(3)(c); Nfld.S.A. s. 73(4)(b)(iii); O.S.A. s. 72(4)(b)(iii); S.S.A. s. 81(7)(c)(iii). Under the Q.S.A. the hold period is 12 months for all securities other than "gilt edged" securities — see Q.S.A. s. 58.

[31]See, for example, A.S.A. s. 109(3)(d); Nfld.S.A. s. 73(4)(b)(iv); O.S.A. s. 72(4)(b)(iv); S.S.A. s. 81(7)(c)(iv).

[32]See Part III A 3 a below with respect to stock dividends.

context of the exempt trade.[33] In these circumstances time for the build up of information about the particular security is not necessary. A hold period with respect to the particular security in these cases would not be necessary given that adequate information for trading in the public domain would already be available or would be provided in a document other than a prospectus. Where the security has been trading in the public domain for some time, there should be adequate information about the security itself. It will be sufficient that the issuer has been a reporting issuer for a sufficient period of time to build up information about the issuer. Thus, in these circumstances the hold-period requirement that the issuer has been a reporting issuer for a 12-month period. However, there is no requirement that the hold-period runs 12 months from the date of the issue of the security since information on the security is available in the prospectus type disclosure or in the public market where the security has previously traded.[34]

c. NO UNUSUAL EFFORT TO PREPARE THE MARKET AND NO
   EXTRAORDINARY COMMISSIONS OR CONSIDERATION

A further set of conditions for resale of securities previously purchased under an exemption is that no unusual effort can be made to prepare the market or create a demand for the securities and no extraordinary commission or consideration can be paid in respect of the trade.[35] These conditions are intended to discourage promotional campaigns which might be used to pressure investors into making purchases and in which representations other than those contained in statutorily required disclosure documents might be made.

---

[33] See Part III A 4 a below with respect to the exemption re amalgamations.

[34] See A.S.A. s. 110(1)-(3); B.C. Rules s. 140(2)(a); Nfld.S.A. s. 73(5); N.S.S.A. s. 77(7); O.S.A. s. 72(5); S.S.A. s. 81(8).

[35] See, for example, A.S.A. s. 109(2)(d), (e); B.C. Rules ss. 140(2)(e), (f), 141(g), (h), and 142(2)(h), (i); Nfld.S.A. s. 73(4); N.S.S.A. s. 77(5)(e); O.S.A. s. 72(4); S.S.A. s. 81(7)(f). This is consistent with the waiting period restrictions (Chapter 4, Part VII D), and the blue sky restrictions on prospectus distributions (Chapter 4, Part VII I).

3. *Underlying Market Efficiency Concept*

As noted in Chapter 2, the efficiency of securities markets in allocating financial capital depends on (i) the amount and accuracy of information available, (ii) the speed at which the information is disseminated to and assessed by the market, and (iii) the extent to which that information comes to be reflected in the prices of securities.

Also, as noted in Chapter 3, one of the purposes of securities regulation emanating from the Kimber Report was to promote public confidence in securities markets by providing information to investors for the purpose of assessing risks and returns associated with securities. The regulation thus assumes that the market is not efficient in making adequate information available. However, the resale rules do assume some degree of efficiency in the market with respect to its ability to respond to the information once it is made available. However, the most that is assumed is that the market is relatively weakly efficient. The market is assumed to respond to the information, under the best of conditions, in a period of 6 months. Under conditions less favourable to market efficiency, the period assumed by some provincial regulation is as much as 18 months.

As noted in Chapter 2, the aggregate value of the securities available for trading will affect the potential for profit from trading and thus the potential to recoup the costs of gathering information about the issuer and about the particular security. The greater the potential to recoup the costs of gathering and assessing information, the greater will be the extent and speed with which the market will respond to information. Accordingly, provinces which provide for variations in the hold period take account of the depth of the market for the securities.

III. EXEMPTIONS AND THEIR UNDERLYING PRINCIPLES

With this concept of the closed system and resale restrictions in mind, Part III examines in more detail the exemptions and resale restrictions that make the closed system work. Exemptions from the prospectus requirement are provided in circumstances in which prospectus disclosure combined with civil liability for misrepresentations is considered unnecessary. In general terms the exemptions are provided in circumstances in which the benefit from prospectus disclosure would not be justified given the costs of prospectus disclosure. This part provides a summary of the main exemptions by fitting them into categories which represent bases for the granting of exemptions.

A. No Need To Know

Many of the exemptions from the prospectus requirement can be justified on the basis that investors do not need to know the kind of information that would be contained in a prospectus. They may not need to know because they are sophisticated investors or have common bonds with the issuer. It is also possible that no new information would be provided by the prospectus, or that the information will be provided in documents other than a prospectus.

1. *Sophisticated Investors*

Some investors may be sufficiently sophisticated to gather information and assess the value of a security without the assistance of information provided in a prospectus. Because of this sophistication compared to the average investor, they can better assess whether the cost of obtaining additional information is justified. They may also be in a position to pressure issuers to provide information. They are likely to be better able to assess the risks and returns associated with a security with available — although perhaps more limited — information, than that contained in a prospectus. Forcing issuers to provide information in a prospectus may well impose substantial costs on the sale of the securities to the sophisticated investors without providing much, if any, benefit to the sophisticated investors. Several exemptions could be said to fit in this category.

a. EXEMPT INSTITUTIONS

Distributions of securities to certain specified institutions are exempt from the prospectus requirement.[36] The primary exempt

---

[36] A.S.A. s. 107(1)(a); B.C.S.A. s. 74(2)(1); M.S.A. ss. 58(1)(a) & 19(1)(c); Nfld.S.A. s. 73(1)(a); N.S.S.A. s. 77(1)(a); O.S.A. s. 72(1)(a); P.E.I.S.A. s. 13(1)(a); S.S.A. s. 81(1)(a). See also Q.S.A. ss. 43, 44. See Yukon Registrar's Order, March 1, 1980, ss. 2 , 3 , 22 and N.B.S.F.P.A. s. 13(12) and s. 7(c).

institutional purchasers are banks, trust companies and insurance companies. The Federal Business Development Bank, Her Majesty in Right of Canada or a Province, a municipal corporation, or public board or commission in Canada are also included in the list of exempt institutional purchasers.[37]

Institutions such as banks, trust companies and insurance companies generally have substantial investments and employ large staffs of people trained in financial analysis and investment management. They also tend to purchase securities in large quantities. The purchase of a large quantity puts these investors in the position to demand that the issuer provide information they need to evaluate the investment. It also gives them an incentive to gather other information they feel they need to evaluate the investment. Their investment expertise gives them a capacity to evaluate the information once they have obtained it. Thus the information that would be provided in a prospectus would likely be information they either already have or are not interested in.[38]

The exemption only applies when the exempt institutional purchaser is purchasing as a principal.[39] If the exempt institution was merely acting as an agent for other investors, then the trade in the security might well involve investors who do need to know the kind of information that would be provided in the prospectus.[40]

A subsequent trade by an exempt institution is deemed to be a distribution unless the specified conditions for resale have been

---

[37] Ibid. Both Ontario and Saskatchewan have added credit unions to the list of exempt institutions. See O.S.A. s. 72(1)(a)(i.1); S.S.A. s. 81(1)(a)(iii.1).

[38] With respect to the sophistication of institutional investors as a reason for the exemption, see D. Johnston & K.D. Rockwell, *Canadian Securities Regulation*, (Toronto: Butterworths, 1998) at 118. In D.L. Johnston, *Canadian Securities Regulation*, (Toronto: Butterworths, 1977) at 192 Johnston also notes that the constitutional difficulties which arise when a provincial agency attempts to regulate federally governed institutions, such as banks, may have contributed to the exempting of such institutions from the legislation.

[39] See the provisions cited *supra* note 36.

[40] Trust companies often act as agents in purchasing securities. Therefore they would not be purchasing as principal. However, they are presumably purchasing with an intent to invest on behalf of those they act for and their sophistication should protect the persons on whose behalf they act. Consequently they are deemed to be purchasing as principal when they are purchasing as agent or trustee for accounts that are fully managed by them — A.S.A. s. 107(2)(a); B.C.S.A. s. 74(1)(a); Nfld.S.A. s. 73(2); N.S.S.A. s. 77(2); O.S.A. s. 72(2); Q.S.A. s. 45; S.S.A. s. 81(2)(a).

met.[41] To resell the security without a prospectus or reliance on an exemption the issuer must be a reporting issuer not in default of its reporting obligations and the requisite hold period must have elapsed to assure an adequate base of information about the issuer and the security.[42]

b. EXEMPT PURCHASERS

There may be institutions other than the specified institutions, such as banks, trust companies and insurance companies, which are sophisticated investors by virtue of the investment expertise they employ and the quantities of securities they are inclined to purchase. Such institutions can apply to be designated as exempt purchasers and trades to these exempt purchasers will then be exempt from the prospectus requirement as long as they are purchasing as principal.[43] Because exempt purchaser status depends on the degree of sophistication of the applicant, the factors which are considered include such matters as the size of investment funds managed, and the expertise of the staff employed by the applicant.[44] The resale restriction that applies to exempt institutions, noted above, also applies to exempt purchasers.[45]

c. LARGE PURCHASES

There is an exemption available where the purchaser makes a large purchase.[46] Where a person pays a large amount for securities

---

[41] A.S.A. s. 109; B.C. Rules 140, 142; Nfld.S.A. s. 73(4); N.S.S.A. s. 77(5) and Reg. s. 132(1); O.S.A. s. 72(4); Q.S.A. s. 5 "distribution" (3); S.S.A. s. 81(6) & (7).

[42] Ibid. With respect to the Q.S.A. conditions see s. 58.

[43] A.S.A. s. 107(1)(c); B.C.S.A. s. 74(2), (3); M.S.A. ss. 58(1)(a) & 19(1)(c); Nfld.S.A. s. 73(1)(c); N.S.S.A. s. 77(1)(c); O.S.A. s. 71(1)(c); Q.S.A s. 44(12); S.S.A. s. 81(1)(c).

Portfolio managers are deemed by most securities acts to act as principal when they purchase or sell as agents for accounts that are fully managed by them. See, for example, A.S.A. s. 107(2)(b); B.C.S.A. s. 74(1)(b); N.S.S.A. s. 77(2)(b); Q.S.A. s. 45. This is done for the same reason as with respect to trust companies noted *supra* note 39.

[44] See D. Johnston & K.D. Rockwell, *supra* note 38, at 118.

[45] See the provisions cited *supra* note 41.

[46] A.S.A. s. 107(1)(d); B.C.S.A. s. 74(2), (4) and B.C. Rules s. 129(1); M.S.A. ss. 58(1)(a), 19(3) & M. Regs. s. 90(1); Nfld.S.A. s. 73(1)(d); N.S.S.A. s. 77(1)(d);

it will be worthwhile to the purchaser to incur the cost of gathering and assessing much more information than that person would be willing to gather and assess if the cost of the acquisition were substantially less. The purchaser's willingness to buy a large amount may put them in a position to demand more information from the issuer. Purchasers who are able to make such large volume purchases are more likely to have made other investments and are thus more likely to have investment experience. They are thus likely to be relatively sophisticated investors. They also have a greater incentive to seek investment advice.[47]

A similar separate exemption is provided when the trade involves the issuance of a security as consideration for assets. So long as the person receiving the security is conveying assets with a fair market value of not less than a specified amount the trade will be exempt.[48] The same resale restriction that applies to exempt institutions and exempt purchasers also applies to large purchases.[49]

O.S.A. s. 71(1)(d) (Reg. s. 32 re contractual right of action in offering memorandum); P.E.I.S.A. s. 13(1)(c); Q.S.A. s. 51; S.S.A. s. 81(1)(d). The level at which a satisfactory degree of sophistication is said to occur is currently deemed to be $97,000. However, some provinces have increased the amount to $150,000. See Nfld. Regs. s. 19 ($100,000); N.S.S.A. s. 77(1)(d) ($150,000); O. Regs. s. 27(1) ($150,000); S.S.A. s. 81(1)(d) ($150,000).

An offering memorandum is required where there is advertising in connection with a distribution under the large purchase exemption — see A. Regs. s. 125; B.C. Rules s. 134(2); Nfld.S.A. s. 73(11); N.S.S.A. s. 77(1)(d); O. Regs. s. 32(2); Q.S.A. s. 51; S. Regs. s. 102(1). See the discussion of offering memoranda under the heading "g. Other Sophisticated Investors" in this chapter.

For a local policy statement on the application of this exemption and its connection to other exemptions, see, for example, O. Pol. 6.1.

[47] Although the exemption might be justified on the grounds noted, it is noteworthy that the Merger Report, *supra* note 3, at 63, para. 5.12, said that this exemption,

"was added to the Act to overcome a reluctance on the part of large sources of capital within Canada and elsewhere which apparently could not be persuaded to apply for the 'exempt purchaser' status."

[48] A.S.A. s. 107(1)(l) ($100,000); B.C.S.A. s. 74(2), (5) ($100,000 Rule s. 129(2)); Nfld.S.A. s. 73(1)(l) ($100,000 Reg. s. 20); N.S.S.A. s. 77(1)(l) ($150,000 Reg. s. 128(1)(d)); O.S.A. s. 72(1)(l) ($150,000 Reg. s. 28); S.S.A. s. 81(1)(m) ($150,000). See also P.E.I.S.A. s. 13(1)(g).

[49] See the provisions cited *supra* note 41.

d. REGISTERED DEALERS

A trade made from one registered dealer to another registered dealer is also exempt as long as the registered dealer making the purchase is acting as principal.[50] Registered dealers must have a designated partner, director or officer who has passed certain specified courses dealing with securities and the securities industry and have a specified amount of previous experience in the securities business. Thus they have a degree of investment sophistication.[51]

Registered dealers relying on the exemption are, of course, not allowed to resell to the investing public without meeting the resale hold period requirements. Thus this trade is subject to the same resale restrictions that apply to exempt institutions and exempt purchasers.[52]

e. SALE TO UNDERWRITERS

Sales made by a person to an underwriter who acts as purchaser or by one underwriter to another underwriter are also exempt.[53] Such trades may be common in the distribution of the securities.[54] For instance, in a bought deal the underwriter would purchase the securities from the issuer. The underwriter would then sell the securities to another underwriter in an underwriting syndicate or to an underwriter who is a member of a banking group. Similarly, the requirements of a standby underwriting may lead to an underwriter purchasing securities from an issuer which the underwriter agreed to take up on a standby basis. That underwriter may then sell the securities to other underwriters in an underwriting syndicate or banking group who also agreed to take up securities on a standby basis.[55]

---

[50] A.S.A. s. 107(1)(u); B.C.S.A. s. 74(2), (6); M.S.A. s. 58(1)(c); Nfld.S.A. s. 73(1)(q); N.S.S.A. s. 77(1)(q); O.S.A. s. 72(1)(q); Q.S.A. ss. 43, 44(9); S.S.A. s. 81(1)(t).

[51] With respect to sophistication as a reason for this exemption see Johnston, *supra* note 38, at 201.

[52] See the provisions cited *supra* note 41.

[53] A.S.A. s. 107(1)(u.1); B.C.S.A. s. 74(2), (15); M.S.A. ss. 58(1)(b) & 19(1)(f); Nfld.S.A. s. 73(1)(r); N.S.S.A. s. 77(1)(r); O.S.A. s. 72(1)(r); Q.S.A. ss. 43, 44(9); S.S.A. s. 81(1)(u). See also Yukon Registrar's Order, March 1, 1980, s. 4.

[54] See Chapter 1, Part IV.

[55] See Johnston & Rockwell, *supra* note 38, at 121.

Persons registered to carry on business as underwriters tend to have a considerable degree of expertise and experience in the securities business. When they commit themselves to buy an issue or do a standby underwriting they put their business and their reputation at risk. They they have a strong incentive to investigate the issuer and assess the value of the security being offered. In short, they are sophisticated investors.[56]

Trades by a person to an underwriter, or by one underwriter to another, usually occur in the context of a distribution of securities to the investing public under a prospectus. The exemption should not allow the distribution to proceed without a prospectus through resales of securities by underwriters. Any resale by the underwriter is deemed to be a distribution without recourse to any resale after meeting such requirements as a hold period and reporting by the issuer.[57]

f. CONSIDERATION TO DEALERS OR UNDERWRITERS

A similar exemption is provided for a trade in a security by an issuer to a registered dealer or registered underwriter as consideration for services performed by the dealer or underwriter in connection with the distribution of securities of the issuer.[58] As noted above, registered dealers and underwriters are involved in the securities business and are presumed to have sufficient investment expertise and experience to assess the value of the securities without the information contained in a prospectus or the protection of the statutory civil liability provision. Registered dealers or underwriters are allowed to resell the securities without a prospectus or reliance on an exemption if they meet the same resale restrictions as noted above with respect to exempt institutions.[59]

---

[56] Ibid.

[57] See, for example, A.S.A. s. 111(1); B.C. Rules s. 142(4); Nfld.S.A. s. 73(6); N.S.S.A. s. 77(10)(a); O.S.A. s. 72(6); S.S.A. s. 2(1)(r)(vi). See Yukon Registrar's Order, March 1, 1980, s. 22.

[58] A.S.A. s. 107(1)(z.1) & Reg. s. 122(b); B.C.S.A. s. 74(2), (23); N.S. Regs. s. 127(f); S.S.A. s. 81(1)(v). See also Q.S.A. ss. 43, 44(9).

[59] See, for example, A. Regs. s. 126(1); B.C. Rules s. 142; N.S. Regs. s. 127(2); S.S.A. s. 81(6).

g. OTHER SOPHISTICATED INVESTORS

There are other exemptions which can be justified in part on the basis that the investors are at least somewhat sophisticated. For example, most provincial securities acts provide an exemption for sales to persons who meet a test of sophistication usually based on the person's net worth and investment experience or on advice from a registered dealer.[60] The test of sophistication serves as some evidence that the investor does not need the protection of the information contained in the prospectus coupled with the civil liability sanction for misrepresentations.

However, the drafters of these provisions were apparently of the view that these tests were insufficient to completely relieve the investor of the need for protection because the provision also requires that the purchaser be provided an offering memorandum.[61] While the offering memorandum is less comprehensive than the prospectus, it provides information similar to that contained in the prospectus.[62] The offering memorandum must also provide the investor with a right to rescission or damages against the issuer or vendor[63] which "reasonably corresponds" to the civil right of action provided

---

[60] See, for example, A.S.A. s. 107(1)(p) & (q) [with a definition of "sophisticated purchaser" in Reg. s. 1(1)(j)]; B.C. Rules s. 128(a), (b) [with a definition of "sophisticated purchasers" in Rules s. 1]; M. Reg. s. 91(a) & (b) and Forms 24 & 25; Nfld.S.A. s. 73(1)(p); N.S.S.A. s. 77(1)(p) [and s. 77(1)(w) with respect to "government incentive security" defined in s. 2(1)(p)]; O.S.A. s. 72(1)(p) [see also Reg. s. 14(f) with respect to "government incentive securities" (defined in Reg. s. 16(2)); and O. Pol. 6.1]; P.E.I.S.A. s. 13(1)(i); Q.S.A. ss. 47, 48; S.S.A. s. 81(1)(s).

Regulations under the B.C.S.A. also provide an exemption where a trade is made by an issuer in a security of its own issue where the purchaser purchases as principal, is a "sophisticated purchaser" and where the aggregate acquisition cost is at least $25,000 [Rules s. 128(b)].

[61] A.S.A. s. 107(1)(p)(iii) & (q)(iii) & Form 43; B.C. Rules s. 128(a)(vi), 128(b)(iv) & Form 43; M. Regs. s. 91(b)(iii) & Form 26; Nfld.S.A. s. 73(1)(p) and 73(22); N.S.S.A. s. 77(1)(p)(v); O. Regs. s. 32(3) [required where the seller is the issuer, an affiliate of the issuer, a control person, or an underwriter]; Q.S.A. s. 47; S.S.A. s. 81(1)(s)(ix).

[62] See, for example, Alta. Form 43; B.C. Form 43; Man. Form 26; N.S. Reg. s. 126.

[63] Note that the contractual right of action is limited to an action against the issuer or vendor and does not extend to other persons who may have been responsible for misrepresentations in the offering memorandum.

by the statute with respect to misrepresentations in a prospectus.[64] However, the offering memorandum is not vetted with the relevant securities commission. Consequently, it can be a less time-consuming and less administratively costly means of distributing securities. Thus the weaker test of sophistication was considered sufficient for a less rigorous scheme of investor protection than that provided by the prospectus clearance process, but not sufficient to avoid the need for at least some investor protection.

The offering of a security under this exemption is not to be accompanied by advertisement nor are promotional expenses to be incurred in connection with the offer.[65] This discourages sales hype and representations other than those made in the offering memorandum and thus covered by the contractual right of action which corresponds to the statutory right of action.

Each purchaser must purchase as principal.[66] This requirement attempts to preclude the use of the exemption as a way to make a broader distribution through a "sophisticated purchaser" acting on behalf of other unsophisticated purchasers.

The number of purchasers must not be more than a specified number.[67] These sophisticated purchaser exemptions vary from

---

[64] A. Regs. s. 127 and Form 43, Item 20; B.C. Rules s. 133(b); M. Regs. s. 91(b)(iii) & Form 26, Item 12 (applies to every person or company who signed the certificates required in the offering memorandum); Nfld.S.A. s. 73(22); N.S.S.A. s. 65(3); O. Reg. s. 32; S.S.A. s. 138. See also Q.S.A. s. 221.

[65] A.S.A. s. 107(1)(p)(v) & (vi) and (q)(v) & (vi); B.C. Rules s. 128(a)(v); with respect to Manitoba this proviso applies to the 15 purchaser exemption in M.Reg. s. 91(a) but not to the 50 purchaser exemption in M.Reg. s. 91(b); Nfld.S.A. s. 73(1)(p)(iii); N.S.S.A. s. 77(1)(p)(iii) [and s. 77(1)(w)(iii) re government incentive securities]; O.S.A. s. 72(1)(p)(iii) [see also Reg. s. 14(f)(iii) re government incentive securities and O. Pol. 6.1]; Q.S.A. s. 47(5); S.S.A. s. 81(1)(s)(vi) & (vii).

[66] A.S.A. s. 107(1)(p)(iv)(A) and (q)(iv)(A); B.C. Rules s. 128(a)(iv); Man. Form 25, para. 2; Nfld.S.A. s. 73(1)(p)(i); N.S.S.A. s. 77(1)(p)(i); O.S.A. s. 72(1)(p)(i); Q.S.A s. 47(1); S.S.A. s. 81(1)(s)(ii).

[67] A.S.A. s. 107(1)(p)(i) & (q)(i) (50 purchasers); B.C. Rules s. 128(a) (50 purchasers); M.Reg. s. 91(a) (15 purchasers) and s. 91(b) (50 purchasers); Nfld.S.A. s. 73(1)(p) (25 purchasers); N.S.S.A. s. 77(1)(p) (25 purchasers) [and 50 purchasers with respect to government incentive securities per s. 77(1)(w)]; O.S.A. s. 72(1)(p) (25 purchasers) [and 50 purchasers with respect to government incentive securities per Reg. s. 14(f) — see also O. Pol. 6.1]; Q.S.A. s. 47 (25 subscribers) [and 50 subscribers with respect to tax shelter securities per s. 48]; S.S.A. s. 81(1)(s) (in Saskatchewan, the limit is a cumulative amount raised under the exemption of up to $1,000,000 instead of a limit on the number of purchasers).

province to province and some have the additional qualification that solicitations are not to be made to more than a specified number of persons.[68] Limits on the number of persons solicited and on the number of ultimate purchasers limits the scale of potential investor loss and its consequent effect on confidence in the market. Also, where the number of persons solicited and the number of ultimate purchasers is limited, the costs associated with clearing a prospectus may not be justified.

To prevent sales to a broader group of persons who are presumed to need the full protection of securities acts, resales of securities purchased under these exemptions are subject to the same resale restrictions that apply to exempt institutions.[69]

2. Common Bonds

Often investors will have no need to know the kind of information contained in a prospectus, or need the withdrawal rights or civil liability protection provided by the Act, because they have common bonds with the issuer. Persons who have common bonds with the issuer are either in a position of having access to information concerning the issuer (and perhaps also some control over decisions of the issuer) or have some relationship to the issuer which reduces the need for protection of the investor.

a. INCORPORATORS AND PROMOTERS

Promoters are persons who take the preliminary steps in the organization of a business venture or in the procurement of financing for the business.[70] Thus promoters usually have an intimate

---

[68] See Nfld.S.A. s. 73(1)(p) (solicitations to no more than 50 persons); N.S.S.A. s. 77(1)(p) (solicitations to no more than 50 persons) [and no more than 75 persons with respect to government incentive securities]; O.S.A. s. 72(1)(p) (solicitations to no more than 50 persons) [and to no more than 75 persons with respect to government incentive securities].

[69] A.S.A. s. 109; B.C. Rules 140, 142; M. Regs. s. 93 provides a hold period with respect to resales of securities purchased under the related persons and sophisticated purchasers exemptions in s. 91 of the regulations; Nfld.S.A. s. 73(4); N.S.S.A. s. 77(5); O.S.A. s. 72(4); S.S.A. s. 81(6), (7). See also Q.S.A. s. 58.

[70] "Promoter" is generally defined in the securities acts as a person who, alone or in concert with other persons, takes the initiative in founding, organizing or substantially reorganizing the business of the issuer or receives, directly or indi-

knowledge of the business and a say in decisions made with respect to the business. They would tend to know the kind of information that would be provided in a prospectus and if a prospectus were issued, they would probably be aware of any material misrepresentations in the prospectus. Thus the cost of preparing a prospectus and providing protection through withdrawal rights and statutory civil liability seems unnecessary in the case of promoters. Accordingly, an exemption is provided where a trade is made by an issuer in a security of its own issue to a promoter of the issuer.[71] An exemption is also provided where the trade is made by a promoter of an issuer, in a security of the issuer, to another promoter.[72]

A similar exemption is provided with respect to incorporators where the trade is considered reasonably necessary to facilitate the incorporation or organization of the issuer.[73] This exemption is limited to a nominal consideration and only five incorporators.[74] The exemption facilitates the organization of the company, which might not otherwise occur if the cost of producing a prospectus was imposed. Facilitating the formation of the company allows it to then raise capital through further issuances of securities which would normally be subject to the prospectus requirement. Usually the incorporators will be persons who are closely connected with the company and thus have access to the kind of information that would be provided in a prospectus. Where the incorporators do not have the protection of common bonds with the issuer, the requirement of only a nominal consideration protects against the downside risk to which the incorporators are exposed.

---

rectly, in connection with a founding, organization or substantial reorganization, 10% or more of a class of the issuer's securities or 10% or more of the proceeds from the sale of a class of the issuer's securities as consideration for services or property or both. However, it does not include commissions for underwriting or property where the person does not otherwise take part in the founding, organizing, or substantial reorganizing of the business. See, for example, B.C.S.A. s. 1(1) "promoter"; O.S.A. s. 1(1) "promoter".

[71] See, for example, A.S.A. s. 107(1)(w); B.C.S.A. s. 74(2)(16); N.S.S.A. s. 77(1)(t); O. Regs. s. 14(c); S.S.A. s. 81(1)(q).

[72] Ibid.

[73] See, for example, A.S.A. s. 107(1)(o); B.C.S.A. s. 74(2), (14); Nfld.S.A. s. 73(1)(o); N.S.S.A. s. 77(1)(o); O.S.A. s. 72(1)(o); S.S.A. s. 81(1)(p). Q.S.A. s. 54 provides an exemption that might be relied on with respect to incorporators.

[74] Ibid. However, an exception is made if the laws of the jurisdiction in which the company is incorporated require a greater number of incorporators or a greater consideration. Under the A.S.A. the limit on the number of incorporators is 15.

Because promoters, and often incorporators, tend to have an intimate knowledge of the business and are involved in procuring financing for the business, they may have access to information about the issuer that is not generally available. Even where the information is available through continuous disclosure filings, the investor will not have the protection of statutory civil liability for misrepresentations. Thus, to provide any missing material information and statutory liability for misrepresentations, resales of securities by promoters or incorporators are deemed distributions subject, in the case of some jurisdictions, to being free of the prospectus requirement if a resale hold period has passed.[75] Thus, where no resale hold period has been provided for, or where a requisite resale hold period has not passed, the promoter must either produce a prospectus or sell under an exemption.

b. CONTROL PERSONS

A "control person" is usually defined as a person who holds a sufficient number of the voting rights attached to voting securities of the issuer to materially affect the control of the issuer.[76] It also includes any combination of persons who jointly exercise voting rights attached to voting securities of the issuer sufficient to materially affect the control of the issuer.[77] Holding, or jointly exercising, more than 20% of the voting rights is usually deemed, in the absence of evidence to the contrary, to be sufficient to materially affect the control of the issuer.[78] Control persons have control over the business decisions of the issuer. They will either run the business themselves or the business will be run by their nominees. Thus they will tend to have access to information concerning the business. Consequently control persons do not need the protection of the Act. An exemption is provided where one control person sells securities

---

[75] A.S.A. ss. 111 and 112(5); B.C. Rules ss. 140, 142(2); Nfld.S.A. s. 73(6); N.S.S.A. s. 77(10); O.S.A. s. 72(6); O. Regs. s. 19(1); S.S.A. s. 81(10). With respect to the Q.S.A. see s. 54 in conjunction with ss. 57-63 and the definition of "distribution" in s. 5 "distribution" (6).

[76] A.S.A. s. 1(c.2); B.C.S.A. s. 1(1) "control person"; Nfld.S.A. s. 2(1)(l)(iii); N.S.S.A. s. 2(1)(l)(iii); O.S.A. s. 1(1) "distribution" (c); P.E.I.S.A. s. 1(b.1)(iii); S.S.A. s. 2(1)(k).

[77] Ibid.

[78] Ibid.

of the issuer (which they control) to another control person of the issuer.[79]

Control persons, because of their ability to exercise control over the issuer, may have access to information that is not generally available. Their trades may also have a significant effect on the value of the securities. Even where information is available through continuous disclosure, it will not be subject to statutory civil liability for misrepresentations. To assure the information is provided with the support of statutory civil liability before the trade occurs, trades by control persons are defined to be distributions.[80] Thus sales by a control person, whether that control person bought from another control person or otherwise, will require a prospectus or reliance on a prospectus exemption. A prospectus exemption for control persons is provided if they meet certain conditions that assure there is adequate disclosure to the public of information about the issuer and about the proposed transaction by the control person.[81]

c. PURCHASE OR REDEMPTION

Where the issuer purchases securities of its own issue or exercises a right to repurchase securities of its own issue from security holders, the trade is exempt.[82] The issuer, through the persons who

---

[79] A.S.A. s. 107(1)(v); B.C.S.A. s. 74(2), (17); N.S.S.A. s. 77(1)(s); O. Regs. s. 14(b)(i); S.S.A. s. 81(1)(r).

[80] A.S.A. s. 1(f)(iii); B.C.S.A. s. 1(1) "distribution" (c); Nfld.S.A. s. 2(1)(l)(iii); N.S.S.A. s. 2(1)(l)(iii); O.S.A. s. 1(1) "distribution" (c); S.S.A. s. 2(1)(r)(iii). See also M.S.A. s. 1(1) "distribution" (b).

[81] The exemptions for control persons vary from province to province. In Ontario, an exemption is provided if the issuer has been a reporting issuer for 18 months, the control person files a notice of intention to sell at least 7 days, and no more than 14 days, in advance of the trade, the control person certifies that they have no knowledge of any material change that has occurred in the affairs of the issuer which has not been generally disclosed nor has any knowledge of any other material adverse information with respect to the current and prospective operations of the issuer which has not been generally disclosed and there is no unusual effort to prepare the market or create a demand for the securities and no extraordinary commission or other consideration is paid in respect of such trade. See, for example, O.S.A. s. 72(7)(b); B.C. Rules 128(d).

[82] A.S.A. s. 107(1)(m.1); B.C.S.A. s. 74(2), (27); N.S. Regs. s. 127(b); O. Regs. s. 14(b)(ii); S.S.A. s. 81(1)(1). Normally the transaction with the issuer would only constitute a distribution where the vendor is a "control person" such that the trade would be a "distribution" (see e.g. O.S.A. s. 1(1)) or where the trade is deemed

manage the issuer, have access to information about the business of the issuer and therefore do not need the protection of securities acts.

As with promoters and control persons there is a concern that the issuer will have access to information that is not generally available and will not be subject to statutory civil liability, for misrepresentations in continuous disclosure documents. To assure disclosure subject to statutory civil liability, a trade by the issuer in securities previously repurchased by it is defined to be a distribution.[83] Thus a resale by the issuer of securities repurchased or redeemed will require a prospectus or prospectus exemption. No right to resell after a prescribed hold period is given, since this might result in a trade on the basis of information either not yet disclosed or contained in continuous disclosure documents without the protection of statutory civil liability which might be appropriate where the vendor is the issuer.

d. FRIENDS AND RELATIVES

An exemption is available where the purchaser is a spouse, parent, brother, sister or child of a senior officer or director of the issuer, or of an affiliate of the issuer, or where the purchaser is a company whose voting securities are beneficially owned by one or more of the spouse, parent, brother, sister or child of a senior officer or director of the issuer or of an affiliate of the issuer.[84] Consistent

---

to be a "distribution" by virtue of the resale restrictions where the securities were sold under a prospectus exemption.

With respect to the Q.S.A. the definition of "distribution" (s. 5) does not cover such trades. Similarly, with respect to the M.S.A. such a trade would not be a "primary distribution to the public" as that term is defined in s. 1(1).

Purchases by issuers of securities of their own issue are regulated under provisions with respect to "issuer bids" — see Chapter 11.

[83] A.S.A. s. 1(f)(ii); B.C.S.A. s. 1(1) "distribution" (b); Nfld.S.A. s. 2(1)(l); N.S.S.A s. 2(1)(l)(ii); O.S.A. s. 1(1) "distribution" (b); S.S.A. s. 2(1)(r)(ii). See also Q.S.A. s. 5 "distribution" (1).

[84] A.S.A. s. 107(1)(p) & (q); B.C. Rules s. 128(a); M. Regs. s. 89 "related purchaser" and s. 91(a) & (b); Nfld.S.A. s. 73(1)(p); N.S.S.A. s. 77(1)(p) [and s. 77(1)(w) with respect to government incentive securities]; O.S.A. s. 72(1)(p) [see also Reg. s. 14(f) with respect to government incentive securities and O. Pol. 6.1]; P.E.I.S.A. s. 13(1)(i); S.S.A. s. 81(1)(z). An exemption of a similar nature is provided in Q.S.A. s. 47.

with the notion behind the common bonds test, the apparent presumption is that the senior officer or director of an issuer, or of an affiliate of an issuer, will see to it that a close relative will not be taken advantage of by the issuer. The senior officer or director is apparently presumed to have sufficient access to information about the issuer, or involvement in the business decisions of the issuer to protect a close relative.[85]

This exemption is provided in conjunction with the exemption for a limited number of sophisticated purchasers discussed above.[86] Thus there is a specified limit on the number of purchasers, and sometimes also a specified limit on the number of persons that can be solicited.[87] The purchasers must purchase as principal and the offer of the securities is not to be accompanied by advertisement or the incurrence of promotional expenses.[88] The degree of protection provided by the close relative's common bond with the issuer is not considered sufficient to eliminate the need for some protection. Disclosure of information similar to that contained in a prospectus must be provided to the purchaser and the purchaser must be given rights substantially similar to the statutory civil right of action for misrepresentations in a prospectus.[89]

To prevent resale of the securities to a broader group of persons presumed to be in need of protection, these trades are subject to the same restrictions on resale as exempt institutions.[90]

3. No New Information

In the case of some trades in securities, investors do not need to know the kind of information that would be contained in a prospectus because the information is already available and disseminated in the marketplace.

---

[85] As Johnston, *supra* note 38, notes, at 222, this exemption borrows from the U.S. experience with "non-public" offerings and "is a cryptic statutory crystallization" of the jurisprudence on the concept of "public". Thus it is based on the concepts of "need to know" and "common bonds" — see *supra* Part II.

[86] See Part III A 1 g.

[87] See *supra* notes 67 and 68.

[88] See *supra* notes 65 and 66.

[89] See *supra* notes 61-64.

[90] A.S.A. s. 109; B.C. Rules 140, 142; M. Regs. s. 93; Nfld.S.A. s. 73(4); N.S.S.A. s. 77(5); O.S.A. s. 72(4); S.S.A. s. 81(6), (7). See also Q.S.A. s. 58.

a. STOCK DIVIDEND

One situation in which a prospectus would provide no new information is a stock dividend. A stock dividend, discussed in Chapter 1 above, is a dividend paid by the distribution of additional stock rather than cash. Where the issuer has distributed securities under a prospectus and has thereafter met its continuous disclosure obligations, or has otherwise met continuous disclosure obligations for a substantial period of time, the prospectus would provide no new information about the issuer or the particular security. Indeed, the owner of the security to whom the stock dividend would go would have already purchased the security with the benefit of either the information contained in the prospectus or continuous disclosure documents. Having access to the information, or having purchased the stock at a price based on the available information, there would be no benefit in replicating the information in a new prospectus.[91] Doing so would involve an unnecessary and wasteful cost. Thus an exemption is provided where the distribution of the security is simply a stock dividend.[92]

A stock dividend might also be paid to persons who purchased the shares under an exemption. These persons were exempt either because they did not need to know the information or they were given information similar to that contained in a prospectus in the form of an offering memorandum or other disclosure document. Consequently, there would be no need to provide information in a prospectus on a further distribution of the same security through a stock dividend. However, as for shares purchased under the original exemption, shares received pursuant to a stock dividend

---

[91] See Johnston, *supra* note 38, at 203-4; V.P. Alboini, *Securities Law and Practice*, 2d ed. (Toronto: Carswell, 1984) at 17-32 to 17-33, and the *Merger Report, supra* note 3, at para. 8.06, with respect to this reason for the exemption.

[92] A.S.A. s. 107(1)(f)(i); B.C.S.A. s. 74(2)(11)(i); M.S.A. ss. 58(1)(a) & 19(1)(h)(i); Nfld.S.A. s. 73(1)(f)(i); N.S.S.A. s. 77(1)(f)(i); O.S.A. s. 72(1)(f)(i); P.E.I.S.A. s. 13(1)(e)(i); S.S.A. s. 81(1)(f)(i). See also Yukon Registrar's Order March 1, 1980, s. 5 and see N.B.S.F.P.A. s. 13(12) and s. 7(e). The exemption also applies, for similar reasons, to other distributions out of earnings or surplus. To discourage promotional schemes and representations other than those contained in the statutorily required disclosure documents, the exemption provides that "no commission or other remuneration is paid or given to others in respect of such distribution except for ministerial or professional services or services performed by a registered dealer". See also Q.S.A. s. 52(2) for a similar exemption.

should be subject to restrictions on resale. Accordingly, there is a resale restriction on the sale of shares received under the stock dividend exemption that is designed to assure that a substantial base of information is available in the market before the shares can be freely traded.[93]

b. DIVIDENDS OR INTEREST USED TO PURCHASE PUBLICLY TRADED SECURITIES

Occasionally plans are made available to security holders that permit them to direct that cash dividends or interest they would be entitled to receive be reinvested in securities of the issuer. Where these securities are publicly traded, with the support of continuous disclosure, information about these securities would already be publicly available and market prices would presumably be based on this information. Securities distributed under these plans would not be major issues intended to finance new business ventures. Thus there would generally be no new material information about the purpose for which the proceeds of the issue would be used. The issuance also would not be determined by the issuer thus alleviating the concern that the issuer may be issuing securities on the basis of undisclosed information indicating that the securities are currently overvalued on the market. There is thus no new information and no pressing need for prospectus disclosure.

The relative dollar value of dividend or interest reinvestment is likely to be small, thereby minimizing the extent of potential loss to the investor. The costs associated with preparing and vetting a prospectus in these circumstances seems unnecessary given the nominal benefit that prospectus disclosure would provide. Thus, there is an exemption where a trade is made by an issuer, in a security of its own issue, under a plan that permits a person, who already holds a security of the issuer, to direct that dividends or interest payable to that person be applied to the purchase of securities of the issuer.[94] The securities of the issuer sold under the exemption must either be publicly traded securities of its own issue or other securities of the issuer that are redeemable at the option

---

[93] A.S.A. s. 110; B.C. Rules ss. 140, 142(3); Nfld.S.A. s. 73(5); N.S.S.A. s. 77(7); O.S.A. s. 72(5); S.S.A. s. 81(8). See also Q.S.A. s. 61.

[94] A.S.A. s. 107(1)(x); B.C.S.A. s. 74(2), (10); N.S.S.A. s. 77(1)(v); Ont. Rule 45-502, para. 2.1; S.S.A. s. 81(1)(cc). See also Q.S.A. s. 52(2).

of the holder of the security. There is an applicable resale restriction that requires that the issuer is a reporting issuer not in default and has been so for a prescribed period of time.[95]

c. RIGHTS OFFERING

There is an exemption for a rights offering.[96] A rights offering, discussed in Chapter 1 above, provides an existing security holder with the right to buy additional securities of the issuer. If the securities are publicly traded as a result of an original distribution under a prospectus or the satisfaction of the requisite resale restriction applicable to an exempt distribution, then there will be a base of information available in the market concerning the securities being offered in the rights offering. Thus there would be little benefit in terms of investor protection in producing the kind of information contained in a prospectus. The risk to the investor in a rights offering would also normally be mitigated to some extent by the usual practice of offering the securities at a discount to the prevailing market price.[97] Thus the cost of producing the prospectus for a rights offering does not seem justified and might substantially deter the use of a rights offering as a method of distributing securities that can reduce the cost of promoting an issue of additional securities of a type that has been previously issued.

A rights offering could be made to security holders who originally purchased the security under an exemption. Thus, it may be the case that there is no outstanding prospectus with respect to the particular security and there may not be an adequate base of information for the securities to become free trading. Consequently, the exemption is subject to a resale restriction which provides for a hold

---

[95] A.S.A. s. 110(3); B.C. Rules ss. 140, 142(3); N.S.S.A. s. 77(7); Ont. Rule 45-502, para. 4.1; S.S.A. s. 81(8). See also Q.S.A. s. 61.

[96] A.S.A. s. 107(1)(h); B.C.S.A. s. 74(2), (7); M.S.A. ss. 58(1)(b) & 19(1)(i); Nfld.S.A. s. 73(1)(h); N.S.S.A. s. 77(1)(h); O.S.A. s. 72(1)(h); S.S.A. s. 81(1)(h). See also Q.S.A. s. 52(1). See Yukon Registrar's Order, March 1, 1980, s. 5 and see N.B.S.F.P.A. s. 13(12) and s. 7(g).

[97] On this point see Ont. Pol. 6.2, VI, 1., which notes that it will be considered not to be in the public interest to allow a rights offering at or above market price, especially where it may discourage some investors from exercising their rights and have the effect of allowing some persons to increase their proportionate interest in the securities of the issuer.

period to ensure an adequate base of information to support public trading in the security.[98]

There may be circumstances in which there is new information that should be provided to security holders. Rights offerings are usually done to raise new funds for investment. Thus the use of the proceeds of the issue may be an important piece of new information. The more significant the proceeds of the issue are, relative to the total assets of the issue, the greater will be the significance of information concerning the proceeds.[99] There may be other information concerning the nature and conditions of the rights offering that may be very significant to the investor. To deal with situations in which there is potentially significant new information that should be known to the investor, or made available in the market, the exemption carries the qualification that the issuer must give notice to the commission of such information as the date, amount, nature and conditions of the proposed trade and the approximate proceeds to be derived by the issuer.[100] The commission then has the right to inform the issuer, usually within ten days, of any objection to the trade.[101]

d. EXERCISE OF CONVERSION, EXCHANGE OR PURCHASE RIGHTS

An exemption is provided where a trade is made by an issuer in a security of its own issue that occurs as a consequence of the exercise by the holder of a right to either purchase securities of the issuer (such as a right under a rights offering), or to convert or exchange a security already held for another security of the issuer (such as a conversion right attached to a bond or debenture).[102]

---

[98] A.S.A. s. 110(3); B.C. Rules ss. 140, 142(3); Nfld.S.A. s. 73(12); N.S.S.A. s. 77(7); O. Regs. s. 19(4); S.S.A. s. 81(8). See also Q.S.A. s. 61.

[99] On this point see O. Pol. 6.2, III, 3., in which it is noted that the Director under the Ontario *Securities Act* will object to a proposed offering if it would result in an increase of more than 25 per cent in the number of outstanding securities of the class to be issued upon the exercise of the rights.

[100] See the provisions cited *supra* note 96. See also Uniform Policy 2-05 with respect to the kind of information required.

[101] See the provisions cited *supra* note 96.

[102] A.S.A. s. 107(1)(f)(iii); B.C.S.A. s. 74(2)(11)(iii); M.S.A. ss. 58(1)(a) and 19(1)(b)(iii); Nfld.S.A. s. 73(1)(f)(iii); N.S.S.A. s. 77(1)(f)(iii); O.S.A. s. 72(1)(f)(iii); P.E.I.S.A. s. 13(1)(e)(iii); S.S.A. s. 81(1)(f)(iii). See also Q.S.A. s. 52(1).

The rights being exercised must be in accordance with the terms and conditions of a previously issued security of the issuer.

If the securities providing the right were previously issued under a prospectus, then a base of information about the issuer and about the security being purchased, or received in conversion or exchange, should be available in the market. Therefore, there is no need for the information to be reiterated in a new prospectus. The cost of the prospectus would not be justified and would likely preclude the use of such purchase or conversion rights if the issuer had to provide a prospectus every time such rights were exercised.

The availability of information in the market should provide a degree of protection to the investor in deciding whether to exercise the right unless the investor is goaded into exercising the right. This latter possibility is discouraged by the requirement that the exemption is only available as long as no commission or other remuneration is paid in respect of the trade, except for administrative or professional services or for services performed by a registered dealer.

4. Information Provided by Documents Other Than a Prospectus

In some situations there is no need to know the information that would be provided in a prospectus because similar information will be provided in other documents.

a. AMALGAMATIONS AND REORGANIZATIONS

For instance, where a security of an issuer is provided in an exchange with another issuer, or security holders of another issuer, in connection with an amalgamation, merger, reorganization or arrangement, the trade is exempt from the requirement to produce a prospectus as long as an information circular, proxy statement or similar disclosure document is provided and the applicable shareholder approval of the transaction is obtained.[103] The information circular required for the shareholder meeting will cover much the same information as would be provided in a prospectus.

---

[103] A.S.A. s. 107(1)(i); B.C.S.A. s. 74(2), (8); M.S.A. s. 58(1)(a) and 19(1)(j); Nfld.S.A. s. 73(1)(i); N.S.S.A. s. 77(1)(i); O.S.A. s. 72(1)(i); S.S.A. s. 81(1)(i). See also Q.S.A. s. 50. See Yukon Registrar's Order, March 1, 1980, s. 6 and see N.B.S.F.P.A. s. 13(12) and s. 7(h).

It could be the case that the issuer of the security traded under this exemption is not a reporting issuer. Since no prospectus would be provided as a consequence of the exemption, the issuer would not become a reporting issuer by making the exempt trade. Without the continuous disclosure that would be required of a reporting issuer, there might not be adequate disclosure to support public trading. To assure an adequate base of continuous disclosure before public trading is allowed to occur there is a resale restriction that deems any subsequent sales to be distributions unless the issuer has been a reporting issuer not in default for a prescribed period.[104]

b. TAKEOVER BIDS

An exemption is provided where an offeror in a takeover bid offers securities of its own issue in exchange for the securities of another issuer.[105] As discussed in Chapter 11 a takeover bid requires the production of a takeover bid circular. The required form for a takeover bid circular provides information specific to the nature of the takeover bid. Where securities are offered by the takeover offeror (or "bidder") the offeror must provide information in the takeover bid circular that is similar to that that would be provided in a prospectus with respect to the securities being offered in exchange for the securities of the offeree issuer.

c. STOCK EXCHANGE EXEMPTION

There is also an exemption where the trade in the securities is made through the facilities of a recognized stock exchange in accordance with the rules of the stock exchange or the requirements of the commission.[106] Instead of producing a prospectus, one must produce a document which is referred to in some provinces as an exchange offering prospectus and in other provinces as a statement of material facts. The exemption is not really an exemption because the exchange offering prospectus or statement of material facts,

---

[104]A.S.A. s. 110; B.C. Rules ss. 140, 142(3); Nfld.S.A. s. 73(5); N.S.S.A. s. 77(7); O.S.A. s. 72(5); P.E.I.S.A. s. 13(1)(f); S.S.A. s. 81(8). See also Q.S.A. s. 60.

[105]A.S.A. s. 107(1)(j); B.C.S.A. s. 74(2), (26); Nfld.S.A. s. 73(1)(j); N.S.S.A. s. 77(1)(j); O.S.A. s. 72(1)(j); S.S.A. s. 81(1)(j).

[106]Alta. Order Feb. 22, 1996; B.C. Blanket Order #95/10 and Local Policy 3-02, Parts 11 and 12; M.S.A. s. 58(3)(b); Nfld.S.A. s. 74(1)(b); N.S.S.A. s. 78(1)(b); O.S.A. s. 73(1)(b); P.E.I.S.A. s. 14.1(b); S.S.A. s. 82(1)(b).

which substitutes for the prospectus, contains information very similar to prospectuses required under the various securities acts. The withdrawal right and civil liability provisions also apply to an exchange offering prospectus, or statement of material facts.[107] The exchange offering prospectus or statement of material facts is usually jointly vetted by the exchange and the relevant securities administrators.

An issuer that has filed an exchange offering prospectus or a statement of material facts and has obtained a receipt for it becomes a reporting issuer. Thus, it will be subject to continuous disclosure requirements which can provide information in support of secondary market trading. Consequently, secondary market trading can proceed as it does with other prospectus offerings without a resale restriction.

B. Facilitate Financing By Smaller Issuers

Some exemptions can, in part, be justified as attempts to facilitate financing by smaller issuers. The cost of producing a prospectus as a proportion of the total proceeds of a distribution is higher for smaller issues than it is for large issues.[108] Therefore, the prospectus requirement may tend to favour larger issuers that float larger issues of securities. Some exemptions appear to be intended to reduce the cost to smaller issuers of distributing securities, while at the same time attempting to limit the exposure of the investing public to reduced regulation in these transactions.

1. *Private Issuers*

An exemption is provided for "private issuers" (or "private companies").[109] A private issuer cannot be a reporting issuer or a mutual

---

[107] Alta. Order Feb. 22, 1996, para. 13.2 making an exchange offering prospectus or prospectus for the purposes of the Act. B.C. Local Policy 3-02, paras. 11.5 and 11.6; M.S.A. s. 58(4); Nfld.S.A. s. 74(2); N.S.S.A. s. 78(2); O.S.A. s. 73(2); S.S.A. s. 82(2).

[108] See J.G. MacIntosh, *Legal and Institutional Barriers to Financing Innovative Enterprise in Canada* (Queen's University, Government and Competitiveness School of Policy Studies, 94-10, 1994) 43-52.

[109] A.S.A. s. 115(a) and s. 66(j); B.C.S.A. s. 75(a) and s. 46(j); M.S.A. ss. 58(3)(a) and 19(2)(i); Nfld.S.A. s. 74(1)(a) and s. 36(2)(j); N.S.S.A. s. 78(1)(a) and s. 41(2)(j);

fund. Its issued and outstanding securities must be subject to restrictions on transfer. Its securities must be beneficially owned, directly or indirectly, by not more than 50 persons. It must also not have distributed any of its securities "to the public". This last restriction on the private issuer retains the notorious words "to the public" that created so much uncertainty for pre-closed system distributions. Thus the jurisprudence on the meaning of the words "to the public", such as in *SEC v. Ralston Purina* and *R. v. Piepgrass*, discussed above,[110] continues to be relevant with respect to the private issuer exemption. The use of the words "to the public" leaves open the possibility of regulating the transaction where the investors in question are considered to be in need of protection.

The restriction on resale will be provided primarily through a restriction on the transfer of the securities which is required to qualify as a "private issuer".[111]

2. Small Number of Friends, Relatives and Sophisticated Investors

The friends, relatives and sophisticated investors exemption (discussed above under subheadings A 1 g and A 2 d) might also be justified on the basis of an attempt to reduce the cost of financing to smaller issuers. The potential loss of confidence in the market due to reduced investor protection is mitigated by a limit on the number of purchasers (and sometimes also on the number of persons solicited) and by a test of sophistication where the investor is not one of the specified relatives of directors or senior officers of the issuer or an affiliate.

3. Regulatory Barriers to Small Firm Finance and Suggested Reforms

Concerns have been raised about the adequacy of small issuer exemptions in addressing the proportionately high cost of com-

---

O.S.A. s. 73(1)(a) and s. 35(2)10; P.E.I.S.A. s. 14.1(a) and s. 2(4)(h); S.S.A. s. 82(1)(a) and s. 39(2)(k). Consider also Q.S.A. s. 54.

[110] See *supra* Part II A 1.

[111] See the definitions of "private issuer" or "private company" in, for example, A.S.A. s. 1(1)(p.1); B.C.S.A. s. 1(1); M.S.A. s. 1(1); Nfld.S.A. s. 2(1)(hh); N.S.S.A. s. 2(1)(ag); O.S.A. s. 1(1); P.E.I.S.A. s. 1(e.1) and P.E.I.C.A. s. 1(e); S.S.A. s. 2(1)(jj.1).

pliance with securities law requirements for small firms.[112] A 1994 study of small business finance suggested, among other things, that seed capital exemptions should not be limited to once in the lifetime of an issuer and that the offering memorandum requirement (requiring substantially the same information as a prospectus) should be removed. It also suggested a complete exemption from the disclosure requirements of securities legislation for issuers with fewer than 50 shareholders and a complete exemption from prospectus requirements for offerings under $2 million. For offerings of between $2 million and $10 million, it suggested a simplified question and answer disclosure format rather than a full prospectus. A further suggestion was the removal of restrictions on the pre-solicitation of prospectus offerings that would allow small issuers to pre-assess the market for the securities before incurring significant prospectus preparation costs. Another suggestion was the shortening of resale hold periods.[113]

The Ontario Securities Commission established a task force on small business finance in 1994. The task force made its final report in 1996.[114] It recommended that the existing private company, prescribed institution (e.g., banks, trust companies, and insurance companies), exempt purchaser, large purchase, seed capital and government incentive exemptions be eliminated and replaced with other exemptions.[115] One such exemption would exempt issuers with 25 or fewer security holders from the prospectus requirement for the distribution of up to $3 million worth of securities over the life of the issuer.[116] For issuers with more than five security holders, use of this exemption would require that investors be given a generic

---

[112]See MacIntosh, *supra* note 108, and *Ontario Securities Commission Task Force on Small Business Financing, Final Report* (Toronto: Queen's Printer for Ontario, 1996) and available in (1996), 19 OSCB 5757 (hereinafter "Small Business Financing Report").

[113]See MacIntosh, *supra* note 108, at 147-50.

[114]*Supra* note 112.

[115]Small Business Financing Report, *supra* note 112, at (1996), 19 OSCB 5765 and 5787-88.

[116]Small Business Financing Report, *supra* note 112, at (1996), 19 OSCB 5765 and 5781-84. The twenty-five security holder limit would be determined according to the number of security holders after giving effect to the financing but excluding "accredited investors" (see below), employees and certain former employees.

information statement four days prior to their investment.[117] The generic information statement would inform potential investors, in general terms, of the information she or he should ask for and assess before making the investment decision.[118] There would be a further exemption for "accredited investors". "Accredited investors" would include a list of prescribed institutions, entities having $5 million or more in assets, persons who (together with their spouse) have a net worth of at least $1 million or net income over a specified threshold and the issuer's management.[119] With respect to these accredited investors there would be no limit on the number of solicitations, the number of purchasers or the number of times the exemption could be relied upon. There would be no requirement to provide a point of sale disclosure document to accredited investors. The report also recommended a reduction in restrictions on securities marketing activities along the lines reflected in Draft National Policy # 43.[120]

C. Regulated Under Another Regulatory Scheme

Several exemptions from the prospectus requirements which relate to the type of security being traded are provided not on the basis that they do not require regulation, but on the basis that they are regulated under another regulatory scheme. One example of

---

[117]Small Business Financing Report, *supra* note 112, at (1996), 19 OSCB 5765 and 5783-84.

[118]The generic information statement might suggest that investors obtain and assess information such as: (i) the business and technical background of senior management; (ii) the composition of the board of directors; (iii) an audited balance sheet for the issuer; (iv) historic financial statements and auditors' reports; (v) the assumptions underlying the forecasts or projections and auditors' reports thereon; (vi) the length of operating history of the issuer; (vii) the possibility of litigation concerning intellectual property or other assets; (viii) plans for the utilization of funds raised through the investment; (ix) whether such funds are sufficient to finance the project; and (x) the liquidity of the security. There would be no requirement for the issuer to provide such information. It would be up to the investor to request that information and, perhaps, choose not to invest if the information were not forthcoming. See Small Business Financing Report, *supra* note 112, at (1996), 19 OSCB 5783.

[119]Small Business Financing Report, *supra* note 112, at (1996), 19 OSCB 5765 and 5784-87.

[120]Ibid.

this type of exemption is mortgages or other encumbrances on property regulated under, for instance, a mortgage brokers act.[121] Similarly, shares or deposits of a credit union normally dealt with under a statute specifically dealing with credit unions are exempt.[122] Cooperative associations could also be said to fit this category.[123]

Another exemption which might, in part, be justified on the basis that securities involved are issued or guaranteed by institutions subject to another regulatory scheme, is the exemption for bonds, debentures or other evidences of indebtedness of, or guaranteed by, banks to which the *Bank Act* applies, loan or trust companies registered under the applicable provincial legislation or insurance companies licensed under the applicable provincial legislation.[124]

D. Safe Investments

There are other exemptions, with respect to certain types of securities, that may be justified in part on the basis that the securities are relatively safe investments. For example, bonds, debentures or other evidences of indebtedness guaranteed by the governments of Canada, the provinces, the United Kingdom or the United States of America or any state, district or commonwealth thereof are

---

[121] See B.C.S.A. s. 75(a) and s. 46(e); Nfld.S.A. s. 74(1)(a) and s. 36(2)(e); N.S.S.A. s. 78(1)(a) and s. 41(2)(e); O.S.A. s. 73(1)(a) and s. 35(2) 5; S.S.A. s. 82(1)(a) and s. 39(2)(f). See also A.S.A. s. 115(1)(a) and s. 66(e); M.S.A. s. 58(3)(a) and s. 19(2)(d).

[122] See, for example, B.C.S.A. s. 75(a) and s. 46(i); M.S.A. s. 58(3)(a) and s. 19(2)(b); Nfld.S.A. s. 74(1)(a) and s. 36(2)(i); N.S.S.A. s. 78(1)(a) and s. 41(2)(i); O.S.A. s. 73(1)(a) and s. 35(2) 9; P.E.I.S.A. s. 14.1(a) and s. 2(4)(g); S.S.A. s. 82(1)(a) and s. 39(2)(j). See also Q.S.A. s. 3(4) and (4.1) to (4.5); Yukon Registrar's Order, March 1, 1980, s. 14.

[123] B.C.S.A. s. 75(a) and s. 46(h); M.S.A. s. 58(3)(a) and s. 19(2)(g); Nfld.S.A. s. 74(1)(a) and s. 36(2)(h); N.S.S.A. s. 78(1)(a) and s. 41(2)(h); O.S.A. s. 73(1)(a) and s. 35(2) 8; P.E.I.S.A. s. 14.1(a) and s. 2(4)(f); S.S.A. s. 82(1)(a) and s. 39(2)(i). See also Q.S.A. s. 3(5). Yukon Registrar's Order, March 1, 1980, s. 13 and N.B.S.F.P.A. s. 13(12) and s. 7(c).

[124] A.S.A. s. 115(a) and s. 66(a)(iii); B.C.S.A. s. 75(a) and s. 46(a)(iv); M.S.A. s. 58(3)(a) and s. 19(2)(a)(iii); Nfld.S.A. s. 74(1)(a) and s. 36(2)(a)(iii); N.S.S.A. s. 78(1)(a) and s. 41(2)(a)(iii); O.S.A. s. 73(1)(a) and s. 35(2) 1(c) and O. Regs. s. 22; P.E.I.S.A. s. 14.1(a) and s. 2(4)(a)(iii); S.S.A. s. 82(1)(a) and s. 39(2)(a)(iii). See also Q.S.A. s. 3(14).

exempt.[125] Similarly, bonds, debentures or other evidences of indebtedness of a municipal corporation in Canada, including debentures issued for vocational school purposes, guaranteed by a municipal corporation in Canada or secured by or payable out of rates or taxes levied under the law of a province on property in the province and collectible by the municipality are exempt.[126] The securities covered by the exemption are debt instruments that are normally less risky than most equity investments. In each of these cases, the issuer or guarantor of the debt securities has a tax base which should provide a reasonable degree of protection to the investor against the risk of insolvency on the part of the issuer.[127]

Bonds, debentures or other evidences of indebtedness of, or guaranteed by, banks, loan or trust companies, or insurance companies are exempt.[128] The exemption does not apply if the bonds, debentures or other evidences of indebtedness are subordinate in right of payment to deposits held by the issuer or guarantor.[129] In Canada these institutions tend to be large, stable institutions subject to restrictions on their investments intended to avoid risky investments by these institutions. In part, their stability is due to their regulation under legislation specific to these institutions.[130] With a large and stable organization standing behind debt instruments, normally having lower risk than equity type investments to begin with, these investments should be relatively safe. Arguably not much

---

[125] A.S.A. s. 115(a) and s. 66(a)(i); B.C.S.A. s. 75(a) and s. 46(a)(i) & (ii); M.S.A. s. 58(3)(a) and s. 19(2)(a)(i); Nfld.S.A. s. 74(1)(a) and s. 36(2)(a)(i); N.S.S.A. s. 78(1)(a) and s. 41(2)(a)(i); O.S.A. s. 73(1)(a) and s. 35(2)1(a); P.E.I.S.A. s. 14.1(a) and s. 2(4)(a)(i); S.S.A. s. 82(1)(a) and s. 39(2)(a)(i) & (i.1). See also Q.S.A. s. 3(1), (15) and s. 41(1).

[126] A.S.A. s. 115(a) and s. 66(a)(ii); B.C.S.A. s. 75(a) and s. 46(a)(iii); M.S.A. s. 58(3)(a) and s. 19(2)(a)(i); Nfld.S.A. s. 74(1)(a) and s. 36(2)(a)(ii); N.S.S.A. s. 78(1)(a) and s. 41(2)(a)(ii); O.S.A. s. 73(1)(a) and s. 35(2)1(b); P.E.I.S.A. s. 14.1(a) and s. 2(4)(a)(ii); S.S.A. s. 82(1)(a) and s. 39(2)(a)(ii). See also Q.S.A. s. 41(2).

[127] There would still be a risk associated with the fluctuation in interest rates, which will affect the value of the bonds, debentures or other evidences of indebtedness. However it is unlikely that any of the issuer specific information contained in prospectus type disclosure would assist the investor with assessing this risk.

[128] See the provisions cited *supra* note 124.

[129] See the provisions cited *supra* note 124.

[130] Consequently this exemption is also justified in part on the basis that the institution is regulated under another regulatory scheme — see Part III C above.

would be gained from the kind of information about the issuer that would be provided in a prospectus.

Other types of exemptions relating to specific securities might also be justified, at least in part, on the basis that they constitute relatively safe investments. For instance, certificates or receipts issued by a trust company or credit union for money received for guaranteed investment might be included in this category.[131] Commercial paper having a term to maturity of not more than 12 months might also be justified in part on the relative safety of the investment.[132] The relatively short period to maturity should, in most cases, limit the degree of default risk associated with this type of security.

E. Promotion of Specific Investments and Social Activities

1. *Educational, Charitable, Religious or Recreational Purposes*

The cost of complying with prospectus requirements could deter the raising of funds for a number of socially desirable activities. Thus an exemption is given with respect to securities sold by an issuer organized exclusively for educational, benevolent, fraternal, charitable, religious or recreational purposes and not for profit.[133] Often

---

[131] A.S.A. s 115(1)(a) and s. 66(b); B.C.S.A. s. 75(a) and s. 46(b); M.S.A. s. 58(3)(a) and s. 19(2)(b); Nfld.S.A. s. 74(1)(a) and s. 36(2)(b); N.S.S.A. s. 78(1)(a) and s. 41(2)(b); O.S.A. s. 73(1)(a) and s. 35(2) 2; P.E.I.S.A. s. 14.1(a) and s. 2(4)(b); S.S.A. s. 82(1)(a) and s. 39(2)(b).

[132] In most provinces the denomination of the commercial paper must also be of a minimum amount suggesting that the basis for the exemption is also in part that the purchaser will be reasonably sophisticated. See, for example, A.S.A. s. 115(1)(a) and s. 66(d) (minimum $50,000); B.C.S.A. s. 75(1)(a) and s. 46(d) (no minimum amount); M.S.A. s. 58(3)(a) and s. 19(2)(c) (minimum $50,000); Nfld.S.A. s. 74(1)(a) and s. 36(2)(d) (minimum $50,000); N.S.S.A. s. 78(1)(a) and s. 41(2)(d) (minimum $50,000); O.S.A. s. 73(1)(a) and s. 35(2) 4 (minimum $50,000); P.E.I.S.A. s. 14.1(a) and s. 2(4)(c) (minimum $50,000); S.S.A. s. 82(1)(a) and s. 39(2)(e) (minimum of $150,000).

[133] A.S.A. s. 115(1)(a) and s. 66(g); B.C.S.A. s. 75(1)(a) and s. 46(g); M.S.A. s. 58(3)(a) and s. 19(2)(f); Nfld.S.A. s. 74(1)(a) and s. 36(2)(g); N.S.S.A. s. 78(1)(a) and s. 41(2)(g); O.S.A. s. 73(1)(a) and s. 35(2) 7; P.E.I.S.A. s. 14.1(a) and s. 2(4)(e); S.S.A. s. 82(1)(a) and s. 39(2)(h). See also Q.S.A. s. 3. See Yukon Registrar's Order March 1, 1980, s. 12.

attached to the exemption are conditions that are presumably intended to remove the incentive to engage in pressure sales tactics. No part of the net earnings of the issuer can accrue to the benefit of a security holder.[134] No commission or other remuneration can be paid in connection with the sale of the securities, and information respecting the securities must be filed with — and be satisfactory to — the relevant securities administrators.[135]

2. Prospecting Expeditions and Prospecting Syndicates

Exemptions are provided with respect to prospecting expeditions and prospecting syndicates in the interests of encouraging the development of primary resources. An exemption is provided with respect to securities issued by a prospector for the purposes of financing a prospecting expedition.[136] It is apparently assumed that the amount of capital involved in a single prospecting expedition will be relatively small and that the approach to investors will be kept simple.[137]

Some acts also provide an exemption for a prospecting syndicate where a prospecting syndicate agreement has been filed and a receipt therefore has been obtained.[138] There are specified required terms for a prospecting syndicate agreement and the agreement substitutes for the prospectus, providing a degree of investor protection without the complexity and cost of complying with the full requirements of prospectus disclosure.[139] Trading in the prospecting syndicate securities is exempt where the sales are made by the

---

[134]See, for example, B.C.S.A. s. 46(g); Nfld.S.A. s. 36(2)(g); N.S.S.A. s. 41(2)(g); O.S.A. s. 35(2) 7; P.E.I.S.A. s. 2(4)(e); S.S.A. s. 39(2)(h).

[135]Ibid.

[136]A.S.A. s. 115(1)(a) and s. 66(k); M.S.A. s. 58(3)(a) and s. 19(2)(j); Nfld.S.A. s. 74(1)(a) and s. 36(2)(k); N.S.S.A. s. 78(1)(a) and s. 41(2)(k); O.S.A. s. 73(1)(a) and s. 35(2)11; P.E.I.S.A. s. 14.1(a) and s. 2(4)(i); S.S.A. s. 82(1)(a) and s. 39(2)(1). See Yukon Registrar's Order, March 1, 1980, s. 16 and N.B.S.F.P.A. s. 13(12) and s. 7(i).

The exemption only applies if the prospector sells the securities.

[137]See Alboini, *supra* note 91, at pp. 14-6.

[138]See, for example, M.S.A. s. 58(3)(a) and s. 19(2)(k), (l); Nfld.S.A. s. 74(1)(a) and s. 36(2)(l), (m); N.S.S.A. s. 78(1)(a) and s. 41(2)(l), (m); O.S.A. s. 73(1)(a) and s. 35(2) 12 and 13; S.S.A. s. 82(1)(a) and s. 39(2)(m), (n).

[139]See, for example, M.S.A. s. 36; Nfld.S.A. s. 52; N.S.S.A. s. 57; O.S.A. s. 51; S.S.A. s. 57.

prospector, or prospectors, with delivery of the prospecting syndicate agreement or where a prospecting syndicate agreement has been filed and the securities are not offered to the public and are sold to not more than 50 persons.[140]

3. *Exchange Issuer Exemptions — B.C.*

The B.C.S.A. has some unique exemptions that apply to "exchange issuers". "Exchange issuers" are defined as issuers whose securities are listed and posted for trading on a stock exchange recognized by the B.C. Securities Commission.[141] Only the Vancouver Stock Exchange has been recognized for this purpose.[142] The additional exemptions provided to exchange issuers apply to the trades by an exchange issuer in securities of its own issue:

(i)   to settle a bona fide debt;[143]

(ii) as consideration for a loan, or loan guarantee;[144]

(iii) as consideration for services performed by a person who is not an insider, or an associate of an insider of the issuer, in connection with the acquisition or disposition of assets or in connection with a private placement to persons not resident in the province;[145]

(iv) to employees of a person providing management services to the issuer where the employee is not induced to purchase by expectation of employment or continued employment with either the issuer or the person providing the management services;[146]

(v)   to up to 24 persons in any 12-month period who are friends or relatives of senior officers or directors of the issuer or an affiliate of the issuer, or which is a company which is

---

[140]See, for example, M.S.A. s. 19(2)(k), (l); Nfld.S.A. s. 36(2)(l), (m); N.S.S.A. s. 41(2)(l), (m); O.S.A. s. 35(2)12,13; S.S.A. s. 39(2)(m), (n).

[141]B.C.S.A. s. 1(1).

[142]B.C. Pol. 3-44.

[143]B.C. Rules s. 128(e).

[144]B.C. Rules s. 128(f).

[145]Ibid.

[146]B.C. Rules s. 128(g).

wholly owned by friends or relatives of senior officers or directors of the issuer or an affiliate of the issuer.[147]

The resale restrictions applicable to exchange issuers are also less restrictive, generally allowing for shorter, or potentially shorter, resale hold periods.[148]

The reduced resale restrictions applicable with respect to exchange issuers in B.C. might be justified, in part, on the basis that trading on the exchange will mean more active trading and therefore a more efficient pricing of securities.[149] The market following and market response to available information may thus be quicker such that the shorter resale hold period restrictions might not adversely affect investor protection. Given the nature of the additional exemptions, the additional exemptions and the associated reduced resale restrictions might also be justified as a method of encouraging venture capital information in the province of British Columbia. However, the exchange issuer exemptions appear to be primarily directed towards promoting the business of the Vancouver Stock Exchange itself.

F. Protection Provided by Active Markets: Prompt Offering Prospectuses, Shelf Offering Prospectuses and "Prep" Procedures

Exemptions are provided where the normal procedures for distribution under a prospectus have been replaced with modified procedures that allow the issuer to have access to Canadian capital markets more quickly than would otherwise be the case. These modified procedures for prospectus disclosure may provide less protection for investors, but are arguably justified on the basis that the efficiency of the market in which the securities are sold provides an adequate degree of substitute protection. The nature of these modified prospectus distribution procedures is dealt with in some detail in Chapter 8.

---

[147] B.C. Rules s. 128(h).

[148] B.C. Rules s. 142(2)(b).

[149] However, the listing requirements of the Vancouver Stock Exchange are not considered particularly stringent and many securities traded on the Vancouver Stock Exchange could be described as being relatively thinly traded.

G. Other Exemptions

The discussion so far has considered many of the exemptions available in the various provincial acts and regulations. However, there are many exemptions contained in the acts and regulations of the various provinces other than those mentioned above. Since this is intended as an introductory text, these other exemptions are left to the reader to pursue.

Exemptions other than those specifically mentioned in provincial acts and regulations may be available. These are provided by securities commissions under their authority to grant exemption orders where it is not prejudicial to the public interest to do so.

1. *Exemption Orders*

There may be instances where a particular transaction being contemplated does not fit within any of the specific exemptions set out in a securities act or the regulations. Nonetheless, the need for prospectus type disclosure may be unwarranted in the context of the transaction. Securities commissions have the power to grant exemptions in these circumstances.[150]

The power of securities commissions to grant an exemption is constrained in that they must be satisfied that to do so would not be prejudicial to the public interest. In making such an assessment, they must exercise their discretion in a manner consistent with the policy underlying the particular securities act. In exercising their discretion, they will thus be inclined to consider the benefits likely to be derived from enforcing the prospectus requirement against the costs of the requirement. In assessing the benefits and costs they will tend to look at considerations similar to those underlying the existing exemptions, such as:

(i) the need of the purchasers to know the kind of information that would be provided by a prospectus;

(ii) any common bonds the purchasers might have with the issuer;

(iii) the extent to which the information that would be provided by a prospectus is already available;

---

[150] A.S.A. s. 116(1); B.C.S.A. s. 76; M.S.A. s. 20; Nfld.S.A. s. 75; N.S.S.A. s. 79; O.S.A. s. 74; P.E.I.S.A. s. 14; O.S.A. s. 263; S.S.A. s. 83.

(iv) the extent to which a market for the securities exists such that available information is likely to be reflected in the market price;

(v) the existence of another regulatory mechanism that will protect investors;

(vi) the degree of risk likely to be associated with investment in the particular securities; and, perhaps also,

(vii) the existence of any policy directed towards promoting the particular type of investment.

If a securities commission grants an exemption, they also have the power to impose terms and conditions upon the exemption as are considered necessary. The terms and conditions may take the form of disclosure which substitutes in part for prospectus disclosure or may take the form of contractual rights of action or withdrawal.

Like the exemptions under the Act, subsequent trades might not fall within the definition of "distribution" but might be made to persons who need to know the kind of information provided by a prospectus. Consequently, terms and conditions which restrict the resale of the securities covered by the exemption order are commonly imposed. The terms and conditions tend to follow the terms and conditions applicable to the exemptions set out in the Act or regulations.

2. Blanket Orders

Securities commissions may find that a particular type of transaction is occuring with sufficient frequency that much of the commission's time spent in hearings could be saved by issuing a blanket order. Where there is a blanket order, the vendor of securities can avoid the need to make an application to the commission for an exemption order if the proposed transaction fits the circumstances of, and meets the conditions described in, the order.

Blanket orders may also be used to effect securities commission policies. For instance, the policy of the Canadian Securities Administrators with respect to prompt offering prospectuses and shelf offering prospectuses, discussed in Chapter 8, has been put into effect in several provinces through blanket orders.

CHAPTER 8

PROMPT OFFERINGS, SHELF OFFERINGS AND PREP PROCEDURES

I. INTRODUCTION

As noted in Chapter 7, there are exceptions to the normal procedures for distributions under a prospectus that allow issuers access to Canadian capital markets more quickly than would otherwise be the case. This chapter looks at these exceptions to the normal procedures, namely, the prompt offering prospectus system ("POP System"), shelf offering prospectuses and the "PREP" procedures. The objective is to provide the reader with an awareness of these substitute prospectus procedures, how they work, and how they are perceived to fit with the overall purpose of securities regulation. Part II considers the POP System. Part III looks at the shelf offering system and Part IV notes the "Prep" procedures. Part V highlights some of the policy issues with respect to these procedures.

II. THE PROMPT OFFERING PROSPECTUS

A. The Problem to Which the POP System Responded

Prior to the introduction of the POP system, the process of preparing and clearing a preliminary prospectus and a prospectus under the regime set out in the securities acts could take in the order of 60 to 75 days.[1] This period could be shortened with respect to offerings in multiple jurisdictions under the procedures set out in National Policy #1. However, even under National Policy #1 it could still take several weeks to clear a prospectus.

This length of time to clear a prospectus might have continued to be considered acceptable if Canadian capital markets operated

---

[1] See R. Steen & R. McKee, "The Prompt Offering Qualification System" Report to the Ontario Securities Commission, March, 1986, [1986] O.S.C.B. 1626, at 1628.

in isolation from the rest of the world. However, developments in capital markets elsewhere in the late 1970s and early 1980s allowed funds to be raised much more quickly outside of Canada. For instance, funds could be raised within a few days in the unregulated Eurodollar market.[2] Funds could also be raised relatively quickly in the U.S. This occurred in part because the Securities and Exchange Commission found it was not able to vet all issues of securities and thus cleared issues on a selective basis.[3] It also occurred in part because of the adoption of a system of "shelf-registration" that allowed a registration statement (a document required for a distribution of securities in the U.S.) to be cleared and filed and then used for up to two years with just pro forma modifications. This allowed securities to be issued immediately at any time over the ensuing two years without having to clear a new registration statement.[4]

With such ready access to funds in foreign markets there was a concern that Canadian securities markets were at a serious competitive disadvantage.[5] To compete with this ready access to funds outside of Canada, and to encourage issuers to raise more funds in Canada, the Canadian Securities Administrators decided to adopt a system for more prompt offerings of securities in Canada. A prompt offering prospectus system (or "POP" system) was first introduced in Canada in 1982.[6]

B. How the POP System Works

The POP system speeds the clearance of the prospectus by allowing the issuer to use an abbreviated, or "short-form" prospectus. The short-form prospectus can be reviewed more quickly by securities administrators than the usual long-form prospectus. The disclosure that would be provided in the usual long-form prospectus (but which is lacking in the short-form prospectus) is provided instead by the build up of a base of disclosure through financial statements,

---

[2] Ibid.

[3] Ibid.

[4] Ibid., at 1629-30.

[5] Ibid., at 1628-30.

[6] See the blanket ruling in Ontario dated October 28, 1982, 4 O.S.C.B. 241B.

proxy circulars, material change reports and a document called an
"annual information form".[7]

1. *The Annual Information Form ("AIF")*

a. THE INITIAL AIF

The first step in providing the disclosure base necessary to allow
the use of a short-form prospectus is the filing of an initial annual
information form ("AIF"). Briefly described, this form provides the
information that would normally be provided in a prospectus concerning the business of the issuer and the people running the
business. It has information about the business of the issuer,[8]
selected financial information,[9] management discussion and analysis

---

[7] The POP System is provided for in NP #47 for all provinces except for
Quebec. In Quebec, an expedited prospectus procedure is provided for in a manner
similar to NP #47 with a simplified prospectus incorporating continuous disclosure
documents by reference and a permanent information record that roughly corresponds to the annual information form referred to in NP #47. See in Quebec see
Q.S.A. ss. 18, 18.1, 19, 64, 84-88 and Q.Reg. ss. 58-62, 164-170.1, Schedules
IV, IX, IX.1, and X, and Pol. No. Q-1.

[8] This information includes information about the incorporation or organization
of the issuer (NP # 47, Appendix A, Contents of AIF, Item 1), a general description
of the issuer's business and its development over the previous five years (Item
2), a narrative description of each industry segment of the business including a
description of the principal products or services of the business, major customers
and significant geographic regions where sales are made, sources and availability
of raw materials, intangible properties such as brand names, copyrights or franchises, the extent to which the business is seasonal, and similarly important matters
concerning other types of businesses such as mining, oil and gas, and banking (Item
3).

[9] NP # 47, Appendix A, Contents of AIF, Item 4. Financial data for the issuer
for its last five completed financial years is to be provided in summary for form
including net sales or total revenues, income or loss before extraordinary items
in total and on a per share and fully diluted per share basis, net income or loss
in total and on a per share and fully diluted per share basis, total assets, total long-
term debt and preferred shares, cash dividends declared per share for each class
of share. The summary must also provide quarterly information for the last eight
quarters on net sales or total revenues, income or loss before extraordinary items
in total and on a per share and fully diluted per share basis, and net income or
loss in total and on a per share and fully diluted per share basis. The AIF must
also describe any restriction that could prevent the issuer from paying dividends
and otherwise describe the issuer's dividend policy. The financial information must
be accompanied by a discussion of factors affecting the comparability of the data

(set out or incorporated by reference),[10] markets for the issuer's securities,[11] and information on the issuer's directors and officers.[12] It may incorporate by reference other information such as the information contained in the issuer's financial statements, proxy circulars and material change reports.[13] The initial AIF is normally vetted by the securities administrator.[14] It can be filed in multiple jurisdictions using the procedure outlined in National Policy #1. An issuer that has securities registered for trading with the U.S. Securities and Exchange Commission may satisfy the AIF requirement by filing, and making available to security holders in Canada, its Form 10K

---

including discontinued operations, changes in accounting policies, significant acquisitions or disposals and major changes in the direction of the business.

[10]Management discussion and analysis ("MD&A") is discussed in Chapter 6, Part VIII. In its MD&A management must discuss and compare the issuer's financial condition, its changes in financial condition and results of operations for the previous two financial years describing the causes for changes in the financial statements from year to year. The results of operations must be explained noting, for instance, any unusual or infrequent events or significant economic changes that materially affected income or loss from operations. MD&A is also forward looking in that, for example, management is asked to describe any known trends or uncertainties that have had or that are reasonably expected to have a favourable or unfavourable impact on revenues or income or loss from operations. The discussion must also consider the liquidity and capital resources of the issuer. The discussion of liquidity focuses on the ability of the issuer to generate adequate amounts of cash (or cash equivalents) when necessary in both the short term and the long term. In the discussion of the issuer's capital resources, management is asked to describe and quantify commitments for capital expenditures as of the end of the most recently completed financial year and note the anticipated source of funds to meet the commitments. They must also quantify uncommitted but necessary expenditures to meet future plans discussed in the MD&A. See NP #47, Appendix A, Schedule 1.

[11]NP #47, Appendix A, Contents of AIF, Item 6. The issuer must identify the exchanges or quotation systems on which the issuer's securities are listed and posted for trading or are quoted.

[12]NP #47, Appendix A, Contents of AIF, Item 7. The AIF must disclose the principal occupations of the directors within the preceding five years, the periods during which each director has served as a director, the expiry date of the term of officer of each director, the percentage of each class of voting securities of the issuer or any of its subsidiaries that the each director and senior officer beneficially owns directly or indirectly or over which control or direction is exercised, and the directors who are members of any executive or audit committee of the issuer.

[13]NP #47, Appendix A, Instructions, para. (1).

[14]NP #47, para. 5.1; and NP #1, Parts 1 and 3.

or 2OF filed with the SEC pursuant to the *Securities Exchange Act of 1934.*[15] Similarly the MD&A requirements can be satisfied by filing the corresponding document filed with the SEC.[16]

b. SUBSEQUENT AIFS

To continue to be eligible to use the POP system, the issuer must file a "Renewal AIF" within 140 days from the end of each financial year of the issuer.[17] This brings the information contained in the AIF disclosure up to date. These subsequent AIFs are subject to selective review by the relevant securities administrators.[18]

2. Short-Form Prospectus

The normal process of filing a preliminary prospectus followed by a final prospectus is followed with the substitution of a short-form preliminary prospectus and a short-form final prospectus.[19] When the issuer seeks to issue securities it produces a preliminary short-form prospectus which is vetted by the relevant securities administrators.[20] This preliminary short-form prospectus contains, for the most part, information about the particular security being issued. For instance, it contains information about the use of the proceeds of the issue, the plan of distribution, whether there will be a market for the particular securities, details about the characteristics or rights attached to the securities and other material facts relating to the issue. The short-form prospectus also incorporates all the other information about the business by reference to the current AIF, financial statements, proxy circular, and material change reports.[21]

The concept behind the short-form prospectus is that because most of the information about the business has already been

---

[15]See NP #47, para. 5.4.

[16]See NP #47, Appendix A, Contents of AIF, Item 5.

[17]NP #47, para. 5.2(1). Under Ont. Pol. 5.10, AIFs must be filed annually by reporting issuers having equity or revenues, as reported in their annual financial statements, of in excess of $10,000,000. See Chapter 6, Part VIII.

[18]NP #47, para 5.2(6).

[19]NP #47, para. 6.3; and NP #1, Parts 2 and 3.

[20]NP #47, para. 6.1(1) and 6.3; and NP #1, Parts 2 & 3.

[21]NP #47, Appendix B, Item 16.

included in the AIF (and in any other disclosure documents incorporated by reference in the AIF), there is a much smaller amount of
information contained in the short-form prospectus and thus a much
shorter document for securities administrators to vet. This allows
securities administrators to vet a preliminary short-form prospectus
in a shorter period of time than a normal preliminary prospectus.
If securities regulators have no comments that the issuer must
respond to, or if responses to the comments can be dealt with
quickly, securities may be distributed in as little as one week from
the filing of the preliminary short-form prospectus.[22]

Once the short-form prospectus has been cleared the final short-
form prospectus can be filed and a receipt therefore obtained. The
securities can then be distributed under the short-form withdrawal
rights and liability for misrepresentations in a prospectus apply with
respect to the short-form prospectus. As well, the issuer must provide
the AIF, financial statements, proxy circulars and other documents
incorporated by reference upon request by prospective investors.[23]

C. The Eligibility Criteria

Not all issuers are allowed to distribute securities under the POP
system. Eligibility criteria for the use of the POP system are designed
to ensure what is considered to be an adequate build up of information about the issuer. They are also designed to ensure that either
the issuer's securities can be readily and fairly priced in securities
markets thereby protecting less sophisticated investors by allowing
them to rely on the market price of the securities as a fair price.
A general set of eligibility criteria are designed to achieve this result.
In addition, there are various alternative criteria designed to achieve
a similar result.

---

[22] NP #1, Item 2. However, if the principal jurisdiction is of the opinion that
the proposed offering is too complex it may notify the issuer within one day of
the filing of the preliminary short-form prospectus that the normal NP #1 prospectus
time periods apply (see NP #1, Item 2(c)).

[23] N.P. #47, Part 8 and Appendix A, item 8(1).

1. *The General Criteria*

a. THE CRITERIA

The general eligibility criteria the POP system are that:[24]

(i) the issuer has been a reporting issuer in the jurisdiction in which it proposes to use the POP system for a period of 12 calendar months prior to the date of filing its initial AIF;[25]

(ii) at the time of filing its AIF the issuer is not in default of any requirement of the Securities Legislation of the jurisdiction in which it proposes to use the POP system;

(iii) the issuer has a "Current AIF"; and

(iv) the aggregate market value of the issuer's "equity securities" listed and posted for trading on a stock exchange in Canada is at least $75,000,000 (the "public float" test).

The aggregate market value of the issuer's equity securities is calculated by multiplying the total number of equity securities for each class of equity securities by the arithmetic average of the closing price of the equity securities of that class on the Canadian stock exchange on which that class of securities is principally traded for the last calendar month of the financial year for which the AIF is filed.[26] In determining the total number of equity securities of each class the issuer, one must exclude those securities beneficially owned[27] or controlled[28] by any person (or by a person together

---

[24] NP #47, para. 4.1.

[25] If the issuer has not been a reporting issuer in the jurisdiction in which it proposes to use the POP system it can still be eligible to use the POP system in the jurisdiction if it has been reporting issuer in another jurisdiction for a period of 12 calendar months and it fills all the continuous disclosure documents it was required to fill in each jurisdiction in which was a reporting issuer for the 12 calendar months prior to the filing of the AIF in the jurisdiction in which it proposes to use the POP system. The issuer must either become a reporting in the jurisdiction in which it proposes to use the POP system or must undertake to file all the subsequent continuous disclosure documents required by that jurisdiction. See NP #47, para. 4.1(1)(a)(ii).

[26] NP #47, para. 4.1(2). If the issuer has filed a Renewal AIF then it has the option of using the last calendar month before the date of filing the Renewal AIF.

[27] This includes direct or indirect beneficial ownership.

[28] NP #47, para. 4.1(2)(a) refers to a person who "alone or together with their affiliates and Associates beneficially own or *exercise control or direction over*" (emphasis added).

with the person's associates[29] or affiliates) that amount to more than 10% of the securities of that class.[30]

If these general eligibility criteria are met, then the issuer can file a POP short-form preliminary prospectus as long as, at the time of filing the preliminary short-form prospectus, or at the time of the issuance of a receipt for the short-form prospectus, the issuer is not in default of any requirement of the act or regulations of the jurisdiction in which it proposes to file a short-form prospectus.[31]

b. THE REASONS FOR THE CRITERIA

The 12-month reporting issuer test, AIF filing and non-default requirements attempt to assure that there is an adequate base of information about the issuer that can be used to assess the value of the securities when they are issued. The requirement of having outstanding listed equity securities (excluding substantial non-trading blocks) with an aggregate value of $75,000,000 is intended to assure there is a sufficient public following for the issuer's securities so that the information provided by the short-form prospectus, AIFs and other continuous disclosure documents will be closely monitored and reflected in the price of the securities that are issued under a short-form prospectus. Major sophisticated investors assessing whether or not it is worthwhile to follow information on a particular issuer's securities are interested in their ability to recoup their information gathering and assessment costs through trading. The ability to recoup these costs is thus based on an assessment of the volume of securities available for trading. Blocks of securities amounting to 10% or more are excluded since they tend not to form part of the regularly traded securities.[32]

---

[29] The term "associate" is defined in NP #47, Part 3. It is essentially the same as the definition of "associate" in, for example, B.C.S.A. s. 1(1); O.S.A. s. 1(1). See Chapter 10 Part III A 3.

[30] NP #47, para. 4.1(2)(a). Some exceptions are made to this exclusion of large block control of equity securities from the public float calculation. For instance, the exclusion does not apply to equity securities held in a pension fund, mutual fund or investment fund unless the portfolio manager is an affiliate of the issuer. See NP #47, para. 4.1(2)(a). Some examples are given in NP #47, note 8a.

[31] NP #47, para. 4.1(3).

[32] In an application by Canron Inc. (1985), 8 O.S.C.B. 3877 Canron did not meet the public float test. However, if the shares of the holder of nearly 20% of the company's shares had been included it would have met the test. It argued

The public float test is intended to provide some assurance of a market following that will cause the information contained in the short-form prospectus and continuous disclosure documents to be quickly incorporated in the price of the security. The requirement that the issuer not be in default of securities legislation requirements provides some assurance that there will be no material gaps in the information available to investors. The expectation is that less sophisticated investors who are less able to assimilate the information will be protected by the establishment of a fair price for the securities by more sophisticated investors who are closely monitoring the information about the particular issuer and its securities.

2. *Alternative Criteria for Certain Issues of Debt or Preferred Shares*

a. THE CRITERIA

Where the issuer does not meet the public float test it can still use the POP system for certain issues of debt or preferred shares.

(i) Non-Convertible Debt or Non-Convertible Preferred Shares

An issuer that does not meet the public float test can issue non-convertible debt or preferred shares if it meets the other general eligibility criteria (i.e., items (i) to (iii) set out in Part II C 1 a above) and:

(i) at the time of filing its AIF the issuer reasonably believes that any non-convertible debt or non-convertible preferred shares that it may issue will receive a provisional approved rating from an approved rating organization;

(ii) at the time of filing its AIF the issuer reasonably believes

---

that the shares should have been included because the holder of the large block did not exercise de facto control over the company and therefore should not have been excluded for the purpose of the public float test. The Commission noted, however, that the control by the insider was not the relevant concern. As the Commission stated,

"[t]he exclusion of [a large block of] shares does not depend on any control exercised by the insider, but is simply to identify those shares which are not actively traded and thus to measure more accurately how widely held an issuer's securities are and the breadth of an issuer's market following." 8 O.S.C.B. 3893 at 3895.

that any non-convertible debt or non-convertible preferred shares that it may issue will not receive less than an approved rating from any approved rating organization;

(iii) at the time of filing a preliminary short-form prospectus the securities to be issued have received a provisional approved rating from at least one approved rating organization; and

(iv) at the time of filing a preliminary short-form prospectus the securities to be issued have not received a provisional or final rating lower than an approved rating from any approved rating organization.

Rating organizations provide ratings of the investment quality of securities such as debt securities and preferred shares. For the purposes of the POP system, the approved rating organizations are C.B.R.S. Inc., the Dominion Bond Rating Service Limited, Moody's Investors Service, Inc., and Standard & Poor's Corporation.[33] NP #47 also sets out the ratings that are "approved" for the POP system for each of these ratings organizations.[34] The approved ratings are ratings of good to high investment quality.

This set of alternative eligibility criteria substitutes a rating by a rating organization for the public float test. The rating involves a careful analysis by the rating organization whose reputation depends on the reliability of its ratings. The rating provides a condensed signal to the market of the risk associated with the particular security and thereby saves other investors and market analysts the costs of replicating the careful analysis done by the rating organization. An approved rating of good quality to highest quality also further assures that the securities constitute a relatively safe investment thus justifying a less rigid regulatory approach.

(ii) Guaranteed Non-Convertible Debt or Non-Convertible Preferred Shares

An issuer may also issue non-convertible debt or non-convertible preferred shares if another issuer that meets requirements (i) to (iii) of the general eligibility criteria noted above guarantees certain obligations connected with the particular debt or preferred share

---

[33] NP #47, Part 3.

[34] Ibid.

issuance.[35] There are four main requirements to these alternative eligibility criteria for the POP system which might be summarized as follows:

(i) as noted above, the guarantor meets requirements (i) to (iii) of the general eligibility criteria;

(ii) the guarantee meets specified requirements;

(iii) the guarantor is not in default; and

(iv) approved rating requirements are satisfied.

The Guarantee

In the case of an issuance of preferred shares, the guarantor issuer must guarantee the payment of any preferred dividend, whether declared or not, within 15 days of the date the issuer is expected to pay the dividend but fails to do so.[36] In the case of an issuance of debt securities, the guarantor issuer must guarantee the payment of principal, or any premium on the principal amount, any interest and any other amounts that may be due within 15 days of the date of failure by the issuer to pay any amount due.[37]

Guarantor Non-Default

At the time of filing of the short-form preliminary prospectus for the debt or preferred shares the guarantor issuer cannot be in default of any requirement of the securities legislation of the jurisdiction in which the short-form prospectus is being filed.[38]

Approved Rating Requirements

The guarantor issuer must have issued and outstanding non-convertible debt securities or non-convertible preferred shares that have received an approved rating from at least one approved rating organization and have not received a rating lower than an approved rating

---

[35] NP #47, para. 4.3(1)(b).

[36] NP #47, para. 4.3(1)(b)(i)(A). The policy statement refers to a dividend that is expected to be paid at fixed regular intervals in a fixed amount or in an amount to be determined by a formula.

[37] NP #47, para. 4.3(1)(b)(i)(B).

[38] NP #47, para. 4.3(1)(b)(ii)(A).

from any approved rating organization.[39] Further, at the time of the filing of the preliminary short-form prospectus, the securities to be issued must have received a provisional approved rating from at least one approved rating organization and must not have received a provisional or final rating lower than an approved rating from any approved rating organization.[40]

Where the future cash flows of the non-convertible debt or preferred shares are guaranteed by another issuer the risk associated with the cash flows ultimately depends on the risk that the guarantor issuer will not be able to fulfill the guarantee. Thus the alternative criteria require that the guarantor not be in default of securities legislation requirements so that there are no gaps in information. The approved rating requirement for the guarantor issuer provides a signal to investors of the risk of non-payment by the guarantor issuer. A further signal of the risk of non-payment by either the issuer or the guarantor is provided by the requirement for a provisional approved rating requirement on the securities to be issued.[41]

(iii) Debt or Preferred Shares Convertible into Eligible Securities

Convertible debt securities or convertible preferred shares may be issued by an issuer that does not meet the general eligibility criteria if:[42]

  (i) the securities are convertible into securities of an issuer that meets the general eligibility criteria;

  (ii) the issuer that meets the general eligibility criteria fully and unconditionally guarantees payment obligations on the convertible debt or convertible preferred shares to be issued;

---

[39] NP #47, para. 4.3(1)(b)(ii)(B).

[40] NP #47, para. 4.3(1)(b)(iii).

[41] This additional approved rating is probably necessary since the rating of the guarantor's debt or preferred shares may not provide complete comfort with respect to the satisfaction of the guarantee. For example, the guarantor's debt securities with the approved rating may be well secured by the assets of the guarantor so that any loss on default to those particular debt securities may be quite low. However, the risk to unsecured creditors, including those making a claim on a guarantee, may be still be quite high. Indeed, the addition of the guarantor may substantially increase the risk to the guarantor's unsecured creditors with only relatively little impact on the risk to secured debt holders.

[42] NP #47, para. 4.3(2).

(iii) at the time of the filing of the short-form prospectus for the convertible debt or preferred shares, the issuer that meets the general eligibility criteria and is not in default of any requirements of the securities legislation of the jurisidiction in which the short-form preliminary prospectus is filed; and

(iv) the approved rating requirement is met.

The approved rating requirements are the same as noted above for guaranteed non-convertible debt or preferred shares. The guarantor issuer must have issued and outstanding non-convertible debt securities or non-convertible preferred shares that have received an approved rating from at least one approved rating organization and have not received a rating lower than an approved rating from any approved rating organization.[43] Further, at the time of the filing of the preiminary short-form prospectus the securities to be issued must have received a provisional approved rating from at least one approved rating organization and must not have received a provisional or final rating lower than an approved rating from any approved rating organization.[44]

As an investor assessing the value of convertible debt or preferred shares one has to be concerned not only with the value of the debt securities or preferred shares assuming there is no conversion, but also with the value of the securities into which the debt securities or preferred shares are convertible (the "underlying securities"). One needs to be able to assess the value of the underlying securities in order to assess the probability that conversion will be worthwhile and the value derived from holding the underlying securities should conversion be worthwhile. The criteria attempt to provide for this. First, an assessment of the value of the underlying securities is provided for by requiring that the general eligibility criteria have to be met for the underlying securities. This is intended to provide a market price for the underlying securities that is established by sophisticated investors on the basis of continuous disclosure concerning the issuer of the underlying securities. Second, the assessment of the value of the convertible debt or preferred shares, assuming no conversion takes place, is facilitated by a guarantee of payment and a market signal of the risk of non-payment on the guarantee in the form of an approved rating for the securities to

---

[43] NP #47, para. 4.3(2)(c).

[44] Ibid.

be issued and the non-convertible debt or preferred shares of the guarantor.

3. Alternative Criteria for "Substantial" Canadian Issuers

There is an alternative set of criteria for issuers that do not meet the normal reporting issuer requirement but are incorporated, continued or organized under the laws of Canada, or a province or territory of Canada, and have a public float of equity securities of $300,000,000 or more.[45] To satisfy the reporting issuer requirement for the general eligibility criteria the issuer must be a reporting issuer for a period 12 months prior to the filing of an AIF in a Canadian jurisdiction. Thus this is an exemption that may be useful for issuers that have not been reporting issuers for the requisite 12 month period before the filing of an AIF. The very significant level public float presumably provides for a sufficiently close market following that a 12 month period of availability of information is not necessary to establish a fair market price. The market is presumably able to assess the information in the newly filed AIF in relatively short order.

D. Implementation of the POP System

Except in the province of Quebec, the POP system set up by NP #47 is implemented in the provinces by way of a blanket order granting an exemption from the normal prospectus requirements of the applicable securities act and regulations. In Quebec, a version of the POP system similar in general approach to that of NP #47 is provided for in the *Securities Act* and Regulations.[46]

E. Exemptions for the POP Eligibility Criteria

The criteria are, of course, an arbitrary attempt to identify a level of disclosure and market following considered sufficient to assure an adequate amount of information and its assimilation by the market. Thus where the issuer comes close to fulfilling the

---

[45] NP #47, para. 4.2.

[46] See in Quebec, see Q.S.A. ss. 18, 18.1, 19, 64, 84-88 and Q.Reg. ss. 58-62, 164-170.1, Schedules IV, IX, IX.1, and X, and Pol. No. Q-1.

requirements and can point to some disclosure or evidence of market following that substitutes for the particular criteria it may be able to obtain an order from a securities commission allowing it distribute securities under the POP system.[47] For instance, one might be able to satisfy the reporting issuer requirement with roughly corresponding disclosure in another jurisdiction or under other regulatory disclosure requirements.[48] Similarly, the issuer may be able to point to other evidence of market following where it does not meet the $75,000,000 public float test.[49]

Securities administrators have also reserved a discretion to refuse to accept an AIF for filing or to refuse to issue a receipt for a short-form prospectus pursuant to NP #47.[50] NP #47 also provides that a securities administrator exercising this discretion give reasons for

---

[47] Securities administrators have reserved a discretion to grant exemptions to the specific requirements of NP #47. See NP #47, paras. 4.5 and 7.3.

[48] For instance, an exception was made with respect to the disclosure requirements in a ruling concerning the Canadian National Railway Company (see (1984), 7 O.S.C.B. 2135). At the time the early version of the POP system required that the issuer be a reporting issuer for a period of 36 months. The company had been a reporting issuer for only 22 months. However, before it became a reporting issuer it had filed annual reports with the Minister of Transport, which were tabled before Parliament, and had filed annual reports and financial statements with the U.S. Securities and Exchange Commission. The Ontario Securities Commission granted an exemption order allowing the Canadian National Railway Company to distribute securities under the POP system. The disclosure to the Minister of Transport and to the SEC arguably served as a reasonable substitute for 36 months of disclosure as a reporting issuer in Ontario.

[49] With respect to the public float test the ruling on an application by Abitibi-Price Inc. is instructive (see (1985), 8 O.S.C.B. 2443). Abitibi did not meet the public float test in its financial statements as of the time required by the policy statement. However, at the time of the application it had met the public float test for a period of ten weeks. The Commission granted the application noting that the company had a wide following in the market owing to its substantial size in terms of sales and assets and its unique position in the forest products industry as the world's largest producer of newsprint.

NP #47, para. 5.2(2) deals with a situation in which the issuer does not meet the public float test either in the last calendar month of its financial year or in the last calendar month before the filing of its Renewal AIF. The issuer can still fill a Renewal AIF and restore its eligibility to use the POP system if it satisfies the public float test during any calendar month before the end of its current financial year.

[50] NP #47, paras. 7.1 & 7.2.

doing so and give the issuer an opportunity to be heard on the matter.[51]

III. THE SHELF OFFERING PROSPECTUS

A shelf offering system was considered by the Canadian Securities Administrators in 1986 and again in 1989.[52] A proposed National Policy was circulated and, after a request for comments, was adapted and became effective on May 10, 1991.[53]

A. The Problem to Which Shelf Offerings Responded

Like the POP system, a system for shelf offerings in National Policy #44 was adopted out of concern for the need for more ready access to capital markets. The claim was that increased market volatility meant that "financing windows" (or periods when capital could be raised on particularly attractive terms) were brief.[54] The adoption of a shelf offering system was intended to "provide more flexibility and reduce the burdens, costs and time pressures for issuers seeking to raise capital under changing market conditions ...".[55] It was also intended to "encourag[e] the raising of capital in the Canadian markets by providing Canadian issuers with procedures now available only outside Canada."[56]

Further, it was argued that some forms of innovative financing techniques were not easily accommodated under the existing prospectus procedures.[57]

---

[51] Ibid.

[52] (1990), 13 O.S.C.B. 2560.

[53] National Policy #44 (hereinafter "N.P #44").

[54] (1990), 13 O.S.C.B. 2560.

[55] Ibid.

[56] Ibid.

[57] Ibid., 2560-61.

B. Description of the Shelf Offering Procedure

1. A Brief Synopsis

The shelf offering procedure increases flexibility and reduces the time for clearance of securities for distribution by allowing the issuer to qualify a prospectus that will apply to a series of distributions of securities under the prospectus over the ensuing two years. To do this the issuer files the short-form prospectus that would be filed under the POP system.[58] However, the short-form prospectus can omit information that would normally be included. The omitted information is information that relates to a specific tranche of securities to be distributed and which will vary from one tranche of securities to another.[59]

When a tranche of the securities cleared under the short-form prospectus is issued, the issuer must provide a prospectus supplement which contains the omitted information.[60] The prospectus supplement will not normally be vetted by securities administrators,[61] but must be filed within two days of the date on which the offering price of the securities is determined or within two days of the first use of the supplement.[62] The distribution of a particular tranche can start whenever the issuer and its underwriters decide it is an appropriate time to issue the securities.

---

[58] N.P. #44, s. 2.3(a). The permission to use the shelf offering procedures in substitution for the normal prospectus procedures is provided, for example, in Ontario by a ruling, dated May 10, 1991.

[59] See infra Part III B 4 a and b.

[60] See infra Part III B 4 c.

[61] In some situations the securities commission reserves the right to review prospectus supplements. For instance, N.P. #44, s. 3.2(c) notes that securities regulatory authorities may require that prospectus supplements for the distribution of derivative securities be pre-cleared. Derivative securities are described as generally including "securities the value of or return from which is based upon the market price, value or return of one or more underlying securities or commodities or upon the level of one or more financial bench marks such as interest rates, foreign exchange rates or stock market indicies"; see the note to N.P. #44, s. 3.2(c).

[62] N.P. #44, s. 3.4(a) & (b).

2. *Eligibility*

To be eligible to use the shelf offering procedures, the issuer must satisfy the eligibility criteria of the POP system.[63] An issuer is also eligible to use the shelf offering procedures if it has obtained an order from a securities regulatory authority that permits it to use the POP system.[64] The shelf offering procedures can be used to offer securities of one basic type such as debt, preferred or common shares.[65] They may also be used by selling security holders, such as control persons, whose trades would constitute a distribution.[66]

3. *Restrictions*

There are some types of offerings for which the shelf offering procedures cannot be used. For instance, the shelf procedures cannot be used for rights offerings.[67] The use of the shelf procedures, for the distribution of derivative securities, the value or return from which depends upon one or more underlying securities or commodities, or upon the level of one or more financial benchmarks such as interest rates, foreign exchange or stock market indices, is also restricted. The use of shelf procedures for derivative securities is subject to prior review by securities regulatory authorities on a case-

---

[63] N.P. #44, s. 3.1(a)(1). This includes the alternative eligibility criteria relating to issues of non-convertible approved rating debt or preferred shares. The POP eligibility criteria are discussed above in Part II C.

If an issuer ceases to satisfy the POP system criteria, it can no longer use the shelf offering procedures. However, the POP System criteria depend, with respect to the public float test, on the issuer's public float in the last month of the fiscal year for its most recently completed annual financial statements. Determining whether the public float test has been satisfied may require that the financial statements be complete. Thus an issuer is given 60 days after the end of its most recently completed financial year to determine whether it has ceased to satisfy the eligibility criteria (either pursuant to the POP system or to an order of a securities commission). If it fails to meet the criteria, any distribution under the shelf offering procedures must stop within 60 days of the end of its most recently completed financial year.

[64] N.p. #44, s. 3.1(a)(2).

[65] N.P. #44, s. 3.2(a).

[66] Ibid.

[67] N.P. #44, s. 3.2(b).

by-case basis.[68] Further, distributions under a shelf offering prospectus are limited to the amount of securities the issuer (or selling security holder) reasonably expects to offer and sell within two years from the date of the filing of the prospectus.[69]

4. *Disclosure*

a. THE ANNUAL INFORMATION FORM

As noted above, to be eligible to use the shelf procedures the reporting issuer will have to comply with the POP system eligibility criteria which requires that the issuer has filed an AIF and has continued to file AIFs as required.[70] The AIF, together with subsequently filed continuous disclosure documents, will provide the disclosure which will allow a distribution to proceed under a prospectus designed to provide information with respect to the particular securities being offered and prospectus supplements designed to provide information particular to the offering of each separate tranche of the securities being offered under the prospectus.

b. THE SHORT-FORM SHELF PROSPECTUS

The short-form prospectus filed under the shelf procedures must set out the aggregate amount of securities to be offered under the prospectus and all information that will not vary from the offering of one tranche of securities under the prospectus to another.[71] A prospectus, or short-form prospectus under the POP system, requires that the plan of distribution of the securities be set out.[72] However, the shelf procedures recognize that different methods of distribution may be appropriate under separate distributions over the two-year life of the shelf prospectus. To provide flexibility in this regard, the shelf procedures allow the issuer to set out two or more alternative methods of distribution.[73]

To the extent the information is not known at the date of the filing of the shelf offering short-form prospectus, there may be

---

[68] N.P. #44, s. 3.2(c) and note 7 of N.P. #44.

[69] N.P. #44, s. 3.2(d).

[70] See Part II C and Part III B 2.

[71] N.P. #44, s. 3.3(a).

[72] See, for example, One. Form 12, Item 2 and N.P. #47, Appendix B, Item 7.

[73] N.P. #44, s. 3.3(b).

omitted from the short-form prospectus filed under the shelf procedures such information as:[74]

(i) the amount of securities to be distributed under each separate tranche of securities distributed under the prospectus;

(ii) maturities, denominations, interest or dividend provisions, purchase, redemption, retraction, conversion, exchange, or sinking fund provisions, or any other special covenants or terms applicable to a particular tranche of securities to be distributed;

(iii) which of any alternative methods of distribution will be applicable to each tranche of securities offered;

(iv) names of any underwriters, conflicts of interest or prospectus certificates of unnamed underwriters, the distribution spread, underwriting fees, discounts and commissions;

(v) the public offering price, delivery dates, legal opinions concerning the eligibility for investment of the securities, statements regarding listing of the securities, actual amount of proceeds or more specific information about the use of proceeds.

This type of information is known as "shelf information".[75] The short-form prospectus must indicate that all such information will be provided in one or more prospectus supplements that will be delivered to purchasers together with the prospectus.[76]

The shelf prospectus must incorporate by reference the latest AIF.[77] It must also incorporate continuous disclosure documents filed since the beginning of the latest financial year in which the latest AIF was filed.[78] It is deemed to incorporate by reference the latest AIF and all continuous disclosure documents filed by the issuer after the date of the prospectus and before the completion, or withdrawal, of the offering.[79]

---

[74] N.P. #44, s. 3.3(c).

[75] N.P. #44, s. 2.1(s).

[76] N.P. #44, s. 3.3(d). See also the statement that must be included in this regard — s. 2.3(b).

[77] N.P. #44, s. 2.4(a).

[78] Ibid.

[79] N.P. #44, s. 2.4(b).

c. PROSPECTUS SUPPLEMENTS

When a tranche of securities is to be distributed under the shelf prospectus, a prospectus supplement must be issued which contains all the information omitted from the shelf prospectus with respect to the particular tranche of securities being offered.[80] It must also include a list identifying and briefly describing any document incorporated by reference which has not been incorporated by reference in the shelf prospectus or in a previous prospectus supplement.[81] The supplement is incorporated by reference into the prospectus, but only for the purposes of the offering of the securities covered by that prospectus supplement.[82]

The supplement may also contain additional information provided it does not describe a material change that has not already been the subject of a material change report or amendment to the shelf prospectus.[83] Where material changes occur, they are simply reported in material change reports without an amendment to the prospectus as long as the material change does not occur during

---

[80] N.P. #44, s. 3.4(a)(1). Where debt or preferred shares are offered, information must normally be provided with respect to earnings and asset coverage ratios. Earnings coverage is the ratio of earnings to interest payment obligations on debt or to interest payment obligations on debt plus dividend preferences on preferred shares. Asset coverage is the ratio of assets to liabilities with respect to obligations to pay the principal amount of debts or the principal amounts of debt plus preferred share redemption values. Under a shelf offering the historical earnings and asset coverage ratios are to be disclosed in the shelf prospectus [N.P. #44 s. 3.6.(a)(1)]. However, at the time of the issue of a particular tranche of securities under the shelf prospectus there may be more up-to-date financial statements which can provide more up-to-date earnings and asset coverage ratios. These more up-to-date figures must be included in the prospectus supplement [N.P. #44, s. 3.4(a)(3) and s. 3.6(a)(2)(i) & (ii)]. Further, the prospectus supplement must provide information on the effect of changes since the last available financial statements as well as information about the effect of the issuance of the particular tranche on earnings and asset coverage ratios [N.P. #44, s. 3.4(a)(3) and s. 3.6].

Similarly, where the dilution effect of a distribution of a tranche of equity securities cannot be determined until the terms of the securities of the particular tranche are set, the supplement must provide information with respect to the dilution effect of the distribution of the particular tranche of securities [N.P. #44, s. 3.4(a)(4) & s. 3.7].

[81] N.P. #44. s. 3.4(a)(7).

[82] N.P. #44, ss. 2.4(c) & 3.4(c).

[83] N.P. #44, s. 3.4(a).

a period when actual offers and sales of securities pursuant to the shelf prospectus are being made. Where a material change occurs while actual offers and sales of securities are being made pursuant to the prospectus, an amendment to the shelf prospectus is required.[84] However, the amendment can take the form of the material change report itself with the addition of prospectus certificates accompanying the amendment indicating that the prospectus, in its amended form, constitutes full, true and plain disclosure.[85]

5. Variable Term Debt Securities

National Policy #44 allows for the creation of a program in which terms of individual debt securities, such as terms to maturity, interest rates and prices, will be determined at the time of sale.[86] The program can be set up in a shelf prospectus or in a supplement to the shelf prospectus.[87] When the maturity, interest rate and pricing of a security is determined, the issuer must provide a "pricing supplement" which sets out these terms and identifies any additional documents to be incorporated by reference into the prospectus that have been filed since the filing of the shelf prospectus or the last prospectus supplement.[88]

6. Non-Fixed Price Offerings

Securities sold under a prospectus following the normal prospectus procedures set out the price of the securities in the final prospectus. Although the price might be altered in a prospectus amendment, this can take time and thus creates some rigidity with respect to changing the price at which securities are offered. National Policy #44 attempts, in a limited way, to provide some flexibility in this regard. It allows for an offering of equity securities at other than a fixed price either through the facilities of an exchange or

---

[84] N.P. #44, ss. 2.5 & 3.8(b)(1).

[85] N.P. #44, ss. 2.5, 3.8(b)(2) and Appendix B ss. 1.1(c), 1.2(c), 2.1(c) and 2.2(c) & (d).

[86] N.P. #44, ss. 2.1(i) & (j), 3.4(b)(1) & (2) and 3.4(f).

[87] N.P. #44, s. 3.4(f).

[88] N.P. #44, s. 3.4(f)(4) & (5).

over-the-counter.[89] However, the issuer must already have securities of the type being offered outstanding.[90]

Although such "non-fixed price" offerings are allowed in order to provide added flexibility, there are some unique problems with disclosure created by allowing such a scheme. Information considered to be important, such as the price, the proceeds of the issue and the compensation of underwriters may not be determinable at the time the securities are issued. To deal with these disclosure problems, the policy sets out special disclosure requirements for the prospectus or prospectus supplement. It requires disclosure as to the commission payable to underwriters, the minimum amount of proceeds to be received by the issuer under a best efforts underwriting, the method of determining the price of the security and where it is to be determined by reference to the market price of the security, or by reference to the market price of a specified security, the latest available market price for the security.[91]

Because of concern with respect to the unique disclosure problems relating to non-fixed price offerings,[92] the offering of equity securities on a non-fixed price basis is limited to 10% of the aggregate market value of the issuer's outstanding[93] equity securities of the class being offered, excluding large block holdings.[94]

---

[89] N.P. #44, s. 2.1(d) and s. 3.5.

[90] N.P. #44. s. 2.1(d).

[91] N.P. #44, s. 3.5(a).

[92] See (1990), 13 O.S.C.B. 2560 at 2562.

[93] The securities counted in determining the aggregate market value is not to include securities held by persons who own, directly or indirectly, or exercise control or direction over more than 10% of the issued and outstanding equity securities of the issuer calculated as of a date 60 days prior to the filing of the prospectus [see N.P. #44, s. 3.5(b)(1)].

[94] N.P. #44, s. 3.5(b). This may provide some assurance that the issue itself will not have a substantial effect on the market price of the securities, with reference to which the price of the securities offered in the non-fixed price offering will be determined. There is also a concern that the person selling the securities might try to influence the market price of the securities with reference to which the offering price of the securities will be determined. To address this concern, issuers are prevented from selling the securities directly. The securities must be sold by an underwriter acting as principal or agent and the underwriter must be named in the prospectus and must sign the prospectus certificates [N.P. #44, s. 3.5(b)(2) & (3)]. Also it must be disclosed (with the benefit of the underwriter's certificate so that it can be enforced) that none of the underwriters and dealers involved

7. Civil Liability

While National Policy #44 modifies the requirements with respect to prospectus disclosure, it does not provide relief from the statutory civil liability or quasi-criminal liability provisions of provincial securities acts.[95] For the purpose of these provisions, the prospectus will consist of the short-form shelf prospectus, any supplements or amendments to that prospectus and all documents incorporated by reference.[96]

As with other prospectuses required under provincial securities laws, prospectus certificates of the issuer and underwriter must be included in the prospectus and must be signed as required under provincial securities laws.[97] To avoid the need to continually re-sign each prospectus supplement, the Policy allows for the use of a "forward looking" certificate which provides that the short-form shelf prospectus in which the certificate appears and all documents incorporated by reference "as of the date of each supplement ..., will constitute full, true and plain disclosure of all material facts ...".[98] However, if preferred, a certificate can be provided with each individual supplement and the method chosen for the provision of an issuer's, promoter's and underwriter's certificate need not be the same.[99]

---

in the distribution, or their affiliates, or anyone acting jointly or in concert with the underwriters, dealers or their affiliates, have over-allotted or will over-allot the securities, or have, or will effect, any transactions which are intended to stabilize or maintain the market price of the securities [N.P. #44, s. 3.5(b)(4)].

[95] N.P. #44, s. 2.6(a).

[96] As of the date of the prospectus, the prospectus must incorporate by reference the latest AIF and all continuous disclosure documents filed by the issuer since the commencement of the issuer's latest financial year in which its latest AIF was filed [N.P. #44, s. 2.4(a)]. Also the latest AIF together with material change reports, interim financial statements, comparative financial statements, the auditor's report and information circulars filed subsequent to the date of the prospectus are all deemed to be incorporated by reference into the prospectus [s. 2.4(b)]. Each prospectus supplement is deemed to be incorporated by reference for the purposes of the offering of securities covered by that prospectus supplement [s. 3.4(c)].

[97] N.P. #44, s. 3.9.

[98] Appendix B, s. 1.1(a). A somewhat modified form of this is provided for underwriters — see Appendix B, s. 1.2(a).

[99] N.P. #44, s. 3.9. For instance, since the underwriter may not be determined at the time of the filing of the shelf prospectus, it may be more practical to have underwriters sign the individual prospectus supplements.

IV. PREP PROCEDURES

A. General Description

The "PREP Procedures" (or post receipt pricing procedures) allow for the pricing of securities to be distributed under a prospectus after a receipt for the final prospectus has been obtained.[100] These procedures are intended to reduce the risk associated with fluctuations in market prices between the time the final prospectus material is provided and the time the receipt for the final prospectus is issued.[101] By reducing this risk, the procedures should reduce the pressure on securities administrators to expedite the issuance of receipts for final prospectuses.[102]

The PREP procedures allow for the filing of a final prospectus that omits the public offering price; the dividend or interest rate; cash underwriting fees, discounts and commissions; the actual amount of proceeds; redemption, purchase for cancellation, conversion and exchange prices and dates; dividend or interest payment dates, record dates and the dates from which dividends or interest accrue; delivery dates, and other terms of the securities dependent upon the offering date or offering price.[103] This omitted information (called the "PREP Information")[104] must be set out in a supplemented prospectus (called the "Supplemented PREP Prospectus") when the price and offering date as determined.[105] The form of

---

[100] In the normal prospectus process the preliminary prospectus need not contain the price and price related information. However, in the normal prospectus process, when the vetting of the preliminary prospectus is complete and all deficiencies have been cleared, the final prospectus submitted for receipt must contain the price and price related information.

[101] See (1990), 13 O.S.C.B. 2560 at 2562 on the introduction of N.P. #44.

[102] Ibid.

[103] N.P. #44, s. 4.3(a).

[104] N.P. #44, s. 2.1(o).

[105] N.P. #44, s. 4.3(b). The Supplemented PREP Prospectus must be filed with the principal securities regulatory authority by no later than the second business day following the date of the determination of the omitted information and, as nearly as practicable, contemporaneously with other applicable securities regulatory authorities. Details on the content of supplemental PREP Prospectus disclosure, issuers and underwriter's certificates, and filing requirements are set out in N.P. #44, ss. 4.3 and 4.4.

the Supplemented PREP Prospectus is the prospectus modified to include the omitted information.[106]

It is expected that offerings using the PREP procedures will be priced shortly after a receipt for the prospectus is obtained.[107] Consequently the price and price related information must be provided within five business days after the receipt for the prospectus is issued.[108] If the omitted information is not provided in a supplemented prospectus within five business days, the information must either be provided in a prospectus amendment or an amended prospectus must be filed to commence a new five business day period.[109]

The changes made to the prospectus by providing the supplemental PREP Information in the Supplemented PREP Prospectus are referred to as the "PREP Changes".[110] These PREP Changes are deemed to be incorporated by reference into the prospectus as of the date of the Supplemented PREP Prospectus.[111] Consequently, statutory civil liability for misrepresentations will extend to the information provided in the Supplemented PREP Prospectus.[112] The Supplemented PREP Prospectus must be delivered to purchasers in lieu of the prospectus and rights of rescission or withdrawal commence from the time of the purchaser's receipt of the Supplemented PREP Prospectus.[113]

B. Eligibility

The PREP procedures may be used by issuers which satisfy the eligibility criteria for the POP system or have equity securities that

---

[106] N.P. #44, s. 4.3(b).

[107] N.P. #44, s. 4.3(d).

[108] Ibid.

[109] Ibid. If PREP information has not been provided in a Supplemented PREP Prospectus or an amended prospectus within 75 days of the date of the receipt for the prospectus, then no distribution of a security under the prospectus may be made.

[110] N.P. #44, s. 4.3(b) and s. 2.1(n).

[111] N.P. #44, s. 4.3(c).

[112] Statutory civil liability is discussed in Chapter 5.

[113] N.P. #44, s. 4.5. As to statutory rights of withdrawal and rescission, see Chapter 4, Part VII E and Chapter 4, Part VIII A 3.

are listed and posted for trading on a recognized stock exchange.[114] Issuers meeting these eligibility criteria may offer securities for cash.[115] Issuers which do not meet the POP system eligibility criteria or do not have securities listed and posted for trading on a recognized stock exchange may still use the PREP procedures to offer non-convertible debt or preferred shares which have an approved rating for cash.[116] The PREP procedures may not be used for rights offerings[117] and the use of the PREP procedures for offerings of derivative securities is assessed on a case-by-case basis due to concern for complex disclosure issues that such offerings may raise.[118]

V. ASSUMPTIONS AND CONCERNS WITH THE POP SYSTEM, SHELF OFFERINGS AND PREP PROCEDURES

A. The Principle Behind the POP System

The POP and shelf systems continue the assumption of the regulatory regime set up prior to the introduction of these systems, namely, that the market is not efficient enough to produce an appro-

---

[114] N.P. #44, s. 4.1. An issuer also satisfies the eligibility criteria if it has obtained a ruling or order from a securities regulatory authority of a province or territory that permits it to use the POP system for the distribution of the securities the issuer intends to distribute under the PREP procedures (see N.P. #44, s. 4.1(b)). The PREP procedures may also be used by selling security holders where the issuer meets the eligibility criteria (see N.P. #44, s. 4.1 and 4.2(a)). The recognized stock exchanges are the Toronto Stock Exchange, the Montreal Exchange, the "Senior Board" of the Vancouver Stock Exchange, the "Exempt Companies" designation of the Alberta Stock Exchange, the New York Stock Exchange, the American Stock Exchange, the National Market System of the National Association of Securities Dealers Automated Quotation System, and the International Stock Exchange of the United Kingdom and the Republic of Ireland Limited. See N.P. #44, Appendix A.

[115] N.P. #44, s. 4.2(a).

[116] N.P. #44, s. 4.2(a). The PREP procedures may also be used for non-fixed price offerings of non-convertible "Approved Rating" debt or preferred shares (see N.P. #44, s. 4.2(b)). The "Approved Ratings" are set out in N.P. #44, s. 2.1(b).

[117] N.P. #44, s. 4.2(c).

[118] N.P. #44, s. 4.2(d).

priate degree of disclosure about securities. This assumption is evident in that the systems are based, in part, on compliance with the mandatory continuous disclosure requirements supplemented with disclosure through the AIF and the short-form prospectus.

The POP and shelf systems are also based on an assumption about the efficiency of the market in disseminating and assessing information once it has been disclosed. The public float test focuses on the extent to which the securities are followed in the market.[119] As noted in Chapter 2,[120] those who specialize in security analysis will not spend a lot of time or incur substantial costs to research a security if there is not a sufficient depth in the market to recoup the costs through trading profits. The public float test is a test based on a rule of thumb used by market analysts in determining whether to follow a particular issuer's securities.[121] Thus the test attempts to identify securities for which the market should be reasonably efficient because the securities will be closely followed. Because the markets for these securities are likely to be reasonably efficient, the information provided through mandatory disclosure should be reflected in the price relatively quickly (at least within the roughly one-week clearance period necessary to issue securities under the POP system).

The protection of unsophisticated investors depends on this market efficiency and the reflection of the information in the price of the security. It is doubtful that the average unsophisticated investor actually reads much of what is in a prospectus that is provided under the normal prospectus disclosure procedures.[122] It is even less likely that they would go to the trouble of gathering and assessing all the information that is incorporated by reference in a short-form prospectus. Thus the protection of the unsophisticated investor under the POP or shelf system does not depend on the investor reading the information and assessing the value of the

---

[119]See G. Emerson, "Short Form Prospectus Offerings in Canada" (November, 1982) cited in Steen and McKee, *supra* note 1, at 20.

[120]Part III A 3.

[121]See Emerson, *supra* note 118.

[122]See, for example, M.H. Cohen, "Truth in Securities Revisited" (1966) 79 Harv. L. Rev. 1340 at 1351-52; H. Kripke, *The SEC and Corporate Disclosure: Regulation in Search of a Purpose* (New York: Law & Business, Inc., 1979), at 22 and 97-98 (citing an SEC Advisory Committee report on corporate disclosure).

security on the basis of that information. Instead it depends on the extent to which the price of the security in the market is a fair reflection of the underlying value of the security.

The POP system, with a clearance period of roughly one week, appears to take a very conservative view of securities market efficiency in light of evidence suggesting that well-traded securities markets respond to information very quickly.[123] On the other hand, the shelf procedures assume the market can virtually instantaneously assimilate information relating to a new issuance of securities.[124] Similarly, the PREP procedures assume the market can virtually instantaneously assimilate information relating to the post receipt pricing of a new issue of securities.

This faith in the efficiency of securities markets for the protection of investors may be somewhat excessive in light of more recent claims by some economists that although the market price may respond quickly to new information, it may not represent a fair estimate of the underlying value of the security. Indeed, there is some evidence that markets may overreact to new information.[125]

B. Concerns With the POP System, Shelf Offerings and PREP Procedures

A wide range of concerns have been noted with respect to the POP system. A few of these concerns are noted below, namely, the concern with respect to due diligence and statutory civil liability for continuous disclosure, and the tendency for the POP system to favour larger issuers and larger underwriters.[126]

---

[123] See the evidence noted in Chapter 2, Part III B.

[124] See the discussion of this assumption in J.N. Gordon and L.A. Kornhauser, "Efficient Markets, Costly Information and Securities Research" (1985) 60 N.Y.U.L. Rev. 761, at 818-23.

[125] See the literature referred to in Chapter 2, note 24.

[126] These concerns and other concerns are discussed in Steen and McKee, *supra* note 1, at pp. 29-45; and in B.A. Banoff, "Regulatory Subsidies, Efficient Markets, and Shelf Registration: An Analysis of Rule 415" (1964) 70 Virg. L. Rev. 135, at 154-84.

1. *Due Diligence and Statutory Civil Liability for Continuous Disclosure*

The idea behind the POP system is to allow for quicker access to securities markets. However, this means a shorter time frame for a due diligence examination. Further, the documents incorporated by reference in the prospectus become part of the prospectus and thus the representations contained in those documents become subject to the statutory civil liability for misrepresentations in a prospectus.[127]

From a practical point of view the added potential liability for misrepresentations in continuous disclosure documents may mean that a greater degree of due diligence work must be done for the preparation of those documents than might otherwise be the case. Also, from a practical point of view, the incorporation of continuous disclosure documents in the prospectus may mean that it is all that much more important to keep the same underwriters, accountants and lawyers involved in the production of the continuous disclosure documents leading up to a distribution under a short-form prospectus, so that a full-blown due diligence examination is not necessary at the time of preparation of the short-form prospectus. The time it could take to conduct a complete due diligence examination might defeat the whole purpose of using the POP or shelf systems, namely, to get quicker access to the capital market.

2. *Favours Larger Issuers*

Another concern with respect to the POP system is that it favours larger issuers. The cost of issuing securities as a percentage of the value of securities tends to decrease as the aggregate value of the issue being sold increases. Thus larger issuers who float larger issues of securities tend to be able to raise capital at lower cost than smaller issuers. The POP and Shelf systems tend to exacerbate this advantage for larger issuers. By allowing larger issuers to access the market more quickly, the risk of fluctuation in market prices to which larger issuers are exposed is reduced. This reduction in the risk of price changes to which larger issuers or their underwriters are

---

[127]Unless, of course, the short-form prospectus or some other disclosure has corrected the misrepresentation before securities are distributed under the short-form prospectus.

exposed allows larger issuers to raise capital at lower cost. This could contribute to a concentration of capital and power.

3. *Favours Larger Underwriters*

The POP system may also tend to favour larger underwriting firms. As noted above, the short time frame for issuing securities under the POP and Shelf systems reduces the risk of fluctuations in the market price associated with the issue. This encourages bought deals since it reduces the risk to the underwriter of being stuck with a large issue of securities, which it can no longer sell at or above the price it paid for them due to a fall in securities market prices in the time between agreeing to buy securities and the time they can be distributed under a prospectus. However, bought deals may favour larger underwriting firms that have the capital to buy and hold large issues of securities.[128]

VI. THE MULTIJURISDICTIONAL DISCLOSURE SYSTEM

A. Reasons for the Multijurisdictional Disclosure System

As noted in Chapter 4, N.I. 71-101 sets up a "multijurisdictional disclosure system" (MJDS) for distributions of securities that are made in both Canada and the United States, or, for a distribution in Canada of securities previously distributed in the U.S. N.I. 71-101 is the Canadian Securities Administrators instrument allowing a security issuance made in compliance with U.S. securities law requirements to be in Canada using a prospectus that conforms to the U.S. securities law requirements supplemented with certain additional Canadian disclosure. Without N.I. 71-101 an issuer of securities in the U.S. that wanted to extend the issuance to Canada would have to produce an entirely new prospectus conforming to the prospectus requirements of Canadian securities law. The cost of complying with the Canadian prospectus requirements might discourage the issuer from extending the issuance to Canada. Thus N.I. 71-101

---

[128] Although syndications of smaller firms might still be able to complete a bought deal, the costs of negotiating the syndicating agreements may make this approach to underwriting a bought deal non-competitive.

attempts to facilitate the extension of a U.S. securities issuance to Canada.[129] Provisions of U.S. securities law provide for a similar system allowing Canadian issuers to issue securities in the U.S. using documents required by Canadian law for a distribution of securities in Canada.[130]

Although a U.S. prospectus requires information that is quite similar to that required by Canadian securities laws, there are several subtle differences in the information required and its presentation. These differences presumably make it difficult for unsophisticated investors to assess and assimilate the information. However, this concern may be alleviated where the information is assessed and assimilated for unsophisticated investors by more sophisticated investors. As with the POP and Shelf systems, it is assumed that a sufficient sophisticated investor review is present where the issuer satisfies a public float test for market following or where the securities have an approved rating.[131]

B. Permitted Offerings Using U.S. Documentation

Thus N.I. 71-101 permits a distribution in Canada on the basis of U.S. prospectus requirements for:

(i) non-convertible debt and non-convertible preferred shares that have an investment grade rating;

(ii) convertible debt and preferred shares that are not convertible for at least one year after issuance, and other securities, as long as the issuer meets a public float test and certain other requirements; and

(iii) certain rights to acquire securities of the issuer.[132]

---

[129] N.I. 71-101 states that the MJDS "is intended to remove unnecessary obstacles to certain offerings of securities of U.S. issuers in Canada ... while ensuring that Canadian investors remain adequately protected".

[130] See the discussion in T.L. Hazen, *Treatise on the Law of Securities Regulation*, 3d ed. (St. Paul, Minn.: West Publishing, 1995) at vol. 1, pp. 134-36. Hazen notes that the original intent of the SEC was to negotiate MJDS agreements, such as the one with Canada, with other countries but that the SEC has since abandoned the MJDS approach in favour of a more generalized series of international disclosure standards.

[131] N.I. 71-101, s. 3.1. On "investment grade" rating, see Companion Policy 71-101 CP, s. 32(2).

[132] N.I. 71-101, s. 3.1(a)(ii)(A).

To issue approved rating non-convertible debt or preferred shares or other securities, the issuer must be a U.S. issuer having a class of securities registered under the U.S. *Securities Exchange Act of 1934* or is otherwise required to make filings similar to those required of a reporting issuer in Canada.[133] The issuer must have made the required U.S. filings for a period of at least 12 calendar months.[134] For other securities, including debt and preferred shares convertible only after one year from the date of issuance, there is a public float test requirement of $U.S. 75,000,000.[135] Debt and preferred shares may be issued under the MJDS by an issuer not satisfying the eligibility requirements for the MJDS if the debt or preferred share obligations are unconditionally guaranteed by a parent issuer that meets the eligibility criteria.[136]

Rights offerings may also be made using U.S. documentation subject to certain additional requirements.[137] For instance, the issuer must have made its reporting issuer type filings in the U.S. for a period of at least 36 calendar months and must have a class of securities listed on the New York Stock Exchange, the American Stock Exchange or the NASDAQ National Market.[138]

C. The Mechanics of an MJDS Offering

A U.S. offering involves the filing of a registration statement with the Securities Exchange Commission (SEC) and the use of a prospectus as a selling document based on the information contained in the registration statement. The SEC can then examine the registration statement for compliance with its requirements and adequacy of disclosure. The distribution can then proceed when the SEC has declared the registration statement effective. Although the process is quite similar to that in Canada, the Canadian process, as noted in Chapter 4, involves the filing of a preliminary prospectus for review followed by the filing of a final prospectus when any deficiencies in the preliminary prospectus have been rectified to the satis-

---

[133] Ibid., s. 3.1(a)(ii)(B).

[134] Ibid., s. 3.1(a)(iii) (36 calendar months for rights offerings, s. 3.1(b)(ii)).

[135] Ibid., s. 3.1(a)(vi) and s. 3.1(c)(ii).

[136] Ibid., s. 3.2.

[137] Ibid., s. 3.1(b).

[138] Ibid.

faction of the securities administrators. To conform to the Canadian prospectus review process N.I. 71-101 requires the issuer to provide a preliminary prospectus.[139] This can take the form of a U.S. prospectus with a supplement containing the additional material required under N.I. 71-101.[140] Where the issuance is being made in both Canada and the U.S., the issuer can leave out information that is unique to the U.S. offering. If the issuance is an issuance only in Canada of securities previous issued in the U.S. the issuer can prepare the prospectus and supplement as if the issuance were also being made in the U.S.

The issuer selects a principal jurisdiction in Canada to review the material filed under N.I. 71-101.[141] The issuer files the preliminary prospectus material with each jurisdiction in Canada where it intends to distribute the securities. The securities regulators in each of those jurisdictions will issue a receipt for the preliminary prospectus when the preliminary prospectus and supporting material have been filed in compliance with N.I. 71-101.[142] A receipt for the prospectus can be obtained from the principal jurisdiction upon the registration statement being declared effective by the SEC.[143] Once a receipt for the prospectus has been obtained from the principal jurisdiction, receipts from the other Canadian jurisdictions can be obtained upon the filing of the prospectus, all documents incorporated by reference in the prospectus and any supporting documentation required by N.I. 71-101.[144] However, a receipt may be refused where the securities administrators in one or more of the Canadian jurisdictions in which the prospectus is filed have reason to believe that there may be a problem with the transaction, the related disclosure or where other special circumstances exist.[145]

---

[139] Ibid., s. 3.4.

[140] Ibid., s. 1.1 "MJDS Prospectus", and Companion Policy 71-101 CP, s. 3.2(5).

[141] Ibid., s. 5.1.

[142] Companion Policy 71-101 CP, s. 3.2(12).

[143] Ibid., s. 3.2(12)(a), (c).

[144] Ibid., s. 3.2(12)(b) & (c).

[145] Ibid., s. 3.2(12).

D. Additional Canadian Disclosure

The additional disclosure requirements include legends to be included with the preliminary prospectus that indicate, among other things, that the preliminary prospectus is not yet final for the purpose of distribution to the public, that the information is subject to completion or amendment and that the disclosure is prepared in accordance with U.S. disclosure laws that may differ from Canadian requirements.[146] The U.S. based financial disclosure in the prospectus must also be reconciled to Canadian generally accepted accounting principles either in the notes to the financial statements or in a supplement to the prospectus.[147] N.I. 71-101 also provides for modified issuer and underwriter certificates to the effect that the prospectus contains full, true and plain disclosure of all material facts.[148]

---

[146] N.I. 71-101, s. 4.3(1).

[147] Ibid., s. 4.6.

[148] Ibid., s. 4.7.

CHAPTER 9

MANDATORY DISCLOSURE AND MERIT DISCRETION: A RECONSIDERATION

I. INTRODUCTION

Chapter 3 noted the purpose of modern securities regulation in Canada. Briefly, the purpose is to protect investors by creating confidence in the market. A key mechanism for creating confidence in the market is disclosure in both the primary and secondary markets for securities. The market itself would not provide this confidence creating disclosure because of the problem of adverse selection.

Chapters 4 through 8 dealt with the mandatory disclosure regime of Canadian securities regulation, which is intended to create confidence in the market and protect investors. This is an appropriate point to pause and reconsider the effect of mandatory disclosure on the prices of securities, before going on to examine other issues in securities regulation. In other words, has the regime of mandatory disclosure had the intended effect on the prices of securities?

The objective in this chapter is to provide the reader with some background for the purpose of addressing this question and suggesting issues that need to be addressed by further research. Part II provides an examination of some evidence on the effects of mandatory disclosure and Part III provides a summary of some different positions which question the need for mandatory disclosure. Part IV briefly notes scepticism as to the benefits of merit discretion.

II. SOME EVIDENCE ON THE EFFECTS OF MANDATORY DISCLOSURE

The evidence of a lack of confidence in the market calling for regulation in both the U.S. and Canada is anecdotal in nature. The anecdotes generally involved evidence of fraud. The legislative response to the problem was to require disclosure. This response was based on the assumption that disclosure would discourage fraud and would improve confidence in the market by improving the base of information on which investors could assess the value of securities.

Studies of the effects of the legislation introduced in the U.S. have since been undertaken. Studies by George Stigler, Greg Jarrell and Carol Simon on the effects of prospectus disclosure and a study by George Benston on mandatory financial disclosure are outlined below.

A. New Issue (or Prospectus) Disclosure

1. *Stigler*

a. ANALYSIS OF PRICE EFFECTS

(i) Method for Analysis of Price Effects

In 1964, George Stigler did a study comparing the pattern of post-issuance price changes for new issues before and after the introduction of U.S. federal laws mandating disclosure for primary distributions of securities.[1] He chose the 1923-28 period for the pre-regulation period and the 1949-55 period for a comparable post-regulation period. He traced the price changes for new issues in each of these periods over five years from the time of issuance. He looked at the ratio of the price at the end of each year after the issuance of the security to the price at which the security was initially issued.

The differences in price changes might have been due to differences in the economy as a whole and its effect on the overall pattern of price changes in the stock market. To adjust for this, Stigler compared the ratio of the price of the security to its issue price to a corresponding ratio for the market (i.e., the ratio of the market index at the end of each year to the market index at the time the security was initially issued).

---

[1] G.J. Stigler, "Public Regulation of Securities Markets" (1964) 37 J. of Bus. 117.

(ii) Results on Price Effects

Stigler found that, except for the third and fourth post-issue years, there were no statistically significant differences in the post-issue price changes of new security issues relative to the market.[2] Stigler's results led him to the conclusion that there was little evidence that mandatory disclosure requirements for the distribution of securities had any effect on securities prices.[3]

b. THE ANALYSIS OF THE EFFECT ON RISK

(i) Method of Analysis of Effect on Risk

Stigler also examined the effect of regulation on the risk of new issues of securities. He used the standard deviation of the price ratios as a measure of the risk associated with the new issues of securities in the 1923-28 period compared with the 1949-55 period.

(ii) Results of Analysis of Effect on Risk

Stigler found significant differences in the variance of the price ratios between the two periods. The variances were much lower in the 1949-55 period.[4] Since variances of the price ratios measured the fluctuation in the price ratios, these variances suggested, as

---

[2] Ibid., at 121. Stigler's test focused on the following ratio:

$$\frac{P_t/P_o}{M_t/M_o}$$

Where P_o is the price of the security at the time of issue of a particular new issue, P_t is the price of the security as measured at the end of each year from the date of issue, M_o is the market index at the date of the issuance of the new issue, and M_t is the market index at the end of each year from the date of issue of the particular new issue. The results of measuring the above ratio with respect to common stocks were as follows:

	Year 1	Year 2	Year 3	Year 4	Year 5
Pre-S.E.C.	.819	.651	.562	.528	.585
Post-S.E.C.	.816	.733	.726	.719	.696

[3] Ibid., at 124.

[4] Ibid., at 121-22. The results with respect to the variance of price ratios, expressed as standard deviations of price ratios, were as follows:

	Year 1	Year 2	Year 3	Year 4	Year 5
Pre-S.E.C.	.437	.467	.437	.485	.651
Post-S.E.C.	.239	.277	.310	.309	.389

Stigler noted, that the apparent effect of the regulation was to "[elim-inate] both unusually good and unusually bad new issues!"[5] Stigler noted that many more new companies used the market in the 1920s than in the 1950s and concluded that a major impact of the regu-lation was to exclude new companies.[6]

2. Jarrell

a. METHOD

Some time after Stigler's study, new techniques were developed for adjusting to differences in overall market effect on prices. New techniques were also developed for measuring the risk associated with particular securities. In a study published in 1981, Greg Jarrell replicated Stigler's analysis using these new techniques.[7] He looked at the performance of new issues between 1926 and 1939 over a five-year period from the date of issue.

b. EFFECTS ON PRICE

Jarrell found that post-regulation issues did better over the first year, while pre-regulation issues did better over the full five-year period. However, these differences were not found to be statistically significant. Jarrell concluded that,

the slightly inferior abnormal return performance of registered, post-SEC new equity issues over five years confirms the finding of Stigler. The mandatory registration of new equity issues did not improve the net-of-market returns over five years to investors who purchased the issues.[8]

c. EFFECTS ON RISK

Jarrell's results were also similar to Stigler's with respect to risk. Jarrell found lower risk on new issues of both equity and debt. He followed up these results with a test on the source of the reduced

---

[5] Ibid., at 122.

[6] Ibid., at 122 and note 7.

[7] G.A. Jarrell, "The Economic Effects of Federal Regulation of the Market for New Security Issues" (1981) 24 J. of Law and Eco. 613. Jarrell used a model known as the Capital Asset Pricing Model as the basis for analysis of returns and risks.

[8] Ibid., at 666.

risk. He found a higher rate of rejections of approval for new issues of securities in characteristically riskier industries such as mining, oil and gas, and merchandising. He also found that privately placed bonds had become riskier than publicly placed bonds, suggesting that regulation had caused issuers of riskier bonds to raise their capital in the unregulated private placement market.[9]

3. Simon

a. METHOD

Carol Simon employed yet more powerful techniques for the analysis of returns and risk in a paper published in 1989.[10] Simon also tested the effect of the *1933 Act on New York Stock Exchange* new issues compared to new issues on regional exchanges. The effect of the 1933 Act on "seasoned" issues (new issues of shares already trading on an exchange) and "unseasoned issues" (new issues of shares that were not previously traded on an exchange) was also examined. The New York Stock Exchange was by far the largest and most active exchange at the time. Consequently, the market for shares trading on the New York Stock Exchange was likely to be more efficient than that on regional exchanges.

b. EFFECTS ON PRICE

Simon found that there was no evidence that, on average, either seasoned or unseasoned issues traded on the New York Stock Exchange were significantly over- or underpriced either before or after the enactment of the 1933 Act.[11] For seasoned issues traded on regional exchanges, there was no evidence that the issues were significantly over- or underpriced on average, either before or after the enactment of the 1933 Act.[12] However, for unseasoned issues traded on regional exchanges, the pre-1933 Act results showed that

---

[9] See Jarrell's conclusions at ibid., 667-69.

[10] C.J. Simon, "The Effect of the 1933 Securities Act on Investor Information and the Performance of New Issues" (1989) 79 Amer. Econ. Rev. 295. Simon's analysis used an Arbitrage Pricing Model which takes account of more potential explanatory factors than does the Capital Asset Pricing Model used by Jarrell.

[11] Ibid., at 305, 313.

[12] Ibid.

such new issues were significantly overpriced. These issues, on average, incurred substantial losses.[13] There was no evidence of such overpricing of new issues of unseasoned shares after the enactment of the 1933 Act.[14]

c. EFFECTS ON RISK

Simon found that risk was significantly reduced for seasoned and unseasoned issues both on the New York Stock Exchange and on regional exchanges after the enactment of the 1933 Act.[15] The differences in risk before and after the introduction of the 1933 Act were most significant for the unseasoned issues on regional exchanges.[16]

B. Secondary Market Disclosure — Financial Statements

George Benston examined the effects of mandatory financial disclosure in the U.S.[17] Before enactment of mandatory financial disclosure in the U.S. in 1934, some New York Stock Exchange firms disclosed sales figures and others did not. Benston traced the effect of mandatory financial disclosure of sales data on the two groups of firms. He hypothesized that if the data was useful to investors in assessing the value of the securities, then there should have been a greater effect on the firms that had not disclosed sales before 1934. The analysis of the effects of mandatory disclosure of sales showed no apparent differences in effect on prices or risk of securities between the two groups. In other words, Benston's analysis revealed no apparent evidence of benefit to investors.[18]

---

[13] Ibid. Tests were conducted to address such concerns as (a) the effects of the severe economic shocks of the depression in the years just prior to the adoption of the 1933 Act, and (b) a possible small firm effect. These effects did not explain the significance of the results with respect to unseasoned issues on regional exchanges — see pp. 306-8.

[14] Ibid., at 305-6, 313.

[15] Ibid., at 309, 313. Simon conducted tests to account for the greater volatility of markets generally in the pre- and post-1933 Act periods and got similar results.

[16] Ibid., at 309-10, 313.

[17] G.J. Benston, "Required Disclosure and the Stock Market: An Evaluation of the Securities Exchange Act of 1934" (1973) 63 Amer. Econ. Rev. 132.

[18] Ibid., at 141-49.

C. Comments on the Studies and Further Evidence

The studies by Stigler, Jarrell, and Benston suggest that securities regulation may be of little or no benefit. Simon's study could be said to have similar implications at least with respect to seasoned and unseasoned securities trading in large and efficient trading markets (such as the New York Stock Exchange) and with respect to seasoned securities on regional exchanges. However, this conclusion has been challenged. In particular, Irwin Friend and Edward Herman challenged Stigler's failure to mention the many types of market manipulation and fraud which, they allege, have been substantially reduced by securities regulation contributing to "sounder capital markets and a better-functioning economy".[19] Their analysis of Stigler's results led them to the conclusion that new issues fared better in the post-regulation period.[20] They also claimed that the evidence of reduced risk associated with new issues in the post-regulation period showed that the regulation did have a beneficial effect. They claimed that the reduced risk was the result of reduced manipulative and fraudulent practices and improved disclosure of the degree of risk, leading to a greater reluctance of investors to invest in the risky new issues.[21]

Benston's test of the effect of mandatory financial disclosure has been criticized on methodological grounds.[22] For instance, it did not compare non-disclosing firms with disclosing firms. Instead it compared firms that engaged in different types of disclosure. The firms that did not disclose sales figures did disclose other financial data, including net income data.[23] Further, the study was criticized on the basis that it did not address the relative quality of disclosure of firms in both groups. Improved quality of disclosure may have affected both groups similarly.[24] As well, Benston's own figures, it

---

[19] I. Friend and E.S. Herman, "The S.E.C. Through a Glass Darkly" (1964) 37 J. of Bus. 382. For another comment on Stigler, see S. Robbins and W. Werner, "Professor Stigler Revisited" (1964) 37 J. of Bus. 406.

[20] Ibid., at 391-92.

[21] Ibid., at 391 and 392-93.

[22] See I. Friend and R. Westerfield, "Required Disclosure and the Stock Market: Comment" (1975) 65 Am. Eco. Rev. 467.

[23] Ibid., at 468.

[24] Ibid.

has been argued, show that risk may have been reduced for both groups of firms after the introduction of financial disclosure requirements.[25]

The evidence provided by Stigler, Jarrell, and Simon may not test the theory that mandatory disclosure increased confidence in the market, thereby reducing the discounting of securities prices due to adverse selection. The tests conducted by Stigler and Jarrell assumed that the purpose of mandatory disclosure was to protect investors against persistently overpricing new issues of securities in securities markets. If there was a tendency of the market to consistently overprice new issues prior to the introduction of mandatory disclosure, then their analysis would have shown prices falling in the years after the issuance of the securities. If the regulation was effective, then it should have reduced the tendency of the market to overestimate the value of new issues and the evidence would have shown less of a fall in the prices of new issues in the years after issuance. The evidence showed no significant differences in the pattern of prices for the pre-regulatory and post-regulatory periods.[26] However, this may only be evidence that the market was correctly pricing securities in both the pre-regulatory and the post-regulatory periods. It says nothing about whether mandatory disclosure improved the value of securities. A new issue that sold for $10 without mandatory disclosure might have sold for $12 with mandatory disclosure. The $2 difference would represent the discount investors may have applied in the non-mandatory disclosure environment for fear that their estimates of value might be based on inadequate or misleading information.[27]

---

[25] Ibid., at 469.

[26] Note however that Simon's results showed that investors were overpricing unseasoned issues on regional exchanges and that this overpricing was not present after the introduction of mandatory disclosure — see *supra* notes 13 and 14 and the accompanying text.

[27] This problem with the hypothesis tested by Stigler and Jarrell is noted in R.T. Smith, "Comments on Jarrell" (1981) 24 J. of Law & Eco. 677, at 679; Easterbrook and Fischel, "Mandatory Disclosure and the Protection of Investors" (1984) 70 Virg. L.R. 669 at 711.

III. SOME CRITIQUES OF SECURITIES REGULATION

The available evidence does not resolve the question of the effect of mandatory disclosure. However, studies such as those by Stigler, Jarrell, Simon and Benston do draw attention to the need to test the effects of mandatory disclosure rather than simply accepting disclosure as the answer to the alleged ills of securities markets. These studies, together with evidence on the efficiency securities markets and the experience of several decades of securities regulation, has led to a reconsideration of mandatory disclosure. Part III canvasses a range of different arguments that have been made with respect to the need for mandatory disclosure.

A. Change in Emphasis

One type of claim that has been made with respect to the existing approach to mandatory disclosure is not that such disclosure is not needed, but rather that there should be a shift in emphasis.

1. *Focus on the Secondary Market and Sophisticated Investors*

For instance, it has been argued that disclosure is directed to the wrong audience and the wrong market. These claims are based on the observation that prospectuses — intended to protect investors — disclose information as required, but bury negative information in lengthy and complex documents filled with boiler plate language designed to mitigate the implications of negative information. It has also been observed that unsophisticated investors rarely read these prospectuses.[28] It has also been suggested that the emphasis on primary market disclosure (that was the focus of early securities laws) is no longer appropriate in today's securities markets, where trading is dominated by secondary market trading.[29] The emphasis should

---

[28] See, for example, M.H. Cohen, "Truth in Securities Revisited" (1966) 79 Harv. L. Rev. 1340 at 1351-52; H. Kripke, *The SEC and Corporate Disclosure: Regulation in Search of a Purpose* (New York: Law & Business, Inc., 1979), at 22 and 97-98 (citing an SEC Advisory Committee Report on Corporate Disclosure).

[29] See, for example, J.C. Baillie, "Securities Regulation in the 70's" in J. Ziegel, ed., *Studies in Canadian Company Law* (Toronto: Butterworths, 1973), at 364 noting Cohen, *supra* note 28.

thus be on continuous disclosure directed to sophisticated investors and to market analysts. Investors will then be protected by sophisticated investors, who cause market prices to reflect the information, and by market analysts who can interpret the information and advise their unsophisticated investor clientele.

Securities laws have arguably responded to some of these criticisms. Securities laws in Canada have become increasingly focused on secondary market disclosure with the post Kimber Report emphasis on continuous disclosure and the development of the closed system with its emphasis on limiting trading to an exempt market until there is an adequate build-up of continuous disclosure. Continuous disclosure has been extended with the addition of material change reports and, for some issuers, annual information forms containing, among other things, management discussion and analysis. These developments also appear to have shifted the focus of securities laws to more sophisticated investors. Where securities are allowed trade outside of the closed market without a prospectus on the basis of continuous disclosure, unsophisticated investors are arguably protected by sophisticated investors who gather and assess the information and trade on it. The unsophisticated investors are protected presumably because trading by sophisticated investors produces a market price that reflects the underlying value of the security. Unsophisticated investors who then pay the market price will be paying a fair price for the security. Similarly, the POP and shelf systems, as noted in Chapter 8, arguably rely on sophisticated investors to gather and assess the continuous disclosure documents incorporated by reference into prospectuses and quickly reflect this information in the price of the securities by their trades.

2. Future-Oriented and Market Disclosure

Another argument that has been made is that the emphasis is on the wrong type of disclosure.[30] This argument draws on evidence suggesting that securities markets are at least weak form efficient and possibly also semi-strong form efficient. Given this evidence,

---

[30] H. Kripke, *supra* note 28. See also R.J. Dennis, "Mandatory Disclosure Theory and Management Projections: A Law and Economics Perspective" (1987) 46 Md. L. Rev. 1197 (arguing for mandatory management disclosure of earnings projections and valuations when control transactions are pending.)

it is argued that the current form of disclosure, which focuses on historical information, provides little information of value to the market.[31] Instead, it is argued, disclosure should focus on future-oriented information.[32]

The claim that the emphasis of the disclosure is wrong also draws on developments in the theory of how securities are valued, noting that the relevant risk to the investor is the market risk and not the firm specific risk which can be reduced through diversification.[33] Existing disclosure concerning the risk of the investment, it is argued, focuses largely on irrelevant firm specific risk.[34] Consequently, it has been suggested that disclosure should focus on aspects of the security which are likely to affect the market risk of the security.[35]

Canadian securities laws have arguably at least partially responded to this suggested change in emphasis. In recent years Canadian securities laws have permitted the disclosure of future-oriented financial information and, for some issuers, have required management discussion and analysis containing a discussion of the issuer's future prospects.

3. Change of Emphasis re Liability and Enforcement

Other arguments relate to the emphasis of existing mandatory disclosure laws on the liability for truthful disclosure and the direction of enforcement efforts with respect to disclosure. Homer Kripke has argued that imposing the statutory standard of care on accountants puts independent accountants on the defensive. This causes them to very conservatively focus on historical information, rather than future information, because the historical information can be more readily verified.[36] Instead, it is argued, the potential liability of independent accountants with respect to future-oriented

---

[31] Ibid., at 83-95, 97.

[32] Ibid., at 12, 97. See also H. Kripke, "A Search for a Meaningful Securities Disclosure Policy" (1975) 31 The Bus. Lawyer 293; and R.J. Dennis, *supra* note 30.

[33] Ibid., at 88-93.

[34] Ibid., at 12-13, 93.

[35] Ibid., at 12-13, 91-95.

[36] Ibid., at 276-82.

"soft" information should be reduced to encourage accountants to proactively assess the future prospects of the issuer.[37]

The argument with respect to enforcement is that securities commission staffs tend to put too much emphasis on confirming compliance with disclosure requirements. Most issuers, it is observed, comply with the disclosure requirements.[38] Perhaps enforcement efforts could be shifted more towards the identification of fraudulent activities with less emphasis on checking disclosure compliance.

4. Agency Cost Emphasis Not Accuracy Enhancement

Another suggested change in the emphasis of securities laws is that securities laws should focus on particular "agency cost" problems and abandon disclosure which focuses on enhancing the accuracy of securities prices.[39] The returns to security holders depend on the efforts of those who control and manage the business from which the returns will derive. The persons controlling and managing the business are effectively the agents of the security holders.[40] One concern the security holders will have is that the managers will not necessarily act in the best interests of the security holders. For instance, managers may not work as diligently as they might, or, worse, they may divert the funds invested by security holders to themselves. A failure of the managers to act in the best interests of the security holders will impose a cost on the security holders. This cost is referred to as an agency cost.

The argument is that mandatory disclosure should be directed primarily to reducing the agency costs that arise due to the risk that the promoters of a business may try to divert investor funds to themselves, their family, their friends or their business associates. Investors, aware of this potential problem, would

> want to know how much of the funds being raised in the offering will go toward the payment of commissions, fees, and similar expenses;

---

[37] Ibid., at 281.

[38] Ibid., at 283-84.

[39] See Paul G. Mahoney, "Mandatory Disclosure as a Solution to Agency Problems" (1995) Univ. of Chicago L.R. 1047.

[40] While they may not be agents of the security holders in the legal sense, they are agents in the sense that their actions affect the interests of security holders and can be said to be acting on behalf of security holder interests.

whether the persons to whom those amounts are being paid have any preexisting relationship with the promoter or directors that might call into question whether the terms reflect arm's length bargaining; and, generally, what other financial interests the promoter, directors, or persons connected with them have in the offering.[41]

Agency information, it is argued, is not costly to produce because it is readily available to the promoter and is limited in scope. It can also be set out with reasonable precision. On the other hand, the kind of information that is relevant to enhancing the accuracy of securities prices is immensely wide in scope. It is hard to say in advance what types of information will be relevant to determining the value of a particular security and the relevant information may vary widely from one type of issuer to another. Thus a mandatory disclosure system that attempts to accommodate a wide range of issuers will result in the disclosure of a great deal of irrelevant information. Many types of information that may be relevant to investors in assessing the value of the securities may not be as important to managers in managing the business. Thus it will include information that will not be readily available to managers and will have to be produced at potentially substantial additional cost.[42]

5. Permitting Silence and Lying

It has also been argued that issuers of securities should be permitted to lie or remain silent in certain circumstances.[43] Suppose an issuer is exploring for minerals on a property that it owns. It discovers potential of a significant lode of ore but it turns out that the probable main vane of ore extends under an adjoining property. The issuer is in the process of negotiating to buy the adjoining

---

[41] Mahoney, *supra* note 39, at 1053.

[42] Ibid., at 1093-94.

[43] See, e.g., J.R. Macey & G.P. Miller, "Good Finance, Bad Economics: An Analysis of the Fraud-on-the-Market Theory" (1990) 42 Stan. L. Rev. 1059 at 1070-76; J.R. Macey & G.P. Miller, "The Fraud-on-the-Market Theory Revisited" (1991) 77 Va. L. Rev. 1001 at 1015; V. Brudney, "A Note on Materiality and Soft Information Under the Federal Securities Laws" (1989) 75 Va. L. Rev. 723 at 733; R.J. Dennis, *supra* note 30 at 1212. See also the discussion of whether issuers should be able to lie and under what conditions in, for example, Ian Ayres, "Back to Basics: Regulating How Corporations Speak to the Market" (1991) Va. L. Rev. 945 and M. Kahan, "Games, Lies, and Securities Fraud" (1992) 67 NYU L. Rev. 750.

property. If it discloses that it has discovered a probable rich vane of ore but that the rich vane of ore extends under the adjoining property, it will probably significantly raise the cost of acquiring the property and thereby reduce the gains to the issuer's security holders. In these circumstances security holders might be better off if the discovery of the ore is not disclosed. If rumours develop about the discovery, security holders might be better off if the issuer denied the existence of the ore even though such a denial would be false.

Canadian securities law accommodates non-disclosure to some extent where the issuing of a press release would be "unduly detrimental to the issuer".[44] Instead the issuer must file a material change report on a confidential basis.[45] However, where rumours persist securities administrators in Canada may require the issuer to disclose and false disclosure could result in penal (and possibly civil) sanctions.[46]

B. No Need for Mandatory Disclosure

1. *Adverse Selection Problem Can be Addressed by the Market*

An argument that mandatory disclosure is unnecessary has been advanced by professors Easterbrook and Fischel.[47] It begins by accepting that there is an "adverse selection" problem that may lead to overinvestment in low quality issues.[48] However, it is observed that steps may be taken to convince investors of the truth of the information.[49]

---

[44] See Chapter 6, Part VII B.

[45] Ibid.

[46] See NP #40 Part E on disclosure in the face of rumours. On the potential sanctions, see Chapter 6, Part IX.

[47] F.H. Easterbrook and D.R. Fischel, *supra* note 27. See also F.H. Easterbrook & D.R. Fischel, *The Economic Structure of Corporate Law* (Cambridge, Mass.: Harvard Univ. Press, 1991) Chapter 11, "Mandatory Disclosure"; see also Beaver, "The Nature of Mandated Disclosure" Report of the Advisory Committee on Corporate Disclosure to the SEC, 95th Congress, 1st Sess. 618-56.

[48] Ibid., at 673-74. See Chapter 3, Part IV B.

[49] Ibid., at 674-77.

a. INDEPENDENT REVIEWS OF ISSUER REPRESENTATIONS

For instance, issuers may get outsiders — such as accountants — to review financial disclosure. The accountants will have a reputation to protect and will thus have an incentive to carefully review the financial disclosure. If the accountants do not carefully review the financial disclosure and it comes to be known that their opinions cannot be relied on, then issuers will be less likely to engage them because they can no longer credibly signal the accuracy of the issuer's disclosure to the market.[50]

Similarly, underwriters engaged to underwrite and market the issue will have an incentive to check the issuer's disclosure; both to reduce their underwriting risk and to preserve their reputation. The underwriter's ability to market an issue of securities will be adversely affected if it develops a reputation for marketing securities that turn out to be losers. If an underwriter develops such a reputation it will have difficulty offering competitive terms in underwriting engagements.[51]

b. PURCHASE OF SHARES BY MANAGEMENT

Issuers may employ other techniques to signal the value of the securities. For instance, management of the issuer may own a substantial portion of the issuer's shares, so that their interests will be aligned with the interests of shareholders. This alignment of the interests of management and shareholders can provide some assurance to investors that management will not be inclined to take advantage of them.[52]

c. TAKING ON DEBT

Similarly, management, whose careers may be closely tied to the continued existence of the issuer, can give some comfort to investors as to the value of the issuer's securities by causing the issuer to take on debt obligations which expose the issuer to a greater risk of bankruptcy. This exposes management to the risk of loss of

---

[50] Ibid., at 675.

[51] Ibid.

[52] Ibid., at 675-76.

their careers and thus gives them an incentive to redouble their efforts to pursue profits for the issuer and its investors.[53]

d. HIGH PAYOUT POLICY

Management of the issuer may also signal some assurance of the value of the issuer by adopting a high payout policy. This forces them to go to the capital market to raise new capital on a regular basis. It thus discourages management from acting against security holder interests because they will have to keep security prices high to raise new capital on favourable terms.[54]

2. Issuers Will Have an Incentive to Make the Appropriate Level of Disclosure

Easterbrook and Fischel note that the use of these techniques by issuers to signal the accuracy of their disclosures and to assure the investors of the value of securities involves costs for the issuer. However, it is argued that the issuer, seeking to maximize its value, will only incur these costs to the extent that the benefit derived from each increment of cost incurred will be at least equal to the cost.[55]

Easterbrook and Fischel suggest that there should be a rule against fraud, since frauds may frustrate these attempts to signal the market about the value of securities and raise the costs of making credible signals to the market about the value of securities.[56] However, they do not support mandatory disclosure. Mandatory disclosure, to the extent that it forces issuers to make disclosures they would not otherwise have made, may cause issuers to make disclosures for which the cost outweighs the benefits. This reduces the value of the issuer to the detriment of all security holders. Thus it is argued that as far as disclosure is concerned, the appropriate type and amount of disclosure should be left to the market to determine.[57]

---

[53] Ibid., at 676.

[54] Ibid.

[55] Ibid., at 684. See also Diamond, "Optional Release of Information by Firms" (1985) 40 J. Fin. 1071.

[56] Ibid., Easterbrook & Fischel, at 677-79.

[57] Ibid., at 684-85. This line of argument is discussed in D.J. Schulte, "The Debatable Case for Securities Disclosure Regulation" [1988] J. of Corp. Law 535;

3. Market Failures as a Justification for Mandatory Disclosure

a. THE MARKET FAILURE ARGUMENTS

Professor John Coffee, Jr. has argued, in response to Easterbrook and Fischel, that mandatory disclosure may be justified because the market may fail to produce the appropriate amount of information.[58] One market failure argument is that securities analysts may be inclined to produce too little information. The other market failure argument is that there is an incentive for investors to invest in the gathering of information to an extent that is excessive with respect to any benefits society may receive from such investment. Mandatory disclosure would serve to reduce such overinvestment in research.

(i) Too Little Information

Coffee has argued that securities information has a "public good" characteristic.[59] A "public good" provides a benefit which one cannot effectively exclude others from using. Thus other persons will have access to and will be able to enjoy the benefit of the public good, but the producer of the public good will be unable to force them to contribute to its cost. In other words, they will "free-ride" on the efforts of the producer of the public good. A producer has less incentive to produce a public good because the producer cannot capture all of the gains enjoyed by others from use of the public good. Less of the good will be produced, even though the benefits that others could derive from the use of the public good would outweigh the costs of producing more of the public good.

Securities information has this public good quality in that, once it is given to a user, there is an incentive to leak the information. Securities analysts cannot obtain the full economic value of their discoveries and thus will engage in less information search and verification.[60] Mandatory disclosure, Coffee argued, reduces the market

---

N. Wolfson, "A Critique of the Securities and Exchange Commission" [1981] Emory Law J. 119. H. Kripke, "A Search for a Meaningful Securities Disclosure Policy" [1975] Bus. Lawyer 292.

[58] J.C. Coffee, Jr., "Market Failure and the Economic Case for a Mandatory Disclosure System" (1984) 70 Virg. L. Rev. 717.

[59] Ibid., at 723-33.

[60] Ibid., at 726.

professional's marginal cost of acquiring and verifying information and thereby increases the amount of securities research and information provided.[61]

Easterbrook and Fischel have acknowledged another possible reason for the production of too little information. Issuers may be inclined to produce too little information because their disclosures reveal information of relevance in assessing the value of the securities of other issuers. The benefit of the disclosure thus accrues to other issuers and not to the issuer who produces the information. If the issuer could capture the gain from the benefits conferred on other issuers by their disclosure, then they would have an incentive to disclose more.[62] However, because they cannot capture the benefits conferred on other issuers, they do not produce the information. Indeed, issuers may be inclined to hold out on providing some forms of disclosure in the hope that other issuers will do it for them. The result is that information, for which the benefits to the market as a whole outweigh the costs, may not be produced. Mandatory disclosure could then be justified as an attempt to encourage cost justified disclosure that would not otherwise be provided.[63]

(ii) Investors Overinvest in Production of Information

Investors in the market may be inclined to spend too much on gathering information because numerous investors have an incentive to gather information on which they can make trading profits. These numerous investors will tend to gather much the same information, each one, in a sense, reinventing the wheel. The cost of producing the same information is thus wastefully incurred many times over. Mandatory disclosure forces the issuer to incur the cost of producing

---

[61] Ibid., at 729.

[62] They would have such an incentive because the increased gain from disclosure would justify greater cost of disclosure.

[63] See Easterbrook and Fischel, *supra* note 27, at 685-87. However, Easterbrook and Fischel note that mandatory disclosure is just one means of dealing with the problem. Markets, they suggest, can also devise ingenious solutions to problems of information (at 687). See also the discussion in Schulte, *supra* note 56, at 538-39. It has, however also been argued that there may be an incentive for issuers to produce too much information — see M.J. Fishman and K.M. Hagerty, "Disclosure Decisions by Firms and the Competition for Price Efficiency" (1989) 44 J. of Fin. 633.

the information and make it available to all investors. Thus the cost of producing the information is incurred once, by the issuer, rather than numerous times by different investors.[64]

b. RESPONSES TO THE MARKET FAILURE ARGUMENTS

The response that has been made by Easterbrook and Fischel to these claims that the market causes issuers to produce too little information and causes investors to overinvest in information gathering is that market mechanisms exist which address these problems. For instance, stock exchanges can address the problem of issuers producing too little information. Issuers have an incentive to join stock exchanges because of (i) the liquidity exchanges provide and (ii) the market signal provided by the reputation of the exchange that makes an issuer's securities more attractive to investors. Stock exchanges, whose business depends on their reputation, have disclosure rules which can address the problem of the issuers' incentive to produce too little information.[65]

The problem of investors incurring excessive costs by duplicating efforts in gathering information may be overstated in that trades by investors affect the price of the security and thereby reduce the profits others might obtain by gathering the same information. Further, by trading on the information they have gathered, investors, to some extent, reveal the information they have gathered, thus obviating the need for others to incur the costs of gathering the information.[66] Also, information intermediaries may reduce the problem of overinvestment in the gathering of information. For instance, underwriters, accountants, engineers, or rating organizations may be engaged by the issuer. These intermediaries examine information with respect to the issuer and convey it to the market by allowing their names to be associated with the issuer's securities, thereby risking their reputation. In doing so they incur the cost of

---

[64]See Coffee, *supra* note 58, at 733. The two claims, that market failures (i) cause too little information to be produced, and (ii) cause too much information production activity, appear inconsistent. Coffee says there is no contradiction in saying that, "[t]he first problem arises because too few companies are followed or are researched inadequately; the second because investigations by one analyst are duplicated by another". [at 734]

[65]Easterbrook and Fischel, *supra* note 27, at 689-90.

[66]Ibid., at 689.

gathering the information once and convey that information to the market in a simple reputation-based signal.[67]

c. SOCIAL GAINS FROM REDUCING SECURITY PRICE INACCURACIES

Inaccurate securities prices are said to cause social losses in several ways.[68] Inaccurate securities prices can affect the allocation of investment funds to productive activities,[69] reduce the liquidity of the market,[70] and increase the risk investors are exposed to.[71] They may produce macroeconomic shocks,[72] impede the proper operation of the market for corporate control,[73] produce inefficient

---

[67] Ibid., at 687-89.

[68] See M. Kahan, "Securities Laws and the Social Costs of 'Inaccurate' Stock Prices" (1992) 41 Duke Law J. 977.

[69] Absent external costs and benefits, a profitable investment project for an issuer of securities will also be one that produces a net gain to society. If a security is overpriced the issuer may raise capital for a project which would be unprofitable. Absent external benefits to society that would not accrue to the issuer, an unprofitable project for the issuer will be one that results in a net social loss to society. Similarly, if a security is underpriced the issuer may not pursue what would otherwise be a profitable investment project thereby forgoing a potential net gain to society. See ibid., Kahan, at 1005-17.

[70] Kahan argues that inaccurate stock prices can make investors reluctant to trade stock and thereby reduce the liquidity of the market. This can result in social losses because reduced volumes of trading can result in higher transactions costs of trading and because such higher transactions costs may discourage otherwise optimal adjustments in investment portfolios. Ibid., at 1017-25.

[71] To risk averse investors, risk is a cost. It is something they would rather avoid. Thus increases in risk increase costs to investors which constitutes a social loss. Inaccuracies in security prices increase the volatility of security prices and thereby increase risk. Ibid., at 1025-28.

[72] For example, a sudden substantial decrease in stock prices can cause investors to have significant perceived reductions in personal wealth. This can affect their consumer spending decisions reducing the aggregate level of consumer spending thus lowering the overall level of economic growth or causing a recession. Ibid. at 1034-35.

[73] A change in who controls a corporation, or other issuer of securities, can be beneficial when it results in an increase in the value of the corporation's assets by deploying them in valuable uses or more effectively managing them. See the discussion in Chapter 11. If the stock of an issuer is undervalued it can encourage a take-over that does not result in any increase in the value of the corporation's assets. This is discussed in more detail in Chapter 11. Similarly, if the stock of an issuer is overvalued it can deter a change in control that might in fact result in an increase in the value of the corporation's assets. Ibid., at 1034-37.

terms in corporate charters,[74] and result in poor decisions by managers as to what investment projects should be pursued.[75]

Disclosure can reduce the costs of information gathering for informed securities traders[76] whose trades help establish securities market prices. The reduced cost of information allows them to gather more information and thereby make more accurate estimates of securities values resulting in trades that produce more accurate securities prices. More accurate securities prices will also attract more informed trading because it reduces risk that may deter some trading.[77]

While market mechanisms may allow some securities price inaccuracies to persist with resulting social losses, this does not necessarily mean that mandatory disclosure is the solution. The question is whether mandatory disclosure can reduce the inaccuracies in a way that results in gains to society that outweigh the costs of mandatory disclosure. It has been argued that by subsidizing the information gathering efforts of informed short-term securities traders mandatory disclosure reduces securities price inaccuracies and increases securities market liquidity resulting in societal gains that outweigh the costs of mandatory disclosure.[78] It is argued that issuers would not voluntarily provide this type of disclosure because, although it would benefit short-term informed traders, it would not benefit longer-term investors. Longer-term investors would not reap

---

[74] If the market is unable to accurately assess the value of some beneficial corporate charter provisions at the time of an initial public offering of a security then the promoter may not have an incentive to put in the beneficial corporate charter terms. Similarly, a promoter may have an incentive to put a term in the corporate charter that favours himself at the expense of investors if the market is unable to accurately assess the negative effect of such a corporate charter term. Ibid., 1038-39.

[75] Inaccurate securities prices can also cause corporate managers to have a mistaken impression of the required rate of return for investment projects they are considering. This may cause them to reject investment projects that result in a net social loss, or possibly, accept investment projects that would result in a social gain.

[76] Informed traders are persons who trade securities making use of available information.

[77] See Nicholas L. Georgakopoulos, "Why Should Disclosure Rules Subsidize Informed Traders?" (1996) 16 Int'l Rev. of Law and Econ. 417, at 423-24.

[78] Ibid., at 425-27.

sufficient gains from trading on increased disclosures to compensate for the added cost of increased disclosure. Because it would not benefit longer-term investors they would not support the expenditure of an issuer's funds on the disclosure of information that would assist informed short-term traders in assessing the value of the issuer's securities. It is argued that longer-term investors will tend to hold a greater portion of the voting securities of an issuer and will therefore dominate in decisions on disclosure by issuers. Issuers will thus choose not to make some forms of disclosure even where disclosure would result in a net social gain from producing more accurate securities prices.[79] In effect, mandatory disclosure forces longer-term investors to subsidize disclosure that increases trading by informed short-term traders resulting in more accurate securities prices and the associated social gains.[80]

The resolution of the collective action problem for the issuer's securities holders, noted above, might not require statutorily imposed mandatory disclosure. A stock exchange could serve to overcome this collective action problem. As noted above, securities holders can benefit from having the issuer's securities listed on a stock or other securities exchange. Issuers thus have an incentive to list their securities on an exchange and the exchange may well overcome this alleged collective action problem by requiring certain forms of disclosure in return for giving the issuer the privilege of having its securities listed on the exchange.[81]

d. STANDARDIZATION OF INFORMATION PRESENTATION

It might also be argued that mandatory disclosure is beneficial to the extent it standardizes the presentation of information.[82] Standardization in the presentation of information can reduce the cost

---

[79] Ibid.

[80] Ibid., at 423-24.

[81] See Easterbrook & Fischel, *The Economic Structure of Corporate Law*, *supra* note 47, at 295 noting that before statutory mandatory disclosure requirements were introduced in U.S. federal law the New York Stock Exchange had an elaborate program requiring detailed disclosure at the time securities were issued as well as required annual disclosure.

[82] Ibid., at 303-4. See also Easterbrook & Fischel, "Mandatory Disclosure", *supra* note 27 at 686-87 and J. Azzi, "Disclosure in Prospectuses" (1991) 9 Co. and Sec. L.J. 205, at 215-16.

to securities market analysts of gathering information and in comparing information between securities issuers. The reduced information costs will permit more gathering and assessing of information and better information comparisons thereby allowing more accurate assessments of securities prices.

Securities exchanges may be able to provide a substantial degree of standardization. In return for the privilege of listing securities on an exchange, issuers can be subjected to substantial amounts of standardized disclosure with formats of presentation that would facilitate comparisons to other issuers. An exchange that has a large number of issuers listed on it would allow for a wide range of comparisons. Two or more exchanges might find it worthwhile to co-operate in the standardization of disclosure and the presentation of disclosure to increase the number of issuers disclosing similar information in similar formats thereby facilitating comparisons. It is thus doubtful that there would be much residual benefit, in terms of information cost savings, to a statutorily imposed form of mandatory disclosure.

C. Interest Group Theories

If one accepts the argument that mandatory disclosure imposes costs that are greater than the benefits derived and is therefore an unnecessary and wasteful expense, then why have mandatory disclosure requirements come into existence? One explanation is that those who supported mandatory disclosure believed erroneously that mandatory disclosure would be beneficial. Another possible explanation is that there were various interest groups that benefited from the imposition of mandatory disclosure that now exists. These interest groups may have benefited even though the net effect was to impose costs that outweighed the benefits to society as a whole.[83]

1. Possible Interest Group Influences

Various interest groups might be considered to have a stake in mandatory disclosure. For instance, accountants may have benefited from the requirement for audited financial disclosure in prospectuses

---

[83] See, for example, S.M. Phillips and J.R. Zecher, *The SEC and the Public Interest*, (Cambridge: MIT Press, 1981) at 17-25, 111-114, and 118-20; D.J. Schulte, *supra* note 57, at 536.

and regular financial statement requirements. Lawyers may have benefited from additional work generated through the increased responsibility for disclosure in prospectuses and through their knowledge of securities regulation.[84] Underwriters may have benefited from additional work generated through their increased responsibility for prospectus disclosure. Various other experts, such as engineers or geologists providing reports on mining or oil and gas properties, may have benefited from additional work generated by their increased responsibility for their reports in prospectus disclosure. Larger issuers may have gained at the expense of smaller issuers to the extent that the costs of prospectus disclosure — as a percentage of the value of an issuer of securities — tend to be higher for smaller issuers.[85] The regulators themselves may have a tendency to protect and expand their regulatory powers once regulation has been introduced.[86]

2. Interests Within Securities Regulatory Organizations

If securities regulators are motivated to protect and expand their regulatory powers they may be inclined to respond to external political forces that affect the degree of support they have for their regulatory activities. They might thus be inclined to provide regulation that is beneficial to groups of persons who can give them the greatest political support. However, securities regulators may also be influenced by interests that are internal to the regulatory organization itself.

The focus on internal interests in the regulatory organization offers an explanation of an extent of regulation and extensiveness of disclosure requirements that may be beyond what industry participants would want. The regulatory organization can be viewed as having diffuse individual interests and attitudes with dispersed informational sources and a loss of control over the organization. A loss

---

[84] See Schulte, *supra* note 57, at 536 and Wolfson, *supra* note 57, at 158.

[85] See Schulte, *supra* note 57, at 536; and Wolfson, *supra* note 57, at 149-56. Evidence of the higher percentage cost for smaller issuers is presented in G.J. Benston, "The Effectiveness and Effects of the SEC's Accounting Disclosure Requirements", H.G. Manne, ed., *Economic Policy and the Regulation of Corporate Securities* (Washington: American Enterprise Institute for Public Policy, 1969), at 60-65 and Phillips and Zecher, *supra* note 83, at 42-51.

[86] See Wolfson, *supra* note 57, at 124-27.

of control over the organization may tend to persist since it is not subject to the kinds of market forces that provide incentives to private enterprises to improve organizational control. The major proponent of this approach, Donald Langevoort, argues that individuals at the Securities Exchange Commission (SEC) in the U.S. tend to maximize their own utility. This utility maximization, he says,

> can readily be understood in terms of that which serves as reward or compensation for certain behavior and runs the gamut from external "bribes" (e.g., promises of future employment in the private sector for key officials) through ego gratification (e.g., favourable publicity) to institutional self-preservation or internal consumption (e.g., enlarged or preserved turf or budget, more leisure time for the staff) − even the sense of pride or satisfaction that comes from doing a task well.[87]

He argues that SEC behaviour will be primarily inner-directed "until external stimuli change in a sufficiently compelling fashion so as to draw a critical mass of attention outward" and will tend toward turf protection and risk avoidance.[88]

Langevoort also argues that the internal interests of the SEC cause it to be reluctant to set out clear rules or standards. This allows it to preserve a broad scope to its discretion. The SEC may have a natural bias towards more regulation and increasingly complex regulation. It is staffed primarily by lawyers who are inclined to make arcane, open-ended and technical rules.[89] These rules serve their interests when they return to private practice since they possess knowledge of these complex rules and will have to be consulted by those seeking to trade in securities markets. This tendency towards ever increasing regulation is consistent with the comment of a former SEC staff member who said that his impression of the measure of performance at the SEC is the amount of new rules one has created over a given period of time.[90]

---

[87] See D.C. Langevoort, "The SEC As a Bureaucracy: Public Choice, Institutional Rhetoric, and the Process of Policy Formulation" (1990) 47 Wash. and Lee L. Rev. 527 at 529-530.

[88] Ibid., at 530.

[89] See ibid., at 531.

[90] See N. Wolfson, *supra* note 57.

3. Use of Rhetorical Conventions

Langevoort also argues that the bureaucratic nature of the SEC has led to a set of rhetorical conventions that serve as a means of forming consensus in the formulation of policy amongst the various divisions of the SEC. According to Langevoort,

> What we have, then, is a highly complex coordination problem: potentially scores of individual negotiations would have to occur to build consensus from a clean slate. This, of course, would be immensely time-consuming (and typically frustrating in a hierarchical setting because other sources of power have a fairly low cost ability to block a significant initiative). Here, it seems, is where rhetorical conventions gain their power. A person charged with formulating or reformulating the initiative is likely to mold the proposal based on rhetoric previously agreed to in earlier negotiations, if only to reduce both the risk and the transactions costs attendant to gaining each successive level of approval. In this way, each new initiative is influenced heavily by the perception of the past.[91]

One example of the kind of rhetoric that may assist in forming a consensus is the claim that individual investors "add depth and liquidity" to the market. Langevoort argues that this rhetoric has been used by the SEC to limit the economic advantage of institutional investors. The increasing significance of institutional investors threatens the basis of securities regulation since it depends on protecting unsophisticated individual investors who have an increasingly less significant role in securities markets. "Adding depth and liquidity" as a rhetorical convention is likely to be supported by brokerage firms that profit from trading by individual investors. The managers of corporations the shares of which are held by a disperse and unorganized group of individual investors rather than concentrated in the hands of institutional investors, are also likely to support this rhetorical convention since their control is enhanced by dispersed and unorganized individual share ownership.

D. Further Research

The empirical evidence to date has not resolved the issue of whether mandatory disclosure has been beneficial in terms of increasing securities prices. It may be difficult for empirical evidence

---

[91] Langvoort, *supra* note 87, at 532-533.

to resolve this issue.[92] However, further analysis of regulated versus unregulated securities markets may yield greater confidence in favour of, or against, mandatory disclosure. The extent to which the regulation shifted riskier securities to unregulated markets is another issue which, it has been suggested, is in need of further research.[93] Who gains and who loses as a consequence of mandatory disclosure needs to be more thoroughly articulated and supported with tests of who gained and who lost on the introduction of mandatory disclosure initially or on subsequent modifications of mandatory disclosure requirements.

IV. MERIT DISCRETION

A. Critique of Merit Discretion

There is also scepticism as to whether merit discretion can benefit investors.[94] According to David Johnston:

> The practical difficulty of course, is that if the [Commission] were to attempt to pass judgment in detail on the viability of the new enterprise, [it] would have to have at [its] disposal a staggering number of highly sophisticated experts from various disciplines. The result would be an economy heavily subject to public regulation, to a much greater extent than Canadians have been accustomed.[95]

Even if substantial blue sky discretion were exercised it might not benefit investors if the effect of it was to foreclose investments in speculative firms. This would reduce competition for established firms in capital markets. Further, investors might be prevented from purchasing shares in successful as well as unsuccessful ventures. For example, in December of 1980 the Massachusetts securities commission barred the first offering of securities in Apple Computer Inc.[96]

---

[92] See Easterbrook & Fischel, *The Economic Structure of Corporate Law, supra,* note 47 at 311-14.

[93] See Simon, *supra* note 10, at 313.

[94] For different views on merit discretion see Campbell, "An Open Attack on the Nonsense of Blue Sky Regulation" (1985) 10 J. of Corp. L. 553 and "Report on State Merit Regulation of Securities Offerings" (1986) 41 Bus. Law 785.

[95] See D. Johnston, *Canadian Securities Regulation* (Toronto: Butterworths, 1977) at 160.

[96] See R. Brealey & S. Myers, *Principles of Corporate Finance,* 2d ed. (1984).

B. An Interest Group Theory of Merit Discretion

An interest group explanation has been given for the development of merit regulation in several states in the United States.[97] The argument is that merit regulation served the interests of small state banks and local state industries and farmers. The small state banks had lost deposits to higher yield debt and equity securities that had grown in popularity. State merit regulation discouraged issues of debt and equity securities thereby reducing the alternatives to deposits as modes of saving. Access to capital for local state businesses and farmers may have been enhanced by excluding competition from out-of-state borrowers. Those with funds to invest would not have the same range of investment options in terms of out-of-state debt and equity securities that were precluded from distribution in the state by state merit regulation. Thus the local investors would have to put more of their investment funds in local bank deposits. Local state banks could thus attract deposits with lower rates of interest than they would have to offer if there was greater competition from out-of-state securities issuers. Local banks could then offer loans to farmers and local state industries at lower rates of interest.

The larger investment banking firms that distributed securities opposed the likely local bias of state merit regulation and the increased administrative burdens it imposed. Firms in industries such as manufacturing firms, railroads and public utilities, that raised significant amounts of capital through bond issues, opposed state merit regulation. Larger out-of-state banks also opposed state merit regulation. Their deposits were not affected by the growth of high yield debt and equity securities, and they also engaged in the securities business including the underwriting of bond issues. In spite of this opposition to merit regulation it was adopted in states where the interests of small state banks, local businesses and farmers outweighed the interests of those opposed to merit regulation.[98]

---

[97] See J.R. Macey & G.P. Miller, "Origin of the Blue Sky Laws" (1991) 70 Texas L.R. 347.

[98] A similar argument might be made with respect to the *Manitoba Sales of Shares Act of 1912*. However, would this argument explain the merit discretion currently left to securities administrators?

CHAPTER 10

INSIDER TRADING

I. INTRODUCTION

To facilitate an understanding of the regulation of insider trading under Canadian securities acts, Part II of this chapter briefly examines the nature of the perceived problem to which the regulation responded. Part III then reviews the regulation of insider trading in Canadian securities acts, focusing on who is prohibited from trading, when the prohibition applies and how it is enforced. Part IV highlights some of the problems encountered in the enforcement of the prohibition of insider trading and Part V seeks to provide an awareness of the debate over whether anyone loses as a consequence of insider trading and whether allowing insider trading has a beneficial or detrimental effect.

II. THE PERCEIVED PROBLEM AND THE APPROACH OF CANADIAN SECURITIES ACTS

The continuous disclosure requirements, discussed in Chapter 6, are intended to provide information in support of secondary market trading. Material changes and material facts relating to each reporting issuer are to be disclosed to ensure equal access to information. Ideally, every trader would have the same access to material information. No trader would have an advantage by virtue of his or her "inside" position. However, this ideal result may not be achieved. First, the reporting issuer may fail to disclose the information, even though it should have been disclosed. Second, information may be undisclosed because it has been kept confidential pursuant to the exception provided in provisions requiring the disclosure of material changes. Third, even if the information has been disclosed, it takes time for that information to be disseminated to the market to an extent sufficient to provide equal access. Consequently, in spite of provisions requiring continuous disclosure, there may be persons who have access to material information which has not been disclosed or widely disseminated in the market.

There is some doubt as to whether trading by persons having superior access to information is good or bad. However, the view reflected in most securities legislation in Canada is that it is improper for persons to make trading profits based on their superior access to information. The basis for this view is that:

> The ideal securities market should be a free and open market with the prices thereon based upon the fullest possible knowledge of all relevant facts among traders. Any factor which tends to destroy or put in question this concept lessens the confidence of the investing public in the marketplace and is, therefore, a matter of public concern.[1]

Insider trading was apparently considered by the Kimber Commission to be a "factor which tends to destroy or put in question" the concept of a "free and open market". If market prices are not based on "the fullest possible knowledge of all relevant facts", then the investor faces the risk of selling for too low a price when there is favourable material information which is undisclosed, and of paying too high a price when there is unfavourable material information which is undisclosed. This risk reduces investor "confidence ... in the marketplace" causing investors to discount the prices they are willing to pay for securities. This discounting of prices in the secondary market will be reflected in primary market securities prices, since investors in that market will take into account the reduced price at which securities can be sold in the secondary market.[2] Reduced prices in the primary market will affect the supply of capital and the allocation of resources.[3]

---

[1] *Report of the Attorney General's Committee on Securities Legislation in Ontario,* March 1965 (the *Kimber Report*) para. 2.02.

[2] See the *Kimber Report, supra* note 1, at paras. 1.11-1.12.

[3] Ibid.

III. CANADIAN SECURITIES ACTS AND THE REGULATION OF INSIDER TRADING

A. What, When, Who and How?

1. *What is Prohibited?*

It is prohibited, with respect to insider trading, to (i) trade on knowledge of material information or (ii) inform others of material information.

2. *When is it Prohibited?*

The notion on which the prohibition of insider trading is based is that trading should be based on equal access to information. Thus trading and informing with respect to knowledge of material information is only prohibited where that information has not been generally disclosed. Where the information has been "generally disclosed", there will be "equal access" to that information.

3. *Who is Prohibited?*

Since the object is to assure that trading is based on equal access to information, persons prohibited from trading or informing are persons having superior access to information. Most Canadian securities acts use the term "special relationship" to describe persons having superior access to information.

A wide variety of persons can become aware of undisclosed information in a variety of ways. Consequently, the definition of "special relationship" is complex and extensive in scope. "Insiders", "affiliates", and "associates" of a reporting issuer are in a special relationship with the reporting issuer.[4] "Insider" is defined to mean a

---

[4] Where the trade is not in securities of a "reporting issuer", the persons involved in the trading are more likely to be able to protect themselves against others having potential superior access to information, either because of the person's sophistication or because of the person's common bond of interest or affiliation.

director[5] or senior officer[6] of an issuer of securities, a person who has control or direction over securities carrying more than 10% of the voting rights of the issuer's outstanding voting securities, a director or senior officer of a person who has control over securities carrying more than 10% of the voting rights on outstanding voting securities of the issuer, and the issuer itself where it has acquired and continues to hold securities of its own issue.[7] "Affiliate" is defined to mean the parent or subsidiary of an issuer or any other issuer that is subject to common control.[8] A person is an "associate" of a reporting issuer if that person is a partner of the reporting issuer, a trust or estate in which the reporting issuer has a substantial beneficial interest (or for which the reporting issuer serves as trustee), or an issuer in respect of which the reporting issuer beneficially owns or controls voting securities carrying more than 10% of the voting rights attached to outstanding voting securities of the issuer.[9]

The definition of "insider" does not include employees or officers other than senior officers. However, officers and employees of a reporting issuer are included in the term "special relationship".[10]

---

[5] Where the issuer is not a company, a director includes any person acting in a capacity similar to that of a director of a company — see A.S.A. s. 1(e.1); B.C.S.A. s. 1(1) "director"; Nfld.S.A. s. 2(1)(k); N.S.S.A. s. 2(1)(k); O.S.A. s. 1; Q.S.A. s. 5; S.S.A. s. 2(1)(q). Corporate statutes often define "director" to mean any person occupying the position of a director by whatever name called; see, for example, C.B.C.A., R.S.C. 1985, c. C-44, s. 2(1); O.B.C.A. s. 1(1).

[6] "Senior officer" is usually defined to mean the chairperson or vice-chairperson of the board of directors, the president, a vice-president, the secretary, the treasurer or the general manager of a company or of any individual performing similar functions for an issuer. It is also generally extended to each of the five highest paid employees of the issuer (including the persons referred to above). See A.S.A. s. 1(w); B.C.S.A. s. 1(1); M.S.A. s. 1(l); Nfld.S.A. s. 2(1)(rr); N.S.S.A. s. 2(1)(ar); O.S.A. s. 1(1); Q.S.A. s. 5; S.S.A. s. 2(1)(tt).

[7] A.S.A. s. 1(i)(iv); B.C.S.A. s. 1(1); M.S.A. s. 108; Nfld.S.A. s. 2(1)(s); N.S.S.A. s. 2(1)(r); O.S.A. s. 1(1); Q.S.A. s. 89; S.S.A. s. 2(1)(w). See also C.B.C.A. ss. 126(1), (2), 131(1).

[8] A.S.A. ss. 2-4; B.C.S.A. s. 1(2); M.S.A. s. 1(2)-(4); Nfld.S.A. s. 2(2); N.S.S.A. s. 2(2)-(4); O.S.A. s. 1(2)-(4); Q.S.A s. 9; S.S.A. s. 2(2)-(4). See also C.B.C.A. s. 2(2).

[9] A.S.A. s. 1(a.1); B.C.S.A. s. 1(1); M.S.A. s. 1(1); Nfld.S.A. s. 2(1)(b); N.S.S.A. s. 2(b); O.S.A. s. 1(1); Q.S.A. s. 5; S.S.A. s. 2(b).

[10] A.S.A. s. 9(c)(i); B.C.S.A. s. 3(c); M.S.A. s. 112(5)(c); Nfld.S.A. s. 77(5)(c); N.S.S.A. s. 82(5)(c); O.S.A. s. 76(5)(c); S.S.A. s. 85(1)(c). See also Q.S.A. s. 189(4).

A person proposing to make a takeover bid or to engage in a reorganization, amalgamation, arrangement or similar business combination with the reporting issuer is likely to have access to material information concerning the reporting issuer. Thus, the definition of "special relationship" includes insiders, affiliates or associates of persons proposing to engage in such transactions with the reporting issuer.[11] Officers or employees of persons proposing to engage in such transactions with the reporting issuer are also included in the definition of "special relationship".[12]

Persons engaged in or proposing to engage in business or professional activities on behalf of a reporting issuer may be given access to information necessary to perform the business or professional engagement. Similarly, persons engaged in a business or professional activity on behalf of another person that is proposing to make a takeover bid for a reporting issuer, acquire a substantial portion of the assets of a reporting issuer or become a party to a reorganization, amalgamation, or arrangement with the reporting issuer, might also obtain access to material information with respect to the reporting issuer for the purposes of their business or professional activities. Thus, any person engaging or proposing to engage in such business or professional activities is also considered to be in a "special relationship" with the reporting issuer.[13] Directors, officers or employees of persons engaged in such business or professional activities may also have access to material information concerning a reporting issuer and are also included in the term "special relationship".[14]

It might happen that a person acquired knowledge of material information while in any of the relationships described above. The person might no longer be in such a relationship. However, the information they acquired while in the relationship may not yet be gen-

---

[11] A.S.A. s. 9(a)(ii); B.C.S.A. s. 3(a)(ii), (iii); M.S.A. s. 112(5)(a)(ii); Nfld.S.A. s. 77(5)(a)(ii), (iii); N.S.S.A. s. 82(5)(a)(ii), (iii); O.S.A. s. 76(5)(a)(ii), (iii); S.S.A. s. 85(1)(a)(ii),(iii). There is no precisely corresponding provision in the Q.S.A.

[12] A.S.A. s. 9(c); B.C.S.A. s. 3(c); M.S.A. s. 112(5)(c); Nfld.S.A. s. 77(5)(c); N.S.S.A. s. 82(5)(c); O.S.A. s. 76(5)(c); S.S.A. s. 85(1)(c).

[13] A.S.A. s. 9(b); B.C.S.A. s. 3(b); M.S.A. s. 112(5)(b); Nfld.S.A. s. 77(5)(b); N.S.S.A. s. 82(5)(b); O.S.A. s. 76(5)(b); S.S.A. s. 85(1)(b). See also Q.S.A. s. 189(4).

[14] A.S.A. s. 9(c)(ii); B.C.S.A. s. 3(c); M.S.A. s. 112(5)(c); Nfld.S.A. s. 77(5)(c); N.S.S.A. s. 82(5)(c); O.S.A. s. 76(5)(c); S.S.A. s. 85(1)(c). See also Q.S.A. s. 189(4).

erally disclosed. For instance, a director or a senior officer might resign and shortly thereafter trade on as yet undisclosed material information that the director or senior officer became aware of while acting as a director or senior officer. Thus persons who know of material information which they acquired knowledge of while in one of the relationships described above, are also considered to be persons in a "special relationship" with the reporting issuer.[15]

There might be others who do not have access to material undisclosed information, but who are informed of such information by persons who do have access to it. These "tippees" are also included in the definition of "special relationship". The definition refers to a person who knows of material information with respect to a reporting issuer where the knowledge was acquired from another person who was in a special relationship and where the tippee knew, or reasonably ought to have known, that the person communicating the information was in a special relationship with the reporting issuer.[16] The definition is such that even a tippee of another tippee can be a person in a "special relationship".[17]

4. How the Prohibition is Enforced

The prohibition of insider trading or informing is enforced through a wide range of sanctions. There are penal sanctions, administrative sanctions, and civil actions for damages or for an accounting to the reporting issuer.

---

[15] A.S.A. s. 9(d); B.C.S.A. s. 3(d); M.S.A. s. 112(5)(d); Nfld.S.A. s. 77(5)(d); N.S.S.A. s. 82(5)(d); O.S.A. s. 76(5)(d); S.S.A. s. 85(1)(d). See Q.S.A. s. 189(4) and (6) which are set in the past tense with respect to the acquisition of privileged information.

[16] A.S.A. s. 9(e); B.C.S.A. s. 3(e); M.S.A. s. 112(5)(e); Nfld.S.A. s. 77(5)(e); N.S.S.A. s. 82(5)(e); O.S.A. s. 76(5)(e); S.S.A. s. 85(1)(e). See also Q.S.A. s. 189(5) and (6).

[17] The definition provides that the other person from whom the information was acquired could be a person who had more direct access to the information, such as a director or officer of the issue, or a person who obtained the information by way of a tip.

a. PENAL SANCTIONS

Canadian securities acts contain penal sanctions for both trading on or informing others of inside information. To obtain a conviction for trading on inside information under most Canadian securities acts, the Crown must prove that:

  (i) the accused was in a "special relationship"[18] with the reporting issuer of the securities;[19]

  (ii) the accused purchased or sold securities of the reporting issuer;[20]

---

[18]See *supra*, notes 4 to 17 and the accompanying text.

[19]A.S.A. s. 119(2); B.C.S.A. s. 86(1)(a); M.S.A s. 112(1); Nfld S.A. s. 77(1); N.S.S.A. s. 82(1)(a); O.S.A. s. 76(1); S.S.A. s. 85(3). Sections 187 and 189 of the Q.S.A. provide a roughly corresponding approach.

The issuer of the securities must be a "reporting issuer". "Reporting issuer" is defined so as to include "persons" (as broadly defined to include individuals, corporations, partnerships, trusts, etc.) who have issued securities which are publicly traded. See the definitions of "reporting issuer", "issuer" and "person" in the A.S.A. s. 1(t.1), (j), (o); B.C.S.A. s. 1(1); Nfld.S.A. s. 2(1)(t), (ee) and (oo); N.S.S.A. s. 2(1)(s), (ad) and (ao); O.S.A. s. 1(1); S.S.A. s. 2(1)(x), (hh) and (qq). See ss. 5 and 68 of the Q.S.A. for definitions of "reporting issuer" and "issuer". Manitoba uses the term "corporation" (see M.S.A. s. 100) for the purposes of the insider trading provisions. The definition is similar to that of "reporting issuers" in other jurisdictions, but is limited to incorporated organizations or associations.

Prince Edward Island, New Brunswick and the Territories do not have provisions on insider trading in their respective securities acts. There are provisions in, for example, the New Brunswick *Business Corporations Act*, S.N.B. 1981, c. B-9.1, as amended, S.N.B. 1983, c. 15, s. 15, s. 83 making insiders liable to compensate direct losses of others where the insider "makes use of any specific confidential information".

[20]See A.S.A. s. 119(2); B.C.S.A. s. 86(1)(c); M.S.A. s. 112(1); Nfld.S.A. s. 77(1); N.S.S.A. s. 82(1)(a); O.S.A. s. 76(1); S.S.A. s. 85(3). See also s. 187 of the Q.S.A. For the purposes of the prohibition against insider trading in several of the securities acts a "security of the reporting issuer" is deemed to include a put, call, option or other right or obligation to purchase or sell securities of the reporting issuer or a security the market price of which varies materially with the market price of the securities of the reporting issuer. See A.S.A. s. 119(1); B.C.S.A. s. 86(1)(d), (e); M.S.A. s. 112(6); Nfld.S.A. s. 77(6); N.S.S.A. s. 82(6)(a); O.S.A. s. 76(6); Q.S.A. s. 189.1 (similar effect); S.S.A. s. 85(2).

(iii) the accused made the purchase or sale with knowledge of material information[21] concerning the affairs of the reporting issuer;[22] and

(iv) that the material information had not been generally disclosed.[23]

To obtain a conviction for informing another of inside information, the Crown must prove that:

(i) the accused person was in a "special relationship" with the reporting issuer;[24]

(ii) the accused informed another person of material information[25] with respect to the reporting issuer;[26] and

---

[21] The legislation generally refers to "material facts" and "material changes". A "material fact" is defined as "a fact that significantly affects, or could reasonably be expected to significantly affect, the market price or value of those securities". See the B.C.S.A. s. 1(1). Similar or identical definitions (generally substituting "would" for the word "could") can be found in other securities acts. See A.S.A. s. 1(l); M.S.A. s. 108(1); Nfld.S.A. s. 2(1)(x); N.S.S.A. s. 1(1)(v); O.S.A. s. 1(1); S.S.A. s. 2(1)(z).

A "material change" is defined as,

"... a change in the business, operations, assets or ownership of the issuer that would reasonably be expected to have a significant effect on the market price or value of any of the securities of the issuer and includes a decision to implement that change made by

(a) senior management of the issuer who believe that confirmation of the decision by the directors is probable, or

(b) the directors of the issuer."

See the B.C.S.A. s. 1(1). Similar or identical definitions can be found in other securities acts. See A.S.A. s. 1(k.1); M.S.A. s. 108(1); Nfld.S.A. s. 2(1)(w); N.S.S.A. s. 1(1)(u); O.S.A. s. 1(1); S.S.A. s. 2(1)(y). The Q.S.A. uses the term "privileged information" which is defined in s. 5 as "any information not yet generally known that could affect the value or the market price of the securities of an issuer".

[22] A.S.A. s. 119(2); B.C.S.A. s. 86(1)(b); Nfld.S.A. s. 77(1); N.S.S.A. s. 82(1)(a); O.S.A. s. 76(1); S.S.A. s. 85(3). The Q.S.A. s. 187 uses the expression "having privileged information".

[23] Ibid. This element is present in the definition of "privileged information" under the Q.S.A. s. 5.

[24] See A.S.A. s. 119(3); B.C.S.A. s. 86(2) and (3); M.S.A. s. 112(2); Nfld.S.A. s. 77(2); N.S.S.A. s. 82(1); O.S.A. s. 75(2); S.S.A. s. 85(4) & (5); Q.S.A. ss. 188, 189. The prohibition against informing also applies to informing by the reporting issuer itself.

[25] See *supra*, note 21.

[26] A.S.A. s. 119(3); B.C.S.A. s. 86(2); M.S.A. s. 112(2); Nfld.S.A. s. 77(2);

(iii) the accused informed another person of the material information before it was generally disclosed.[27]

The prohibitions with respect to informing typically permit the defence that the information was given in the necessary course of business of the reporting issuer.[28] There is a defence with respect to both the trading and informing offences that the person reasonably believed that the material information had been generally disclosed.[29] There are also specific exemptions from liability in situa-

---

N.S.S.A. s. 82(2); O.S.A. s. 76(2); S.S.A. s. 85(4), (5); Q.S.A. s. 188.

[27] Ibid. This aspect is present in the definition of "privileged information" in s. 5 of the Q.S.A.

[28] A.S.A. s. 119(3); B.C.S.A. s. 86(2); M.S.A. s. 112(2); Nfld.S.A. s. 77(2); N.S.S.A. s. 82(2); O.S.A. s. 76(2); S.S.A. s. 85(4); Q.S.A. s. 188(2). B.C.S.A. s. 86(2) also adds a defence with respect to the necessary course of business of the person in the special relationship.

[29] A.S.A. s. 119(6); B.C.S.A. s. 86(4); M.S.A. s. 112(4)(a); Nfld.S.A. s. 77(4); N.S.S.A. s. 82(4); O.S.A. s. 76(4); S.S.A. s. 85(6)(a); Q.S.A. s. 187(1) and s. 188(1). Both M.S.A. s. 112(4)(b) and A.S.A. s. 119(6)(b) provide the defence that the material fact or change was known or ought reasonably have been known to the purchaser. The A.S.A. also provides for a series of defences with respect to trading on inside information such as that the person who made the trade did not have "actual" knowledge of the material information, acted on behalf of a person that did not have knowledge of the material information or that the purchase was pursuant to a legal obligation to do so [see A.S.A. 119(5)]. The N.S.S.A. also provides the defence that the defendant did not make use of the material information in purchasing or selling the securities.

Given that these provisions carry criminal sanctions, it is likely that the accused's burden of proof is only such as to raise a reasonable doubt with respect to concluding that they could not have reasonably believed that the material fact or material change had been generally disclosed. If it required proof on a balance of probabilities of a reasonable belief that the information had been generally disclosed, it might be considered contrary to s. 11(d) of the *Canadian Charter of Rights and Freedoms* (see *R. v. Dubois*, [1985] 2 S.C.R. 350, [1986] 1 W.W.R. 193, 41 Alta. L.R. (2d) 97, 48 C.R. (3d) 193, 22 C.C.C. (3d) 513, 23 D.L.R. (4th) 503, 18 C.R.R. 1, 66 A.R. 202, 62 N.R. 50; *R. v. Oakes*, [1986] 1 S.C.R. 103, 50 C.R. (3d) 1, 24 C.C.C. (3d) 321, 26 D.L.R. (4th) 200, 19 C.R.R. 308, 14 O.A.C. 335, 65 N.R. 87; *R. v. Vaillancourt*, [1987] 2 S.C.R. 636, 60 C.R. (3d) 289, 39 C.C.C. (3d) 118, 10 Q.A.C. 161, 81 N.R. 115; *R. v. Holmes*, [1988] 1 S.C.R. 914, 27 O.A.C. 321, 85 N.R. 21; *R. v. Whyte*, [1988] 2 S.C.R. 3, 64 C.R. (3d) 123, 42 C.C.C. (3d) 97, 29 B.C.L.R. (2d) 273, 6 M.V.R. (2d) 138, 86 N.R. 328, [1988] 5 W.W.R. 26. S. 68(4) of the B.C.S.A. requires an accused to prove "on the balance of probabilities" that they reasonably believed that the material fact or material change had been generally disclosed.) This "reverse onus" provision may be contrary to s. 11(d) of the *Canadian Charter of Rights and Freedoms* (see the cases noted

tions where the person can be said not to have taken advantage of the knowledge of the undisclosed material information.[30]

There is a separate prohibition against informing in the case of a proposed takeover bid, reorganization, amalgamation, merger, arrangement or similar business combination with a reporting issuer, or in the case of a proposed acquisition of a substantial portion of the property of a reporting issuer.[31] A defence is available where the giving of the information is necessary to effect the takeover, business combination or acquisition.[32] The defence that the person reasonably believed that the material information had been generally disclosed is also available.[33]

---

above, especially *R. v. Oakes* and the views of Dickson C.J.C. at [1986] 1 S.C.R. 132-33). It might be said to be demonstrably justifiable under s. 1 of the Charter.

[30]See, for example, A.S.A. s. 119(5), (6) and s. 171(2); B.C. Rules s. 161; M. Regs. s. 44.1; Nfld. Regs. s. 149D; N.S. Regs. s. 181; O. Regs. s. 175.

Exemptions for persons purchasing or selling securities with knowledge of undisclosed information are provided where, for instance:

(i) the person who bought or sold only knew of the material information by virtue of the knowledge of the director, officer, partner, employee or agent and where the decision to make the trade was made by a director, officer, employee or agent who had no knowledge of the material information and was not advised on the basis of that material information by those having knowledge of it;

(ii) the person bought or sold as agent in response to an unsolicited order not made on advice based on the material information given by the person acting as agent;

(iii) the person bought or sold as agent in response to an order given before the person had knowledge of the material information; or

(iv) the person bought or sold pursuant to an automatic dividend reinvestment plan or purchase plan entered into before the person had knowledge of the material information;

There is also an exemption with respect to trading or informing where the person proves that they reasonably believed that the person traded with or informed knew of the undisclosed material information.

[31]A.S.A. s. 119(4); B.C.S.A. s. 86(3); M.S.A. s. 112(3); Nfld.S.A. s. 77(3); N.S.S.A. s. 82(3); O.S.A. s. 76(3); S.S.A. s. 85(5).

[32]Ibid.

[33]A.S.A. s. 119(6); B.C.S.A. s. 86(4); M.S.A. s. 112(4); Nfld.S.A. s. 77(4); N.S.S.A. s. 82(4); O.S.A. s. 76(4); S.S.A. s. 85(6)(a).

b. CIVIL ACTIONS

Canadian securities acts generally provide for an action for damages against a person trading on material inside information by the person with whom the trade was made.[34] As with the penal sanction,[35] the elements that the plaintiff must show are

(i) the defendant was in a "special relationship"[36] with the reporting issuer;[37]

(ii) the defendant purchased or sold securities[38] of the reporting issuer;

(iii) the defendant made the purchase or sale with knowledge of material information about the reporting issuer;[39] and

(iv) that the material information had not been generally disclosed.

---

[34]See A.S.A. s. 171(1); B.C.S.A. s. 136(2); M.S.A. s. 113(1); Nfld.S.A. s. 134(1); N.S.S.A. s. 142(1); O.S.A. s. 134(1); S.S.A. s. 142(1); Q.S.A. s. 226 (referring to ss. 187 and 189 with respect to the elements that must be proved). There are also provisions for such an action in most Canadian corporate law statutes (e.g., C.B.C.A. s. 131; B.C.C.A. s. 129; O.S.C.A. s. 138). These provisions generally require that the insider "make use of specific confidential information". Problems with proving this (see Simmonds, *infra*, note 68, Buckley, *infra*, note 67), probably make these provisions less likely to lead to a successful action. Consequently, the focus herein is on the provisions of provincial securities acts.

Common law actions against directors and officers are also possible. Although such actions have long been thought to be virtually impossible on the basis of a rather broad interpretation of *Percival v. Wright*, [1902] 2 Ch. 421, 71 L.J. Ch. 846 as authority for the proposition that directors and officers owe their fiduciary duties to the corporation and not to shareholders, more recent cases suggest that in some situations ("special facts") there may be a duty to shareholders (see, e.g., *Coleman v. Myers*, [1977] 2 N.Z.L.R. 225; *Dusik v. Newton* (1985), 62 B.C.L.R. 1 (B.C.C.A.) (cf. *Roberts v. Pelling* (1981), 16 B.L.R. 150, 130 D.L.R. (3d) 701) and the obiter comments in *Nir Oil Ltd. v. Bodrug* (1985), 18 D.L.R. (4th) 608 (Alta. C.A.)).

[35]See the securities acts provisions cited *supra* notes 19 to 22.

[36]See *supra*, notes 4 to 17 and the accompanying text.

[37]See *supra*, note 19 with respect to the definition of "reporting issuer".

[38]The provision also extends to the purchase or sale of puts, calls, options, or derivative securities (the market price of which varies materially with the market price of any securities of the reporting issuer). See A.S.A. s. 171(11); B.C.S.A. s. 136(1); M.S.A. s. 112(6); Nfld.S.A. s. 134(8); N.S.S.A. s. 142(8); O.S.A. s. 134(8); S.S.A. s. 85(2).

[39]See *supra*, note 21 with respect to the definition of "material fact" and "material change" which together constitute "material information".

As with the penal sanction, there is a defence of reasonable belief that the material information had been generally disclosed.[40] There is an additional defence that the plaintiff knew of the undisclosed material information or that the plaintiff ought reasonably have known of it.[41] There are also specific exemptions from liability in situations where the person can generally be said not to have taken advantage of the information.[42]

Similarly, Canadian securities acts also generally provide that an action for damages can be brought against a person who informed another of the inside information.[43] The action can be brought by anyone who sold securities to or purchased securities from a person who obtained the inside information from the informer. The elements that the plaintiff must prove are again similar to those that the Crown must prove to obtain a conviction against an informer. They are that[44]

(i) the defendant is the reporting issuer, was in a "special relationship" with the issuer, or was a person proposing to make a takeover bid, became a party to a reorganization, amalgamation, merger, arrangement or similar business combination with the reporting issuer or proposing to acquire a substantial portion of the property of a reporting issuer;

(ii) the defendant informed another person of material information with respect to the issuer; and

---

[40]See A.S.A. s. 171(2)(a); B.C.S.A. s. 136(2)(c); M.S.A. s. 113(1)(a); Nfld.S.A. s. 134(1)(a); N.S.S.A. s. 142(1)(a) & (2)(a); O.S.A. s. 134(1)(a); S.S.A. s. 142(1)(a); Q.S.A. s. 187(1). Applying the burden of proof in civil actions, the onus on the defendant in establishing this defence should be proof on the balance of probabilities rather than simply having to introduce a reasonable doubt as in a criminal action.

[41]See A.S.A. s. 171(2)(b) (Section 172(2) also provides the additional defences noted *supra*, note 29, with respect to the penal provision for insider trading) B.C.S.A. s. 136(2)(d); M.S.A. s. 113(1)(b); Nfld.S.A. s. 134(1)(b); N.S.S.A. s. 142(1)(b); O.S.A. s. 134(1)(b); S.S.A. s. 142(1)(b). No such defence is specifically set out in the Q.S.A. The burden of proof, in the context of the civil action, will be for the defendant on the balance of probabilities rather than simply raising a reasonable doubt as in a criminal action.

[42]See *supra* note 30.

[43]See A.S.A. s. 171(3); B.C.S.A. s. 136(3); M.S.A. s. 113(2); Nfld.S.A. s. 134(2); N.S.S.A. s. 142(2); O.S.A. s. 134(2); S.S.A. s. 142(2); Q.S.A. s. 227 (with reference to ss. 188 and 189 as to what must be proved).

[44]Ibid.

(iii) the information was given before the material information was generally disclosed.

The defences are the same as those that apply to an action for damages against a person trading on inside information, with the additional defence that the information was given in the course of business of the issuer, or, in the context of a proposed takeover bid, business combination or acquisition, the information given was necessary to effect the takeover bid, business combination or acquisition.[45] In assessing the damages, the court is to consider the difference between the price at which the plaintiff bought or sold the securities and the average market price over the 20 trading days after the general disclosure of the information.[46] However, the court may consider any other measure of damages it considers relevant in the circumstances.[47]

c. ACTIONS BY OR ON BEHALF OF THE REPORTING ISSUER

The issuer of the securities traded can bring an action against an insider, affiliate or associate of the issuer where that person has either traded with knowledge of or informed another person of material information that has not been generally disclosed.[48] The issuer must show that the person was an "insider", "affiliate", or "associate" of the issuer, that the person either bought or sold securities

---

[45]See A.S.A. s. 171(4); B.C.S.A. s. 136(3)(d) to (g); M.S.A. s. 113(2)(d) to (g); Nfld.S.A. s. 134(2)(d)-(g); N.S.S.A. s. 142(2)(d)-(g); O.S.A. s. 134(2)(d)-(g); S.S.A. s. 142(2)(d) to (g); Q.S.A. s. 188(2). With respect to information given by a person in a special relationship with the reporting issuer, the B.C.S.A. s. 119(3)(f) also provides as a defence that the information was given in the course of business of the person in the special relationship with the reporting issuer. The O.S.A. provides that the disclosure must have been in the "necessary course of business" in order to establish the defence. There is also a defence where the person proves that they reasonably believed that the person who was informed already knew of the undisclosed material information. See the provisions cited *supra* note 30.

[46]See A.S.A. s. 171(9); B.C.S.A. s. 136(7); M.S.A. s. 113(6); Nfld.S.A. s. 134(6); N.S.S.A. s. 142(6); O.S.A. s. 134(6); S.S.A. s. 142(6). S. 226 and 227 of the Q.S.A. simply refer to "the harm suffered".

[47]See A.S.A. s. 171(10); B.C.S.A. s. 136(7); M.S.A. s. 113(6); Nfld.S.A. s. 134(6); N.S.S.A. s. 122(6); O.S.A. s. 131(6); S.S.A. s. 142(7).

[48]See A.S.A. s. 171(5); B.C.S.A. s. 136(5); M.S.A. s. 113(4); Nfld.S.A. s. 134(4); N.S.S.A. s. 142(4); O.S.A. s. 134(4); S.S.A. s. 142(4). A roughly corresponding action is provided for in s. 228 of the Q.S.A. A similar action is provided for in most Canadian corporate law statutes – see *supra*, note 34.

with knowledge of material information or informed another of the material information, and that they did so before the information was generally disclosed.[49] The action is for an accounting to the issuer for any benefit or advantage received by the insider, affiliate, or associate or by the tippee.[50] The defences are a reasonable belief that the information had been generally disclosed,[51] and, with respect to informing, that the giving of the information was necessary in the course of business of the issuer.[52]

Where the reporting issuer fails to bring or continue an action, the securities commission, or, a person who was a security holder at the time of the transaction, or who is currently a security holder, can bring an application for leave to bring an action, or continue an action, in the name of and on behalf of the issuer to enforce the duty to account.[53] The court may make an order requiring the commission or authorizing a person or the commission to commence or continue an action on behalf of the reporting issuer.[54] The court may make such an order where it is satisfied that the commission or security holder has reasonable grounds for believing that the reporting issuer has a cause of action and the reporting issuer has failed to diligently prosecute an action commenced by it or has failed to commence an action within 60 days of being requested to do so by the commission or security holder.[55] The discretion which

---

[49] Ibid. Under the Q.S.A. the persons to which an action for accounting applies is a much broader group set out in s. 189.

[50] Ibid.

[51] A.S.A. s. 171(6); B.C.S.A. s. 136(5); M.S.A. s. 113(4); Nfld.S.A. s. 134(4); N.S.S.A. s. 142(4)(c); O.S.A. s. 134(4); S.S.A. s. 142(4); Q.S.A. ss. 187(1), 189.1.

[52] Ibid. The Q.S.A. provision for accounting to the issuer does not make reference to the provision in s. 188 dealing with "disclosure" of privileged information. However it does refer to s. 189.1 which prohibits "use" of privileged information. S. 189.1 does not specifically provide a defence with respect to giving information in the necessary course of business. The B.C.S.A. s. 119(5) also provides a defence of the necessary course of business of the insider, affiliate or associate.

[53] See A.S.A. s. 172(1); B.C.S.A. s. 137(1); M.S.A. s. 114 (allows a security holder to apply for an order to have the commission bring an action); Nfld.S.A. s. 135(1); N.S.S.A. s. 143(1); O.S.A. s. 135(1); S.S.A. s. 143(1); Q.S.A. ss. 229, 233.

[54] A.S.A. s. 172(1); B.C.S.A. s. 137(1); M.S.A. s. 114(1); Nfld.S.A. s. 135(1); N.S.S.A. s. 143(1); O.S.A. s. 135(1); Q.S.A. ss. 229, 233; S.S.A. s. 143(1).

[55] Ibid.

is left to the court would allow it to take into account other factors, such as whether pursuing the action would be in the best interests of the reporting issuer. The court is also empowered to order the reporting issuer to pay all costs properly incurred by the person or securities commission commencing or continuing an action on behalf or the reporting issuer.[56]

d. ADMINISTRATIVE SANCTIONS

There are also several administrative sanctions that might be applied in the context of insider trading or informing.

(i) Cease Trade Orders

A securities commission may make a cease trade order against a person who has engaged in insider trading or informing.[57] A temporary order can be made pending a hearing on a cease trade order for a longer period.[58]

(ii) Removal of Exemptions

Exemptions to which persons involved in insider trading or informing might be entitled can be removed where a securities administrator or commission considers it in the public interest to do so.[59]

(iii) Prohibition from Acting as a Director or Officer

In some provinces the commission, where it is considered to be in the public interest, may order that a person resign from their

---

[56]See A.S.A. s. 172(6), (7) & (8); B.C.S.A. s. 136(4), (5) & (6); s. 114 of the M.S.A. simply provides that the court may make an order for commencing or continuing the action on such terms as the judge thinks fit; Nfld.S.A. s. 135(4), (5) & (6); N.S.S.A. s. 143(4), (5) & (6); O.S.A. s. 135(4), (5); S.S.A. 143(4), (5) & (6); Q.S.A. s. 232.

[57]See A.S.A. s. 165(1)(b); B.C.S.A. s. 161(1)(b); M.S.A. s. 148(1); Nfld.S.A. s. 127(1); N.S.S.A. s. 134(1)(b); O.S.A. s. 127(1), (2); S.S.A. s. 134(1); Q.S.A. s. 265.

[58]See B.C.S.A. s. 161(2); M.S.A. s. 148(2); Nfld.S.A. s. 127(3); N.S.S.A. s. 134(2); O.S.A. s. 127(5); S.S.A. s. 134(3).

[59]A.S.A. s. 165(1)(c); B.C.S.A. s. 161(1)(c); Nfld.S.A. s. 128; N.S.S.A. s. 134(1)(c); O.S.A. s. 127(1)3; Q.S.A. s. 264; S.S.A. s. 134(1)(a).

position as a director or officer or prohibit a person from becoming a director or officer.[60]

(iv) Administrative Penalty

In some provinces the commission, after a hearing, may also apply an administrative penalty for a contravention of the Act.[61]

e. INSIDER REPORTING

According to the Kimber Report, the risk to confidence in securities markets due to improper insider trading required a two-fold remedy. One remedy recommended was a sanction against those who engaged in insider trading.[62] The other remedy recommended was reporting of insider trades.[63] The reporting requirement was said to be the primary requirement. Disclosure of insider trades would, it was said, deter insider trades because insiders would be less likely to engage in improper insider trading when they knew their trades would be disclosed.[64] Disclosure, it was said, would also lead to greater confidence in the securities market.[65] The recommendations of the Kimber Report with respect to reports of trades by insiders have, for the most part, been followed in Canadian securities acts. The reporting requirements are discussed in Chapter 6, Part VI with respect to secondary market disclosure requirements.

IV. ENFORCEMENT PROBLEMS

According to the Kimber Report, allowing insider trading would "put into question" the concept of a free and open securities market and thereby "[lessen] the confidence of the investing public in the marketplace".[66] Thus insider trading should be deterred and the

---

[60]See A.S.A. s. 165(1)(e); B.C.S.A. s. 161(1)(d); N.S.S.A. s. 134(1)(d); O.S.A. s. 128(3) 7 & 8 (allows court to make such an order); S.S.A. s. 134(1)(h).

[61]See B.C.S.A. s. 162; N.S.S.A. s. 135; S.S.A. s. 135.1.

[62] *Kimber Report, supra* note 1, at para. 2.04.

[63] Ibid.

[64] Ibid.

[65] Ibid., para. 2.02.

[66] Ibid.

prohibition of insider trading is presumably directed at such deterrence.

However, the current means of enforcing the prohibition against insider trading is plagued by a number of problems. To begin with, it can be difficult to detect insider trading. Even if insider trading is detected, there are impediments in the currently available means of enforcement that may allow incidents of insider trading to escape without any sanction being imposed. These detection and enforcement problems may account for the relative paucity of cases dealing with insider trading.[67] These detection and enforcement problems may also account for (a) the widely-held view that a substantial amount of trading on inside information does occur without detection or the imposition of sanctions and (b) empirical evidence suggesting that trading on inside information does occur.[68]

A. Detection Problems

The first hurdle in detecting the presence of insider trading is the identification of trading which may have involved trading by insiders on undisclosed information. For instance, substantial changes in trading volumes or prices may indicate the presence of insider trading, particularly where these changes occur just prior to announcements of significant information concerning the issuer.

Once suspicious trading is identified, one must identify the persons who did the trading. This will often require tracing back orders through the records of brokers to the persons who traded. This trace may simply reveal trading done through nominee

---

[67] The relative paucity of cases is noted in R.L. Simmonds, "Penal Liability for Insider Trading in Canada: Commission des Valeurs Mobilières du Quebec v. Blaikie" (1988)14 C.B.L.J. 477 at 477; F.H. Buckley, "How to do Things with Inside Information" (1977-78) 2 C.B.L.J. 343, at 344.

[68] There is evidence of profits from insider trading based on studies of insider trading reports. See, for example, J. Jaffe, "Special Information and Insider Trading" (1974) 47 J. of Bus. 410; J. Jaffe "The Effect of Regulation Changes on Insider Trading" (1974) 5 Bell J. of Eco. and Mgnt. Sci. 93; J.E. Finnerty, "Insiders and Market Efficiency" (1976) 31 J. of Fin. 1141; H.N. Seyhun, "Insiders Profits, Costs of Trading and Market Efficiency" (1986) 16 J. of Fin. Eco. 189; H.N. Seyhun, "The Information Content of Aggregate Insider Trading" (1988) 61 J. of Bus. 1; D.J. Fowler and C.H. Rorke, "Insider Trading Profits on the Toronto Stock Exchange" (1988) 5 Can. J. Admin. Sci. 13; J.M. Suret and E. Cormier, "Insiders and the Stock Market" (1990) 3(2) Can. Investment Rev. 87.

accounts. Further tracing may be required to identify the true beneficiary of the trading. This can be especially problematic where the nominee account turns out to be a numbered bank account of an offshore bank having a policy of non-disclosure of client affairs.[69] The growing internationalization of securities markets is also making it possible to engage in insider trading from jurisdictions with weaker insider trading laws and resisting the application of the laws of jurisdictions with stricter insider trading laws when trading in the jurisdiction with weaker insider trading laws.[70]

Thus detection of insider trading is not without difficulties. Consequently not all incidents of insider trading will be detected. A penalty in excess of the profits earned from insider trading may be required to effectively deter insider trading given this imperfect detection.[71]

B. Enforcement Problems

Once insider trading is detected, there are, as discussed in Part III, several possible avenues through which a sanction may be imposed on persons who traded on or informed others of the undisclosed material information. There are penal sanctions, administrative sanctions, and civil actions. There are problems with each of these mechanisms for the enforcement of the prohibition against insider trading.

---

[69]See, for example, G.R. Raifman, "The Effect of the U.S.-Swiss Agreement on Swiss Banking Secrecy and Insider Trading" (1983) 15 L. & Pol. of Intl Bus. 565; D.L. McNew, "Blocking Laws and Secrecy Provisions: Do International Negotiations Concerning Insider Trading Provide a Solution to Conflicts in Discovery Rules" (1989) 26 Cal. W.L. Rev. 103.

[70]See C.J. Smith, "Extraterritorial Enforcement of Rule 10b-5: Insider Trading in the International Equities Market" (1988) 12 Suffolk Transnational L.J. 83, at 107-21.

[71]If insider trading is primarily motivated by the profits the insider expects to derive from trading on undisclosed information, then it can only be deterred by taking away the expected profits. If the penalty is just equal to the profit then the insider will only have the profit taken away when they are caught. On occasions when they are not caught (because detection and enforcement are not perfect) they will keep the profit. The ability to profit on those occasions when they are not caught and only lose the profit made when they are caught will leave an incentive to continue to trade on undisclosed information. Thus a penalty which is greater than the profit obtained by the insider on those occasions where the insider is caught will be required to deter insider trading.

1. Circumstantial Evidence

One problem with each enforcement mechanism is that the evidence required to prove an offence or make out the claim will often be circumstantial in nature. Where there has been trading by persons other than tippees, there will usually be corporate records providing direct evidence of a "special relationship". There may be direct evidence of trading available through records of brokers. There may also be direct evidence of material information through some form of subsequent disclosure such as in a material change report, financial statement, proxy circular or other report. However, unless there is a fortuitous admission by the defendant, proof of knowledge of the material information by the defendant will depend on circumstantial evidence.

Where the defendant is an informer, or a tippee who has traded, proof of the informing by the informer and receipt of the information by the tipper will, without the benefit of an admission on the part of either the informer or the tippee, depend on circumstantial evidence. Circumstantial evidence will be required to prove the communication as well as the content of the communication.

The *Bennett* case is a good example of this.[72] Louisiana Pacific Corporation, a U.S. company which had been interested in a take-over of Doman Industries Ltd., a British Columbia company. Bill Bennett, a former premier of British Columbia, and his brother Russell Bennett, who were friends of Herb Doman, had borrowed heavily to invest in Doman Industries around the time Louisiana Pacific had first expressed an interest in a takeover of Doman Industries. On the morning of November 4, 1988, the president of Louisiana Pacific phoned Herb Doman, the president of Doman Industries, to advise him that Louisiana Pacific was no longer interested in the takeover. A few minutes later there was a call from the Doman Industries offices in Duncan, B.C. to the McIntosh Centre in Kelowna, B.C. where the Bennetts had their offices. This was confirmed by long distance phone records. However, these phone records did not indicate who were the parties to the phone conversation. Within minutes of the phone call to the McIntosh Centre, the Bennetts had disposed of their substantial shareholdings in Doman Industries. The evidence that Doman had informed the Ben-

---

[72] *R. v. Bennett*, [1989] B.C.J. No. 1884.

netts of the withdrawal of the takeover offer and that the Bennetts knew of a material fact that had not been generally disclosed was circumstantial. In the quasi-criminal proceedings that followed the B.C. Provincial Court trial judge held that the Crown had not proved its case.

2. Penal Sanctions, the Burden of Proof and Compellability

There are additional problems with respect to penal sanctions. The burden of proof is proof beyond a reasonable doubt. The defendant cannot be compelled as a witness and thus cannot be examined or cross-examined as to their knowledge of the material information, whether they communicated with or informed another person of the information, or whether they received the information from another person.[73]

3. Civil Action for Damages

Civil actions by persons who traded with the insider are likely to be rare because of the costs of detection and the costs of instituting an action. Identifying insider trading might in part be accomplished through an analysis of insider reports. However, these apply to "insiders" only and thus cover only a limited scope of persons included in the term "special relationship".[74] Determining whether one traded with an insider may require access to the records of brokers. Even if access were available, the cost of analyzing these documents on the chance that one might have traded with an insider is often likely to be prohibitively costly. Recouping the costs of the action may depend on success in the action and thus there will be no guarantee that the costs of the action will be recovered. Even if the costs of the action are recovered, the costs of detecting the insider trading may not be. Consequently, a person is only likely

---

[73] For example, none of the accused in the *Bennett* case, *supra* note 72 testified. Thus the Crown could not get direct evidence as to who spoke to whom or what the content of the conversation was. There may also be a problem with being able to sufficiently specify a charge where numerous events over a prolonged period may indicate a pattern of insider trading, but where no single clearly identifiable event would be sufficient to constitute insider trading.

[74] See the discussion of "insider" and "special relationship" in Part III A 3 and the discussion of insider reporting requirements in Chapter 6, Part VI.

to pursue a claim for damages where there is a relatively large potential damage award and a relatively high probability of success.

4. *Civil Action for Accounting*

The costs of detection and the costs of an action may also deter the reporting issuer from bringing an action for accounting. Furthermore, those in control of the reporting issuer may be reluctant to take action against persons with whom they work, socialize or conduct business on a daily basis.

An accounting for profits would be made to the issuer and not to a security holder. A security holder would thus only share in the award to the extent of that security holder's interest in the issuer. The security holder's costs may not be fully compensated even if an order for costs was made.[75] Consequently, a security holder may not have much incentive to bring an action for accounting on behalf of the issuer.

Whether a securities commission can be expected to bring an action on behalf of a reporting issuer for an accounting will depend on the resources the securities commission has to monitor insider trading and pursue the enforcement of infractions. Given other obligations of commissions with respect to vetting prospectuses, dealing with various exemption applications, and so on, there may be limited resources available for the monitoring and enforcement of insider trading violations.

An order of the court must be obtained by a security holder or a securities commission to bring an action for accounting on behalf of the issuer.[76] A judge may be inclined not to make the order where it is not in the interests of the issuer to do so.[77] Given the costs of the action and likelihood of success, it may not be in the best interests of the issuer to bring the action.

5. *Administrative Sanctions*

As with actions for an accounting sought by a securities commission on behalf of a reporting issuer, the use of administrative

---

[75] The legal cases covered by such an order would not, for instance, cover the time and effort expended by the individual in bringing the action.

[76] See Part III A 4 c.

[77] See Part III A 4 c.

sanctions against insider trading may be limited by the resources available to securities commissions to monitor and enforce insider trading violations.

C. Summary

The problems identified above are not unique to the enforcement of a prohibition against insider trading. The enforcement of the prohibition of insider trading, like the enforcement of many other prohibitions, will be imperfect. However, these problems appear to be quite pronounced with respect to the current means of enforcing the prohibition of insider trading.[78] Given the potentially quite high costs of both detection and enforcement, one might ask whether the potential benefits of attempting to enforce a prohibition of insider trading can possibly outweigh the costs.[79] The challenge, if we continue to believe that insider trading should be prohibited, is to create new mechanisms of enforcement that will improve enforcement and more effectively deter insider trading.

V. A RECONSIDERATION OF THE POLICY REGARDING INSIDER TRADING

Although the law currently reflects the view that insider trading should be prohibited, there are those who are of the view that insider trading should not be prohibited. Two lines of argument that

---

[78] In the United States in the 1980s, the SEC devoted a substantially greater amount of resources to the enforcement of insider trading sanctions. The average number of cases brought per year increased more than six fold. A statute was passed in 1984 which, for the first time, allowed penalties of up to three times the profit from insider trading. There were several high profile cases in which insider trading sanctions were successfully enforced. However, empirical tests of the profits from insider trading prior to and after these changes showed that the profits from insider trading did not go down as a result of the increased enforcement efforts or the higher potential penalties. See H. Nejat Seyhun, "The Effectiveness of Insider-Trading Sanctions" (1992) 35 J. of Law and Econ. 149.

[79] The *Bennett* case is a good example of the potential costs of enforcement. Having detected a potential incident of insider trading, the enforcement process involved numerous court appearances over a wide variety of issues over a ten year period at, no doubt, considerable cost. The saga is reviewed in D. Johnston & K.D. Rockwell, *Canadian Securities Regulation*, 2d ed. (Toronto: Butterworths, 1998) 323-26.

question the need for a prohibition of insider trading are discussed below.

A. Do Investors Lose as a Consequence of Insider Trading?[80]

Although the presence of undisclosed information may cause investors to pay too much or sell for too little, which may lessen confidence in the marketplace, it is not clear that any investor, or group of investors, suffers a loss due to insider trading. Trading in securities markets is usually anonymous. Consequently, an investor does not know whether or not the person on the other side of the transaction is an insider. The investor may well engage in the trade regardless of whether or not there is insider trading.

For instance, where the investor places a "market order",[81] the broker would make the trade at the prevailing market price regardless of whether an insider was trading or not. Thus while a lack of disclosure may cause the investor to suffer a loss, the loss occurs whether or not an insider trades.[82]

---

[80]As to whether anyone loses as a result of insider trading, see, for example, M.P. Dooley, "Enforcement of Insider Trading Restrictions" (1980) 66 Va.L.Rev. 1, at 33, 36, 55, 68; H.G. Manne, *Insider Trading and the Stock Market* (New York: Free Press, 1966); K.E. Scott, "Insider Trading: Rule 10-5, Disclosure and Corporate Privacy" (1980) 9 J. of Legal Studies 801, at 807, 809; W.S. Wang, "Trading on Material Nonpublic Information on Impersonal Stock Markets: Who is Harmed and Who Can Sue Whom Under SEC Rule 10b-5?" (1981) 54 So. Cal. L. R. 1217; W.J. Carney, "Signalling and Causation in Insider Trading" (1987) 36 Cath. U. L. Rev. 863.

[81]A "market order" is an order placed to buy or sell a security immediately at the best current price.

[82]Johnston & Rockwell, *supra* note 79, say that the claim that insider trading is a victimless crime is a "weak argument" against the prohibition of insider trading. They say that "[t]he fact that the insider did not intend to harm person A does not lessen A's loss". This counter argument seems to miss the point. The point is not that the insider did not intend to harm "person A". The point is that the insider trade does not cause A's loss. "A" would have suffered the loss whether or not there had been an insider trade. Although A would not have traded if A had known the information the insider knew, the fact remains that there will be some undisclosed information from time to time and that A will make a trade on a less than fully informed basis regardless of whether an insider trades. In other words, the prohibition of insider trading will do nothing to prevent A's loss.

However, it can be argued that in certain instances trading by insiders on undisclosed information does cause a loss to an investor. It is possible that even a trade on an "at-the-market" order can be caused by insider trading. Trades on "limit orders"[83] may also be caused by insider trading. It is also argued that there is a loss to all persons who traded in the opposite direction to an insider.

1. *"Market Orders"*

It might be argued that a "market order" was caused by insider trading. For instance, undisclosed favourable information may indicate that a share, currently trading for $18 per share on the basis of publicly available information, is worth about $22 per share. Increased demand due to insider trading on the basis of undisclosed favourable information might put upward pressure on the price. If the price rises to $20, an investor unaware of the undisclosed favourable information may think the shares are worth about $18 per share on the basis of currently available information and may therefore be inclined to place an "at-the-market" sell order. The investor will have sold a share worth $22 per share for just $20, thus losing $2 per share. Similarly, undisclosed unfavourable information may indicate that shares, currently trading at $18 per share on the basis of publicly available information, are worth only about $14 per share. An increased supply of shares due to sales by insiders may put downward pressure on the price. If the price falls to $16 per share, an investor, unaware of the undisclosed unfavourable information, may think the shares are worth $18 per share and may therefore be inclined to place a market order to buy. The investor will have bought a share worth $14 per share for $16 per share, thus losing $2 per share.

There is another way in which insider trading may be said to cause market orders. Purchases by insiders may lead to subtle price and volume changes. An investor may interpret these changes as an indicator of favourable information and be induced to buy the shares. Insider trading would have thus caused the trade. However, the investor will not suffer a loss. When the information is disclosed, the price will rise further and the investor will benefit. Similarly,

---

[83] A "limit order" is an order to buy or sell at a specific price or at a better price.

sales by insiders may lead to subtle price and volume changes that may be interpreted as an indicator of unfavourable information. This may cause an investor to sell. Insider trading will have caused the sale. However, the investor will not suffer a loss. When the information is disclosed, the price will fall further and the investor will have been caused to sell before the full drop in the price.

2. *"Limit Orders"*

Where a limit order is placed, it may happen that the trade which caused the loss would not have occurred but for trades by insiders. For instance, an investor might place a limit order for the sale of a share when the price exceeds $20 at a time when the shares are trading at $18 per share. Purchases by an insider on the basis of undisclosed information suggesting a price of something in excess of $22 per share may cause the trade on the limit order to occur when it otherwise might not have. First, at the time of the trade the insider's bid may be the only available offer at a price in excess of $20. Second, the trades by the insider will increase the demand for the security, thereby putting upward pressure on the price. Third, the increased trading volume and price increase as a result of insider trades may be interpreted by the market as a signal of favourable information about the issuer, which may lead to further upward pressure on the price. Each of these may cause a trade to occur on a limit order at $20 per share when it otherwise would not have. In this sense a trade by an investor who placed a limit order could be said to have been caused by trades by one or more insiders.

Even if insider trading causes a trade by an investor making a limit order, it may not cause any harm to the investor. If the information had been released, the price would have increased and the order might have been executed at $20 per share without insider trading. Unless the investor could cancel the limit order in time, the sale might still occur for a price of at least $2 less than what it otherwise might have.

3. *Persons Trading in the Opposite Direction*

It has also been argued that the causal link is simply the non-disclosure of information. For instance, by buying shares on undisclosed favourable information, the insider benefits while all those who trade in the opposite direction (i.e., sell) will lose by selling the shares for less than they would be worth if the information were disclosed. The class of persons trading in the opposite direction to the insider could be quite large. It includes persons who would have traded at the predisclosure price whether or not the information was disclosed.

B. Is Insider Trading Detrimental or Beneficial?[84]

In *Diamond v. Oreamuno*[85] it was argued that insider trading would have an adverse impact on an issuer's reputation. This could cause a devaluation of the issuer's securities making future financing more expensive.[86] In *Insider Trading and the Stock Market*[87] Henry Manne argued, conversely, that issuers actually benefit from permitting insider trading. Insider trading, he said, provides a superior form of compensation for rewarding good performance by management of the issuer.[88]

---

[84] This summary of academic literature on the detrimental or beneficial effects of insider trading is drawn primarily from F.H. Easterbrook, "Insider Trading as an Agency Problem" in J.W. Pratt and R.J. Zechauser, eds., *Principals and Agents: The Structure of Business* (Boston: Harvard Business School Press, 1985), Chapter 4, 82-100. See also F.H. Easterbrook & D.R. Fischel, *The Economic Structure of Corporate Law* (Cambridge, Mass.: Harvard University Press, 1991), Chapter 10. There is a substantial volume of literature on this issue. See, for example, Manne, *supra* note 80; H.G. Manne, "Insider Trading and the Law Professors" (1970) 23 Vand. L. Rev. 547; D.W. Carlton and D.R. Fischel, "The Regulation of Insider Trading" (1983) 35 Stan. L. Rev. 857; R.A. Schotland, "Unsafe at Any Price: A Reply to Manne, Insider Trading and the Stock Market" (1967) 53 Virg. L. Rev. 1425; V. Brudney, "Insiders, Outsiders and Informational Advantages under the Federal Securities Laws" (1979) 93 Harv. L. Rev. 322; S. Levmore, "Securities and Secrets: Insider Trading and the Law of Contracts" (1982) 68 Virg. L. Rev. 117; J.D. Cox, "Insider Trading and Contracting: A Critical Response to the Chicago School" [1986] Duke L. J. 628; D.D. Haddock and J.R. Macey, "A Coasian Model of Insider Trading" (1985/86) 80 N.W.U.L. Rev. 1449; W.J. Carney, *supra* note 80.

[85] 24 N.Y. 2d 494, 248 N.E. 2d 910, 301 N.Y.S. 2d 78 (1969).

[86] The link between insider trading and the issuer's reputation was not articulated. Several arguments that link insider trading to the value of an issuer's securities are discussed below in response to Manne's argument that insider trading may actually benefit the issuer.

[87] H.G. Manne, *supra* note 80.

[88] Ibid., at 123-68.

1. *Superior Compensation*

a. MANNE'S ARGUMENT

Ownership is often separated from control in widely-held issuers. Shareholders own the issuer and managers control it. Managers' interests may diverge from shareholder interests. Managers, not having a significant ownership interest in the issuer, may not have a strong incentive to pursue profit without some form of compensation that gives them an incentive to pursue profits consistent with the interests of the issuer's security holders.

Allowing insider trading, Manne argued, provides a method of compensation that tends to align the interests of managers and shareholders.[89] Managers have an incentive to perform well because they can profit by trading on inside knowledge of their good performance. Manne argued that this method of compensation was more closely tied to rewarding good performance than other compensation techniques such as bonuses or stock options.[90]

b. RESPONSES TO MANNE AND REPLIES

(i) Windfalls

Critics of the claim that insider trading helps align manager and shareholder interests have argued that insider trading payoffs are not well linked to performance. Some insiders may be aware of good performance even though they did not bring it about. Their insider trading gain is not a reward for good performance but simply a windfall from being aware of good performance due to their position in the company. There may also be good or bad events with respect to the issuer which are beyond the control of insiders. Nonetheless insiders will profit from trading on the information. They thus profit not from good performance but from a mere windfall.[91]

Arguments in reply note that no compensation device is perfect in matching performance and reward. For some types of performance, insider trading may be a better compensation technique for matching rewards to performance. Although some insiders may benefit from good performance they did not bring about, it is argued

---

[89] Ibid.

[90] Ibid.

[91] See Easterbrook, *supra* note 84, at 84.

those who do provide the good performance are more likely to profit due to their more immediate access to the information. Furthermore, even though there may be gains from good and bad events not connected to performance, the issuer may benefit from allowing insider trading because it would provide an incentive to seek out information. The early identification of good or bad news would benefit the issuer by allowing for quicker response or adaptation.[92]

Other compensation techniques, such as salaries, bonuses, and stock options, could be used to reward good performance and penalize poor performance. Performance could be assessed after a period of time. Salaries, bonuses and the like could be adjusted in response to the assessed performance. However, the assessment of performance requires information which can be costly to gather. Insider trading provides compensation which is contingent on performance and does not require the costly gathering of information to assess performance.[93]

(ii) Perverse Performance Incentives

Another critique of the claim that insider trading is a compensation technique that aligns the interests of managers and owners is that there could be a perverse incentive with respect to management performance. Although there could be an incentive to perform well and profit from trading on advance knowledge of good performance, there would also be an incentive to perform poorly and profit through insider trades on advance knowledge of the poor performance. Managers could short sell[94] the securities of the issuer, reveal information concerning their poor performance and then buy

---

[92] See Easterbrook, *supra* note 84, at 84.

[93] See Easterbrook, *supra* note 84, at 83-84; Manne, *supra* note 80, at 134-39.

[94] A short sale is the sale of securities one does not currently own. Brokers can support such sales by supplying the securities required to settle the transaction out of their own inventory. The client is obliged to buy back the securities to replace those supplied to complete the short sale transaction. The short seller can gain where the security price falls between the date of the short sale and the date the short seller purchases the security to replace securities supplied to settle the short sale transaction.

back the securities after the price falls in response to the news of poor performance.[95]

Although there is a potential perverse incentive, the counter-argument is that it is unlikely that most managers will persist in such a strategy. The careers of managers may well be closely tied to the organization and they may be disinclined to persist in a poor performance strategy that would put the organization's existence in jeopardy.[96]

(iii) Hoarding

A further critique is that allowing insider trading will give managers an incentive to hoard information to permit them to capitalize on insider trading opportunities. Hoarding of information by lower level managers will retard the transfer of information to higher levels of management. This will impede the response of the issuer to new information. The impeded response to new information will make the issuer less efficient, thereby reducing the value of the issuer.[97]

However, the counter-argument is that hoarding, if it occurs, does not justify a restriction on insider trading by higher management. Furthermore, if it does occur and is bad for firms, then why don't firms ban insider trading by lower level managers? Indeed, if prohibiting it was profitable for the firm, then firms might be able to offer higher salaries to managers in return for their agreement not to engage in insider trading.[98]

(iv) Moral Hazard

Allowing insider trading may also create a "moral hazard".[99] Managers allowed to trade on inside information have greater oppor-

---

[95] See, for example, S. Levmore, *supra* note 84, at 149; R.A. Schotland, *supra* note 84, at 1453-54.

[96] See, for example, Carlton and Fischel, *supra* note 84, at 872, 873-74.

[97] See Easterbrook, *supra* note 84, at 84-85 citing R.J. Haft, "The Effect of Insider Trading Rules on the Internal Efficiency of the Large Corporation" (1982) 80 Mich. L. Rev. 1051, at 1053-60.

[98] See Easterbrook, *supra* note 84, at 85 citing R.A. Dye, "Insider Trading and Incentives" (1984) 57 J. of Bus. 295.

[99] "Moral hazard" is said to arise when a person does not bear the full risk of loss associated with his or her beheviour and thus does not have the incentive

tunities for profit the greater the variation in the price of the securities of the issuer. They thus have an incentive to make decisions that lead to higher business risk and thus greater fluctuations in the prices of the issuer's securities. Managers will be inclined to take on higher risk than the security holders because, it is argued, they do not face the loss that security holders do. Security holders, being the owners of the issuer, will bear the loss should the issuer become bankrupt. Managers in widely-held issuers do not face the same risk of loss due to bankruptcy because they are not the owners of the issuer.[100]

One response to the moral hazard argument is that managers do suffer a loss on bankruptcy even if they do not share in the ownership of the issuer. Their careers, and thus much of their personal wealth, is tied to the success of the issuer. Loss of the issuer could mean a substantial loss for most managers. Indeed, managers may be much more inclined to shun risk than shareholders who can diversify by holding portfolios of securities and thereby reduce their exposure to risk. Insider trading may be to the benefit of issuer security holders by encouraging managers to take greater risks than they otherwise would. This would realign management risk-taking preferences with those of the issuer's diversified security holders.[101]

(v) Adverse Selection

Firms hiring managers will have less than perfect information as to the quality of managers they hire. Managers may have difficulty signalling the quality of their management abilities. This may result in errors in the selection of managers. Insider trading may allow good quality managers to signal their quality by their willingness to accept such a compensation package. Not allowing insider trading

---

to take all cost justified precautions against the loss. In the case of insider trading, the manager's incentive may indeed be to exacerbate the risk.

[100] See Easterbrook, *supra* note 84, at 86-87 citing discussions of the problem in, for example, F.H. Easterbrook, "Insider Trading, Secret Agents, Evidentiary Privileges, and the Production of Information" (1981) Supreme Court Rev. 309, at 332-33 and R.W. Leftwich and R.E. Verrecchia, "Insider Trading and Managers' Choice Among Risky Projects" (University of Chicago Center for Research in Security Prices Working Paper No. 63, revision July 1983).

[101] See Easterbrook, *supra* note 84, at 86-87 citing Dye, *supra* note 98.

would remove a potentially valuable technique for overcoming a lack of information as to the quality of managers.[102]

The counter that has been made to this adverse selection argument is that the acceptance of payments through insider trades contingent on the success of the issuer does not necessarily clearly identify a manager as a skilled manager. A manager willing to accept such compensation may merely be an optimistic or overconfident manager.[103] Further, since managers are likely less able to diversify their career investment in the issuer than the issuer's security holders (who can hold diversified portfolios), managers accepting compensation contingent on insider trading opportunities will face more risk from fluctuations in the issuer's security prices than the issuer's security holders will. This suggests that the level of compensation for risk managers would require would be greater than the amount the issuer's security holders would be willing to pay.[104]

2. More Efficient Pricing

a. THE ARGUMENT

Information may be permitted to remain undisclosed where premature disclosure would be detrimental to the issuer. However, as Henry Manne also argued,[105] allowing insider trading may cause

---

[102] See D.W. Carlton and D.R. Fischel, *supra* note 84, at 871-72. The use of insider trading as part of a manager's compensation package may also cause good quality risk averse managers to go to firms offering a pure fixed salary compensation package even where their economic value is higher with the firm offering a combination of fixed salary and insider trading. Furthermore, the use of insider trading as part of the compensation package may attract risk preferrant managers. As to whether this would be good or bad, see the dicussion of moral hazard above. Although these problems may arise with the use of insider trading as part of the compensation package, it does not necessarily mean that insider trading should be prohibited. Firms could be left to weigh the benefits of the signalling of quality by allowing insider trading with the costs of deterring good quality managers from joining the firm and the costs of attracting risk preferrant managers. For a discussion of the adverse selection problem see Easterbrook, *supra* note 84, at 87-89.

[103] See N.L. Georgakopoulos, "Insider Trading as a Transactional Cost: A Market Microstructure Justification and Optimization of Insider Trading Regulation" (1993) 26 Connecticut L. Rev. 1 at 4.

[104] Ibid.

[105] See, for example, H.G. Manne, "Insider Trading and the Law Professors" (1970) 23 Vanderbilt L. Rev 547, at 565-78. See also H.K. Wu, "An Economist

market prices to reflect undisclosed information more quickly than would be the case if insider trading were prohibited. Trades by insiders and by others interpreting insider trades can put pressure on the price to move in the direction it would if the undisclosed information were disclosed.[106] Thus insider trading facilitates the efficient allocation of capital by causing security prices to more accurately reflect information relating to security values.

b. RESPONSES

One criticism of the argument that insider trading improves the accuracy of security prices is that it is unlikely to have a significant effect on security prices. Insider trades themselves, it is argued, probably only have a small and insignificant impact on the price of a security.[107] Delays in reporting of insider trades delay non-insider trades in response to knowledge of insider trading.[108] The relatively transitory and insignificant impact of insider trading on security prices and trading volumes will provide very little basis for non-insiders to identify and interpret the price and volume changes as indicators of undisclosed information and trade accordingly.[109] Thus, it is argued, the overall effect of insider trading on the prices of securities is likely to be insignificant.

Looks at Section 16 of the Securities Exchange Act of 1934" (1968) 68 Col. L. Rev. 260.

[106] Trades by insiders put some pressure on prices to move in the direction they would if undisclosed information were disclosed. Also non-insiders might interpret evidence of insider trading, or just evidence of changes in trading patterns, as indications of undisclosed information. They may trade on the basis of this and put further pressure on prices to move in the direction they would if the undisclosed information were disclosed. See, for example, R.J. Gilson and R.H. Kraakman, "The Mechanisms of Market Efficiency" (1984) 70 Virg. L. Rev. 549, at 630-31.

[107] See, for example, R. Brealey, *An Introduction to Risk and Return from Common Stocks*, 2d ed. (Oxford: Basil Blackwell, 1983), at 35-44; F.H. Easterbrook, *supra*, note 100, at 335-36; Gilson and Kraakman, *supra* note 106, at 630.

[108] See the discussion of insider reporting requirements in Chapter 6, Part VI. See also Gilson and Kraakman, *supra* note 106, at 630.

[109] Gilson and Kraakman describe this kind of trading by market participants in response to price and volume changes as "derivatively informed" trading. They argue that because derivatively informed trading operates slowly and often sporadically, it is a relatively inefficient mechanism for adjusting market prices in response to information and thus is unlikely to have much effect on the efficiency of securities prices (see Gilson and Kraakman, *supra* note 106, at 572-79, 631).

In direct contrast to the claim that insider trading leads to a more efficient pricing of securities, it has been argued that a prohibition of insider trading can lead to a more efficient pricing of securities.[110] The argument is that the profits that insiders make from their informed trading reduces the profits that other non-insider informed traders, such as sophisticated institutional investors, make from their trades. The reduced profits for these non-insider informed traders reduces their incentive to gather information and to trade. This, it is argued, reduces the liquidity of the market and the speed with which prices respond to new information.

c. THE IMPLICATIONS OF PRE-REGULATION NON-PROHIBITION

(i) The Argument

Prior to the development of laws prohibiting insider trading in North America, issuers did not impose prohibitions on insider trading. It has been suggested that if insider trading was really bad for these issuers, then they would have prohibited it. The fact that they did not is said to be evidence for the claim that allowing insider trading is beneficial for issuers.[111]

(ii) Responses and Replies

Persistent Advantage Taking

One reason offered for the failure of issuers to prohibit insider trading is that the management of issuers benefits from insider trading and thus could not be expected to prohibit it.[112]

However, if insider trading was really bad for the issuer, managers could benefit by prohibiting insider trading. This would

---

[110]See Georgakopoulos, *supra* note 103. For similar arguments and related discussions of the transactions cost imposed on uninformed traders in securities markets see, e.g., Note, "Insider Trading in Junk Bonds" (1992) 105 Harv. L. Rev. 1720; L.M. Ausubel, "Insider Trading in a Rational Expectations Economy" (1990) 80 Am. Econ. Rev. 1022; L.R. Goldstein & P. Milgrom, "Bid, Ask and Transaction Prices in a Specialist Market with Heterogeneously Informed Traders" (1985) 14 J. Fin. Econ. 71; M. Manove, "The Harm from Insider Trading and Informed Speculation" (1989) 104 Q.J. Econ. 823.

[111]See, for example, Easterbrook, *supra* note 84, at 90. See also Carlton and Fischel, *supra* note 84, at 858-60.

[112]See, for example, Brudney, *supra* note 84, and Haft, *supra* note 97, at 1058.

increase the value of the issuer. The increased value could be shared between security holders and managers. Security holders could receive greater returns and managers could receive larger salaries or other forms of compensation. Both managers and security holders would benefit and would thus have an incentive to prohibit trading if it were bad for the issuer. At least one might expect existing or senior managers to prohibit insider trading by new or junior managers.[113]

If insider trading was bad for issuer performance, then a competitor might be able to enter the market with a prohibition of insider trading and outperform an issuer which allowed insider trading. Issuers allowing insider trading might then be forced out of the market. Similarly, if insider trading was bad for issuer performance, then the prices of the securities of an issuer that allowed insider trading would tend to fall. A competitor with a prohibition of insider trading might then be able to sell securities at higher prices and thus face lower financing costs. Issuers allowing insider trading might then be forced out of the market.[114]

Non-Prohibition May Indicate High Enforcement Costs

Evidence that issuers did not ban insider trading before the development of legal rules banning insider trading may not be evidence that insider trading was not bad for issuers. It may simply indicate that it was too costly to enforce a prohibition against insider trading. In other words, a prohibition of insider trading might have been beneficial were it not for the cost of enforcement. Enforcement costs may have outweighed any benefits that might have been derived from the prohibition of insider trading. Thus a prohibition would not have been worthwhile.[115]

High enforcement costs may account for the earlier lack of legal rules prohibiting insider trading. However, enforcement costs may have fallen with the development of the computer which reduced the cost of monitoring trading to identify unusual trading patterns indicative of possible insider trading. This reduction in enforcement

---

[113] See, for example, Easterbrook, *supra* note 84, at 90. See also Carlton and Fischel, *supra* see 84, at 857-58.

[114] See Easterbrook, *supra* note 84, at 90-91.

[115] Ibid., at 91-92.

costs may account, in part, for the development of laws prohibiting insider trading.[116]

But why didn't the reduction in enforcement costs cause issuers to ban insider trading? Was it necessary to have a publicly enforced prohibition of insider trading?

A Public Enforcement Advantage

One suggestion for the need for public enforcement is that there are economies of scale in the enforcement of a prohibition of insider trading. The cost of enforcement by a single issuer with respect to trading in its securities may be proportionately greater than the cost of enforcement with respect to trading in the securities of many issuers. If this is the case, some kind of joint enforcement scheme would be appropriate.[117]

However, the existence of economies of scale in enforcement does not, of itself, necessarily imply that a public enforcement scheme is necessary. A stock exchange could provide for joint enforcement. The stock exchange could provide enforcement for all issuers listed on the exchange. Benefits from the prohibition of insider trading net of the costs of joint enforcement, which could be charged by the exchange in its listing fee, would be one reason for obtaining a listing on the exchange.[118]

There is, however, an added institutional reason for public enforcement. In spite of reduced enforcement costs with the assistance of computer monitoring and joint enforcement, the rate of detection appears to be quite low. This implies that a relatively high penalty and possibly imprisonment may be necessary to effectively deter insider trading. Private agreements which allow a party to the agreement to exact a penalty on the other party are generally not upheld by courts. Thus public enforcement may be necessary to exact the kinds of penalties required to effectively deter insider trading.[119]

---

[116] Ibid., at 93.

[117] Ibid.

[118] Ibid.

[119] Ibid., at 93-94.

C. An Interest Group Explanation of the Prohibition of Insider Trading

Part B above considers the question of whether there is a public benefit to the prohibition of insider trading. If it is true that the prohibition of insider trading is not beneficial then the question is, how did the prohibition of insider trading come about? Were there, for instance, some private benefits to particular interest groups that gave them an incentive to lobby for the prohibition against insider trading? Further, why did these private interest groups succeed in prohibiting insider trading over resistance by other interest groups that incurred losses as a result of the prohibition of insider trading?

One such private interest group argument claims that market professionals, such as securities analysts that make a living by gathering and assessing information on securities and profiting by trading on that information, coalesced to demand a prohibition of insider trading.[120] A simple way of understanding this is to consider the order of access to new information. Insiders, such as directors, officers and related persons, would, in many situations, be the first to have access to new information relevant to the value of an issuer's securities. If they are free to trade on this information their trades will disperse much of the profit that subsequent traders can make on the information. Market professionals, who make it their business to be on top of new information about securities, will be the next in line to acquire the information. However, the potential for them to profit on the information is reduced to the extent that insiders have already traded on the information and thereby have caused prices to move closer to the market price that will prevail after the information becomes widely available. The argument then is that these market professionals constitute a better organized and more concentrated group with a more substantial stake in the prohibition

---

[120]See D.D. Haddock & J.R. Macey, "Regulation on Demand: A Private Interest Model, With an Application to Insider Trading Regulation" (1987) 30 J. of Law & Econ. 311. It is also argued that insiders may support insider trading restrictions that discourage the use of arbitrageurs by take-over bidders. Bidders can reveal a proposed bid to arbitrageurs who will take up shares ahead of the public announcement of the bid and then tender under the bid. This gives the bidder greater assurance of the success of the bid. Insiders would support insider trading restrictions that would discourage this use of arbitrageurs and thereby reduce the potential for successful hostile take-over bids.

of insider trading than insiders and uninformed traders. Thus they will exert a much stronger influence in the political process concerning the regulation of insider trading.

It is worth noting the public interest counter argument to this noted above. Prohibiting trades by insiders and increasing profits to informed traders such as market professionals can increase market liquidity and the speed of response of market prices to new information which can be to the benefit of market professionals, uninformed traders and insiders alike.[121]

D. Summary

Although the law in Canada reflects the view that insider trading should be prohibited, there is some doubt as to whether anyone loses as a consequence of insider trading and some question as to whether or not insider trading might indeed be beneficial in terms of increasing the values of securities and the efficiency of capital markets. Many competing assumptions are made in the debate over these questions. There is very little empirical evidence available to sort out these competing assumptions. Empirical research testing many of these assumptions would be a useful contribution to the literature on insider trading.[122] If indeed there is no public benefit to a prohibition of insider trading then the presence of such a prohibition might be explained by the gains that such a prohibition may provide to one or more influential interest groups.

Perhaps the focus on efficient performance by issuers and efficient capital market prices does not capture the full picture. The aversion many people have to allowing insider trading may be due to a sense of a distributional consequence of insider trading that they find unacceptable. Even though the anonymous market may make it difficult to articulate who loses, there is a sense that the

---

[121] Insiders can benefit because the increased market liquidity and accuracy of prices reduces the risk for both market professionals and uninformed traders. This makes the issuer's securities more valuable and thereby reduces the cost of capital for issuers. This allows issuers to expand their investments and reap greater returns out of which insiders can be compensated.

[122] This is not to say that there has not been a considerable amount of empirical work done on insider trading. However, the available empirical evidence is directed primarily at identifying the presence of trading by insiders leading to abnormal profits. See *supra* note 74.

insider's gain is obtained at someone's expense. A sense of equity with respect to the distribution of gains may dictate that either the insider be precluded from making such gains or should be required to somehow compensate those at whose expense the gain was made.

CHAPTER 11

TAKEOVER BID AND ISSUER BID REGULATION

I. INTRODUCTION

The objective of this chapter is to provide a background for relating the regulation of takeover bids and issuer bids to the problems the regulation was intended to respond to. The background, coupled with a summary of the legislation, should provide assistance in understanding how and when takeover bid and issuer bid regulation applies. Part II deals with takeover bid regulation and Part III deals with issuer bid regulation.

II. TAKEOVER BID REGULATION

A takeover bid is a method of obtaining control over a corporation, and became popular in the 1960s. As the popularity of this acquisition technique grew, there were several complaints about the problems that it created for the shareholders to whom takeover bids were made.[1]

Some background is necessary to begin to understand what takeover bid regulation regulates. Subpart A provides a background on what takeovers are, how they are effected, and what a takeover bid is. Subpart B provides a summary of possible motivations for takeovers and subpart C provides a summary of the problems takeover bid regulation was said to address at the time it was introduced. With this background in mind, the regulation on takeover bids is briefly summarized. The chapter also briefly notes the debate over whether takeover bids should be regulated.

---

[1] See *infra*, Part II C.

A. Background[2]

1. *What Is a Takeover?*

The expression "a takeover" simply refers to a change in the control over management of the issuer or firm. A takeover, or change in control, of a widely-held corporation may be structured in any of several different ways.

a. METHODS OF EFFECTING A TAKEOVER

The takeover may be effected by way of a proxy contest in which a dissident shareholder, or group of shareholders, seeks the proxies of other shareholders to obtain control over sufficient votes to change the board of directors and thereby change the management. The takeover may occur as a result of an amalgamation whereby two corporations are combined to form a new corporation. The takeover can be effected by the purchase of all the assets of the firm to be taken over.

A takeover can also be effected by an acquisition of shares to give the acquirer of the shares sufficient voting power to exercise control over the target. The acquisition of sufficient shares may be done through the purchase of a controlling block of shares (or a few significant blocks of shares that together amount to a controlling block), or, by purchasing the shares of numerous shareholders through a general offer to all, or most shareholders, to buy shares.

b. FRIENDLY AND HOSTILE TAKEOVERS[3]

A takeover can be done in a friendly or hostile manner.

(i) Friendly

In a friendly takeover, target management supports the takeover. An acquirer may approach target management or target man-

---

[2] For further background discussion of takeovers and takeover bids see, for example, W.A. Klien and J.C. Coffee, Jr., *Business Organization and Finance: Legal and Economic Principles*, 2d ed. (Westbury, New York: The Foundation Press Inc., 1996) at 180-90; R.C. Clark, *Corporation Law* (Boston: Little, Brown & Co., 1986), at 531-46; R.J. Gilson, *Law and Finance of Corporate Acquisitions* (Mineola, New York: The Foundation Press, Inc., 1986), at 255-498.

[3] See Klien and Coffee, *supra* note 2, at 181.

agement may approach a potential acquirer. A friendly overture suggesting some kind of benefits from combining the two companies may be made. For instance, Grand Piano Co. may identify Upright Piano Co. as being a company with which it could profitably combine. Grand Piano Co. could then approach Upright Piano Co. management suggesting a possible profitable combination. After further discussions and negotiations, an arrangement between the two companies may be worked out.

(ii) Hostile

On the other hand, the takeover bid may be hostile. In a hostile takeover, target management does not support the takeover. The acquirer makes a "takeover bid" for the shares of the target.

2. What Is a "Takeover Bid" (or "Tender Offer")?

A takeover bid (which, in the U.S., is referred to as a "tender offer") is a general offer to all or most shareholders to purchase shares of a particular issuer, the result of which will be that the offeror (or "bidder") will obtain sufficient shares to control the offeree issuee (or "target"). A takeover bid can be either a "share exchange offer", a "cash offer" or a combination of a share exchange offer and a cash offer. In a share exchange offer, the offeror offers shares of the offeror (or a related company) in exchange for shares of the offeree. In a cash offer, the offeror offers to pay cash for shares tendered under the bid. It is also possible to have a combined cash and share offering in exchange for shares of the target.

For example, Acquisitions Ltd. might make an offer to SlowGrow Ltd. shareholders to buy SlowGrow common shares. The offer may be at a modest premium over the prevailing market price. Acquisitions Ltd. might offer two Acquisitions Ltd. preferred shares (worth $10 per share) in exchange for every SlowGrow Ltd. common share (worth $15 per share) tendered by SlowGrow shareholders or it might simply offer to pay cash (e.g., in the amount of $20 per share) for each share tendered.

B. Motivations for Takeovers[4]

Generally takeovers are not done on a whim. They are undertaken because there is some expected gain from the takeover. Understanding the motivations for takeovers provides insight into types of takeovers which are most likely to be affected by takeover bid regulation.

1. Inefficient Management

One reason that a takeover may be profitable is that target management may be inefficient. An acquirer can gain by taking over control of the target and then replacing the inefficient management.

2. Synergy

Another motivation for a takeover is that it may produce synergistic gains. A synergistic gain is said to occur when the value of the combination of the assets of two firms is greater than the sum of the value of the two firms if they remain independent. The assets and skills of the personnel of the two firms may gel in such a way that the combined result is worth more than the sums of the values of the two firms if they remain separate.

3. Market Power

A combination of two firms in a given industry may increase their market power. That is, they may be able to reduce competition by combining and thus gain from the higher price they could charge.

4. Tax Considerations

There can also be tax gains from combining firms. The most common source of gain from combining two companies is that one company may have losses that they may never be able to use or will not be able to use in the near future. A gain can be derived from combining with a profitable company that can then apply the other company's tax loss to its profits.

---

[4]See Klien and Coffee, *supra* note 2, at 187-90; Clark, *supra* note 2, at 533-45; Gilson, *supra* note 2, at 257-498.

5. *Undervaluation*

If a company's shares are undervalued in the market, an acquirer can reap gains by buying the company. In effect it is speculating on the value of the company. The acquirer believes the shares are worth more and the market will soon discover this and the share price will increase, or they have some information about the company that the market does not have. They buy up the shares and then release the information to the market or wait until the market adjusts to reflect a higher price for the shares. It's like buying a house for $120,000 when you know you can sell it within a week for $150,000.

6. *Empire Building/Managerialism*

Management acquires other firms in order to enhance the size of their firm and obtain for themselves either increased prestige or greater compensation.

7. *Looting*

Some of the rhetoric behind the enactment of takeover bid regulation in the U.S. was based on the notion that corporations were being "looted". In the U.S. the *Williams Act* amended the *Securities Exchange Act of 1934* to add provisions regulating tender offers.[5] The Act was named after Senator Williams, who, complaining that tender offers were being used to destroy venerable old corporations that were pillars of American society, proposed an early draft of the legislation.[6] These corporations, he complained, were being taken over by others who would sell the assets and wind up the corporation.

This kind of activity may indeed provide some social benefits. It may be that the assets would be better used in other endeavours. The acquirers are simply reallocating the assets to more highly valued uses. The assets have yet to be allocated to more highly valued uses because target management have chosen not to liq-

---

[5] Williams Act, Pub. L. No. 90-439, 82 Stat 459 (1968), codified as am. 15 U.S.C. 78m (d)-(e), 78n (d)-(f) (1968).

[6] See the comments of Senator Williams, 11 Cong. Rec. 27248-49, October 22, 1965.

uidate, probably being reluctant to surrender their livelihood. In other words, this really is just a specialized case of inefficient management.

On the other hand, this kind of takeover may not provide any social benefits. The takeover might be motivated by an attempt to buy control and then use that control to divert corporate assets to the acquirer at the expense of the non-acquirer shareholders remaining after the takeover. In other words, the acquirer liquidates the company by selling off the assets to a related company at less than fair market value. Similarly, the acquirer might divert shareholder wealth by buying out any minority interest remaining after the takeover bid for less than the fair value of the minority shares.

8. *Hubris*

Another motivation for a takeover bid is the acquirer's belief that the takeover will produce a gain. The acquirer thinks there will be a gain for any of the foregoing reasons, but has simply misjudged the situation. This explanation for takeovers has been advanced to explain anecdotal evidence that takeovers do not turn out as well as expected, and some empirical evidence that suggests that, on average, takeovers result in net losses to acquirers.

C. Reasons for Takeover Bid Regulation

Takeover bid regulation responded to problems raised in those situations where the acquirer would make a hostile takeover bid which was open for only a short period of time. The hostile takeover bid was often made in a manner euphemistically referred to as a "Saturday Night Special". Notionally, the idea was to make a bid on a Saturday night when the market was closed and say that tenders under the bid would be accepted only until 11:00 a.m. Monday morning. The acquirer's broker would open a book for the receipt of tenders on the Monday morning. Those shareholders who had tendered their shares by 11:00 a.m. would have their shares taken up. While bid periods were not typically this short, they were commonly not open for more than a few days. This had two main advantages for the acquirer: (i) it cut out competing bids; and (ii) it precluded target management from engaging in defensive tactics designed to prevent the takeover (i.e., takeover bid defences). All cash offers were typically used to avoid the delay that would be caused by the need to clear a prospectus in order to offer shares in a share exchange offer.

Concerns with respect to takeover bids were noted in the Kimber Report,[7] and in U.S. Congressional and Senate reports and academic literature at the time of the adoption of federal laws regulating takeovers in the U.S.[8] The main concerns are briefly noted below.

1. Insufficient Information/Gap in Disclosure Requirements

Offeree shareholders would often have nothing more than an offer, which could be from an unknown source since the offeror would often make the offer through a third party. The offerer shareholder would thus have no way of knowing whether the offer was a good offer or whether they should (i) take what was being offered and get rid of their shares, (ii) hold on to their shares in the hope of sharing in the gain the offeror expected to generate, or (iii) hold on to the shares in the hope of receiving a subsequent higher offer.

It was also noted that this lack of disclosure was a "gap" in securities law. Disclosure would have been required if there was a share exchange offer and bidders, it was argued, should not be able to avoid disclosure simply by making a cash offer.

2. Insufficient Time to Respond

Since offers were only open for a short period of time, offeree shareholders were typically forced to respond very quickly. Offeree shareholders needed more time to respond and they needed time to assess the information they should be given.

3. "First-Come First-Served" Offers Put Undue Pressure on Shareholders to Tender Early

When bids were made for less than all the shares of a target, they were often made on a "first-come first-served" basis. For

---

[7] *Report of the Attorny General's Committee on Securities Legislation*, March 1965 (the *Kimber Report*), at paras. 3.01 to 3.25.

[8] See U.S.C. Congressional and Administrative News, 1968, p. 2811; House Report No. 1711, July 15, 1968.

example, suppose 60% of the shares were sought and suppose 80% of the shares were tendered. The offeror would take up 60% by taking up shares in the order in which they were tendered. If the shares had been selling at $10 per share and the offer was for $12 per share, a shareholder, keen on getting in on the deal, would be under pressure to tender early.

4. Lock-Up of Tendered Shares

Once shares were tendered without any withdrawal rights, they were unavailable for tender under a subsequent bid. For instance, if the shares were selling for $10 and an offer was made at $12 on a first-come first-served basis, a shareholder who tendered early to get the $12 offer would not be able to tender the shares under a competing bid at $14. The shares could not be tendered under the $14 bid if they had already been tendered under the initial $12 bid. The shares were said to be "locked-up". In fact, the pressure to tender early coupled with the "lock-up" on tendered shares was said to discourage competing bids since by the time competing bidders were prepared to make a bid, the majority of the shares might have already been locked-up by the first bidder.

5. Unequal Consideration

Another common practice was to increase the consideration under the bid and not pay it to the shareholders who tendered prior to the increase. For example, a bidder might bid $12 for just 60% of the shares at a time when the shares were trading for $10 per share. If the bidder only got tenders of 40% of the shares, it might increase the bid to $13 to try to get the additional 20%. On obtaining sufficient shares, the bidder would pay $12 per share for the first 40% which were tendered before the increase in consideration and pay $13 per share on the additional 20%. This was seen as being unfair to offeree shareholders who tendered under the $12 bid.

There was also a concern that the acquirer might seek the shares of a controlling shareholder or a group of persons jointly controlling the corporation rather than making a bid to all shareholders. The controlling shareholder or group might then obtain a premium for their shares while the remaining shareholders were left with no premium at all. It was argued that this was unfair to the shareholders to whom offers were not made.

6. *Looting*

"Looting" was also cited as a reason for takeover bid legislation. There was a concern that venerable corporate pillars of American society were being taken over and destroyed by the winding up of these corporations.[9] There was also a concern that acquirers could take less than all the shares of the target corporation and then, using the control position they had obtained, force minority shareholders to sell their shares at less than fair market value in a post-takeover amalgamation. Similarly, acquirers might take advantage of minority shareholders by usurping corporate opportunities or selling assets of the target at less than fair market value to related corporations.

7. *Other Concerns*

The concerns discussed above were the main concerns noted in the academic literature and the various background reports. However, there were other concerns that the legislation also responded to. For instance, a shareholder might tender under a cash offer that the bidder was subsequently forced to renege on because the bidder had failed to obtain adequate financing for the purpose of taking up and paying for shares tendered under the bid. A similar concern was that the bidder, in the circumstances of a takeover bid, was making a "take it or leave it" offer. In doing so the bidder was inclined not to put any stringent obligations on itself with respect to such matters as the taking up of shares tendered or the due date for payment on the shares.

Other concerns have also arisen with respect to the takeover bid process since the original takeover bid legislation was enacted. For instance, offerors, unbeknownst to the market or to offeree shareholders, might influence the success of the offer by buying shares in the market during the bid period. Further, offerors who had effectively abandoned their bids might take up shares tendered

---

[9]See the comments of Senator Williams, 11 Cong. Rec. 27248-49, October 22, 1965.

under the bid and sell them in the market at prices influenced by their bid or might tender the shares under a competing bid prior to the expiry of their own bid.[10]

D. An Outline of Takeover Bid Regulation

Takeover bid regulation can be broken down into these elements: basic rules, when the rules apply, and anti-avoidance provisions. The basic rules governing takeover bids respond to the concerns noted under subheading C. The rules respond to the concerns with respect to bids identified as "takeover bids" subject to exemptions. Over the years since its initial enactment, there have been attempts to avoid the application of takeover bid regulation. This has led to the enactment of anti-avoidance provisions. Subsequent reviews of takeover bid regulation led to amendments designed to expand the potential for competing bids for target shares and to further protect target shareholders from being forced to surrender their shares for less than fair market value in post-takeover amalgamations.

1. The Basic Rules

In response to the perceived problems noted above, takeover bid legislation provides for the production of information, time to assess that information, the preclusion of first-come first-served offers, withdrawal rights to avoid the lock-up of shares, and the payment of equal consideration for shares tendered.

a. PROVIDES INFORMATION – DISCLOSURE REQUIREMENTS

Firstly, the legislation requires that where a takeover bid is made, a bid circular must be sent to all holders in the province of the secu-

---

[10] The concern here was that the offeree shareholder who tendered and whose shares were taken up under the first bidder's bid would not be able to tender under the competing bid.

rities sought.[11] The takeover bid circular must also be filed with the commission and sent to the offerer issuer.[12]

The content of a takeover bid circular includes information that would presumably be useful to offerer shareholders in deciding whether to tender their shares. The takeover bid circular provides information to assist the offeree shareholder in deciding whether to offer the shares at the offer price or hold on to the shares in the hope of (i) sharing in the gain that would accrue after the change in control or (ii) getting a subsequent competing offer. The takeover bid circular must provide the following information:[13]

(i) the name of the offeror;

(ii) the name of the offeree issuer;

(iii) ownership and trading in offeree issuer shares by the offeror or insiders of the offeror;

(iv) the method and time of payment for the shares of the offeree issuer;

(v) the source of any funds to be used for payment;

(vi) arrangements between the offeror and the directors or senior officers of the offeree issuer;

(vii) whether the offeror intends to purchase shares subject to the bid in the market;

(viii) information indicating a material change in the offeree issuer since the last interim or annual financial statement of the offeree issuer;

(ix) material facts relating to the offeree issuer; and

(x) appropriate prospectus information if the offer is a share exchange offer.

The shareholders are then given further information by way of a directors' circular, which must be provided within ten days of the

---

[11] The legislation requires that a circular containing prescribed information be circulated to holders of shares subject to the bid within the province. See A.S.A. ss. 137(1), 137.2, Alta. Rules s. 177, and Form 31; B.C.S.A., s. 108, B.C. Rules s. 177, Form 32; M.S.A. s. 89(1), M. Regs. s. 101 and Form 29; Nfld.S.A. s. 99, Nfld. Regs. s. 163, Form 31; N.S.S.A. s. 104, N.S. Regs. s. 189, Form 32; O.S.A., s. 98, O. Regs. s. 189(a), and Form 32; Q.S.A. s. 128, Q. Regs. s. 176, and Schedule XI; S.S.A. s. 107(1), S. Regs. s. 152(1), and Form 29.

[12] See A.S.A. s. 140; B.C.S.A. s. 110; M.S.A. s. 91, Nfld.S.A. s. 101, N.S.S.A. s. 106; O.S.A. s. 100; Q. Regs. s. 180; S.S.A. s. 109.

[13] See the Forms noted, *supra* note 11.

making of the takeover bid.[14] The directors must give reasons for (i) their recommendation to accept or reject a bid, or (ii) not making a recommendation.[15]

The directors' circular provides offeree shareholders with information relating to the bid. It is information that the directors have control over. For instance, information must be provided with respect to responses to the bid such as:[16]

(i) a merger or reorganization;

(ii) a sale of a material amount of assets of the issuer;

(iii) an issuer bid or other acquisition of issuer shares; or

(iv) a material change in capitalization or dividend policy.

With respect to the recommendation, a directors' circular includes other information that would indicate any interest the directors or senior officers have in the transaction including:[17]

(i) their ownership of and trading in securities of the offeree issuer;

(ii) whether they have accepted or intend to accept the offer;

(iii) any arrangement or agreement between the offeror or offeree issuer and the directors or senior officers of the offeree issuer to make a payment to directors or senior officers owing to loss of office upon the takeover;

(iv) interests of directors or senior officers of the offeree issuer in any material contract to which the offeror is a party; and

(v) any information indicating a material change in the affairs of the offeree issuer or any material facts about the offeree issuer known to the directors.

---

[14]See A.S.A. ss. 138, 139.1, Alta. Rules s. 178 and Form 32; B.C.S.A., s. 109, B.C. Rules s. 177, Forms 34 and 35; M.S.A. s. 90(1), M. Regs. s. 103, and Form 31; Nfld.S.A. s. 100, Nfld. Regs. s. 165, Form 33; N.S.S.A. s. 105, N.S. Regs. s. 191, Form 34; O.S.A., s. 99, O. Regs. s. 189(c), (d), and Forms 34 and 35; Q.S.A. s. 134, Q. Regs. s. 177, and Schedule XII; S.S.A. s. 108(1), S. Regs. s. 152(3), (4) and Forms 30 and 31.

[15]A.S.A. s. 138(2); B.C.S.A. s. 109(2); M.S.A. s. 90(2); Nfld.S.A. s. 100(2); N.S.S.A. s. 105(2); O.S.A. s. 99(2); Q.S.A. s. 134; S.S.A. s. 108(2).

[16]See the Forms noted *supra*, note 14.

[17]See the Forms noted *supra*, note 14.

There is potential civil liability for false statements or omissions in a takeover bid circular or a directors' circular.[18] The scheme of these civil liability provisions is similar to that of the civil liability provision for misrepresentations in a prospectus.[19]

b. TIME TO ASSESS THE INFORMATION – MINIMUM BID PERIOD

Securities can be deposited under a takeover bid for a minimum of 21 days from the date of the bid.[20] Where there is a variation of the bid, the bid period is extended by ten days.[21]

c. FIRST-COME FIRST-SERVED OFFERS NOT ALLOWED – PRO RATA TAKE-UP

The 21-day period would not be of much use if offerer shareholders could be pressured to tender early under a first-come first-served offer. Consequently, first-come first-served offers are not allowed. Instead, where the bid is for less than all the shares and where a greater number of shares than requested are deposited under the bid, they must be taken up pro rata.[22] For example, if the bid was for 600,000 shares and 800,000 shares were tendered, then three-quarters of the shares tendered by each shareholder would have to be taken up regardless of when the shares were tendered.

---

[18] A.S.A. s. 169; B.C.S.A. s. 132; M.S.A. s. 97; Nfld.S.A. s. 131; N.S.S.A. s. 139; O.S.A. s. 131; Q.S.A. ss. 222-225.1; S.S.A. s. 139.

[19] See Chapter 5 above.

[20] See A.S.A. s. 135(c); B.C.S.A. s. 105(b) and B.C. Rules s. 180(a); M.S.A. s. 86(c); Nfld.S.A. s. 96(b); N.S.S.A. s. 101.2; O.S.A., s. 95.2; Q.S.A. s. 147.3; S.S.A. s. 104(3).

[21] A.S.A. s. 137.1(2); B.C.S.A. s. 108(5) and B.C. Rules s. 180(f); M.S.A. s. 89(5); Nfld.S.A. s. 99(5); N.S.S.A. s. 104(5); O.S.A. s. 98(5); Q.S.A. s. 147.8; S.S.A. s. 107(5). However, where the variation is simply a waiver of a condition on a bid for which the consideration consists solely of cash, there is no mandatory extension of the bid period – see A.S.A. s. 137.1(3); B.C.S.A. s. 108(6); M.S.A. s. 89(6); Nfld.S.A. s. 99(6); N.S.S.A. s. 104(6); O.S.A. s. 98(6); Q.S.A. s. 147.8; S.S.A. s. 107(6).

[22] See A.S.A. s. 135(i); B.C.S.A. s. 105(g); M.S.A. s. 86(g); Nfld.S.A. s. 96(g); N.S.S.A. s. 101.7; O.S.A. s. 95.7; Q.S.A. s. 147.2; S.S.A. s. 104(8).

d. LOCK-UP PREVENTED – WITHDRAWAL RIGHTS

With the pro rata take-up provision it would generally not make sense for an offeree shareholder to tender early. However, to protect those shareholders who do tender early there is also a rule preventing the lock-up of shares. Shares cannot be taken up for 21 days and shares deposited within the 21-day period can be withdrawn at any time prior to the end of the 21-day period.[23] If there is a variation in the bid,[24] the withdrawal right is extended by 10 days unless the shares have already been taken up,[25] or the variation is simply an increase in the consideration offered[26] or a waiver of a condition on a cash bid.[27]

e. UNEQUAL CONSIDERATION IS NOT ALLOWED

In response to the concern that a controlling shareholder or group of shareholders might be made an offer to the exclusion of others, provincial securities legislation requires that a takeover bid be made to all holders in the province of the securities sought.[28]

The legislation also sets out the principle that the offeror must offer the identical consideration to all members of the class of equity securities sought.[29] Where the consideration under the bid is increased, the consideration must be paid on all securities taken up whether deposited before or after the increase.[30]

---

[23] See A.S.A. s. 135(e)-(g); B.C.S.A. s. 105(d)-(f) and B.C. Rules s. 180(b)-(d); M.S.A. s. 86(d)-(f); Nfld.S.A. s. 96(d)-(f); N.S.S.A. s. 101(4)-(6); O.S.A. s. 95.4-.6; Q.S.A. s. 147.5; S.S.A. s. 104(5)-(7).

[24] See A.S.A. s. 137.1; B.C.S.A. s. 108(5); M.S.A. s. 89(5); Nfld.S.A. s. 99(5); N.S.S.A. s. 104(5); O.S.A. s. 98.5; Q.S.A. s. 147.8; S.S.A. s. 107(5).

[25] See A.S.A. s. 135(f); B.C.S.A. s. 105(e)(i); M.S.A. s. 86(e)(i); Nfld.S.A. s. 96(e)(i); N.S.S.A. s. 101(5)(a); O.S.A. s. 95.5ii; Q.S.A. s. 147.5; S.S.A. s. 104(6)(a).

[26] See A.S.A. s. 135(f); B.C.S.A. s. 105(e)(ii); M.S.A. s. 86(e)(ii); Nfld.S.A. s. 96(e)(ii); N.S.S.A. s. 101(5)(b); O.S.A. s. 95.5ii; Q.S.A. 147.5; S.S.A. 104(6)(b).

[27] See A.S.A. ss. 135(f), 137.1(3); B.C.S.A. s. 108(6); M.S.A. s. 89(6); Nfld.S.A. s. 99(6); N.S.S.A. s. 104(6); O.S.A. s. 98(6); Q.S.A. s. 147.5; S.S.A. s. 107(6).

[28] See A.S.A. s. 135(a); B.C.S.A. s. 105(a); M.S.A. s. 86(a); Nfld.S.A. s. 96(a); N.S.S.A. s. 101(1); O.S.A. s. 95.1; Q.S.A. ss. 127, 128; S.S.A. s. 104(2).

[29] See A.S.A. s. 136(1); B.C.S.A. s. 107(1); M.S.A. 88(1); Nfld.S.A. s. 98(1); N.S.S.A. s. 103(1); O.S.A. s. 97(1); Q.S.A. s. 145; S.S.A. s. 106(1).

[30] See A.S.A. s. 136(3); B.C.S.A. s. 107(3); M.S.A. s. 88(3); Nfld.S.A. s. 98(3); N.S.S.A. s. 103(3); O.S.A. s. 97(3); Q.S.A. s. 146; S.S.A. s. 106(3).

Similarly, the bidder, or anyone acting jointly or in concert with the bidder, is not allowed to enter into collateral agreements with shareholders, the effect of which is to give one or some shareholders a greater consideration than other shareholders would receive.[31]

f. LOOTING – FORMAL VALUATION REQUIREMENTS

(i) Corporate Law Constraints

Although a concern for looting was one of the motivating concerns for takeover bid legislation, the legislation initially did not specifically deal with the problem of an acquirer subsequently taking advantage of minority shareholders. However, to the extent the legislation deterred takeovers, it may have reduced the extent of takeovers done for the purpose of looting. The main sources of protection against looting are provided for in statutes of incorporation. In particular, appraisal rights with respect to post-takeover amalgamations provide some protection to target shareholders against a forced post-takeover sale of their shares at less than fair market value.[32] Corporate statutory oppression remedies and fiduciary duties coupled with easier access to derivative actions provide some degree of protection against the usurpation of corporate opportunities or sales of assets to entities related to the acquirer at less than fair market value.[33]

(ii) Formal Valuations

Recent amendments to provincial securities laws do provide an added measure of protection against looting. These require that a "formal valuation" of the offeree issuer be provided in the bid circular in certain circumstances.[34]

---

[31] See A.S.A. s. 136(2); B.C.S.A. s. 107(2); M.S.A. s. 88(2); Nfld.S.A. s. 98(2); N.S.S.A. s. 103(2); O.S.A. s. 97(2); Q.S.A. s. 145 (the commission can approve such an agreement where it is not made for the purpose of increasing the consideration to a particular offeree); S.S.A. s. 106(2).

[32] See, for example, A.B.C.A. s. 184; B.C.C.A. s. 207; O.B.C.A. s. 185; C.B.C.A. s. 190.

[33] See, for example, A.B.C.A. s. 234; B.C.C.A. s. 200; O.B.C.A. s. 248; C.B.C.A. s. 241.

[34] A. Rules s. 171(2); B.C. Rules s. 162(2); M. Regs. s. 94(2); Nfld. Regs. s. 156(2), (3); N.S. Regs. s. 182(2), (3); O. Regs. s. 182(2), (3); Q. Regs. s. 183; S. Regs. s. 146(1).

One circumstance in which a formal valuation is required is where the offeror anticipates that a "going private transaction" will follow a takeover bid.[35] A "going private transaction" is defined as an amalgamation, arrangement, consolidation, or other transaction proposed by an issuer and in which a holder of a security participating in the earnings of the issuer may be terminated without the consent of the security holder.[36] The transactions set out in the definition of a "going private transaction" are the kinds of transactions most commonly cited as methods by which acquirers forced minority shareholders to accept less for their shares than they were worth.

Another circumstance in which a formal valuation is required is where the offeror in a takeover bid is an insider[37] of the issuer or any associate[38] or affiliate[39] of the offeree issuer.[40] In these circumstances, referred to as "insider bids", there is a concern that minority shareholders may be unfairly dealt with due to a conflict of interest or informational or other advantage the offeror may have by reason of its relationship to the issuer.[41]

---

[35] A. Rules s. 171(1)(b); B.C. Rules s. 162(2)a(ii); M. Regs. s. 94(3)(b); Nfld. Regs. s. 156(3)(b); N.S. Regs. s. 182(3)(b); O. Regs. s. 182(3)(b); Q. Regs. s. 183; S. Regs. s. 146(1)(b).

[36] A. Rules s. 170(a); B.C. Rules s. 162(1); M. Regs. s. 94(1); Nfld. Regs. s. 156(1); N.S. Regs. s. 182(1)(b); O. Regs. s. 182(1); Q. Regs. s. 183 (refers to transformation into a closed company or its equivalent); S. Regs. s. 145(b).

This does not apply where the offeror substitutes an interest of equivalent value in a participating security of the issuer or of a successor to the business or of another issuer that controls the offerer issuer. It also does not apply to the acquisition of securities pursuant to a statutory right of acquisition such as under CBCA s. 206.

[37] A. Rules s. 170(b) & (c); B.C. Rules 162(1); M. Regs. s. 94(1); Nfld. Regs. s. 156(1); N.S. Regs. s. 182(1)(d); O. Regs. s. 182(1); Q. Regs. s. 183; S. Regs. s. 145(c).

[38] A. Rules s. 170(b) & (c); B.C. Rules 162(1); M. Regs. s. 94(1); Nfld. Regs. s. 156(1); N.S. Regs. s. 182(1)(d); O. Regs. s. 182(1); Q. Regs. s. 183; S. Regs. s. 145(d).

[39] A. Rules s. 170(b) & (c); B.C. Rules s. 162(1); M. Regs. s. 94(1); Nfld. Regs. s. 156(1); N.S. Regs. s. 182(1)(d); O. Regs. s. 182(1); Q. Regs. s. 183; S. Regs. s. 145(d).

[40] A. Rules s. 171(1)(a); B.C. Rules s. 162(2)a(i); M. Regs. s. 94(3)(a); Nfld. Regs. s. 156(3)(a); N.S. Regs. s. 182(3)(a); O. Regs. s. 182(3)(a); Q. Regs. s. 183; S. Regs. s. 146(1)(a).

[41] O. Pol. 9.1, Part I 1 3.

The "formal valuation" is a valuation carried out by an independent valuer as of a date not more than 120 days before the date of the takeover bid, with appropriate adjustments for material intervening events and without any downward adjustments to reflect the fact that the offeree shareholders do not or will not form part of a controlling interest.[42] This allows the offeree shareholder to compare the bid price to the price that might be offered in a post-takeover amalgamation.[43]

(iii) Ontario Policy 9.1

Ontario Policy 9.1 (OP 9.1) provides further protections against potential looting of minority shareholders. OP 9.1 applies where a bidder obtains sufficient shares to get control of an issuer and then attempts to use that control position to remove minority shareholder interests (i.e., a "going private transaction"). OP 9.1 also applies where there is a takeover bid by an insider of an issuer who may have more information about the value of the securities of an issuer and may therefore be in a position to take advantage of other shareholders. In addition to particular disclosure and valuation requirements, OP 9.1 recommends that the transaction be reviewed by an independent special committee. In the case of a going private transaction, OP 9.1 requires that the transaction be approved by minority shareholders.

Special Committee Review

Where an issuer that has security holders resident in Ontario is the subject of a going private transaction or an insider bid, OP

---

[42] A. Rules s. 171(2); B.C. Rules s. 162(4); M. Regs. s. 94(4); Nfld. Regs. s. 156(4); N.S. Regs. s. 182(4); O. Regs. s. 182(4); Q. Regs. s. 183; S. Regs. s. 146(2).

The formal valuation can be made up as of a date more than 120 days before the takeover as long as the valuer has no reasonable grounds to believe there has been any intervening event materially affecting the value of the securities — see A. Rules s. 171(3); B.C. Rules s. 162(5); M. Regs. s. 94(5); Nfld. Regs. s. 156(5); N.S. Regs. s. 182(5); O. Regs. s. 182(5); Q. Regs. s. 183; S. Regs. s. 146(3). Guidance on the independence of the values and on valuation procedures is set out in O. Pol. 9.1, Part VI.

[43] See, for example, O.S.C. Pol. 9.1, Part VI 1 1. The valuation may provide a sense of fair value that might be obtained on the exercise of appraisal rights upon dissenting to a post-takeover amalgamation. Additional requirements (such as an assessment by a committee of independent directors or minority approval of going private transactions) are set out in O. Pol. 9.1.

9.1 provides that the issuer should consider a review of the trans-action by a special committee. The role of the special committee is to safeguard against an interested party taking unfair advantage of minority shareholders.[44] According to OP 9.1, the special com-mittee should consist of directors who are independent from the interested party.[45] A director would not normally be considered independent where the director is an employee of the interested party, or an insider, associate or affiliate of an interested party.[46] A director who may benefit from the issuer bid in a way that is different from minority security holders or who would end up with a material interest in the issuer would also not be considered inde-pendent.[47] A director is also not normally considered to be inde-pendent where the director is, or was in the previous five years, an employee of the valuer or an insider, associate or affiliate of the valuer who is performing the formal valuation for the issuer.[48]

Minority Approval

Where an issuer that has security holders resident in Ontario is the subject of a going private transaction or an insider bid, OP 9.1 also provides that the issuer obtain approval of the transaction from a majority of the minority shareholders. Minority shareholder approval is determined by excluding the votes of the issuer, the person or company (or persons or companies acting together) who control the issuer, and any person or company that is controlled by the issuer or by a person or company who controls the issuer.[49] Where the minority shareholders are to receive something other than just cash for their shares or where they are to receive something less than the amount determined in the formal valuation of the shares, then the approval must be by two-thirds of the minority share-holders.[50] Otherwise the approval required is a simple majority.[51]

---

[44] OP 9.1, s. 27.1.

[45] Ibid.

[46] OP 9.1, s. 27.3.

[47] Ibid.

[48] Ibid.

[49] OP 9.1 s. 2.2(7) "interested party", s. 2.2(10) "minority approval" and s. 2.2(14) "related party".

[50] OP 9.1 s. 31.

[51] Ibid.

g. OTHER CONCERNS DEALT WITH

The concern that offeree shareholders may end up as creditors of an offeror which has failed to adequately finance a takeover bid that includes cash consideration is addressed by requiring that the offeror make adequate arrangements prior to the bid to ensure full payment for all securities that the offeror has to acquire.[52]

The potential for delinquent take-up of and payment for tendered shares is dealt with by a requirement that shares be taken up within ten days of the expiry of the bid.[53] Shares are to be paid for not more than three days after they are taken up.[54]

To assist target shareholders in assessing the likelihood of success of the bid, and to prevent the bidder from influencing the success of the bid through open market purchases, the bidder's purchases of shares during the bid period is restricted. The bidder can only purchase a maximum of 5% of the outstanding offeree issuer shares of the class subject to the bid. The intention to make such purchases must be announced in the takeover bid circular, the purchases must be made through the facilities of a recognized stock exchange and a press release with respect to the purchases must be made at the close of business of the exchange on each day on which shares have been purchased. This control on and disclosure of purchases permits the market and target shareholders to keep track of the bidder's ownership of offeree issuer shares, thus facilitating the assessment of the likelihood of the success of the bid.[55] To allow the market to adjust after the announcement of the takeover bid, the bidder cannot commence its purchases until the third day following the

---

[52]See A.S.A. s. 135.1; B.C.S.A. s. 106; M.S.A. s. 87; Nfld.S.A. s. 97; N.S.S.A. s. 102; O.S.A. s. 96; Q.S.A. s. 147; S.S.A. s. 105.

[53]A.S.A. s. 135(k); B.C.S.A. s. 105(i); B.C. Rules s. 180(e); M.S.A. s. 86(i); Nfld.S.A. s. 96(i); N.S.S.A. s. 101(9); O.S.A. s. 95.9; Q.S.A. s. 147.6; S.S.A. s. 104(10).

Furthermore, once shares are taken up under the bid, any shares subsequently deposited under the bid must be taken up within ten days — see, for example, O.S.A. s. 95.11.

[54]A.S.A. s. 135(l); B.C.S.A. s. 105(j); M.S.A. s. 86(j); Nfld.S.A. s. 96(j); N.S.S.A. s. 101(10); O.S.A. s. 95.10; Q.S.A. s. 147.6; S.S.A. s. 104(11).

[55]A.S.A. s. 134(2), (3); B.C.S.A. s. 101(2), (3); M.S.A. s. 85(2), (3); Nfld.S.A. s. 95(2), (3); N.S.S.A. s. 100(2), (3); O.S.A. s. 94(2), (3); Q.S.A. s. 142; S.S.A. s. 103(2), (3). The information required in the press release is set out in, for example, O. Regs. s. 188.

date of the bid.[56] To deal with concerns about sales during the bid period, bidders are restricted, during the bid period, from selling, or tendering under a competing bid, shares taken up under the bid.[57]

2. When the Rules Apply

a. THE DEFINITION OF "TAKEOVER BID"

The rules are, of course, intended to apply when there is a takeover bid. In other words, the rules apply when there is an offer for shares that will result in a change in control over the offeree issuer. However, there is no simple definition of a change in control for all potential offeree issuers. For instance, it might be defined as an acquisition of more than 50% of the voting rights. However, for some issuers there could be a change of control upon an acquisition of substantially less than 50% of the voting rights.

One approach would be a case-by-case assessment of whether a given acquisition results in a change in control. However, this approach would leave a great deal of uncertainty about when the rules apply. Another approach would be to set a level at which it would be assumed that *de facto* control of the offeree issuer would be obtained. The legislation took the latter approach. It deemed a takeover to have occurred upon the acquisition of 20% of the voting rights attached to securities of an issuer. Thus a "takeover bid" was defined to occur upon an offer to acquire voting shares which resulted in the offeror owning or controlling 20% or more of the voting shares.[58]

More recently the definition has been extended. Although the concerns over takeover bids arose in the context of bids for voting shares resulting in changes in control, similar issues of lack of information, lack of time, first-come first-served offers, unequal consideration and the lock-up of shares could occur in offers for non-voting shares as well as for voting shares. Thus "takeover bid" is defined

---

[56] A.S.A. s. 134(3); B.C.S.A. s. 101(3); M.S.A. s. 85(3); Nfld.S.A. s. 95(3); N.S.S.A. s. 100(3); O.S.A. s. 94(3); Q.S.A. s. 142; S.S.A. s. 103(3).

[57] A.S.A. s. 134.1(4), (5); B.C.S.A. s. 104(1), (2); M.S.A. s. 85(8), (9); Nfld.S.A. s. 95(8),(9); N.S.S.A. s. 100(8), (9); O.S.A. s. 94(8),(9); Q.S.A. s. 143; S.S.A. s. 103(9), (10).

[58] Originally the threshold applied to shares carrying voting rights. See *The Securities Act, 1966*, S.O. 1966, c. 42, s. 80(g).

to mean an "offer to acquire"[59] voting or equity securities held by a person in the province where the result of the acquisition will be that the offeror will end up owning[60] 20% or more of the outstanding shares of a class of voting or equity securities.[61]

b. EXCEPTIONS TO THE APPLICATION OF THE TAKEOVER BID RULES

With the broad definition of "takeover bid" (noted above) it is easy to see that it would apply to a wide range of transactions — not all of which would raise the kinds of concerns that takeover bid regulation was originally intended to deal with. For instance, if a person holds 51% of the sole voting class of shares, sufficient to exercise control over the corporation, it would be a "takeover bid" if that person offered to acquire even a single additional share. Consequently, there are exceptions for transactions for which the application of takeover bid rules is considered inappropriate.

(i) Stock Exchange Bids

Takeover bids made through the facilities of a stock exchange are generally regulated by the stock exchange.[62] Such bids are

---

[59] An "offer to acquire" is defined to include an offer to purchase securities, a solicitation of an offer to sell securities or an acceptance of an offer to sell securitities — see A.S.A. 131(1)(l); B.C.S.A. s. 92(1); M.S.A. s. 80(1); Nfld.S.A. s. 90(g); N.S.S.A. s. 95(1)(g); O.S.A. s. 89(1); S.S.A. s. 98(1)(e).

[60] This includes securities which are beneficially owned or over which control or direction is exercised by the offeror or anyone acting jointly or in concert with the offeror — see "offeror's securities" in A.S.A. s. 131(1)(o); B.C.S.A. s. 92(1); M.S.A. s. 80(1); Nfld.S.A. s. 90(1)(j); N.S.S.A. s. 95(1)(j); O.S.A. s. 89(1); Q.S.A. s. 111; S.S.A. s. 98(1)(h).

[61] Amendments extended the definition of "takeover bid", and thus the application of takeover bid rules, to a threshold of 20% of the voting or equity securities of a class. "Equity security" is defined as any right to participate in the earnings of the issuer and the assets of the issuer upon the liquidation or winding up of the issuer. See the definitions of "equity security" and "takeover bid" in A.S.A. s. 131(1)(d), (r); B.C.S.A. s. 92(1); M.S.A. s. 80(1); Nfld.S.A. s. 90(1)(c), (l); N.S.S.A. s. 95(1)(c), (e); O.S.A. s. 89(1); Q.S.A. s. 110 (the Q.S.A. definition of "takeover bid" is limited to "a class of voting securities"); S.S.A. s. 98(1)(j) and s. 2(1)(s).

[62] TSE By-law s. 23.01 — s. 23.13; ME Rule 12, 12001-12012; VSE Rule B.4.0, B.4.01-B.4.13; ASE By-law s. 24.01 — s. 24.13.

exempt from the rules in provincial securities acts,[63] but are subject to similar stock exchange rules.[64] The stock exchange rules are subject to review by the securities commission and are generally consistent with the approach of the securities acts.[65]

The stock exchange rules require that a notice be provided by the offeror containing information similar to that required by a takeover bid circular under securities acts. The notice must be filed with the applicable exchange, or exchanges, and must be distributed to registered holders of the class of securities subject to the bid in Canada and otherwise the terms of the bid must be communicated by advertising in the manner approved by the applicable exchange. The details of the offer must be disseminated through the news media in the form of a press release. The offeree directors must also issue a press release recommending, with reasons, acceptance or rejection of the bid or indicating, with reasons, that they are not making a recommendation. The press release must contain other information that covers some of the same informational items that would be included in a directors' circular under the securities acts. The exchange rules also provide for pro rata take-up of shares where more than the number of shares sought are tendered.

A book for the receipt of tenders on a stock exchange can be opened on the 21st calendar day day after the date on which notice of the stock exchange bid is accepted by the exchange. An offeror cannot attach any conditions to a stock exchange takeover bid other than a condition as to the maximum number of shares sought and making the bid conditional on no action by the Director of Investigation and Research under the *Competition Act.*

(ii) "Normal Course" Purchases

The definition of "takeover bid" would mean that any purchase by a person holding 20% or more of a class of equity securities would constitute a "takeover bid" and trigger the application of takeover bid rules, even if the purchase does not affect the control

---

[63] A.S.A. s. 132(a); B.C.S.A. s. 98(1)(a); M.S.A. s. 84(1)(a); Nfld.S.A. s. 94(1)(a); N.S.S.A. s. 99(1)(a); O.S.A. s. 93(1)(a); Q.S.A. s. 119; S.S.A. s. 102(1)(a).

[64] A.S.A. s. 133.1; B.C.S.A. s. 100; M.S.A. s. 84(4); Nfld.S.A. s. 94(4); N.S.S.A. s. 99(4); O.S.A. s. 93(4); Q.S.A. s. 119; S.S.A. s. 102(5).

[65] A.S.A. s. 53; B.C.S.A. s. 29(1)(a); M.S.A. s. 139(2); Nfld.S.A. s. 24(2); N.S.S.A. s. 30; O.S.A. s. 21; Q.S.A. ss. 177-80; S.S.A. s. 21(6).

of the issuer. To allow a holder of 20% or more of a class of shares to make modest purchases, an exemption is provided for what are referred to as "normal course" purchases. Normal course purchases are purchases of not more than 5% of the securities of a class provided that[66] (i) the purchase price does not exceed the market price,[67] and (ii) only 5% are purchased in any one-year period. In other words, up to 5% of the outstanding securities of a class can be purchased each year without triggering the takeover bid rules.

(iii) Control Block Purchase

The definition of "takeover bid" would preclude any attempt to acquire control by acquiring a control block. If the offeror would end up with 20% of the "equity securities" of a class, it would be a "takeover bid". However, transfers of control may well be beneficial for the target corporation's shareholders.[68] Some transfers of control might not occur if the controlling shareholder, or group of controlling shareholders, is not offered a premium on the sale of control. Thus some transfers of control through sales of control blocks ought to be allowed.[69]

There is a view, however, that the person, or group of persons, selling control should not be entitled to a premium for their controlling interest. It has been argued, for instance, that control is a corporate asset and thus belongs to all shareholders.[70] Accordingly, the premium for the sale of control should be shared equally amongst the shareholders.

---

[66] A.S.A. s. 132(1)(b)(i); B.C.S.A. s. 98(1)(b); M.S.A. s. 84(1)(b); Nfld.S.A. s. 94(1)(b); N.S.S.A. s. 99(1)(b); O.S.A. s. 93(1)(b); Q.S.A. s. 126; S.S.A. s. 102(1)(b).

[67] "Market Price" is defined, in the normal case where there is trading on a public market which provides a closing price, as the simple average of the closing price for each business day on which there was a closing price over the previous twenty days — see A. Rules s. 172(1); B.C. Rules s. 163; M. Regs. s. 95(1); Nfld. Regs. s. 157(1); N.S. Regs. s. 183(1); O. Regs. s. 183(1); S. Regs. s. 147(1).

[68] See the discussion of the motivations for takeovers, *supra* Part II B.

[69] See the discussion in F.H. Easterbrook and D.R. Fischel, "Corporate Control Transactions" (1982) 91 Yale L.J. 698.

[70] See, for example, D.C. Bayne, "A Philosophy of Corporate Control" (1963) 112 U. Pa. L.R. 22; W.D. Andrews, "The Stockholders Right to Equal Opportunity in the Sale of Shares" (1965) 78 Harv. L. Rev. 505.

Provincial securities acts attempt to achieve a balance between these two competing views. Transfers of control through the sale of control blocks for a premium are allowed as long as the premium is not substantial. If the premium is substantial, then the bid must be made to holders of shares of the class sought. The level at which a premium is considered substantial for these purposes is 15% above the prevailing market price.

To effect this result, provincial securities acts provide an exemption from the application of the takeover bid rules where an offer is made to 5 or fewer persons, an offer is not made generally to security holders of the class of equity securities sought, and the offer price does not exceed the market price of the securities by more than 15%.[71]

This also allows shareholders who hold a control block of shares some room to deal with their shares and allows some transfers of control through the sale of control blocks. By limiting the control premium to 15%, however, transfers of control through control block purchases will not be very common. The holders of controlling share blocks will likely attach some value to their control position and will not be inclined to surrender control without a substantial premium. By discouraging changes in control through control block purchases, the legislation may discourage takeovers which are beneficial both from the point of view of target shareholders and of society.

(iv) Closely-Held Company Exemption

Shareholders in closely-held companies often have share transfer restrictions that would prevent the types of takeover bids that caused the kinds of problems which takeover bid regulation responded to. Also shareholders in a closely-held company usually have access to the kind of information that would be provided in a takeover bid circular. Thus the costs of preparing a takeover bid circular and otherwise complying with the takeover bid regulations would not be justified. Consequently, an exemption from the takeover bid regulations is provided where the number of security holders of the class sought is less than 50, the bid is not for the shares of a reporting

---

[71]See A.S.A. s. 132(1)(c); B.C.S.A. s. 98(1)(c); M.S.A. s. 84(1)(c); Nfld.S.A. s. 94(1)(c); N.S.S.A. s. 99(1)(c); O.S.A. s. 93(1)(c); Q.S.A. s. 123; S.S.A. s. 102(1)(c).

issuer, and there is no published market for the securities that are the subject of the bid.[72]

(v) Limited Relevance to Jurisdiction

A takeover bid may have limited application in a particular province if the bid involves very few shareholders representing a small percentage of the outstanding shares of the class sought and who are resident in the province. If the bid is made in compliance with similar laws of another jurisdiction respecting takeover bids, then the concerns noted above with respect to takeovers will be dealt with and confidence in the market will be protected. Consequently, there is no need to subject the bid to the additional costs of complying with the takeover bid regulations of the particular province to the extent that such regulations are inconsistent with the regulations of the primary jurisdiction. Indeed, forcing compliance with the regulations of the particular province might discourage the sale of shares of issuers outside the province to residents of the province.

In recognition of this problem, an exemption to the takeover bid regulations is provided where (i) less than 2% of the securities of the class sought are held by persons resident in the province, (ii) there are fewer than 50 holders of the securities resident in the province, (iii) the bid is made in compliance with the laws of another recognized jurisdiction, and (iv) material relating to the bid is sent by the offeror to all shareholders of the class sought resident in the province.[73]

---

[72] A.S.A. s. 132(1)(d); B.C.S.A. s. 98(1)(d); M.S.A. s. 84(1)(d); Nfld.S.A. s. 94(1)(d); N.S.S.A. s. 99(1)(d); O.S.A. s. 93(1)(d); Q.S.A. s. 122; S.S.A. s. 102(1)(d). In determining whether there are 50 holders of securities of the class sought, one can exclude holders who are, or were, in the employment of the offeree issuer or an affiliate of the offeree issuer. Such persons are likely to have access to or knowledge of information relevant to deciding whether or not to tender their shares. The requirement that there be no published market and that the shares are not shares of a reporting issuer will tend to limit the group of persons from whom securities are being purchased to persons who are relatively sophisticated investors, have common bonds with the issuer or have access to information (see the discussion of the closed system, *supra*, Chapter 7).

[73] A.S.A. s. 132(1)(e); B.C.S.A. s. 98(1)(e); M.S.A. s. 84(1)(e); Nfld.S.A. s. 94(1)(e); N.S.S.A. s. 99(1)(e); O.S.A. s. 93(1)(e); Q.S.A. s. 121; S.S.A. s. 102(1)(e).

(vi) Exemption Applications

As in other areas governed by provincial securities acts, it is recognized that the exemptions specifically provided for may not cover unforeseen or unique situations that should be exempt from the broad scope of the legislation. Thus provincial securities acts allow for an application to the commission for an exemption from the takeover bid regulations where such an exemption would "not be prejudicial to the public interest".[74]

3. Anti-Avoidance Provisions

Takeover bid regulation may be costly to comply with and may create impediments to effecting takeovers through either a general offer to offeree shareholders or private agreements with controlling shareholders for substantial premiums. Not surprisingly, therefore, there have been attempts to avoid the application of takeover bid regulation. Some of these avoidance techniques were anticipated in the original legislation. Other avoidance techniques have since been responded to in amendments to the legislation.

a. ACTING JOINTLY OR IN CONCERT

One simple technique for avoiding the application of takeover bid legislation is to cooperate with another person in the purchase of shares. For instance, three persons, each currently owning no shares of a particular offeree issuer, might agree that each will offer to buy 17% of the shares of a class of that offeree issuer. If the shares are voting shares, the three persons might agree to vote the shares jointly. With joint control over 51% of the voting shares, this would constitute a change in control. However, since none of the three persons ends up owning 20% or more of the shares of the offeree issuer, there will be no "takeover bid" as that term is defined in provincial securities acts.

A similar technique would be to offer to acquire some amount of shares that would result in ownership of less than 20% of the shares of a class of voting shares, but agree with some other person

---

[74] A.S.A. s. 144(2)(c); B.C.S.A. s. 114(2)(c); M.S.A. s. 95(2)(c); Nfld.S.A. s. 105 (2)(c); N.S.S.A. s. 110(2)(c); O.S.A. s. 104(2)(c); Q.S.A. s. 263 (not "detrimental to the protection of investors"); S.S.A. s. 113(2)(c).

who already owns shares of the offeree issuer to jointly vote the shares. The acquisition of shares, coupled with the agreed-upon joint voting, may result in a change in control of the offeree issuer and thus may lead to the problems takeover bid regulation was intended to deal with. However, since the offer to acquire will not lead to ownership of 20% or more by the offeror, there will be no "takeover bid" as that term is defined in provincial securities acts.

Consequently, in determining whether the "offeror's securities" constitute 20% or more of the class, the "offeror's securities" include the securities of anyone acting jointly or in concert with the offeror.[75] "Acting jointly or in concert" is left to be determined according to the common meaning of the term.[76] However, specific situations that will amount to "acting jointly or in concert" are set out. "Affiliates" or "associates" are deemed to be joint actors as well as anyone with whom the offeror has an agreement, commitment or understanding for the acquisition of shares of the same class or with whom the offeror has an agreement, commitment or understanding to jointly exercise voting rights.[77]

b. RIGHTS TO ACQUIRE SECURITIES IN THE FUTURE

Another way of avoiding the "takeover bid" definition would be to buy options which grant a right to buy securities of the class being sought in the bid or to buy securities carrying a right to be converted into securities of the class of securities sought. "Takeover bid" is defined as an "offer to acquire" shares resulting in ownership of 20% or more of the shares of a class.[78] The exercise of such

---

[75] A.S.A. s. 131(5); B.C.S.A. s. 95(2); M.S.A. s. 81(2); Nfld.S.A. s. 91(2); N.S.S.A. s. 96(2); O.S.A. s. 90(2); Q.S.A. s. 111; S.S.A. s. 99(2).

[76] The acts provide that "it is a question of fact as to whether a person is acting jointly or in concert with an offeror" — A.S.A. s. 131.1; B.C.S.A. s. 96; M.S.A. s. 82; Nfld.S.A. s. 92; N.S.S.A. s. 97; O.S.A. s. 91; Q.S.A. s. 111; S.S.A. s. 100.

[77] A.S.A. s. 131.1(c); B.C.S.A. s. 96(1); M.S.A. s. 82; Nfld.S.A. s. 92; N.S.S.A. s. 97; O.S.A. s. 91; Q.S.A. s. 111; S.S.A. s. 100. "Associates" are usually defined to include such persons as an issuer in which the person owns more than 10% of the outstanding voting securities, partners of the person, trusts in which the person serves as a trustee or has a substantial beneficial interest, and relatives — see, for example, B.C.S.A. s. 1(1); O.S.A. s. 1(1) 2. "Affiliates" include subsidiaries, parent issuers, or issuers which have a common parent to the particular person — see, for example, B.C.S.A. s. (1)(2); O.S.A. s. 1(2).

[78] See *supra* 59-61.

rights might not constitute a "takeover bid" since it would probably not be construed as an "offer to acquire".[79]

To deal with this possible avoidance technique, securities acts generally provide that the offeror, or any person acting jointly or in concert with the offeror, is deemed to own securities which it can acquire by exercising a conversion right or some other right to acquire the security, within sixty days of the date for which the offeror's ownership of securities is being assessed.[80]

c. DIRECT OR INDIRECT OFFERS

There may be any number of techniques by which an offeror can attempt to avoid the application of takeover bid rules by not making the offer directly for the shares of the intended target. For instance, the offeror may want to offer a controlling shareholder, Jones, a premium in excess of the 15% allowed under the exemption, but does not want to have to make an equivalent offer to all other shareholders as would be required if a premium in excess of 15% were offered. A simple way to do the transaction without making an offer for shares of the intended target would be to have Jones incorporate a holding company and transfer ownership of the shares of the intended target to the holding company in exchange for shares of the holding company. The holding company would then have control over the target. The offeror could then make an offer to Jones for the shares of the holding company and end up with control over the holding company and thereby have control over the intended target.[81] No offer would have been made to shareholders of the intended target. To deal with such avoidance techniques, there is a broad anti-avoidance provision whereby an offer to acquire securities, or to exercise control or direction over securities, includes a

---

[79] An "offer to acquire" is defined to include an offer to purchase, or a solicitation of an offer to sell, securities or an acceptance of an offer to sell securities — see, for example, B.C.S.A. s. 92(1); O.S.A. s. 88(1). See *supra* note 59.

[80] A.S.A. s. 131(2)-(4); B.C.S.A. ss. 94, 95(1), (3); M.S.A. ss. 80(3), 81; Nfld.S.A. ss. 90(3), 91; N.S.S.A. ss. 95(3), 96; O.S.A. ss. 89(3), 90; Q.S.A. ss. 111, 112; S.S.A. s. 98(3), 99.

[81] The offeror could rely on the closely-held company exemption to avoid the application of takeover bid regulation to the offer to acquire shares of the holding company from Jones. The closely-held company exemption is discussed in Part II D 2 b iv above.

direct or indirect offer to acquire securities, or to exercise control or direction over securities.[82]

d. LINKED BIDS

All shareholders subject to a takeover bid to which takeover bid regulation applies are to receive identical consideration. However, an offeror might provide a greater consideration to some shareholders by acquiring shares, either before or after the formal bid to all shareholders, pursuant to private agreements in reliance on the private agreement exemption.[83] To prevent this technique for avoiding the requirement of providing identical consideration, the offeror must offer consideration equivalent to, and on the same basis as, the highest consideration paid per security by the offeror in any transaction in the previous 90 days which was not generally available to shareholders of the class of securities sought in the bid.[84] The offeror must also offer to acquire the same percentage of securities as was purchased from the vendor in any of the private transactions in the 90 days prior to the formal takeover bid.[85]

With respect to transactions after the expiry of the formal takeover bid, the offeror cannot acquire securities of the class subject to the bid for 20 business days after the expiry of the bid except by way of a transaction that is generally available to shareholders of the class subject to the bid and on terms identical to the terms of the formal takeover bid.[86]

4. *"Early Warning" Disclosure*

Any person acquiring control over 10% of the securities of a class of voting or equity securities must issue and file a press release

---

[82] A.S.A. s. 131(4)(b)(ii); B.C.S.A. s. 97; M.S.A. s. 83; Nfld.S.A. s. 93; N.S.S.A. s. 98; O.S.A. s. 92; Q.S.A. s. 114; S.S.A. s. 101.

[83] The private agreement, or control block purchase, exemption is discussed in Part II D 2 b iii above.

[84] A.S.A. s. 134.1(2); B.C.S.A. s. 103(1); M.S.A. s. 85(5); Nfld.S.A. s. 95(5); N.S.S.A. s. 100(5); O.S.A. s. 94(5); Q.S.A. s. 142.1; S.S.A. s. 102(6).

[85] Ibid.

[86] A.S.A. s. 134.1(1); B.C.S.A. s. 103(2); M.S.A. s. 85(6); Nfld.S.A. s. 95(6); N.S.S.A. s. 100(6); O.S.A. s. 94(6); Q.S.A. s. 144; S.S.A. s. 102(6).

identifying the person and the extent of their control over the voting securities.[87]

On each subsequent increase by 2% in the proportion of the securities of that class of voting securities the person controls, the person must again issue a press release and file a report with the commission.[88]

This has the effect of giving the target corporation an early warning of any potential takeover and can signal to others the potential gain from acquiring the target. This will increase the potential for competing bids and will allow target management more time to engage in defensive tactics.

5. Applications to a Securities Commission or Court

Applications can be made to a securities commission for an order restraining the distribution of any record used in connection with a takeover bid, requiring an amendment to or variation of any record used or issued in connection with a takeover bid, or directing any person to comply with or cease contravening the takeover bid requirements.[89] The commission may also proceed to make such orders on its own motion. An "interested person" may apply to court for an order compensating an applicant, rescinding a transaction with any interested person, requiring the disposition of securities acquired, prohibiting the exercise of voting rights, requiring the trial of an issue or making any other order the court thinks fit where it is satisfied that a person has not complied with the takeover bid requirements.[90]

---

[87] See A.S.A. s. 141; B.C.S.A. s. 111; M.S.A. s. 93; Nfld.S.A. s. 102; N.S.S.A. s. 107; O.S.A. s. 101; Q.S.A. s. 147.11; S.S.A. s. 110.

[88] Ibid., with respect to the Q.S.A., see s. 147.12.

[89] A.S.A. s. 144; B.C.S.A. s. 114; M.S.A. s. 95; Nfld.S.A. s. 105; N.S.S.A. s. 110; O.S.A. s. 104; Q.S.A. ss. 263-65, 272.1; S.S.A. s. 113.

[90] A.S.A. s. 145; B.C.S.A. s. 115; M.S.A. s. 96; Nfld.S.A. s. 106; N.S.S.A. s. 111; O.S.A. s. 105; S.S.A. s. 114. See also Q.S.A. s. 233.1.

E. Takeover Bid Defences and Takeover Bid Regulation

1. *Some Typical Defences*

Takeover targets may attempt to block a takeover or encourage competing bids for the target through a wide variety of defensive tactics. For instance, the target may issue new shares into friendly hands to defeat the controlling interest of the bidder. The target may seek a so-called "white knight" (an acquirer who is more acceptable to the target often because the white knight will not replace target management). The target may make a bid for its own shares (an "issuer bid"), competing with the outstanding hostile bid.

The target may attempt to discourage the bidder by selling off the asset or assets which the bidder is primarily seeking. This is sometimes referred to as a "crown jewel" defence. Instead the target might grant an option to a third party to buy the "crown jewel" at an exceptionally low price in the event that the hostile bidder's bid succeeds. Another technique is to enter into a "bust-up fee" arrangement with the white knight bidder.[91] Under this arrangement if the white knight's bid does not succeed, the target must pay an exorbitant sum to the white knight. Thus if the hostile bidder's bid succeeds, the hostile bidder will have acquired a controlling interest in a company with a substantial debt and therefore worth far less than the hostile bidder would have at first perceived.

The target may also attempt to defeat or delay the bid by commencing litigation and seeking an injunction until the litigation is resolved. This kind of defence is sometimes referred to as a "show stopper" defence. Litigation might be in the form of an alleged competition law violation or more generally in the form of an alleged violation of takeover bid regulations.

There are also a number of takeover defences that can be set up in advance to discourage takeover bids generally or to assure that takeovers occur on the terms dictated by the target (often through terms dictated by target management). For instance, a company might create a class of so-called "poison pill preferred"

---

[91] A "bust-up fee" or "lockup" has been criticized in M. Kahan & M. Klausner, "Lockups and the Market for Corporate Control" (1996) 48 Stan. L. Rev. 1539, arguing that "the prospect that a lockup may be granted to a 'white knight' bidder reduces both the number of actual hostile takeovers and the disciplinary effect of the takeover threat."

shares and distribute them to existing shareholders by way of a stock dividend. These preferred shares are typically convertible into common shares of the target and allow the holder of the preferred shares to redeem the shares if a bidder acquires some specified percentage (usually in the order of 30%) of the voting rights in the target. The right to redeem is often also conditional on the successful bidder not effecting an amalgamation within a specified period of time (e.g., 120 days). The redemption price is often set to ensure that the shareholder receives a fair price for the shares. For instance, it is sometimes set as the highest price paid for the target common or preferred shares during the previous 12-month period.[92]

Where the acquirer does effect a post-takeover bid amalgamation, the poison pill preferred shares are often given an entitlement to equivalent substitute shares in the amalgamated corporation. The conversion right usually given on the preferred shares would then "flip-over" to the amalgamated corporation, giving the preferred shareholder the right to convert the preferred shares into the common shares of the amalgamated corporation.[93] Such "flip-over" plans are intended to ensure that the shareholder is not forced out at an unfair price in a post-takeover amalgamation.

The creation of a class of poison pill preferred shares requires shareholder approval. This can be avoided with another type of poison pill plan known as a "poison rights plan". The right is usually distributed to the target shareholders as a dividend. In the event that a bidder acquires more than a specified percentage of the target voting rights (e.g., 20%) and then effects an amalgamation with the target, the right "flips-over" into a right to buy the shares of the amalgamated corporation at a price that is usually set up to be a very low price for the amalgamated corporation's shares. There are also often provisions for the holders of the rights to buy the shares of the target at a very low price if the acquirer obtains control of the target and does not effect a post-takeover amalgamation but instead engages in various self-dealing transactions with the target

---

[92] See M. Lipton, ed., *Takeover Defenses and Director's Liabilities* (Philadelphia: American Law Institute, 1986) at 95-96. See also G. Coleman, "Poison Pills In Canada" (1988)15 C.B.L.J. 1, at 1-2 and J.W. Forsyth, "Poison Pills: Developing a Canadian Regulatory and Judicial Response" (1991) 14 Dal. L.J. 158.

[93] Ibid., Lipton.

corporation.[94] The poison rights plan is generally intended to encourage the bidder to enter into negotiations with the target.[95] The rights are usually redeemable by the company at a nominal price for a short period after accumulation of the specified percentage of the voting rights by a bidder. This allows the board to remove the effect of the rights if it negotiates an acceptable arrangement with the bidder.[96]

Takeover bid regulation tends to encourage the use of defensive tactics of the type that are used in response to a bid. It does this, in part, by allowing time, through the bid period requirement, for the target management to respond to the takeover bid. It also facilitates white knight type defences by ensuring that target shares will be available for competing bids through the prevention of first-come first-served bids (due to pro rata take-up requirements) and through the lock-up of shares (due to withdrawal rights).

2. Validity of Takeover Bid Defences

Where a takeover threatens the replacement of target management, target management may have a strong incentive to resist the takeover. This may cause target management to engage in defensive tactics that are not in the interests of the target's security holders. The law in this area has been developing rapidly in recent years. The law is briefly canvassed below.

a. THE "PROPER PURPOSE" TEST

One approach which has been applied to deal with takeover defences, but which appears to be losing favour, is the "proper purpose" test. Under the proper purpose test, the court identifies the power under which the directors purported to act, considers

---

[94] Ibid., Lipton at 96-100. Some poison rights plans also provide for rights to buy shares of the target at low prices if the bidder acquires more than some specified percentage of the target. In this way the rights can take effect without a post-takeover amalgamation or self-dealing transaction — see Coleman, *supra* note 92, at 2.

[95] Ibid., Lipton 96-100.

[96] For a policy discussion on poison pill plans see, for example, J.G. MacIntosh, "The Poison Pill: A Noxious Nostrum for Canadian Shareholders" (1989)15 C.B.L.J. 276.

the nature of the purposes for which the power was intended and the "primary" or "substantial" purpose for which the power was used. If the substantial purpose for which the power was used is inconsistent with the nature of the purposes for which the power was intended, then the power is said to have been exercised for an "improper purpose". The current leading Anglo-Canadian authority for this approach is the case of *Howard Smith v. Ampol Petroleum.*[97]

b. THE "BEST INTERESTS" TEST

In *Teck Corporation v. Millar*[98] Mr. Justice Berger of the B.C. Supreme Court, after reviewing the law with respect to the proper purpose test, said that the proper purpose test was inconsistent with the general discretion of the directors to act in the best interests of the corporation. Mr. Justice Berger held that the acts of directors would be improper if they did not act in the best interests of the corporation. In setting out how the determination of whether the directors acted for a proper purpose was to be made, Mr. Justice Berger said,

> I think the Courts should apply the general rule in this way: The directors must act in good faith. Then there must be reasonable grounds for their belief. If they say that they believe there will be substantial damage to the company's interests, then there must be reasonable grounds for that belief. If there are not, that will justify a finding that the directors were actuated by an improper purpose.[99]

Teck Corporation v. Millar has been referred to with approval in a number of subsequent cases.[100]

---

97 [1974] A.C. 821, [1974] 1 All E.R. 1126. See also *Bonisteel v. Collis Leather* (1919), 45 O.L.R. 195, 15 O.W.N. 465 (H.C.); *Mills v. Mills* (1938), 60 C.L.R. 150 (Aust. H.C.); and *Hogg v. Cramphorn Ltd.*, [1967] Ch. 254, [1966] 3 All E.R. 420.

98 (1972), 33 D.L.R. (3d) 288, [1973] 2 W.W.R. 385 (B.C.S.C.).

99 33 D.L.R. (3d) 288 at 315-16, [1973] 2 W.W.R. 385 at 414.

100 *Shield Development Co. v. Snyder,* [1976] 3 W.W.R. 44 at 62-64; *Olsen v. Phoenix Industrial Supply Ltd.* (1984), 27 Man. R. (2d) 205 at 209; *Re Olympia & York Enterprises Ltd. v. Hiram Walker Resources Ltd.* (1986), 59 O.R. (2d) 254 at 268, 271-72, 37 D.L.R. (4th) 193 at 207, 210-11 (H.C.), aff'd (1986), 59 O.R. (2d) 280, 37 D.L.R. (4th) 219 (Div. Ct.); *Re Royal Trustco Ltd. (No. 3)* (1981), 14 B.L.R. 307 at 314-15; *Dixon v. Merland Explorations Ltd.* (1984), 50 A.R. 353, at 361-62; *Northern & Central Gas Co. v. Hillcrest Collieries Ltd.,* [1976] 1 W.W.R. 481 at 551; *First City Financial Corp. v. Genstar Corp.* (1981), 33 O.R. (2d) 631, 125 D.L.R. (3d) 303 (H.C.).

A much more restrictive version of the best interests test was set out by the

3. Reasonable in Relation to the Threat Posed and Shareholder Approval

In *Producers Pipelines Inc.*[101] the Saskatchewan Court of Appeal considered the adoption of a poison rights plan and an issuer bid by Producers Pipelines Inc. The decision of the majority of the court reviewed the law in Canada and concluded that it did "not conflict with the business judgment rule developed in the United States". The majority stated that the business judgment rule in the United States,

> recognizes that in a take-over situation, the directors will often be in a conflict of interest situation, and, in implementing a poison pill defence strategy, the directors must be able to establish that (a) in good faith they perceived a threat to the corporation, (b) they acted after proper investigation, and (c) the means adopted to oppose the takeover were reasonable in relationship to the threat posed.[102]

The majority held that the test developed in *Teck Corporation v. Millar* did not go far enough in giving principles for determining whether or not the defensive strategy was reasonable in relation to the threat posed. The court concluded that,

> when a corporation is faced with susceptibility to a take-over bid or an actual take-over bid, the directors must exercise their powers in accordance with their overriding duty to act bona fide and in the best interests of the corporation even though they may find themselves, through no fault of their own, in a conflict of interest situation. If, after investigation, they determine that action is necessary to advance the best interests of the company, they may act, but the onus will be on them to show that their acts were reasonable in relation to the threat posed and were directed to the benefit of the corporation and its share-holders as a whole, and not for an improper purpose such as entrenchment of the directors.[103]

Nova Scotia Supreme Court trial division in *Exco Corporation v. Nova Scotia Savings and Loan* (1987), 35 B.L.R. 149, 78 N.S.R. (2d) 91, 193 A.P.R. 91 (T.D.). The court stated, at 35 B.L.R. 261, that the directors must show that they acted in a way that was consistent with the best interests of the company and inconsistent with any other interests. This was criticized as being too stringent a test in *820099 Ontario Inc. v. Harold E. Ballard Ltd.* (1991), 3 B.L.R. (2d) 123 (Ont. H.C.), aff'd (1991), 3 B.L.R. (2d) 113 (Ont. Dist. Ct.).

[101] *347883 Alberta Ltd. v. Producers Pipelines Inc.*, [1991] 4 W.W.R. 577 (Sask. C.A.).

[102] Ibid., at 594.

[103] Ibid., at 595.

The majority of the court also noted that defensive actions should, wherever possible, be put to the shareholders for approval. Since the shareholders have the right to decide to whom and at what price they will sell their shares, defensive action must interfere as little as possible with that right. Accordingly, any defensive action should be put to the shareholders for prior approval where possible, or for subsequent ratification if not possible.[104]

Further, the court noted that "[d]efensive tactics that result in shareholders being deprived of the ability to respond to a take-over bid or to a competing bid are unacceptable."[105]

The *Producers Pipelines* case has been applied in a number of subsequent cases.[106] However, in *CW Shareholding Inc. v. WIC Western International Communications Ltd.*[107] it was held that the *Producers Pipelines* case went too far to the extent that it put the onus on the directors of the target to justify their actions. It was held that the directors of the target should be protected by the business judgment rule. If the *CW Shareholding* approach is followed the onus will be on complainants to show that the directors of the target acted in a way that was not reasonable in relation to the threat posed.

4. National Policy No. 62-202

The majority decision in *Producers Pipelines Inc.* was heavily influenced by National Policy #38, the virtually identically worded forerunner to N.P. No. 62-202. In N.P. No. 62-202 the Canadian securities regulatory authorities have noted that shareholders of the

---

[104] Ibid., at 595.

[105] Ibid., at 595. For a comment on the *Producers Pipelines* case see R. Yalden, "Controlling the Use and Abuse of Poison Pills in Canada: *347883 Alta. Ltd. v. Producers Pipelines Inc. (Saskatchewan)*" (1992) 37 McGill L.J. 887.

[106] See *Hamelin v. Seven Mile High Group Inc.* (1994), 89 B.C.L.R. (2d) 298, 4 C.C.L.S. 210 (C.A.); *Rooney v. Cree Lake Resources Corp.*, [1998] O.J. No. 3077; *Dixon v. First Heritage Savings Credit Union*, [1993] B.C.J. No. 3037 (B.C.S.C.); *Remington Energy Ltd. v. Joss Energy Ltd.*, [1993] A.J. No. 1043 (Alta. Q.B.); *CW Shareholding Inc. v. WIC Western International Communications Ltd.*, [1998] O.J. No. 1886. See also *Rogers Communications Inc. v. MacLean Hunter Limited et al.* (1994), 2 C.C.L.S. 233; and *Primex Investments Ltd. v. Northwest Sports Ltd.* (1995), 13 B.C.L.R. (3d) 300.

[107] [1998] O.J. No. 1886.

offeree company should be free to make fully informed decisions in the context of takeover bids. They also note their concern that certain defensive measures have the effect of denying shareholders the ability to make such fully informed decisions and of frustrating an open takeover bid process. In the view of the Canadian securities regulatory authorities, unrestricted auctions produce the most desirable results in takeover bids. Thus tactics that encourage auctions are considered acceptable. However, the Canadian securities regulatory authorities note in N.P. No. 62-202 that they might take action where the tactics are likely to deny or severely limit the ability of the shareholders to respond to a takeover bid.

The Canadian securities regulatory authorities advise in N.P. No. 62-202 that they are prepared to examine target company tactics in specific cases to determine whether they are abusive of shareholder rights. They also note that prior shareholder approval of corporate action would, in appropriate cases, allay concerns that company tactics are abusive of shareholder rights. In particular, they suggest that tactics that may come under scrutiny if undertaken during the course of a bid or immediately prior to a bid would include, for instance, the issuance, granting of an option on, or the purchase of a significant percentage of securities of the target, or the sale or purchase or granting of an option on assets of a material amount. To enforce this intrusion into what has otherwise traditionally been a fiduciary duty issue in corporate law, the securities administrators would presumably use their wide discretionary powers to impose cease trade orders or remove exemptions on the grounds that it is "in the public interest" to impose such sanctions.[108]

---

[108] For a discussion of N.P. #38, the forerunner to N.P. No. 62-202, see S.M. Beck and R. Wildeboer, "National Policy 38 as a Regulator of Defensive Tactics" (1987) Meredith Memorial Lectures 119; R.L. Simmonds, "Changing the Regulation of Defensive Tactics in Canada" (1987) Meredith Memorial Lectures 157; and J.P. Lowry, "Monitoring Defensive Tactics Against Takeover Bids – The Role of the Ontario Securities Commission" [1994] J. of Bus. Law 99. For an application of N.P. #38 (Now N.P. No. 62-202), that struck down a poison rights plan after it had "outlived its usefulness" in terms of inducing competing bids or increasing the bid price, see *Re Canadian Jorex Limited* (1992) 15 O.S.C.B. 257.

5. Securities Commission Response to Poison Pills

The Ontario Securities Commission has considered the use of poison pill plans as a takeover defensive tactic in several cases.[109] The general approach of the Commission in these cases has been to ask, in line with National Policy #38, whether the poison pill plan has outlived its usefulness in terms of promoting an auction for the shares of the target issuer. If the poison pill plan has outlived its usefulness then the Commission can impose a cease trade order. In most cases involving a poison rights plan the cease trade order would prevent target shareholders from exercising the rights.

To determine whether a poison pill plan has outlived its usefulness the Commission asked whether:[110]

(i) the outstanding bids can proceed if the rights plan is not removed;[111]

(ii) keeping the rights plan in place will lead to any further enhancement of the existing bid or bids;

(iii) continuance of the rights plan will lead to further bids; and

(iv) the plan has been approved by the target's shareholders.

In considering whether outstanding bids can proceed if the plan is not removed the Commission may look at whether management has made it clear that the bid will proceed if the minimum conditions for the bid have been met.[112] In considering whether the continuance of the rights plan will lead to further the bids, the Commission may consider the period of time since the original bid. The longer the time since the original bid, the less likely it is that there will be further competing bids. It has also looked at the number of out-

---

[109]See *Re Canadian Jorex Limited* (1992), 15 OSCB 257; *Re Lac Minerals Ltd. and Royal Oak Mines Inc.* (1994), 17 OSCB 4963; *Re MDC Corporation and Regal Greetings & Gifts Inc.* (1994), 17 OSCB 4971; *Re CW Shareholdings Inc. and WIC Western International Communications Ltd.* (1998), 21 OSCB 2899.

[110]See *Re Lac Minerals Ltd. and Royal Oak Mines Inc.* (1994), 17 OSCB 4963 at 4968; and *Re MDC Corporation and Regal Greetings & Gifts Inc.* (1994), 17 OSCB 4971 at 4979-80.

[111]In *Re Canadian Jorex Limited* (1992), 15 OSCB 257 the Commission was of the view that the outstanding bid would not proceed unless the plan was removed.

[112]See, e.g., *Re Lac Minerals Ltd. and Royal Oak Mines Inc.* (1994), 17 OSCB 4963 at 4969.

standing bids.[113] The more bids there are the less likely it is that continuing the plan will lead to additional bids. The Commission may also consider the number of other potential bidders that have been contacted and are still considering a bid and whether other bids are still being sought.[114]

In considering shareholder approval, the Commission may also look to the timing of the approval of the plan. If the approval is close to the time of the takeover it suggests that the plan may have been adopted to block a particular bid.[115] The Commission may also consider the degree of institutional participation in the shareholder approval.[116] The apparent assumption is that non-institutional shareholders are assumed to be relatively ill-informed about the consequences of poison pill plans and may be duped by target management into adopting a plan that is not in their interests. On the other hand, institutional shareholders are likely to be better informed about the consequences of a poison pill plan and their support suggests that the plan may be beneficial for the target shareholders.

F. The Takeover Bid Regulation Policy Debate

All of the reasons which were noted above for takeover bid regulation can be tied to the notion of confidence in the market. Concern that there might be a lack of information and time with respect to a decision to tender should a takeover bid materialize may cause investors to discount the value of shares. Fear that, if a takeover

---

[113]See, e.g., *Re MDC Corporation and Regal Greetings & Gifts Inc.* (1994), 17 OSCB 4971 at 4978.

[114]See, e.g., *Re Lac Minerals Ltd. and Royal Oak Mines Inc.* (1994), 17 OSCB 4963 at 4970 and *Re MDC Corporation and Regal Greetings & Gifts Inc.* (1994), 17 OSCB 4971 at 4979.

[115]In *Re CW Shareholdings Inc. and WIC Western International Communications Ltd.* (1998), 21 OSCB 2899 the Commission issued a cease trade order with respect to a poison rights plan that was put into place without the approval of the shareholders and in the face of a bid for shares of the issuer. The Commission would only allow such a plan to continue to operate if it was being used to prevent a coercive bid (i.e., one that would leave offeree shareholders little choice but to tender under the bid). *Re Canadian Jorex Limited* (1992), 15 OSCB 257 was also a case in which the plan was adopted in the face of an actual bid and which had not been approved by shareholders.

[116]See *Re MDC Corporation and Regal Greetings & Gifts Inc.* (1994), 17 OSCB 4971 at 4978.

bid were made, shares tendered may become locked up with the risk that the shares may not be paid for, either at all or in timely fashion, may also cause investors to discount the value of shares. The potential for not sharing in a premium paid for control acquired from one or a few may also cause investors to discount the value of shares. The reduced value of shares, if these concerns were not addressed by takeover bid regulation, would result in reduced allocations of savings to investment, higher financing costs and a related reduction in economic growth. By addressing the various concerns that prompted takeover bid regulation, takeover bid regulation promotes confidence in this market.

However, it has been argued that takeover bid regulation should be repealed on the basis that it has the perverse effect of reducing the value of shares. Proponents of takeover bid regulation have made a series of responses to the arguments against takeover bid regulation and there have been various suggestions as to other methods of regulating takeover bids.

1. *The Argument Against Takeover Bid Legislation*

As noted above, there are several possible motivations for takeovers. Some takeovers may be socially beneficial, such as takeovers to replace inefficient managements and takeovers that produce synergistic gains. These takeovers are said to be socially beneficial because they lead to more efficient uses of society's scarce resources.

The takeover bid may be a particularly effective takeover technique where the motivation for the takeover is the replacement of inefficient management. A management that faces replacement upon a takeover is unlikely to cooperate in an amalgamation. Proxy contests are not generally a very effective technique for replacing a corporation's management where the corporation's shares are widely held.[117] The takeover bid allows the bidder to obtain sufficient control to replace an existing management without the need of a proxy contest or cooperation from the existing management.

By facilitating the replacement of inefficient management, takeover bids allow assets to be allocated to more efficient uses.

---

[117]See, for example, D.R. Fischel, "Efficient Capital Market Theory, the Market for Corporate Control, and the Regulation of Cash Tender Offers" (1978) 57 Tex. L. Rev. 1, at 6.

The threat that management may be replaced through takeover bids encourages management to be more efficient and act more in accord with the interests of the corporation's security holders rather than in their own interests.[118] However, it is argued that takeover bid regulation tends to deter takeover bids and thus discourages takeovers that replace inefficient management and otherwise encourage management to behave efficiently.[119]

There are several aspects of takeover bid regulation that may tend to deter takeovers. The disclosure requirements may give competing bidders useful information in formulating competing bids. The minimum bid period of 21 days allows time for competing bidders to gather and assess information concerning the target and to prepare a competing bid. It also gives the target time to engage in defensive tactics that may further encourage competing bids. The pro rata take-up requirement together with withdrawal rights ensure that shares will be available for tender under competing bids. This increased potential for competing bids is said to put upward pressure on the price of target shares, thus reducing the gains to be obtained by bidders from making takeover bids.[120]

There is some empirical evidence in support of the alleged deterrent effect of takeover bid regulation.[121] First, there is evidence

---

[118]See R. Grabowski, I. Mathur & N. Rangan, "The Role of Takeovers in Increasing Efficiency" (1995) 16(3) Managerial and Dec. Economics 211 for evidence in support of the claim that the threat of takeover makes managements more efficient.

[119]The main proponents of these arguments against takeover bid regulation and target defensive tactics are F.H. Easterbrook and D.R. Fischel. See, for example, D.R. Fischel, "Efficient Capital Market Theory, the Market for Corporate Control, and the Regulation of Cash Tender Offers" (1978) 57 Tex. L. Rev. 1; F.H. Easterbrook and D.R. Fischel, "The Proper Role of a Target's Management in Responding to a Tender Offer" (1981) 94 Harv. L. Rev. 1161. See also A. Schwartz, "Search Theory and the Tender Offer Auction" (1986) 2 J.L. Eco. & Org. 2; and H. Manne, "Mergers and the Market for Corporate Control" (1965) 73 J. of Pol. Econ. 110.

[120]See Easterbrook and Fischel, *supra* note 119, at 1175-76.

[121]There is a considerable volume of empirical evidence on takeovers. There are also several reviews of the empirical evidence with respect to takeovers. For recent reviews of the empirical evidence on takeovers, see G.A. Jarrell, J.A. Brickley and J.M. Netter, "The Market for Corporate Control: The Empirical Evidence Since 1980" (1988) 2 J. of Eco. Perspectives 49; R. Romano, "A Guide to Takeovers: Theory, Evidence and Regulation" (1992) 9 Yale J. on Reg. 119 and R.J. Daniels, "Stakeholders and Takeovers: Can Contractarianism be Compassionate" (1993) 43

of increased takeover bid premiums upon the introduction of takeover bid regulation.[122] Second, there is evidence of increased returns to targets and reduced returns to bidders in takeover bids after the introduction of takeover bid regulation.[123] Third, there is evidence that litigation initiated by targets during the minimum bid period delays takeovers and encourages competitive bidding.[124] Fourth, there is evidence that firms with announced acquisition programs experienced significant decreases in value on the introduction of takeover bid regulation.[125] Fifth, there is some evidence that the number of takeovers declined more than the number of acquisitions after the introduction of the *Williams Act*.[126] Sixth, to the extent takeover bid regulation increases competitive bidding in the ways described above, there is evidence that such increased competition

---

U. of T. L.J. 315. See also B. Espen Eckbo, "Mergers and the Market for Corporate Control: the Canadian Evidence" (1986) 19 Can. J. of Eco. 236; and M.C. Jensen and R.S. Ruback, "The Market for Corporate Control: the Scientific Evidence" (1983) 11 J. of Fin. Eco. 5. The format of the discussion of the empirical evidence is taken primarily from the presentation in the paper by Romano, *supra*.

[122] See Romano, *supra* note 121, at 158 citing M. Bradley, A. Desai and E.H. Kim, "The Rationale Behind Interfirm Tender Offers: Information or Synergy?" (1983) 11 J. of Fin. Eco. 183; G.A. Jarrell and M. Bradley, "The Economic Effects of Federal and State Regulation of Cash Tender Offers" (1980) 23 J. of Law and Eco. 371, at 389-90; and G. Jarrell, "The Wealth Effects of Litigation by Targets: Do Interests Diverge in a Merge?" (1985) 28 J. of L. and Eco. 151. But see K. Nathan and T. O'Keefe, "The Rise in Takeover Premiums: An Exploratory Study" (1989) 23 J. of Fin. Eco. 101 suggesting the increase did not occur until several years after the introduction of the *Williams Act*; and J. Franks and R. Harris, "Shareholder Wealth Effects of Corporate Takeovers: The U.K. Experience 1955-1985" (1989) 23 J. of Fin. Eco. 225 finding that takeover premiums also increased in the U.K.

[123] See, for example, R. Smiley, "The Effect of the Williams Act and Other Factors on Transactions Costs in Tender Offers" (1975) 3 Ind. Org. Rev. 138; Jarrell and Bradley, *supra* note 122, at 387-98; and P. Asquith, R.F. Brunner and D. Mullins, Jr., "The Gains to Bidding Firms from Merger" (1983) 11 J. of Fin. Eco. 121, at 133 and 138.

[124] See Jarrell, *supra* note 122.

[125] K. Schipper and R. Thompson, "The Impact of Merger-Related Regulations on the Shareholders of Acquiring Firms" (1983) 21 J. of Accting. Res. 184; and K. Schipper and R. Thompson, "Evidence of the Capitalized Value of Merger Activity for Acquiring Firms" (1983) 11 J. of Fin. Eco. 85.

[126] See Jarrell and Bradley, *supra* note 122.

reduces returns to bidding firms.[127]

2. Counterarguments by Proponents of Takeover Bid Regulation

Counterarguments by proponents of takeover bid regulation note that takeovers may not be socially beneficial. Furthermore, they claim that there may be social benefits to encouraging competitive bidding in takeovers.[128]

a. NON-SOCIALLY BENEFICIAL TAKEOVERS

Proponents of takeover bid regulation have argued that takeovers may be motivated by gains to be derived by bidders that do not produce a corresponding gains to society as a whole. For instance, the gains derived by bidders may simply be due to the undervaluation of target shares, gains from reduced competition, or

---

[127] There is evidence that increased competition in takeover contests, which may result from takeover bid regulation, reduces shareholder wealth — see S. De, M. Fedenia & A.S. Triantis, "Effects of Competition on Bidder-Returns" (1996) 2(3) J. of Corp. Fin. 261. There is also evidence that a competitive bid from a "white knight" is met with an immediate and strongly negative market reaction concerning the first bidder's shares — see A. Banerjee & J.E. Owers, "The Impact of the Nature and Sequence of Multiple Bids in Corporate Control Contests" (1996) 3(1) J. of Corp. Fin. 23.

[128] A leading proponent of the need for takeover bid regulation, although not necessarily in its current form, is L.A. Bebchuk. See, for example, L.A. Bebchuk, "The Case for Facilitating Competing Tender Offers" (1982) 95 Harv. L. Rev. 1028 (hereinafter "Facilitating Competing Tender Offers"); and L.A. Bebchuk, "Toward Undistorted Choice and Equal Treatment in Corporate Takeovers" (1985) 98 Harv. L. Rev. 1693 (hereinafter "Undistorted Choice"). See also R.J. Gilson, "A Structural Approach to Corporations: The Case Against Defensive Tactics in Tender Offers" (1981) 33 Stan. L. Rev. 819; J.C. Coffee, Jr., "Regulating the Market for Corporate Control: A Critical Assessment of the Tender Offer's Role in Corporate Governance" (1984) 84 Colum. L. Rev. 1145; and R. Lüttman, "Changes of Corporate Control and Mandatory Bids" (1992) 12 Int'l Rev. of Law & Econ. 497. For reviews of the debate, see C.S. Ingram, "An Overview and Economic Analysis of Tender Offers and Management's Response to Takeover Threats" (1989) 54 Missouri L. Rev. 953; J.G. Howard, "Takeover Defences: A Reappraisal" (1990) 24 U.B.C. L. Rev. 53, at 57-63; S. Deakin & G. Slinger, "Hostile Takeovers, Corporate Law, and the Theory of the Firm" (1997) 24 J. of Law & Soc. 124; and I. Ramsay, "Balancing Law and Economics: the Case of Partial Takeovers" [1992] J. of Bus. Law 369.

the expropriation of wealth from others such as taxpayers or target employees, creditors, customers, or minority shareholders.[129]

(i) Undervaluations

Takeover bids, it has been suggested, may simply be used to acquire the shares of targets that are currently undervalued. This may provide some social benefit by causing the market price to more accurately reflect the value of the target's activities and thereby improve the efficiency of allocation of savings to investment. However, it is argued that this social gain is not as great as the gain to the bidder from capitalizing on the undervaluation. Therefore, there may be an incentive for bidders to engage in takeover bids to an extent which is not justified by the social gains from such takeover bids.[130]

Given the substantial evidence for the claim that reasonably well traded markets are semi-strong form efficient, it seems unlikely that undervaluations can account for takeover premiums in the order of 30 to 50%. Furthermore, if undervaluation was the cause of a substantial number of takeovers, one would expect to find that target share prices would remain at a higher level after a takeover bid which revealed that the shares were undervalued even if the target was not acquired. However, studies show that target share prices fall to their pre-bid levels after an unsuccessful takeover bid.[131]

It has also been argued that the market tends to focus on short-term gains and does not fully reflect the value of long-term investments that target management may be pursuing. The bidder may gain by acquiring the target and shifting its investments to short-term investments that are more likely to be reflected in the market price.[132] The available evidence does not support this potential

---

[129] See Romano, *supra* note 121, at 133-52. With respect to theories of potential expropriation in particular see Daniels, *supra* note 121, at 317-25.

[130] See, for example, Bebchuk, "Facilitating Competing Tender Offers", *supra* note 128, at 1047. See also the discussion in Romano, *supra* note 121, at 143-45.

[131] See Romano, *supra* note 121, at 144 citing P. Asquith, "Merger Bids, Uncertainty and Shareholder Returns" (1983) 11 J. of Fin. Eco. 51; Bradley, Desai and Kim, *supra* note 122; and Jarrell, *supra* note 122.

[132] See the discussion in Romano, *supra* note 121, at 144-45. See also J. Stein, "Takeover Threats and Managerial Myopia" (1988) 96 J. of Pol. Econ. 61.

undervaluation of long-term investments. For instance, targets tend to be in industries with low investments in long-term research and development.[133] There is no significant difference in the research and development activities of target firms and acquirer firms.[134] After an acquisition, research and development expenditures tend to either increase or remain unchanged.[135] Furthermore, the market tends to respond favourably to capital expenditures and announced increases in research and development expenditures.[136]

(ii) Reduced Competition

Takeovers may simply be due to gains in market power from reduced competition. Reduced competition has been shown to lead to net social efficiency losses. Thus takeover bid regulation deterring such takeovers should be beneficial.[137]

Reduced competition in an industry should lead to increased stock prices for firms in the industry due to the gains to be derived from the potential for charging higher prices. However, studies of the stock prices of competitors of acquirers and targets have not shown increased prices due to takeovers reducing competition in the industry.[138] This suggests the takeovers may have been moti-

---

[133] See Romano, *supra* note 121, at 145 citing B. Hall, "The Effect of Takeover Activity on Corporate Research and Development" in A. Auerbach, ed., *Corporate Takeovers: Causes and Consequences* (Chicago: University of Chicago Press, 1988), 69.

[134] Ibid.

[135] Ibid.

[136] See Romano, *supra* note 121, at 145, citing S.H. Chan, J. Martin and J. Kensinger, "Corporate Research and Development Expenditures and Share Value" (1990) 26 J. of Fin. Eco. 255; and J. McConnell and C. Muscarella, "Capital Expenditure Decisions and Market Value of the Firm" (1985) 14 J. of Fin. Eco. 399.

[137] That takeover bids may be motivated by market power gains was noted in Bebchuk, "Facilitating Competing Tender Offers", *supra* note 128, at 1047. See the discussion in Romano, *supra* note 121, at 142-43. As to the effects on various corporate stakeholders such as creditors, employees and suppliers, see Daniels, *supra* note 121.

[138] See B. Espen Eckbo, "Horizontal Mergers, Collusion and Stockholder Wealth" (1983) 11 J. of Fin. Eco. 241; B. Espen Eckbo, "Mergers and the Market Concentration Doctrine: Evidence from the Capital Market" (1985) 58 J. Bus. 325; and R.S. Stillman, "Examining Antitrust Policy Towards Horizontal Mergers (1983) 11 J. of Fin. Eco. 225.

vated by gains other than gains from reduced competition. There is also no evidence of increased sales margins in related industry takeovers.[139]

(iii) Empire Building or Managerialism

Acquirer managements may engage in takeovers to satisfy their own objectives, such as increased power or prestige or decreased risk through diversification, rather than the objectives of the firm's security holders. Such takeovers, while satisfying acquirer management objectives, generally would not produce broader social efficiency gains from more efficient uses of resources.[140]

Decreased risk through diversifying takeovers may be of benefit to some shareholders. However, it is not a benefit they could not produce for themselves through holding a diversified portfolio of investments.[141] There may be some net benefits to risk reducing diversification through relieving managers' stress from the threat of bankruptcy in exchange for which managers may be willing to accept lower compensation. It may also protect management skills with respect to particular businesses built up over the years (their "human capital") from being dissipated in a forced liquidation on bankruptcy. Thus there may be net gains to security holders and net social efficiency gains from diversification.[142]

There is evidence of a positive correlation between acquirer returns and acquirer management's share ownership indicating that returns are lower where acquirer management share ownership is low and thus where acquirer management incentives to act in the interests of shareholders is weakest.[143] There is also evidence that

---

[139]See Romano, *supra* note 121, at 143, citing P. Healey, K. Palepu and R. Ruback, "Does Corporate Performance Improve After Mergers?" National Bureau of Economic Research Working Paper No. 3348.

[140]See Bebchuk, "Facilitating Competing Tender Offers", *supra* note 128, at 1047; R. Marris, "A Model of the 'Managerial' Enterprise" (1963) 77 Q. Journal of Eco. 185.

[141]See R. Brealey and S. Myers, *Principles of Corporate Finance* (New York: McGraw-Hill, 1981), at 662-63.

[142]See Romano, *supra* note 121, at 147.

[143]See Romano, *supra* note 121, at 149, citing W. Lewellen, C. Loderer and A. Rosenfeld, "Merger Decisions and Executive Stock Ownership in Acquiring Firms" (1985) 7 J. of Accting & Eco. 209.

acquirer returns are lower the less independent (or more management controlled) the acquirer's board is.[144] This suggests that managers who are not as well monitored by independent directors may have more of a tendency to engage in less beneficial takeovers. This evidence is consistent with acquirer managerial self-interest in the motivation for takeover.

(iv) Hubris

Takeovers are not socially beneficial if they occur simply because the acquirer has a mistaken belief that the takeover will generate gains.[145] Takeover bid regulation which deters takeovers may be beneficial if most takeovers are motivated by mistaken beliefs in potential gains. Evidence of negative returns to bidders in the 1980s tends to support this "hubris" hypothesis.[146] There is also evidence that bidders overpay in takeovers.[147] However, evidence that there are net gains to takeovers when bidder losses are combined with target gains suggests that pure hubris cannot explain all takeovers.[148]

(v) Expropriation Theories

The takeover gains may not be due to socially efficient improved uses of target assets, but may simply be due to opportunistic expropriations from taxpayers, or target customers, employees or minority shareholders. Tax gains may come from, for instance, combining a

---

[144]See Romano, *supra* note 121, at 149, citing J. Bird and R. Hickman, "Do Outside Directors Monitor Managers? Evidence from Tender Offer Bids", manuscript, Washington State University. See also Z.Z. Zantout & M. O'Reilly-Allen, "Determinants of Corporate Strategy and Gains of Acquiring Firms" (1996) 11(1) J. of Accounting, Auditing & Finance 119 finding that the probability of engaging in a diversification program decreases when the board of directors is dominated by outsiders.

[145]On the hubris hypothesis, see R. Roll, "The Hubris Hypothesis of Corporate Takeovers" (1986) 59 J. Bus. 197.

[146]See, for example, M. Bradley, A. Desai and E.H. Kim, "Synergistic Gains from Corporate Acquisitions and Their Division Between the Stockholders of Target and Acquiring Firms" (1988) 21 J. of Fin. Eco. 3. See also Jarrell, Brickley and Netter, *supra* note 121, at 53.

[147]See, for example, N. Varaiya, "The 'Winners Curse' Hypothesis and Corporate Takeovers" (1988) 9 Managerial and Dec. Eco. 209.

[148]See Bradley, Desai and Kim, *supra* note 122.

firm having sufficient income to take advantage of operating losses or depreciation allowances that another firm does not have sufficient income to take advantage of. Approximately 20% of mergers and takeovers in the United States have potential tax gains. These gains appear to represent approximately 10% of the value of target firms.[149] This is substantially less than takeover premiums in the order of 30 to 50%.

A takeover bidder may, it is argued, behave opportunistically by breaking implicit contracts with labour. These implicit contracts may involve such things as dismissals or layoffs of employees or reversions of pension surpluses by acquirers that target management, having a long-standing relationship with employees, may be unwilling to undertake.[150] Evidence of labour turnover suggests that most turnover occurs in middle and top management and not at the level of plant production employees.[151] There is also evidence of increased employment and wages after takeovers.[152] Pension fund reversions occur in about 14% of takeovers and average about 10 to 13% of takeover premiums.[153]

Another suggested source of expropriation is from the acquirer's creditors. In order to finance the takeover, the acquirer may take on increased debt (or "leverage"). This increased debt increases the risk of bankruptcy and thereby increases the risk of existing debt.

---

[149]See A. Auerbach and D. Reishus, "The Impact of Taxation on Mergers and Acquisitions" in A. Auerbach, ed., *Mergers and Acquisitions* (Chicago: University of Chicago Press, 1988) 69 cited in Romano, *supra* note 121, at 14-17. The tax saving may also be brought about through increased leverage (increasing debt) and capitalizing on the deduction of interest. This tax motivation and its potential consequences for various corporate stakeholders is discussed in Daniels, *supra* note 121, at 27-29.

[150]See Romano, *supra* note 121, at 137-42. See also Daniels, *supra* note 121, at 318-21, which expands on the kinds of monetary and psychic costs imposed on employees by mass layoffs.

[151]See F. Lichtenberg and D. Seigel, "Productivity and Changes in Ownership of Manufacturing Plants" (1987) Brookings Papers on Economic Activity 643 (Washington, D.C.: Brookings Institute), cited in Romano, *supra* note 121, at 22.

[152]Ibid. See also C. Brown and J. Medoff, "The Impact of Firm Acquisitions on Labor" in A. Auerbach, ed., *Corporate Takeovers: Causes and Consequences* (Chicago: University of Chicago Press, 1988), 9.

[153]J. Pontiff, A. Shleifer, M. Weisbach, "Reversions of Excess Pension Assets After Takeovers" (1990) 21 Rand J. of Eco. 600. The evidence on the effects of takeovers on employees is also reviewed in Daniels, *supra* note 121, at 9-12.

This increased risk for existing debt lowers the value of the existing debt.[154] There is some evidence of a decrease in the value of acquirers' bonds from leveraged takeovers. However, the estimated average decrease in value of approximately 2.5% is not sufficient to account for the size of takeover premiums. The size of the decrease in the value of bonds does not appear to depend on the total amount of outstanding debt.[155]

The expropriation from minority shareholders is said to come from the kinds of looting discussed above, namely, post-takeover amalgamations or reorganizations in which minority shareholders are forced out at unfair prices or other transactions in which acquirers can transfer target wealth to themselves.[156] In the takeover bid, shareholders may be pressured into accepting the bid not because the bid is a reasonable bid, but because they do not want to be left out of the bid and be subject to a post-takeover force-out at an unfair price.[157]

---

[154] See Romano, *supra* note 121, at 136-37. See also Daniels, *supra* note 121, at 323-24.

[155] See Romano, *supra* note 121, at 137, citing P. Asquith and T. Wizman, "Event Risk, Covenants, and Returns in Leveraged Buyouts" (1990) 27 J. of Fin. Econ. 195; D. Denis and J. McConnell, "Corporate Mergers and Security Returns" (1986) 16 J. of Fin. Eco. 143. See also the summary of the evidence in Daniels, *supra* note 121, at 323-24. Lenders can respond to this potential expropriation by having protective covenants in their loan agreements or bond indentures. For instance, bondholders may be entitled to sell their bonds back to the issuer at a predetermined price in the event of a takeover. Shareholders can gain from such covenants to the extent bondholders demand lower rates of interest in return for such covenants. However, managements may benefit from the takeover deterrent effect of such covenants. Empirical evidence suggests that both a bondholder protection and takeover deterrent effect are involved in the design of such bondholder takeover protection covenants. See M. Kahan & M. Klausner, "Antitakeover Provisions in Bonds: Bondholder Protection or Management Entrenchment?" (1993) 40 UCLA Law Rev. 931.

[156] Concerns with respect to post-takeover amalgamations at unfair prices (or "front-end loaded two tier takeovers") were noted in V. Brudney and M.A. Chirelstein, "Fair Shares in Corporate Mergers and Takeovers" (1974) 88 Harv. L. Rev. 297, at 336-37 and E.F. Greene and J.J. Junewicz, "A Reappraisal of Current Regulation of Mergers and Acquisitions" (1984) 132 U. Pa. L. Rev. 647, at 676-81.

[157] See, for example, Bebchuk, "Undistorted Choice", *supra* note 128, at 1717-33 and W.J. Carney, "Shareholder Coordination Costs, Shark Repellants and Takeout Mergers: The Case Against Fiduciary Duties" [1983] Am. Bar Found. Res. J. 341.

Evidence that minority share interests (left after a takeover) tend to continue to retain the price increase associated with takeover bid premiums suggests that this form of expropriation, or looting, is not prevalent.[158] However, there is some evidence of favourable reactions to corporate charter amendments that provide some assurance of a fair price in any post-takeover amalgamation or reorganization.[159]

b. SOCIAL EFFICIENCY BENEFITS OF COMPETITIVE BIDDING

Proponents of takeover bid regulation point not only to the potential negative social efficiency consequences of takeovers, but also to the potential social efficiency benefits of promoting competitive bidding in takeovers. For instance, it has been argued that promoting competitive bidding in takeovers promotes the efficient use of assets by allocating the target's assets to the bidder that can make the "best" (most "highly-valued") use of the target's assets.[160] The highest valuing user of the target's assets will win in the competitive bidding process because it will be willing to bid the highest price. It will be willing to bid the highest price because it will be able to make greater gains from its better use of the assets than other bidders. However, it has also been argued that the allocation to the highest valuing user can occur without competitive bidding through a subsequent transfer of the target assets by the initial takeover bidder.[161]

Other claims for social efficiency benefits from promoting competitive bidding include encouraging initial investments in potential

---

[158] See P. Dodd and R. Ruback, "Tender Offers and Stockholder Returns" (1977) 5 J. of Fin. Eco. 351, at 361-71. Evidence on post-takeover minority freeze-outs also does not support claims that looting is a substantial source of takeover gains to bidders. Announcements of going-private "minority freezeouts" transactions are associated with statistically significant gains to shareholders of over 30%. See H. DeAngelo, L. DeAngelo and E.M. Rice, "Going Private: Minority Freezeouts and Stockholder Wealth" (1984) 27 J. of Law & Eco. 367.

[159] See, for example, G.A. Jarrell and A. Poulsen, "Shark Repellants and Stock Prices: The Effects of Antitakeover Amendments Since 1980" (1987) 19 J. of Fin. Eco. 127.

[160] See, for example, Bebchuk, "Facilitating Competing Tender Offers", *supra* note 128, at 1048 and Gilson, *supra* note 128, at 872.

[161] See F.H. Easterbrook and D.R. Fischel, "Auctions and Sunk Costs in Tender Offers" (1982) 35 Stan. L. Rev. 1, at 14.

targets, encouraging target managers to search for acquirers, and encouraging useful exchanges of information by encouraging negotiated amalgamation transactions rather than non-negotiated takeover bids.[162]

3. Some Alternative Approaches to Takeover Bid Regulation

a. THE "UNDISTORTED CHOICE" OR "SOLE SHAREHOLDER" APPROACH

The concerns that prompted takeover bid regulation might be summarized as a concern that the unregulated takeover bid process puts pressure on shareholders to tender on terms they might freely choose to accept were it not for this pressure.[163] If shareholders were to consider the transaction as if they were a single person selling an asset, then they would consider whether the bid price would be greater than the value of the asset. The vendor of the asset might consider the value of the asset to be greater than the bid price and therefore may expect higher subsequent bids. The single vendor could then refuse to accept the bid.

A shareholder in a takeover bid is not in the position of a single vendor comparing the bid price to the value of the asset. Instead, the shareholder in a takeover bid cannot compare the bid price to the value of their share in the target if it remains independent. The shareholder must also consider the value received by not tendering and instead continuing to hold the securities of the target in the event of a successful bid. Thus the shareholder in a takeover bid is not comparing the bid price to the value of the shares of the target, but is comparing the bid price received if they tender to a composite of the value of the shares of the target if the bid does not succeed

---

[162]See Bebchuk, "Facilitating Competing Tender Offers", *supra* note 128, at 1049-50; and Lüttman, *supra* note 128. There is competing evidence on whether target management defensive tactics benefit target shareholders. See, e.g., S. Thosar, "Tender Offers and Target Management Responses: Managerial Entrenchment versus Stockholder Interest Revisited" (1996) 31 Fin. Rev. 87 suggesting significantly higher post-tender offer gains where target management resists a takeover. But see J. Saint-Pierre, J.M Gagnon & J. Saint-Pierre, "Concentration of Voting Rights and Board Resistance to Takeover Bids" (1996) 3 J. of Corp. Fin. 45, a study using Canadian data, finding poor target performance and blocks of shares held by directors associated with a higher probability of target management resistance as evidence of managerial entrenchment.

[163]See Bebchuk, "Undistorted Choice", *supra* note 128, at 1717-33.

and the value of the shares of the target if the bid succeeds and they do not tender. With the potential for a post-takeover amalgamation at a price lower than the value of the shares in the independent target, this composite price is less than the value of the shares of the target. The shareholder may thus choose to tender even though the bid price is less than the value of the shares of the target.[164]

A suggested form of takeover bid regulation to deal with this "distorted" choice would be to have shareholders provide two separate responses to a takeover bid. Shareholders would vote for or against the takeover bid succeeding and note separately whether they would tender their shares under the bid. This approach would isolate the shareholders' decision to sell the target from uncertainty associated with the success or failure of the bid. In considering whether to vote for or against the success of the bid, they could compare the bid price to the value of the shares of the target. Thus they would make the decision in an undistorted fashion on the same basis as any other vendor of assets.[165]

b. A CORPORATE CHARTER APPROACH

As noted above, takeovers may provide social efficiency gains through the replacement of inefficient management. They may also provide synergistic gains. These potential gains encourage the search for targets that will yield such gains. Takeover bid regulation which promotes competitive bidding raises takeover bid premiums, thereby reducing the gains from takeovers and the incentive to search for potential targets. However, as noted above, there may be allocative gains from competitive bidding in that it allocates target assets to their most highly valued use. Thus allocative gains from promoting competitive bidding run contrary to the gains from search.

There are also costs to consider. Preparing bids in a competitive bidding process is costly. Thus promoting competitive bidding is costly. Without competitive bidding, the allocation of target assets to the highest-valuing user may have to occur through retransfers of target assets after the initial takeover. This may also be a costly process. In sum, in assessing the promotion of competitive bidding

---

[164] Ibid.

[165] Ibid., at 1747-64.

in takeovers one must consider the gains from search, the allocative gains from promoting competitive bidding, the costs of promoting competitive bidding, and the costs of retransfers of target assets.

By adjusting the shareholding level at which takeover bid regulation would apply, the degree of disclosure and the minimum bid period, takeover bid regulation could control the degree of competitive bidding to reach an optimal balance between the gains from search for targets, allocative gains from competitive bidding, costs of competitive bidding and costs of potential retransfers. However, if this optimal balance varies from one takeover situation to another, the regulation may not achieve the appropriate balance for some takeovers. Consequently, an approach which varies from one situation to another may be appropriate.

The optimal balance may vary from one takeover situation to another for a variety of reasons. First, the gains from the search for targets may depend, in part, on the importance of the takeover process for encouraging management to behave efficiently in the interests of security holders. Where, for a given issuer, the ownership structure of the issuer, or its capital, labour and product markets are relatively effective at controlling management, the threat of takeover will be of less significance. The gains from search for such an issuer as a potential target will be lower.

Second, the allocative gains from competitive bidding may vary from one issuer to another. In some cases, different bidders may derive quite different values from acquiring targets. This might be the case, for instance, where the takeover will produce synergistic gains. In these circumstances, there would be potential allocative gains from promoting competitive bidding. In other cases, the variation in the value different bidders could derive may be very small. This might be the case where the takeover gain comes from the replacement of an inefficient target management. In these circumstances, adding bidders to the auction is less likely to provide much in the way of allocative gains.[166]

Third, the costs of competitive bidding will depend, in part, on the cost of gathering and assessing information about the target. In some cases the quantity and complexity of the information, and the cost of gathering and assessing it, will be greater than in other cases.

---

[166]See, for example, P. Cramton and A. Schwartz, "Using Action Theory to Inform Takeover Regulation" (1991) 7 J. of Law, Eco. & Org. 27, at 47.

Similarly, the information gathering and assessment costs associated with retransfers are likely to vary, depending on the nature of the assets involved.

One way of achieving flexibility in the design of takeover bid regulation to respond to the variation in the optimal degree of competitive bidding would be to allow issuers to design their own takeover bid regimes. They could do this through the adoption of a "poison pill" provision in their constating documents which would come into effect if the bidder, or bidders, did not comply with the target issuer's own takeover bid rules. Issuers could then set rules which would respond to their own unique circumstances.

The management of potential targets may have an incentive to protect their own positions and may therefore be inclined to adapt overly restrictive takeover bid provisions. This concern would be exacerbated where a takeover bid has already been made. However, management would also have an incentive to ensure the success of the issuer through having the highest possible prices for its securities and thus the lowest possible cost of financing. This would provide an incentive for the adoption of techniques that would discourage management from resisting takeovers in ways which are not conducive to shareholder interests. They would thus be discouraged from adopting overly restrictive takeover bid rules.[167] A management employment contract which compensated man-

---

[167] There are numerous studies on the effects of poison pill adoptions on firm share prices with mixed results. Some studies find that adoptions of some types of poison pill plans reduce share prices while other types of poison pill plans result in positive or insignificant share price responses. See, e.g., S. Datta, M. Iskandar-Datta, "Takeover Defenses and Wealth Effects on Securityholders: The Case of Poison Pill Adoptions" (1996) 20(7) J. of Banking & Finance 1231; R. Comment & G.W. Schwert, "Poison or Placebo? Evidence on the Deterrence and Wealth Effects of Modern Antitakeover Measures" (1995) 39(1) J. of Fin. Econ. 3; J.M. Mahoney, C. Sundaramurthy & J.T. Mahoney, "The Differential Impact on Stockholder Wealth of Various Antitakeover Provisions" (1996) 17(6) Managerial & Dec. Econ. 531; J.M. Mahoney & J.T. Mahoney, "An Empirical Investigation of the Effect of Corporate Charter Antitakeover Amendments on Stockholder Wealth" (1993) 14(1) Strategic Management J. 17; A. Akhigbe & J. Madura, "Impact of Anti-Takeover Amendments on Corporate Performance" (1996) 6 Applied Fin. Econ. 519; P.H. Malatesta & R.A. Walking, "Poison Pill Securities: Stockholder Wealth, Probability and Ownership Structure" (1988) 20 J. Fin. Econ. 347; M. Ryngaert, "The Effect of Poison Pill Securities on Shareholder Wealth" (1988) 20 J. of Fin. Econ. 377; Securities and Exchange Commission, Office of the Chief Economist, *The Effects of Poison Pills on the Wealth of Target Shareholders* (October 23, 1986).

agement upon replacement after a takeover could be adopted by the issuer to deter excessive management resistance to a takeover bid.[168]

c. OTHER ALTERNATIVES

There may be other alternatives to regulating takeover bids which provide shareholders with adequate information about a bid and time to assess the information, but would reduce the potential deterrent effect. For instance, disclosure with a minimum bid period, pro rata take-up of tendered shares, withdrawal rights, rules for the timing of payment for shares taken up and the adequacy of financing to pay for shares taken up could be provided with a preclusion of competing bids and target defensive tactics designed to block the takeover. Specific regulation could be directed to the potential negative aspects of takeovers (noted under subheading 2 above) without deterring the takeovers that produce benefits such as synergistic gains or the replacement of inefficient management.

III. ISSUER BID REGULATION

A. Reasons for Issuer Bid Regulation

When an issuer makes a bid for its own securities, it may do so on the basis of an information advantage or on the basis of a conflict of interest between the interests of management of the issuer, or a person or persons in control of the issuer, and the interests of the issuer itself or the offeree security holders under the bid.[169] As with takeover bids, there is a concern that confidence in the market will be weakened if such transactions proceed without adequate disclosure and time to assess the information and without

---

[168] See R.A. Lambert and D.R. Larker, "Golden Parachutes, Executive Decision Making and Shareholder Wealth" (1983) 7. J. of Accting. & Eco. 179 finding evidence of stock price gains on the adoption of golden parachutes. But see P.L. Hall & D.C. Anderson, "The Effect of Golden Parachutes on Shareholder Wealth and Takeover Probabilities" (1997) 24 J. of Bus. Fin. & Acctng. 445 finding that shareholders experience a decrease in wealth on the adoption of a "golden parachute".

[169] See, for example, O. Pol. 9.1, s. 1.3.

assurance that such transactions proceed in a manner which is fair and which is perceived to be fair.[170]

B. The Basic Rules

Because the concerns with respect to issuer bids are similar to those with respect to takeover bids, issuer bids are subject to many of the same basic rules that govern takeover bids. Where an issuer bid is made, it must be made to all holders in the province of the securities sought.[171] An "issuer bid circular" must be delivered along with the bid.[172]

The issuer bid circular provides information that would presumably be useful to the issuer's security holders in deciding whether to tender their shares. The circular must include the significant aspects of the bid, such as the name of the issuer, the securities sought, the dates on which the issuer bid will commence and close, the consideration offered, and the method of acquisition.[173] The circular also includes other information that may be relevant to deciding whether to tender, such as:

(i) the method and time of payment of the consideration;

(ii) the source of funds for payment;

(iii) the reasons for the issuer bid and any plans for a going private transaction;

(iv) the markets on which the securities currently trade, the trading volumes and price range of the securities over the previous twelve months, the market price of the securities before the announcement of the bid, and any change in the principal markets on which the securities will trade after the bid;

(v) the ownership of and trading in shares by directors and senior officers of the issuer and any person holding more

---

[170] Ibid., s. 1.1.

[171] A.S.A. s. 135(a); B.C.S.A. s. 105(a); M.S.A. s. 86(a); Nfld.S.A. s. 96(a); N.S.S.A. s. 101(1); O.S.A. s. 95.1; Q.S.A. s. 127 and s. 147.20; S.S.A. 104(2).

[172] A.S.A. s. 137(1); B.C.S.A. s. 108(1) and 110(6); M.S.A. ss. 89(a), 91(3); Nfld.S.A. ss. 99(a), 101(3); N.S.S.A. ss. 104(1), 106(3); O.S.A. ss. 98(1), 100(3); Q.S.A. ss. 128, 133, 147.20; S.S.A. ss. 107, 109(4).

[173] A. Form 34; B.C. Form 33; Man. Form 30; Nfld. Form 32; N.S. Form 33; O. Form 33; Que. Schedule XIV; S. Form 32.

than 10% of any class of equity securities of the issuer or by any person acting jointly or in concert with the issuer;

(vi) whether directors, senior officers, persons holding more than 10% of the equity securities of the issuer, or persons acting jointly or in concert with the issuer will receive any direct or indirect benefits from accepting or refusing to accept the issuer bid and whether any of them propose to accept the issuer bid and the number of securities they propose to tender;

(vii) any proposals for material changes including plans to amalgamate, liquidate the issuer, sell, lease or exchange all or a substantial portion of its assets, or change its corporate structure, management or personnel;

(viii) details of any agreements or arrangements between the issuer and any person with respect to any securities of the issuer in relation to the issuer bid;

(ix) prospectus type disclosure with respect to any securities to be given as consideration under the bid; and

(x) other material facts not previously generally disclosed which would reasonably be expected to affect the decision of security holders of the issuer to accept or reject the offer.

Most Canadian securities acts provide for statutory civil liability for misstatements or omissions in an issuer bid circular. The issuer, its directors, any person signing the certificate required on the circular[174] and any experts who have given their consent with respect to the use of a report or excerpt from a report prepared by them are subject to the statutory civil liability for misstatements or omissions in an issuer bid circular.[175]

Other provisions with respect to issuer bids are similar to those for takeover bids. For instance, the bid must remain open for a minimum of 21 days with extensions of 10 days for variations in the bid.[176] Where the bid is for less than all the outstanding securities of the class and more than the number of securities sought

---

[174] Ibid.

[175] A.S.A. s. 169(3); B.C.S.A. s. 132; M.S.A. s. 97(3); Nfld.S.A. s. 131(3); N.S.S.A. s. 139(3); O.S.A. s. 131(3); S.S.A. s. 139(3). There is a provision for rescission in Q.S.A. s. 222.

[176] See *supra* note 20 and 21.

is tendered under the bid, then the securities must be taken up pro rata.[177] Lockups of shares are prevented by withdrawal rights in the same manner as with respect to takeover bids.[178] Unequal consideration is precluded by the requirement that the bid be made to all security holders of the class in the province,[179] and the requirement that equal consideration be offered to all holders of securities of the class sought.[180]

From the date of an issuer's bid until its expiry, the issuer is restricted from making acquisitions of its own securities subject to the bid otherwise than through the bid itself.[181] Sales by the issuer of securities subject to the bid are also not allowed during the bid period.[182] As with takeover bids, the issuer is required to make adequate arrangements prior to the bid to ensure that the required funds will be available to effect payment in full for all the securities for which the issuer has offered to pay cash or partly cash.[183]

C. Exemptions from Issuer Bid Requirements

There are a number of exemptions from the issuer bid requirements. These exemptions are generally provided where the concerns that motivated the regulation of issuer bids are not likely to be present, where the benefits are small given the limited number of issuers affected or their likely close connection to the issuer, where issuer bid regulation interferes with other potentially beneficial arrangements or where the regulation is effected through another regulatory mechanism.

---

[177] See *supra* note 22.

[178] See *supra* notes 23-27.

[179] See *supra* note 28.

[180] See *supra* notes 29-30.

[181] A.S.A. s. 134(2); B.C.S.A. s. 102; M.S.A. s. 85(4); Nfld.S.A. s. 95(4); N.S.S.A. s. 100(4); O.S.A. s. 94(4); Q.S.A. ss. 141, 147.20; S.S.A. s. 103(4).

[182] A.S.A. s. 134.1(4), (5); B.C.S.A. s. 104; M.S.A. s. 85(8), (9); Nfld.S.A. s. 95(8), (9); N.S.S.A. s. 100(8), (9); O.S.A. s. 94(8); Q.S.A. ss. 143, 147.20; S.S.A. s. 103(9), (10).

[183] A.S.A. s. 135.1; B.C.S.A. s. 106; M.S.A. s. 87; Nfld.S.A. s. 97; N.S.S.A. s. 102; O.S.A. s. 96; Q.S.A. ss. 147, 147.20; S.S.A. s. 105.

1. Pre-Arranged Acquisitions

For instance, an exemption is provided where the securities are purchased, redeemed or otherwise acquired in accordance with terms of the security, allowing the issuer to acquire the securities without the consent of the owners of the securities or where the securities are acquired to meet sinking fund requirements.[184] Similarly, there is an exemption where the purchase, redemption or other acquisition of the securities is required by the statute under which the issuer was incorporated, organized or continued or by the instrument under which the securities were created.[185] In these situations the acquisition of the securities is determined in advance and is thus not likely to be susceptible to management taking advantage of the issuer or a control person to the disadvantage of offeree security holders.

2. Security Holder Controlled Acquisition

There is an exemption where the securities carry a right of the security holder to require the issuer to redeem the security holder's securities.[186] The potential for a purchase to be to the disadvantage of the security holder is not as likely to occur when the security holder controls the decision of the issuer to redeem or repurchase.

3. Employee Security Ownership

An exemption for the purchase from current or former employees of the issuer gives the issuer flexibility in setting up security ownership incentive schemes for its employees.[187] If there

---

[184] A.S.A. s. 133(a); B.C.S.A. s. 99(a); M.S.A. s. 84(3)(a); Nfld.S.A. s. 94(3)(a); N.S.S.A. s. 99(3)(a); O.S.A. s. 93(3)(a); S.S.A. s. 102(4)(a), (b). See also Que. s. 147.21.

[185] A.S.A. s. 133(b); B.C.S.A. s. 99(b); M.S.A. s. 84(3)(b); Nfld.S.A. s. 94(3)(b); N.S.S.A. s. 99(3)(b); O.S.A. s. 93(3)(b); S.S.A. s. 102(4)(c). See also Q.S.A. s. 147.21.

[186] A.S.A. s. 133(c); B.C.S.A. s. 99(c); M.S.A. s. 84(3)(c); Nfld.S.A. s. 94(3)(c); N.S.S.A. s. 99(3)(c); O.S.A. s. 93(3)(c); S.S.A. s. 102(4)(d). See also Q.S.A. s. 147.21(1).

[187] A.S.A. s. 133(d); B.C.S.A. s. 99(d); M.S.A. s. 84(3)(d); Nfld.S.A. s. 94(3)(d); N.S.S.A. s. 99(3)(d); O.S.A. s. 93(3)(d); S.S.A. s. 102(4)(e).

is a public market for the securities, there are restrictions on the exemption. The consideration paid cannot exceed the published market price and the aggregate number of securities (or aggregate principal amount in the case of convertible debt securities) cannot in any 12-month period exceed 5% of the securities of the class issued and outstanding at the beginning of the 12-month period.[188]

4. *Private Companies*

An exemption is provided for private companies.[189] The issuer cannot be a reporting issuer and there can be no published market for the securities subject to the bid. Furthermore, the number of holders of securities of the issuer, exclusive of those in the employment of the issuer or an affiliate of the issuer, or who were former employees of the issuer or affiliate and who were, and still are, security holders of the issuer, cannot be more than 50. In these cases, the benefits from issuer bid regulation are limited given the limited number of security holders involved and the security holders in such relatively closely-held companies are likely to have a sufficiently close connection to the issuer that they are less likely to be taken advantage of. The costs of compliance for smaller issuers is also likely to be proportionately higher than it is for larger issuers.

5. *De Minimis Exemption*

There is a de minimis test with respect to the effect on security holders in the province. Where the number of holders in the province of securities of the class subject to the bid is less than 50, the securities held by such holders constitute less than 2% of outstanding securities of the class, and the bid is made in compliance with laws recognized by the particular securities authorities for the purposes of issuer bids, then there is an exemption from compliance with the particular province's issuer bid requirements.[190] In these

---

[188] A.S.A. s. 133(d); B.C.S.A. s. 99(d); M.S.A. s. 84(3)(d); Nfld.S.A. s. 94(3)(d); N.S.S.A. s. 99(3)(d); O.S.A. s. 93(3)(d); S.S.A. s. 102(4)(e).

[189] A.S.A. s. 133(g); B.C.S.A. s. 99(g); M.S.A. s. 84(3)(g): Nfld.S.A. s. 94(3)(g); N.S.S.A. s. 99(3)(g); O.S.A. s. 93(3)(g); Q.S.A. ss. 122, 147.20; S.S.A. s. 102(4)(h).

[190] A.S.A. s. 133(h); B.C.S.A. s. 99(h); M.S.A. s. 84(3)(h); Nfld.S.A. s. 94(3)(h); N.S.S.A. s. 99(3)(h); O.S.A. s. 93(3)(h); Q.S.A. ss. 121, 147.20; S.S.A. s. 102(4)(i).

All material relating to the bid that is sent to offeree security holders must

circumstances, the benefits of issuer bid regulation are likely to be small and the offeree security holders will be protected by the laws of the recognized jurisdiction.

6. Stock Exchange Issuer Bids

An exemption is provided where the issuer makes the bid through the facilities of a stock exchange recognized for the purposes of making issuer bids.[191] The stock exchanges recognized have their own issuer bid requirements that are very similar to those of the securities acts that restrict issuer bids.

7. Normal Course Purchases

An exemption is also provided to allow the issuer to make so-called "normal course" purchases. An issuer can purchase up to 5% of the outstanding securities of a class in any 12-month period without having to comply with the issuer bid requirements. The issuer must publish a notice of intention to make such purchases and the securities must be purchased in the open market.[192]

8. Exemption Order

The securities commission can also grant an exemption from the issuer bid requirements where it would not be prejudicial to the public interest to do so.[193]

---

also be sent to the security holders in the particular province and filed in the particular province.

[191] A.S.A. s. 133(e); B.C.S.A. s. 99(e); M.S.A. s. 84(3)(e); Nfld.S.A. s. 94(3)(e); N.S.S.A. s. 99(3)(e); O.S.A. s. 93(3)(e); Q.S.A. ss. 120, 147.20; S.S.A. s. 102(4)(f).

[192] A.S.A. s. 133(f); B.C.S.A. s. 99(f); M.S.A. s. 84(3)(f); Nfld.S.A. s. 94(3)(f); N.S.S.A. s. 99(3)(f); O.S.A. s. 93(3)(f); S.S.A. s. 102(4)(g). See also Que. s. 147.21(2).

[193] A.S.A. s. 144(2)(c); B.C.S.A. s. 114(2)(c); M.S.A. s. 95(2)(c); Nfld.S.A. s. 105(2)(c); N.S.S.A. s. 110(2)(c); O.S.A. s. 104(2)(c); Q.S.A. s. 263; S.S.A. s. 113(2)(c).

CHAPTER 12

SECURITIES INDUSTRY REGULATION

I. INTRODUCTION

The objective of this chapter is to provide a brief overview of the regulation of persons involved in the securities industry in a way that will allow the reader to begin to understand this regulation in terms of the problems it seeks to address. This should provide a base for further reading on the regulation of securities market actors.

Part II notes who the various persons involved in the securities industry are. This is a necessary preamble to understanding the types of problems (discussed in Part III) to which the regulation responds. Part IV then provides an outline to the regulation of these persons in terms of the problems noted in Part III.

II. SECURITIES INDUSTRY PARTICIPANTS

Before outlining the problems to which the regulation of the securities industry responds, it is useful to note who the persons involved in the securities industry are and what it is they do. The securities industry is said to perform two basic functions. First, it brings together persons seeking funds and persons who have surplus funds to invest. The securities industry performs this first function through the underwriting and distribution of new issues of securities. Second, it provides a liquid market for the trading of outstanding securities.[1] The securities industry participants who perform these functions are underwriters, brokers, dealers and advisors. These persons, and the related definitions in Canadian securities acts, are briefly described below.

---

[1] See *The Canadian Securities Course* (Toronto: The Canadian Securities Institute, 1987), at 56.

A. Underwriters

Underwriters are formally in the business of underwriting, or insuring, the sale of an issue of securities. For example, they may provide this insurance by purchasing the issue and reselling it themselves or through a standby underwriting.[2] More generally, they are involved in assisting in the issuance of securities and may simply provide services in the form of marketing the issue, often on what is known as a "best efforts underwriting".[3] Securities firms also engage in the underwriting function by participating in underwriting syndicates or in banking groups, whose members may agree to purchase part of an issue of securities in a bought deal or part of an unsold portion of an issue of securities in a standby underwriting.

Most Canadian securities acts define "underwriter" to include the activities described above. "Underwriter" is typically defined to mean a person or company who agrees to purchase securities with a view to distributing them, or who offers for sale or sells securities in connection with a distribution.[4] The definition typically includes a person or company who has a direct or indirect participation in any such distribution.[5]

B. Brokers and Dealers

Brokers are persons or firms who act as agents in the buying and selling of securities. In their capacity as brokers they do not themselves take ownership of the securities. Instead they facilitate transactions in securities by acting as a link between buyers and sellers of securities.

---

[2] See Chapter 1, Part IV.

[3] Ibid.

[4] A.S.A. s. 1(y); B.C.S.A. s. 1(1); M.S.A. s. 1(1) "underwriter"; Nfld.S.A. s. 2(1)(tt); N.S.S.A. s. 2(1)(2)(at); O.S.A. s. 1(1); S.S.A. s. 2(1)(ww).

[5] Ibid. There are a series of persons or companies who are exempt from the definition of underwriter. For instance, "underwriter" does not include "a person or company whose interest in the transaction is limited to receiving the usual or customary distributor's or seller's commission payable by an underwriter or issuer". Thus members of a selling group who sell a portion of an issue of securities simply on a customary commission basis should not fall within the definition of underwriter. See, for example, A.S.A. s. 1(y)(iii); B.C.S.A. s. 1(1) "underwriter" (d-g); M.S.A. s. 1(1) "underwriter"; Nfld.S.A. s. 2(1)(tt); N.S.S.A. s. 2(2)(at); O.S.A. s. 1(1); S.S.A. s. 2(1)(ww).

Dealers in securities are persons or firms who trade in securities for their own account. That is, they buy and sell securities on their own behalf without the assistance of a broker. They buy securities in the market and hold them in inventory for resale. This helps maintain a market in the securities held.

Securities firms generally trade in securities both as brokers and as dealers. In other words, they buy and sell securities on their own behalf and on behalf of others.

Canadian securities acts generally do not make a distinction between brokers and dealers. Both functions are normally covered under the term "dealer". "Dealer" is typically defined to mean a person or company who trades in securities in the capacity of principal or agent.[6]

C. Advisors

Advisors provide investment advice. The term is typically defined to mean a person or company engaging in or holding himself or herself out as engaging in the business of advising others as to investing in or buying or selling securities.[7] For the purposes of regulation, the function of advising is often broken down into the categories of investment counselling, market commentaries or portfolio management.[8]

1. *Investment Counselling*

Investment counselling involves providing continuing investment advice to individual clients on the basis of the particular needs or objectives of the individual client.[9]

---

[6] A.S.A. s. 1(d); B.C.S.A. s. 1(1) "dealer"; M.S.A. s. 1(1) "broker-dealer"; Nfld.S.A. s. 2(1)(i); N.S.S.A. s. 2(1)(i); O.S.A. s. 1(1); Q.S.A. s. 5 "dealer"; S.S.A. s. 2(1)(n).

[7] A.S.A. s. 1(a); B.C.S.A. s. 1(1); M.S.A. s. 1(1) "securities advisor"; Nfld.S.A. s. 2(2)(a); N.S.S.A. s. 2(1)(a); N.W.T.S.A. s. 1 "securities advisor"; O.S.A. s. 1(1); Q.S.A. s. 5 "advisor"; S.S.A. s. 2(2)(a); Y.S.A. s. 1 "securities advisor".

[8] A. Rules s. 17; B.C. Rules s. 8; Nfld. Regs. s. 87; N.S. Regs. s. 14; O. Regs. s. 98; Q. Regs. ss. 190-194; S. Regs. s. 11.

[9] A. Rules s. 17; B.C. Rules s. 8(b); M.S.A. s. 1(1); Nfld. Reg. s. 87(b); N.S.S. Reg. s. 14(a); N.W.T.S.A. s. 1; O. Regs. s. 99; S. Regs. s. 11(b); Y.S.A. s. 1.

2. *Market Commentaries*

Investment advice is also given in the form of market commentaries through direct advice or through publications or writings which are not tailored to the needs of specific clients. Persons who provide advice in this form are typically referred to in Canadian securities acts as "securities advisors".[10]

3. *Portfolio Management*

An investor may give a person or company a discretionary authority to manage the investor's portfolio of investments. A person or company given such authority is referred to as a "portfolio manager" and Canadian securities acts include portfolio managers as one of the subcategories of advisors.[11]

D. Securities Firms

Securities firms generally engage in most, or all, of the activities described above.[12] Competitive pressures in the offering of financial services has led to efforts of financial institutions to offer a broader range of financial services. Financial institutions such as banks, trust companies and insurance companies have been expanding their securities related activities such that they are engaged in many of the activities described above.

III. PROBLEMS IN SECURITIES INDUSTRY ACTIVITIES

Individuals and companies involved in providing underwriting services or brokerage services, or who deal in securities, or advise with respect to investment in securities often come into contact with

---

[10] A. Rules s. 17; B.C. Rules s. 8(c); M.S.A. s. 1(1); Nfld. Regs. s. 87(d); N.S. Regs. s. 14(c); N.W.T.S.A. s. 1; O. Regs. s. 99; Q.S.A. s. 5 "advisor"; S. Regs. s. 11(d).

[11] A. Rules s. 17; B.C. Rules s. 8(a); Nfld. Regs. s. 87(c); N.S. Regs. s. 14(b); O. Regs. s. 99; S. Regs. s. 11(c).

[12] See *The Canadian Securities Course* (Toronto: The Canadian Securities Institute, 1987), at 56.

members of the investing public. Investors may not be capable of assessing the quality of the services of securities industry participants they are dealing with or the risks associated with dealing with securities industry participants.

If investors cannot fully assess quality of securities industry participants, the problem of adverse selection, discussed in Chapters 3 and 9, may plague the activities of securities industry participants just as it is said to affect primary and secondary market trading in securities. The less financially responsible, less honest, and less competent securities industry participants (who can operate at lower cost) may drive more financially responsible, more honest and more competent securities industry participants out of the securities industry. The risk of substantial loss from dealings with less financially responsible, less honest and less competent securities industry participants may, in the long-run, cause investors to discount the value of the services provided by industry participants or the value of the securities themselves. In short, investors will "lose confidence" in securities markets.

Securities industry participants and investors alike would thus benefit from the increased value of securities industry activities that could accrue if the financial responsibility, honesty and competence[13] of securities industry participants was, to some degree, increased. However, they need to overcome the incentive for securities industry participants to profit from the lower costs associated with lesser degrees of financial responsibility, honesty and competence. Regulation that sets and enforces standards of financial responsibility, honesty and competence is the means by which, it is hoped, this perverse incentive can be avoided.

The concerns with respect to financial responsibility, honesty and competence, and the problems related thereto are discussed below.

A. Financial Responsibility and the Risk of Securities Firm Business Failures

In transactions between securities firms and their clients, securities firms are often in a position of owing money to their clients.

---

[13] This "triumvirate of values" is borrowed from M.Q. Connelly, "The Licensing of Securities Market Actors", in *Proposals for a Securities Market Law for Canada* (Ottawa: Ministry of Supply and Services, 1979) 1269, at 1273.

Clients are thus, from time to time, creditors of securities firms. They would typically be unsecured creditors who may get little or none of the amounts owing to them in the event of bankruptcy. Similar problems may occur where the securities firm misappropriates clients' funds or securities held in trust.

There may, however, be an incentive to operate the securities firm with as little initial capital investment as possible. This would put more of the risk of business failure onto persons such as the client-creditors of the firm and thereby lower the risk and cost of engaging in the particular securities business.

B. Honesty

There is a risk that persons and companies involved in the securities business may be inclined to pursue their own interests at the expense of others. This inclination manifests itself in a number of ways, including conflicts of interest, market manipulation, and pressure selling.

1. Conflicts of Interest

Whenever a securities market actor may gain from acting in some way that is contrary to a client's interests there is a conflict of interest. Also, given the range of services provided by securities firms, they are often in the position of serving two or more clienteles that have competing interests. Conflicts of interest can arise in a wide variety of circumstances, some of which are discussed below.

a. CHURNING

Brokers generally charge a fee on a commission basis. The commission is usually a percent of the total amount of each trade the broker performs on behalf of the client. The more trades there are, the greater the fees that can be earned by the broker. Thus there is an incentive for the broker to recommend trades which may not be in the client's best interests. The same incentive exists for a dealer which earns its income from the spread between the price at which it buys securities and the price at which it sells them. More trades with a given positive spread will lead to greater income. This incentive to encourage more trades than is in the client's best interests is known as "churning".[14]

b. FRONT RUNNING

A broker or dealer may obtain a large order for securities that may affect the price of the securities when executed. The broker or dealer then has an incentive to execute an order on behalf of itself before executing the client's order. Similarly, a broker or dealer may have an incentive to hold back several orders, which together would be likely to influence the price, and trade on its own behalf before executing the orders of clients. Such trading by a broker or dealer on its own behalf before executing a previous order from a client is known as "front-running".

c. USE OF INSIDE INFORMATION

Members of securities firms, with their knowledge of the securities markets in which capital is raised for investment, often serve as advisors to, or on the boards of directors of issuers of securities. In serving in these capacities they often become aware of material information about the issuer which remains undisclosed. Of course, if they trade on the information, or inform others of the information, they can be subject to the various sanctions with respect to insider trading or informing. However, even if they don't trade or inform with respect to the information, they are put in a difficult position of conflict with respect to their clients. For instance, if the information they obtain is unfavourable, then, in the interests of their clients, they should recommend selling the issuer's securities or, where they manage a client's account, they should sell the issuer's securities on behalf of the client. This, however, would arguably be contrary to their duty to the issuer. It would also involve taking advantage of undisclosed material information, which might, according to the argument for prohibiting insider trading, breed a lack of confidence in the market.

---

[14]See J. M. Vaughan, "Private Actions for the Broker's Churning of a Securities Account" (1975) 40 Mo. L. Rev. 281.

d. RELATED PARTY TRANSACTIONS AND OTHER CONFLICTS OF
INTEREST

Securities firms may be in a position to engage in underwriting, trading, advising, portfolio management, investment analysis, and referral activities in ways that favour persons with whom they have some connection or relationship. For instance, the securities firm may be influenced by an issuer which has a controlling interest in the securities firm. That influence may lead the securities firm to exercise its portfolio management discretion in favour of the issuer by purchasing the issuer's securities contrary to the best interests of the client. It may lead to advising in favour of the purchase of the issuer's securities or touting of the issuer's securities, even where the purchase may not be in the best interests of the firm's clients.

Securities firms which act as dealers (buying and selling securities on their own behalf) may often have substantial interests in particular securities. *Burke v. Cory*[15] is an example of the kind of problem that can arise. The broker who advised the purchase of the securities and produced pamphlets containing glowing reports about the securities was in fact the promoter of the issuers in question and, therefore, had a considerable interest in being able to sell the securities and inflate the market price of those securities. Similarly, securities firms which act as underwriters or receive a commission for the sale of new issues also have an interest in the securities being sold under the issue. A conflict of interest may also affect the decision on how to allocate limited investment opportunities among clients.

2. *Market Manipulation*

There are numerous ways in which the market price of a security can be manipulated. A person may attempt to manipulate the price and profit from trades with foreknowledge of the manipulations and their effect on the price. Two market manipulation techniques, "wash sales" and "scalping", are discussed below.[16]

---

[15] (1959), 19 D.L.R. (2d) 252 (Ont C.A.).

[16] Other market manipulation techniques are discussed in L. Kryzanowski, "Manipulation of Share Prices" in L. Sarna, ed., *Corporate Structure, Finance and Operations* (Toronto: Carswell, 1982) Vol. 2, 265.

a. WASH SALES

If a person enters corresponding buy and sell orders for the same security the transaction is referred to as a "wash sale". The transaction can give the appearance of more trading in the security than there otherwise would have been. If the trade is made at a price greater or lower than the prevailing market price it can give the appearance of either an increase or a decrease in price and may, for a period of time, affect the price at which subsequent trades occur.[17] The person who made the wash sale, and knows the price to be artificially inflated or deflated, can gain from selling securities at the artificially high price or buying securities at the artificially low price.

b. SCALPING

Scalping involves buying securities just before touting the security in some form of investment news media and then selling the security upon the price increase in response to the touting. A similar technique might be employed to cause the market price to fall and engage in trading to profit from the falsely deflated price of the security.

3. *Pressure Selling*

The art of selling, some would say, occasionally involves, in the hands of some salespersons, techniques which are ethically questionable. The salesperson might make wholly unfounded claims about the value of the security, which would be difficult for the purchaser to verify. The salesperson might promise extraordinary gains which never materialize. They might make a personal — but unenforceable — guarantee that the security will be repurchased at a given price, that the purchase price of a security will be refunded, that the price will increase to or not fall below a certain amount, or that the future marketability of the security is guaranteed because it will eventually become listed and posted for trading on an exchange.

Some securities sales persons, allegedly skilled in the techniques of selling relatively worthless securities to persons not particularly

---

[17] R.J. Gilson and R.H. Kraakman, "The Mechanisms of Market Efficiency" (1984) 70 Virginia L. Rev. 549, at 579-88.

interested in investing, or persons whose savings are otherwise held in more secure investments, have been known to set up shop for the purpose of contacting unsuspecting and gullible potential investors. Such shops are referred to as "boiler room" operations. When these operations were effectively closed down in Canada, they moved offshore to sell apparently worthless, or extremely risky, Canadian securities to unsuspecting and gullible foreigners.[18]

C. Professional Competence

Investors may not be able to fully assess the competence of the persons offering securities services such as portfolio administration, advising, or brokerage. Consequently, investors suffer losses by unknowingly engaging persons who provide a poor quality of service. Furthermore, a lack of competence increases the risk of business failure and the consequent losses to clients.

IV. AN OUTLINE OF SECURITIES INDUSTRY REGULATIONS

A. Registration

1. *Who Must Register*

Securities legislation in Canada regulates the various securities market actors by requiring them to register. Thus the legislation provides that no person shall trade in securities, underwrite issuances of securities or give advice with respect to investments in securities unless the person is registered.[19] A person who trades, underwrites or advises without registration can be subject to penal sanction.[20] Registrants are subject to regulatory requirements and noncom-

---

[18]See "Boiler Rooms Full of Canadians from St. Kitts to Switzerland", *Globe and Mail*, Feb. 10, 1987, pp. B1, B2; and "Canadian Run Stock Scam Triggers Probe by Ireland", *Globe and Mail*, June 13, 1988, p. B11.

[19]A.S.A. s. 54(1); B.C.S.A. s. 34(1); M.S.A. s. 6; N.B.S.F.P.A. s. 5(1); Nfld.S.A. s. 26(1); N.S.S.,A. s. 31(1); N.W.T.S.A. s. 4; O.S.A. s. 25(1); P.E.I.S.A. s. 2; Q.S.A. s. 148; S.S.A. s. 27(1); Y.S.A. s. 3.

[20]A.S.A. s. 161(1)(c); B.C.S.A. s. 155(1)(d); M.S.A. s. 136(1)(c); N.B.S.F.P.A. s. 41(1); Nfld.S.A. s. 122(1)(c); N.S.S.A. s. 129(1)(c); N.W.T.S.A. s. 49(c); O.S.A. s. 122(1)(c); P.E.I.S.A. s. 28(1); S.S.A. s. 131(3)(c); Y.S.A. s. 46(c).

pliance with these requirements can lead to reprimand or suspension, cancellation or restriction of registration.[21]

2. Subcategories of Registrants

There are various subcategories of registrants. A person may be registered as a dealer or as a salesperson, partner, director or officer of a securities firm which is registered as a dealer.[22] A person who advises can be registered as an advisor or as a partner or officer of a registered advisor.[23]

There are several subcategories of dealers. These subcategories vary from province to province but generally include the categories of "broker", "investment dealer", "mutual fund dealer", "scholarship plan dealer", "securities dealer" and "security issuer".[24] A "broker" is usually defined as a person who trades in the capacity of principal or agent and is a member of a recognized stock exchange in the particular province.[25] An "investment dealer" is usually defined as a person who trades as principal or agent and is a member of the Investment Dealers' Association of Canada.[26] A "mutual fund dealer" is defined as a person who trades exclusively in the securities of mutual funds.[27] A "scholarship plan dealer" is a person who trades

---

[21] A.S.A. s. 56(1); B.C.S.A. s. 144(1)(f); M.S.A. s. 8(1); N.B.S.F.P.A. s. 12(1)(c); Nfld.S.A. s. 28(1); N.S.S.A. s. 33(1); N.W.T.S.A. s. 10(1); O.S.A. s. 127(1)1; P.E.I.S.A. s. 3(5), 7; Q.S.A. s. 152; S.S.A. s. 134(1)(i) & (j); Y.S.A. s. 8.

[22] A.S.A. s. 54(1)(a); B.C.S.A. s. 34(1)(a); M.S.A. s. 6(1)-(3); N.B.S.F.P.A. s. 5(1)(a); Nfld.S.A. s. 26(1)(a); N.S.S.A. s. 31(1)(a); N.W.T.S.A. s. 4; O.S.A. s. 25(1)(a); P.E.I.S.A. s. 2(1); S.S.A. s. 27(1)(a); Y.S.A. s. 3.

[23] A.S.A. s. 54(1)(c); B.C.S.A. s. 34(1)(c); M.S.A. s. 6(6),(7); Nfld.S.A. s. 26(1)(c); N.S.S.A. s. 31(1)(c); N.W.T.S.A. s. 35; O.S.A. s. 25(1)(c); P.E.I.S.A. s. 2(1)(d); S.S.A. s. 27(1)(c); Y.S.A. s. 30.

[24] These categories are set out in A. Rules s. 16; B.C. Rules s. 6; Nfld. Regs. s. 86; N.S. Regs. s. 13; O. Regs. s. 98; P.E.I. Regs. s. 28 (has several subcategories of "brokers", which include many of the terms other provinces include in their subcategories of "dealers". For example, P.E.I. includes "Mutual fund dealer" and "Scholarship Plan dealer" under s. 28 as types of brokers); Q. Regs. s. 192; S. Regs. s. 10.

[25] Ibid.

[26] Ibid.

[27] Ibid. "Mutual funds" are dealt with in Chapter 13.

exclusively in scholarship or educational plans.[28] "Securities dealers" are persons who trade in securities generally in the capacity of principal or agent.[29] "Securities issuers" are issuers who trade in securities for the purposes of distributing securities of their own issue and solely for their own account.[30]

There are also several categories of advisor. These categories vary from province to province but generally include "investment counsel", "portfolio managers", and "securities advisors".[31] An "investment counsel" is a person who engages in the business of advising others as to the investing in or buying of specific securities, or who engages in giving continuous advice as to the investment of funds on the basis of the particular objectives of each client.[32] A "portfolio manager" is a person who manages the investment portfolio of clients through discretionary authority granted by clients.[33] "Securities advisors" are persons who hold themselves out as engaging in the business of advising others through direct advice or through publications as to the investing in or buying or selling of specific securities where the advice is not purported to be tailored to the needs of specific clients.[34]

Exemptions from the registration requirements for some persons (discussed in Part IV A 7 below) may create opportunities for persons such as banks, trust companies, insurance companies and non-residents, to be involved in the securities business without being subject to the same regulatory requirements that others are. Ontario and Newfoundland responded to this by introducing a system of

---

[28] Ibid. These plans provide funds to finance the education of the beneficiary of the plan, normally at the post-secondary level, if the beneficiary advances to education at that level. The plans are usually sold to the parents of young children.

[29] Ibid.

[30] Ibid.

[31] A. Rules s. 17; B.C. Rules s. 8; M.S.A. s. 1(1); Nfld. Regs. s. 87; N.S. Regs. s. 14; N.W.T.S.A. s. 1; O. Regs. s. 99; Q. Regs. ss. 190-194; S. Reg. s. 11; Y.S.A. s. 1.

[32] A. Rules s. 17(b); B.C. Rules s. 8(b); Nfld. Reg. s. 87(b); N.S. Reg. s. 14(a); O. Regs. s. 99(2); S. Reg. s. 11(b).

[33] A. Rules s. 17(a); B.C. Rules s. 8(a); Nfld. Regs. s. 87(c); N.S. Regs. s. 14(b); O. Regs. s. 99(3); S. Regs. s. 11(c).

[34] A. Rules s. 17(c); B.C. Rules s. 8(c); M.S.A. s. 1(1); Nfld. Regs. s. 87(d); N.S. Regs. s. 14(c); N.W.T.S.A. s. 1; O. Regs. s. 99(4); S. Regs. s. 11(d); Y.S.A. s. 1.

"universal registration". This system of universal registration involves additional categories of registrants. The term "financial intermediary dealer" includes banks, trust companies, credit unions and co-operative corporations engaging in trading in securities for other than investment purposes.[35] The term "foreign dealer" is used to describe dealers subject to foreign control.[36] The term "international dealer" describes dealers that carry on business as a dealer in a country other than Canada,[37] and the term "limited market dealer" is used to include dealers who, but for the regulations, would not have been required to register for trading pursuant to exemptions provided in the Act.[38] The registration requirement subjects these dealers to securities regulatory requirements and the regulations impose restrictions on the securities market activities of these persons.[39]

3. *Application for Registration and the Discretion of the Administrator*

A person or company intending to act in one of the categories described above, for which no exemption applies, must file an application for registration in a prescribed form.[40] These forms ask a series of questions assessing the financial responsibility, integrity and competence of the applicant. The administrator, who has the power to grant registration, has broad discretion. The administrator shall grant registration "where in the opinion of the [administrator] the applicant is suitable for registration and the proposed registration ... is not objectionable".[41] The administrator can also impose terms and conditions on the registration.[42] If the applicant's registration

---

[35] See O. Regs. s. 98; Nfld. Regs. s. 86.

[36] Ibid.

[37] Ibid.

[38] Ibid.

[39] See O. Regs. ss. 204-11; Nfld. Regs. ss. 169-75.

[40] A.S.A. s. 59; B.C.S.A. s. 34(2); M.S.A. s. 10; N.B.S.F.P.A. s. 9(1); Nfld.S.A. s. 30; N.S.S.A. s. 35; N.W.T.S.A. s. 5; O.S.A. s. 29; O. Regs. s. 129, Forms 3 & 4; O. Regs. s. 195 and Form 2; S.S.A. s. 31; Y.S.A. s. 9.

[41] A.S.A. s. 55(1); B.C.S.A. s. 35(1); M.S.A. s. 7(1); N.B.S.F.P.A. s. 12(2)(b); Nfld.S.A. s. 27(1); N.S.S.A. s. 32(1); N.W.T.S.A. s. 6(1); O.S.A. s. 26(1); P.E.I.S.A. s. 3(1); Q.S.A. s. 151; S.S.A. s. 28(1); Y.S.A. s. 4.

[42] A.S.A. s. 55(2)(a); B.C.S.A. s. 36; M.S.A. s. 7(3); N.B.S.F.P.A. s. 12(1)(f);

is refused, or if terms and conditions are imposed, the applicant must be given an opportunity to be heard.[43]

4. Renewals of Registration

Registrations are generally automatically suspended one year from the date they were granted.[44] The registrant must apply for renewal in advance of the time of suspension.[45] The applicant has a right to be heard if a renewal of registration is refused.[46] Applications for renewal allow for an updating of all changes in the information filed as of the last application for registration or renewal thereof.[47]

5. Continued Fitness for Registration

It is through registration that the various regulatory requirements governing securities industry participants are primarily enforced. Securities commissions, after giving the registrant an opportunity to be heard, may suspend, cancel, restrict or reprimand a registrant

---

Nfld.S.A. s. 27(2); N.S.S.A. s. 32(2); N.W.T.S.A. s. 6(2); O.S.A. s. 25(2); P.E.I.S.A. s. 3(4); Q.S.A. s. 152; S.S.A. s. 28(2)(a); Y.S.A. s. 5.

[43] A.S.A. s. 55(3); B.C.S.A. s. 35(3), 36(2); M.S.A. s. 7(2); N.B.S.F.P.A. s. 3(2) (appeal to Lieutenant Governor in Council); Nfld.S.A. s. 27(3); N.S.S.A. s. 32(3); N.W.T.S.A. s. 13 (appeal to Supreme Court); O.S.A. s. 26(3); Q.S.A. s. 317; S.S.A. s. 28(3); Y.S.A. s. 16 (application to the Supreme Court).

[44] A. Rules s. 49(1); B.C. Rules s. 67 (2 years for most types of registrants); M. Regs. s. 4(3) (salesperson's registration expires on the date the employer's registration expires); N.B. Regs. 7(1); Nfld. Regs. s. 116(1); N.S. Regs. s. 46(1); N.W.T.S.A. s. 7(1); O. Regs. s. 130(1); P.E.I. Regs. s. 43(1); Q. Regs. s. 199 (valid until cancelled); S.S.A. s. 36; Y.S.A. s. 6.

[45] A. Rules s. 49(2); M. Regs. s. 4(4); N.B. Regs. s. 7(1); Nfld. Regs. s. 116(3); N.S. Regs. s. 46(2); N.W.T.S.A. s. 7(2); O. Regs. s. 130(3) (at least 30 days prior to suspension); P.E.I. Regs. s. 43(2); S.S.A. s. 36(2); Y.S.A. s. 6.

[46] A.S.A. s. 55(3); B.C.S.A. s. 35(3); M.S.A. s. 7(2); N.B.S.F.P.A. s. 3(2) (appeal to Lieutenant Governor in Council); Nfld.S.A. s. 27(3); N.S.S.A. s. 32(3); N.W.T.S.A. ss. 10(2), 13 (appeal to the Supreme Court); O.S.A. s. 26(3); Q.S.A. s. 317; S.S.A. s. 28(3); Y.S.A. s. 16 (appeal to the Supreme Court).

[47] A. Rules s. 48 (see also A.S.A. s. 63); B.C. Rules s. 68 (and B.C.S.A. s. 42); M. Regs. s. 4(4); N.B. Regs. s. 7(1); Nfld. Regs. s. 117(2) & 118(2) & Forms 5 & 6; N.S. Regs. ss. 47(2) & 48(2) & Forms 5 & 6; N.W.T.S.A. s. 7(2); O. Regs. ss. 132(2) and 133(2) and Forms 5 & 6; P.E.I. Regs. s. 45(2); S. Regs. ss. 43, 44 and Forms 5 and 6; Y.S.A. s. 6.

where the commission is of the opinion that it is in the public interest to do so.[48] Commissions are given the power to suspend registration on an interim basis where the delay necessary for a hearing would be prejudicial to the public interest.[49] Violations of the securities laws of any jurisdiction or of a recognized self-regulatory organization are considered, in principle, to be prejudicial to the public interest and may thus affect the registrant's continued fitness for registration.[50]

6. Surrender of Registration

As noted above, securities market actors, in their dealings with clients, may become financially obligated to their clients. Consequently, there is a concern for the registrant leaving its financial obligations undischarged. Accordingly, provisions for the voluntary surrender of registration provide that the commission (or executive director) may accept such voluntary surrenders subject to such terms and conditions as it may impose where it is satisfied that the financial obligations of the registrant to its clients have been discharged and the surrender of the registration would not be prejudicial to the public interest.[51]

7. Exemptions from the Registration Requirement

In some situations the problems posed by the activities of securities market actors may not be present. In other situations the problems may not be of sufficient magnitude to justify the costs of registration and compliance with the regulations. Consequently there are exemptions from the registration requirement.

---

[48] A.S.A. s. 56(1); B.C.S.A. s. 161(1)(f); M.S.A. s. 8(1); N.B.S.F.P.A. s. 12(1)(c); Nfld.S.A. s. 28(1); N.S.S.A. s. 33(1); O.S.A. s. 127(1) 1; P.E.I.S.A. s. 3(5); Q.S.A. s. 152; S.S.A. s. 134(1)(i) & (j).

[49] Generally the hearing must be held within 15 days. A.S.A. s. 21; B.C.S.A. s. 161(2); M.S.A. s. 8(2); N.B.S.F.P.A. s. 23(2) (interim injunction on *ex parte* application of the Administrator to the court); Nfld.S.A. s. 28(2); N.S.S.A. s. 33(2); N.W.T.S.A. s. 22(3) (*ex parte* application to court by the Registrar); O.S.A. s. 127(5); S.S.A. s. 134(3); Y.S.A. s. 19 (*ex parte* application to Court by the Registrar).

[50] See National Policy #17.

[51] A.S.A. s. 57; B.C.S.A. s. 41; Nfld.S.A. s. 28(3); N.S.S.A. s. 33(3); O.S.A. s. 27(1); Q.S.A. s. 153; S.S.A. s. 29.

Generally the exemptions can be said to fit within broad categories according to the reasons for granting the exemptions.[52] The broad categories considered below are exemptions for isolated trades by persons who are not engaged in the securities business, exemptions for activities that are regulated under some other regulatory scheme and exemptions on the basis that the persons involved in the trading are relatively sophisticated.

This section does not describe all of the exemptions available. Instead, it puts exemptions into broad categories in order to focus on the basis for the exemptions. This should facilitate an understanding of other exemptions the reader may wish to pursue and an understanding of when exemption orders may be obtained and the kinds of arguments that could be made in order to obtain such exemptions.

a. ISOLATED TRADES BY PERSONS WHO ARE NOT IN THE SECURITIES
BUSINESS

If a trade is made by a person who does not engage in any of the businesses carried on by securities industry participants (who are the focus of the regulation), then the trade is not likely to create the kind of problems that the regulation was designed to address. Consequently, requiring persons to register and comply with the regulatory requirements for registrants would be unnecessary. Compliance might also be costly and likely to impede the transaction since the cost of compliance would not be amortized over numerous future trades, as it would be in the case of persons regularly engaged in the business of trading in securities.

(i) Executors, Administrators, Trustees, etc.

The work of executors, administrators, guardians, trustees, assignees, receivers, custodians, or liquidators might be substantially constrained by the costs of compliance with the regulations. They also generally do not act for a large clientele of investors whom they are likely to become financially obligated to. These trades are usually not done on an ongoing basis, but are instead done for the period necessary to accomplish the purpose of their appointment.

---

[52] The categories adopted herein constitute just one of several possible categorizations.

Thus these activities are less likely to raise the kinds of problems encountered with respect to those who regularly engage in trading. The exemptions for these persons might also be considered in the category below with respect to regulation under other regulatory schemes, since these persons are usually subject to regulation under other statutes. Consequently, there is an exemption for trades by executors, administrators, etc.[53]

(ii) Bank Realizations

A trade made by a lender in a security that has been pledged or mortgaged as collateral for a bona fide debt is also exempt from the registration requirement.[54] In making such trades lenders will not be engaged in trading in the same sense as a broker or dealer. The lender will be acting on its own behalf and thus will not be acting on behalf of a client with whom conflicts of interest and financial obligations may arise. The lender will also presumably not be carrying an inventory of the particular security and engaging in ongoing buying and selling of the particular security. Thus concerns with respect to such dealing in securities will either not be present or will not be as pronounced.

(iii) Trades Under Prospectus Exemptions

The prospectus exemptions mentioned in Chapter 7 involve trades by persons who are not normally engaged in the business of trading in securities on behalf of others. These trades are not likely to raise the kinds of problems to which the regulation of securities industry participants is addressed. Consequently, there are a series of exemptions from the registration requirement for trades in which there are corresponding exemptions from the prospectus requirement.[55]

---

[53] A.S.A. s. 65(1)(a)(i); B.C.S.A. s. 45(2)(1); M.S.A. s. 19(1)(a); N.B.S.F.P.A. s. 7(a); Nfld.S.A. s. 36(1)(a); N.S.S.A. s. 41(1)(a); N.W.T.S.A. s. 2(f); O.S.A. s. 35(1)(l); P.E.I.S.A. s. 2(3)(a); S.S.A. s. 39(1)(a)(i); Y.S.A. s. 2(f).

[54] A.S.A. s. 65(1)(g); B.C.S.A. s. 45(2)(19); M.S.A. s. 19(1)(d); N.B.S.F.P.A. s 7(d); Nfld.S.A. s. 36(1)(g); N.S.S.A. s. 41(1)(g); N.W.T.S.A. s. 2(e); O.S.A. s. 35(1), (7); P.E.I.S.A. s. 2(3)(e); S.S.A. s. 39(1)(f); Y.S.A. s. 2(e).

[55] See, for example, A.S.A. s. 65(1); B.C.S.A. s. 45(2); M.S.A. s. 19(1); Nfld.S.A. s. 36(1); N.S.S.A. s. 41(1); O.S.A. s. 35(1), O. Regs. ss. 148-151; P.E.I.S.A. s. 2(3); Q.S.A. s. 157; S.S.A. s. 39(1).

(iv) Exempt Advisors

Some persons are exempt from registration in the advisor category. For instance, registration as an advisor is not required for a lawyer, accountant, engineer, or teacher.[56] Similarly, registration as an advisor is not required for a registered dealer, or any partner, employee or officer of a registered dealer.[57] Also, registration is not required for a publisher of, or writer for, any bona fide news magazine (or business or financial publication of general and regular paid circulation which is distributed only to persons who have paid for the publication) who gives advice only through the publication, has no interest in the securities on which the advice is given and receives no commission or other consideration for giving the advice.[58]

These exemptions only apply where the performance of the service as an advisor is solely incidental to the person's principal business or occupation.[59] The notion again is presumably that the person only occasionally provides what might be considered to be advice and does so in the context of conducting another business. They are thus not regularly involved in the business of giving advice and the requirement of compliance with the registration requirements and related regulations might impose an unreasonably high and constraining cost on the incidental advice given. The administrative cost of granting registration, not to mention the exceptional cost likely to be associated with any attempt to enforce the regula-

---

[56] A.S.A. s. 64(b)(iv); B.C.S.A. s. 44(2)(c); M.S.A. s. 18(b); Nfld.S.A. s. 35(b); N.S.S.A. s. 40(b); O.S.A. s. 34(b); P.E.I.S.A. s. 2(5)(b); Q.S.A. s. 156(1); S.S.A. s. 38(1)(a)(iv). The terms "lawyer", "accountant", "engineer", and "teacher" are not defined. Presumably a person fits within one of these groups if they have been licensed as such by the relevant provincial government (see D.L. Johnston, *Canadian Securities Regulation*) (Toronto: Butterworths, 1977), at 120.

[57] A.S.A. s. 64(b)(v); B.C.S.A. s. 44(2)(e); M.S.A. s. 18(c); Nfld.S.A. s. 35(c); N.S.S.A. s. 40(c); O.S.A. s. 34(c); P.E.I.S.A. s. 2(5)(c); Q.S.A. s. 156(2); S.S.A. s. 38(a)(v).

[58] A.S.A. s. 64(c); B.C.S.A. s. 44(2)(f); M.S.A. s. 18(d); Nfld.S.A. s. 35(d); N.S.S.A. s. 40(d); O.S.A. s. 34(d); P.E.I.S.A. s. 2(5)(d). Q.S.A. s. 156.1; S.S.A. s. 38(1)(a)(vi). Just who would constitute a "publisher" is not entirely clear. See Johnston, *supra* note 56, at 121-22.

[59] A.S.A. s. 64; B.C.S.A. s. 44(3); M.S.A. s. 18; Nfld.S.A. s. 35; N.S.S.A. s. 40; O.S.A. s. 34; P.E.I.S.A. s. 2(5); Q.S.A. s. 156; S.S.A. s. 36(1)(a).

tions with respect to the incidental giving of advice, would likely not be matched by any benefit that might be derived.[60]

(v) Trades by Individual Investors

The definition of "trade" in most Canadian securities acts includes a disposition of a security for valuable consideration and includes any act in furtherance of such a disposition. Thus any individual investor who seeks to sell a security with the assistance of a broker or to a dealer might be considered to be trading. Of course, the law is intended to protect — not regulate — these persons. Accordingly, there is an exemption for trades by such persons where they act solely through an agent who is a registered dealer.[61]

(vi) Other Isolated Trades

There is a general exemption for isolated trades "where the trade is not made in the course of continued and successive transactions of a like nature, and is not made by a person or company whose usual business is trading in securities."[62] The reason for this exemption is presumably that concerns with respect to the business of securities market actors do not arise, or are not significant, with respect to isolated transactions where the person engaging in the transaction is not normally involved in the business of trading in securities.

b. REGULATED UNDER A SEPARATE REGULATORY SCHEME[63]

Certain types of investments that would otherwise likely fall within the meaning of the word "security" are excluded from the

---

[60] The exemptions with respect to the professions might also be justified, in part on the basis that these professions are governed by a separate scheme of regulation that attempts to assure the integrity and competence of persons practicing in the profession.

[61] A.S.A. s 65(1)(j); B.C.S.A. s. 45(2), (7); M.S.A. s. 19(1)(g); N.B.S.F.P.A. s. 5(4); Nfld.S.A. s. 36(1)(j); N.S.S.A. s. 41(1)(j); N.W.T.S.A. s. 2(a); O.S.A. s. 35(1), (10); P.E.I.S.A. s. 2(3)(h); S.S.A. s. 39(1)(j); Y.S.A. s. 2(a).

[62] A.S.A. s. 65(1)(b); B.C.S.A. s. 45(2)(3); M.S.A. s. 19(1)(b); N.B.S.F.P.A. s. 7(b); Nfld.S.A. s. 36(1)(b); N.S.S.A. s. 41(1)(b); O.S.A. s. 35(1), (2); P.E.I.S.A. s. 2(3)(b); S.S.A. s. 39(1)(b).

[63] See also Johnston, *supra* note 56, at 127.

application of the registration requirement.[64] For instance, trading in these "securities" would not be a violation of the registration requirement leading to penal sanction since the particular security is exempt from the application of securities laws. Exemptions with respect to particular types of securities might be justified, in some cases, on the basis that trading in that type of security is regulated under other, perhaps more appropriate, regulatory regimes and thus need not be regulated under securities legislation.

For instance, an exemption given for certificates and receipts issued by a trust company registered under provincial legislation governing such companies[65] might be justified on the basis that the appropriate place to deal with concerns arising from dealings with the investing public in respect of such securities is in the legislation governing trust companies. Similarly, mortgages or other encumbrances upon real or personal property (other than those relating to a bond, debenture or similar obligation) are often exempted from the registration requirement as long as they are offered for sale by a person registered or exempted from registration under legislation dealing with mortgage brokers.[66] Legislation dealing directly with the integrity and competence of mortgage brokers might be a more appropriate place to deal with the regulation of trading in such securities.

c. SOPHISTICATED/COMMON BOND CUSTOMER EXEMPTIONS

Some exemptions might be justified on the basis that the persons involved in the trading are likely to be relatively sophisticated and thus not in need of the protection of the regulations governing securities industry participants. For instance, trades in commercial paper with less than one year duration and in specified minimum amounts are usually exempted under Canadian securities acts. The persons

---

[64] O.S.A. s. 35(2). Some of these exemptions were also dealt with in the context of exemptions from the prospectus requirement in Chapter 7. See also A.S.A. s. 66; B.C.S.A. s. 46; M.S.A. s. 19(2); N.B.S.F.P.A. s. 7(c); Nfld.S.A. s. 36(2); N.S.S.A. s. 41(2); P.E.I.S.A. s. 2(4); Q.S.A. s. 154; S.S.A. s. 39(2).

[65] A.S.A. s. 65(1)(y.2); B.C.S.A. s. 46(b); M.S.A. s. 19(1)(c)(ii); N.B.S.F.P.A. s. 7(c); Nfld.S.A. s. 36(2)(b); N.S.S.A. s. 41(2)(b); N.W.T.S.A. s. 2(c); O.S.A. s. 35(2); S.S.A. s. 39(2)(a)(iii); Y.S.A. s. 2(c).

[66] A.S.A. s. 66(e); B.C.S.A. s. 46(e); M.S.A. s. 19(2)(d); Nfld.S.A. s. 36(2)(e); N.S.S.A. s. 41(2)(e); O.S.A. s. 34(2), (5); S.S.A. s. 39(2)(b).

who trade in commercial paper in these volumes tend to be large companies and banks who might be expected to be capable of investigating – and who would find it worthwhile to investigate – the integrity and financial responsibility of the persons they are dealing with.

Other exemptions might be justified on the basis that the persons involved in the trade have close enough contact to the vendor of the securities that they can assess the character of the person they are dealing with and the merit of the security involved in the transaction. For instance, where trades are made in the securities of private companies, the person making the trade is exempt from the registration requirement as long as the securities are not offered for sale to the public.[67] The test of "to the public" will consider the "need to know" of the persons buying and the "common bonds" of the persons buying with the issuer. Where these tests are met, the person buying the security will presumably have some knowledge of the trustworthiness and financial responsibility of the vendor.[68]

d. SAFE SECURITY

There are several types of securities for which trading is exempt from the registration requirements. Some of these are exempt ostensibly on the basis that the securities are relatively safe securities, such that trading in them is less likely to raise concerns regarding the professional competence of the trader or a conflict of interest.[69] Other securities are exempt from the registration requirement

---

[67] O.S.A. s. 35(2), (10). This exemption might also be justified on the basis of the transaction being an isolated transaction. Presumably the persons involved in the trade are not regularly engaged in the business of trading in securities. A.S.A. s. 66(j); B.C.S.A. s. 46(j); M.S.A. s. 19(2)(i); Nfld.S.A. s. 36(2)(j); N.S.S.A. s. 41(2)(j); P.E.I.S.A. s. 2(4)(h); Q.S.A. s. 3(2); S.S.A. s. 39(2)(k); Y.S.A. s. 2(g).

[68] A similar "common bonds" type of exemption is an exemption for the issuance of securities by a mining company in exchange for mining claims. See O.S.A. s. 35(2), (14). This exemption might, of course, also be justified on the basis that the transaction is an isolated transaction in which the person disposing of the securities is not regularly engaged in the business of trading in securities. See also A.S.A. s. 66(1); Nfld.S.A. s. 36(2)(n); N.W.T.S.A. s. 2(k); N.S.S.A. s. 41(2)(n); Y.S.A. s. 2(k).

[69] For instance, debt instruments of governments or municipal corporations might be said to be exempt for these reasons. See Chapter 7, Part III D.

because concerns regarding trading in the securities are addressed by other regulatory mechanisms.[70] Still other securities are exempt from the registration requirement in the interests of promoting socially beneficial activities or facilitating smaller issuers.[71]

8. A Cautionary Note

Chapters 4 and 7 looked at the prospectus requirement and exemptions from that requirement. In assessing the application of securities legislation to a transaction, one should not stop with the prospectus requirement. Since a distribution will involve a trade in a security, and since trading in securities requires registration, one should also ask whether there is an exemption from the registration requirement.

B. Response to Concerns Regarding Securities Market Actors

The perceived problems with respect to the businesses of trading, underwriting and advising are the subject of a wide range of regulatory responses. The regulatory responses to each of the problems outlined above are discussed below. Some of the regulatory provisions discussed below respond to more than one of the problems outlined above.

1. Financial Responsibility/Business Failure

There are several aspects of the regulation of securities market actors that might be said to respond to the problem of business failure. The minimum net free capital requirement, a bonding requirement, a compensation fund, the know your client rule, and requirements for professional competence might all be said to respond, in part, to the problem of business failure.

---

[70] For instance, mortgages offered for sale by a person registered under the *Mortgage Brokers Act* (see, for example, B.C.S.A. s. 32(e)) or equivalent act might be said to be exempt for this reason. See Chapter 7, Part III C.

[71] For instance, securities issued for benevolent fraternal, charitable or religious purposes or securities of private issuers not offered for sale to the public, or offered to finance a prospecting expedition. See Chapter 7, Part III E.

a. MINIMUM NET FREE CAPITAL

There is a minimum net free capital requirement for applicants in order to be registered.[72] It requires that assets less liabilities be above a specified minimum amount. The intention is to ensure that registrants who begin to engage in acting on behalf of others have sufficient funds to meet obligations to clients as they develop.

b. BOND

The securities regulator may require the registrant to post a bond in the amount considered necessary to provide protection to the registrant's clients.[73]

c. COMPENSATION FUND

Dealers must also contribute to a compensation fund that is to provide protection in the event of a business failure.[74] Members of the Montreal, Toronto, Alberta and Vancouver Stock Exchanges as well as members of the Investment Dealers Association of Canada contribute to the National Contingency Fund. There is no limit on the amount of a claim under the Fund and the Fund has retained the right to levy further charges on members when it is required.

d. KNOW YOUR CLIENT

Brokers must know the identity, credit-worthiness and reputation of their clients to ensure that the clients can meet their obligations.[75] The idea is that since brokers and dealers are often in the position of extending credit to clients, they ought to be careful about the credit risks that they accept.[76]

---

[72] A. Rules s. 23; B.C. Rules ss. 19, 20; Nfld. Regs. s. 95; N.S. Regs. s, 23; O. Regs. s. 107; P.E.I. Regs. s. 34; Q. Regs. ss. 207-12; S. Regs. s. 19.

[73] A. Rules s. 25; B.C. Rules s. 21; M.S.A. s. 7(4); N.B.S.F.P.A. s. 10(1), Regs. s. 6; Nfld. Regs. s. 96; N.W.T. Regs. s. 8(1); N.S. Regs. s. 24; O. Regs. s. 108; P.E.I.S.A. s. 5, Regs. s. 35; Q. Regs. s. 213; S. Regs. s. 20; Y. Regs. s. 7.

[74] See, for example, A. Rules s. 28; B.C. Rules s. 23; Nfld. Regs. s. 98; N.S. Regs. s. 27; O. Regs. s. 110; Q. Regs. s. 215; S. Regs. s. 23.

[75] See, for example A. Rules s. 30(4); B.C. Rules s. 48; N.S. Regs. s. 31(4); O. Regs. s. 114(4); P.E.I. Regs. s. 38; Q. Regs. s. 235; S. Regs. s. 26(4).

[76] In the *W.D. Latimer Co. Ltd.* case [March, 1975] O.S.C.B. 103, Latimer Co. allowed a direct line to be installed in the offices of a person named Gould.

e. COMPETENCE

To obtain a licence to trade in securities as a broker, dealer or underwriter, or to act as a securities advisor, certain educational and apprenticeship requirements (intended to assure a minimum level of competence) must be met. In part, the idea of requiring a minimum level of competence is to ensure that those engaged in the business have some ability to run the business and are thus not as likely to go bankrupt. In other words, the business may go bankrupt because of a downturn in the market (protection against consequent losses being provided by the other techniques), but it should not go bankrupt due to incompetence.

2. Honesty and Integrity

a. CONFLICTS OF INTEREST

(i) Churning

A broker who provides investment counselling or manages a client's investments is in a fiduciary relationship with the client. Indeed, with respect to the management of a client's portfolio, the broker is the client's agent. The broker has a duty not to engage in a transaction which creates a conflict of interest. Nor is the broker permitted to make secret profits or profit at the expense of their client. Where a broker "churns" an account to make profits by taking extra commission, they breach a fiduciary duty to the client. Consequently, the client will be able to take an action to rescind the commissions on any of the trades.

This civil remedy may be inadequate. It requires that the client be able to understand that this is the problem and be able to catch the broker in the act. In order to reduce this problem securities regulations provide that investment counsel and portfolio managers may

---

Gould used the line to place orders to be executed by Latimer in trades to nominee accounts in other brokerage firms (i.e., they were manipulating the market through wash sales). The accounts with the brokerage houses were on a delivery against payment basis; that is, the brokerage houses were to deliver the stock (stock certificates) to a bank for the nominee account who would pay for the security on behalf of the nominee upon delivery of the stock certificate. The brokers who had made orders for the stock had to suffer the loss for failure to verify the credit-worthiness of their clients in the nominee accounts.

not base their fees on the value or volume of transactions initiated for the client.[77]

(ii) Front Running

Front running may constitute a fraud within the meaning of s. 380 of the *Criminal Code*. By benefiting from a client's confidential information, front running would constitute a breach of fiduciary duty.

(iii) Inside Information

National Policy #18 provides that where one is a director or officer of a company, or acts in an advisory capacity, the first duty is to the company and one ought to be cautious that inside information is not disclosed to the registrant firm of which they are a member.

(iv) Related Party Transactions and Other Conflicts of Interest

Several provinces have passed regulations which impose extensive conflict of interest disclosure requirements and other restrictions on the activities of registrants in order to address the problem of registrants conducting their business in ways that favour persons with whom they have some relationship, connection, or association, but which are potentially contrary to the interests of the registrant's clients. Restrictions are imposed on acting as an underwriter or selling group member, trading as principal or agent, advising, exercising account or portfolio discretion, recommending securities, or jointly offering financial services with a bank, trust company, credit union or insurer. These restrictions are imposed in certain specified circumstances where a conflict of interest would be likely to arise.[78]

The circumstances in which potential conflicts of interest are presumed to arise are defined through the use of such terms as "related", "connected" and "associated". Persons are said to be

---

[77]See, for example, A. Rules s. 31; Nfld. Regs. s. 103(2); N.S. Regs. s. 32(2); O. Regs. s. 115(2); Q. Regs. s. 240; S. Regs. s. 27(2).

[78]See generally B.C. Rules ss. 75-85; Nfld. Regs. ss. 183-97; N.S. Regs. ss. 59-75; O. Regs. ss. 219-33; Q. Regs. ss. 230.1-49.1.

"related" to one another where one influences the other, both influence the same third person, or both are influenced by the same third person.[79] A person is said to "influence" another person if the person, either alone or in combination with others, can exercise a controlling influence over the management and policies of the other person through beneficial ownership of, or direction or control over voting securities, securities convertible into voting securities or securities currently carrying a right to acquire either voting securities or securities convertible into voting securities.[80] A person is deemed to be able to exercise a controlling influence over another person if the person beneficially owns or exercises control or direction over (or has a right to acquire or convert into) securities constituting more than 20% of the outstanding securities of any class or series of voting securities of that other person.[81]

A person is considered "connected" to a registrant where the person (or someone related to that person) is indebted to, or has some other relationship with, the registrant, a person related to the registrant, or a director, officer or partner of the registrant or of a person related to the registrant. The term "connected" applies to an initial distribution of securities issued or held by the person connected to the registrant where a reasonable purchaser of the securities would question whether the registrant and the person were independent.[82]

A registrant is not allowed to act as an underwriter or selling group member in connection with an issue of securities by the registrant, or issued or held by a related party or connected party of the registrant unless certain conditions are met. Briefly stated, the conditions are that the prospectus or some other document contains disclosure of the relationship, an independent underwriter (i.e., not "related" or "connected" to the issuer or seller) underwrites a spec-

---

[79] B.C. Rules s. 75(2); Nfld. Regs. s. 183(1); N.S. Regs. s. 59(1)(g); O. Regs. s. 219(1); Q. Regs. s. 230.1.

[80] B.C. Rules s. 75(3); Nfld. Regs. s. 183(1); N.S. Regs. s. 59(1)(d); O. Regs. s. 219(1); Q. Regs. s. 230.1.

[81] B.C. Rules s. 75(4); Nfld. Regs. s. 183(4); N.S. Regs. s. 59(4); O. Regs. s. 219(4); Q. Regs. s. 230.4.

[82] B.C. Rules s. 75(1), (2); Nfld. Regs. s. 183(1), (2); N.S. Regs. s. 59(1)(a), (2); O. Regs. s. 219(1), (2); Q. Regs. ss. 230.1, 230.2.

ified portion of the issue and the underwriter's certificate on the prospectus is signed by the independent underwriter.[83]

Restrictions apply to trading, the exercise of disccretion, advising or recommending where there is a conflict due, for instance, to the issuance of a security by a person related or connected to the registrant or a trade in a security of the registrant or a person related to the registrant.[84] Trading as principal or agent in such circumstances requires disclosure of the nature of the potentially conflicting relationship or connection before the transaction and a confirmation of the transaction that indicates that the trade involved the particular potential conflict.[85] An exercise of discretion with respect to an account or portfolio in such circumstances is subject to obtaining written consent to the exercise of the discretion after prior disclosure of the potential conflict of interest.[86] Advising in such circumstances requires disclosure orally or in writing[87] and recommendations in such circumstances requires that the recommendation appear in a regularly distributed circular or pamphlet that discloses the nature of the potential conflict.[88] Registrants who engage in any of the

---

[83] B.C. Rules s. 78; Nfld. Regs. s. 188; N.S. Regs. s. 64; O. Regs. s. 224. See also Q. Regs. s. 236.1.

[84] See generally the provisions cited infra notes 85 to 89. In B.C. the restrictions extend to situations where, for instance, any director, officer, partner, salesperson or employee of the registrant who participates in the activities knows of a conflict with an "associated party of the registrant" or with a connected person who is a control person of the issuer of the security. A person is an "associated party of the registrant" if the person is "related" to the registrant, is a partner of the registrant, or is a director, officer, salesperson or employee of the registrant or of a related party of the registrant. A trust or estate is also an "associated" person if any of the persons described above serves as trustee or has a substantial beneficial interest in the trust or estate. Also, a relative of any of the persons described above who lives in the same home is considered an "associated" person. See B.C. Rules ss. 75(1), 79, 81, 82 and 83.

[85] B.C. Rules ss. 79, 80; Nfld. Regs. ss. 189, 190; N.S. Regs. ss. 65, 66; O. Regs. ss. 225, 226. See also Q.S.A. s. 234.3.

[86] B.C. Rules s. 82; Nfld. Regs. s. 191(2)(b); N.S. Regs. s. 67(2)(b); O. Regs. s. 227(2)(b). See also Q.S.A. s. 236.

[87] B.C. Rules s. 81; Nfld. Regs. s. 191(2)(a); N.S. Regs. s. 67(2)(a); O. Regs. s. 227(2)(a).

[88] B.C. Rules s. 83; Nfld. Regs. s. 192; N.S. Regs. s. 68; O. Regs. s. 228. See also Q. Regs. s. 237.1. National Policy #25 also requires that advisors disclose any interest they have in securities referred to in any publication, circular, pamphlet, or ad, or in the sale or purchase of securities, including any commission, financial

above transactions in the prescribed circumstances where potential conflicts are presumed to arise must file a conflict of interest statement with the relevant securities administrators.[89]

The regulations of some provinces also prohibit loans made from a client's discretionary account or portfolio to the registrant, a partner of the registrant, a person related to the registrant, a director, officer, salesperson, or employee of the registrant, or the associates of any such persons.[90]

The conflict of interest rules also give securities administrators the power to prevent or restrict "networking arrangements".[91] A "networking arrangement" is an arrangement between a registrant and an insurer or a savings institution (such as a bank, trust company or credit union) in which the registrant offers for sale to the public a combination of securities and goods or services, part of which consists of goods or services provided by the savings institution or insurer. A "networking arrangement" also includes a situation in which the registrant cooperates with the savings institution or insurer in the joint offering for sale of securities and goods or services, including paying the savings institution or insurer or its employees a commission for referring clients to the registrant to whom the registrant sells securities or goods and services.[92] Where the registrant plans to enter into a networking arrangement it must give notice to the securities administrator of the intention at least 30 days before entering into the networking arrangement and the securities administrator then has 30 days to object to the networking arrangment subject to giving the registrant an opportunity to be heard.[93]

Conflicts that may arise in the allocation of limited investment opportunities are addressed through a requirement that investment

---

arrangements, or other remuneration they may expect to receive if their recommendations are followed.

[89] B.C. Rules s. 77; Nfld. Regs. s. 187; N.S. Regs. s. 63; O. Regs. s. 223. See also Q. Regs. s. 234.2.

[90] B.C. Rules s. 82(3); Q.S.A. s. 168.

[91] B.C. Rules s. 84; Nfld. Regs. s. 193; N.S. Regs. s. 69; O. Regs. s. 229; Q. Regs. s. 236.3.

[92] B.C. Rules s. 84; Nfld. Regs. s. 183(1); N.S. Regs. s. 59(1)(e); O. Regs. s. 219(1); Q. Regs. s. 230.1.

[93] B.C. Rules s. 84; Nfld. Regs. s. 193; N.S. Regs. s. 69; O. Regs. s. 229. See also Q. Regs. s. 236.3.

counsel and portfolio managers develop policies for the allocation of investments where investment opportunities are limited.[94] These policies are to be filed with the relevant securities administrators and provided to the client.

b. MARKET MANIPULATION

(i) Wash Sales

The problem of wash sales is dealt with in s. 382 of the *Criminal Code*. Proof of an "intent to create a false or misleading appearance of active public trading in a security or with intent to create a false or misleading appearance with respect to the market price of a security" is required for a conviction under s. 382.

(ii) Scalping

Brokers must disclose any intention to trade as principal when they issue a circular, letter or ad regarding the security in which they intend to trade.[95] The disclosure must be in the circular, letter or ad itself. Scalping and other market manipulation frauds are dealt with in s. 380 of the *Criminal Code*. This requires a showing of fraudulent intent.

c. PRESSURE SELLING

Provincial securities acts deal with pressure selling in the context of a distribution of securities in part by having a period of time (called the "waiting period") between the receipt for the preliminary prospectus and the receipt for the final prospectus.[96] Selling activities during the waiting period are constrained. During the waiting period one can only identify the security, its price, and where it can be bought, give out the preliminary prospectus, and solicit expressions of interest in the purchase of the security.[97] This is intended to dis-

---

[94] See, for example, A. Regs. s. 31(1); Nfld. Regs. s. 103(1); N.S. Regs. s. 32(1); O. Regs. s. 115(1); S. Regs. s. 27(1).

[95] A.S.A. s. 71; B.C.S.A. s. 51; M.S.A. s. 70; Nfld.S.A. s. 40; N.S.S.A. s. 45; O.S.A. s. 39; Q.S.A. s. 163; S.S.A. s. 45.

[96] See Chapter 4, Part VII.

[97] There are limits on the type of advertising allowed during the waiting period — see Chapter 4, Part VII.

courage issuers, underwriters and brokers from making unfounded glowing claims about the securities in an attempt to prod the investor into buying the security. Instead, any information provided by issuers, underwriters and brokers should be information contained in the preliminary prospectus and prospectus and thus subject to the statutory civil sanction for misrepresentations in a prospectus.

Furthermore, the purchaser has a right to withdraw from a purchase within 2 days of receiving the final prospectus.[98] This withdrawal right gives the investor an opportunity to examine the material in the prospectus and a chance for reflection or "cooling off".

Securities acts also prohibit attending at a residence or telephoning to any residence for the purpose of effecting a trade.[99] In other words, the individual has to come to the broker or dealer first. This is intended to discourage door-to-door and telephone sales techniques which might be inclined to pressure investors into making purchases.

Securities acts also prohibit certain types of representations that might be used to tease an unsuspecting client into an investment they wouldn't otherwise make. Specifically, the following representations are prohibited:[100] (i) a promise to resell or repurchase or refund

---

[98] A.S.A. s. 106; B.C.S.A. s. 83(3); M.S.A. s. 64; Nfld.S.A. s. 72; N.S.S.A. s. 76; O.S.A. s. 71; P.E.I.S.A. s. 8.16(2); Q.S.A. s. 30; S.S.A. s. 79(3).

[99] A.S.A. s. 69; B.C.S.A. s. 49; M.S.A. s. 68; N.B.S.F.P.A. s. 28; Nfld.S.A. s. 38; N.S.S.A. s. 43; N.W.T.S.A. s. 33; O.S.A. s. 37; S.S.A. s. 43; Y.S.A. s. 28.

[100] A.S.A. s. 70; B.C.S.A. s. 50; M.S.A. s. 69; N.B. Regs. s. 16; Nfld.S.A. s. 39; N.S.S.A. s. 44; O.S.A. s. 38; S.S.A. s. 44.

Alberta has passed a *Financial Consumers Act*, S.A. 1990, c. F-9.5 (proclaimed in force May 1, 1991 except for ss. 9, 21, 23-25) amended by S.A. 1998, c. F-1.05 which imposes certain duties on consumers and suppliers with respect to life insurance policies that provide for a cash surrender value, interest bearing cash balances, mutual fund units, term deposits, investment certificates, and guaranteed investment certificates. Consumers are obligated, for instance, to provide information that they know or should know would have a significant effect on advice provided by a supplier of the above noted financial products (s. 5). The consumer is also obligated to become reasonably well-informed about the financial product, obtaining and reviewing information about the product and making a sensible decision about investing in it (s. 5). Failure of the consumer to fulfill the obligations can be considered in assessing or apportioning damages (s. 7). Suppliers of the above noted financial products are obligated to provide a suitable financial product based on the information given by the consumer (s. 8). The supplier is also required to

the purchase price of a security, (ii) an undertaking as to the future value or price of the security, or (iii) that the security will be listed and posted for trading or that a listing application has been made.

3. *Professional Competence*

Individuals seeking registration as advisors, broker-dealers, or investment counsel must complete courses provided by certain associations such as the Canadian Securities Institute, the Investment Dealers Association, and the Institute of Chartered Financial Analysts.[101] There are also minimum apprenticeship periods. Approval of persons for registration may be delegated to private associations such as the VSE and the Investment Dealers Association of Canada.[102]

For instance, to become a registered dealer one needs to (i) complete the Canadian Securities Course, (ii) complete the Canadian Investment Finance Course, (iii) complete the first year of the Canadian Financial Analysts Course, and (iv) have done financial analysis for at least five years with three of those years under the supervision of an advisor responsible for the administration of investment portfolios having an aggregate value of at least $1m. The purpose of these requirements is to ensure that persons who engage in the securities business have some knowledge of, and experience in, the business.

Brokers and advisors must also know their clients before giving advice to or managing the portfolio of a particular client.[103] They are supposed to know the investment needs and objectives of the client in order to give advice or make decisions that are consistent with the client's needs and objectives.

---

give the consumer information with respect to such matters as rights for redemption, cancellation, compensation for loss, commissions to be received by an agent, and premiums or fees payable by the consumer (s. 8). The Act provides for an action by a "consumer organization" (s. 28) and by the Director under the Act (ss. 28, 36). The Act also gives the Director investigatory power and the power to order compliance with the Act (ss. 29-35).

[101] See, for example, A. Rules ss. 41-45; B.C. Rules ss. 60-63 (and B.C. Pol. 3-22); Nfld. Regs. ss. 111, 112; N.S. Regs. ss. 41, 42; O. Regs. ss. 124, 125; P.E.I. Regs. s. 39; S. Regs. ss. 37, 38.

[102] See, for example, B.C. Pol. 3-22.

[103] See *supra* Part IV B 1 d. See also the provisions of the Alberta *Financial Consumers Act*, referred to *supra* note 100.

C. Enforcement

There are several avenues for enforcement of the regulation of securities market actors. There are potential penal sanctions, and a range of administrative sanctions and possible civil actions.

1. *Penal Sanctions*

As noted in Part B above, fraudulent market manipulation techniques are dealt with under the *Criminal Code*. There are also penal sanctions for many of the provisions of the securities acts and their accompanying regulations.[104]

2. *Administrative Sanctions*

A key means of sanctioning securities market actors is the cancellation, restriction, or suspension of registration.[105] Securities administrators could also impose an injunction or compliance order,[106] a cease trade order,[107] or removal of exemptions.[108]

3. *Civil Actions*

There are also several possible common law bases for civil actions. For instance, in acting contrary to the interests of clients, the various securities market actors could be found to be in breach of contractual obligations to clients, leading to actions for damages or specific performance. Securities market actors will often be in a fiduciary relationship with their clients such that they must act with due care, consistent with the prevailing professional standard,

---

[104] A.S.A. s. 161; B.C.S.A. s. 155; M.S.A. s. 136; N.B.S.F.P.A. ss. 5(2), 41; Nfld.S.A. s. 122(c); N.W.T.S.A. s. 49(1)(c); N.S.S.A. s. 129(1)(c); O.S.A. s. 122(c); P.E.I.S.A. s. 28, s. 2; Q.S.A. s. 202; S.S.A. s. 131(3)(c); Y.S.A. s. 49(1)(c).

[105] See *supra* note 53.

[106] A.S.A. s. 164; B.C.S.A. ss. 157, 161(1)(a); M.S.A. s. 152; Nfld.S.A. s. 126; N.S.S.A. s. 134(1)(a); O.S.A. s. 127(1) 1; Q.S.A. s. 272.1; S.S.A. s. 133.

[107] A.S.A. s. 165(1)(a); B.C.S.A. s. 161(1)(b); M.S.A. s. 148; Nfld.S.A. s. 127; N.S.S.A. s. 134; N.W.T.S.A. s. 37; O.S.A. s. 127(1) 2; Q.S.A. ss. 265, 266; S.S.A. s. 134(1)(b); Y.S.A. s. 37.

[108] A.S.A. s. 165(1)(c); B.C.S.A. s. 161(1)(c); M.S.A. s. 19(5); Nfld.S.A. s. 128; N.S.S.A. s. 134(1)(c); O.S.A. s. 127(1) 3; Q.S.A. s. 264; S.S.A. s. 134(1)(a).

in the best interests of their clients and not take secret profits or put themselves in a position where they are in conflict of interest. A breach of these fiduciary duties could lead to an action for an injunction or an accounting for profits or benefits received.

CHAPTER 13

MUTUAL FUNDS

I. INTRODUCTION

Mutual funds are subject to the securities law requirements discussed in previous chapters. However, there are several special securities law requirements for mutual funds set out in provincial securities acts, regulations, and policy statements. There has been an enormous growth in both the number and total dollar volume of mutual funds in Canada in recent years. From 1982 to 1994, the number of mutual funds grew from 91 to 799.[1] The total asset value of mutual funds grew from $4.07 billion in 1982 to $130.5 billion in 1994.[2] Consequently, mutual funds have taken on a much greater significance in Canadian securities markets and in Canadian securities law in recent years. The purpose of this chapter is to provide a brief background on mutual funds and a brief outline of special requirements for mutual funds under provincial securities laws.

II. BACKGROUND ON MUTUAL FUNDS[3]

A. Open-End (or Mutual) Funds and Closed-End Funds Distinguished

There are two types of investment funds — closed-end funds and open-end funds. Closed-end investment funds sell securities to

---

[1] See the Investment Funds Institute of Canada Historical Overview chart reproduced in schedule one to the Stromberg Report (*Regulatory Strategies for the Mid-90's: Recommendations for Regulating Investment Funds in Canada* (Canadian Securities Administrators, January 1995)).

[2] Ibid.

[3] For further background on mutual funds, see *The Canadian Securities Course*, (Toronto: The Canadian Securities Institute, 1995) Chapter 7; and J.C. Francis and E. Kirzner, *Investments: Analysis and Management*, 3rd ed., (Toronto: McGraw-Hill Ryerson, 1988), Chapter 26.

investors to raise funds which are then invested by the closed-end fund issuer in the securities of other securities issuers. The securities sold by closed-end funds to investors generally cannot be redeemed by investors. Instead the investor wishing to liquidate his or her investment would sell the closed-end fund security to another investor.

The open-end fund, or "mutual fund", also sells securities to investors to create a fund for investment in a portfolio of securities of other securities issuers. However, the open-end fund's securities can be redeemed by investors wishing to liquidate their investment in the fund.[4] Securities in a mutual fund are redeemed at the "net asset value" per share of the fund. The net asset value of the fund is the market value of all of the assets of the fund (which consists primarily of the securities of other securities issuers) less the liabilities of the fund.

B. Mutual Fund Organization

Mutual funds are organized as trusts or as incorporated companies. The fund employs a custodian. The fund may also employ a fund manager to manage the fund's business and a distributor to distribute the fund's securities and deal with the fund's investors. The management and distribution functions may be provided by the promoters of the fund itself.

---

[4] "Mutual fund" is defined in the B.C.S.A. s. 1(1) as including,

"an issuer of a security that entitles the holder to receive on demand, or within a specified period after demand, an amount computed by reference to the value of a proportionate interest in the whole or in a part of the net assets, including a separate fund or trust account, of the issuer of the security"

See also A.S.A. s. 1(m.1); Nfld.S.A. s. 2(1)(aa); N.S.S.A. s. 2(1)(z); O.S.A. s. 1(1); P.E.I.S.A. s. 1(d.3); S.S.A. s. 2(1)(dd). Under the M.Regs. s. 1 "mutual fund company" is defined as a company designated by the Director as a mutual fund company. Under the Q.S.A. s. 5 "mutual fund" is defined as a company issuing shares which must, on request of the holder, redeem them at their net asset value. The N.B.S.F.P.A., N.W.T.S.A. and the Y.S.A. contain no specific provisions on mutual funds.

1. *The Manager*

The mutual fund manager supervises the fund's investment portfolio.[5] The mutual fund manager maintains a portion of the fund in cash and liquid investments in order to meet demands for the redemption of shares, make new portfolio purchases, and pay dividends. The manager prepares the fund's prospectus and the fund's reports. The manager is also responsible for the calculation of the net asset value of the fund.

2. *Distribution*

A mutual fund may engage a securities firm to act as a distributor or may use the "in-house" sales force of the fund's promoter.[6] The distributor's representatives are involved in explaining the nature of the fund to clients and in dealing with various client matters with respect to the mutual fund. The distributor is compensated through sales charges pursuant to a distribution contract.

3. *Custodian*

Mutual funds are required to appoint a custodian because of the temptations that may be present given the large amounts of

---

[5] Under the B.C.S.A. s. 1(1) "mutual fund manager" is defined as "a person who provides investment advice under a management contract".

Under N.P. #39, s. 1.01(8) a "manager" of a mutual fund is defined as

"a person or company who has the power or responsibility to direct the affairs of the mutual fund but does not include a person or company who is not associated with the promoter or trustee of the mutual fund and whose duties are limited to managing the investment portfolio of the mutual fund and the provision of investment advice in connection therewith".

Other statutes define a "mutual fund contract" (or "management contract") as a contract under which a mutual fund is, for valuable consideration, provided with investment advice alone or together with administrative or management services. See, for example, A.S.A. s. 1(k); Nfld.S.A. s. 2(1)(v); N.S.S.A. s. 2(1)(u); O.S.A. s. 1(1); S.S.A. s. 115(1)(d).

[6] Under the B.C.S.A. a "mutual fund distributor" is defined as "a person distributing a security under a distribution contract". A "distribution contract" is defined as "a contract under which a mutual fund or its legal representative grants to a person the right to purchase the securities of the mutual fund for distribution or to distribute the securities of the mutual fund on behalf of the mutual fund." See, for example, A.S.A. s. 1(g); B.C.S.A. s. 1(1); Nfld.S.A. s. 2(1)(n); N.S.S.A. s. 2(1)(n); O.S.A. s. 1(1); S.S.A. s. 115(1)(b).

liquid funds in mutual fund portfolios.[7] A trust company or a bank is appointed as a custodian to (a) receive funds from investor purchases of the mutual fund's securities, (b) hold the mutual fund's portfolio securities, (c) receive income from dividends on or sales of portfolio securities, and (d) arrange for payment of dividends declared by the mutual fund, payment on shares redeemed by mutual fund investors and payment for securities purchased by the mutual fund for its portfolio.

C. Types and Advantages of Mutual Funds

1. Types of Mutual Funds

Mutual funds are designed with a wide variety of investment objectives to meet the various investment needs of the investing public. Some of the different types of funds are briefly described below.[8]

a. INCOME FUNDS

There are "income funds" which invest in shares and bonds paying substantial dividends and interest. Speculative investments are avoided. The objective of the fund is to provide the investor with a secure stream of income.

b. MORTGAGE FUNDS

Mortgage funds hold groups of mortgages, usually consisting of first mortgages with relatively short terms to maturity. With relatively short terms to maturity on first mortgages, the volatility of the value of the fund is kept to a minimum. Thus the goal of these funds is to provide income in a relatively safe investment.

c. BOND FUNDS

Bond funds consist of a portfolio of bonds with the object of providing a stream of income from a relatively safe investment.

---

[7] See, for example, J.C. Baillie and W.M.H. Grover, *Proposals for a Mutual Fund Law for Canada*, Consumer and Corporate Affairs, Vol. 1, 69.

[8] The types of funds noted, as well as other types of funds, are discussed in *The Canadian Securities Course, supra* note 3, at 7-3 to 7-7; and in Francis and Kirzner, *supra* note 3, at 759.

d. DIVIDEND FUNDS

Dividend funds consist of a portfolio of preferred shares and common shares that have a history of consistent dividend payments. These funds take advantage of the dividend tax credit.

e. GROWTH FUNDS

There are "growth funds" that invest primarily in common shares and take some risks in the expectation of obtaining higher returns. These funds may appeal to investors who are willing to accept greater risk for greater potential returns and who would prefer to receive income in the form of capital gains rather than interest or dividends.

f. BALANCED FUNDS

The objective of "balanced funds" is to obtain a combination of capital appreciation, income and security of investment. This is provided through a combination of fixed-income securities (such as bonds) and share holdings which yield a combination of both dividend income and capital gains.

g. ASSET ALLOCATION FUNDS

Asset allocation funds give a wide discretion to the portfolio manager to adjust the portfolio among equity, money market instruments and fixed income securities (such as bonds) in response to changes in the economy.

h. MONEY MARKET FUNDS

"Money market funds" invest in short-term investments such as treasury bills, short-term government bonds and commercial paper. The objective is to earn high rates of return from low-risk, short-term investments. These funds are especially popular when interest rates are unusually high.

i. SPECIALTY FUNDS

"Specialty funds" concentrate their investments in a defined industry, geographic area, or segment of the capital market. These funds tend to be of a more speculative nature. They are less diversified and may be subject to great volatility due to swings in the particular industry or the economy of the particular geographic area. Specialty funds concentrating in the securities of foreign markets are also subject to currency exchange rate fluctuations.

j. INTERNATIONAL FUNDS

International funds invest in a portfolio of securities from different countries. They can provide international diversification and allow for adjusting the portfolio to concentrate on markets offering the best prospects. They are, however, subject to the risk of currency fluctuations.

k. REAL ESTATE FUNDS

There are also "real estate funds" that invest in real property. These investments may be in income-producing properties or in more speculative real estate holdings.

l. ETHICAL FUNDS

A more recent type of fund is an "ethical fund" which avoids investing in the securities of issuers which are more inclined to be involved in environmental degradation or which profit from the sales of such things as weapons, alcohol or tobacco.

2. *Advantages of Mutual Funds*

Mutual funds provide a number of advantages for investors who lack investment knowledge and experience and who lack sufficient funds to buy a diversified investment portfolio. Mutual funds provide professional investment management and pool the funds of investors to buy a diversified portfolio. There are, as noted above, a variety of funds to meet various investment needs and the right to redeem mutual fund securities at the net asset value per share of the mutual fund provides liquidity for the investor.[9]

---

[9] These and other advantages are noted in *The Canadian Securities Course, supra* note 3, at 7-9 to 7-10.

D. Purchases and Redemptions

1. *Methods of Buying Mutual Fund Securities*

Mutual fund securities can be purchased through lump sum cash purchases, accumulation purchase plans, or through dividend reinvestment.

a. LUMP SUM

Mutual fund securities can be purchased through lump sum payments. There is normally a minimum amount that must be purchased with minimums ranging from $50 to $1,000. Sales charges, discussed below, are included in the purchase price and the sales charge percentage is usually subject to a declining scale for larger lump sum purchases. Short-term trading penalties are often applied to discourage investors from frequent trading which can subject the fund to excessive administrative expenses.

b. PURCHASE PLANS

Mutual funds often provide accumulation purchase plans, or "contractual plans", for investors who do not have sufficient funds to make the larger investments necessary to reduce sales charge percentages. These plans allow investors to make periodic payments, often in varying amounts, or commit the investor to buy shares in stipulated amounts at specified times over several years.

c. DIVIDEND REINVESTMENT

Mutual funds often provide for the purchase of mutual fund shares by reinvesting dividends declared by the mutual fund.

2. *Sales Charges*

Some mutual funds charge a sales charge at the time of purchase by the investor.[10] The purchase price per share or unit of the mutual fund is the net asset value per share plus the sales charge. The sales

---

[10] Other funds use management and administrative fees instead of a sales charge. Other funds charge only a nominal administrative fee at the time of purchase and levy instead a redemption fee at the time of redemption. See *The Canadian Securities Course, supra* note 3, at 7-12.

charge percentage is usually expressed as a percentage of the offering price or the net asset value per share.[11] Because the administrative costs associated with a purchase tend to be relatively fixed, the sales charge percentage is reduced for progressively larger purchases.

There are "front-end load" plans under which sales charges are based on projected deposits over the term of the purchase plan, but which apply the charge mostly to deposits in the early stages of the plan (e.g., over the first year) with lower charges applying to later deposits. "Level-load" plans spread the sales charge evenly over deposits made over the term of the purchase plan and charge a termination fee for terminating the plan prior to the end of the plan's term. "Rear-end load" plans charge small administrative fees at the time purchases are made and apply the brunt of the charges at the time of redemption.

E. Mutual Fund Fees

In addition to sales charges, there are other fees charged for the operation of mutual funds.

1. Trailer / Service Fees

Trailer, or service, fees are fees that a mutual fund manager may pay to individuals or organizations that have sold the mutual fund units. The fee is intended to compensate sales persons or organizations for the cost of providing services such as investment and tax advice and other services related to the investor's mutual fund investment. These fees are based on the value of the particular mutual fund held by clients of the salesperson or organization and are usually in the range of 0.25% to 0.5% per year.[12]

---

[11] The offering or purchase price is determined as follows:

$$\text{Offering or Purchase Price} = \frac{\text{Net Asset Value per share}}{100\% \text{ less } \% \text{ Sales Charge}}$$

See The *Canadian Securities Course, supra* note 3, at 7-13.

[12] See the *Canadian Securities Course, supra* note 3, at 7-13.

2. *Management Fees*

Mutual funds also charge management fees against the fund that cover the cost of managing the fund's portfolio of investments. These fees can vary widely often depending, in part, on the nature of the fund.

3. *Other Expenses*

In addition to management fees, there are other expenses such as brokerage fees for transactions to make changes in the mutual fund portfolio, audit and legal fees, custodial fees, and the provision of information to the mutual fund's investors.

III. THE DISTRIBUTION OF MUTUAL FUND SECURITIES

The distribution of mutual fund securities involves the disposition of securities for valuable consideration and thus constitutes a "trade" in the securities of the mutual fund. Consequently the persons distributing securities of mutual funds must be registered for trading.[13] Since the sale of mutual fund securities will be a "distribution", the mutual fund issuer must file and obtain a receipt for a preliminary prospectus and a prospectus.[14]

The distribution of mutual fund securities differs from the distribution of the securities of other issuers in several respects. First, mutual fund securities are not all sold over a given distribution period, but are offered on a continuous basis with investors making lump sum purchases at different points in time or spreading purchases over time under a purchase plan. Second, a full prospectus has been viewed as too complicated a document for the typical mutual fund investor.[15] Consequently Canadian securities laws provide for a simplified prospectus, or allow for a summary statement, to be used as a document for distribution. Third, the structure of the mutual fund business, the nature of the mutual fund

---

[13] Registration for trading is discussed in Chapter 12.

[14] The requirement to file a preliminary prospectus and a prospectus in order to distribute securities is discussed in Chapter 4. Exemptions from the prospectus requirement are discussed in Chapter 7.

[15] See Baillie and Grover, *supra* note 7, at 25.

contract with its investors and the generally less sophisticated nature of mutual fund investors create unique disclosure issues with respect to mutual funds. The discussion below summarizes the prospectus requirements, clearance procedures and the unique disclosure issues relating to mutual funds.

A. The Mutual Fund Prospectus

1. *Prospectus or Simplified Prospectus Option*

A mutual fund has the option of filing a prospectus under the normal prospectus procedures[16] or filing an abbreviated prospectus known as a simplified prospectus.[17] To use the simplified system, the mutual fund files a preliminary simplified prospectus and a preliminary annual information form.[18] The preliminary simplified prospectus and preliminary annual information form are reviewed together[19] in accordance with the securities legislation in force in each province or territory where the simplified prospectus is filed.[20] The filing may be made under National Policy #1, and National Policy #30, with respect to the processing of seasoned prospectuses, also applies.[21]

---

[16]Special forms are provided for mutual fund prospectuses — see, for example, Alta. Form 15; B.C. Form 15; Man. Form 12; Nfld. Form 15; N.S. Form 15; Ont. Form 15; Sask. Form 16.

Some provinces provide for an abbreviated version of the prospectus, known as a "summary statement", to be used as the document for distributions to investors. The full prospectus must still be filed. See A.S.A. s. 93(1), A. Rules s. 78 and Form 15A; Nfld.S.A. s. 64(3), Nfld. Regs. s. 21 and Form 15A; N.S.S.A. s. 68(3), N.S. Regs. s. 86(5) and Form 15A; O.S.A. s. 63, O. Regs. s. 33 and Form 16; P.E.I. Regs. s. 3.

[17]The use of a simplified prospectus is provided for in N.P. #36. N.P. #36 s. 1.2 provides that the simplified prospectus option is not available for a mutual fund which invests in real property or which constitutes a commodity pool programme.

The B.C.S.A. s. 61(3), B.C. Rules ss. 100, 101 and Forms 50 and 51 provide for a "short form of prospectus" and an "annual information form" similar to N.P. #36.

[18]N.P. #36, s. 4.1. See also B.C. Rules ss. 100(2), 101(3).

[19]N.P. #36, s. 6.1.

[20]N.P. #36, s. 4.5.

[21]N.P. #36, ss. 6.2 and 6.3.

2. The Simplified Prospectus

The simplified prospectus is intended to be a concise presentation of information in plain language.[22] It contains information on matters such as:[23]

(i) the name and formation of the issuer, and a brief description of the issuer's business;

(ii) risk factors relating to the securities offered;

(iii) a description of the securities offered (including such matters as dividend rights, voting rights, liquidation rights, and redemption rights);

(iv) the method of determining the sales price, redemption price and sales and redemption charges;

(v) the method of distribution;

(vi) responsibility for principal functions such as the management of the issuer, its investment portfolio, investment analysis, recommendations and decisions, etc.;

(vii) management fees and other expenses;

(viii) investment objectives and practices;

(ix) dividends, dividend reinvestment and other distributions to security holders;

(x) the tax consequences to security holders of dividends or other distributions, redemptions, etc.

It must also disclose other material facts.[24] The simplified prospectus must also contain a statement of the purchaser's statutory rights of

---

[22] N.P. #36, Sch. A, General Instruction. See also, for example, B.C. Form 50, General Instruction. A similar description is used in the forms for summary statements — see the general instructions in Alta. Form 15A; Nfld. Form 15A; N.S. Form 15A; Ont. Form 16; Que. Schedule V, Item 2.

[23] N.P. #36, Schedule A. See also B.C. Form 50. Similar items are required for summary statements used as the document for distribution of mutual fund securities under the normal prospectus procedures as out in the securities acts and regulations of some provinces — see, for example, Alta. Form 15A; Nfld. Form 15A; N.S. Form 15A; Ont. Form 16; P.E.I. Regs s. 21; Que. Schedule V.

[24] N.P. #36, Sch. A, Item 15. See also B.C. Form 50, Item 15. Subject to N.P. #36, the Ontario approach is to allow for a "summary statement" (Form 16) to be used as a selling document in addition to a full prospectus (Form 15) to be filed with the Director. The full prospectus would contain "other material facts" (Form 15, Item 28). The summary statement requires a certificate which states that the summary statement contains no untrue statement of a material fact and

withdrawal, rescission or damages to the extent applicable provincial laws provide for such rights.[25]

Investors are to be provided with information on the tax saving features of investments in a mutual fund where the mutual fund's securities qualify for retirement savings plans, deferred profit sharing plans or other savings plans under the *Income Tax Act* (Canada). The qualification for tax saving must be disclosed in the prospectus together with any limitations imposed by the *Income Tax Act* on the portion of such plans that may be invested in the securities of the mutual fund without subjecting the plans to taxes or penalties under the *Income Tax Act*.[26] A mutual fund prospectus may not disclose that its securities qualify as investments for pension funds, insurance companies, trust companies or loan companies unless the mutual fund satisfies securities administrators that such disclosure is not misleading.[27]

The simplified prospectus must have a cover statement indicating that it incorporates by reference and is accompanied by audited annual statements for the fund for its last completed financial year.[28] It is to contain an introductory statement to the effect that it is a concise statement of the relevant information, but that additional

---

does not omit to state a material fact. See also Alta. Form 15, Item 28 and Form 15A, Item 18; Man. Form 12, Item 26; Nfld. Form 15, Item 28, Form 15A, Item 18; N.S. Form 15, Item 28 and Form 15A, Item 18; Que. Schedule V, Item 15; Sask. Form 16, item 28.

[25] N.P. #36, Sch. A, Item 17. See also B.C. Form 50, Item 17. Similar statements of the purchaser's rights must be provided in summary statements used under the prospectus procedures provided for in the act and regulations of some provinces — see, for example, Alta. Form 15A, Item 17; Nfld. Form 15A, Item 17; N.S. Form 15A, Item 17; Ont. Form 16, Item 17; Que. Schedule V, Item 17.

Statutory rights of rescission with respect to purchases of mutual fund securities are given for purchases of less than specified amounts. The right to rescind expires 48 hours after purchase or 60 days after purchase in the case of a contractual plan. See, for example, A.S.A. s. 174; B.C.S.A. s. 139; Nfld.S.A. s. 137; N.S.S.A. s. 145; O.S.A. s. 137; S.S.A. s. 145.

[26] N.P. #39, s. 2.02.

[27] N.P. #39, s. 2.03.

[28] N.P. #36, Sch. A, Item 1. See also B.C. Form 50, Item 1. Similar statements must be provided in summary statements provided for under the act and regulations of some provinces — see, for example, Alta. Form 15A, Item 1; Nfld. Form 15A, Item 1; N.S. Form 15A, Item 1; Ont. Form 16, Item 1; P.E.I. Regs. s. 21(4); Que. Schedule V, Item 2.

information is contained in the annual information form, financial statements and other documents that are required to be filed with securities administrators in each province or territory.[29] The introductory statement goes on to note that the statements in the annual information form are incorporated by reference into the simplified prospectus and thus are subject to statutory civil liability.[30]

3. The Annual Information Form

Where the mutual fund uses the simplified prospectus procedure, the additional information referred to in the introductory statement to the simplified prospectus includes:[31] (i) the annual information form and (ii) other information required to be filed pursuant to the laws of each province or territory in which the simplified prospectus is filed (including the most recent audited annual financial statements, interim audited financial statements, material change reports and information circulars). These documents, together with the simplified prospectus, are said to constitute the mutual fund's "permanent information record".[32] The simplified prospectus must also contain a statement to the effect that a copy of the permanent information record will be provided to the purchaser on request.[33]

The annual information form provides the information contained in the simplified prospectus and contains additional information.[34]

---

[29] N.P. #36, Sch. A, Item 2. See also B.C. Form 50, Item 2. For similar requirements in summary statements, see Alta. Form 15A, Item 1; Nfld. Form 15A, Item 1; N.S. Form 15A, Item 1; Ont. Form 16, Item 1 (with respect to a "summary statement" — see supra, note 16); P.E.I. Regs. s. 21(4); Que. Schedule V, Item 2.

[30] Ibid. See also N.P. #36, s. 3.5. N.P. #36, s. 4.4 notes that the simplified prospectus is a prospectus within the meaning of the securities legislation of the various provinces and territories.

[31] N.P. #36, s. 32.1. See also B.C. Rules s. 100(2); Que. Schedule X.

[32] N.P. #36, s. 2.1. See also B.C. Rules s. 100(3); Q.S.A. s. 108.

[33] N.P. #36, Item 2. See also B.C. Rules s. 105 and Form 50, Item 2. The annual information form must also contain an undertaking to provide the other documents constituting the permanent information record on request — N.P. #36, s 3.3 (see also B.C. Rules s. 101(2)).

There is a similar requirement with respect to summary statements. The purchaser can request a copy of the full prospectus. See, for example, Alta. Form 15A, Item 1; Nfld. Form 15A, Item 1; N.S. Form 15A, Item 1; Ont. Form 16, Item 1; Que. Schedule V, Item 2.

[34] N.P. #36, Sch. B. See also B.C. Form 51.

In particular it provides additional information with respect to the mutual fund issuer and the persons associated with it and provides additional information pertaining to redemption price, method of distribution and responsibility for such matters as the management of the issuer, management of the issuer's investment portfolio, the distribution of its securities, and so on.[35]

4. Pro-forma Simplified Prospectus and Pro-forma Annual Information Form

Since the simplified prospectus is a prospectus for the purposes of applicable securities legislation, the time periods for lapse of the prospectus and the filing of a pro-forma simplified prospectus apply.[36] Since mutual fund securities are distributed on a continuous basis, a pro-forma simplified prospectus, together with the more extensive disclosure in a pro-forma annual information form, will have to be filed 30 days before the end of the 12-month period following the date a receipt for the simplified preliminary prospectus was given.[37] The pro-forma simplified prospectus and pro-forma annual information form must reflect material changes in the affairs of the mutual fund.[38] However, the Canadian Securities Administrators have noted that the simplified prospectus need only be revised where it is necessary to reflect material changes in the affairs of the mutual fund and they note that they anticipate that it will normally not be necessary to revise the simplified prospectus annually.[39] If a material change does occur prior to the lapse of the simplified prospectus, the simplified prospectus and the annual information form must be amended and a receipt for the amendment must be obtained.[40]

---

[35] Ibid.

[36] N.P. #36, s. 4.4.

[37] A.S.A. s. 97; B.C.S.A. s. 70; M.S.A. s. 56; Nfld.S.A. s. 63; N.S.S.A. s. 67; O.S.A. s. 62; P.E.I.S.A. s. 8.9; Q.S.A. ss. 33-35; S.S.A. s. 71.

[38] The pro-forma prospectus must comply with the requirements of the act and regulations with respect to the form and content of a prospectus. This requires disclosure of all material facts. See, for example, B. C. Rules s. 99.

[39] N.P. #36, s. 4.6.

[40] N.P. #36, s. 4.7. See also Chapter 4, Part VII F on the amendment of the prospectus.

IV. INVESTMENT REQUIREMENTS, RESTRICTIONS AND PRACTICES

To a large extent the regulation of mutual funds under securities laws in Canada has been effected through policy statements. Enforcement with respect to these policy statements is primarily through the power of securities administrators to refuse to issue a receipt for a prospectus or through the exercise of the power to impose administrative sanctions such as cease trade orders and the removal of exemptions.[41] These policy statements regulate, among other things, the investments of mutual funds, certain changes in mutual funds, contractual purchase plans, sale and redemption of mutual fund securities, management fees and custodianship. The regulation of investment requirements, investment restrictions and investment practices of mutual funds is discussed below.

A. Initial Investment in a New Mutual Fund

National Policy #39 imposes a minimum initial investment requirement before the mutual fund can begin operating. The initial investment must be at least $150,000 provided by the manager of the mutual fund, or by the portfolio advisor, promoter or sponsor of the fund or their directors, officers or shareholders. Securities of the fund are not to be redeemed unless an additional $500,000 is raised from other investors. If the initial investment has not been provided, then the minimum amount of $500,000 must be subscribed through a best efforts offering.[42]

B. Investment Restrictions

1. *Conflict of Interest Restrictions*

The mutual fund might, without knowledge of the investing public, use funds raised from investors to make investments in persons related to those involved in the management of the fund. Such investments would raise a conflict of interest between the per-

---

[41] The available administrative sanctions are summarized in Chapter 14.

[42] N.P. #39, s. 3.01. The organization costs for the mutual fund are to be borne by the promoter, sponsor or manager and they are not to be reimbursed by the mutual fund — see N.P. #39, s. 3.02.

sonal interest of those involved in the management of the fund and their duty to act in the best interests of the fund.

Consequently, most provincial securities acts prohibit mutual funds from making investments by way of a loan to any officer or director of the mutual fund, its manager, or distributor, or any of their associates, or any individual where the individual, or an associate of the individual, beneficially owns more than 20% of the voting rights attached to outstanding voting securities of the mutual fund, or its manager or distributor.[43]

Most provincial securities acts provide several other similar restrictions. For instance, a mutual fund must not knowingly make an investment in any person that beneficially owns more than 20% of the voting rights attached to outstanding voting securities of the mutual fund or its manager or distributor.[44] The mutual fund cannot knowingly make an investment in an issuer in which an officer or director of the mutual fund, its manager or distributor, or a person, or group of persons, who beneficially owns more than 20% of the voting rights attached to outstanding voting securities of the mutual fund, has a significant interest.[45] A mutual fund is not to knowingly make an investment in an issuer in which it alone, or together with one or more other mutual funds under common management, beneficially owns more than 20% of the voting rights attached to out-

---

[43] A.S.A. ss. 151, 152(1); B.C.S.A. ss. 120, 121(1); Nfld.S.A. ss. 111, 112(1); N.S.S.A. ss. 118, 119(1); O.S.A. ss. 110, 111(1); S.S.A. ss. 119, 120(1).

[44] A.S.A. s. 152(2); B.C.S.A. s. 121(2); Nfld.S.A. s. 112(2); N.S.S.A. s. 119(2); O.S.A. s. 111(2); S.S.A. s. 120(2).

[45] A.S.A. s. 152(2)(c); B.C.S.A. s. 121(2)(c); Nfld.S.A. s. 112(2)(c); N.S.S.A. s. 119(2)(c); O.S.A. s. 111(2)(c); S.S.A. s. 120(2)(c).

"Significant interest" is defined as a person who beneficially owns more than 10% of an issuer, or, in the case of a group of persons, the group beneficially owns more than 50% of an issuer. See, for example, A.S.A. s. 151(1)(b); B.C.S.A. s. 120(2)(b); Nfld.S.A. s. 111(b); N.S.S.A. s. 118(b); O.S.A. s. 110(2)(a); S.S.A. s. 119(1)(b).

A person or group of persons owning beneficially (directly or indirectly, individually or collectively) voting securities carrying more than 20% of the voting rights attached to all outstanding voting securities of the issuer is referred to in most acts as a "substantial security holder" — see, for example, A.S.A. s. 151(1)(c); B.C.S.A. s. 120(2)(c); Nfld.S.A. s. 111(c); N.S.S.A. s. 118(c); O.S.A. s. 110(2)(b); S.S.A. s. 119(1)(c).

standing voting securities of the issuer.[46] A mutual fund is also not to knowingly enter into a contract or any other arrangement in which it becomes directly or indirectly liable or contingently liable in respect of an investment in or to any person in whom it is prohibited from making the investments described above.[47] Applications can be made to the relevant securities commissions for relief from these restrictions on the basis that the investment or contract represents the "business judgment of responsible persons uninfluenced by considerations other than the best interests of the mutual fund" or on the basis that it is in the best interests of the mutual fund.[48]

A mutual fund is also not to make an investment where any of the persons in whom the mutual fund, its manager or distributor are prohibited from making an investment will receive a fee or other compensation. An exception is made where the fees are paid under a contract disclosed in the prospectus or where the commission, on application by the mutual fund, so orders on the basis that it would not be prejudicial to the public interest to do so.[49] A mutual fund manager must file a report within 30 days of the end of the month for each mutual fund managed by the mutual fund manager with respect to transactions with persons whom the mutual fund, its manager or distributor are prohibited from transacting.[50]

There are also special conflict of interest rules that apply where the manager of the mutual fund is a registered dealer.[51] Such a mutual fund is not to knowingly make an investment in any class of securities of any issuer for which the dealer-manager has acted

---

[46] A.S.A. s. 152(2)(b); B.C.S.A. s. 121(2)(b); Nfld.S.A. s. 112(2)(b); N.S.S.A. s. 119(2)(b); O.S.A. s. 111(2)(b); S.S.A. s. 120(2)(b).

[47] A.S.A. s. 153; B.C.S.A. s. 122; Nfld.S.A. s. 113; N.S.S.A. s. 120; O.S.A. s. 112; S.S.A. s. 121.

[48] A.S.A. s. 154; B.C.S.A. s. 123; Nfld.S.A. s. 114; N.S.S.A. s. 121; O.S.A. s. 113; S.S.A. s. 122.

[49] A.S.A. s. 156; B.C.S.A. s. 124; Nfld.S.A. s. 116; N.S.S.A. s. 123; O.S.A. s. 115; S.S.A. s. 124.

[50] A.S.A. s. 158(1) and Form 38; B.C.S.A. s. 126, Form 39; Nfld.S.A. s. 118(1) and Form 37; N.S.S.A. s. 125(1) and Form 39; O.S.A. s. 117, Form 39; S.S.A. s. 126(1) and Form 36.

[51] A registered dealer may act as a manager of a mutual fund where securities authorities are satisfied that the dealer-manager has one or more persons who are directly responsible for the portfolio management of the mutual fund who would qualify as an investment counsel and portfolio manager (see N.P. #39, s. 4.01).

as underwriter in the previous 60 days or of which any partner, director, officer or employee of the dealer-manager, or its affiliates or associates, is an officer or director.[52] The dealer may purchase securities from a mutual fund it manages, or sell securities to a mutual fund it manages, as long as when it purchases from a mutual fund it manages, it pays not less than the bid price on any public quotations in common use, and when it sells securities to a mutual fund it manages, it sells at not more than the ask price for the securities on public quotations in common use.[53]

2. Investment Restrictions

There are several restrictions on the kinds of investments that mutual funds can make. These are apparently directed to assuring that the fund remains what the investor presumably anticipates, namely, that the fund is a vehicle for investing in securities of issuers and does not exist for the purpose of making other types of investments or controlling other issuers. The restrictions are also directed at reducing the risk to which the portfolio will be exposed.

For instance, mutual funds, without the approval of securities administrators, are not permitted to invest in real estate,[54] write options (other than covered clearing corporation call options),[55] or purchase or sell commodities or commodity futures contracts or options.[56] Mutual funds are not to make investments where they

---

[52]N.P. #39, s. 4.02. These restrictions do not apply with respect to securities issued or guaranteed by the Government of Canada or a province or by an agency of the Government of Canada or a province. The underwriting restriction does not apply where the dealer-manager acts solely as a member of a selling group and distributes not more than 5% of the securities underwritten. The restrictions with respect to issuers in which partners, directors, officers or employees of the dealer-manager or its affiliates or associates serve as directors or officers does not apply where the partner, director, officer or employee does not participate in the formulation of investment decisions made on behalf of the mutual fund, does not have access prior to implementation of investment decisions made on behalf of the mutual fund and does not influence investment decisions made on behalf of the mutual fund.

[53]N.P. #39, s. 4.03.

[54]N.P. #39, s. 2.04(2).

[55]N.P. #39, s. 2.04(6).

[56]N.P. #39, s. 2.04(10).

end up with more than 10% of any class, or series of a class, of securities of an issuer nor purchase securities for the purpose of exercising control or management of an issuer of securities.[57] A mutual fund is not to have more than 10% of its net assets invested in any one issuer.[58] It is not to have more than 10% of its total assets invested in gold or gold certificates,[59] nor in securities which are subject to share transfer restrictions.[60] It is not to have more than 10% of its net assets invested in clearing corporation options or warrants or rights.[61] There are restrictions on the purchase of mortgages[62] and there are restrictions on investment in the securities of other mutual funds.[63]

There are further restrictions on the investment practices of a mutual fund. For instance, a mutual fund may not, without prior approval, invest more than 10% of its net assets in liquid investments, purchase securities on margin, sell securities short, engage in the business of underwriting securities, lend money other than through the purchase of debt obligations, lend portfolio securities, guarantee the securities or obligations of any other person, purchase securities through other than normal market facilities unless the purchase price approximates the prevailing market price or is negotiated on an arm's length basis.[64] Without the prior approval of securities authorities,

---

[57] N.P. #39, s. 2.04(1)(b), (8).

[58] N.P. #39, s. 2.04(1)(a).

[59] N.P. #39, s. 2.04(9).

[60] N.P. #39, s. 2.04(5).

[61] N.P. #39, s. 2.04(7). This does not prevent it from investing in securities that have warrants attached thereto or buying securities offered in units consisting in part of warrants or rights or acquiring warrants or rights that are issued to the mutual fund as a holder of a security — see N.P. #39, s. 2.04(7).

[62] N.P. #39, s. 2.04(3), (4).

[63] N.P. #39, s. 2.04(11). There are exceptions to this, such as where there are provisions to deal with conflicts of interest and avoid the duplication of management fees and sales charges and these are described in the prospectus — see N.P. #39, s. 2.04(11). The securities administrators recommend that prior approval of investment in other mutual funds be obtained from the securities administrators. This prior approval is required where the mutual fund invests more than 10% of its net assets in other mutual funds or where it holds more than 10% of any class, or series of a class, of securities of another mutual fund — see N.P. #39, s. 2.04.

[64] N.P. #39, s. 2.05. "Liquid investments" are defined as investments which may not be disposed of, in a marketplace where such investments are normally

mutual funds are not to borrow money or pledge their assets except as a temporary measure for the purposes of meeting redemption requests.[65] Investment in certain permitted derivative securities is allowed for hedging purposes and other purchases of derivative securities and forward contracts is permitted subject to certain restrictions.[66]

3. Investment in Mortgages and Hypothecs

National Policy #29 provides restrictions on investments by mutual funds in mortgages where more than 10% of its portfolio is invested in mortgages. For instance, it provides for minimum amounts of funds to be invested in liquid assets such as cash or deposits at banks or trust companies, debt securities valued at market or guaranteed by the federal government or provincial governments, or money market instruments.[67] It restricts investment in mortgages on raw or undeveloped land, mortgages other than first mortgages, mortgages secured by unappraised property, and mortgages for more than 75% of the fair market value of the property unless the mortgage is insured.[68] There are also limitations on the amounts can be invested in mortgages with the limitation based on the net assets of the fund,[69] and there are restrictions with respect to the terms to maturity of the mortgages.[70] There are also conflict of interest restrictions with respect to investment in mortgages.[71]

There are extensive disclosure requirements for mutual funds investing more than 10% of their portfolio in mortgages. Disclosure is required with respect to such matters as the method of determining

---

purchased and sold and public quotations in common use in respect thereof are available, at an amount at least equal to the amount at which such investments are valued for the purpose of determining the net asset value of the mutual fund (N.P. #39, s. 2.06).

[65] N.P. #39, s. 2.05(1). Furthermore, any such permitted borrowings are not to exceed 5% of the net assets of the mutual fund (N.P. #39, s. 2.05(1)).

[66] N.P. #39, s. 2.07.

[67] N.P. #29, s. III.(l).

[68] N.P. #29, s. III.(2).

[69] N.P. #29, s. III.(2.1)(h).

[70] N.P. #29, s. III.(2.1)(g).

[71] N.P. #29, ss. III.(2.1)(i) and III.(2.4).

the value of the mortgages, types of mortgages held and the applicable interest rates, terms to maturity, geographical distribution of the mortgages, and the status of mortgages having amounts which are more than 90 days in arrears.[72]

C. Disclosure of Investment Practices

The prospectus of the mutual fund must disclose its investment restrictions and practices. The "standard investment restrictions and practices", of the type described above, need not be set out in the prospectus. The prospectus need only state that the mutual fund has adopted the standard investment restrictions and practices, that they are incorporated by reference into the prospectus and that a copy of them will be provided on request. Any investment restrictions and practices in addition to, or approved variances from, the standard investment restrictions and practices must be set out in the prospectus.[73]

Where the mutual fund intends to invest in foreign securities, concentrate its investments in a particular class or kind of industry, invest a specific portion of its assets in a particular type of security or invest in property other than securities it must state this in its prospectus.[74]

V. APPROVAL OF CHANGES

National Policy #39 imposes requirements designed to give protection to mutual fund investors with respect to fundamental changes to the mutual fund. Such changes are subject to either approval by securities administrators or by the mutual fund security holders or both.

A. Approval by Securities Administrators

Prior approval of securities administrators is required for a change of the manager of a mutual fund, a change in control of

---

[72] N.P. #29, s. IV.

[73] N.P. #39, s. 2.08.

[74] N.P. #39, s. 2.01.

the manager of the mutual fund or a change in the custodian of the assets of a mutual fund where there has been or is to be a change in the manager, or the control of the manager, of the mutual fund.[75]

B. Approval by Securities Holders

Approval by security holders is required for a change in the manager of the mutual fund, any change in the fundamental investment objectives of the mutual fund, any change of auditors, any decrease in the frequency of calculating the net asset value of the fund, and any other matter for which security holder approval is required by the constating documents of the mutual fund, by the laws applicable to the mutual fund or by any agreement to be submitted to the security holders.[76] Approval is also required for a change in any contract, or the entering into of a new contract, which will result in a change in the basis for the calculation of fees or expenses charged to the mutual fund which could result in an increase in charges to the mutual fund.[77]

Unless the constating documents of the mutual fund, the laws applicable to the mutual fund, or any agreement provide for a greater majority, approval is effected by a majority of the votes cast by the mutual fund security holders at a meeting called for the purpose

---

[75] N.P. #39, s. 9.01. Approval is not required for a change in the mutual fund manager where the change is simply to an affiliate of the existing manager (N.P. #39, s. 9.01(1)). Section 9.02 of N.P. #39 also provides for a system for multi-jurisdictional approval with the mutual fund making application in the jurisdiction in the province where the mutual fund is managed and sending a copy to the other jurisdictions where it sells its securities. The principal jurisdiction will contact the securities administrators of the other jurisdictions for their comments.

[76] N.P. #39, s. 6.01. The approval of a change of the mutual fund manager is not required where the change is simply to an affiliate of the existing manager (N.P. #39, s. 6.01(b)).

[77] N.P. #39, s. 6.01(a). The approval is not required where the mutual fund contracts at arm's length and with parties other than the manager of the mutual fund, or its associates or affiliates, or where the mutual fund has neither a sales charge nor redemption fee (other than a redemption fee for redemptions effected within 90 days of the purchase of the securities of the mutual fund) as long as the prospectus notes that the security holders will be given at least 60 days' notice before the effective date of any change that could result in an increase in charges to the mutual fund and such notice is actually given (N.P. #39, s. 6.03).

of considering the change.[78] There must be 21 days' notice for the meeting and compliance with the applicable proxy solicitation requirements.[79]

VI. CONTRACTUAL PLANS

Where a mutual fund provides for a contractual plan that allows the investor to build up an investment in the mutual fund through a series of purchases over a specified period, the sales charges on the plan are often more heavily taken out of the earlier payments to the plan. With most of the payments made having gone to cover sales charges in the early stages of the plan, an investor who redeems securities in the early stages of the plan could end up having very little of their investment returned. To protect investors from surprises of this kind, National Policy #39 sets out restrictions on the rate of sales charges and provides the investor with withdrawal rights.

Where sales charges on any periodic payment under a contractual plan exceed the maximum sales charges that would apply to a single lump sum purchase then several restrictions apply. First, the payments must be scheduled in equal amounts on a weekly, monthly, quarterly, half-yearly or yearly basis, provided that a double or a triple instalment may be required as the first payment.[80] Second, the sales charges levied against any payment to be made in the first 12 months of the plan must not exceed 50% of the individual payments under the plan and the remaining payments made under the plan must, to the extent reasonably practicable, be levied at an equal rate.[81] The total sales charges levied during the term of the plan are not to exceed 12% of the face amount of the plan.[82]

The minimum withdrawal rights specified must allow the planholder to withdraw from the plan at any time within 60 days of

---

[78] N.P. #39, s. 6.03.

[79] N.P. #39, s. 6.04.

[80] N.P. #39, s. 10.01(1).

[81] N.P. #39, s. 10.01(2). A higher total amount of sales charges can be deducted in the second year where the sales charges in the first year do not exceed 50% of the payments scheduled to be made in the first year and as long as the percentage deducted from any payment for sales charges does not exceed the percentage deducted from any previous payment and the total sales charges levied during the term of the plan do not exceed 12% of the face value of the plan.

[82] Ibid.

receipt of the confirmation of the initial payment. Upon withdrawal the planholder is entitled to receive a refund equal to the amount of all sales charges paid in respect of the plan, plus all payments scheduled to be made and actually made during the first 60 days of the plan and, with respect to prepayments of additional payments scheduled to be made under the plan, the net asset value of the securities purchased for the planholder.[83]

After 60 days from the plan date and up to 365 days after the plan date, the planholder is to continue to be entitled to rescind their obligations under the plan. Where the planholder exercises the right of rescission during this period they are entitled to receive a refund equal to the net asset value of securities purchased under the plan plus the amount by which the sales charges exceed 30% of the payments scheduled to be made and actually made under the plan up to the end of the 365-day period.[84]

The withdrawal rights are to be set out in the mutual fund prospectus and in the copy of the contractual plan, a document supplied with the contractual plan, or in the confirmations of purchases of securities made during the first 60 days of the plan.[85]

VII. SALE AND REDEMPTION

There are provisions in National Policy #39, with respect to sales and redemptions of mutual fund securities, that are directed to ensuring that funds invested through a distributor are received promptly by the mutual fund. The provisions are also directed to ensuring that during the period from the delivery of funds by the investor to the time of receipt by the mutual fund the risk of loss of an investor's funds is reduced and interest on the investor's funds accrues to either the investor or the mutual fund. Furthermore, the provisions seek to ensure that interest earned on an investor's funds during the period from the acceptance by the mutual fund of the investor's order for redemption to the time of receipt of such funds

---

[83] N.P. #39, s. 10.03(a). The refund of the net asset value of securities purchased with prepayments can be limited to the amount of the prepayments.

[84] N.P. #39, s. 10.03(b).

[85] N.P. #39, s. 10.03.

by the investor accrues to the benefit of the mutual fund.[86] To accomplish these objectives there are provisions requiring that transmittal of orders for the purchase or redemption of securities be expedited, setting out time restrictions for the acceptance or rejection of orders to purchase securities, determining the time of pricing for sales and redemptions and the frequency of determining net asset value, setting a maximum time for payment of the issue price of securities, and setting out trust requirements for distributors.[87]

Orders received by sales representatives for the purchase or redemption of mutual fund securities are to be transmitted to the principal office of the principal distributor of the mutual fund's securities in the shortest time possible and no later than the same day they are received.[88] A right to accept or reject an order must be clearly set out in the prospectus and a decision to accept or reject an order to purchase securities must be made promptly, and in any event, within two days of receipt of the order.[89] Where an order is rejected all monies received with the order must be returned promptly.[90]

The purchase price for the purchase or redemption of securities is set according to the next determination of net asset value after the receipt of the order.[91] The net asset value is to be determined at least once each week unless the shareholders approve of a longer period of up to one month.[92] The period for the payment of the issue price by the investor is to be as short as possible and is not to exceed five days from the date of the determination of the issue

---

[86]N.P. #39, s. 11.01.

[87]See generally N.P. #39, ss. 11 and 12.

[88]N.p #39 s. 11.02.

[89]N.P. #39, s. 11.03.

[90]Ibid.

[91]N.P. #39, s. 11.04(1). The mutual fund is deemed to receive an order for the purchase or redemption of securities when the order is actually received by the mutual fund at its principal office or at the principal office of the principal distributor of the mutual fund, or at such other office as may be designated for that purpose (see N.P. #39, s. 11.04(2)). Setting the price for a purchase or redemption according to the time of an earlier determination of net asset value is considered unacceptable (see N.P. #39, s 11.04(3)).

[92]N.P. #39, s. 11.05.

price.[93] If the issue price is not paid within the five-day period, the mutual fund is deemed to have received an order for redemption.[94] The redemption proceeds are to be applied to reduce the amount owing on the purchase and if the redemption proceeds exceed the purchase price, the excess belongs to the mutual fund.[95] If the redemption proceeds are less than the price of the securities, then the difference is a debt of the principal distributor which the principal distributor is entitled to collect from the dealer who took the order.[96]

Monies received by the principal distributor for investment in mutual fund securities or on redemption of mutual fund securities must be separately accounted for and deposited in interest-bearing trust accounts with interest accruing on the accounts to be paid to the mutual fund at least once a month.[97] The amounts are not to be used to finance operations of the principal distributor.[98] Monies may only be withdrawn from the trust accounts for the purpose of remitting amounts to be invested to the mutual fund, to pay redemption proceeds to investors and to pay sales or service charges to which the principal distributor may be entitled.[99] The monies received for the purchase of securities are to be paid to the mutual fund as soon as possible and in any event by the second business day after they are received.[100] The principal distributor must not transfer, pledge, encumber or otherwise deal with the securities of a mutual fund that it holds in safekeeping for investors except according to the terms of a written agreement between the principal distributor and the investor.[101] Similar provisions extend these trust obligations to any dealer that participates with a mutual fund or a principal distributor of a mutual fund in the distribution of securities of the mutual fund.[102]

---

[93] N.P. #39, s. 11.07(1).

[94] N.P. #39, s. 11.07(3).

[95] Ibid.

[96] Ibid.

[97] N.P. #39, s. 12.01(1), (4).

[98] N.P. #39, s. 12.01(2).

[99] N.P. #39, s. 12.01(3).

[100] N.P. #39, s. 12.01(5).

[101] N.P. #39, s. 12.06(6).

[102] N.P. #39, s. 12.03.

Security holders of mutual funds are to be provided at least annually with a statement outlining the procedures to be followed by a security holder to redeem securities of the mutual fund.[103] Payments for redemptions are to be made within five business days of the date of the determination of the net asset value for the purpose of the redemption.[104] With the prior written consent of the security holder, payment of the redemption price can be satisfied by the delivery of portfolio securities of the mutual fund.[105]

VIII. MANAGEMENT FEES

The management fees of a mutual fund cannot be charged on an incentive basis without prior approval of securities administrators.[106] Where it is proposed that an incentive fee is to be charged, there must be an appropriate benchmark or relevant index against which performance is to be measured and this benchmark must be satisfactory to the securities administrators.[107] National Policy #39 also requires that it be provided that if the benchmark is not met in any period, no incentive fee is to be paid until the performance of the mutual fund has equalled or exceeded the benchmark on a cumulative basis.[108]

The financial statements of the mutual fund must set out the fees and other expenses of the mutual fund in appropriate detail and must set out in tabular form a management expense ratio for each of the last five completed financial years.[109] The management expense ratio is determined by dividing the sum of all fees and expenses other than commissions and brokerage fees, interest charges and taxes, by the average net asset value of the fund for the financial year.[110]

---

[103] N.P. #39, s. 13.01.

[104] N.P. #39, s. 13.01(1)

[105] N.P. #39, s. 13.03.

[106] N.P. #39, s. 8.02.

[107] Ibid.

[108] Ibid.

[109] N.P. #39, s. 8.03(1), (5).

[110] N.P. #39, s. 8.03(1), (4).

IX. CUSTODIANSHIP

The portfolio securities of a mutual fund must be held by a custodian and must be held in Canada.[111] Only certain specified institutions are allowed to act as custodians. The specified institutions are Canadian chartered banks, or a subsidiary of a Canadian chartered bank having shareholders' equity of not less than $10,000,000 and trust companies incorporated under the laws of Canada or a province of Canada and having shareholders' equity of not less than $10,000,000 or a subsidiary of such a trust company having shareholders' equity of not less than $10,000,000.[112] Where the mutual fund holds foreign securities, they may be held through sub-custodians outside of Canada.[113]

Where registered securities are not registered in the name of the mutual fund, there must be provision in the records of the custodian or sub-custodian indicating that beneficial ownership of the securities is vested in the mutual fund.[114] Where the securities are held in bearer form, they must be designated or segregated by the custodian or sub-custodian, or their nominees, so as to establish that the beneficial ownership of the securities is vested in the mutual fund.[115] Securities may be held in a book-based system by a depository institution, such as the Canadian Depository For Securities, in which the beneficial ownership of securities is identified with bookkeeping entries and transfers are made without physical delivery of security certificates.[116] Where securities are held in this form,

---

[111] N.P. #39, s. 7.01(1), (2).

[112] N.P. #39, s. 7.02.

[113] N.P. #39, s. 7.01(3). Only specified institutions are allowed to act as subcustodians. The specified institutions are those that can act as custodians (these are described in N.P. #39, s. 7.02) or banking institutions or trust companies, or their subsidiaries, that are incorporated under the laws of a country other than Canada which are regulated by that other country and the institution or its subsidiary acting as a sub-custodian has shareholders' equity of not less than $100,000,000 (see N.P. #39, s. 7.03). Provision must be made with the sub-custodian preventing any further sub-delegation, providing for similar terms and conditions of custodianship as between the custodian and the mutual fund and for the enforcement of the terms of the sub-custodianship agreement (see N.P. #39, s. 7.01(3)).

[114] N.P. #39, s. 7.01(5).

[115] Ibid.

[116] N.P. #39, s. 7.01(9).

the depository institution does not thereby become a custodian of the mutual fund's portfolio securities.[117]

National Policy #39 specifies certain provisions that must be included in the custodianship agreement and in sub-custodianship agreements. For instance, the agreement with the custodian or subcustodian may not allow the custodian or sub-custodian to mortgage, pledge, hypothecate, charge, or have any lien or other security interest in the portfolio securities of the mutual fund except a lien with respect to the payment of custodianship fees or expenses.[118] The custodianship agreement must provide that the custodian must meet a minimum standard of care, namely, that in safekeeping or dealing in the portfolio securities of the mutual fund, it exercise the degree of care which it gives to its own property of similar kind being kept by the custodian.[119] A copy of the custodianship agreement or any sub-custodianship agreements must be delivered to the securities administrators upon request.[120]

X. ADVERTISING

National Policy #39 also contains provisions with respect to advertisements and sales communications. These provisions are intended to deal with potential misleading statements in mutual fund advertising or sales communications. It is also intended to standardize the method of calculation of performance information so that data comparing mutual funds can be included in sales communications in a way that is less likely to be misleading.[121]

XI. INSIDER TRADING

No person who has access to information concerning the investment program of a mutual fund can purchase or sell securities of an issuer for that person's own account where the portfolio secu-

---

[117] Ibid.

[118] N.P. #39, s. 7.01(7).

[119] N.P. #39, s. 7.01(6).

[120] N.P. #39, s. 7.01(11).

[121] See N.P. #39, s. 16. The provisions under s. 16 are lengthy and detailed and thus are beyond the scope of this introductory text.

rities of the mutual fund include securities of that issuer and where the information is used by the person for his, her or its direct benefit or advantage.[122] Where a person engages in the purchase or sale of securities in such circumstances, the person is subject to penal sanction[123] and is liable to account to the mutual fund for any benefit or advantage received or receivable.[124]

XII. PRIVATE MUTUAL FUNDS

Private mutual funds are exempt from the regulations discussed above.[125] A private mutual fund is typically defined as a mutual fund having not more than 50 security holders, has never sought to borrow money from the public, does not pay or give any remuneration for investment, management or administration advice in respect of trades in securities, except normal brokerage fees, and all of its members are required to make contributions in proportion to the securities each holds for the purpose of financing its operations.[126] A private mutual fund is frequently defined under provincial securities acts to include a mutual fund that is administered by a trust company and consists of a "common trust fund".[127]

---

[122] A.S.A. s. 160; B.C.S.A. s. 111; M.S.A. s. 113(3); Nfld.S.A. s. 120; N.S.S.A. s. 127; O.S.A. s. 119; Q.S.A. ss. 190, 191; S.S.A. s. 128.

[123] A.S.A. s. 161(1)(e); B.C.S.A. s. 138(1)(c); M.S.A. s. 136(1)(c); Nfld.S.A. s. 122(1)(c); N.S.S.A. s. 129(1)(c); O.S.A. s. 122(1)(c); Q.S.A. s. 202; S.S.A. s. 131(3)(c).

[124] A.S.A. s. 171(7); B.C.S.A. s. 119(4); M.S.A. s. 113(4); Nfld.S.A. s. 134(3); N.S.S.A. s. 142(3); O.S.A. s. 134(3); Q.S.A. s. 228; S.S.A. s. 142(3).

[125] A.S.A. s. 66(c), 115(1)(a); B.C.S.A. s. 32(c), 58(1)(a); Nfld.S.A. s. 36(2)(c), 74(1)(a); N.S.S.A. ss. 41(2)(c), 78(1)(a); O.S.A. ss. 35(2), 3, 73(1)(a); S.S.A. ss. 39(2)(c), 82(1)(a).

[126] See, for example, A.S.A. s. 1(q); B.C.S.A. s. 1(1); Nfld.S.A. s. 2(ii); N.S.S.A. s. 2(1)(ah); O.S.A. s. 1(1); S.S.A. s. 2(1)(kk).

[127] See, for example, A.S.A. s. 1(q)(ii); B.C.S.A. s. 1(1); Nfld.S.A. s. 2(ii); O.S.A. s. 1(1).

XIII. MUTUAL FUND SALES PRACTICES

A. Background

Several questionable sales practices developed with the exceptional growth in mutual funds. Concerns about these sales practices were addressed in a report of the Investment Funds Institute of Canada in 1991.[128] This was followed by the introduction of a voluntary code in October of 1991. An extensive review of mutual funds was then undertaken by the Ontario Securities Commission. A report, known as the Stromberg Report, was released in 1995.[129]

B. Mutual Fund Sales Practice Concerns

The Stromberg Report identified several questionable mutual fund sales practices. These sales practices raised conflict of interest concerns in which sales incentives encouraged advice given to investors on mutual fund purchases and sales that would be in the interests of the advisors or salespersons rather than in the interests of the investor. Several of these questionable sales practices are briefly described below.

1. *Trailer Fees*

For example, it became common for mutual funds to pay a service fee or "trailer fee" to mutual fund salespersons based on a percentage of the net asset value of an investor's interest in the particular mutual fund. The fee was payable on an ongoing basis for as long as the investor kept the investment in the mutual fund. The trailer fees were said to be necessary to support ongoing services that sales representatives provided, such as monitoring the performance of their client's investment funds, providing tax advice, and answering inquiries about client accounts.[130] These trailer fees could

---

[128]See (1998) OSCB 770.

[129] *Regulatory Strategies for the Mid-'90s: Recommendations for Regulating Investment Funds in Canada* (Ontario Securities Commission, January 1995). The report was prepared by Ontario Securities Commission Commissioner Glorianne Stromberg.

[130]It seems odd that charges for such services should be paid by mutual funds rather than directly by the clients being served. In fact, in spite of the trailer fee paid, these investment services were often provided by the mutual fund managers

vary from one mutual fund to another. Thus mutual fund sales-persons might be tempted to recommend that a client shift her or his investment from a low trailer fee fund to a higher trailer fee fund, even though the change in the mutual funds invested in was not appropriate for the particular client. Similarly, a high trailer fee may tempt a salesperson not to recommend a change in the mutual funds invested in even where such a change was in the interests of the client.[131]

2. Reciprocal Commissions

Another way in which mutual funds compensated sales represen-tatives was to have the mutual fund managers direct orders for pur-chases and sales of securities for the mutual fund portfolio through sales representatives. Sales representatives would then forward these orders to the trading department of their firm.[132] The brokerage commissions for these trades would then be split between the firm and the sales representative. The volume of orders that would be directed through a particular sales representative was based on the amount of the mutual fund securities sold by that sales represen-tative. This practice raised questions as to whether mutual fund man-agers were executing mutual fund portfolio transactions in the most efficient manner.[133] It could also raise conflicts of interest between sales representatives and their clients if the sales representative rec-ommended a particular mutual fund on the basis that it provided greater potential commissions from mutual fund portfolio trading than some other mutual fund.

---

themselves with the costs included in their management fees. Investors were thus effectively paying twice for the services. See the Stromberg Report, *supra* note 1, at 56.

[131] On the use of trailer fees see the Stromberg Report, *supra* note 129 at 55-59.

[132] Another technique was to have the mutual fund manager place the order directly with the trading department and also call the sales representative to advise that the order had been placed and to advise of the portion of the order that was attributed to the particular sales representative. See the Stromberg Report, *supra* note 129, at 61.

[133] Stromberg Report, *supra* note 129, at 60-63.

3. *Marketing Incentive Programs*

The Stromberg Report also noted the use of marketing incentive programs in which sales representatives could earn points based on the amount or value of securities of a particular mutual fund they sold. The points earned could then be redeemed for products or services by presenting the invoice for the product or service to have it paid by the mutual fund.[134]

4. *Trailer Fee Split Payments*

Trailer fees are normally paid to the sales representative's firm. However, a variation on this developed. Part of the trailer fee would be held back in a pool of funds that individual sales representatives could draw on for the purchase of products or services for their own use. Some sales representatives allegedly did not report the receipt of these products or services as income for tax purposes.[135] As with other sales practices, this technique could taint investment advice where the sales representative was tempted by how generous one mutual fund organization's split payments were compared to those of another.

5. *Trips and Other Non-Cash Sales Incentives*

Mutual fund organizations often provided expense paid trips for sales representatives. These were trips to conferences, seminars or trade shows that could provide useful information to sales representatives in advising their clients. However, a related practice that developed was to have these trips provide the opportunity to add on vacations at little or no cost.[136] To the extent these opportunities depended on the amount or value of sales of a particular mutual fund by individual sales representatives, it may have influenced the advice they gave to mutual fund investors.

---

[134] Ibid., at 63.

[135] Ibid., at 64.

[136] Ibid., at 65-66.

6. *Cooperative Advertising*

Another way in which mutual fund organizations compensated sales firms or individual sales representatives was to pay for all or a portion of the promotional activities of the firms or individuals. Promotional expenses covered included such things as the cost of preparing and sending newsletters, the preparation of a business plan or the cost of space at a trade show.[137] The degree to which a mutual fund organization offered to pay such expenses might have influenced the mutual fund investment advice provided to investors.

7. *Bonus Commissions*

Bonus commissions might also be paid to sales representatives based on the amount or value of sales of a particular mutual fund by individual sales representatives.[138] Differences in the amounts of such payments by different mutual fund organizations could result in investment advice based on the bonus a sales representative would receive rather than the best interests of the investor.

8. *Reimbursement of Expenses*

Payments were being made, in some cases, to compensate securities firms or their representatives for expenses incurred by them in the running of their business.[139] This could influence advice given in the choice of a mutual fund investment for an investor.

C. Response to Mutual Fund Sales Practice Concerns

In response to the Stromberg Report, the Investment Funds Institute of Canada prepared a revised code of conduct for the mutual fund industry. However, there was no self-regulatory organization which could make the code applicable to all distributors of mutual fund securities. Consequently the Investment Funds Institute of Canada recommended that the code be reflected in Canadian

---

[137] Ibid., at 67.

[138] Ibid., at 68.

[139] Ibid., at 69.

securities regulation.[140] The Ontario Securities Commission responded with a draft rule in August of 1996.[141] An amended version of this became National Instrument 81-105 which was issued with a Companion Policy 81-105CP.

National Instrument 81-105 sets out a general prohibition on mutual fund sales practices and then permits a number of sales practices subject to certain restrictions. It then requires disclosure of the compensation of distributors and dealers, their sales practices, and the relationship between the mutual fund organization members,[142] participating dealers and their representatives in terms of the equity interests they have in each other.

1. *The Broad Prohibition of Certain Sales Practices*

The NI takes the common securities regulatory approach of making a very broad prohibition but then providing a number of exceptions. It begins by prohibiting any member of a mutual fund organization from paying money to, or providing a non-monetary benefit to, a dealer or dealer representative in connection with the distribution of securities of the mutual fund.[143] It also prohibits any member of a mutual fund organization from reimbursing expenses incurred by a mutual fund dealer or representative in connection

---

[140] See (1998) 21 OSCB 770-71.

[141] (1996) 19 OSCB 4734.

[142] The members of the organization of a mutual fund are the manager of the fund, its principal distributor, its portfolio advisor or an affiliate of any of these persons. It also includes a person organized by the mutual fund as a vehicle to fund payment of commissions to participating dealers and that has a right to arrange for the distribution of mutual fund securities. See NI 81-105, s. 1.1.

[143] NI 81-105, s. 2.1(1). The provisions refer to "participating dealers" although this term is not defined in the NI or in NP #39. A "representative" of a participating dealer means a partner, director, officer, salesperson or employee of the participating dealer and any company through which one of the above provides services to the participating dealer. See NI 81-105, s. 1.1. The phrase "in connection with the distribution of securities" is considered to include anything done in furtherance of the sale, distribution or marketing of the securities of a mutual fund. Thus promotional activities relating to the investment in securities or mutual funds generally, or educational activities concerning financial, investment or retirement planning are included in the activities to which the prohibition relates. See Companion Policy 81-105CP, s. 4.1.

with the distribution of securities of the mutual fund.[144] A member of a mutual fund organization is also prohibited from making, or representing that it will provide a payment, non-monetary benefit or reimbursement of an expense conditional on the sale of a particular amount or value of securities of one or more mutual funds by a dealer or dealer representative, or that is conditional on a particular amount or value of securities of one or more mutual funds held in the accounts of clients of the dealer or dealer representative.[145] Similarly, dealers and their representatives are prohibited from accepting payments, non-monetary benefits or reimbursements of expenses from a mutual fund or members of a mutual fund organizations in connection with the distribution of securities of the mutual fund.[146]

2. Permitted Sales Practices

A number of exceptions to these broad prohibitions are provided.[147] Several of these exceptions are discussed below.

a. COMMISSIONS

The NI allows a payment by a member of a mutual fund organization to a dealer if the obligation to make the payment arises at the time of the trade in the mutual fund and the prospectus of the mutual fund discloses the range of rates of commissions that may be paid and how they will be calculated.[148] The rate of commission cannot be increased based on increases in the amount or value of securities of the mutual fund sold, increases in the amount or value of mutual fund securities held in accounts of clients of the dealer, or for a particular part of the year in which the commission is paid or earned.[149]

---

[144] Ibid.

[145] Ibid., s. 2.1(2).

[146] Ibid., s. 2.2(1).

[147] The broad prohibitions in NI 81-105, ss. 2.1 and 2.2 are subject to the sales practices permitted by Parts 3 and 5 of the NI. See ss. 2.1(2) and 2.2(2).

[148] NI 81-105, s. 3.1(a) and (b).

[149] Ibid., s. 3.1.

b. TRAILER FEES

The NI permits the payment of a trailer fee if it is based on the aggregate value of securities of the mutual fund held in the accounts of clients of the dealer.[150] However, the obligation to make the payment must arise after the time of the trade and thus not as a direct consequence of the trade.[151] The prospectus must disclose the range of rates of trailer fees that may be paid and how the fees will be calculated.[152] The method of calculation of trailer fees and the time periods used in determining the amount of trailer fees must be the same for all dealers.[153] Further, the rate of the trailing commission cannot increase based on increases in the amount or value of securities of the mutual fund sold, increases in the amount or value of securities of the mutual fund held in the accounts of clients of the dealer, or for a particular period of the year in which the trailing commission is paid or earned.[154]

c. COOPERATIVE MARKETING PRACTICES

The NI also allows for cooperative marketing practices to continue subject to specific constraints. A member of a mutual fund organization may pay a dealer the direct costs incurred by the dealer with respect to a sales communication, investor conference or investor seminar prepared or presented by the dealer.[155] However, the primary purpose of the marketing activities must be to promote or provide educational information concerning the mutual fund (or family of related mutual funds).[156] The dealer must provide the mutual fund organization member with invoices for, or receipts evidencing payment of, direct costs incurred in these marketing activities.[157] The direct costs of the dealer paid by all mutual funds cannot exceed 50% of the total direct costs incurred by the dealer.[158]

---

[150] Ibid., s. 3.2(1).

[151] Ibid., s. 3.2(1)(a).

[152] Ibid., s. 3.2(1)(b).

[153] Ibid., s. 3.2(1)(c).

[154] Ibid., s. 3.2(1)(d).

[155] Ibid., s. 5.1.

[156] Ibid., s. 5.1(a).

[157] Ibid., s. 5.1(c).

[158] Ibid., s. 5.1(d).

Where the direct costs of dealer marketing activities are being paid for by mutual fund organization members, the sales communication literature must disclose the identity of all parties paying a portion of the dealer's costs.[159] Similarly, in the case of a conference or investor seminar, those attending must be informed in writing of the identity of all parties paying a portion of the dealer's costs.[160]

Where a dealer puts on a conference or seminar that is directed more generally to financial planning, investment in securities, or mutual fund industry matters, a member of the mutual fund organization may pay up to 10% of the dealer's direct costs as long as the aggregate amount of direct costs paid by members of mutual fund organizations do not exceed 66% of the total direct costs. The selection of representatives to attend the conference must be made by the dealer uninfluenced by any member of a mutual fund organization contributing to the direct costs and the conference or seminar must be held in Canada or the continental United States.[161]

d. MUTUAL FUND CONFERENCES OR SEMINARS

Members of mutual fund organizations may continue to allow dealer representatives to attend conferences or seminars organized and presented by members of the mutual fund organization, as long as the primary purpose of the conference or seminar is the provision of educational information about financial planning, investing in securities, mutual fund industry matters or educational information about the mutual fund or family of mutual funds.[162] The selection of dealer representatives must be made exclusively by the dealer uninfluenced by any member of the mutual fund organization and the conference must be held in Canada, the continental United States or, where the primary purpose is to provide information about the investments or activities carried on by the mutual fund, a location where the portfolio advisor of the mutual fund carries on business.[163] No member of the organization of the mutual fund can pay any travel, accommodation or personal incidental expenses asso-

---

[159] Ibid., s. 5.1(e).

[160] Ibid.

[161] Ibid., s. 5.5.

[162] NI 81-105, s. 5.2(a).

[163] Ibid., s. 5.2(b) and (c).

ciated with the attendance of the representative at the conference or seminar.[164] The costs of the organization and presentation of the conference or seminar must also be reasonable in relation to the purpose of the conference or seminar.[165]

e. PAYMENTS OF REPRESENTATIVE CONFERENCE, SEMINAR OR COURSE REGISTRATION FEES

A mutual fund organization member may pay the registration fees for a representative for a conference, seminar or course that is not put on by the mutual fund if the conference, seminar or course is primarily for the purpose of providing educational information about financial planning, investing in securities, mutual fund industry matters or mutual funds generally.[166] The dealer must provide invoices for, or receipts evidencing payment of, the registration fees and the selection of representatives must be made by the dealer uninfluenced by members of the mutual fund organization.[167] The conference or seminar must be held in Canada or the continental United States.[168] Similar restrictions are imposed with respect to the payment of registration fees for conferences, seminars or courses put on by the Investment Funds Institute of Canada, the Investment Dealers Association of Canada or other trade or industry association.[169]

f. NON-MONETARY BENEFITS

The provision of non-monetary benefits, such as products or services, may still be provided by a member of a mutual fund organization to a representative of a dealer. However, the non-monetary benefit must be of a promotional nature and be of a minimal value.[170] Mutual fund organization members may engage in promo-

---

[164] Ibid., s. 5.2(d).

[165] Ibid., s. 5.2(e).

[166] Ibid., s. 5.3(a).

[167] Ibid., s. 5.3(b) and (c).

[168] Ibid., s. 5.3(d).

[169] Ibid., s. 5.4(1).

[170] Ibid., s. 5.6. "Non-monetary benefits" includes any goods, services or other benefits and include such things as domestic or foreign trips, food, beverages, accommodation, entertainment, tickets to concerts, theatre or sporting events, gifts and non-cash gratuities, computer hardware and software. However, "non-monetary

tional activities that result in non-monetary benefits to representatives as long as the provisions of such benefits is not so extensive or frequent as to cause a reasonable person to question whether the provision of the benefits or activities improperly influence the investment advice given by the representative.[171] In the case of business promotional activities, the mutual fund organization members may not pay for the travel, accommodation or personal incidental expenses associated with the attendance of the representative at the activities.[172]

g. RECIPROCAL COMMISSIONS

Mutual fund organization members cannot influence how or if a dealer will allocate a brokerage commission to any representative of the dealer.[173] Mutual fund organization members also cannot advise a representative of a dealer that a particular portfolio transaction of the mutual that is to be directed to the dealer.

Mutual fund organization members cannot direct a portfolio transaction to a dealer as an inducement or reward for the sale of the mutual fund's securities, or for having maintained particular levels of the mutual fund's securities in the accounts of the dealer's clients.[174] There is a corresponding restriction on a dealer. A dealer may not solicit or execute portfolio transactions for a mutual fund as an inducement or reward for the sale of the mutual fund's securities, or for having maintained particular levels of the mutual fund's securities in the accounts of the dealer's clients.[175]

---

benefits" does not include goods and services provided by mutual fund organizations to facilitate the marketing of securities of the mutual fund, such as brochures, or educational material. Computer software that is designed to assist in determining which mutual funds of the mutual fund organization are most appropriate for a dealer's client is not considered a non-monetary benefit. Also, computer software designed to facilitate the electronic interface between the dealer and mutual fund organization members is considered a non-monetary benefit. However, financial planning software of a more general nature would likely be considered a non-monetary benefit. See Companion Policy 81-105CP, s. 4.2.

[171] Ibid., s. 5.6(a).

[172] Ibid., s. 5.6(b).

[173] Ibid., s. 6.1(1).

[174] Ibid., s. 6.1(4).

[175] Ibid., s. 6.1(5).

Mutual fund organization members can only direct a portfolio transaction through individuals designated by the dealer as the institutional representatives of the dealer.[176] In other words, mutual funds are supposed to execute their portfolio transactions using the most efficient method rather than breaking up a large transactions in order to allocate the benefits of brokerage fees amongst the persons selling mutual fund securities. There is a corresponding restriction on dealers. A dealer must execute the portfolio transaction through an individual designated by the dealer as an institutional representative of the dealer.[177]

h. OTHER SALES PRACTICES

The NI also puts restrictions on certain other sales practices such as commission rebates by dealers,[178] financial assistance to dealers or representatives by mutual fund organization members,[179] and charitable donations by mutual funds on behalf of dealers or representatives.[180]

3. Prospectus and Point of Sale Disclosure

Mutual funds must provide in their prospectus (or simplified prospectus) a complete description of the compensation payable by members of the organization of the mutual fund to their principal distributors or dealers.[181] They must also disclose the sales practices

---

[176] Ibid., s. 6.1(2).

[177] Ibid., s. 6.2.

[178] Commission rebates involve payments of investor redemption fees by dealers or representatives when an investor switches mutual fund investments. The NI sets out certain disclosure requirements if commission rebates are offered. See NI 81-105, s. 7.1.

[179] A mutual fund cannot provide financial assistance to a dealer or dealer representative and dealers and representatives cannot solicit or accept financial assistance from mutual funds. An exception is made where the financial assistance is provided by a Canadian financial institution in the ordinary course of its business if there are no conditions attached to the providing of the financial assistance that are designed to promote the distribution of particular mutual funds. See NI 81-105, s. 7.2.

[180] A mutual fund cannot make a charitable donation for which the tax credit will accrue to a dealer or dealer representative. See NI 81-105, s. 7.3.

[181] NI 81-105, s. 8.1(1)(a).

followed by the members of the organization of the mutual fund for the distribution of the securities of the mutual fund.[182]

The prospectus (or simplified prospectus) must also disclose equity interests that any member of the organization of the mutual fund has in a dealer, that a dealer and its associates have, in aggregate, in any member of the organization of a mutual fund, and that any individual representative of a participating dealer (and his or her associates) have, in aggregate, in any member of the organization of a mutual fund.[183] A similar disclosure of such equity interests must be set out in a document delivered to a purchaser for each trade of a security of a mutual fund.[184] The participating dealer must obtain the prior written consent of the purchaser to the trade after the purchaser has received the equity interest disclosure document.[185]

---

[182] Ibid., s. 8.1(1)(b).

[183] Ibid., 8.2(1). An exception is made for a member of the organization of a mutual fund which is not a reporting issuer (see s. 8.2(2)).

[184] Ibid., s. 8.2(3). However, the document need not be provided if the purchaser has made a previous purchase for which the equity disclosure document has been provided and the information in the document has not changed (see NI 81-105, s. 8.2(5)).

[185] NI s. 8.2(4). However, the consent is not required if the purchaser has made a previous purchase for which the equity disclosure document has been provided and the information in the document has not changed (see NI 81-105, s. 8.2(5)).

CHAPTER 14

ENFORCEMENT MECHANISMS

I. INTRODUCTION

The object of this chapter is to provide a summary of the various sanctions provided for under securities legislation and an overview of the administrative mechanisms for enforcing securities laws. The chapter begins, in Part II, with a review of the sanctions available under securities legislation. Parts III and IV provide an overview of the review and appeal procedures and of powers for investigations and audits.

II. SANCTIONS

A. Securities Acts

Enforcement of the provisions of securities legislation is generally provided through a variety of techniques. These include penal sanctions, administrative sanctions, and statutorily created civil causes of action.

1. *Penal Sanctions*

Securities legislation in Canada typically specifies a range of offences for which penal sanctions are provided.

a. OFFENCES

(i) False Statement to Administrators, Investigators or Auditors

It is an offence for a person to make a false statement in evidence or information required to be given under the applicable securities laws to securities administrators or to a person appointed under the legislation to make an investigation or audit.[1]

(ii) Failure to File

It is an offence for a person to fail to file or send a record required to be filed or sent, or to not file or send the record within the required period of time.[2]

(iii) Misrepresentation

Making a statement in any record required to be filed or sent which is a misrepresentation in light of the circumstances in which it is made and at the time it is made also constitutes an offence.[3]

(iv) Contravention of Act or Regulations

Some securities acts provide that any contravention of the act or the regulations constitutes an offence.[4] Other acts set out particular provisions, contravention of which constitutes an offence. These acts also usually provide that an offence is committed where one contravenes regulations which specify that contravention of the regulation constitutes an offence.[5] The provisions (contravention of which constitutes an offence) usually include, for instance, the failure (a) to register for trading, underwriting or advising, (b) to comply with restrictions on registrants such as calling or telephoning at a residence or making prohibited representations, (c) to file a prospectus as required, (d) to report material changes or provide insider trading reports, (e) to comply with the takeover bid requirements,

---

[1] A.S.A. s. 161(1)(a); B.C.S.A. s. 155(1)(a); M.S.A. s. 136(1)(a); Nfld.S.A. s. 122(1)(a); N.S.S.A. s. 129(1)(a); N.W.T.S.A. s. 49(1)(a); O.S.A. s. 122(1)(a); S.S.A. s. 131(3)(a); Y.S.A. s. 46(1)(a).

[2] A.S.A. s. 161(c.1); B.C.S.A. s. 155(1)(b); N.B.S.F.P.A. s. 21(4); P.E.I.S.A. s. 17(3) (failure to furnish required information); O.S.A. s. 195(3).

[3] A.S.A. s. 161(1)(b); B.C.S.A. s. 155(1)(c); M.S.A. s. 136(1)(b); Nfld.S.A. s. 122(1)(b); N.S.S.A. s. 129(1)(b); N.W.T.S.A. s. 49(1)(b); O.S.A. s. 122(1)(b); P.E.I.S.A. s. 15(2); Q.S.A. s. 196; S.S.A. s. 131(3)(b); Y.S.A. s. 46(b).

[4] M.S.A. s. 136(1)(c); N.B.S.F.P.A. s. 41; Nfld.S.A. s. 122(1)(c); N.S.S.A. s. 129(1)(c); N.W.T.S.A. s. 49(1)(c); O.S.A. s. 122(1)(c); P.E.I.S.A. s. 28; Q.S.A. ss. 202, 203; S.S.A. s. 131(3)(c); Y.S.A. s. 46(1)(c).

[5] See, for example, A.S.A. s. 161(1)(d), (e); B.C.S.A. s. 155(1)(d), (f).

or (f) to solicit proxies as required or to send required proxy circulars.[6]

(v) Failure to Comply with a Decision Made Under the Act

Securities administrators are typically given a wide range of powers to make decisions. A failure to comply with a decision made under the act is also specified as an offence under several securities acts.[7]

(vi) Insider Trading or Informing

As noted in Chapter 10, there are penal sanctions for trading on or informing others of material changes or material facts that have not been generally disclosed.[8]

b. SANCTIONS

The penal sanctions include fines for persons other than individuals and fines or imprisonment for individuals.[9] The potential sanctions vary substantially from jurisdiction to jurisdiction. For instance, the potential fine under the A.S.A., the B.C.S.A., the M.S.A., the Nfld.S.A., the N.S.S.A., the O.S.A., and the S.S.A. is $1,000,000. However, the potential imprisonment for an individual is 5 years less a day under the A.S.A., 3 years under the B.C.S.A., 2 years under the M.S.A., the Nfld.S.A., the N.S.S.A., the O.S.A. and the S.S.A. Under the N.B.S.F.P.A. and the P.E.I.S.A. the sanction against an individual is a potential fine of $1,000 for a first offence and $2,000 for a second offence and potential imprisonment for up to 6 months. Under the P.E.I.S.A. the fine for a company is up to $25,000 and under the N.B.S.F.P.A. the fine for a company is up to $5,000. Under the Q.S.A. the fine is from $1,000 to $20,000 for an individual

---

[6] See the provisions cited *supra*, note 5.

[7] A.S.A. s. 161(1)(c); B.C.S.A. s. 155(1)(e); M.S.A. s. 136(1)(d); Nfld.S.A. s. 122(1)(d); N.S.S.A. s. 129(1)(d); N.W.T.S.A. s. 49(1)(d); P.E.I.S.A. s. 24 (failure to comply with requirement of the Director of Corporations); Q.S.A. s. 195(1); S.S.A. s. 131(3)(d); Y.S.A. s. 46(1)(d).

[8] See Chapter 10, Part III A 4 a.

[9] A.S.A. s. 161(1); B.C.S.A. s. 155(1); M.S.A. s. 136(1); N.B.S.F.P.A. s. 41; Nfld.S.A. s. 122(1); N.S.S.A. s. 129(1); N.W.T.S.A. s. 49(1); O.S.A. s. 122(1); P.E.I.S.A. s. 28; Q.S.A. s. 202; S.S.A. s. 131(3); Y.S.A. s. 46(1).

and $1,000 to $50,000 for persons other than individuals. Under the N.W.T.S.A. and the Y.S.A. the sanction is a fine of up to $25,000 for companies and the sanction for individuals is a fine of up to $2,000 and imprisonment for up to 1 year.

c. DUE DILIGENCE DEFENCES

Some of the provincial offence provisions provide for due diligence defences to some of the specified offences. For instance, under the B.C.S.A., there is a due diligence defence to the charge of making a misrepresentation in evidence or information submitted to securities administrators or an investigator or auditor, and a due diligence defence to the charge of making a misrepresentation in any record required to be filed or sent. A person is not guilty of these offences if the person shows that they did not know and − in the exercise of reasonable diligence could not have known − that the statement was a misrepresentation.[10] The provision of a due diligence defence for these offences implies there is no due diligence defence for the other offences listed in the offence provisions. The lack of words suggesting an intentional element in other offence provisions suggests that they are "absolute liability" offences. Absolute liability offenses that impose on individuals a sanction of imprisonment, or possibly also the potential for imprisonment for nonpayment of fines, may be in violation of s. 7 of the *Canadian Charter of Rights and Freedoms*.[11]

d. APPLICATION TO OFFICERS, DIRECTORS AND OTHERS

The statutory offence provisions also typically provide that where a person other than an individual commits an offence under the act, an officer or director of that person who authorizes, permits or acquiesces in the commission of the offence commits the same offence.[12]

---

[10] A.S.A. s. 161(3); B.C.S.A. 155(3); M.S.A. s. 136(2); Nfld.S.A. s. 122(2); N.S.S.A. s. 129(2); N.W.T.S.A. s. 49(2); O.S.A. s. 122(2); S.S.A. s. 131(4); Y.S.A. s. 46(2).

[11] See, for example, *R. v. Wholesale Travel Group Inc.*, [1991] 3 S.C.R. 154; *Re B.C. Motor Vehicle Act*, [1985] 2 S.C.R. 486; and *R. v. Vaillancourt*, [1987] 2 S.C.R. 636.

[12] A.S.A. s. 161(4) (includes directors of a company or any other person); B.C.S.A. s. 155(4) (the provision also extends to employees and agents); M.S.A.

e. LIMITATION PERIODS

The acts also typically provide for limitation periods that apply to the enforcement of the offence provisions. The limitation period under the A.S.A. and B.C.S.A is 6 years.[13] Ontario has a five year limitation. Under the Nfld.S.A. and N.S.S.A. the limitation period is 1 year for proceedings in court and 2 years for proceedings brought before the commission with the time running from the time the facts upon which the proceedings are based first came to the knowledge of the commission.

f. COSTS OF INVESTIGATION

Some of the acts also provide that a person convicted of an offence under the act is liable for the costs of the investigation of the offence.[14]

2. Administrative Sanctions

a. TYPES OF ORDERS

Under most Canadian securities laws securities administrators are given the power to make a wide range of orders to encourage compliance with the securities act or regulations.

(i) Compliance

Securities administrators are typically given the power to order that a person comply with, or cease contravening, a provision of the act or regulations or a decision of the securities administrators.[15]

---

s. 136(3); N.B.S.F.P.A. s. 41(1); Nfld.S.A. s. 122(3); N.S.S.A. s. 129(3); N.W.T.S.A. s. 49(3); O.S.A. s. 122(3); Q.S.A. s. 205; S.S.A. s. 131(5); Y.S.A. s. 46(3).

[13] A.S.A. s. 167; B.C.S.A. s. 159; M.S.A. s. 137 (2 years); N.B.S.F.P.A. s. 41(4) (6 months); Nfld.S.A. s. 129; N.S.S.A. s. 136; N.W.T.S.A. s. 50(2) (2 years); O.S.A. s. 129.1 (5 years); Q.S.A. s. 211 (5 years); S.S.A. s. 136 (6 years); Y.S.A. s. 47(2) (2 years).

[14] A.S.A. s. 167.1; B.C.S.A. s. 160; M.S.A. s. 28; N.B.S.F.P.A. s. 25(2); N.S.S.A. s. 135A; N.W.T.S.A. s. 23; P.E.I.S.A. s. 29; Q.S.A. s. 212; S.S.A. s. 19; Y.S.A. s. 49.

[15] A.S.A. s. 164 (an application to court); B.C.S.A. s. 161(1)(a) (the provision also applies to a by-law, rule, policy or decision of a stock exchange or self-regulatory organization); M.S.A. s. 152 (an application to court), s. 62; N.B.S.F.P.A. s. 23 (an application to court); Nfld.S.A. s. 126 (an application to court); N.S.S.A. s. 134(1)(a) (the provision also applies to a by-law, rule, policy or decision of a stock exchange

(ii) Cease Trade

Another important administrative power is the power to order that all persons, class of persons, or particular persons cease trading in a specified security or class of securities.[16]

(iii) Denial of Exemptions

Important exemptions are provided from the application of securities acts with respect to registration, prospectus filing requirements and takeover bid regulations. Securities administrators typically have the power to remove these exemptions with respect to the persons specified in an order by the securities administrator.[17] The removal of these exemptions can have a significant impact on, for instance, the business of a registrant, financing by an issuer, persons involved in private placements or persons engaged in acquisitions.

(iv) Resignation or Prohibition from Acting as a Director or Officer

Some securities acts also give securities administrators a power to order that a person resign from a position as a director or officer of an issuer or be prohibited from becoming or acting as a director or officer of an issuer.[18]

(v) Prohibition of or Required Dissemination of Information

Under some securities acts the securities administrators are specifically given the power to (a) order that a registrant or issuer be prohibited from disseminating to the public the information specified in the order, (b) require the registrant or issuer to disseminate the information specified in the order, or (c) require a registrant or issuer

---

or self-regulatory organization); O.S.A. s. 128 (an application to court); Q.S.A. s. 272.1; S.S.A. s. 133.

[16] A.S.A. s. 165; B.C.S.A. s. 161(1)(b); M.S.A. s. 148; N.B.S.F.P.A. s. 18; Nfld.S.A. s. 127; N.S.S.A. s. 134(1)(b); N.W.T.S.A. s. 37; O.S.A. s. 127 2; P.E.I.S.A. s. 19; Q.S.A. s. 265; S.S.A. s. 134(1)(b); Y.S.A. s. 32.

[17] A.S.A. s. 165(1)(c); B.C.S.A. s. 161(1)(c); M.S.A. s. 19(5); Nfld.S.A. s. 128; N.S.S.A. s. 134(1)(c); O.S.A. s. 127 3; P.E.I.S.A. s. 13(2); Q.S.A. s. 264; S.S.A. s. 134(1)(a). There is no similar provision under the N.B.S.F.P.A., N.W.T.S.A., or the Y.S.A.

[18] A.S.A. s. 165(1)(d), (e); B.C.S.A. s. 161(1)(d); N.S.S.A. s. 134(1)(d); S.S.A. s. 134(1)(h).

to amend information specified in the order before it is distributed to the public.[19]

(vi) Reprimand of Registrant or Suspension, Cancellation or Restriction of Registration

Securities administrators also have the power to order that a registrant be reprimanded, or that a person's registration be suspended, cancelled or restricted.[20]

b. PROCEDURE

The administrative orders noted above can generally be made on a temporary basis without a hearing, where the securities administrator considers that the length of time required to hold a hearing could be prejudicial to the public interest.[21] The application of a temporary order is typically limited to 15 days,[22] but the administrator can order an extension of the order until a hearing can be held.[23] A hearing is required before the imposition of a final order.[24]

c. ADMINISTRATIVE PENALTY

The B.C.S.A., S.S.A. and the N.S.S.A. provide for an administrative penalty of up to $100,000 to be paid to the securities commission, pursuant to an order of the securities commission, where

---

[19] A.S.A. s. 165(1)(f), (g); B.C.S.A. s. 161(1)(e); N.S.S.A. s. 134(1)(e); S.S.A. 134(1)(g).

[20] A.S.A. s. 56; B.C.S.A. s. 161(1)(f); M.S.A. s. 8; N.B.S.F.P.A. ss. 22, 23; Nfld.S.A. s. 28; N.S.S.A. s. 33; N.W.T.S.A. s. 10; O.S.A. s. 127 1 and 6; P.E.I.S.A. ss. 18, 19; Q.S.A. s. 273; S.S.A. s. 134(1)(i), (j); Y.S.A. s. 8(2).

[21] A.S.A. s. 21; B.C.S.A. s. 161(2); M.S.A. s. 148(2); Nfld.S.A. ss. 127(3), 128(2); N.S.S.A. s. 134(2); O.S.A. s. 127(5), (6); S.S.A. s. 134(3).

[22] Ibid.

[23] A.S.A. s. 21(3); B.C.S.A. s. 161(3); M.S.A. s. 148(2); Nfld.S.A. ss. 127(3), 128(2); N.S.S.A. s. 134(3); O.S.A. s. 127(7); S.S.A. s. 134(3).

[24] See, for example, A.S.A. s. 165(3); B.C.S.A. s. 161(1); M.S.A. s. 148(2); Nfld.S.A. ss. 127(3), 128(2); N.S.S.A. s. 134(1); O.S.A. s. 127(4); S.S.A. s. 134(3). Section 164 of the B.C.S.A. gives the commission or the superintendent the power to make a cease trade order without a hearing where a person fails to file a record that is required to be filed or furnished, or fails to file or furnish adequate information in a record that is required to be filed or furnished. The order applies until the person files or furnishes the required information.

it is determined, after a hearing, that a person has contravened a provision of the act or the regulations or a decision made under the act.[25] The power of a provincial legislature to give a securities commission jurisdiction to order such a penalty, and the burden of proof required in making the determination are questions that may need to be resolved in the application of this "administrative" penalty.

d. THE SCOPE OF THE ADMINISTRATIVE POWERS

Securities commissions are given the power to impose sanctions, such as cease trade orders and removal of exemptions, where it "considers it to be in the public interest" to do so. The scope of these powers has been interpreted quite broadly.

In *Re C.T.C. Dealer Holdings Ltd. et al. and Ontario Securities Commission et al.*[26] it was argued that this discretion was not intended to be exercised in the absence of a concurrent breach of the act, regulations, or policy statements. To interpret the section differently, it was argued, would "confer an unprecedented, unjustified, unintended and unreviewable discretion on the Commission. It would place the Commission 'above the Law'".[27]

A unanimous bench of Ontario Divisional Court rejected this contention noting that other sections of the Ontario Act conferred a discretion on the Commission only where there was a breach of the Act. This implied that the broader "public interest" discretion was not to be so confined. Further, the court noted that the discretion of the Commission was fettered by the words "in the public interest" and thus the Commission was not "above the law". The court stated that,

> Were the Commission ever to use its discretion in the irresponsible fashion suggested by appellants, it would be subject to prompt correction in this court. Thus, if the Commission were to label something as contrary to the public interest in the absence of any evidence to support that view, it would have misused its jurisdiction. Similarly, if the Commission were to act *mala fide*, perversely, maliciously, arbitrarily or capriciously it would have misused its powers, and be open

---

[25] B.C.S.A. s. 162; N.S.S.A. s. 135; S.S.A. s. 135(1).

[26] 59 O.R. (2d) 79, 35 B.L.R. 117, 23 Admin. L.R. 285, 37 D.L.R. (4th) 94, 21 O.A.C. 216 (Div. Ct.), aff'g (1987), 10 O.S.C.B. 857, 35 B.L.R. 56, leave to appeal to the Ont. C.A. refused (1987), 35 B.L.R. xx (note) (C.A.).

[27] 59 O.R (2d) 95.

to correction in this court. But when the Commission has acted *bona fide*, with an obvious and honest concern for the public interest, and with evidence to support its opinion, the prospect that the breadth of its discretion might someday tempt it to place itself above the law by misusing that discretion is not something that makes the existence of the discretion bad *per se*, and requires the decision to be struck down.[28]

Courts have also generally exhibited a reluctance to interfere with the decisions of securities commissions. This was also noted in *Re C.T.C. Dealer Holdings Ltd. and Ontario Securities Commission,*

> Out of respect for the expertise of the Commission, for the weight of the responsibility it bears, and for the stature it has achieved in the industry it is called upon to regulate, the courts have repeatedly expressed the view that its actions should not lightly be interfered with.[29]

In *Re C.T.C. Dealer Holdings Ltd.* the Commission imposed an obligation to include a non-voting class of shares in a takeover bid for a separate class of voting shares. Such an obligation was consistent with the apparent intent of a provision of the articles of Canadian Tire Ltd., but the takeover bid had been structured so as to avoid the application of the provision. The takeover bid was not clearly contrary to the statute itself. The Commission's cease trade order thus effectively imposed an obligation not clearly imposed by the act itself. On the other hand, while it appears that a commission may have some authority to impose obligations beyond those expressly set out in the act, it also appears that it cannot impose obligations that are inconsistent with the wording of the act.[30]

---

[28] 59 O.R. (2d) 97. See also *Gordon Capital Corp. v. Ontario Securities Commission* (1991), 50 O.A.C. 258 (Div. Ct.) in which it was held that the scope of the commissions discretion with respect to "the public interest" was limited only by the general purpose of the act and that the commission did not commit an error of law in rejecting the appellant's due diligence defence.

[29] 59 O.R. (2d) 89.

[30] In *Re Calpine Resources Inc.* (1992), 66 B.C.L.R. (2d) 257, 96 D.L.R. (4th) 137 (B.C.C.A.), a majority of the B.C. Court of Appeal found that the extension of the timely disclosure obligation to "material facts" by National Policy #40 was inconsistent with the act. The timely disclosure obligation in the act was confined to "material changes" and the expression "material fact" was used in conjunction with the prohibition against insider trading and informing. Thus there appeared to be a deliberate choice of the legislature not to extend the application of the timely disclosure obligation to "material facts" and an attempt by the Commission

3. *Civil Sanctions*

There are also statutory civil sanctions for rescission or damages for a failure to deliver a prospectus (discussed in Chapter 4),[31] a misrepresentation in a prospectus (discussed in Chapter 5),[32] and a misrepresentation in a takeover bid circular or directors' circular (noted in Chapter 11).[33] There are also civil actions for compensation or an accounting in respect of insider trading or informing (discussed in Chapter 10).[34] There is an action for rescission with respect to a failure by a registered dealer to make required disclosure in the context of margin contracts, or a failure of a registered dealer to make required disclosure with respect to acting as principal in a trade (discussed in Chapter 12).[35]

B. Common Law Civil Actions

There are also potential common law civil actions for rescission or damages with respect to misrepresentations in prospectuses or other disclosure documents and with respect to transactions which are in violation of securities acts.[36] There may also be civil actions with respect to brokers, advisors and portfolio managers for breach of contract, for negligence or for breach of fiduciary duties.

III. REVIEW AND APPEAL PROCEDURES

A. Review of Decisions by Securities Commissions

Several provincial securities acts create securities commissions that act, in part, as a tribunal to which decisions of the administrator

---

to extend the timely disclosure obligation to "material facts" was therefore contrary to the act. While the decision of the B.C. Court of Appeal was reversed on appeal to the Supreme Court of Canada ([1994] 2 S.C.R. 557), Mr. Justice Iacobucci, speaking for the court, noted that the Commission's policy-making role is limited in that their policies cannot be elevated to the status of law ([1994] 2 S.C.R. 596).

[31] Chapter 4, Part VIII A 3.

[32] Chapter 5, Part III.

[33] Chapter 11, Part II D 1 a.

[34] Chapter 10, Part III A 4 b.

[35] Chapter 12, Part IV C 3.

[36] These actions are discussed in Chapter 4, Part VIII; Chapter 5, Part II; and Chapter 6, Part X B.

of the act can be appealed.[37] Under the N.B.S.F.P.A., P.E.I.S.A., N.W.T.S.A. and Y.S.A. the administrative responsibilities are assigned to government officials or administrators appointed under the act.[38]

Where the act creates a securities commission, persons directly affected by decisions of the administrator can appeal to the commission.[39] The commission may confirm the decision of the administrator or make any other decision it considers proper.[40] The commission may grant a stay of the decision under review until it has made its review.[41]

Notice of certain specified types of decisions made by the administrator must be given to the commission.[42] The commission is empowered to convene a hearing to review any of these decisions if it chooses to do so.[43] This allows the commission to establish policy and monitor the implementation of its policies with respect to the most significant aspects of the administration of the act and regulations.[44]

Reviews by a commission will typically be of a judicial nature involving the rights of persons affected by the decisions under

---

[37] See Chapter 3, Part V C with respect to securities commissions and administrators. The administrator of the various acts is referred to as the "Director" in Manitoba, Newfoundland, Nova Scotia, Ontario and Saskatchewan, and the "Executive Director" in Alberta and British Columbia.

[38] See Chapter 3, Part V C.

[39] See, for example, A.S.A. s. 24(1); B.C.S.A. s. 165(3) (by notice in writing to the commission within 30 days of the mailing of the notice of the decision by the superintendent); M.S.A. s. 29(1); Nfld.S.A. s. 9(2); N.S.S.A. ss. 6(1), 25(2); O.S.A. s. 8(2) (within 30 days of the mailing of the notice of the decision); Q.S.A. s. 322; S.S.A. s. 10(2).

[40] A.S.A. s. 25(3); B.C.S.A. s. 165(4); M.S.A. s. 29(2); Nfld.S.A. s. 9(3); N.S.S.A. ss. 6(2), 25(3); O.S.A. s. 8(3); S.S.A. s. 10(3).

[41] See, for example, A.S.A. s. 25(5); B.C.S.A. s. 165(5); Nfld.S.A. s. 9(4); N.S.S.A. s. 25(4); O.S.A. s. 8(4); Q.S.A. s. 323; S.S.A. s. 10(5).

[42] See, for example, B.C.S.A. s. 165(1) (notice with respect to refusal, suspension, termination, restriction or imposition of conditions on registration, refusal of a receipt for a prospectus, halt trading orders, imposition of administrative orders, refusal of exemption from registration or prospectus requirements); Nfld.S.A. s. 9(1); N.S.S.A. s. 25(1); O.S.A. s. 8(1) (notice with respect to refusals of registration and refusals to issue a receipt for a prospectus); S.S.A. s. 10(1).

[43] See, for example, B.C.S.A. s. 165(2); Nfld.S.A. s. 9(1); N.S.S.A. s. 25(1); O.S.A. s. 8(1); S.S.A. s. 10(1.1). See also Q.S.A. ss. 309, 310.

[44] See V.P. Alboini, *Securities Law and Practice*, (Toronto: Carswell, 1984), at 5-2.

review. Consequently, the requisite degree of fairness or natural justice must be met. Thus the review normally involves a hearing, of which reasonable notice must be given and at which the parties would usually be represented by counsel.

B. Appeal of Decisions of Administrators

Any person directly affected by a decision of the commission, other than decisions with respect to exemptions from prospectus requirements, or also, under some acts, exemptions from registration requirements,[45] can appeal the decision of the commission to a court.[46] The court may grant a stay of the decision of the commission until the disposition of the appeal.[47] The court is empowered to direct the commission to make any decision or do any act the commission is authorized and empowered to do under the act or regulations and the commission is required to act accordingly.[48] However, where new material with respect to the matter comes forward, or where there is a significant change in the circumstances with respect to the matter, the commission may make any further decision it considers appropriate.[49] Any such further decision is also subject to appeal to the court.[50]

---

[45]See, for example, A.S.A. s. 26(1); B.C.S.A. s. 167(1); Nfld.S.A. s. 10(1); N.S.S.A. s. 26(1); S.S.A. s. 11(1). Under N.W.T.S.A. s. 13 if registration is refused, suspended or cancelled there is an appeal to the Supreme Court which may confirm, reverse or modify the decision.

[46]See, for example, A S.A. s. 26(1) (to the Court of Appeal); B.C.S.A. s. 167(1) (to the Court of Appeal); M.S.A. s. 30(1) (to the Court of Queen's bench); Nfld.S.A. s. 10(l) (Supreme Court Trial Division); N.S.S.A. s. 26(1) (Trial Division); O.S.A. s. 9(1) (to the Divisional Court); Q.S.A. s. 324 (to three members of the Provincial Court); S.S.A. s. 11(1) (Court of Appeal).

[47]See, for example, B.C.S.A. s. 167(2); M.S.A. s. 30(8); Nfld.S.A. s. 10(2); N.S.S.A. s. 26(2); O.S.A. s. 9(2); Q.S.A. s. 329; S.S.A. s. 11(8).

[48]A.S.A. s. 26(6)(c); B.C.S.A. s. 167(3); M.S.A. s. 30(6); Nfld.S.A. s. 10(5); N.S.S.A. s. 26(5); O.S.A. s. 9(5); S.S.A. s. 11(6).

[49]See, for example, B.C.S.A. s. 167(4); M.S.A. s. 30(7); Nfld.S.A. s. 10(6); N.S.S.A. s. 26(6); O.S.A. s. 9(6); S.S.A. s. 11(7).

[50]Ibid.

In the other jurisdictions that do not create securities commissions, the decisions of the administrator can be appealed to the court on questions of law or as to the jurisdiction of the administrator.[51]

IV. INVESTIGATIONS AND AUDITS

Provisions under the securities acts are made for investigations and audits to facilitate the administration and enforcement of the acts. Powers are given under the securities acts for the appointment of a person to conduct an investigation and make a report.[52] The investigators are given broad powers to conduct their investigation, including summoning and enforcing the attendance of witnesses, and compelling witnesses to give evidence under oath and produce records.[53] Powers are also provided for the appointment of a person to conduct an audit of the financial affairs of a reporting issuer, a registrant, mutual fund custodian or self-regulatory organization.[54] The person appointed is given the power to examine books of account, securities, cash, documents, bank accounts, and records of every description for the purposes of conducting the examination.[55]

---

[51] See, for example, N.B.S.F.P.A. s. 37(3) (appeal to the Court of Appeal upon leave of a judge of the Court of Queen's Bench given upon a petition made within 15 days of the making of the decision appealed from), s. 3(2) and s. 4.1 (appeal re refusal of registration to a person appointed by the Lieutenant Governor in Council); N.W.T.S.A. s. 13 (appeal to Supreme Court re refusal, suspension or cancellation of registration), s. 38 (appeal re cease trade order); Y.S.A. s. 32(4) (appeal to Supreme Court re cease trade order), s. 16 (appeal refusal, suspension or cancellation of registration to Supreme Court).

[52] A.S.A. ss. 28, 30-33; B.C.S.A. ss. 142-49 (order can be made by the commission or the Minister); M.S.A. ss. 22, 23, 25; N.B.S.F.P.A. s. 21; Nfld.S.A. ss. 12-14, 16; N.S.S.A. ss. 27-29, 29B; N.W.T.S.A. s. 18; O.S.A. ss. 11-13, 15; P.E.I.S.A. s. 17; Q.S.A. ss. 239, 247, 292; S.S.A. ss. 12-14,16; Y.S.A. s. 18.

[53] A.S.A. s. 29; B.C.S.A. ss. 143 and 144; M.S.A. s. 22(3), (4); N.B.S.F.P.A. s. 21; Nfld.S.A. s. 12(3), (4); N.S.S.A. s. 27(2), (3); N.W.T.S.A. s. 18(3); O.S.A. s. 11(3), (4); P.E.I.S.A. s. 17(1), (2); S.S.A. s. 12(4), (5); Y.S.A. s. 18(2).

[54] A.S.A. s. 48; B.C.S.A. s. 153; M.S.A. s. 35; N.B.S.F.P.A. ss. 29, 30; Nfld.S.A. s. 19; N.S.S.A. s. 29E; N.W.T.S.A. s. 41; P.E.I.S.A. s. 21 (books may be inspected by the Director of Corporations or their representative); Q.S.A. ss. 241-43; S.S.A. s. 20; Y.S.A. s. 35.

[55] Ibid.

V. ORDERS TO FREEZE PROPERTY

In certain circumstances orders can be made to freeze a person's property in the jurisdiction. For instance, where, in respect of a person, an investigation is proposed, ongoing or has been concluded, an administrative order (such as a cease trade order) is proposed or has been made, or criminal proceedings are about to be or have been instituted, an order can be made requiring a person to continue to hold any funds, securities or other property that it holds on deposit and which belongs to the person subject to the investigation, order or proceeding. The securities commission (or, under some acts, the administrator) can also order that the person subject to the investigation, order, or proceeding refrain from withdrawing any funds, securities, or other property or to hold all funds, securities or other property of clients or others in trust for an interim receiver or trustee.[56]

VI. CHARTER ISSUES

There have been very few challenges to securities law under the *Canadian Charter of Rights and Freedoms*.[57] The *Charter* challenges that have been brought so far have been largely unsuccessful.

In *Bennett v. B.C. (Securities Commission)*,[58] the petitioners sought orders that would have prohibited a hearing by the B.C. Securities Commission. One of the grounds for relief was based on s. 7 of the *Charter*, which provides that "everyone has the right to life, liberty and security of the person and the right not to be deprived thereof except in accordance with the principles of fundamental justice." The B.C. Court of Appeal held that it was premature to make the orders requested when there was, as yet, no deprivation of life, liberty and security of the person but only a possibility of such a deprivation.[59] Even if the Commission found against the petitioners, the remedies

---

[56] A.S.A. s. 37; B.C.S.A. s. 151; M.S.A. s. 26; N.B.S.F.P.A. s. 24; Nfld.S.A. s. 17; N.S.S.A. s. 29C; N.W.T.S.A. s. 24(1); O.S.A. s. 126; P.E.I.S.A. s. 20; Q.S.A. s. 249; S.S.A. s. 135.4; Y.S.A. s. 20(1).

[57] *Canada Act 1982* (U.K.), 1982, c. 11.

[58] (1992), 94 D.L.R. (4th) 339 (B.C.C.A.), affirming (1991), 82 D.L.R. (4th) 129 (S.C.), leave to appeal to S.C.C. refused (1992), 97 D.L.R. (4th) vii.

[59] 94 D.L.R. (4th) 355.

that the Commission might impose would not necessarily have led to such a deprivation.[60]

In *B.C. (Securities Commission) v. Branch*,[61] the petitioner claimed that his s. 7 and s. 13 *Charter* rights were being violated by having to testify against his interests. The Supreme Court of Canada weighed the public interest in enforcing securities laws to protect investors against the individual's right to protection from self-incrimination. The court held that the burden of proof is on the witness to show that there is no legitimate purpose in compelling his or her testimony. Further, the witness has the protection that the testimony cannot be used to incriminate him or her in a subsequent proceeding.[62]

In *Branch*, the protection against unreasonable search or seizure in s. 8 of the *Charter* was also considered. The court considered the petitioner's expectation of privacy in the context of the business of securities trading compared with the regulatory needs expressed in securities regulation. The court concluded that the expectation of privacy is relatively low in the context of securities trading since it is widely known and accepted that the industry is extensively regulated.[63] Further, documents produced in the course of a business which is highly regulated have a lesser privacy right than do documents that are personal in nature.[64] The court also considered the nature of the seizure authorized by the *Securities Act* and concluded that it is one of the least intrusive of the possible methods which might be used to obtain documentary evidence.[65]

It has also been held that the protections for an accused charged with an offence under s. 11 of the *Charter* do not apply to cease trade orders.[66]

In spite of the relatively few securities cases dealing with *Charter* issues there are many potential applications of the *Charter* to secu-

---

[60] Ibid.

[61] [1995] 2 S.C.R. 123, 123 D.L.R. (4th) 462.

[62] 123 D.L.R. (4th) 476-79.

[63] 123 D.L.R. (4th) 485-87.

[64] 123 D.L.R. (4th) 488.

[65] 123 D.L.R. (4th) 487.

[66] *Holoboff v. Alberta (Securities Commission)* (1991), 80 D.L.R. (4th) 603 (Alta. C.A.).

rities legislation.[67] Many important securities law *Charter* issues are yet to be litigated.

---

[67] See D. O'Connor & F. Kristjanson, "Securities Law and the Charter" in *Securities Law in the Modern Financial Marketplace*, Special Lectures of the Law Society of Upper Canada (Toronto: De Boo, 1989) 497 at 504-16.

BIBLIOGRAPHY

Adams, S.N., "Raising Capital for Small Issuers: Private Placements and Distribution Restrictions" in *Securities Law in the Modern Financial Marketplace*, Special Lectures of the Law Society of Upper Canada (Toronto: De Boo, 1989) 237-46.

Alboini, V.P., "Due Diligence and the Role of the Securities Lawyer" (1982) 6 *Canadian Business Law Journal* 241.

————, *Ontario Securities Law* (Toronto: De Boo, 1980).

————, *Securities Law & Practice*, 2nd ed. (Toronto: Carswell, 1984).

Alince, P. and L. Sarna (eds.), *Insider trading: a Canadian legal manual* (Montreal: Jewel Publications, 1990).

Anand, A., "Fairness at what Price?: An Analysis of the Regulation of Going-Private Transactions in OSC Policy 9.1" (1998) 43 *McGill L. J.* 115-137.

Anisman, P., et al., *Proposals for a Securities Market Law for Canada*, 3 vols. (Ottawa: Consumer and Corporate Affairs Canada, 1979).

Anisman, P., "Legitimating Lawmaking by the Ontario Securities Commission: Comments on the Final Report of the Ontario Task Force on Securities Regulation", in *Securities Regulation: Issues and Perspectives, Queen's Annual Business Law Symposium 1994* (Scarborough, Ont.: Carswell, 1995), 1-77.

Anisman, P., "Offering Corporations and Corporate Governance: A Proposal to Amend the Ontario Business Corporations Act, 1982" (1989) 15 *Canadian Business Law Journal* 223-34.

————, "Takeover Bid Legislation in Canada: The Definitions, Exemptions and Substantive Requirements" (1972) 11 *Western Ontario Law Reports* 1.

————, *Takeover Bid Legislation in Canada, A Comparative Analysis* (Don Mills, Ont.: CCH Canada, 1974).

————, "The Commission as Protector of Minority Shareholders" in *Securities Law in the Modern Financial Marketplace*, Special Lectures of the Law Society of Upper Canada (Toronto: De Boo, 1989) 451-95.

————, "The Proposals for a Securities Market Law for Canada: Purpose and Process" (1981) 19 *Osgoode Hall Law Journal* 329.

Apple, B.N., *Filing of Prospectus by Mining Companies under Section 38 of the Securities Act* (Ontario: Ontario Securities Commission, January, 1964)

Baer, M.G., Comments on [a paper by David A. Brown and Janet A. Holmes]: "The Empty Seat at the Boardroom Table", in *Securities Regulation: Issues and Perspectives: Queen's Annual Business Law Symposium 1994* (Scarborough, Ont.: Carswell, 1995), 414-416.

Baillie, J.C., and Grover, W.M.H., "Discovery-Type Procedures in Security Fraud Prosecutions" (1972) 50 *Canadian Bar Review* 496.

————, "Securities Regulation in the Seventies", in J.S. Ziegel, ed. *Canadian Company Law*, vol. 2 (Toronto: Butterworths, 1973) 343.

————, "The Protection of the Investor in Ontario" (1965) 8 *Canadian Public Administration* 172-268, 325-432.

————, *Proposals for a Mutual Funds Law for Canada* (Ottawa: Information Canada, 1974).

Baillie, J.C., "Investor Protection Plans" in *Securities Law in the Modern Financial Marketplace*, Special Lectures of the Law Society of Upper Canada (Toronto: De Boo, 1989) 77-92.

————, "The Protection of the Investor in Ontario" (1965) 8 *Canadian Public Administration* 172 and 325.

Ballard, J., Comments on [Paul M. Moore's paper]: "The Role of Regulation: A Case Study on the Emerging Regulation of Derivative Products", in *Securities Regulation: Issues and Perspectives: Queen's Annual Business Law Symposium 1994* (Scarborough, Ont.: Carswell, 1995), 499-501.

Banwell, P.T., "Proposals for a National Securities Commission" (1969) 1 *Queen's Law Journal* 3.

Baxter, I.F.G., and Johnston, D.L., "New Mechanics for Securities Transactions" (1971) 21 *University of Toronto Law Journal* 336.

————, "Transfer of Investment Securities – Some Current Proposals" (1972) 10 *Osgoode Hall Law Journal* 191.

Baxter, M., "The fiduciary Obligations of Directors of a Target Company in Resisting an Unsolicited Takeover Bid" (1988) 20 *Ottawa L. Rev.* 63-115.

Beck, H.L., "The Legal Aspect" in Morin and Chippindale, ed., *Acquisitions & Mergers in Canada* (Toronto: Methuen, 1970) 186.

Beck, S. and R. Wildeboer, "National Policy 38 as a Regulator of Defensive Tactics (Hostile Takeover Bids)" [1987] Meredith Mem. Lect. 119-139.

Beck, S.M., "Comment on *Ames et al. v Investo-Plan Ltd. et al.*" (1974) 52 *Canadian Bar Review* 589.

————, "Of Secretaries, Analysts and Printers: Some Reflections on Insider Trading" (1984) 8 *Canadian Business Law Journal* 385.

————, "Recent Trends in Securities Regulation" in *Securities Law in the Modern Financial Marketplace*, Special Lectures of the Law Society of Upper Canada (Toronto: De Boo, 1989) 1-8.

Beck, S.M., "Gatekeepers and the Commission: The Role of Professionals in the Regulatory System", in *Securities Regulation: Issues and Perspectives, Queen's Annual Business Law Symposium 1994* (Scarborough, Ont.: Carswell, 1995), 239-263.

Bertrand, M., Comments on [René Sorell's paper] "Supervision of Self-Regulatory Organizations in Ontario's Securities Market", in *Securities Regulation: Issues and Perspectives: Queen's Annual Business Law Symposium 1994* (Scarborough, Ont.: Carswell, 1995), 192-196.

Bird, R.W., "Corporate Mergers and Acquisitions in Canada" (1968) 18 *University of New Brunswick Law Journal* 16.

Blake, S., "Hydra? What Hydra?": [Comments on James Douglas's paper: Dispelling Fears of a Hydra: Toward Defining a Constructive Role for the Regulator in Enforcement Proceedings], in *Securities Regulation: Issues and Perspectives, Queen's Annual Business Law Symposium 1994* (Scarborough, Ont.: Carswell, 1995), 226-232.

Boreham, G., "Three Years After Canada's Little Bang" (Sept. 1990) 97 *The Canadian Banker & ICB Review* No. 5, 7-15.

Braithwaite, W.J., "Comment on Healy: National Policy Statement

No. 41" in *Securities Law in the Modern Financial Marketplace*, Special Lectures of the Law Society of Upper Canada (Toronto: De Boo, 1989) 379-84.

Braithwaite, W.J., "Who is Best Suited to Introduce Corporate Governance Reform and Mutual Fund Governance Reform?", in *Securities Regulation: Issues and Perspectives: Queen's Annual Business Law Symposium 1994* (Scarborough, Ont.: Carswell, 1995), 277-320.

Bray, H.S., "Recent Developments in Securities Administration in Ontario: The Securities Act, 1966", in J.S. Ziegel, ed., *Canadian Company Law*, vol. 1 (Toronto: Butterworths, 1967) 415.

Brown, D.A. & J.A. Holmes, "The Regulation of Financial Institutions: The Empty Seat at the Boardroom Table", in *Securities Regulation: Issues and Perspectives: Queen's Annual Business Law Symposium 1994* (Scarborough, Ont.: Carswell, 1995), 341-413.

Buckley, F.H., "Small Issuers under the Ontario Securities Act, 1978: A Plea for Exemptions" (1979) 29 *University of Toronto Law Journal* 309.

Cameron, W. Walter, "Securities Legislation, Administration and Marketing in the Province of Ontario, 1956" *Bulletin of Ontario Securities Commission Bulletin* (Nov. 1956), 4.

———, "Securities Legislation, Administration and Marketing in the Province of Ontario," *Bulletin of Ontario Securities Commission*, Sept. 1954, 2. This article appeared as "Regulation and Distribution of Securities in Ontario", (1954) 10 *University of Toronto Law Journal* 199.

Canada and the Provinces, *Report of the Canadian Committee on Mutual Funds and Investment Contracts* (Ottawa: Queen's Printer, 1969) ("Mutual Funds Report").

Canadian Securities Law Reporter, 4 vols. (Toronto: CCH Canada Ltd., 1991).

Canada, *Minister of Consumer and Corporate Affairs. Proposals for a Securities Market Law for Canada*, 3 vole. (Ottawa: 1979).

———, *Proposals for a New Business Corporation's Law for Canada*, vols. I and II (Ottawa: Queen's Printer, 1971).

———, *Royal Commission on Banking and Finance: Report* (Ottawa: Queen's Printer, 1964) ("Porter Report").

————, *Royal Commission on Canada's Economic Prospects: Final Report* (Ottawa: Queen's Printer, 1958) ("Gordon Report,").

Canadian Institute, "The securities business in the global environment" (Toronto: Canadian Institute, 1987).

Canadian Securities Institute, *The Canadian Securities Course* (Toronto: Canadian Securities Institute, 1995).

Carr J., A. Milne and S.M. Turnbull, "Greenline Investors Service: Shall We Keep Brokers and Banks Apart?" (1983) 8 *Canadian Business Law Journal* 257.

Caty, J.C., Comments on [Ed Waitzer's paper] "Coordinated Securities Regulation: Getting to a More Effective Regime", in *Securities Regulation: Issues and Perspectives: Queen's Annual Business Law Symposium 1994* (Scarborough, Ont.: Carswell, 1995), 136-138.

Chorney, N.A., *Index to Canadian Securities Cases*, 2nd ed. (Toronto: Law Society of Upper Canada, Dept. of Continuing Education, 1980).

Clark, S.D.A., "Impact of the Securities Act on Financing a Corporation", in *Business Law 1986-1987* (Law Society of Upper Canada Bar Admission Course Materials) (Toronto: Carswell, 1986) 113-28.

Coleman, J.G., "Take-over Bids, Insider Bids and Going-Private Transactions — Recent Developments" in *Corporate Law in the 1980s*, Special Lectures of the Law Society of Upper Canada (Toronto: De Boo, 1982) 155-214.

Committee to Study the Requirements and Sources of Capital and the Implications of Non-Resident Capital for the Canadian Securities Industry. *Report*, Toronto Stock Exchange (May, 1970) ("Moore Report").

Condon, M.G., "Alternative Accountabilities: Examples from Securities Regulation" in *Accountability for Criminal Justice* (Toronto: U. of Toronto Press, 1995) 239-267.

————, Comments on [Stanley Beck's paper]: "Gatekeepers and the Commission: The Role of Professionals in the Regulatory System", in *Securities Regulation: Issues and Perspectives: Queen's Annual Business Law Symposium 1994* (Scarborough, Ont.: Carswell, 1995), p. 264-269.

Conway, G.R., *The Supply of and Demand for Canadian Equities*. (Toronto: Toronto Stock Exchange, 1970).

Courtright, J., *Securities Regulation of Take-over Bids in Canada* (Carswell, 1985).

Courtwright, J.T.D., "Securities Regulation of Take-over Bids in Canada" (Calgary: Carswell, 1985).

Cranston, R.R., "Comment on *Green v Charterhouse Group*" (1974) 32 *University of Toronto Faculty Law Review* 175.

Crawford, H.P., "Insider" (1965), 8 *Canadian Bar Journal* 400.

Crawford, P., "A Vision of the Securities Law Practitioner as Legal, Business and Social Architect" in *Securities Law in the Modern Financial Marketplace*, Special Lectures of the Law Society of Upper Canada (Toronto: De Boo, 1989)133-43.

Creber, G.E., "Take-Over Bids, Insider Trading and Proxy Requirements", in *Developments in Company Law*, Special Lectures of the Law Society of Upper Canada (Toronto: De Boo, 1968) 235.

Davies, Ward & Beck, *Canadian Securities Law Precedents* (Toronto: Carswell, 1989).

Derby, W. and C.C. Gagnon, "The Consequences of Incomplete Disclosure under the B.C. Securities Act" (1996) 54 *Advocate* 91-101.

Dey, P.J., "Exemptions Under the Securities Act of Ontario" in *Corporate and Securities Law*, Special Lectures of the Law Society of Upper Canada (Toronto: De Boo, 1972) 127.

————, "Securities Reform in Ontario: The Securities Act, 1975" (1975) 1 *Canadian Business Law Journal* 20.

————, "New Instruments in Public Financing" in *Securities Law in the Modern Financial Marketplace*, Special Lectures of the Law Society of Upper Canada (Toronto: De Boo, 1989) 215-69.

Dialogue with the OSC, 1990: Current Developments in Securities Regulation (Toronto: Insight Educational Services, 1990).

Douglas, J., "Dispelling Fears of a Hydra: Toward Defining a Constructive Role for the Regulator in Enforcement Proceedings", in *Securities Regulation: Issues and Perspectives: Queen's Annual Business Law Symposium 1994* (Scarborough, Ont.: Carswell, 1995), 209-225.

Drinkwater, D.W., W.K. Orr and R. Sorell, *Private Placements in Canada* (Toronto: Carswell, 1985).

Duggan, W.M., "The Function of the Ontario Securities Commission" *Canadian Journal of Accountancy* 55 (March 1957).

Emerson, H.G., "Business Finance Under the Closed System of the Ontario Securities Act: Statutory Scheme and Pitfalls" in *Corporate Law in the 1980s*, Special Lectures of the Law Society of Upper Canada (Toronto: De Boo, 1982) 29-102.

————, "An Integrated Disclosure System for Ontario Securities Legislation", in J.S. Ziegel, ed., *Canadian Company Law*, vol. 2 (Toronto: Butterworths, 1973) 400.

English, J.T., "Corporate Acquisition – General Considerations" in J.S. Ziegel, ed., *Canadian Company Law*, vol. 1 (Toronto: Butterworths, 1967) 603.

Evans, J.L., "Co-ordinated Regulation of Securities and Financial Markets" in *Securities Law in the Modern Financial Marketplace*, Special Lectures of the Law Society of Upper Canada (Toronto: De Boo, 1989) 67-75.

Eyton, T.J., "Let the Current Reform Process Work its Will" [Comments on William Braithwaite's paper: Who is best suited to introduce corporate governance reform and mutual fund governance reform?], in *Securities Regulation: Issues and Perspectives: Queen's Annual Business Law Symposium 1994* (Scarborough, Ont.: Carswell, 1995), 338-340.

Farrar, J., "Business Judgment and Defensive Tactics in Hostile Takeover Bids" (1989) 15 *Can. Bus. L. J.* 15-42.

Forbes, R.F. and D.L. Johnston, *Canadian Companies and the Stock Exchanges* (Don Mills: CCH Canada, 1979).

Forget, M.V., "Les Bilans dans le Prospectus", 88 *Canadian Chartered Accountant* 481 (June, 1966).

French, H.L., *International Law of Take-Overs and Mergers: United States, Canada, and South and Central America* (Westport, Conn: Quorum Books, 1986)

Fullerton, D.H., *The Bond Market in Canada* (Toronto: Carswell, 1962)

Garrod, D.R., "Securities Regulation – 1996 Update: Materials prepared for a ... Seminar held in Vancouver, B.C. on May 9, 1996" (Vancouver: Continuing Legal Education Society of B.C., 1996).

Geller, J.A., Comments on [a paper by David A. Brown and Janet A. Holmes]: "The empty seat at the boardroom table", in *Securities Regulation: Issues and Perspectives: Queen's Annual Business*

Law Symposium 1994 (Scarborough, Ont.: Carswell, 1995), 417-420.

Getz, L., "Alberta Proxy Legislation" (1970) 8 *Alberta Law Review* 18.

————, "The Structure of Shareholder Democracy" in J.S. Ziegel, ed., *Canadian Company Law*, vol. 2 (Toronto: Butterworths, 1973).

Reports of Leon Getz to the Minister of Consumer and Corporate Affairs of British Columbia and to the Ontario Securities Commission of an Investigation into Various Matters Including Trading in the Securities of Kaiser Resources Limited (KRI) and British Columbia Resources Investment Corporation (BCRIC) (Victoria: Minister of Consumer and Corporate Affairs, 1980)

Gillen, M., "Capital Market Efficiency Assumptions: An Analytical Framework with an Application to Disclosure Laws" (1994) 23 Cdn. Bus. L. J. 346-78.

————, "Economic Efficiency and Takeover Bid Regulation" (1986) 24 *Osgoode Hall L.J.* 919-959.

————, "Proposed Changes to Provincial Takeover Bid Legislation: Deterrence Without Protection" (1991) 25 U.B.C. Law Rev. 129.

————, "Sanctions Against Insider Trading: A Proposal for Reform" (1991) 70 Cdn. Bar Rev. 215-43

————, "Takeover Bid Auctions: Analysis and Implications", Proceedings of the Twenty-First Annual Meeting of the Western Decision Sciences Institute, 1992.

————, "Takeover-bid Auctions" (thesis) (Toronto, 1987).

Giroux, L., "Liability for Improper Insider Trading in Quebec" (1988) 5 *Bus. & L.* 34-35.

Girvan, G.M., "Developments in Financing Techniques: Securitization of Financial Assets" (1987-88) 2 *Review of International Business Law* 61-74.

Goulet, G., "A Comparative Analysis of Constitutional Aspects of Securities Regulation in Canada and Australia" [microform] (Ottawa: National Library of Canada, 1991).

Grafstein, L., "Whose Company Is It, Anyway?: Recent Developments in Canadian Takeover Law" (1988) 46 *University of Toronto Faculty Law Review* 522-41.

Grant, D.W., "Cooperative Securities Regulation" A Partnership of

Direct Government Regulation and Self-regulation: [Comments on René Sorell's paper: Supervision of Selfregulatory organizations in Ontario's Securities Market], in *Securities Regulation: Issues and Perspectives: Queen's Annual Business Law Symposium 1994* (Scarborough, Ont.: Carswell, 1995) 197-202.

Greenwood, A., "The Chinese Wall doctrine: Substantive Legal Theory or Rule of Evidence?" (1989) 3 *R.I.B.L.* 271-306.

Gresham, Julia E., "The POP System, Dissemination and Civil Liability: A Proposed Alternative to the Closed System" *Securities Law in the Modern Financial Marketplace*, Special Lectures of the Law Society of Upper Canada (Toronto: De Boo, 1989) 385420.

Groia, J. & C. Olesen, "Hercules v. the Hydra and O.S.C." [Ontario Securities Commission] Encore?: [Comments on James Douglas's paper: Dispelling Fears of a Hydra: Toward Defining a Constructive Role for the Regulator in Enforcement Proceedings], in *Securities Regulation: Issues and Perspectives: Queen's Annual Business Law Symposium 1994* (Scarborough, Ont.: Carswell, 1995) 233-238.

Grover, W. and N. Cheifetz, "Federal Regulation of Securities Activities of Banks and Other Financial Institutions" *Securities Law in the Modern Financial Market Place*, Special Lectures of the Law Society of Upper Canada (Toronto: De Boo, 1989) 9-25.

Guttman, E. and T.P. Lemke, "The Transfer of Securities in Organized Markets: A Comparative Study of Clearing Agencies in the United States of America, Britain and Canada" (1981) 19 *Osgoode Hall Law Journal* 400.

Guy, P., "Take-over Bids: the New Rules" [1987] Meredith Mem. Lect. 107-110.

Halperin, S., "Levelling the Playing Field" (1992) 125 *C.A. Mag No.* 1, 37-42.

Harley, D.M., "Central Depository System for Securities" (1983) 7 *Canadian Business Law Journal* 306.

————, "Central Depository System for Securities" in *Corporate Law in the 1980s*, Special Lectures of the Law Society of Upper Canada (Toronto: De Boo, 1982) 383-99.

Hay, C.T., "Exchange of Information Among Canadian Provincial and American Securities Commissions" (1988) 2 *Review of International Business Law* 219-24.

Hayden, Gerald, Jr., "The Development of the Ontario Follow-up Offer Rule and Its Reform" (1985) 23 *University of Western Ontario Law Review* 49-65.

Healy, Priscilla H., "National Policy Statement No. 41: The First Year" in *Securities Law in the Modern Financial Marketplace*, Special Lectures of the Law Society of Upper Canada (Toronto: De Boo, 1989) 355-77.

Huberman, D., "Winding-Up of Business Corporations" in J.S. Ziegel, ed., *Canadian Company Law*, vol. 2 (Toronto: Butterworths, 1973) 273.

Iacobucci, F. and D.L. Johnston, "The Private or Closely-Held Corporation" in J.S. Ziegel, ed., *Canadian Company Law*, vol. 2 (Toronto: Butterworths, 1973) 68.

Iacobucci, F., "The Business Corporations Act, 1970: Creation and Financing of a Corporation and Management and Control of a Corporation" (1971) 21 *University of Toronto Law Journal* 416-40 and 543-75.

Janisch, H.N., Comments on Philip Anisman's paper [Legitimating Lawmaking by the Ontario Securities Commission] in *Securities Regulation: Issues and Perspectives: Queen's Annual Business Law Symposium 1994* (Scarborough, Ont.: Carswell, 1995), p. 78-83.

Janisch, Hudson N., "Reregulating the Regulator: Administrative Structure of Securities Commissions and Ministerial Responsibility" in *Securities Law in the Modern Financial Marketplace*, Special Lectures of the Law Society of Upper Canada (Toronto: De Boo, 1989) 97-119.

Jeffers, W.J., "Expanding Securities Regulation in Ontario" 163 Commercial and Financial Chronicle 1218 (March 7, 1946)

————, "Ontario's Financial Regulation Under New Securities Act" 162 *Commercial and Financial Chronicle* 2876 (Dec. 13, 1945).

Johnston, D.L., "Case Comment on *Green v The Charterhouse Group*" (1973) 51 *Canadian Bar Review* 676.

————, "Exemptions from Sales Disclosure in Regular Financial Statements: Courts, Tribunals, and Business Judgments" (1973) 23 *University of Toronto Law Journal* 215.

————, "Insider Trading Liability: A Comparison of U.S. and Ontario Legislation", *Ontario Securities Commission Bulletin* (Sept, 1968) 199.

_____, "Public Offering Companies and Non-Public Offering Companies Under the Ontario Business Corporations Act, 1970" (1971-72) 5 *Ottawa Law Review* 1.

Johnston, P.M., "Alberta Securities Law Simplified: A Layman's Guide to Securities Law and Regulation in Alberta" (Calgary, P.M. Johnston; 1996).

Jordan, C., "Securities Law: Proposed Multidurisdictional Disclosure System Between Canada and the United States" (1990) 4 *Canada-U.S. Business Law Review* 141-46.

_____, "U.S. Takeover Defences – In the Canadian Context" (1988) 2 *Review of International Business Law* 205-18.

Kimber, J.R. and L. Lowe, "The Toronto Stock Exchange" in *Corporate and Securities Law*, Special Lectures of the Law Society of Upper Canada (Toronto: De Boo, 1972) 193.

Kramer, M.E., "The Treatment of Crown Corporations Under Provincial Securities Legislation: The Role of Crown Immunity" (1986) 2 *Administrative Law Journal* 68-76.

_____, "The Treatment of Crown Corporations under Provincial Securities Legislation: The Role of Crown Immunity (Part II)" (1987), 3 *Administrative Law Journal* 2-6.

Lampe, J., Comments on [Stanley Beck's paper]: "Gatekeepers and the Commission: The Role of Professionals in the Regulatory System": Why Us?, in *Securities Regulation: Issues and Perspectives: Queen's Annual Business Law Symposium 1994* (Scarborough, Ont.: Carswell, 1995), 273-275.

LaRochelle, L., F.J. Pepin and R.L. Simmonds, "Bill 85, Quebec's New Securities Act" (1983) 29 *McGill Law Journal* 88.

LaRochelle, L., M. Brunet and R. Simmonds, "Continuing Securities Reform in Canada: Amendments to Quebec's Act" (1986) 11 *Canadian Business Law Journal* 147-70.

Le Pan, N., Comments on [Ed Waitzer's paper] "Coordinated Securities Regulation: Getting to a More Effective Regime", in *Securities Regulation: Issues and Perspectives: Queen's Annual Business Law Symposium 1994* (Scarborough, Ont.: Carswell, 1995), 139-144

Lennox, O.E., "Administration Under the Securities Act of Ontario" 72 *Canadian Chartered Accountant* 525 (June 1958).

_____, "Securities Legislation and Administration" in *Company*

Law, Special Lectures of the Law Society of Upper Canada (Toronto: De Boo, 1950) 81.

Libin, B.R., "Securities Aspects of Specialized Financing" (1980) 19 *Alberta Law Review* 43.

Lococo, R., S. Magidson and D. Wakefield, "Insider Trading Rules Tightened" (1988) 5 *Bus. & L.* 33-34.

Lortie, P., "The Regulation of Take-Over Bids in Canada: Premium Private Agreement Transactions", *Report of the Securities Industry Committee on Take-over Bids* (Ottawa: The Committee, 1983).

MacIntosh, J., "Corporate Governance in Canada: a Broad-Brush Assessment:" [comments on William Braithwaite's paper: Who is Best suited to introduce Corporate Governance Reform and Mutual Fund Governance Reform?], in *Securities Regulation: Issues and Perspectives: Queen's Annual Business Law Symposium 1994* (Scarborough, Ont.: Carswell, 1995) 321-332.

MacIntosh, J., "International Securities Regulation: of Competition, Cooperation, Convergence and Cartelization" (Toronto: Cdn. Law and Economics Association, 1996).

MacIntosh, J., "Securities Regulation and the Public Interest: of Politics, Procedures, and Policy Statements (Part 1)" (1994) 24 *Can. Bus. L. J.* 77-120.

MacIntosh, J., "Securities Regulation and the Public Interest: of Politics, Procedures, and Policy Statements (Part 2)" (1994) 24 *Can. Bus. L.J.* 287-314.

Mackenzie, M.A., Comments on [a paper by David A. Brown and Janet A. Holmes]: "The Empty Seat at the Boardroom Table", in *Securities Regulation: Issues and Perspectives: Queen's Annual Business Law Symposium 1994* (Scarborough, Ont.: Carswell, 1995), 421-426.

Makens, H.H., "An American State-Federal Perspective on the Proposals" (1981) 19 *Osgoode Hall Law Journal* 424.

Mann, M.D., "International Legal Assistance in Securities Law Enforcement: Status and Perspective" (1987) 1 *Review of International Business Law* 1.

Martel, J., Comments on [Ed Waitzer's paper] "Coordinated Securities Regulation: Getting to a More Effective Regime", in *Securities Regulation: Issues and Perspectives: Queen's Annual Business Law*

Symposium 1994 (Scarborough, Ont.: Carswell, 1995), p. 145-163.

May, A.W., "Ontario Revises Its Securities Act" 162 *Commercial and Financial Chronicle* 1230 (Sept. 13, 1945).

McDermott, R., "Directors' Fiduciary Duties in the Face of Take-over Bids: A Practical Framework (Parts 1-2)" (1989) 4 *S.C.R.R.* 274-278.

McTague, C.P., "Regulating Canadian Security Markets" 164 *Commercial and Financial Chronicle* 1934 (Oct. 17, 1946).

―――――, "Self Government for Canadian Security Dealers", 164 *Commercial and Financial Chronicle* 81 (July 4, 1946).

Medland, C.E., "Regulation and Ownership of Market Intermediaries in Canada", *Report of the Joint Securities Industry Committee on behalf of the Albert, Montreal, Toronto and Vancouver Stock Exchanges and the Investment Dealers Association of Canada* (Toronto: The Committee, 1984)

Menzel, D.G.C., "Corporate Reorganizations and Amalgamations" in *Developments in Company Law*, Special Lectures of the Law Society of Upper Canada (Toronto: De Boo, 1968) 273.

Moore, P.M., "The Role of Regulation: A Case Study of the Emerging Regulation of Derivative Products", in *Securities Regulation: Issues and Perspectives: Queen's Annual Business Law Symposium 1994* (Scarborough, Ont.: Carswell, 1995), 427-498.

Morin, D.B. and Chippendale, W., eds., *Acquisitions and Mergers in Canada* (Toronto: Methuen, 1970).

Moyer, P., "The Regulation of Corporate Law by Securities Regulators: A Comparison of Ontario and the United States" (1997) 55 *U.T. Fac. L. Rev.* 43-76.

Mulvey, T., *Company Capitalization Control: Report Upon Securities Legislation in Canada and Elsewhere by the Undersecretary of State (Canada)* (Ottawa: 1913)

―――――, "Blue Sky Law" (1916) 36 *Canadian Law Times* 37.

Myhal, P., "Some Observations on the 'Usual' Anti-Dilution Provisions" (1990) 17 *Canadian Business Law Journal* 283.

Nantel, D., "La Commission des Valeurs Mobilieres du Quebec", 89 *Canadian Chartered Accountant* 123 (August, 1966).

Neufeld, E.P., *The Financial System of Canada: Its Growth and Development* (Toronto: Macmillan, 1972).

Nickerson, M., "Securities Regulation — Follow-Up Bids — Securities Act, R.S.O. 1980, c. 466, s. 91" (1984) 62 *Canadian Bar Review* 688.

Nixon, S.E., "The Preparation of Canadian Corporate Prospectuses", 83 *Canadian Chartered Accountant* 345 (November, 1963).

O'Connor, C.E., "The Securities Act in Operation: Public and Private Distribution of Securities in Ontario" in *Corporate Law in the 1980s*, Special Lectures of the Law Society of Upper Canada (Toronto: De Boo, 1982) 103-53.

O'Connor, D. and F. Kristjanson, "Securities Law and the Charter" in *Securities Law in the Modern Financial Marketplace*, Special Lectures of the Law Society of Upper Canada (Toronto: De Boo, 1989) 497-516.

O'Connor, V., "Pezim v. British Columbia (Superintendent of Brokers): Material Fact or Material Change?: A Distinction with a Difference" (1993) 10 *Bus. & L.* 21-24.

Ontario. *Report of the Committee on Commodities Trading*, (Toronto: Queen's Printer, 1975) ("Bray Report")

Legislative Assembly Select Committee on Company Law: Report on Mergers, Amalgamations and Certain Related Matters (Toronto: Queen's Printer, 1973) ("Hodgson Report").

Report of the Minister's Committee on Franchises Dealing with Referral Sales, Multi-Legal Sales and Franchises (Toronto: Queen's Printer, July 1971) ("Grange Report").

Legislative Assembly Select Committee on Company Law: Report on Cooperatives (Toronto: Queen's Printer, 1971).

Legislative Assembly Select Committee on Company Law: Report on Credit Unions (Toronto: Queen's Printer, 1969).

Royal Commission Appointed to Inquire into the Failure of Atlantic Acceptance Corps Ltd. Report, 4 vols. (Toronto: Queen's Printer, 1969) ("Hughes Report.").

Royal Commission on Civil Rights: Report, 5 vols. (Toronto: Queen's Printer, 1968-71) ("McRuer Report"}

Legislative Assembly Select Committee on Company Law: Interim Report (Toronto: Queen's Printer, 1967) ("Lawrence Report"}

Royal Commission to Investigate Trading in the Shares of Windfall Oils and Mines Ltd.: Report (Toronto: Queen's Printer, 1965) ("Kelly Report").

Committee on Securities Legislation in Ontario: Report (Toronto: Queen's Printer, 1965) ("Kimber Report").

Ontario Securities Commission, "A Regulatory Framework for Entry into and Ownership of the Ontario Securities Industry" (Toronto: The Commission, 1985).

————, "New Requirements Under O.S.C.", 75 *Canadian Chartered Accountant* 141 (August, 1959).

————, *An Introduction to Investing in Securities* (Toronto: OSC, 1987)

————, *Report of the Securities Industry Ownership Committee* (Toronto: OSC, 1972)

Osode, P.C., "Insider Trading Regulation: The Theoretical and Policy Foundations" (Ottawa: National Library of Canada, 1995).

Palmer, E.E., "Directors Powers and Duties," in J.S. Ziegel, ed., *Canadian Company Law*, vol. 1 (Toronto: Butterworths, 1967) 365.

Palmer, K.B., "Securities Legislation in Canada" 20 *Journal of Comparative Legislation and International Law*, 3rd series 230 (1938).

Pascutto E. and D.P. Iggers, "The Role of Commission Staff" in *Securities Law in the Modern Financial Marketplace*, Special Lectures of the Law Society of Upper Canada (Toronto: De Boo, 1989) 421-50.

Peters, J.R., *Economics of the Canadian Corporate Bond Market* (Montreal: McGill-Queen's University Press, 1971)

Pincus, S., "Insider Trading Rules in Ontario" (Part 2) (1988) 3 *S.C.R.R.* 129-131.

Pincus, S., "Insider Trading Rules in Ontario" (Part 1) (1988) 3 *S.C.R.R.* 124-128.

Pincus, S., "New Insider Trading Rules in Ontario" in *Corporate structure, finance and operations* (Toronto: Carswell, 1988) 199-211.

Ponder, D., "Continuous Disclosure and Insider Trading (Parts 1-2)" (1989) 4 *S.C.R.R.* 263-274.

Porteous, J.G., "The Securities Act" (1945) 5 *Rev. du Barreau* 328.

Prichard, M., "Proposed SEC Rules for Multi-Jurisdictional Disclosure System" July 1990) 4 *Canada-U.S. Business Law Review* 68-73 (Toronto: Carswell, 1991).

Quebec. Department of Financial Institutions: Companies and Cooperatives, *Study on the Securities Industry in Quebec* (Interim Report, 1971; Final Report, 1972, Quebec City Official Publisher) ("Bouchard Report").

Study Committee on Financial Institutions-Report (Quebec City: Official Publisher, 1969).

Queen's Annual Business Law Symposium, *Securities Regulation: Issues and Perspectives* (Scarborough: Carswell, 1995)

Raffin, L. and D.W. Stephen, "Participation in the British Columbia Securities Market" (1987) 1 *Review of International Business Law* 305-10.

Ratner, D.L., "Self-Regulatory Organizations" (1981) 19 *Osgoode Hall Law Journal* 368.

Reid, R.F., "The Role of the Courts: Is Judicial Review Effective for Specialized Agencies?" in *Securities Law in the Modern Financial Marketplace,* Special Lectures of the Law Society of Upper Canada (Toronto: De Boo, 1989) 517-23.

Report of Committee of the OSC on the Problems of Disclosure Raised for Investors by Business Combinations and Private Placements (Toronto: Ontario Securities Commission, 1970) ("Merger Report").

Report of Commissioner D.S. Beatty on Matters Related to the Financing of Mining Exploration and Development Companies (Toronto: OSC, 1968) ("Beatty Report").

Report of the Attorney General's Committee on Securities Legislation in Ontario (Toronto: March, 1965) (Kimber Report).

Report of the Royal Commission to Investigate Trading in the Shares of Windfall Oils and Mines Ltd (September, 1965).

Riley, J.A., Comments on [Paul M. Moore's paper]: "The Role of Regulation: A Case Study on the Emerging Regulation of Derivative Products", in *Securities Regulation: Issues and Perspectives: Queen's Annual Business Law Symposium 1994* (Scarborough, Ont.: Carswell, 1995), 502-508.

Rodier, A.R., "Prospectus Disclosure Under the Proposed Securities Act in Ontario: Problems in a Changing Environment" (1985) 23 *University of Western Ontario Law Review* Rev. 21.

Roman, A., "E.A. Manning Ltd. v. Ontario (Securities Commission)" (Case Comment), (1995) 32 *Admin. L.R.* 22-27.

Romano, S., "Self-regulation in the Securities Industry: a Regulatory Perspective" (1996) 17 *Can. Compet. Rec. No. 1* 35-47

Rosenfeld, W.P., "Corporate Acquisitions" (1972) Special Lectures of the Law Society of Upper Canada 367.

Salvatori, P.E., "Silk Purse or Sow's Ear: What is a Valuable Security?" (1980) 11 *Manitoba Law Journal* 91.

Sawiak, G.V., *The Toronto Stock Exchange: A Procedural Guide for Companies and Their Professional Advisors* (Scarborough: Butterworths, 1986).

Scarlett, J.D., "Universal Registration Under the Securities Act: History and Implementation" in *Securities Law in the Modern Financial Marketplace,* Special Lectures of the Law Society of Upper Canada (Toronto: De Boo, 1989) 145-79.

Shaw, D.C. and T.R. Archibald, *The Management of Change in the Canadian Securities Industry* (Toronto: Toronto Stock Exchange, 1972-76).

Shay, R., Comments on [René Sorell's paper] "Supervision of Self-Regulatory Organizations in Ontario's Securities Market", in *Securities Regulation: Issues and Perspectives: Queen's Annual Business Law Symposium 1994* (Scarborough, Ont.: Carswell, 1995), 203-207.

Simmonds, R.L., "Director's Negligent Misstatement Liability in the New Scheme of Securities Regulation in Ontario" (1979) 11 *Ottawa Law Review* 633; reprinted in *Corporate Structure, Finance and Operation* (Toronto: Carswell, 1980).

———, "Financial Planners: A Securities Law Primer" in *Securities Law in the Modern Financial Marketplace,* Special Lectures of the Law Society of Upper Canada (Toronto: De Boo, 1989) 181-98.

Sinclair, J.D., Comments on [Paul M. Moore's paper]: "The Emerging Regulation of Derivatives: The New Soviet Republic?", in *Securities Regulation: Issues and Perspectives: Queen's Annual Business Law Symposium 1994* (Scarborough, Ont.: Carswell, 1995), 509-518.

Smart, J.C. & J.C. Baillie, Comments on [Philip Anisman's paper] "Legitimating Lawmaking by the Ontario Securities Commission: Comments on the Final Report of the Ontario Task Force on Securities Regulation", in *Securities Regulation: Issues and Perspectives: Queen's Annual Business Law Symposium 1994* (Scarborough, Ont.: Carswell, 1995), 84-90.

Smith, S.E., "Stockbrokers' Bankruptcies" (1933) 3 *Dominion Law Reports* 1.

Sorell, R., "Offering Memoranda under the Ontario Securities Act, 1978" (1980) 4 *Canadian Business Law Journal* 467.

Sorell, R., "Supervision of Self-Regulatory Organizations in Ontario's Securities Market", in *Securities Regulation: Issues and Perspectives: Queen's Annual Business Law Symposium 1994* (Scarborough, Ont.: Carswell, 1995), 165-202.

Stevens, G. and S.D. Wortley, "Murray Pezim in the Court of Appeal: Draining the Lifeblood from Securities Regulation" (1992) 25 *U.B.C.L. Rev.* 331-340.

Stokes, M., "The Usefulness of 'law and economics': Analysis of Takeover Bids" (Toronto: 1987).

Stransman, J.M. and A.A. Greenwood, "Provincial Regulation of Securities Activities of Banks and Other Federal Financial Institutions: the Ontario Perspective" in *Securities Law in the Modern Financial Marketplace*, Special Lectures of the Law Society of Upper Canada (Toronto: De Boo, 1989) 27-65.

Strother, R.C., "Income Tax Disclosure in Prospectuses and Other Securities Documents" (1987) 39 Canadian Tax Foundation 44:1-44:44.

Sullivan, D.F., "New Developments in Corporate Financing" (1988) 40 *Canadian Tax Foundation* 20:1-20:48.

Thomforde, F.H., "Administrative Enforcement Powers and Procedures Under the Proposed Securities Market Law" (1981) 19 *Osgoode Hall Law Journal* 381.

Thompson, A., "Part 14 of the New Securities Act: 'Due Diligence' Comes to B.C." (1988) 22 *University of British Columbia Law Review* 279-313.

Thomson, C.R., "Concepts and Procedures in Hearings Before the Ontario Securities Commission" in *Corporate and Securities Law*, Special Lectures of the Law Society of Upper Canada (Toronto: De Boo, 1972) 95.

Toronto: The Task Force, "Responsibility and Responsiveness: Interim Report of the Ontario Task Force on Securities Regulation" (1994).

Turner, J., Comments on [Stanley Beck's paper]: "Gatekeepers and the Commission: The Role of Professionals in the Regulatory

System", in *Securities Regulation: Issues and Perspectives: Queen's Annual Business Law Symposium 1994* (Scarborough, Ont.: Carswell, 1995), 270-272.

University of Ottawa, "Canadian Securities Regulation" (Toronto: Insight Press, 1994).

Vesely, G. and R. Roberts, "Takeover Bids: Selected Tax, Corporate, and Securities Law Considerations" (1991) 43 *Can. Tax Found.* 11:1-11:47.

Voore, M. and M. Matheson, "Securities Regulation of Publicly Traded Companies: Disclosure and Reporting Compliance" in *Corporate Structure, Finance and Operations* (Scarborough: Carswell, 1996) 91-141.

Waitzer, E.J. & A. Sahazizian, "Coordinated Securities Regulation: Getting to a More Effective Regime", in *Securities Regulation: Issues and Perspectives: Queen's Annual Business Law Symposium 1994* (Scarborough, Ont.: Carswell, 1995), 101-128.

Walsh, M.H., The Role of the Regulator: [comments on William Braithwaite's paper: Who is Best suited to introduce Corporate Governance Reform and Mutual Fund Governance Reform?], in *Securities Regulation: Issues and Perspectives: Queen's Annual Business Law Symposium 1994* (Scarborough, Ont.: Carswell, 1995), 333-337.

Walter, J.E. and J.P. Williamson, "Organized Securities Exchanges in Canada" (1960) 15 *Journal of Finance* 307.

Ware, J.G., "The Role of the Trustee Under Trust Indentures" (1968) 26 *University of Toronto Faculty Law Review* 45.

Watson, A.G., "The Auditor's Part in Prospectuses", 82 *Canadian Chartered Accountant* 415 (June, 1963).

Whitehead, "The Work of the Ontario Securities Commission," in *Canadian Boards at Work*, J. Willis, ed. (Toronto: Macmillan, 1941) 48.

Whyte, J.D., Comments on [Philip Anisman's paper] "Legitimating Lawmaking by the Ontario Securities Commission: Comments on the Final Report of the Ontario Task Force on Securities Regulation" in *Securities Regulation: Issues and Perspectives: Queen's Annual Business Law Symposium 1994* (Scarborough, Ont.: Carswell, 1995), 91-99.

Williamson, J.P., "Mining Accounts, Could We Have Better Disclosure for Investors?", 83 *Canadian Chartered Accountant* 415 (June, 1963).

_____, "Securities Regulation — A Canadian S.E.C.?" (1964) 29 *The Business Quarterly* 54.

_____, "Securities Regulation: A Review of Some Current Problems", 27 *The Business Quarterly* 31 (Fall, 1962).

_____, "Take-Over Bids and Insider Trading" (1963) 28 *The Business Quarterly* 47.

_____, "Securities Regulation: Their Effect on Canadian Industrial Financing", 69 *Canadian Banker* 27 (Spring, 1962).

_____, *Securities Regulation in Canada* (Toronto: University of Toronto Press, 1960) and Supplement (Ottawa 1966).

Ziegel, J.S., "Constitutional Aspects of Canadian Companies", in J.S. Ziegel, ed., *Canadian Company Law*, vol. 1 (Toronto: Butterworths, 1967) Chapter 5, 149.

Ziegel, J.S., ed., *Studies in Canadian Company Law*, 2 vol. (Toronto: Butterworths, 1967 and 1973).

Ziegel, J.S., "Must we Settle for Second Best?" Comments on Ed Waitzer's paper: [Coordinated Securities Regulation: Getting to a More Effective Regime], in *Securities Regulation: Issues and Perspectives: Queen's Annual Business Law Symposium 1994* (Scarborough, Ont.: Carswell, 1995), 129-135.

INDEX

ABBREVIATED PROSPECTUS
see SHORT-FORM PROSPECTUS

ACQUISITIONS
see TAKEOVERS

ACTING JOINTLY OR IN CONCERT
meaning of term, 386–387

ACTORS
see SECURITIES MARKET ACTORS

ADMINISTRATORS
see also SECURITIES COMMISSIONS
blue-sky discretion, 135–137
decisions and rulings
appeal to court, 510–511
failure to comply, 501
generally, 98
review by Commission, 508–509
generally, 88–89
mutual fund changes, approval,
477–478
policy statements, 96

ADVERSE SELECTION
concept, 84
confidence in market connection, 86
insider trading, effect, 352–353
securities markets, in, 85–86
securities regulation as response, 87

ADVERTISING
mutual funds, 485

ADVISORS
see also SECURITIES MARKET
ACTORS
investment counsel
see INVESTMENT COUNSEL
market commentaries
see MARKET COMMENTARIES
portfolio managers
see PORTFOLIO MANAGERS
registration
see REGISTRATION
securities advisors
see SECURITIES ADVISORS

ANNUAL INFORMATION FORM (AIF)
general, 202–205

mutual funds
pro-forma, 470
requirements, 469–470
prompt offerings
initial, 261–263
subsequent, 263
shelf offerings, 277

APPEALS
administrators, from, 510–511
securities commissions, from, 510

APPROVED RATINGS
POP system, 267–268, 269–270

ASSET BACKED SECURITIES, 19

AUDITORS
see also EXPERTS
misrepresentation in prospectus liability,
155

AUDITS
enforcement powers, 511–514

BANK LOANS
described, 4–5

BANK REALIZATIONS
isolated trades, registration exemption,
438–441

BANKING GROUPS
underwriting firms, 23

BEARER FORM CERTIFICATES
see also SHARE CERTIFICATES
exchange process, 29–33

BENSTON STUDY
mandatory disclosure, effects, 300

BEST INTERESTS TEST
takeover bid defences, 394

BIDS
see TAKEOVER BIDS

BLANKET ORDERS
exempt trades, granting, 258
Securities Commissions, 97–98

BLUE-SKY DISCRETION
administrators, 135–137
critique of, 321
interest group theory, 322

BONDS
see DEBENTURES, 5–7

BORROWING
see DEBT FINANCE

BOUGHT DEAL
distribution of securities, 21–22
POP system encourages, 288–289

BROKERS
see also DEALERS; SECURITIES
MARKET ACTORS
churning
see CHURNING
clearing agencies, use, 34–35
depository corporations, 35
front running
see FRONT RUNNING
inventories, 35
over-the-counter trades, 38
using, 25

BULLETINS
Securities Commissions, 98

CALLS
bonds or debentures, 6
preferred shares, 11

CANADA SAVINGS BONDS
see GOVERNMENT SECURITIES

CAPITAL MARKET EFFICIENCY
see SECURITIES MARKET EFFICIENCY

CASH DIVIDENDS
see DIVIDENDS

CEASE TRADE ORDERS, 390

CERTIFICATES
see SHARE CERTIFICATES

CHANGES
material changes, 193–198
mutual funds, 477–479
proposed changes, 199

CHARITABLE ORGANIZATIONS
exempt trades, 253–254

CHARTER IMPLICATIONS
securities regulation, 512–514

CIRCULARS
see TAKEOVER BID CIRCULARS

CLEARANCE PERIOD
distribution of securities, 130

CLEARING AGENCIES
function, 34–35, 37

CLOSED SYSTEM CONCEPT
concept described, 217
diagram, 218
provincial regulation statutes, 77, 98
resale restrictions
see RESALE OF SECURITIES
response to uncertainty and gaps, 217
trading outside
disclosure requirements, 217–218
resale restrictions, 219–221
trading within, 217
weaknesses in preclosed system,
214–216
continuous disclosure, 216
uncertainty, 214–216

CLOSED-END INVESTMENT FUNDS
described, 42

COMMENT LETTER
distribution of securities, 130

COMMERCIAL PAPER
described, 5

COMMISSIONS
see SECURITIES COMMISSIONS

COMMON BOND INVESTORS
see also INVESTORS IN SECURITIES
friends and relatives, 239–240,
248–250
registration exemptions, 442–443

COMMON SHARES
see also SHARES
dividend rights, 8–9
liquidation rights, 9
voting rights, 8

COMPENSATION
see SUPERIOR COMPENSATION

CONFIDENCE-IN-THE-MARKET
see also SECURITIES MARKETS
adverse selection and, 84–86
allocation of savings, 82–83
method of achieving, 83–84
primary and secondary, link, 82
promoting, 82

CONFIDENTIAL REPORTING
material information, 199, 201–202
proposed changes, 200–201

CONFLICTS OF INTEREST
mutual funds, restrictions, 471–474

CONSIDERATION
see also SUPERIOR COMPENSATION

CONSOLIDATIONS
see AMALGAMATIONS

CONSTITUTIONAL DIVISION OF POWERS
see also SECURITIES REGULATION
federal powers, 69
provincial powers
    property and civil rights, 67–68
    scope, 68–69

CONSTITUTIONAL IMPLICATIONS
securities regulation, 512–514

CONTINUOUS DISCLOSURE
see also DISCLOSURE; MANDATORY
    DISCLOSURE; SECONDARY
    MARKET DISCLOSURE
benefits, 170–171
financial statements, 172–173
see FINANCIAL STATEMENTS
information circulars
see PROXY CIRCULARS
insider reports
see INSIDER REPORTS
primary purpose, 170–171
proxy circulars
see PROXY CIRCULARS
reporting issuers,
see REPORTING ISSUERS
sanctions
    common law, 211–212
    penal, 208–209
    statutory civil, 209–211
secondary market, 170
summary, 173
timely disclosure
see TIMELY DISCLOSURE

CONVERSION
bonds, 6–7

COOLING-OFF PERIOD
purchase of securities, 132

CREDIT LINES
see REVOLVING LINES OF CREDIT

DEALERS
see also SECURITIES MARKET
    ACTORS
investment
see INVESTMENT DEALERS
professional competence, 90

registration
see REGISTRATION
scholarship plans
see SCHOLARSHIP PLAN DEALERS
securities
see SECURITIES DEALERS

DEBENTURES
described, 5–6
features
    call, 6
    convertible, 6–7
    sinking funds, 6
    warrants, 7
government
see GOVERNMENT SECURITIES
trading, 40

DEBT FINANCE
see also EQUITY FINANCE
bank loans, 4–5
bonds or debentures, 5–7
call feature, 6
commercial paper, 5
funding source, 1–2
sinking fund, 6
trade credit, 4

DEFENCES
due diligence
see DUE DILIGENCE DEFENCE
misrepresentations in prospectus,
    142–167
takeover bids,
see under TAKEOVER BIDS

DEFICIENCY LETTER
see COMMENT LETTER

DEPOSITORY CORPORATIONS
functions, 35–36, 37

DERIVATIVE SECURITIES, 15–19

DETRIMENTAL INFORMATION
reporting, 200

DIRECT ISSUE
distribution of securities, 20–21

DIRECTORS' CIRCULARS
see also TAKEOVER BIDS CIRCULARS

DIRECTORS' LIABILITY
prospectuses, 154, 159–161, 164

DISCLOSURE
see also MANDATORY DISCLOSURE
closed system concept
see CLOSED SYSTEM CONCEPT
continuous disclosure
see CONTINUOUS DISCLOSURE

DISCLOSURE – *(cont'd)*
history of securities regulation, 74–77
multi-jurisdictional offerings, 134
mutual funds, investment practices, 477
prospectus requirements,
    see PROSPECTUSES
secondary market
    see SECONDARY MARKET
    DISCLOSURE
takeover bids
    early warning, 389–390
    timely
    see TIMELY DISCLOSURE

DISCOUNTING
value of securities, 48

DISTRIBUTION OF SECURITIES
see also SALE OF SECURITIES;
    TRADES IN SECURITIES
control persons, 126–127
deemed on resale, 127
definition, 124–127
exempt distributions
    see EXEMPT DISTRIBUTIONS
methods
    best efforts underwriting, 22
    bought deal, 21–22
    direct issue, 20–21
    offer to sell, 21–22
    private placement, 21
    standby underwriting, 22
    summary, 23–24
    underwriters, through
    see UNDERWRITING
primary market trading, 24–25
process, 128–137
prospectus requirements
    see PROSPECTUSES
securities not previously issued,
    124–125
securities returned to issuer, 125–126
treasury stock, 126

DIVIDEND REINVESTMENT
see also DIVIDENDS

DIVIDENDS
see also STOCK DIVIDENDS
common shares, 8–9
preferred shares
    cumulative rights, 10
    participation rights, 10–11
reinvestment
    see DIVIDEND REINVESTMENT

DUE DILIGENCE DEFENCE
see also DEFENCES
auditors, 162–163
cases considering, 157–164

directors and officers, 159–161
expertised portion, 158
lawyer's role, 164–167
POP offerings, 288
shelf offerings, 288
underwriters, 162

EFFICIENCY
see SECURITIES MARKET EFFICIENCY

ENFORCEMENT MECHANISMS
administrative sanctions, 503–507
audits, 511–514
civil sanctions, 508
constitutional implications, 512–514
freeze orders, 512
investigations, 511–514
penal sanctions, 499–503
review and appeal procedures,
    508–511

EQUITY FINANCE
see also DEBT FINANCE
common shares, 8–9
funding source, 1–2
limited partnership units, 13–14
options, 13
preferred shares, 9–11
restricted shares, 11–12
rights, 12–13
share capital, 7–8
units of securities, 13–14

EXCHANGE RIGHTS
see CONVERSION

EXCHANGE TRADING
see STOCK EXCHANGE TRADING

EXECUTIVE COMPENSATION,
    183–185

EXECUTORS
see TRUSTEES

EXEMPT DISTRIBUTIONS
see also DISTRIBUTION OF
    SECURITIES; EXEMPTION
    ORDERS; EXEMPTIONS
closed system concept
    see CLOSED SYSTEM CONCEPT
modified procedures, 256
no need to know
    common bonds, 235–238
    information elsewhere, 245–247
    no new information, 240–245
    sophisticated investors, 227–235
other exemptions
    blanket orders, 258
    exemption orders, 257–258
    regulated elsewhere, 250–251

resale restrictions
see RESALE OF SECURITIES
safe investments, 251–253
smaller issuers, 247–248
specific activities
  charitable, 253–254
  educational, 253–254
  exchange issuers, 255–256
  prospecting expeditions, 254–255
  prospecting syndicates, 254–255
  recreational, 253–254
  religious, 253–254

EXEMPTION ORDERS
see also EXEMPT DISTRIBUTIONS;
  EXEMPTIONS
granting, 257–258

EXEMPTIONS
disclosures
see EXEMPT DISTRIBUTIONS
orders
see EXEMPTION ORDERS

EXPEDITIONS
see PROSPECTING EXPEDITIONS AND
  SYNDICATES

EXPERTS
prospectus liability, 155, 158

FEDERAL SECURITIES COMMISSION,
  78

FEES
see MANAGEMENT FEES

FINANCIAL RESOURCES
optimal allocation
  cost not excessive, 83
  investor protection, link, 81
  method of achieving, 83–84
  savings, 83
  securities regulation, purpose, 80–81

FINANCIAL STATEMENTS
annual statements, 175–176
exemptions
  conflict of laws, 178
  consistency of reporting, 179
  deviation from GAAP, 177–178
  general power, 179
  specific omissions, 178
interim statements, 176
preparation according to GAAP,
  176–177

FINANCING
debt finance
see DEBT FINANCE

equity finance
see EQUITY FINANCE

FIRMS
see SECURITIES FIRMS

FORMAL VALUATION
see also VALUATION OF SECURITIES
takeover bids, requirements, 375–377

FRAUD
fraud on the market doctrine, 211–212
prospectus disclosures, 146–147
secondary market disclosures, 211–212
securities regulation, history, 74–75

FREEZE ORDERS
enforcement powers, 512

FUNDAMENTAL ANALYSIS
valuation of securities, 51

FUTURE ORIENTED FINANCIAL
  INFORMATION, 103–104

GOING PRIVATE TRANSACTIONS
defined, 376
minority approval, 378
special committee review, 377–378
takeover bid, after, 376

GOVERNMENT SECURITIES
overview, 14–15
safe investments, 251–253

HISTORY OF SECURITIES
  REGULATION
Canada
  fraud prevention, 74–75
  interprovincial cooperation, 77–78
  Kimber report, 76–77
  Merger report, 77
  prospectus disclosure, 75–76
summary, 78–79
United Kingdom, 70–73
United States, 73–74

HOLD PERIOD
resale restrictions, 223–225

HUBRIS
takeover motivation, 366, 407

INCORPORATORS
exempt trades, 235–237

INFORMATION
detrimental
see DETRIMENTAL INFORMATION
inside
see INSIDE INFORMATION
material
see MATERIAL INFORMATION

INFORMATION CIRCULARS
see PROXY CIRCULARS

INSIDE INFORMATION
see also INSIDER TRADING

INSIDER BIDS
see also TAKEOVER BIDS
minority approval, 373
special committee review, 373

INSIDER REPORTS
see also INSIDER TRADING
disclosure requirements, 191–192
enforcement means, 338
insider, defined, 191

INSIDER TRADING
see also INSIDE INFORMATION;
INSIDER REPORTS
enforcement of prohibitions
administrative sanctions, 337–338
civil actions, 333–335
penal sanctions, 329–332
reporting, 282
reporting issuers, by, 335–338
enforcement problems
administrative sanctions, 343–344
circumstantial evidence, 341–342
civil accounting sanctions, 343
civil damage actions, 342–343
detection, 339–340
penal sanctions, 342
summary, 344
insider, defined, 191, 325–326
interest group theory, 358
perceived problem, legislative approach,
323–324
policy reconsideration
do investors lose, 345–347
is it detrimental, 348–357
market liquidity, 355
summary, 359–360
prohibitions
how, 328–338
what, 325
when, 325
who, 325–328
proposed changes, 200–202
reporting requirement
see INSIDER REPORTS

INTEREST GROUP THEORY
mandatory disclosure, 317–321

INTEREST IN PROPERTY
see also SECURITIES
security, inclusion in definition,
110–111

INTEREST RATE CAPS, 18–19

**INTERNATIONALIZATION OF
SECURITIES MARKETS**, 43–46

INVESTIGATIONS
enforcement powers, 511–514

INVESTMENT CONTRACTS
see also SECURITIES
meaning of term, 111–120
security, inclusion in definition,
110–111

INVESTMENT DEALERS
see also DEALERS

INVESTMENT FUNDS
closed-end
see CLOSED-END INVESTMENT
FUNDS
open-end
see MUTUAL FUNDS

INVESTMENTS
see SAFE INVESTMENTS; SECURITIES

INVESTOR PROTECTION
cost not excessive, 83
method of achieving, 83–84
resource allocation, link, 81
securities regulation, purpose, 79–80

INVESTORS
institutional, 43

INVESTORS IN SECURITIES
banks, 41
common bonds
see COMMON BOND INVESTORS
individuals, 43
investment funds, 42–43
life insurance companies, 42
pension funds, 42
protection
see SOPHISTICATED INVESTORS
trust companies, 41

ISSUER BID REGULATION
see also TAKEOVERS
basic rules, 416–418
exemptions
de minimis test, 420–421
employee security ownership,
419–420
exemption order, 421
normal course purchases, 421
owner controlled acquisitions, 419
pre-arranged acquisitions, 419
private companies, 420
stock exchange bids, 421
reasons for, 415–416

ISSUERS OF SECURITIES
see also SECURITIES ISSUERS
exchange issuers
see EXCHANGE ISSUERS (B.C.)
misrepresentations, strict liability defences,
153–154
non-profit
see NON-PROFIT ISSUERS
prospectus form, 101–102
reporting issuers
see REPORTING ISSUERS
smaller
see SMALLER ISSUERS
takeover bid target, 362–363

JARRELL STUDY
mandatory disclosure, effects, 298–299

KIMBER REPORT
investor protection, 80
optimal allocation of resources, 80–81
primary and secondary market
confidence, link, 82
public confidence, 82
securities regulation, history, 76

LAWYERS
prospectus preparation, role, 164–167

LICENCES
see REGISTRATION

LIMITATIONS
misrepresentation actions, 156

LIQUIDATION
common shares, rights, 9

**MANAGEMENT DISCUSSION AND
ANALYSIS,** 202–205

MANAGERIALISM
see EMPIRE BUILDING

MANAGERS
portfolio
see PORTFOLIO MANAGERS

MANDATORY DISCLOSURE
see also DISCLOSURE
change in emphasis
agency cost emphasis, 306–307
future-oriented, 304–305
liability and enforcement, 305–306
market risk, 304–305
permitting silence and lying,
307–308
secondary market, 303–304
sophisticated investors, 303–304
effect
comments, 301–302
critiques, 303–321
new issue disclosure, 296–300
secondary market disclosure, 300
further research, 320–321
interest group theory, 317–320
blue-sky discretion, 322
generally, 317–320
rhetorical conventions, 320
within securities regulatory
organizations, 318–319
need for
adverse selection problem, 308–310
market failures, 311–317
reducing security price inaccuracies,
314–316
standardization of information
presentation, 316–317
prospectus disclosure,
see PROSPECTUSES

MANNE'S ARGUMENT
insider trading benefits
efficient pricing, 353–357
superior compensation, 349–353

MARGIN TRADING, 39–40

MARKET COMMENTARIES
see also ADVISORS

MARKET MANIPULATION
see SECURITIES MARKETS

MATERIAL CHANGES
reporting requirements, 193–198
proposed changes, 199

MATERIAL FACTS
see also STATEMENT OF MATERIAL
FACTS
defined, 103, 197–198
prospectus disclosure, 103
timely disclosure, 194–197

MATERIAL INFORMATION
see also MATERIAL CHANGES;
MATERIAL FACTS
reporting requirements
confidential reporting, 199,
201–202
determination, 197–198
detrimental information, 199–200
material changes, 193–194, 201
material facts, 194–197
process of disclosure, 202
proposed changes, 200–201

MEMORANDA OF UNDERSTANDING,
97

MERGERS
see AMALGAMATIONS

MERIT DISCRETION
see BLUE-SKY DISCRETION

MISREPRESENTATIONS IN PROSPECTUS
common law position
    contractual claims, 145–146
    tort claims
        fraud, 146–147
        negligence, 147–149
documents incorporated by reference, 211
due diligence defence
    see DUE DILIGENCE DEFENCE
other statutory sanctions, 167–168
statutory civil liability
    defences, 152–155
    due diligence defence, 156–167
    elements, proof, 150–151
    expansion on common law, 149–150
    persons liable, 151–152

MULTI-JURISDICTIONAL DISCLOSURE SYSTEM, 134, 289–293

MUTUAL FUNDS
advantages, 462
advertising, 485
asset allocation funds, 461
bond funds, 460
changes, approval
    securities administrators, 477–478
    securities holders, 478–479
closed-end funds distinguished, 457–458
contractual plans, 479–480
custodianship, 484–485
dividend funds, 461
fees
    management fees, 465, 483
    service fees, 464
    trailer fees, 464
growth of, 457
initial investment, 471
insider trading, 485–486
international funds, 462
investment practices, disclosure, 477
investment restrictions
    conflicts of interest, 471–474
    mortgages and hypothecs, 476–477
    types of investments, 460–462
management fees, 483
mortgage funds, 460, 476–477
open-ended fund, 42, 457–458
organization
    custodian, 459–460
    distribution, 459
    manager, 459

point of sale disclosure, 497–498
private mutual funds, 486
prospectus requirements
    annual information form, 469–470
    options, 466
    pro-forma, 470
    simplified prospectus, 466–469
purchases, 463
sale and redemption, 480–483
sales charges, 463–464
sales practices
    bonus commissions, 490
    commissions, 488, 490, 496
    conferences, 494–495
    co-operative advertising, 490
    course registration fees, 495
    expenses reimbursement, 490
    marketing incentive programs, 489
    non-cash sales incentives, 489
    permitted practices, 492–497
    prohibition of, 491–492
    reciprocal commissions, 488, 496
    seminars, 494–495
    trailer fees, 487, 493
    trailer fee split payments, 489
    trips, 489
types, 460–462

NATIONAL INSTRUMENTS, 94

NATIONAL POLICY NO. 41
see SHAREHOLDER COMMUNICATION

NEGLIGENT MISSTATEMENT
see also MISREPRESENTATIONS IN PROSPECTUS
prospectus, 147–149

NON-CONVERTIBLE DEBT
POP system eligibility
    approved ratings, 267–268, 269–270
    criteria, 265–266
    exemptions, 272–274
    reasons, 266–267
shelf-offering eligibility, 276

NON-CONVERTIBLE PREFERRED EQUITY
POP system eligibility
    approved ratings, 267–268, 269–270
    criteria, 265–266
    exemptions, 272–274
    reasons, 266–267
shelf offering eligibility, 276

NON-FIXED PRICE OFFERINGS
shelf prospectus, 280–281

NON-PREFERRED EQUITY
POP system eligibility
    criteria, 265–266
    exemptions, 272–274
    reasons, 266–267
shelf offering eligibility, 276

NON-PROFIT ISSUERS
see also ISSUERS OF SECURITIES

OFF THE EXCHANGE TRADING
see also STOCK EXCHANGE TRADING;
    TRADING IN SECURITIES
bonds and debentures, 38–39
over-the-counter trades, 38
private trades, 37
upstairs market, 37

OFFER TO SELL
see BOUGHT DEAL

OFFERING MEMORANDUM
sophisticated investors, provision,
    233–235

OPEN-END INVESTMENT FUNDS
see MUTUAL FUNDS

OPTIONS
overview, 13
stock index options, 17–18

POISON PILLS
securities commission response,
    398–399

POLICY STATEMENTS
securities commissions
    jurisdiction to make, 93
    local, 92
    national, 91–92
    uniform, 92

PORTFOLIO MANAGERS
see ADVISORS

POST RECEIPT PRICING
    PROCEDURES
see PREP PROCEDURES

PREFERRED SHARES
see also SHARES
call provisions, 11
cumulative dividend rights, 10
participation rights, 10–11
redemption, 11
retraction rights, 11

PRELIMINARY PROSPECTUS
see also PROSPECTUSES
amendment, 130
filing, 128

vetting, 128–130

PREP PROCEDURES
concerns with, 287
eligibility, 284–285
exempt distribution, 256
general description, 283–284

PRICES
see VALUATION OF SECURITIES

PRO RATA TAKE-UP
takeover requirements, 373

PROFIT SHARING AGREEMENTS
see also SECURITIES

PROMPT OFFERING PROSPECTUS
    (POP)
see also PROSPECTUSES
assumptions behind system, 285–287
concerns with
    civil liability, 288
    favours larger issuers, 288–289
    favours larger underwriters, 289
eligibility criteria
    exemptions, 272–274
    non-convertible, 268–269
    non-preferred, 267–268
exempt distribution, 256
procedure
    AIF, 261–263
    short-form prospectus, 263–264
reason for system, 259–260
set-up of system, 260–261

PROPOSED CHANGES
confidential disclosure, 199
insider trading, 201–202
reasonably probable confirmation,
    200–201

PROSPECTING EXPEDITIONS AND
    SYNDICATES
exempt trades, 254–255

PROSPECTUSES
see also MANDATORY DISCLOSURE
amendment
    final, 132–133
    preliminary, 130–131
blue-sky discretion, 135–137
clearance period, 130
comment letter, 130
contents, overview, 101–104
deficiency letter, 130
delivery, time, 132
exchange offerings
    see EXCHANGE OFFERING
        PROSPECTUS

PROSPECTUSES – *(cont'd)*
exemptions
  see EXEMPT DISTRIBUTIONS
failure to deliver
  administrative sanctions, 138–139
  civil sanctions, 139
  penal sanction, 137–138
failure to file
  administrative sanctions, 140
  civil sanctions, 140–143
  penal sanction, 140
full, true and plain disclosure, 102–103
future oriented financial information
  see FUTURE ORIENTED FINANCIAL
    INFORMATION
lapse, 132–133
material facts, 103
misstatements or omissions
  see MISREPRESENTATIONS IN
    PROSPECTUS
modified procedures
  exempt trades, 256–257
prep procedures
  see PREP PROCEDURES
prompt offering
  see PROMPT OFFERING
    PROSPECTUS (POP)
shelf offering
  see SHELF OFFERING PROSPECTUS
multi-jurisdictional offerings, 134
  see also MULTI-JURISDICTIONAL
    DISCLOSURE SYSTEM
mutual funds, 466–469
national offerings, 133
persons signing, liability, 154
preliminary prospectus,
  see PRELIMINARY PROSPECTUS
refusal, 135–137
simplified prospectus
  see SIMPLIFIED PROSPECTUS
waiting period, 128, 130–131
when required, 105–106

PROVINCIAL REGULATION
  see also SECURITIES REGULATION
blanket orders and notices, 93, 96,
  97–98
bulletins, 98
closed system statutes, 77, 98
decisions and rulings, 98
policy statements
  local statements, 92
  national statements, 91
  uniform statements, 92
regulatory bodies
  commissions and administrators,
    88–89
  self-regulatory organizations, 89–91
securities acts, 87

securities regulations, 88
variations, 98–99

PROXY CIRCULARS
annual information form
  see ANNUAL INFORMATION FORM
    (AIF)
automatic exemptions
  beneficial owner requests, 186–187
  de minimis, 15, 185
  registrants, 186–187
  similar law compliance, 185–186
discretionary exemptions
  adequate justification, 187–189
  conflict of laws, 187
executive compensation
  see EXECUTIVE COMPENSATION
information required, 182–185
management discussion and analysis
  see MANAGEMENT DISCUSSION AND
    ANALYSIS
overview, 180
solicitation requirements, 181–182

PUBLICLY TRADED SECURITIES
reinvestment in, exempt trade,
  242–243

PURCHASE RIGHTS
  see also RIGHTS OFFERINGS
exercise
  exempt trade, 244–245

RECREATIONAL ORGANIZATIONS
exempt trades, 253–254

REDEMPTION
  see also CALLS
preferred shares, 11

REGISTERED DEALERS
  see DEALERS

REGISTERED SHARE CERTIFICATES
  see also SHARE CERTIFICATES
exchange process, 29–30

REGISTRATION
application for, 435–436
bond, posting, 445
competency requirements, 446, 453
continued fitness, 436–437
exemptions
  common bond customers, 442–443
  isolated trades, 438–441
  safe securities, 443–444
  separate regulatory scheme,
    441–442
  sophisticated customers, 442–443
granting, discretionary, 435–436
minimum net free capital, 445

renewal, 436
subcategories of registrants, 433–435
surrender, 437
who must register, 432–483

RELATIVES
exempt trades, 239–240, 248–250

RELIGIOUS ORGANIZATIONS
exempt trades, 253–254

REORGANIZATIONS
exempt trades, 245–246

REPORTING ISSUERS
see also ISSUERS OF SECURITIES
continuous disclosure, 173–175
default, in, effect, 221–223
financial statements
see FINANCIAL STATEMENTS
insider reports, 191–192
trades without prospectus or exemption,
221–223

RESALE OF SECURITIES
see also TRADES IN SECURITIES
deemed distribution, 127, 221
exempt institutions, by, 227–229
exempt purchasers, by, 229
market efficiency, underlying concept,
226
outside closed market, 217–219
registered dealers, by, 231
returned securities, 125–126
underwriters, by, 231–232
without prospectus or exemption
hold period, 223–225
no unusual effort, 225
reporting issuer not in default,
221–223

RESCISSION
misrepresentations, re, 145–146, 151,
156

RESOURCES
see FINANCIAL RESOURCES

RESTRICTED SHARES
see also SHARES
rights, 11–12

RETRACTION
preferred shares, 11

REVOLVING LINES OF CREDIT
described, 4

RIGHTS OFFERINGS
see also PURCHASE RIGHTS
granting, equity finance, 12–13

RISK
generally, 49
Jarrell study, 298–299
Simon study, 299–300
Stigler analysis, 296–298
systematic, 49–50
unsystematic, 49–50

RULES
see SECURITIES COMMISSION RULES

SAFE INVESTMENTS
exempt trades, 251–252
registration exemptions, 443–444

SALE OF SECURITIES
see also DISTRIBUTION OF
SECURITIES; TRADES IN
SECURITIES
control persons, by, 126–127
cooling-off period, 132
mutual funds, 480–483
purpose, 1–3, 20
resales
see RESALE OF SECURITIES
underwriting
see UNDERWRITING
units, 14
valuable consideration, 121–122
waiting period, during, 130–131

SANCTIONS
see ENFORCEMENT MECHANISMS

SECONDARY MARKET DISCLOSURE
see also CONTINUOUS DISCLOSURE
continuous nature, 170
mandatory disclosure, effects, 303–304

SECURITIES
see also SECURITIES MARKETS
asset-backed
see ASSET BACKED SECURITIES
catch-all provisions, 110–111
common types, 3–20
debt
see DEBT FINANCE
definition, 106–109, 120–121
depository corporations
see DEPOSITORY CORPORATIONS
derivative
see DERIVATIVE SECURITIES
distribution
see DISTRIBUTION OF SECURITIES
equity
see EQUITY FINANCE
government
see GOVERNMENT SECURITIES
interest in property
see INTEREST IN PROPERTY

SECURITIES – *(cont'd)*
investment contract
  see INVESTMENT CONTRACTS
investors
  see INVESTORS IN SECURITIES
issue, definition, 124–125
merits, assessment, 135–137
profit sharing agreements
  see PROFIT SHARING AGREEMENTS
sale
  see SALE OF SECURITIES
trading
  see TRADING IN SECURITIES
types
  common types, 3–20
units, 14
valuation
  see VALUATION OF SECURITIES
variable term
  see VARIABLE TERM DEBT
  SECURITIES

SECURITIES COMMISSION RULES,
94

SECURITIES COMMISSIONS
blanket orders
  see BLANKET ORDERS
bulletins, 98
cease trade orders
  see CEASE TRADE ORDERS
chief administrative officers
  see ADMINISTRATORS
compliance orders
  see COMPLIANCE ORDERS
decisions and rulings, 98
exemption orders,
  see EXEMPTION ORDERS
freeze orders
  see FREEZE ORDERS
policy statements, 91–92, 93–94, 96
review powers, 91
sources of law, 88–89
structure, 88–89

SECURITIES ISSUERS
  see DEALERS; ISSUERS OF
  SECURITIES

SECURITIES MARKET ACTORS
advisors
  see ADVISORS
brokers
  see BROKERS
business failures
  problems, 427–428
  regulatory response, 444–446
dealers
  see DEALERS
described, 423–426

enforcement of regulations
  administrative sanctions, 454
  civil actions, 454–455
  penal sanctions, 454
financial responsibility
  problems, 427–428
  regulatory response, 444–446
honesty
  problems, 428–451
  regulatory response, 446–453
professional competence
  problems, 432
  regulatory response, 453–455
registration
  see REGISTRATION
securities firms
  see SECURITIES FIRMS
underwriters
  see UNDERWRITERS

SECURITIES MARKET EFFICIENCY
  see also SECURITIES MARKETS
anomalous evidence, 60
Canada, 63
chaos theory, 56 note 14
factors affecting, 54
forms of efficiency
  evidence favouring, 58
  semi-strong form, 56–57
  strong form, 57–58
  weak form, 55–56
framework for analysis, 65–66
fundamental efficiency, 60–61
informational efficiency, 60–61
joint hypothesis problem, 58–60
meaning of term, 53–54
noise theory, 61–62
price as an average of value
  estimates, 53

SECURITIES MARKETS
background, 1–46
closed market
  see CLOSED SYSTEM CONCEPT
confidence-in-the-market
  see CONFIDENCE-IN-THE-MARKET
efficiency
  see SECURITIES MARKET EFFICIENCY
failures
  businesses, 427–428, 444–446
  major investors, 41–43
manipulation
  see MARKET MANIPULATION
unusual effort to prepare, 225

SECURITIES REGULATION
  see also PROVINCIAL REGULATION
adverse selection, response, 84–86
charter implications, 512–514

constitutional division of powers, 67–69
enforcement
  see ENFORCEMENT MECHANISMS
history
  see HISTORY OF SECURITIES
  REGULATION
purpose
  confidence in the market, 82–83,
    83–87
  investor protection, 47, 79–80
  methods of achieving, 83–84
  not at excessive cost, 83
  resource allocation, 80–81
regulation, other, effect, 250–251
scope, 98–99
sources of provincial law, 87–92
variation between jurisdictions, 98–99

SEDAR
  see SYSTEM FOR ELECTRONIC
  DOCUMENT ANALYSIS AND
  RETRIEVAL ("SEDAR")

SHARE CERTIFICATES
  see also SHARES
bearer form certificates, 29–30
depository corporations, 35–36
registered form, 33–34

SHAREHOLDER COMMUNICATION,
  189–191

SHARES
  see also EQUITY FINANCE
additional share rights, 12–13
certificates
  see SHARE CERTIFICATES
common shares
  see COMMON SHARES
options
  see OPTIONS
overview, 7–8
preferred shares
  see PREFERRED SHARES
restricted shares
  see RESTRICTED SHARES
warrants
  see WARRANTS

SHELF OFFERING PROSPECTUS
  see also PROSPECTUSES
civil liability, 282
concerns with
  civil liability, 287
  favours larger issuers, 288–289
  favours larger underwriters, 289
disclosure
  AIF, 277
  prospectus supplements, 279–280

short-form prospectus, 277–278
  eligibility, 276
  non-fixed price offerings, 280–281
  reason for system, 274
  restrictions, 276–277
  synopsis of procedure, 275
  variable term debt, 280

SHORT SELLING, 40

SHORT-TERM PROSPECTUS
  see also PROSPECTUSES
prompt offerings, 263–264
shelf offerings
  certificate, 282
  contents, 277–278
  supplements, 279–280

SIMON STUDY
mandatory disclosure, effects, 299–300

SIMPLIFIED PROSPECTUS
  see PROSPECTUSES

SINKING FUNDS
  see also DEBT FINANCE
bonds or debentures, 6

SMALLER ISSUERS
  see also ISSUERS OF SECURITIES
exempt trades
  private issuers, 247–248
  small number investors, 248

SMALL FIRM FINANCE
regulatory barriers, 248–250
suggested reforms, 248–250

SOLE SHAREHOLDER APPROACH
  see UNDISTORTED CHOICE

SOPHISTICATED INVESTORS
  see also INVESTORS IN SECURITIES
exempt institutions, 227–229
exempt purchasers, 229
large purchases, 229–230
offering memorandum, provision,
  233–235
other investors, test, 233–235
registered dealers, 231
registration exemptions, 442–443
small issuers, exempt trades,
  233–235, 248
underwriters, 231–232

STATEMENT OF MATERIAL FACTS
  see also MATERIAL FACTS

STIGLER STUDY
mandatory disclosure, effects, 296–298

STOCK DIVIDENDS
see also DIVIDENDS
described, 8–9

STOCK EXCHANGE TRADING
see also OFF THE EXCHANGE
TRADING; TRADING IN
SECURITIES
bearer certificate, diagram, 30
clearing and depository institutions
diagram, 32
communication, 28–29
computerization, 36–37
development, 25–27
elements, 27–28
exempt trades, 246–247
payment, 29
registered certificate, diagram, 31
simplifying process
broker inventories, 35
certificate depositories, 35–36
clearing agencies, 34–35
generally, 34
transfer of ownership
bearer form, 29
registered form, 33–34

STOCK EXCHANGES
generally, 89–90
review by securities commission, 91
trading on
see STOCK EXCHANGE TRADING

STOCK INDEX OPTIONS, 17–18

SYNDICATES
prospecting
see PROSPECTING EXPEDITIONS AND
SYNDICATES
underwriting, 22–23

**SYSTEM FOR ELECTRONIC
DOCUMENT ANALYSIS AND
RETRIEVAL ("SEDAR")**, 205–208

TAKEOVER BID CIRCULARS
requirements, 370–373

TAKEOVER BID REGULATION
see also TAKEOVERS
anti-avoidance provisions
acting jointly or in concert, 386–387
future rights, 387–388
indirect offers, 388–389
linked bids, 389
bidder purchases, 379–380
cease and desist orders, 390
defensive tactics, encouragement, 393
disclosure requirements, 370–373
early warning disclosure, 389–390

exceptions
applications for, 386
closely-held companies, 384–385
control block purchases, 383–384
limited relevance, 385
normal course purchases, 382–383
stock exchange bids, 381–382
formal valuations, 375–377
full payment, 379
issuer bids
see ISSUER BID REGULATION
minimum bid period, 373
policy debate
alternative approaches, 411–415
argument against, 400–403
counterarguments, 403–411
pro rata take-up, 373
reasons for
insufficient info, 367
insufficient time, 367
lock-up, 368
looting, 369
other concerns, 369–370
undue pressure, 367–368
unequal consideration, 368–369
restraining orders, 390
time limits, 379–380
unequal consideration, prohibition,
374–375
withdrawal rights, 374

TAKEOVER BIDS
see also TAKEOVERS
circulars
see TAKEOVER BID CIRCULARS
competitive bidding, social benefits,
410–411
defences
National Policy No. 62–202,
396–397
reasonableness, 395–396
shareholder approval, 396
typical, 391–393
validity, 393–394
defined, 380–381
description, 363
insider
see INSIDER BIDS
regulation
see TAKEOVER BID REGULATION

TAKEOVERS
bids
see TAKEOVER BIDS
court intervention, 390
defences
see under TAKEOVER BIDS
defined, 362
friendly, 362–363

going private transactions after, 376
hostile, 363
issuer bids
see ISSUER BID REGULATION
methods of effecting, 362
motivations for, 364–366
non-socially beneficial
empire building, 406–407
expropriation theories, 407–410
hubris, 407
reduced competition, 405–406
undervaluations, 404–405

TARGETS
takeover bids, 362–363

TECHNICAL ANALYSIS
valuation of securities, 51–52

TENDER OFFERS
see TAKEOVER BIDS

TENDERED SHARES
lock-up, 368, 374

TIMELY DISCLOSURE
see also CONTINUOUS DISCLOSURE;
MANDATORY DISCLOSURE
confidential reporting, 199
determination, 197–198
detrimental information, 199–200
material changes, 193–194
material facts, 194–197
process of disclosure, 202
proposed changes, 200–202
purpose, 192–193

TRADE CREDIT
described, 4

TRADES IN SECURITIES
see also DISTRIBUTION OF
SECURITIES; SALE OF SECURITIES
behalf of others, 122
brokers
see BROKERS
closed system
see CLOSED SYSTEM CONCEPT
definition, 121–124
furtherance of, 123–124
insider trading
see INSIDER TRADING
major investors, 41–43
off exchange
see OFF THE EXCHANGE TRADING
open-ended nature, 124
overview, 25–28
pre-sale activities, 123–124
primary market trading, 25
resales
see RESALES OF SECURITIES

sale for valuable consideration,
121–122
secondary market trading, 25
securities not previously issued,
124–125
short selling
see SHORT SELLING
stock exchange
see STOCK EXCHANGE TRADING

TRANSFER AGENTS
registered share certificates, 33

TREASURY BILLS
see GOVERNMENT SECURITIES

UNDERWRITERS
see also SECURITIES MARKET
ACTORS; UNDERWRITING
prospectus liability, 154, 158, 162

UNDERWRITING
see also UNDERWRITERS
agreement, 22
banking groups, 23
best efforts underwriting, 22
bought deal, 21–22
exempt sales, 231–232
market out clauses, 21–22
offer to sell, 21–22
process, diagram, 24
selling group, 23
standby underwriting, 22
syndicated underwriting, 23

UNITS
bundles of securities, 14
limited partnerships, 13–14

UNIVERSAL REGISTRATION,
434–435

VALUATION OF SECURITIES
approaches
fundamental analysis, 51
technical analysis, 51–52
discounting, 48
fundamental elements, 51
price as an average of estimates, 53
risk
generally, 49
systematic and unsystematic, 49–50
application, 53–60
source of value, 47–48

VARIABLE TERM DEBT SECURITIES
see SECURITIES

VENTURE CAPITAL FINANCE
see SMALL FIRM FINANCE

VOTING
common shares, 8

WARRANTS
bond feature, 7

WITHDRAWAL RIGHTS
takeover bids, 374